"The best guidebook to adventure in

"Best book on Mexico. Carl Franz
. . . is really priceless."

"It's the best guide to visiting and living in Mexico that has ever
been published."

—Oakland *Tribune*

"The text is whimsically refreshing, the sketches clever and the
presentation expertly detailed. Be careful after reading it
because a resident could mistake you for a native."

—*Los Angeles Times*

"Will often be imitated . . . but unlikely surpassed."

—Mexico City *News*

"This is no ordinary travel book but a very loving and accurate
picture of what the traveler might see, if only given the chance."

—*High Times*

"If you are planning on a Mexican safari, this book is more necessary than your toothbrush or dictionary."

—*New Mexican*

"It's like having a funny, trusted, and well-traveled friend along
to show you the ropes."

—Amazon.com

"This is a 'must' for anyone interested in Mexican travel: highly
recommended."

—*Midwest Book Review*

to Joy

the PEOPLE'S GUIDE to
MEXICO

Wherever You Go... There You Are!!

CARL FRANZ

Editing by
Lorena Havens & Steve Rogers

John Muir Publications
Santa Fe, New Mexico

John Muir Publications, P.O. Box 613, Santa Fe, NM 87504

Printed in the United States of America.
Eleventh edition. First printing August 1998.

ISBN 1-56261- 419-3
ISSN 1099-5315

Illustrated by Glen Strock, Toby Williams and Nancy Gale
Typesetting by Melissa Tandysh
Production by Marie J.T. Vigil
Printed by Publishers Press

Distributed to the book trade by
Publishers Group West
Berkeley, California

Portions of this book were previously published in *The People's Guide to Camping, Backpacking & Boating in Mexico*; *The People's Guide to R.V. Camping in Mexico*; *The People's Guide Travel Letter* and *The Tour Express Insiders Guide to Mexico* and are used here by permission of the authors.

Table of Contents

Cover, Illustrations and Graphics:

GLEN STROCK

Special Thanks:

Toby Williams, for contributions marked TW
Peter Aschwanden, for Day of the Dead cartoons, and
Nancy Gale, for Mayan temple, Chichen Itza

ACKNOWLEDGMENTS

Editing and Research: Lorena Havens, Steve Rogers, Linda Reybine, Lety Hall, Stephanie Hopkinson, David Eidell, Beatriz

Index: Lorena Havens and Steve Rogers

Encouragement, Suggestions, Criticism and more: Ken Luboff, Eve Muir, Susan Fiksdal, Tom Scott, Dr. Matt Kelly, Lic. Napoleon Negrete, Nacho and Teresa Espinosa, Mauro Lopez, Felicia and family, Sergio Legaretta, Olan and Lois Adams, Dianna Delling, Martha Brewster

Design and Layout: Lorena Havens, Kimberly Brown

Proofreading: Stephanie Hopkinson

Lorena and I sincerely thank those of you who have taken the time to write us about your travels in Mexico. Your letters not only provide much-appreciated moral support but they also contribute valuable information that we pass on to other readers through regular revisions of this book and *The Peoples Guide Travel Letter*. *"¡Qué le vaya bien!"* to you all.

THE PEOPLE'S GUIDE
Twenty-Fifth Silver Anniversary Edition

In late December of 1972, I stood nervously on the sidewalk in front of Cody's, a popular bookstore on Berkeley's Telegraph Avenue. As a small crowd gathered, Steve and Lorena tore open a heavy carton and spread newly printed copies of *The People's Guide to Mexico* across a brightly patterned Mitla blanket. In addition to the apprehension every author suffers when birthing a book, we were also experiencing serious financial suspense. Three years of travel through Mexico and Central America had left us nearly penniless. With two unruly parrots and a road-weary VW van to feed, we were counting on the *People's Guide* to provide us with enough gas money to escape the big city.

While Steve and I wrung our hands in a parody of anxious fatherhood, Lorena's luminous, post–Summer-of-Love smile soon attracted curious browsers. Within minutes she sold the first copy. To my delight there was no further need to "pitch" our wares. Like hungry customers crowded around a busy taco stand, the word spread favorably from one person to another—"It's some kind of really far-out travel book on Mexico!"

Within an hour our pockets were stuffed with cash. *"Caramba!"* Steve cried as he ripped open a second box. "I can't believe it! It works! They like it!" Lightheaded with excitement, we passed out books and frantically made change.

Needless to say, we had no premonition that the success of the "PG" would keep the book in print for more than twenty-five years, through many expansions, revisions, upheavals and editions. When our friend and publisher John Muir (the late author of the classic *How to Keep Your Volkswagen Alive*) mused that our book might sell as many as 25,000 copies in its lifetime, I dismissed his prediction as completely reckless.

Once the book was finished we hit the road again, continuing to roam from one corner of North America to another. It would take a computer to trace our path: according to our sometimes hazy memories, Lorena and I have lived in over eighty places, from southern Guatemala to British Columbia and Alaska. In the early Seventies, Steve and the parrots headed for the mountains of Oregon while Lorena and I took up residence in San Miguel de Allende. There I completed one of my favorite projects, *The People's Guide to Camping, Backpacking and Boating in Mexico*, followed a few years later by *The On & Off the Road Cookbook*. Meanwhile, Steve was not gathering moss. In addition to importing folk art, Steve, Tina Rosa and their daughter Churpa produced two well-regarded books, *The Shopper's Guide to Mexico* and *Mexico in 22 Days*. Next came another collaboration with Steve, *The People's Guide to RV*

Camping in Mexico. The book didn't attract quite as much attention as the reunion of the Beatles, but we enjoyed it almost as much.

By the mid-Eighties, even our parents finally gave in to our nomadic lifestyle and quit asking when we intended to settle down and get "real" jobs. It was apparent that in spite of its rather offhanded conception, the tail was vigorously wagging the dog: *The People's Guide to Mexico* had led us toward ill paid but very rewarding careers in travel writing, importing, guiding and alternative publishing.

Today, as we wrap up this Twenty-Fifth Silver Anniversary Edition, we can only shake our heads—in both gratitude and amazement—at the impact the *People's Guide* has had on our lives. Though we can't thank each of our readers personally, please know that your support over the years has been our main inspiration to keep the book alive and up to date.

A Different Kind of Guidebook

This book is about Mexico. But it's also about living, traveling and taking things as they come in a foreign country. And it's about driving conditions and health and how to cross the border. It's about drinking the water without getting sick and how to enjoy yourself regardless of how close you are to the nearest "recommended" tourist attraction.

It is not about which hotels to stay in or the most interesting villages to visit. The purpose of this book is to teach you how to find out those things for yourself.

Many books have been written about Mexico under the guise of "guidebooks" that, in reality, are nothing more than compilations of hotels, restaurants and nightclubs, along with a few tips about where to buy authentic handicrafts that almost look as if they came from Mexico and not Taiwan. That type of guidebook, actually a directory, tells you that Mexico can put you up in reasonable style and comfort, in air-conditioned rooms with sterilized meals, for less than it would cost at home. These books don't guide you *to* Mexico—they guide you away from it.

Traveling is difficult at times; nothing much is familiar when we get to wherever we're going. For many people this is a strain. Because they don't understand everything that is happening, they try to diminish the experience, to make it unimportant and less real.

This is when you hear the panicky tourist say, "Well, how much is that in *real* money?" or "Let's get some *real* food for a change." They've just lost contact, both with Mexico and with themselves.

One of the main purposes of this book is to show the traveler how to accept, as calmly as possible, the sights and experiences of a strange place. It began, in fact as a series of anecdotes I'd written for friends about various adventures we (Lorena, Steve, myself and others) had had in Mexico. Our friends enjoyed the stories, but their inevitable reaction was, "Fine for you but what about me? Can I get along?" To back up our assurances that they could indeed make it on their own, we began compiling detailed information about the country. Some of that information isn't positive or cheery, but we wanted our friends to know what they were really headed for, not just what a travel agent would like them to believe.

Guidebooks tend to stress fun and ignore problems. In this book, however, you'll get all the information. Warnings and precautions should make your trip easier and more enjoyable, rather than nerve-wracking. And when you ask others how their trip went, take "horror" stories with a grain of salt. "Had a great time but . . ." is a favorite opening. These are the stories you hear most often because they are the ones people most enjoy telling. No one wants to admit that they went to Mexico and were bored stiff, though surely that must happen on occasion.

When you feel nervous while traveling, either out of ignorance of what's happening or out of fear of what you've heard might happen, you cut yourself off from experience—good or bad. You communicate in only one sense: defensively. That's why tourists often speak to "natives" in tones one would use to address a lamppost. When you are relaxed you can communicate, even if it's just a quick smile or a passing greeting.

Which brings up one of the main purposes of this book: to help travelers be both aware and appreciative of what they see and experience, and to lessen the impact, not only on them but on the places and people they travel to see. Keeping the mutual shock to a minimum will benefit all of us. So remember, please:

Wherever you go . . . there you are!

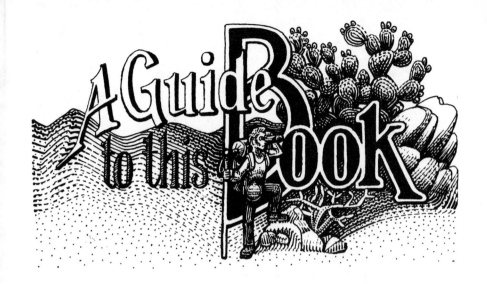

A Guide to this Book

There's really only one way to use a book of this type effectively: as you need it. There are sections you may never need and never read and others that you'll use as a continual reference.

If you know nothing about Mexico or just wonder, then you might like to read it all before leaving. As you travel, specific questions will come to mind. "What's the word for motor oil?"; "How do I order coffee?"; "Where do I get my tourist card?" Keep the book handy; it should provide the answers.

Use the Table of Contents and Index liberally. If the order of chapters doesn't seem logical, you're right; it isn't. But neither is Mexico.

The Spanish words and phrases in the text and Appendix were included to help you out, not to teach you the language. Anyone with a genuine interest in communicating will—or should—buy a dictionary and basic grammar book. The Spanish I've included is not necessarily logical or even according to the rules, but it represents the reality of Mexico versus the tourist agency image. I've yet to hear a Mexican say, "Would you please fill my car's gasoline tank, sir?" It's a hell of a lot easier for both you and the attendant if you say, *"Lleno, por favor,"* (Full, please), and leave it at that.

I suggest that you take extensive notes as you travel, either in a book or on paper that can be kept between these pages: maps to hot springs, a special campsite, the name of a strange fruit or a cheap hotel. When you meet others on the road, exchange this information. After you've returned home, show your book to friends interested in Mexico; they might like to copy your notes or question you on specific points of the book's content.

This book was designed to be useful for an entire trip, not just one part of it. Draw in it, use it for a hot pad, make corrections, rip out pages, glue in new ones, waterproof it, do anything—just use and enjoy it; that's what it's for.

"While we are abroad, let us not exhibit vain tricks and trances."

> — Pierre Delattre
> *Tales of a Dalai Lama*

"Boy, when you cross that Rio Grande, you in *another country!*"

> —Texas border patrolman

TRAVELING IN MEXICO

Planning your trip • A travel routine • Where to go? • How to get there: drive or take the bus or train; air travel • Using a travel agent • Travel packages: choosing a travel package, specialty travel packages • Tours: selecting the perfect tour, what is the actual cost of the tour, trip cancellation insurance, should we tip the guide • Traveling with friends • Traveling alone • Traveling with kids: food and health, toys, language, enrolling children in schools, babysitters

Planning Your Trip

I visited Mexico for the first time in 1964. On that journey, my friend Steve Rogers sparked my curiosity—and my career as a travel writer—with an unforgettable initiation into the "real" Mexico. Using an outdated road map and an alarmingly thin stack of traveler's checks, we pointed Steve's shiny new Volvo sedan away from Seattle's chilling rain and down Highway 99 to San Diego, Tijuana, Guaymas and Mazatlán, then south and east across the Sierra Madre to Mexico City, Puebla, Veracruz, Villahermosa and the Yucatán Peninsula.

Having lived and studied in Mexico as a college exchange student, Steve was eager to share his discoveries about this marvelous country and its people. Pounding the steering wheel for emphasis, he held forth on topics ranging from the proper pronunciation of Tzintzuntzán to his favorite enchilada recipes. What I thought would be a brief vacation south of the border became a combination tire-burning, transcontinental marathon and total immersion course in Mexican travel.

In the Mérida market I traded my tennis shoes for huaraches and my winter coat for a hammock. As usual, Steve was ecstatic but already restless; according to a friendly truck driver, the highway now continued eastward through Yucatán and Quintana Roo, all the way to the Caribbean. "Land's end!" he exulted, tossing the map into the back seat.

Several adventures later, we finally reached the beach at Puerto Juárez. Ignoring my whines of "Are we there yet?" Steve's eyes now fastened on an offshore island.

Stuffing a few clothes into a laundry bag, we ditched the exhausted Volvo in a coconut plantation and jumped aboard the first boat to Isla Mujeres. There, in a setting that struck me as remarkably like Paradise, I was finally able to relax. For about two days . . .

Then, a lobster dinner in a thatched restaurant turned into an invitation to stay with a Mayan family, which in turned blossomed into friendship and further invitations: to work in their taco stand, visit relatives, drink horchata, help with chores and eventually, to become part of the family, exploring even more remote corners of the Yucatán Peninsula, visiting jungle villages, buying pigs, corn, furniture, chickens.

Our two-week Christmas vacation in search of the sun gradually lengthened into a winter-long odyssey. Before it was over, we would push on even farther, well beyond the limits of our maps, our money and sometimes our common sense. As it happened, the adventure didn't end when we finally returned to the States.

I'd dropped out of college to join Steve on that first landmark journey, too dazzled by daydreams of Mexico to worry about the consequences of giving up my student draft deferment. The mess in Vietnam soon became desperate, however, and six months after thumbing my nose at the draft, I was pounding a drill field with a rifle on my shoulder, a self-proclaimed "prisoner of war" in a Navy boot camp.

I wouldn't regain my freedom for four endless years. Once out of uniform, however, I didn't waste time before heading back to Mexico again. Lorena joined us, chucking her job as society editor for a small-town Alaskan newspaper. The rest, as they say, is history and is described throughout this book.

For some people much of the enjoyment of a trip is in the advance planning: they haunt libraries and bookstores, send off for brochures and itineraries, draw lines and x's on maps and consult astrological charts for a propitious departure date. Others are militantly casual about long journeys; they get out of bed one morning, stuff a toothbrush and a change of clothes into a flight bag and head off in a generally southerly direction. Whichever style suits you best, read over and give some thought to the following pages before saying anything like, "We're going to hitchhike to Perú" or "I think a two-week, 10,000-mile bus ride would be just what the doctor ordered."

Locate a map of Mexico so you can gloat over all the places you'll be visiting and conjure up a few armchair adventures. This will help pull you through the tedium of packing and the daily despair of leaving for work. Unfortunately, this can also lead to unforeseen difficulties.

Unless you are adept at interpreting the map, you will tend to look at Mexico in terms of miles rather than actual geography. "On the second day," you say authoritatively, puffing clouds of smoke into your wife's eagerly respectful face, "we'll cross—hack! cough!" and you tap the map with the pipe stem, "this range of mountains!" On closer examination you might discover that you've just casually pointed to over four hundred miles of one-lane dirt road, jammed with trucks and interrupted by several slow ferries. Obviously, on the evening of the second day you're not going to be where you'd so confidently planned. If this upsets you, you're on your way to greater irritations when the remainder of your carefully contrived schedule goes completely to pieces.

"The schedule is Veracruz Monday and Mérida on Tuesday!" you say emphatically, accelerating to an appropriately schedule-meeting, nerve-shattering speed. As the countryside blurs by, you feel the muscles knot in the back of your neck. Your friends are staring rigidly at the highway in front of the car. You are having fun?

If your time is limited, you'll be tempted to travel great distances at a marathon pace in order to see as much as possible. We've met a discouraging number of people who were so exhausted and spaced-out from driving or riding thousands of miles in a few days that they thought only of finding a hotel room and mustering up strength for the return trip. The most lasting impression these people have of Mexico is smelly gas stations, lousy breakfasts with cold coffee, hotel lobbies and ragged kids trying to shine their shoes whenever they slumped onto a park bench.

It may be glamorous to say to friends, "Why, we visited over twenty archaeological sites, fifteen cities, nine beaches and seventeen native markets . . . in ten days!" but if your trip is for pleasure, make it that—not an ordeal.

Personal interests and energy level are very important. Many travelers fail to take them into account, however, and instead force themselves into the type of trip they assume they should be making.

A good example of this is the Church-Ruin-Runaround, usually two or three weeks of frantic cathedral-gazing and temple-crawling that leave the tourist completely exhausted. I find historical monuments only slightly more interesting than bridges and tunnels.

Another trap is the I-am-a-camera routine. Victims can be seen with their Instamatics and videocams grafted to their faces, madly capturing miles of overexposures. These photos and jerky videos will eventually send their friends and relatives into trances of stupefying boredom.

When we first went to Mexico, our idea of traveling was to cover as many miles as we could between dawn and collapse, usually about midnight. We traveled through the country so quickly that I often thought the place we'd been yesterday was the destination for today.

The return was equally frantic; when we finally stepped out of the car in the US, we were ankle-deep in snow and wearing sandals. My memories of that trip are slightly surreal: beautiful sand beach, diarrhea and wondering where in the hell we were but not really caring.

Our hectic pace on that trip taught us a basic fact about traveling: it costs money. Following this brainstorm it soon became clear that the longer the stops were, the longer the trip could be. This rather obvious fact is the basis for our present travel routine. We can't afford to do a great deal of moving around, especially when traveling in a vehicle. We compute how many miles we can afford to travel and then break that up according to how much time can be spent on the trip.

Our plan, for example, might be to travel for six months, spending a month or more in each of several places. When making long stops we either camp or rent a house or apartment. If traveling by car, we park and try to forget that it's there. We use buses, cabs or walk to the local market for groceries and to see the local sights. It is really quite amazing how your expenses decrease when you stop moving.

When we've tired of a place, we repack our bags and move on to another.

This routine is modified by stops at markets, rivers, ruins or any other diversion that tempts us. When driving, we travel three or four hundred miles only on a very hard day and a hundred miles or less when in a really low-key mood.

After we adopted this type of travel and living routine, we were not surprised to find that others had discovered it too. In fact, there is a large community of people who are able to spend a great deal of time traveling and living in Mexico on little money.

A Travel Routine

A travel routine is not a schedule and should not be allowed to insidiously evolve into one. A travel routine is a loose plan that helps you enjoy a trip more by taking into consideration such things as your stamina, your mode of travel, what you want to do with your time, how much money you have, etc.

"We usually splurge when it comes to a hotel room." "I don't like to drive; I take the bus instead." "We stop whenever we see pyramids, no matter where it is." These people have established at least a very basic travel routine and, though they may not be aware of it as a "routine," they do know that it makes their traveling more enjoyable.

Schedules, on the other hand immediately put you in the position of *having* to do something.

Indulge yourself. If your true interests are lounging in sidewalk cafés or sitting on warm beaches, staring mindlessly out to sea, then do it. Throw away your guidebooks and leave the camera in the closet. You can buy professional videos in a tourist shop and spin great stories about your explorations and adventures; no one will know the difference.

Where to Go

Where to go and how to get there? are questions that reduce many would-be-travelers to fits of map-shredding and random dart-throwing. Shall we drive to Mexico City, or fly to Veracruz, or take the bus to Guadalajara? Or fly to La Paz and take the ferry from there to Mazatlán? Or . . . ? The choices and combinations seem infinite and the final decision may be made on a whim rather than logically. On my first trip to Mexico I went directly to Topolobampo, for the simple reason that its name stuck in my mind like a snatch of a song and wouldn't go away until I'd actually seen the place.

Assuming that you haven't got the foggiest idea of a destination, the most important consideration should be what you want to do. My own answer to this varies from snorkeling, birding and hiking to prowling bookstores and Indian markets. As far as Lorena is concerned, Chichén Itzá, *fiestas* and the Museum of Anthropology come second to soaking up enough sun.

Our plans also depend greatly on the season. I prefer the beach in the wintertime, when the sand isn't so hot that it grills the soles of your feet. In the summer, we look for mountains, the higher and cooler the better.

The first rule of thumb after deciding on a destination is *never take your decision seriously*: if something else comes up that seems better, drop plan A and try plan B. If you're relaxed and adventurous, you'll probably work right through the alphabet and hit plan Z: two months playing Humphrey Bogart in a jungle hut might suddenly take precedence over your original plan to study Aztec culture and Spanish grammar.

Read guidebooks and ask friends for advice, keeping in mind, of course, that both the books and your friends are full of exaggerations, misinformation and white lies. I've often heard and read descriptions of places I've been to that sounded more like Shangri-La than reality. The disappointment may be great, but don't let it get you down. When we find that the super-cheap colonial hotel with fine food is actually an adobe version of the Holiday Inn, or the picturesque sleepy village is staging a week-long brass band competition, we just move along, knowing that something better isn't far off.

How to Get There

One of your most important decisions is how to travel: bus or car? plane or train? hitchhike or tour group? People with cars, camper vans or RVs may automatically plan to drive to Mexico. Others casually take the plane when a slower, less expensive train trip might be more enjoyable. It is important to keep in mind that your trip begins the minute you step out the front door. Every effort should be made to enjoy all of it, from beginning to end.

If your trip will be for less than a month the obvious choice is probably public transportation. Mexico's public transportation system is very extensive and very cheap; some type of bus, cab or truck runs over almost every mile of road, including some you don't want to take your car on.

Drive or Take the Bus or Train?

Mile for mile, Mexico certainly rates as one of the most varied and interesting countries in the world. It is also huge, with startling regional variations in culture, climate and terrain. As we'll discuss later in the book, this rich variety is tremendously exciting, but it doesn't make trip planning easy. Any decent road map will show you that Mexico's network of toll roads and freeways, secondary highways, rural *terracerias* (gravel roads) and *brechas* (rough dirt roads) would take lifetimes to explore.

In our experience, the best reason to drive your own vehicle is the ability to make spur-of-the-moment turns and twists, and to investigate this fascinating country at your own pace. Every crossroads becomes an opportunity instead of a frustration. We call this the "coin toss method of travel planning." When another tourist mentions a little-known *fiesta* in the village of Santa Teresa—you can say "Heads! Let's do it!" rather than, "I wish we'd known but . . . maybe next trip?"

Yes, driving is a big expense and a big responsibility, but if you're like us and prefer the outdoors to cities, driving is definitely the best way to "get away from it all" in Mexico. Whether it's a day trip for bird watching or an early morning jungle walk, there's no doubt that a personal vehicle is more convenient than cabs or buses. By the same token, an itinerary that takes in small off-the-beaten-track hotels, campgrounds, rural *posadas* and eco-lodges can be challenging to follow by public transportation.

(As a compulsive collector of baskets and exotic, oddly shaped souvenirs, Lorena also insists that I remind you how much wonderful stuff can be stuffed into the back seat of your groaning VW Bug.)

Have you heard too many scare stories about driving in Mexico to take the risk? Does the thought of crossing the border, with all that red tape, give you second thoughts about taking the family car or RV? If so, read this book through before making a final decision. Pay special attention, of course, to the descriptions of driving conditions—once you get used to Mexico's style of driving, I think you'll find that it's a lot easier (at least outside of Mexico City) than you expected. (If you'd like the support and company of a guided RV caravan, see *Camping: RV Caravans*.)

In an effort to encourage drivers and to soothe tourists' nerves, the Mexican government offers entry information, brochures on many aspects of travel in Mexico and referrals via a toll-free number: call 800-446-3942 (800-44-MEXICO) and ask for the latest update. This is an excellent info line, unlike the phone number we published in the previous edition, which has become a sex hotline. They also have a Fax-on-Demand service at 541-385-9282. Press 1 to get a menu of all their documents. For additional information, read the discussion of border crossings in *Red Tape and the Law*.

Air Travel

If you will be traveling to Mexico by public transportation, check out the prices and alternatives very carefully. Competition has driven air, train and bus fares to wonderful lows, but many of the best offers can be complicated and confusing. You may find, for example, that a special half-price flight departs only on alternate Mondays at two in the morning for people over the age of forty willing to fly standby in the cargo hold.

Many low-cost air fares are for round trip, minimum stay. The advantages of saving money may not justify the limits imposed on your itinerary, especially if you like to take things as they come rather than in a neat plan. Tempting side trips and diversions have a way of appearing in Mexico and it's a shame to have to pass them up.

The option of going wherever you please and by any means is one of the greatest advantages of traveling without a car. On a recent trip we drove a pickup truck to the border, put it in a storage lot and then traveled by train, switched to a bus, then to a local *cooperativo* truck and from that to a small boat. The boat dropped us off in the middle of nowhere and we finally reached another bus after a great deal of hitching on boats and walking. Trips such as this require a complete lack of schedules. The sense of freedom more than compensates for any inconveniences encountered.

Using a Travel Agent

First of all, don't expect a travel agent to arrange Mexican bus and train reservations. Unless the agent has an unusually good knowledge of Mexico and exceptional patience, they won't handle public transportation other than by air.

A good, experienced travel agent can be very helpful, but too many agents automatically push more expensive flights (with higher commissions), withholding information on the real deals unless the customer is willing to badger them. I once got a bargain by turning down the suggestion to fly, telling the agent I'd already checked on the bus and knew it was far cheaper. He hammered away at his computer and eventually managed to "discover" an air fare that was actually cheaper than the bus (taking into consideration food on the 50-hour ride).

To save even more money, tell the agent you're willing to go off-season, in midweek and late at night. Does a resort in Baja sound just about as good as a beach in Cancún or Oaxaca? Tell your travel agent you'll take anything, anywhere, just as long as it is in Mexico and the price is right.

Considering that travel agents work on small commissions already built into the price of airline tickets and travel packages, or charge medest fees, their services are not expensive. Using an agent also gives you a measure of protection against fraud and major disappointment, especially if you pay with a credit card. In case your package trip or airfare bargain really is too good to be true, a travel agent has more leverage when seeking a rebate than a single customer.

As for travel offers that must be paid in cash—this is the trademark of the fly-by-night operator. Stay away; such deals are seldom worth the risk.

Travel Packages: Too Good to Be True?

Open the travel section of your Sunday newspaper and the ads scream out, "Cancun 5 Days 4 Nights $329 INCLUDES AIR!" Like any sensible person trying to massage an overstrained vacation budget, prices like this give your checkbook a warm, pleasurable tingle. On the other hand, your grandmother's favorite travel agent has sworn a blood oath that the lowest round-trip fare available to Cancún that includes a seat belt is $439. You naturally have to ask yourself, "Are these prices real or is this a scam? Can we afford to take a chance on one of these travel packages?"

Over the years we've met a considerable number of people who credit package travel with introducing them to Mexico. When you're trying to convince Aunt Jo and Uncle Milton to trade their snow shovels for a few weeks of winter sun, the predictable comforts and reassuring convenience of a travel package can be just the ticket to overcome their skepticism.

First-timers and anxious, would-be visitors to Mexico especially benefit from package travel. Anxiety about where you'll stay when you arrive in a foreign country—and how you'll get from the airport to a hotel—is a burden for inexperienced travelers.

Considering the price and convenience, there's little doubt that a good travel package can benefit people with very limited free time. This is especially true if you can travel spur-of-the-moment and take advantage of last-minute deals and closeouts. Shop carefully: to the travel industry, trip packages are a commodity to be bought and sold, often at drastically reduced prices, just like a sack of potatoes.

Most readers of this book will consider package travel to be far too commercial for their taste, about as authentic and appealing as microwaved tamales. There's little doubt that many package trips to "Resort Mexico" won't show you the heart of the country or the true character of its people. After all, if your firsthand experience of the United States is limited to a four-day frenzy at Knott's Berry Farm, it might be difficult to take the country seriously.

At its worst, package travel presents Mexico as a garish caricature, a loud, Spanish-accented cartoon directed by jaded, wisecracking guides and cynical Mexicans. On the other hand . . . travel packages are definitely cheap!

First of all, remind yourself that there's still no such thing as a free lunch. Low-priced package trips are assembled by a travel wholesaler, who makes a classic capitalist profit by dealing in high volume and generally lower quality. This doesn't mean that you won't get good value for your money—but please don't expect truffles if you've paid for tacos.

The wholesaler assembles a package trip by negotiating rock-bottom prices for airfare and hotel rooms. Amazing deals can be had when you reserve hundreds or even thousands of coach seats and hotel room-nights at a single whack. (One wholesaler confided to us that they paid as little as $10 a night for off-season beachfront rooms.) Similar high-volume deals are cut with transfer operators—the people who shuttle tourists back and forth from the airport to their hotel—as well as sightseeing guides and tour operators, restaurants and anyone else who contributes a product or service to the travel package.

Once the wholesaler puts a price on the ready-made vacation it is offered to legions of travel agents. Wholesalers seldom sell directly to the public. Booking a package involves time-consuming paperwork and one-on-one consultation, the stock-in-trade of the travel agent, who earns a commission on each package.

Choosing a Travel Package: Roulette Anyone?

The more you know about Mexico, the easier it will be to choose a travel package. If this is your first trip, however, you can still do better than tossing a coin or asking a stranger, "I want to go to Mexico. What do you suggest?"

The best and most obvious way to select a package trip is to ask a trusted person who has already been-there-and-done-that for a recommendation. This person may or may not be your travel agent. In fact, it is always advisable to ask if your travel agent has personally visited the "property" (agent jargon for the hotel you'll stay in).

When asking for suggestions, keep in mind that package travel has a mixed reputation. If your neighbor's father-in-law insists on blaming the refried beans for his embarrassing parasailing experience in Puerto Vallarta last year, don't jump to conclusions.

A good travel agent will offer a range of package trips and help you to match a trip to your budget and interests. Some packages can also be customized, allowing you to select from a variety of hotel and sightseeing options.

If your needs in food and lodging can be satisfied by "three hots and a cot," consider a bare-bones package. Ask for a package with airfare and hotel room, but few if any additional frills and services. If you prefer making your own way, but have limited time, such a package makes it easy to arrange a cheap, semi-independent trip to Mexico. For example, you could fly into a Pacific resort on a package, and then spend your time exploring the surrounding region by cab, bus or bicycle. Even though your hotel room is included in the package, you can probably overnight elsewhere on a side trip and still come out ahead.

Check the restrictions on your travel package carefully. Is it possible to return on a later flight, in case you decide to extend your trip beyond the package's normal limits? What will it cost to change your return ticket?

Once you've made a tentative selection, clarify a few details about the travel package:

Where is the hotel located? This can be a vital question, since "convenient to the airport" also means that you'll be staying miles out of town. That may be fine if you prefer quieter surroundings. But . . . is there a free shuttle or frequent public bus service to town, or will you be paying for taxis?

What kind of room are you actually booking? Be very clear about this. One of the most common complaints about package travel is that the customer's hotel room doesn't meet their expectations. Does your room overlook the swimming pool or the alley? Hotels might try a "bait and switch" but in most cases the traveler's disappointment comes from wishful thinking. When you book a cheap, cramped "standard" room don't expect to stay in the spacious Junior Suite splashed across the cover of a glossy brochure.

If you're unsure, ask in advance if you can upgrade to a better room at a reasonable cost once you arrive in Mexico.

Specialty Travel Packages

So-called "specialty packages" are an alternative for more adventurous travelers. Some small hotels, inns, eco-lodges and off-the-beaten-track resorts also offer packages. These might have a theme—bird watching, diving, horseback riding or hiking—or offer comfortable accommodations and expert guides in remote, unusual places.

In terms of price, service and satisfaction, most specialty packages are a far cry from the mass tourism, cut rate style of the cheapest travel packages.

Tours

Lorena and I began leading occasional tours to Mexico in 1985. Our goal was simple: we'd not only cover the considerable costs of researching and updating this book, but the work would be fun and financially rewarding. With a little luck and enough Pepto Bismol, we might even get rich. (Steve also liked the idea of being a tour guide—for about two days. He promises to write up the story of rescuing his first client, The Mad Housewife, from the roof of the Uxmal Visitor's Center just as soon as his hands stop shaking.)

At first glance, visiting Mexico in the company of a tour group might seem contrary to the theme of this book. For many years, my own feeling was that organized tours were about as tempting as a city council meeting on a warm autumn evening. Why pay someone to nursemaid you through Mexico when you could explore the country just as well or better on your own, and at much less cost? Come to think of it, the very idea of being "guided" reminded me too much of school children being escorted across intersections by play-cops.

My change of heart began when I received an invitation to explore off-the-beaten-track Mayan ruins on a tour led by a well-known archaeologist. Reasoning that I'd get a rare opportunity to visit remote and little-known sites—for free—I swallowed my doubts and signed up.

This two-week expedition gave me an excellent taste of the highs—and extreme lows—that even a well-organized tour group can experience. Instead of the "canned" experience I expected, our tour had more than its share of sudden turns and genuine surprises. In addition to on-the-spot translations of Mayan hieroglyphs and tantalizing insider gossip on prominent Mayanists, we were treated to frequent lectures on topics ranging from pre-Hispanic masonry techniques to ritual penis piercing. The tour's scholarly tone was balanced by serious camping and jungle-bashing. I vividly recall the thrill of entering a vast, jungle-cloaked city previously known to only a handful of archaeologists and tomb robbers—and I'll never forget the horrendous gauntlet of heat, insects, mud wallows and thorns we endured to reach it.

I eventually realized a well-led, thoughtfully organized tour offers its clients many years of experience in compressed form. Tours are especially appropriate if your time is limited or you have a specific interest such as birding, archaeology, diving, pottery, architecture, etc. Outdoor trips that require special equipment such as river rafting and kayaking can also be difficult and expensive to arrange on your own.

It is good, of course, to dream of buying a dugout canoe and paddling down the Río Usumacinta, or to get out the map and dream of spending a week in the Sierra de Oaxaca, visiting Mixtec weavers in remote villages. When it comes right down to it, however, how many people have the time, patience and determination to turn these daydreams into day-by-day itineraries? Well-managed tours are like icebergs: 90 percent of the preparation and organization is hidden beneath the surface. An independent traveler might do a day trip on the Usu or ride a second-class bus through the Oaxaca mountains, but the difficulty of organizing more ambitious adventures often lies beyond our grasp.

Keep in mind, too, that a tour group actually shares the cost of travel arrangements and services that would break the budget of most independent travelers. As a guide, I can use our group's combined buying power to charter bush planes into the ruins of Bonampak, or to pay an outrageous (but worthy) speaking fee to a famous Mexican painter. On our own, Lorena and I would never be able to afford such interesting but expensive experiences.

Selecting the Perfect Tour

Shopping for a tour isn't quite the same as buying a used car, but considering how much money you'll spend and how far you'll travel, it pays to lift the hood, so to speak, and kick the tires. The best way to do this is to ask for references from past clients, and to ask pertinent questions about the tour itself.

Whenever possible, speak directly with the tour's organizer or principal guide. If you book through a travel agent, allow plenty of time for your questions and answers to be relayed to the tour operator before you make a final commitment.

The best tour operators are happy to answer questions, especially if the tour will be physically challenging. On specialized trips, the operator should also want detailed information and answers from you. Health and physical condition are primary concerns on most adventure and camping tours. As wonderful as whitewater rafting may look on the Discovery Channel, the reality of a Class V adrenaline rush is definitely not for everyone.

Be honest about your own limitations. Within an hour of beginning a six-day trek into the Copper Canyon, it became obvious that one of our clients was seriously lame. It wasn't until she hobbled into our first night's camp, however, that Susan would admit that she'd long suffered from a sciatic nerve problem. Her desire to make the trek was so strong that she'd convinced herself the pain could be ignored or simply overcome. Evacuating her was not only difficult and inconvenient, but Susan forfeited the full cost of the tour.

A word about that overworked, over-hyped buzzword "eco-tourism": for some tour operators, eco-tourism is nothing but another flavor of bait to hang on a marketing hook. If the trip you're considering uses "eco" in any way, it is fair to ask for further clarification.

What impact does the tour actually have on the people and places you'll visit? What benefits does the tour bring beyond pumping a few pesos into the local economy? Are contributions to authentic projects and organizations included in the tour price? Do local people interact with the group on more than a token basis, or is their role mainly to pose for photos, wait on tables and give service?

What Is the Actual Cost of the Tour?

Although I firmly believe that independent, budget-minded travelers tend to have more personal contact with Mexico, and more "authentic" experiences than those who travel at a four- and five-star level, this doesn't necessarily apply to guided tours. In fact, you do "get what you pay for" on most tours. The higher the cost, the more satisfied you should be with the accommodations, meals, special services and guides. In short, if I was considering a tour, I'd go for the best I could afford, rather than the cheapest.

Saving a few hundred bucks by booking the lowest-priced tour can backfire in more ways than one. Generously assuming that the quality of the guiding on both the lower-cost tour and the more expensive tour is equal, it stands to reason that the lesser-priced tour will cut corners somewhere. You'll probably find, for example, that many meals are not included, and accommodations average less than three stars.

Ask for an estimate of additional, out of pocket expenses. The cost of admissions to private museums, gardens, reserves, concerts and special events can add up quickly. Less expensive tours tend to pass these by, or present them as "options" or "add-ons." By the time you chip in for additional meals and incidentals, the money you thought to save by taking a cheaper tour looks like wishful thinking.

Pay more than passing attention to the experience and background of your guide. If the guide is not a native of the country, does she speak Spanish? How long has she been working or traveling in Mexico? What are her special interests and training?

It is unrealistic to expect instant, unequivocal answers to every question, but the guide should have more than casual knowledge of the language and country. I've found that younger American river guides who work in Mexico during their winter off-season often exhibit amazing pecs and bubbling enthusiasm—but you're lucky to get more than a blank stare if you ask about Mexico's customs, culture or wildlife.

Worse yet, inexperienced guides may pretend to know more than they do—I call this "ego-tourism"—or cover themselves in a protective smokescreen of inane small talk and stale jokes. On the other hand, a guide with genuine expertise can transform the most mundane itinerary into a journey of constant discovery.

Trip Cancellation Insurance

If there's any doubt that you might not be able to make the tour you've chosen, buy cancellation insurance. I'd sooner risk my safety on a surly mule than take a chance of forfeiting my money because illness, family problems, severe weather or some other out-of-the-blue event caused me to miss the tour.

The night before Lorena and I were to lead a van tour in the Yucatán, one of our clients canceled because her son was convinced we'd be killed and eaten by Mexican bandits. When all of our reassurances were in vain, we reminded her that it was far too late for a refund. "I know it's crazy," she lamented. "But he's so worried that he's going to reimburse me for the entire cost."

Should We Tip the Guide?

To most Americans, the subject of tipping is about as awkward as talking about sex. Tour clients often discuss tipping in whispered asides and go through elaborate contortions to offer their tips as discreetly as possible. Others blithely ignore tipping or assume that tips are included in the price of the tour.

The policy of most tour operators is that tipping is appreciated but not required. In other words, tips are not included in the price of the tour. If you've been given a good tour rather than just being taken for a ride, a tip for the guide and other tour staff (cook, boat handlers, muleskinners, etc.) is definitely indicated.

How much?: This is literally the "64 Dollar Question." Good service probably merits a tip of up to 5 percent of the tour's cost. For example, on a tour price of $1,500 per person, a couple might give tips (for the entire staff) of $90 to $150. In practice, however, few groups are this generous, even when they've had the proverbial trip-of-a-lifetime. A more realistic figure for the $1,500 tour is probably a tip of $25 to $75 per couple (less than 3 percent).

Guides also receive gifts in lieu of cash tips. Spare camping gear, pocket knives, clothing and leftover books are undoubtedly welcome, but considering that wages for most guides are less than flipping burgers, cash is a better way to express your appreciation.

To simplify tipping when there's a tour staff, just give the money to the principal guide and ask that it be distributed. Most tours have a formula for divvying tips that is carefully adhered to.

If you've been given special service by one or more of the staff, include their gratuity with the group tip, then personally thank them with something extra—cash or a gift.

Traveling with Friends

Unless you prepare for your trip with the utmost secrecy—load the car at night and slip away without a word—you might very well be faced with whether or not to take along a friend (or friends).

Let's imagine that you are standing in your driveway, looking critically at the packing job you and Linda have just completed. A friend approaches.

"Hey man, you actually got all of that junk in there! Might even have room for another person. Hey! Hey!"

You stand mute; Linda is making noncommittal motions that indicate the decision to take Harold or leave Harold is up to you.

"Hey, Phil," he says, "I could pay part of the gas."

That does it; you aren't exactly loaded with money.

"OK. How much have you got?"

"Twenty-seven bucks!" Harold says, grinning from ear to ear at the thought of making the trip. Money is no object; he's willing to blow the whole wad.

Later: "Hey, Phil," Harold says with a slight look of embarrassment, "I'd like you to meet Laura . . . "

"Sure, OK. Just try to be here by nine tomorrow. I want to get on the road before lunch."

Harold sighs with relief and as they're leaving he shouts back eagerly, "Laura's got some money, too! About $17!"

As you're walking into the house to tell Linda, she meets you and says, "Robert just called. He's changed his mind. They'll be by this evening so we can go over the plans."

You look back at the car, a '78 Volkswagen van that is beginning to blow oil, and you mentally cram in six people, thinking of all the things you will have to leave behind.

"Oh, well!" you say, "might as well start repacking."

Traveling with a group of friends can lead to problems, but it doesn't have to.

If you'll be traveling with other people, everyone should participate in trip planning. This avoids the inevitable, "Well, you said . . ." when things don't go exactly according to plan.

Final decisions should be made while everyone is sober, relaxed and feeling good. Soft music and loose, comfortable clothing, sharp pencils, clean maps, good lighting and snacks will all contribute to successful planning sessions.

Common goals or interests are important. Your friends may not share your passion for collecting orchids or touring bordellos. So, *before* leaving, agree to what everyone vaguely wants to do and absolutely doesn't want to do.

Money can destroy even the best traveling relationships. When everyone in the group has a more or less equal amount of and attitude toward money, sharing expenses and being economical will be much easier.

A good system of sharing or pooling funds should be devised so that no one pays an unjust portion of the bills. The most accurate and reliable method is to appoint a book-keeper to keep a written account of all expenses and periodically conduct a settling up.

We do this in a small notebook, tied by a string to the dashboard of the car or carried in a shirt pocket. Whenever anyone spends something for the group, the person who paid it records it in the book or tells the bookkeeper. Every few days the entries are totaled and divided by the number in the group. Individual contributions are then compared to the average debt and those who paid in less make it up to those who paid in more.

If you take a car, tell your passengers how much you estimate will have to be spent on gas, oil changes and insurance. People who have never driven long distances usu-ally don't realize how expensive it will be. If you expect them to help pay any repair bills, let everyone know before you leave, *not* after the engine has blown up and the car is in the shop.

Passengers should do as much as possible to ease the burden on the car owner. They can do this by sharing the driving, checking the oil, cleaning the windshield and so on.

Let's imagine once again that you're Phil. You have been unofficially designated the group leader because you own the car and had two years of high-school Italian.

The trip to the border has been uneventful; several gallons of oil needed and a few flats fixed, but nothing major has gone wrong. Now everyone has finally stopped hold-ing their breath each time you pump the brakes. After the border crossing, you've made a straight shot into central Mexico.

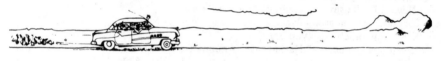

T.W.

The scene opens at breakfast in a small restaurant. Everyone is discussing what to do that day.

"I'd like to look for that hot springs someone told us about!"

"How about visiting a few churches?"

"Why not check out the market?"

"Let's just go somewhere and relax!"

"I thought we were going to head over to Veracruz today?"

The suggestions get thicker and more insistent, but nothing has been resolved by the time the bill arrives.

In Mexico, it is customary for one person to pay for everything and settle up later, but some group members have other ideas.

"I had one egg and coffee and that's all"

"You ate my beans, but I had some of your eggs. How much is that?"

"Who's paying for the tortillas?"

"I ate four of those rolls. How much are they?"

"You owe me for lunch yesterday, but I owe Phil for gas. Let's see, if you pay Laura for the suntan oil and I'll pay Harold for . . ."

In desperation, you pay the entire bill and tell everyone to forget it. On the way back to the car, discussion of the day's plans continues.

"He said ask near the plaza. Everyone knows where the hot springs are."

"I really want to get one of those baskets."

"Oh, wow, I can just feel that sand and that water!"

Harold and Laura have gone ahead and are standing by the car, attempting to con-verse with a cop.

"What's up?" you ask, fearing the worst.

"I think he wants us to move the car."

Everyone piles in, trying to find somewhere to sit amidst the sleeping bags, packs and old potato-chip bags. The inside of the car is like a furnace and before you can reach into your pocket for the key, the usual comments fly from the back seat.

"Let's get moving! I can hardly breathe back here."

"Hey, would you mind opening your window?"

"I think this cop is trying to take our license plate off."

That last comment speeds you along, but instead of the mighty roar of the engine, all you hear is the whir of the starter.

"Not again!"

"I thought you fixed that before we left!"

"He *is* taking our license plate off!"

After convincing the cop (with a bank note) that you're not parked illegally, you delve into the engine, getting grease all over your last clean shirt.

"OK, where to?" you ask agreeably, after you've got the beast started.

"I don't care," comes the chorus.

"Well," you say, somewhat piqued at the sudden lack of interest in the day's events, "*someone* decide."

"It's up to you, Phil," someone says, magnanimously throwing it all in your lap.

"Whatever you say, man."

"Doesn't matter to me."

Harold makes the decision when he announces that he really needs another bathroom, *fast* . . . his second trip in the last fifteen minutes. It is pushing 11 a.m. and you notice a tic in your left eye.

Harold comes out of the gas station, wobbling slightly, and sags into the front seat.

"Wow," he gasps, "that place was enough to gag a maggot!"

You decline comment. Harold has become extremely fastidious since crossing the border.

A few hours later everyone has cheered up (after a nap while you were driving), and they eagerly discuss your decision to visit Veracruz. Even Harold seems to have revived and he actually mentions eating again.

Laura hands you a warm, fizzy Coke and you tune the radio to a great *ranchera* station. It's hotter than hell in the crowded car, but everyone suddenly feels really glad to be there.

"Oh, well," you say to yourself, "I suppose we'll work it out."

Traveling in groups with more than one vehicle can be extremely frustrating.

For example: You stop to take a leak. You're just about finished when your friends overtake you and stop.

"What's wrong?" they ask.

"Taking a leak," you say, discreetly leaning against your back fender.

"Oh, OK," and off they go.

A few miles later you see them in a gas station.

"Don't you need gas?" they ask.

"Not yet, still got half a tank."

You wait impatiently for fifteen minutes while they check the oil, wash the windows and fill the tank. Ten minutes after leaving the station they pull over.

"What's wrong?"

"Taking a leak," they say.

"Oh," you say, "Why didn't you do it in the gas station?"

"Forgot."

Using signals between vehicles while driving is a good method of maintaining communications *if* you can work out a reasonably foolproof system.

Our experiences with signals between vehicles usually go something like this:

Steve: "Dammit! Why don't they stop? I signaled four times."

They finally pull over.

Steve: "Why didn't you stop when I signaled?"

"I thought you were blinking your lights to speed up."

Steve: "No, I was giving you the 'rest stop' signal."

"I thought that was two honks and a left-turn signal."

Steve: "No, of course not! That's the 'stop at the next gas station' signal."

"Oh no, it isn't! 'Stop for gas' is four fingers pointed up and a right-turn signal."

Steve: "Is it? I thought that was 'are you hungry?' "

"I'm not hungry. We just ate."

Steve: "Do you know what this signal is?" He is beating his fists on his forehead.

"No, what is it?"

Steve: "It's the 'meet you in Oaxaca next month' signal."

If you are traveling in more than one vehicle and find that it isn't working as smoothly as you'd planned, there's just one sensible thing to do—part company.

Since most of these problems arise while driving, it's easier to meet somewhere than to stick close together on the road. The meeting can be at the end of each day, at the end of a week or at some specific location with no definite time.

If you agree to meet in or near a town, just leave a stamped letter or postcard at the post office, advising your friends where to find you (See *A to Z: Post Office and Mail*). The standard devices used to signal friends in the States—paper plates nailed to trees, flashy signs, etc.—are apt to be taken down by curious kids as soon as you're out of sight. Messages left at bars, stores and gas stations rarely get delivered.

When traveling with people you don't know very well, don't be afraid to strike off again on your own. Traveling can strain even well-established relationships, and it's far better to face the problem rather than to ignore it in the hope that it will just go away. Friends of ours, for example, found that their long-awaited "dream trip" turned into a minor nightmare because their two teenaged children wouldn't give them a moment's peace. The problem was solved by simple arrangement: the parents would escort the kids to the bus station and see them off to the next town along their route, agreeing to meet at a hotel they'd selected from a guidebook. When their kids were gone, the folks drove by themselves, trying to arrive at the meeting place within a few hours of the kids. The parents got privacy and peace and their children learned to be more independent and self-reliant.

Some people are natural loners and refuse to travel with others, but it is also not unusual to meet people on their own who really wish that they weren't. They have a tendency to latch onto a companion like a second shadow. The most casual conversation can suddenly turn into a partnership.

"Where you headed?"

"South."

"Gee, me too."

"Hmmm."

"How far?"

"Never can tell. Mmmm."

"You said it. Got your ticket?"

"Well . . ."

"Me either. I'm just hanging loose. You know?"

"Hmmm."

"Hey, I've got an idea! Why don't you and I . . . ?"

Ordinary, normal-looking people may suddenly display completely disagreeable or bizarre behavior. I once traveled, briefly, with a fellow who claimed that his body hardly required any food. We were traveling by bus down the length of Mexico and I took advantage of the opportunity to rediscover regional dishes. We always took a table together, though my new friend would never order so much as a glass of water. His routine began when my food appeared.

"Hey, wow, what is that stuff?"

"It's called *asadero*," I said, plunging my fork into the long flour tortilla oozing with rich melted cheese. His eyes fastened on my plate as though it were a crystal ball.

"Hey, do you mind if I taste that thing?" he asked as if the food were some sort of laboratory specimen that required identification. I pushed the plate across the table.

"That's not too bad." He took a second huge bite to confirm the analysis. "Kind of spicy, though," he said, casually sucking down half of my orange juice in one greedy swallow.

"You could order one," I suggested. "They aren't expensive."

"Oh, no!" he said, "I'm not hungry. It's not the money, it's just that I don't require as much food as most people." His hand worked idly across the table and began plucking at the chopped lettuce. I quickly stabbed my fork into the salad, but not before he'd filched the sliced tomato.

This scene was repeated over the *mole* sauce, which took several bites before he reached a final verdict—"weird stuff!"—the breakfast of *chilaquiles*, the lunch of *enchiladas*, various samplings of bread, tortillas, hot sauces and whatever drink I'd ordered. When he said, "Hey, does that taste like *real* coffee?" and reached for my Nescafé, I realized that our paths were about to separate.

Another apparently normal person turned out to be a walking collection of worry and paranoia. "Sure hope this train doesn't derail and kill us all. If it does I hope I die instead of being maimed. Which would you prefer?" The simple act of drinking a beer and watching the sunset from the dining car brought on dire comments on alcoholism, food poisoning, excess cosmic ray exposure, night blindness and the futility of hope.

We parted company soon after. His final comment when I told him where I was headed was: "Well, sure hope you make it." Doubt was heavy in his voice, though my alleged destination was no more than a few blocks away.

We were driving through a tiny village on the remote Gulf Coast of Yucatán many years ago when the sound of our car brought people scurrying from their houses. One of them, tall, bearded and obviously not a Mexican, ran to the car and shouted desperately, "Are you Americans? Do you speak English?"

We hesitated before answering, fearing that he might be totally insane. All the others in the village looked happy and calm. "Right out of an old late-night movie," I thought, expecting to hear a voice with a heavy British accent say, "Gone starkers, I'd say; jungle madness."

We told him that we were Americans and he cried eagerly, "Thank God! Can you get me out of here?"

The prospect of being stuck with a madman didn't appeal to us so we stalled a bit and asked what was wrong.

"I'll tell you," he said. "I came here several months ago looking for privacy. A village like this seemed to be perfect; no other Americans, none of the things that distract you from reading and thinking and relaxing. I rented a house and moved in."

He paused and surveyed the group of smiling faces around him, his neighbors. "Then these people," and he indicated a crowd, "started visiting me, bringing food and inviting me to their homes and *talking* to me day in and day out. Finally, I couldn't take it any more. I started hiding in the house during the day. But they pounded on the door to ask if I was sick. It's no use; they just won't let me alone. I hate to be unfriendly to them, but I have to get out of here!"

A few minutes later, he threw a hastily packed bag into the car and we left, followed by a pack of friendly children, chased by friendly dogs and waved sadly away by friendly villagers.

Traveling Alone

When you want to travel with someone but can't find a companion, don't let the prospect of traveling alone in Mexico stop you. Don't be afraid—you really will be safe. Lots of people do it, from high school kids to elderly ladies.

If the thought is still too much for you, you can be reasonably sure that you'll meet someone else who is alone and who will want to combine forces.

Traveling alone has many advantages. It is much easier to learn and speak Spanish and to become involved with Mexicans when you're alone. Most attractive to me is the sense of freedom and independence that comes with being entirely on my own. It is, quite frankly, a feeling of power; there are no arguments, even from loved ones. As Steve puts it, you are finally boss-of-the-games. If you don't like the looks of a place you can just move along, and if you're feeling lazy you stop, even though the world's most unbelievable tourist attraction may be just up the road.

When I'm traveling alone it seems that I involve myself in side trips that I'd otherwise pass up. "Do you want to visit my uncle with me for a few days?" Why not? There's no one else to consult or consider and I don't much care where I sleep. Changing my mind is also easier if I don't have to convince anyone but myself that it's a Good Idea. When I step off the bus during a brief rest stop and suddenly feel compelled to grab my bag and stay for awhile, it's entirely up to me; the bus driver certainly doesn't care.

Traveling alone requires a certain degree of self-reliance and level-headedness that some people have most of the time and the rest of us have some of the time. When by myself, I am much more careful with my money and personal possessions. I even pay more attention to what I eat: after all, getting sick when you've got someone there to cool your fevered brow with damp cloths and to hustle fresh orange juice can be almost pleasant; when you're alone it isn't so nice.

There are disadvantages to traveling alone. Single travelers tend to be more susceptible to emotional stress and you may feel an exaggerated sense of strain from normal problems in dealing with a foreign language and customs. A tiring day may become an exhausting one. Throw in a long train ride and a case of indigestion and the lone tourist may wonder if it's all worth it or not.

Single travelers often complain that they don't have anyone to bounce ideas off of or to compare impressions with. "Am I the only person in Mexico who thinks tortillas taste like cardboard?" "Should I blow my money on this handwoven blanket or save it to visit Monte Albán?"

Doubt usually leads to conservative decisions, but it may just as well go the other way: "Ah, the hell with it, you only live once!" The latter reflects my attitude toward decisions that don't directly affect my health or sanity. If, for example, I get a sudden whim to change my route and visit a new place, I do it. What's the difference? On the other hand, if it's whether or not to have just one more little drink before walking back to your hotel through dark side streets, pay up and leave.

Should things begin to get too weird while you're alone, it's time to slow down or stop completely. Don't panic; everything will be all right after a nice session of our Traveler's Therapy: locate a pleasant place to spend the night and rent a room. Don't fret over the price, even if it seems a little steep.

Now go up to your room and take off your clothes. Get into the shower or tub and use up all of the hot water. Dry off and move to the bed. Lie down. Put the pillow over your head. Breathe deeply. Scream a little if you must, but don't overdo it.

Lie in this position for at least an hour, thinking of clouds, ice cubes or gentle breezes. When you're ready to face the world again, get up, put on your clothes and stroll calmly out of the room. The secret is to move and think *slowly*, to respond to people and events with the same serene, deliberate manner that you do at home. When a shoeshine boy races up and begins tugging at your arm, banging his shine kit against your sore knee, don't shriek obscenities or raise your hand: just fix him with an unyielding but benevolent smile and whisper, "*No, gracias.*"

Now glide on down the street, absorbing the scenery. Cross at the proper intersections to avoid nerve-shattering near misses. Find a pleasant café or park bench. Sit down. Let it all flow around you. Buy a newspaper. It doesn't matter what language it's in; it is just something to occupy your hands. Don't you feel better already?

This is a good meditation to perform before making any decisions about what to do next or where to go. Single travelers are prone to impetuous changes in location. It is not unusual to hear of people who spent their entire vacation riding buses aimlessly from one end of the country to the other, waiting for that flash of inspiration or chance meeting that will give them a reason to stop.

Any place that is regularly visited by tourists will have a hotel, restaurant or bar where foreigners congregate. This can provide relief from traveling alone: an opportunity to exchange news, advice, reading material and diarrhea remedies. You might also pick up a ride or a traveling companion. By asking others you'll learn of similar meeting places in other towns.

You can maintain independence but still meet other travelers and join them for short periods of time—a side trip or just a meal, for example. Women traveling alone will find the "gringo circuit" helpful as insulation against relentless male attention and machismo (see *¡Viva Mexico!: Machismo*).

One of the hazards of traveling alone is encountered by those using public transportation: the dreaded Empty Seat. Unless precautions are taken it may be filled by a cigar-smoking octopus, a screaming baby, a drunk, a chatterbox or some other threat to your peace of mind.

The solution is quite simple: put something in the seat (assuming seats are not assigned) which gives the impression that it is already occupied. As the other passengers move down the aisle, wait until you see someone who looks compatible as a seatmate. The others can be fended off with a combination of significant looks at the object in the empty seat, lies (yes, it's occupied . . . by my paperback novel), scowls, glares or leers. My beard usually protects me from the fearful mother-with-two-children-in-arms. When a likely prospect appears, just pick up the decoy from the seat and smile sincerely, luring them in. (Women, see *Safety* and *¡Viva Mexico! Machismo*.)

Traveling with Kids

Traveling with children or babies in Mexico doesn't have to be more of a hassle than it is anywhere else.

After the initial shock of entering a foreign country has diminished, children are remarkably blasé about where they are. It is important, however, that parents respect their children's interests as well as their own. The trip should be arranged for the amusement and benefit of all concerned, from the father's passion for Mayan relics to the child's love of playing on the beach.

I am often asked by nervous parents if it is safe to take their children to Mexico. It's not only safe, but can actually make parts of the trip much easier for everyone.

Children are natural icebreakers; when you enter a small village, just send the kid out into the street and within minutes your welcome will be assured. Mexicans lavish attention on their children and are very considerate to gringo kids, especially if the child is timid or just plain scared.

A friend of ours made a long trip to Mexico with his eight-year-old daughter, the first time he'd ever tried traveling with a child. When I asked him how things worked out, he answered, "It was like having a diplomatic passport." He explained that all the people he normally expected to be cool toward him (he is tall, with a fierce black beard and long hair) completely ignored his appearance and treated him like a loyal and devoted parent. He and his daughter were given special attention in restaurants, escorted to the head of the line in the train station and generally treated like VIPs.

"I even got a better deal on souvenirs," he laughed. "I just let her do the bartering."

This reaction to children is very common and the younger the children are, the more helpful other people are. A woman traveling with a small baby told us that whenever she wanted to speed up a border crossing she gave the little tyke a pinch and his squalling was better than having a personal friend in the President's office.

Lorena and I had been camped on a beach for quite a while, and one day we decided that it was my turn to make a trip to town for the mail. The minute I walked into the post office I realized that I'd made a serious error: weeks of sun and salt water had been rather hard on my clothes and I'd forgotten to comb my hair for a few days. The clerk gave me a hard, suspicious look and demanded my identification before he'd hand over our letters. I explained that I'd left my tourist card at camp, but his only reaction was to remind me that I was legally required to carry it at all times.

I wandered away, snarling and spitting; that long-awaited check for a million dollars might be in there! What if it were returned marked NO FORWARDING ADDRESS?! I was leaning against a wall, racking my brain for a solution, when a voice said, "*Ola. ¿Qué tal?*"

I looked up to find a Mexican acquaintance and his wife smiling at me curiously. "Oh, I'm fine, thanks," I said, shaking hands and absentmindedly patting one of their older children on the head. We exchanged the usual pleasantries and were about to go our separate ways when inspiration struck.

"Hey, Francisco," I said, "Would you mind if . . . *pues* . . . would your wife mind if I, uh, held the baby for a minute?"

Francisco gave me a hard look; we'd spent enough time together to know our respective ideas on birth and population control. Had I spent a little too much time in the sun? His wife tightened her grip on the tiny bundle in her arms, looking to her husband for protection.

"Just a minute," I cooed, reaching for the baby with a cheery, sane smile. I knew I was taking advantage of their politeness, embarrassing them into doing something that seemed strange, but I had to have that check! A million green ones; hell, I'd buy them a nursery school!

The baby didn't know the difference. I just hoped the guy with my letters wouldn't question the discrepancy in our complexions; little Tomasito was pretty dark. His parents were looking at each other with mixed amusement and fright as I ducked into the post office.

The clerk recognized me at once; his face congealed into an unyielding mask. I didn't say a word, just edged up to the window and gave him a quick flash of the baby. His mouth dropped open. I chucked it under the chin a couple of times. It drooled. The clerk's eyes came up and looked into mine. He smiled.

"Thanks a lot," I said a few minutes later, transferring the baby back to his anxious mother. I scanned eagerly through the packet of letters that had been forwarded from home: an invitation to join a book club, an appeal for donations to protect small rodents along a polluted river system and a seed catalog.

Single mothers will find that having a child cuts down on unwanted attention from men. Motherhood is sacred in Mexico; husbands and marriage licenses are just frills.

Most of the following advice and comments on traveling with children came from innumerable conversations with parents and children and letters from readers. The almost-unanimous conclusion was that a child should not be left at home unless the parents are making the trip specifically to get away by themselves or the kid has a serious health problem. Here, then, is what they have to say:

Food and Health
Health problems are a major source of worry for parents, especially when traveling. Careful attention should be paid to small children, particularly those in the grab-all-eat-all stage.

Because infants can't move around much or get into major mischief, they are easier to travel with than toddlers. Keep babies off the floor and out of the dirt.

Health care is cheap in Mexico; if your baby gets sick you should have no trouble finding a doctor (see *Health*).

If you are expecting a child, you might want to have the birth occur while you're in Mexico. There are two good reasons for doing this: it costs substantially less for medical care, and the child becomes a dual citizen of Mexico and the U.S. As a citizen of Mexico, the baby can legally own land or a business, an idea the parents might find attractive. (See *Live and Retire* for information on buying land in Mexico.)

Children are notoriously picky eaters so the sudden change to Mexican food may be difficult for them. There are many dishes, however, that will satisfy kids who demand something other than *mole poblano* for lunch. (See *Restaurants and Typical Foods*.)

Baby bottles can be filled with fresh juices, and most juice-stand operators will make purees of fresh fruits and vegetables if you ask. People in restaurants will go out of their way to heat baby bottles or to prepare a special dish for your child.

Baby foods and formulas of all types, from pablum to familiar brands of canned and bottled vegetables, meats and fruits, are available throughout the country. Keep in mind that Mexico has a high birth rate and the care and feeding of babies is a huge industry. Small food mills that will puree a single food or cooked dish are also useful.

Disposable diapers (*panuelos desechables*) are sold in drugstores and supermarkets.

Carry a piece of mosquito netting large enough to drape over a baby's cradle or bed, particularly if you will be staying in cheaper hotel rooms or camping out.

Toys

If you are on the road with a child, you'll find that simple games, puzzles and small toys will interest the kid much more than the passing scenery.

For those who are old enough, a personal map can be a great treat. I recall one young boy who constantly pestered his parents with questions about what city they were in. The poor kid really wanted to know, but his folks didn't realize that a simple road map would have more than satisfied him. "It doesn't make any difference" was their standard reply to his questions.

A good supply of comic books may not enrich the child's mind, but the same could be said for the father's copy of *Hustler*. Although children's books in English are available in a few of the largest cities, bring plenty if your child is an avid reader.

Children's books and school texts in Spanish are excellent language aids for both kids and older folks. Many familiar books and comic books are also translated into Spanish.

If your kid is addicted to a familiar object, such as the classic Peanuts blanket, take it along. A favorite cup, bowl or plate may make the difference when serving the child a piece of fried iguana.

Should your child find it difficult to play with Mexican kids, don't get upset; it will only increase the kid's apprehension. Simple toys and non-verbal games will usually bridge the communication gap.

Frisbees, puzzles, marbles, kites, balls, jacks, jump ropes, tops, coloring books, modeling clay, etc., are almost universal, in one form or another. Expensive toys may cause problems of jealousy. Large, unbreakable toys are good for smaller kids.

Toys are available in the market place and many of the handmade wooden ones make excellent gifts for adults as well. There are also many types of plastic toys and small pottery imitations of regular dishes and other kitchen utensils.

Carnivals, circuses and fairs are common and inexpensive. Public playgrounds and amusement parks are located in most large towns.

Language

Sudden exposure to a foreign language can be unnerving for anyone, and children may be particularly baffled by the change. Fortunately, they also adapt very quickly. The speed with which most kids pick up Spanish is amazing; they'll learn in days what it takes the rest of us weeks and months to cram into our heads—and we'll never match the natural sound and flow of their pronunciation. Tongue-tied parents often come to rely on their children for translations.

Give your children a push in the right direction by teaching them basic Spanish words and polite phrases. This will give them a feeling of independence and self-importance that helps to break barriers of shyness and timidity.

The learning process won't always be fun; one little gringo sobbed to his mother that no matter how many times he said something in English to his new friends, they didn't seem to hear him. He felt like the Invisible Boy until he began to pick up a few simple Spanish words and phrases.

Another child rebelled against his mother's efforts to teach him how to ask for food and yelled, "I can't speak Spanish! I can't say 'tortilla'!" Needless to say, he pronounced *tortilla* like a native.

Children often don't understand the concept of another language until they've heard it spoken and have time to accept that it is real. A three-year-old, after two days on the train, turned to her parents and said accusingly, "You didn't tell me *everybody* talks Spanish." By the end of their trip she didn't know the difference between the two languages and used half and half.

If your child's initial reaction to Spanish is negative, don't make a big deal out of it. I remember a little boy who had driven his parents to distraction because he absolutely refused to speak a word of Spanish. One day I saw him playing in the sand with some Mexican kids and decided to eavesdrop.

They were engrossed in their play, with the Mexican children babbling back and forth in Spanish. It took me a few minutes to realize that the gringo kid was completely involved in whatever game they'd invented, though he was acting out a private and entirely different fantasy than the others.

If you're staying in one spot for awhile you might want to enroll your child in a Mexican school.

Enrolling Children in School

Foreign children do study in Mexico's public schools, but if classrooms are overcrowded, they may not be admitted unless arrangements are made well in advance of a term. For those going beyond the sixth grade, an evaluation test is required (in Spanish). Most foreigners enroll their kids in private bilingual schools.

Reminiscing about her childhood experience as the lone gringa in a rural Mexican public school, Steve's daughter Churpa says, "I barely spoke the language, and instead of being the poor kid in Oregon, I was now the rich kid, possibly even a worse stigma. In Spanish my name, Churpa, literally means 'sucker.' Plus, after spending the better part of the winter running around half-naked on the beach, I had the reputation of being 'the gringa who didn't wear underwear'.

"Somehow this didn't turn out as bad as one might expect. The school, sprawled on a hilltop, with its missing windows and bare cement floors, had the look of a long forgotten government project. The teacher was a pretty young woman who I couldn't hear at all over the sound of about seventy kids packed into a cement echo chamber. I did, however, pick up a lot of Spanish on the playground and in the street. This accounts for my proficiency with slang and horrible grammar. Overall, my memories of those days are as fond as possible."

Babysitters

Many parents, especially those without partners, say that Mexico is like traveling in a vast day-care center. Mexicans are very casual about having another kid around the house. In homes that can afford a maid or cook, the children are often placed under her care and one or two more probably won't be noticed.

A woman traveling with her five-year-old son told us that after she rented a house in a small town and had met the neighbors, her boy all but disappeared. When she wanted him back she just walked down the street until she was directed to whichever family was entertaining him that day. Stories such as this are very common. And then there's the very strange-but-true story of the woman who decided that her children were happier in Mexico and left them with the neighbors . . . permanently.

Leaving your children with someone else doesn't mean that you're abandoning them. You may, in fact, be doing everyone a big favor. Kids tend to tire quickly of traveling, especially when hopping from one town or tourist attraction to the next. Many children tell us that they'd rather stay at the beach while their folks go off on side trips by themselves. Don't be afraid to consider this alternative just because you're in a new country. If nothing else you might find some gringos willing to babysit.

We left our palm hut and its beautiful isolated beach and moved on south, hoping to travel into Central America before the summer rains. That day and evening were typical of many we spent while traveling in our VW van.

I sat between Steve and Lorena on an improvised bench of blankets stacked on a case of empty soda bottles, my back supported by a bulky tent and a large bundle of clothing. By twisting my legs to the right to avoid the gear shift, by pressing them downward to avoid the tape deck, by supporting myself with an arm behind each seat and by craning my head around the mirror—generally contorting my entire body—I was able to sit quite comfortably for as long as fifteen minutes.

Then Steve would turn to me and shout over the roar of the decaying muffler and the thumping beat of the music, "Anything cold to drink back there?"

There always was and he certainly knew it; he just couldn't seem to ask for it out-right. Instead Steve used this thinly worn ploy, my cue to move from my long-sought-after position of comfort and lean back for a *refresco*. But it wasn't merely a matter of reaching into a handy open case. No, we had them in the icebox. I could either turn around in the seat, jostling both Steve and Lorena severely, or lie on my back and reach a twisted arm around to open the icebox door. This was no easy feat. With my fingers barely clutching the handle I would slowly pull the door open and attempt to extract the slippery bottles, one by one, without causing a general landslide.

This, of course, was seldom successful. I would then climb over the seat, shovel the bottles and ice and whatever else had fallen out back into the box, close the door and crawl back into the front. After I'd handed out the drinks and taken a few sips, Lorena would give her line in the play:

"Steve, if you see a wide spot, I have to take a leak."

"My God!" I thought. "A Wide Spot! Some mythical pull-off designed especially for bird-bladdered tourists by the Mexican Highway Department." I gnashed my teeth qui-etly as we pulled to a stop, three minutes after my acrobatics with the sodas. While Lorena sat in the bushes, I opened the side doors of the van and attempted to restore some sort of order to the icebox. As a precaution, I put a good stock of liquid refresh-ments in the front seat. After that clever piece of planning, I had only to lift myself and allow one of them to reach into the case beneath me.

A few miles later, Steve announced that he was hungry. Some people say such things casually, meaning it as a statement of condition: not necessarily to be reacted to immedi-ately, just something to keep in the back of one's mind should a restaurant appear. But Steve is different. "I'm hungry" is for him a statement of absolute existence, of total irrefutable fact. This great all-consuming Hunger cannot be delayed. Like the lighting of a fuse, the time between the igniting statement and fatal destruction is not long.

His eyes began to move nervously about the front of the van. "Isn't there anything to eat up here?" came the plaintive query.

"No," I said wearily, anticipating the next line.

"Well, how about in the back?" he asked with perfect timing, knowing quite well that the back was jammed with food, all carefully and deeply packed away.

"I don't think there's anything very accessible back there," I stalled.

We drove on for a few minutes, Steve watching the road closely for any sign of a café, restaurant or vendor. I sat quietly, dreading the inevitable. It didn't take long.

"*I have got to have something to eat!*" Steve suddenly cried. "I don't care if it's only a lousy scrap of stale tortilla!" he continued, hammering out the words on the steering wheel with his hand. "I have just got to have *something!*"

My cue. Sighing deeply I began the tortuous climb over the seat, knowing only too well that I would probably be back there for an hour rooting through boxes, bags and icebox, preparing a meal for that cavernous, insatiable mouth.

"Find anything?" Steve asked, glancing back greedily before my feet had hit the floor.

"Hold on, dammit!" I snapped. "I'm not an acrobat!"

He turned back to the job of driving, but I felt his eyes on the rearview mirror, watch-ing my every movement, appraising the possible food value of everything I touched. I found a few pieces of bread and a box of dried-up miscellaneous vegetables. "What the hell?" I thought, "he'll eat it." A thick coating of gooey peanut butter, several slices of pungent onion and a slab of hard green tomato, all topped with a generous serving of slightly rancid mayonnaise. Steve gobbled it up, licking his fingers of every smear and crumb. I waited.

"Any more?"

An avocado, badly bruised and overripe. He smacked his lips as he tossed the pit onto the floor. "What else have you got back there?"

"How about a roast beef sandwich, order of fries and a cup of coffee?" I sneered, handing him a mushy banana that we had had for days.

Steve laughed at my joke, gorging down the banana and throwing the skin into the back.

"Thanks," I said, picking the peel off my knee.

"For what?" he answered, as usual oblivious to anything not actually involving the ingestion of food. Garbage is nothing; he does not recognize its existence. It is in a class with trees and rocks and other inedible things.

"Forget it. Never mind," I muttered gloomily, wondering when this meal would end.

"How about that pineapple we got yesterday?" he called, apparently bottomless.

"Are you serious?" I yelled. "If you think I'm going to cut up an entire pineapple, you're out of your mind!"

With that question settled, he went into the second part of his routine: "Let's stop at the next restaurant, then, because I'm still hungry."

I agreed, knowing that until he had eaten from a plate, with a fork, he would never be satisfied or silenced. Half an hour later we came to a café and screeched to a stop.

After our usual meal of beans, rice and tortillas, we were back on the highway. Steve, suddenly tired, warned us to keep an eye out for a camping place. I mentally moved the stage equipment and adjusted the lights for the next scene.

"How about that?" Lorena said, pointing in the twilight to a sheltered clearing in a beautiful grove of trees.

"What? Where?" Steve asked, sleepily driving on.

"There was a good spot back there," I said, knowing it was hopeless.

"I didn't see it until it was too late," Steve said, adding, "Oh, what the hell? There'll be something better up ahead."

He was occasionally correct in his predictions and we'd agree while sitting around a blazing fire that it was lucky we hadn't stopped in a less desirable place earlier. But other nights that better camping spot never materialized and we'd find ourselves on the highway long after dark, heads heavy with fatigue, tempers ground to a raw edge against the swaying motion of the van as we rolled endlessly around dark mountain curves. The night jealously hid all of the wide spots, side roads, fields, dumps and clearings that had been so plentiful earlier. Would we ever find a place?

"There's a road!"

Steve, reacting quickly to Lorena's shout, stopped the van and backed slowly to a vague turnoff. We bounced and bumped down a dark winding trail, peering desperately into the thick brush on each side for a parking space. We traveled on without success for half an hour when the road widened abruptly and ended in a small grassy clearing.

We stopped, then sat in dazed silence, the sound of the engine still echoing in our ears like the pounding of a distant surf. Mosquitoes hummed anxiously against the windows. Steve switched on the radio and began a careful search for gospel music, a nightly ritual while on the road. We sat quietly, listening to the reedy sound of Brother Bob's Country Choir, crackling and wavering as it floated down from some pious Southern state to this deserted Mexican back road. Lorena revealed a bag of peanuts she'd hoarded away since Guaymas. We nursed them for as long as possible, letting that good gospel sound mellow our nervous systems before going to sleep.

"This world is not my home, I'm just a-passing through.
My treasures are laid up, somewhere beyond the blue."

THE BEST OF MEXICO

Wherever you go • A mercifully brief lesson in geography and climate • The seasons: winter or summer, the rainy season, camping in the rainy season, the dry season, the hurricane season • Baja California • Copper Canyon • Pacific Beaches • Central Mexico: the Colonial Heartland • The Gulf Coast • The Indian Highlands: Oaxaca and Chiapas • The Yucatán Peninsula • The Ruta Maya

●●

Wherever You Go . . .

For years I've resisted the temptation to point travelers toward specific places in Mexico. In fact, this may be the only travel guide published that didn't mention a single specific hotel or restaurant. How, then, did we get away with calling this book *The People's Guide to Mexico*?

Although our subtitle, *Wherever You Go, There You Are*, has a humorous ring to it, there's a shred of hard-earned wisdom there, too. Experience has taught us that there's far more to travel than just moving from one place to another. Travel literally changes us, sometimes dramatically, whether we want to change or not. One of the most exciting things about Mexico is our sense of discovery, that "first time" thrill of encountering new places, people and experiences. By not including specific place names in earlier editions of the *People's Guide*, I hoped to preserve that thrill and to encourage readers to explore Mexico for themselves, rather than traveling in follow-the-leader style. (This no-name policy also saved thousands of hours of additional legwork, but that's another story. . . .)

Why, then, do we include our favorite itineraries and place names in this edition? The answer is simple: we gave in to reader demand. Over the years, so many *People's Guide* readers have asked us to provide such information that we decided it was worth a try. We sincerely hope, however, that you'll use these itineraries as starting points for your own adventures, not as inflexible, step-by-step route plans. Lorena and I have a strict rule about itineraries in Mexico: take them one day at a time and never take them seriously. If we're distracted by a fiesta or tempted to take an unscheduled side trip, the itinerary is immediately changed.

Each trip described here covers a major region of Mexico, with up to a thousand miles of travel. If you can possibly swing it, double or even triple the time you allow for these itineraries. Avoid at all costs the "If-this-is-Tuesday-it-must-be-Tehuantepec" syndrome and the habit of traveling too far or too fast. I can't stress enough the importance of altering the itinerary to suit your own interests. When tired, slow down. When you find a place you don't want to leave, toss out the itinerary and *don't leave*.

In addition to Steve's considerable experience and our own independent travels by car and bus, Lorena and I have traveled most of these itineraries while leading small group van tours. We haven't included detailed information such as bus timetables, since this is widely available in the usual guidebooks. (Our guidebook suggestions are included in the *For More Information* chapter.)

By the way, remember that archaeological sites are open from 8 a.m. to 5 p.m., seven days a week, and that admission to ruins and museums is free on Sunday. Most, but not all, museums close on Monday.

Finally, I hope you'll share your own experiences, observations and favorite places with us for future editions of this book and *The People's Guide Travel Letter*. Please write to us at P.O. Box 179, Acme, WA 98220 or send an email to mexico@peoplesguide.com. or visit our web page at <http://www.peoplesguide .com/mexcio>.

A Mercifully Brief Lesson in Geography and Climate

Mexico is *big*, about one-fifth the size of the United States or Canada, covering over 760,000 square miles. Mexico includes two vast peninsulas (Baja and Yucatán) and over 6,000 miles of shoreline along the Gulfs of Mexico and California, as well as the Caribbean Sea and Pacific Ocean. In cross-section, Mexico is also high: most of the country is 3,000 feet or more in elevation. There are several major mountain ranges and peaks soaring to more than 17,000 feet.

Mexico's climate is as varied as the topography, with deserts so arid they may not see rain for years at a time, and dripping, eternally moist tropical rain forests. There are four distinct temperature zones within the country, from the low, humid southern *tierra caliente* (hot land) to temperate, cold and even *helada* (frozen).

Though much of northern Mexico is dry and thorny, there are vast pine and oak forests, lowland savannahs, immense wetlands, lagoons, jungles and deserts of several types. When such factors as climate, altitude, vegetation and topography are all shuffled together, the country is revealed as a collection of more than fifty distinct regions, a complex geographic jigsaw puzzle that defies simple description.

Travelers will find that Mexico's diversity not only translates into sudden, dramatic changes in scenery and weather, but it also affects the people. In the state of Oaxaca, for example, the daily lives and language of highland Mixtec Indians are quite different from the Zapotecs of the central valleys or the mixed-blood mestizos of the coastal fishing communities. Though their differences are as obvious as those between Americans and Germans, these diverse groups are separated by only a few hours' travel.

Higher altitudes mean cooler temperature. Mexico is made up of highlands and lowlands, with steep, narrow transitions between the two. In summer the highlands are temperate and the lowlands are quite hot. In winter, the lowlands become temperate and the highlands surprisingly cool, especially at night. For example, at 5,000 feet elevation, Guadalajara's climate is often described as "eternal spring" or "Mediterranean." At 7,000 feet, however, nighttime temperatures in winter will drop into the 20s and 30s around Mexico City. In summer, Mexico City's high altitude means daytime temperatures are in the moderate 70s and 80s.

In winter, temperatures go from cool in the north to hot in the south. Northern and eastern Mexico (including the Yucatán) are strongly influenced by winter weather systems from the U.S. and Canada. Cooling effects are commonly felt as far south as Mexico

A. Sierra Madre Occidental; **B.** Vizcaino Desert; **C.** Magdalena Plain; **D.** Bolson de Mapimi; **E.** Sierra Madre Oriental; **F.** Volcano Zone; **G.** Sierra Madre Del Sur; **H.** Sierra Madre de Chiapas; **I.** Sierra Norte de Chiapas; **J.** Yucatán Peninsula; **K.** Bolson de Mayran

City, with occasional heavy snows in Chihuahua and the north-central mountains. These same storms will affect the Pacific beaches as far south as Guaymas and Mazatlán, though Puerto Vallarta is usually reliably warm. Depending on your luck, the entire Baja Peninsula can be quite cool in January and February.

Eastern Mexico, including most of the Yucatán Peninsula and the entire Gulf of Mexico, is swept by winter *nortes* ("northers") from the American Midwest. The Gulf of Mexico is also the country's wettest region. The Gulf's "dry" season is never entirely dry. It comes in late winter and lasts only a few months.

Roughly speaking, the warmest winter weather is on the Pacific coast south of Manzanillo, including Ixtapa-Zihuatanejo, Acapulco, Puerto Escondido, Huatulco and Salina Cruz.

The Seasons

Winter or Summer?
Although they share the same winter and summer seasons as the U.S. and Canada, people in southern Mexico and Central America usually refer to the dry season (our winter) as *verano* (summer) and the rainy season (our summer) as *invierno* (winter).

The Rainy Season
Summers are rainy and winters are dry. Mexico's rainy season is from mid-May or June through October, but it seldom pours heavily until late summer. Except for wetter tropical areas and the Gulf of Mexico, summer rains are usually brief but intense. A typical rain will come in the afternoon or at night and be followed by clear or partly cloudy skies. In our experience, mid-August through mid-October is the wettest time of year.

During *las aguas* (rainy season, "the waters") we find the lowlands too hot and humid for comfort. In the desert, summer rain is infrequent and afternoon temperatures will be quite high.

Fortunately, there are many places to visit during the rainy season that have year-round access to all-weather roads. With a good umbrella and fast-drying shoes, travel in the rainy season is quite enjoyable. (In most cases, it rains only for a short time in the afternoon, even at the height of the rainy season.)

Camping in the Rainy Season
The rainy season is a particularly beautiful time in Mexico, but it definitely complicates camping. Anticipate that a lot of rain, even for a short time, can turn a dusty creekbed into a raging river and a shallow pond into a lake. Steve learned this one the hard way, when he and his van were nearly swept away in a "dry" riverbed. Other campers haven't been so lucky.

Park or camp where you won't be isolated by the first heavy cloudburst. Can you reach an all-weather road once the rains begin? When in doubt, carry extra food. Creeks that rise overnight usually drop just as quickly, so be patient.

The rain may begin with a few afternoon drizzles or it will come dramatically, with a torrential downpour. In many remote areas, the rainy season brings genuine isolation, when the only contact with the outside world is by foot or canoe and sometimes only by radio. Food becomes scarce and those too poor to stockpile ahead have to endure real hardship.

We always question the local people closely when the rainy season approaches and establish: 1. the condition of the roads after the rains begin, 2. alternate routes out of the area, 3. the earliest date that the area has been isolated, and 4. if it was cut off temporarily or for the entire rainy season.

The Dry Season

The dry season, *las sequias*, begins in late October but doesn't really show its effects on vegetation until mid-winter.

The end of the dry season is often the hottest time of year. The month of May can be especially warm in the dry central highlands, southern Mexico and Yucatán. On the other hand, May can also be perfect on the Pacific beaches from Manzanillo to Mazatlán and in Baja.

The Hurricane Season

The hurricane season is in summer and autumn. Although hurricanes have struck as late as December, the greatest chance of a *ciclon* is from late summer to mid-autumn. Hurricane Gilbert, one of the most destructive storms in history, struck Mexico in mid-September of 1988.

Hurricanes frequently strike close together. Even those that only glance off Mexico can bring torrential rainfall to a significant portion of the country. Roads are cut, food is scarce and you may face great discomforts and even danger. Unless you regularly listen to a shortwave radio or closely follow Mexican newspapers, don't expect much, if any, warning. *The News*, an English-language paper printed in Mexico, gives weather forecasts, but the paper is available only in tourist areas and larger cities.

Should you find yourself in the likely path of a hurricane, don't even think about riding it out in a palm-front hut, a beachfront condo or the local *cantina*. Go to high ground, as far from the beach as possible. In addition to heavy flooding and mudslides, a hurricane uproots trees, particularly coconut palms, and flying limbs, roofs and junk can fill the air.

Our friend David Eidell has survived direct hits from several Mexican hurricanes. If you must ride out the storm, David advises you to take refuge in an interior hotel room or basement. "Fill as many containers as possible with drinking water. Close all windows, blinds or drapes. To avoid shattering glass you may have to hide in the bathroom or crouch under a mattress. Never leave an exposed hotel room. Flying glass, lawn furniture, signs and roof tiles can be fatal.

"Hurricanes usually last four to six hours. If you must 'make your break,' do so while the winds are calmed in the central 'eye' of the storm. You may have only six to ten minutes of calm or as much as thirty minutes. Once the eye of a hurricane passes, however, the winds accelerate almost instantly to full strength! The wind will also return in the opposite direction from which it originally came, so take this into account when choosing a hideout. There's nothing like a sudden gust at 150 miles per hour to take your breath away!"

To sum it up, my favorite time of year in Mexico is from mid-October, when the rainy season ends and the temperatures quickly moderate, through January, February and early March. The sky and vegetation have been thoroughly washed, the harvests are in and the weather tends to be very settled. Of course, springtime is also very pleasant, especially on the Pacific coast. Then again, May is wonderful in Mulege and June is ideal in . . .

Although no one can really predict the weather, there are two weather oddities in

Mexico that are worth noting. The first comes in late July or early August (usually) and is called *la canicula,* loosely, "dog days." This is a period of a few weeks when normal summer rains stop and are replaced by hot and dry weather.

The other side of the weather coin comes in early January, when it suddenly rains in the middle of the dry season.

Once again, if you don't like the weather, take advantage of Mexico's varied climates by moving along until you find a place that is more agreeable.

BAJA CALIFORNIA

A different feeling • Driving: conditions and precautions • Buses, hitching, planes and ferries • Money • Shopping • Camping, fishing and diving • Red tape

A Different Feeling

Several years ago I met a turtle fisherman from southern Baja who was vacationing with relatives in mainland Mexico. After a few shots of tequila he began ranting about the attractions of life in Baja, describing it as a veritable paradise on earth. At that time the peninsula was still divided into a southern territory and a northern state. Like the territory of Quintana Roo, the Baja was considered one of Mexico's last frontiers.

"What makes it so different?" I asked, surprised to hear him claim that he found the mainland of Mexico to be like another country.

"Different?" he said, "Well, I'll tell you." He lifted his glass for a long drink, then slapped it back down on the bar, empty. "We've got about 2,000 kilometers of desert and mountains between us and southern California and another few hundred kilometers of *mar abierto* [open sea] between us and Mexico. We're an island!"

Baja California's isolation has now ended due largely to the opening in 1973 of the Transpeninsular Highway, and regular passenger jet and ferry service. But in spite of increased accessibility and tourism, Baja still remains distinctly different. Hundreds of years of isolation created a way of life that can't be erased by a two-lane highway.

Imagine a narrow, sparsely populated desert island almost a thousand miles in length, cut off from the rest of the world until the mid-Seventies. Now connect the north end of this island to California with a single two-lane highway and the south end to Mexico with a few small vehicle/passenger ferries. This, along with a mere handful of towns, thousands of miles of beaches and seemingly endless deserts, is Baja California.

Until it was opened to overland tourism by the Transpeninsular Highway, Baja was a vast, exclusive reserve for well-heeled American sportsmen and off-road driving buffs. Fly-in resorts catered to celebrity anglers, the wealthy and fanatical fishermen.

Baja now has been opened to the rest of us. Judging from the numbers of tourists who visit the peninsula every year, it is clearly living up to its reputation as an outdoor paradise. There are several factors that make Baja particularly attractive to campers.

In fact, Baja's popularity is due in great part to the character of its people. Most campers, myself included, feel much safer there than at home. Crime is so low that Steve says, "Even the cops are mellow!" With the nagging exception of a few gas stations, swindles are uncommon. As in mainland Mexico, the vast majority of people have "old-fashioned" values of honesty and hospitality.

Baja's Pacific shore includes several huge, seafood-rich lagoon systems and hundreds of miles of empty beaches. In addition to beachcombing, surf fishing and birding, campers can observe the annual winter migration of hundreds of gray whales from the Bering Sea to Magdalena Bay.

On the east coast of the peninsula, the Gulf of California, also known as the Sea of Cortez or Vermillion Sea, has some of the best fishing, kayaking and beach camping in the world. Because the Sea of Cortez has little or no surf, it is ideal for small boats and sailboarding. Be wary of strong, sudden winds, however. Snorkeling and scuba diving are also very good, especially in the southern "Los Cabos" (Capes) region.

Although most of Baja is quite arid, there are dramatic variations in landscape and vegetation from one area to another. The west coast, for example, is considerably cooler and more moist than the eastern shore, along the Sea of Cortez. In winter, heavy snows blanket the northern peaks and chilly winds sweep across the upper portions of the peninsula. Wind, in fact, is the region's greatest drawback.

Driving: Conditions and Precautions

Baja can be an easy drive or it can be a killer; it all depends on how well prepared you are and what you want to subject yourself and your vehicle to. When the Transpeninsular Highway was completed, but not yet officially opened, Lorena and I drove its entire length, about 1,050 miles, in a twenty-year-old station wagon, badly overloaded and suffering from terminal fatigue. We never got stuck, never ran out of gas and never had to perform any miracles of mechanical improvisation. It was just a long drive. A few years before that, however, we almost left a VW van to bleach its bones in a deep sand trap, right in the middle of what was supposedly a road. It took a large group of dune buggy maniacs to rescue us. They shrugged off our experience as just another typical Baja driving incident.

So what can you expect? If you're driving anything—car, truck, motor home or motorcycle—that isn't designed or modified for very tough off-road travel, you won't have any trouble in Baja *as long as you stay on the highway and paved arterials*. When you're off the pavement, you're in the realm of the Baja 1,000 road race: no road signs, no road maintenance and, sometimes, no road at all. It's sand pits, sharp rocks, unbelievably steep grades, washouts, slides, teeth-cracking ruts, blow-outs, breakdowns and uncertain supplies of gas, water and food. In other words, it's a four-wheel-drive Disneyland, the mecca of untold thousands of drivers eager to challenge themselves and their vehicles against something more exciting than a logging road or the local gravel pit.

Anyone contemplating more than a few miles on one of Baja's typical back roads should consult one of the excellent information sources described in the *For More Information* chapter at the end of this book. Getting well into the boondocks can be an exciting adventure, but the hazards are very real. More than one motorist has lost it all, from their supposedly tough truck to their lives, by not making adequate preparations and observing the necessary precautions.

The greatest hazard on the Transpeninsular Highway is driving too fast. Slow down! Once you've driven this highway for a few miles you'll appreciate this warning: the road is two narrow lanes, with poorly banked curves and few, if any, shoulders. Cattle wander across it without restriction and at night livestock and wild animals are constant hazards. In the clear desert air the glare from oncoming headlights is intense, and because of the restricted passing room and abrupt shoulders, close calls are inevitable.

Drive cautiously and don't drive at night. There are too many drivers from southern California, determined to relive the thrills of the Baja 1,000, with a few cases of beer on the back seat and three days off work.

Whenever it rains in Baja you can expect a very quick accumulation of run-off to cross the highway. There are many *vados* (dips), most marked with depth sticks. Check these carefully if water is running and when in doubt about driving through, don't. The water drops as quickly as it rises and a few minutes can make the difference between flooding your car or a safe crossing. These *vados* are also very hazardous to vehicles traveling at high speeds; they'll put you into orbit like a downhill ski jump.

Gasoline is available along the main highway and unless you go into the back country, the days of strapping several five-gallon cans to the bumpers are long past. A gas can is always a good idea, however, if only to help out the person who forgot theirs and to tide you over during random shortages.

A jug of water should always be carried, both for the radiator and for drinking. Driving in the summertime is very hot; many people recommend driving only in the morning and evening.

Car repairs can be a problem, especially if you need parts. Parts and repairs are available in La Paz, but in smaller towns you'll have to rely mostly on the mechanic's ingenuity and luck. When in doubt, carry spares. If you're driving a vehicle that can't be repaired in Baja without special tools or parts, it's best to make some arrangement with a friend to ship you whatever is needed in case of a serious breakdown.

There is regular Green Angel service along the main highway and other tourists are particularly helpful. The tradition of mutual aid continues to be a part of travel in Baja.

Buses, Hitching, Planes and Ferries

Regular first-class bus service is available along the entire length of the Transpeninsular Highway, though only a few buses run each way. The trip from Tijuana to La Paz takes just under twenty-four hours. It is a fast, easy ride and quite cheap.

Off the main road, bus service is irregular to nonexistent; most small towns and villages rely on cabs and cooperative sharing of expenses for a private vehicle to get back and forth.

Hitching isn't difficult on the main roads, but back roads are another story entirely. I met a European hitchhiker who claimed to have spent three days traveling a hundred-mile stretch of deserted desert road, including walking almost half of it. This sounds reasonable, especially when you consider that on some roads, the passing of a vehicle is so unusual that it almost rates a commemorative celebration.

Don't count on getting a ride *out* if someone has offered to give you one *in*. We met another optimistic hitcher who got to the end of the line, took one long look and decided to go somewhere else. There was just one problem: he was at the end of the road and there was no traffic. Fortunately, the rancher who had given him a lift had extra chores that needed doing; a week later, the rancher drove out and was able to take the hitchhiker with him.

The hazards of hitching in arid and hot regions can't be stressed enough. Baja is not the place to get stranded or lost in. Be careful. (See *Getting Around: Hitching.*)

For many years private planes were the most practical means of transportation in Baja and they still serve a great many areas. Ranchers use them to fly in equipment or to visit the dentist, and tourists like to drop out of the sky for a quick weekend of sport fishing and margarita guzzling.

Regularly scheduled flights to La Paz, Loreto and Los Cabos from many points in the U.S. and Mexico are available. Check with a travel agent to see if bargain fares are being offered. A travel agent should also be able to tell you about flights to other towns. Many resorts in Baja offer package deals in conjunction with airlines. (See *Traveling in Mexico: Travel Packages.*)

Ferry service between Baja and mainland Mexico is quite good. They carry everything from walk-on passengers to semi trucks and passenger buses. (See *Getting Around: Ferries.*)

Money

Exchange your money at a bank; few business establishments, especially those regularly dealing with tourists, will give a good exchange rate. Because banks are few and far between, I always carry more cash than I normally would. When you get away from the main road or towns, small change will be difficult to find, so break large bills at the bank or in stores. (See suggestions on concealing money and valuable papers in *Packing Up*.)

American dollars are widely accepted by businesses in Baja, but coins and bills larger than twenties may be refused.

Shopping

Food is more expensive in Baja than on the mainland. Much of the fresh food is imported from the mainland, and canned and dry goods often come from California. Local fruits and vegetables are available in season, but the supply is far below the demand. The wonderful market places of Mexico are not found on the peninsula, though La Paz and San José del Cabo have small ones. Bartering is almost unknown.

American-style *supermercados* are located in Guerrero Negro, La Paz and Cabo San Lucas.

Grocery stores are found in small towns and many now have a CONASUPO outlet (see *Markets and Stores: CONASUPO*), though it may be inside a movable trailer and not a permanent building. The concept of traveling stores is not new to Baja; many of the isolated *ranchos* and villages still rely on a pickup truck (or boat) that follows a regular route. These people also sell to tourists, especially in popular camping areas. They offer everything from cabbages to canned beer and may also double as mail carriers and buyers for homemade cheese (a specialty in some parts), homegrown produce and fresh and dried fish.

La Paz is the commercial center of the lower peninsula and if you need something, whether it's a souvenir (almost all are from the mainland) or a fishing lure, your best chance to find it will be there. Even then, however, you may be out of luck; it is basically a small town, in spite of tourism.

Camping, Fishing and Diving

Even the thought of camping in Baja gives me an almost uncontrollable urge to drop this computer and head for a deserted beach, to sit in the sand for a few weeks and watch the pelicans and man-o'-war birds enjoying one of the greatest seafood smorgasbords on earth.

Baja offers everything from mountain trout fishing and hiking in the north to fantastic deep-sea fishing and beach lounging in the south. In between, there's shell collecting, exploring, rock climbing, whale watching and hot spring stewing, not to mention bird watching, boating, some surfing, hunting and general goofing off.

The abundance and variety of life in the Sea of Cortez has long been the object of slack-jawed awe by anyone who has fished or gone diving there. It is certainly no exaggeration; once you've stood on a beach, watching schools of game fish beating the water to a froth just a few feet in front of you, the attraction of Baja becomes a compulsion. This profusion of life, however, has its limits. For example, the *totuava*, a gigantic type of sea bass that formerly delighted anglers, is now virtually fished out.

Baja seems to inspire waste in a certain type of person, whether it's a commercial fisherman who keeps only the best of the catch and throws the rest to the sharks or a gringo who can't resist just one more hour of fishing, though half of the fish hooked may be injured or die. "I threw 'em back" doesn't mean much if they go straight to the bottom for the crabs to feed on.

Baja is vulnerable to the depredations of the tourist; clams are already disappearing in many popular camping beaches. Unless self-restraint is practiced, the problem of overfishing won't be solved until there is no fishing left at all.

Red Tape

A tourist card is not required for those visiting the border zone, but anyone traveling south must have one. The immigration checkpoint is just north of Ensenada, near the fish market. You shouldn't have any trouble spotting it.

Permits for your car and other vehicles are not required unless you intend to cross over to the mainland. These permits are issued at the border or in La Paz. Ask for directions; it's a small town and the government office is easy to locate. (For more details see *Red Tape and the Law: Car Permits* and *Getting Around: Ferries*.)

COPPER CANYON

Climate • Food • Accommodations • Train • Buses and hitching • Money • Hiking: guides, exploring essentials, maps and directions • The Tarahumara • Suggested itineraries

"There are places that have great strength for one that knows how to understand and feel. They are places of unique power that comes out of the depths of the earth. It can be a place apart, somewhere in the fields, in the mountains, surrounded by rocks or boulders, at the entrance of a cave, at the high summit or at the rim of a canyon. . . ."

—Romayne Wheeler, *Life Through the Eyes of a Tarahumara*

As a writer, traveler and incurable romantic, I have a special affection for northwestern Mexico and the state of Chihuahua, especially that portion of the Sierra Madre known as the Copper Canyon. Like many other daydreamers and do-it-yourself adventurers, I feel an irresistible attraction to this "Last Frontier" of canyons, mesas and vast, forested *sierras*. With genuine *vaqueros* and Tarahumara Indians at virtually every

bend, not to mention ancient Spanish missions and lost silver mines, what more could a restless middle-aged boy ask for?

Although it lies just a few hundred miles south of the U.S. border, the *Barranca del Cobre* gets only superficial attention from tourists and travel writers. The reasons for this oversight are largely practical: for all of its attractions, travel here has never been easy. An early, bone-weary writer aptly described the rugged *barrancas* when he said, "Inaccessibility was the principal feature of the country."

A hundred years later, there are still only two convenient ways to penetrate these forbidding *sierras*: via the spectacular train route from Los Mochis to Chihuahua City or over the serpentine *Gran Vision* (Great View) highway. There are many tortuous, tire-busting Jeep roads, and thousands of miles of trails passable only on foot or by saddle animal. In true Old West fashion, trains of pack mules haul food, passengers and freight between isolated villages and *ranchos*. Burros heavily outnumber tour buses and though you'll see a few satellite dishes beside log cabins, turn-of-the-century customs and conditions still prevail.

Every writer who visits the "titanic mountains" of the Sierra Madre brags that the Copper Canyon is several times larger and even deeper than the Grand Canyon of Arizona. However impressive this may be, statistics can't convey the face-to-face impact of the *barranca*. Once you've peered into a mile-deep gorge, it is easy to appreciate why descriptions of the Copper Canyon sometimes teeter on the edge of hysteria. An early Mexican historian complained that, "Upon frequently ascending and descending steep and sudden slopes, in which each step of the mule all but suspends one over the abyss, one sees the imminent risk of falling and smashing into a thousand pieces. One cannot believe that this can be called a 'trail' and that it leads to a place inhabited by civilized people."

In fairness to Arizona's magnificent but solitary "Big Ditch," the area popularly known as the Copper Canyon is actually made up of several major canyons, including the huge Sinforosa, Urique, Batopilas and Copper Canyons. This system of canyonlands is a territory the size of one of our western states, easily large enough to be called a *country* of grand canyons. It is also one of the earth's richest and most diverse ecosystems, with pine and oak forests, rivers, mountain ranges and remote plateaus. Add a widely scattered population of Tarahumara Indians, prospectors and Mexican ranch families to a delightful range of climate zones and you've got . . . paradise?

Climate

One of western Chihuahua's greatest attractions is the dramatic variety of its climate. Many tourists are pleasantly surprised to find that the Sierra Madre is definitely not a desert. In fact, you can expect occasional rain in both summer and winter. Hikers should be prepared for sudden temperature and weather changes. If it rains heavily, rivers will rise as much as twenty feet in a very short time.

Summer in the Sierra will be moderately warm and quite pleasant. Starting in late autumn and continuing through Easter, nighttime temperatures in the pine-and-oak highlands around Creel (the *tierra fria* or "cold country") often dip below freezing. Snow is not uncommon during the coldest months. (The snow melts quickly, but you'll welcome a hat, gloves and warm clothes.)

To beat the chill, simply go down into the canyons. Snow can blanket the high forests while a few miles away—and *down*—orange groves bloom in the canyon bottoms. Follow the age-old wisdom of the Tarahumara, who use the region's abrupt topography to their advantage by moving to the high country in summer and into the warm canyons in winter.

Later, from early May through October, the sun will turn the narrow canyons into solar ovens. This is the cue for the Tarahumara—and savvy tourists—to move upward again into the agreeably fresh and cool highlands.

Food

The Sierra Madre menu features "cowboy cuisine" and not much else. Typical *norteño* fare runs heavily to beef, beans, cheese, potatoes, eggs, tortillas and *estofado* (hash). If you're desperate for a burger, you'll find relief in Creel and even Batopilas. Vegetarians should pack a lot of snacks.

Accommodations

There are comfortable lodges and well-established tourist hotels in and around Cerocahui, Batopilas, Divisadero and Creel, but in the rest of the Sierra, accommodations tend to be Spartan and low budget. Hotels vary in value, so don't be shy about inspecting the room or looking for something better. Typical rooms will be clean but very plain. Expect lumpy mattresses, stiff blankets, cement bag pillows and a single light bulb too weak for bedtime reading. The bath—or outhouse—will probably be shared. Experience the delights of travel in the nineteenth century!

The most interesting accommodations are found in various lodges. These range from pleasantly rustic log cabins to a lavishly restored Victorian-era *hacienda* in Batopilas. They aren't cheap, but considering the high overhead in this region, most lodges give fair value. Lodge rates often drop during the summer off-season.

Train

James Russell, editor of *Rail Travel News*, rated the Copper Canyon as North America's "most scenic train ride" in the January/February 1995 issue of *EcoTraveler* magazine.

To take advantage of daylight hours and the best canyon views, ride the train from west (Los Mochis) to east (Creel, Chihuahua City). On the other hand, if you do catch the train in Chihuahua City, make every effort to overnight along the way.

Regardless of what your travel agent or guidebook may say, don't expect to find a dining car on the first-class Chihuahua Al Pacifico (Copper Canyon train). In fact, even though you'll probably buy a first-class ticket, don't expect true "first-class" service. Pack a good lunch, as well as drinking water and toilet paper.

The Copper Canyon train is reasonably punctual, but its route is sometimes blocked by rockfalls, landslides, mudflows, avalanches, snow and stubborn cattle. Delays can stretch from several hours to one or even two days. When rain or snow threatens to fall, Lorena always boards the train lugging a huge *lonche* ("lunch" or provisions) and at least three paperback novels.

A tourist quizzed the manager of the Sierra Madre Lodge near Creel about the punctuality of the Copper Canyon train.

"Very often the train arrives exactly on time," the manager stated emphatically. "Exactly, *exactly* on time!

There was a long pause.

"But . . . unfortunately," the manager smiled broadly, "it is sometimes yesterday's train that arrives here exactly on time."

Robbers have sometimes struck the train, mainly during the peak Christmas and Easter seasons. Don't be alarmed if you see heavily armed guards, or even the occasional bullet hole in a window. The risk is low, but if I were lucky enough to have large amounts of cash, I wouldn't carry it on the train, nor would I display expensive cameras or costly jewelry. In the unlikely event of a robbery, be calm, quiet and cooperative. In other words, don't argue; just fork over the loot.

Buses and Hitching

Bus service in the sparsely populated Sierra Madre is adequate, but don't expect frequent service. For example, there are just three weekly buses from Creel to Batopilas. (See *The*

Copper Canyon by Bus in the Itineraries section, below.) Hitching is common, and many drivers expect to be paid for thumbed rides.

Money

U.S. greenbacks (not coins) spend almost as easily in the Copper Canyon as Mexican pesos. I strongly recommend that you bring a good supply of small U.S. bills, especially ones. Observe the Mexican custom of always paying with the largest possible bill and hoarding your change.

Hiking

• **Guides:** Keep in mind that some of the best hiking in the Copper Canyon is within easy reach. You don't have to make "killer" treks to find unforgettable views and fine scenery. For better or worse, an absence of hiking maps and detailed information tends to concentrate visitors on just a few better-known trails. If you'd like to make ambitious treks, explore for rare birds and cave dwellings, or enjoy hidden viewpoints that few outsiders have seen, plan to hire a guide.

One caveat: you'll probably be approached by local guides who drive vans and Chevrolet Suburbans. As friendly, talkative chauffeurs, these men can be quite useful, since some hiking areas are easiest to reach by hired vehicles. As hiking guides, however, most of them are hopeless.

Your best choice is to hire a local wrangler, a Tarahumara farmer or a Mexican *ranchero*. Some of these men are living encyclopedias of Copper Canyon trails and lore.

To find a reliable guide, ask your hotel manager or approach a storekeeper, woodcutter or some mature, well-established person. (In remote country, kids and younger adults are usually tongue-tied or too inexperienced to deal with total strangers. This is especially true of the Tarahumara.)

Another alternative is to join an organized trek led by an outfitter. Given that all you're expected to do is carry a daypack and gush enthusiastically over the views and refried beans, this is a tempting way to go. (For more information on van- and burro-assisted treks into the Copper Canyon, contact The People's Guide Experience™ at 612 Bellevue Way N.E., Suite 219, Bellevue, WA 98004; telephone: 425-455-1996; fax: 425-455-1980; or e-mail: solsierra@dbug.org)

Compared to well-documented trails in the U.S., the responsibility and uncertainty associated with planning a hike in the Sierra Madre can be intimidating. Remember, however, that in the Copper Canyon both the "burden" and the genuine joy of discovery still await you. When in doubt, consider that old muleskinner's saying, "You have to go to get there!"

• **Exploring essentials:** Get the best boots and hiking socks you can afford—I'm convinced that the cost is more than compensated by dramatic improvements in traction, support and comfort. Most trails are rough, with loose rocks, scree and crumbly volcanic tuff, or slippery with pine needles and oak leaves. Sport sandals and running shoes are simply not adequate for canyon trails.

Bring several one-quart canteens or equivalent water sacks, water purification filters or chemicals, baseball cap and/or sombrero, sunscreen and inflatable pillow.

In terms of clothing, err on the side of warmth, especially if you'll be traveling between November and April. Take a set of long underwear and plan on layering. When I'm knocking around the Sierra Madre highlands, I carry a light, highly compactable down-filled sleeping bag and vest, a warm cap and a pair of gloves. Many bitter nights in caves, cabins, train depots and unheated hotel rooms have taught me that a sleeping bag is my best chance for a warm snooze. (A hot water bottle is also a great way to thaw your feet and ease the ache of tense, tired muscles.)

Take light rain gear—the summer rainy season is June to October but I've experienced one- to three-day showery periods in virtually every "dry" month, with the possible exception of May.

• **Maps and directions:** Thousands of miles of unmarked trails make a mockery of both maps and "dead reckoning." I use topos but I also count on local advice, guides and good luck to lead me from one point to another. In addition, I carry a simple compass for seat-of-the-pants orienting and an expensive Swiss altimeter to satisfy my morbid curiosity about gains and losses in trail elevation.

To find your way, you'll need basic Spanish phrases, a dictionary and sign language. Away from town, asking for directions is best described as *"problemático."* Many of the people you'll meet on the trail are bashful, Rarámuri-speaking Tarahumara. Smile, say *"Kwirá!"* ("Hello") and then try sign language.

• **The Tarahumara:** Although this country is very sparsely inhabited, you'll occasionally encounter the Tarahumara, especially while hiking. It is important to understand that many Tarahumara are so shy that they prefer not to talk to strangers. When meeting on the trail, for example, it is not unusual for Tarahumara women and children to slip away or to firmly turn their backs and refuse to speak. Never impose by taking photographs or approaching occupied dwelling caves and cabins without invitation.

In places where tourists are more common, Tarahumara women may offer beautifully woven baskets, dolls, drums and other small handicrafts for purchase. I encourage you to buy from them, as it provides their families with a small but very important cash income. By the way, *bartering is not a Tarahumara custom.*

• **Beggars:** Nothing unsettles a tourist like the outstretched hand of a beggar. Unfortunately, tourists often encourage children and even adults to beg by distributing treats, money and small novelties. This problem is now appearing in the Copper Canyon, where begging was virtually unknown. (Begging should not be confused with the Tarahumara custom of *korima*, neighborly sharing with those in need.) (See *¡Viva Mexico!: Beggars and Con Artists.*)

If you'd like to help people, donations left with the Jesuit Mission Store, next to the bank in Creel, help support Tarahumara schools and health clinics in the region. Money, medicines and basic school supplies are especially useful. (Don't bring clothing; the Tarahumara are swamped with castoffs.)

Suggested Itineraries

Planning a trip into the Sierra Madre is complicated by a lack of "infrastructure" and a dearth of reliable information. I've listed three itinerary options below, followed by a more detailed, place-by-place description. Whichever itinerary you follow, do your best to make at least one side trip by bus or hired vehicle to the deeper canyon bottoms at Batopilas (from Creel) or Urique (from Bahuichivo). The roads to these ancient mining villages provide views that rival and even surpass those seen from the train.

1. The Copper Canyon train: Take the train across the Sierra Madre, preferably from west to east, that is, from Los Mochis to Chihuahua, overnighting and making side trips along the way. This is the route taken by at least ninety percent of the visitors to the Sierra Madre. Fly or bus to Los Mochis and spend the night before the train trip.

Catch the early morning train at either Los Mochis or nearby El Fuerte—train to Bahuichivo and side-trip to Cerocahui and Urique—continue by train from Bahuichivo to Divisadero and Creel—hiking, biking and side trips to Cusarare, Arareco, Sisoguichic and Batopilas—train or bus to Chihuahua for local sightseeing. Bus or fly to El Paso and home.

2. The Copper Canyon loop: Start in El Paso and bus or drive to Chihuahua City. From Chihuahua, continue on by train (or bus) to Creel, a small mountain town ideally situated for side trips on foot and mountain bike. Local van tours are also available, so plan on spending at least one or two days here. From Creel continue west to Los Mochis (no bus; you must take the train). Spend one or two nights in El Fuerte (near Los Mochis) and then return on the train to Creel.

To return to El Paso, Texas, take the "back door" (by car or bus) from Creel to Madera (good hiking and the Cuarenta Casas archaeological site), and on to Nuevo Casas Grandes and Paquime (ruins and museum). If you like fine pottery, take local gravel roads to the village of Mata Ortiz (highly recommended). Then back to El Paso.

• A smaller loop variation: Drive or bus from Chihuahua City to Ciudad Cuauhtemoc, and from there to La Junta and Basaseachic Falls National Park. Continue north on Highway 16 to Madera, Casas Grandes, Janos and Ciudad Juárez— or, double-back to the east on Mex 10 to El Sueco, and from there go south again to Chihuahua City on Mex 45.

By the way, with the exception of the train trip from Creel to Los Mochis these loops follow good secondary roads and are easily done in a rental car.

• The Copper Canyon by bus: Many people don't realize just how easy and inexpensive a trip into the Sierra Madre can be if you take the bus. Start by taking a cross-border Greyhound bus from El Paso, Texas, directly to the huge terminal in Juárez, Mexico (about an hour).

Before reaching the Juárez terminal, the driver's assistant may offer to radio ahead and reserve a seat for you on the first available bus to Chihuahua. He will make the reservation and even issue the ticket, at no additional charge. This is very convenient; I usually step off the cross-border bus and onto a departing Chihuahua-bound bus (about five hours) without even entering the terminal.

The bus to Chihuahua City from Juárez stops for a baggage and immigration inspection about fifteen miles south of the border. Tell the driver you need a tourist card—it shouldn't take more than a few minutes to run inside to the Migración office. (A tourist card is absolutely required to visit Mexico beyond the border zone, so be sure you get one.) If there's a delay or the driver is impatient, he may leave you here and let you catch the next bus after you've gotten your tourist card. This is fine, but keep your ticket handy and be sure to take your baggage off the bus.

In Chihuahua's splendid *terminal de autobuses*, look for Estrella Blanca, the only bus line to Creel (four to five hours). If you're not in a hurry, there's also a daily 7 a.m. train from Chihuahua to Creel and Los Mochis.

3. Drive to Creel from Hermosillo: Passenger cars regularly travel these isolated but decent secondary roads. Once you get to Creel, do a round trip (with stopovers) on the train to Mochis or follow the Gran Vision highway south all the way to Parral. By the time you read this, there'll probably be a paved connection from Parral to the Pacific coast near Culiacan.

4. Only for the stout-of-heart: An unmarked four-wheel-drive route goes from Los Alamos, Sonora, all the way to Bahuichivo and Creel. The directions are very complicated. Please visit our website at <http://www.peoplesguide.com/mexico> for further details.

• **Los Mochis and El Fuerte:** The western terminus of the Chihuahua Al Pacifco (Copper Canyon train) is in Los Mochis, a busy city with a good market and seafood restaurants. We much prefer to board the train (and overnight) in the small, authentically colonial village of El Fuerte, about an hour east. If you do stay in Los Mochis, Lorena insists that you check out her namesake, the Hotel Lorena, a three-star alternative to the usual tourist places, that is well regarded by many travelers.

• **Bahuichivo:** The train is met by the Urique bus and shuttles from Cerocahui. The village has both an expensive lodge and cheap, unheated rooms, but I'd check out the Paraíso del Oso, a family-style eco-lodge and campground in beautiful surroundings near Cerocahui. The owner encourages independent hiking and camping, and doesn't disdain visitors on a budget.

• **Urique:** A couple of hours beyond Cerocahui by bus, the village lies at the bottom of the Urique Canyon, beside the Urique River. (If you suffer motion sickness, consider medication for this serpentine descent.)
There are several Spartan hotels and one good campground, known simply as "Tom's" or "Lo de Tomás." Owned by two Americans, this is the place to find peace and quiet (the village is noisy) as well as information on hiking and trail conditions. Plan on spending a couple of full days and two or three nights around Urique.

• **Divisadero** loosely means "overlook." For nearly all of the Copper Canyon's visitors, this brief, twenty-minute train stopover is the main point of their trip. The views are high and so, comparatively speaking, are the rates for lodging here. Still, if you're going to splurge, a room on the canyon rim is the place to do it.
Directions for a very steep, "killer" hike from Divisadero *down* into the canyon can be found locally.

• **Creel:** This dusty rail and logging town of about 4,000 inhabitants is re-styling itself into a regional tourist center and Copper Canyon "gateway." Creel's small shops, budget hotels and ho-hum restaurants make a good base for explorations into several outlying canyons and interesting highland communities. Three places are particularly noteworthy: the Tarahumara-owned and -operated eco-reserve of Arareco (San Ignacio), with its lake, campground and amazing rock formations; the mission and waterfall at Cusárare; and Batopilas.

• **Batopilas** is a small, colonial-era mining town wedged into the bottom of the precipitous Batopilas Canyon. Hire a van or catch the three-times-a-week "Dramamine Express" bus from Creel. There are several modest hotels and the upscale, outrageously decorated Riverside Lodge.
Several of the trails out of Batopilas go up, up, *up* to distant mesas and remote ranches. Trails to the west and south can lead to opium and marijuana patches. For

your safety and peace of mind, I strongly advise that you take a reliable local guide. (Three excellent choices are Juan Cruz, Manuelito Gil and Trinidad Rodriguez.)

• **Chihuahua City:** Chihuahua is an attractive city, with an upbeat, friendly atmosphere that deserves more of a look than most people give it. I suggest a walking and taxi tour that takes in the city's market, museums and historical sites. Stroll the open-air pedestrian mall (across from the cathedral), visit the Cultural Institute, and shop for saddles, quirts, chaps, sombreros and pointy-toed boots—this is serious cowboy country so the selection is incredible. The city also has some very tempting bakeries.

If you're headed into the Sierra Madre, take a few minutes to exchange U.S. dollars or traveler's checks into Mexican pesos at one of the convenient banks or *casas de cambio* (money exchange shops) in the downtown area.

• **Other places of interest: Basihuare** (on the way to Batopilas), the historic Jesuit center of **Sisoguichic**, and the area around **Divisadero** all have excellent scenery and potential for great hiking (but virtually no hikers). **San Rafael** and **Temoris**, both on the train route to Los Mochis, see very few visitors and would also be interesting places to lay over for a day or more.

PACIFIC BEACHES

Climate zones • *"Resort Mexico"* • *Itinerary suggestions: Mazatlán, Puerto Vallarta to Manzanillo, Michoacán, Ixtapa-Zihuatanejo, Acapulco, Puerto Escondido*

Lorena affirms that "every good trip to Mexico begins or ends at the beach . . . and the best trips do both!" You don't need a crystal ball to predict that Mexico's Pacific beaches will one day be recognized as the world's finest "riviera." Development of such prime beachfront real estate is inevitable, yet whenever I'm dismayed by the destruction that "progress" has wreaked, I remind myself that Acapulco, Puerto Vallarta and other resorts are still just minor intrusions on this fabulous 2,000-plus-mile coastline. With everything from palm-lined beaches, tropical sunsets and off-beat fishing villages to bargain prices, easy access and excellent weather, it is small wonder that travelers easily confuse Mexico's Pacific coast with nirvana.

Climate Zones

One of the Pacific coast's main attractions is its relatively stable climate, especially during the winter-spring "high" travel season. For all of the hype about Cancún's "eternal spring," you'll actually find that the Pacific coast (especially southward from Manzanillo) has the country's most dependable warm weather.

To help refine your search for the perfect beach, I divide the Pacific coast into three climate zones:

1. South from tiny Puerto Peñasco to Mazatlán you're actually on the Sea of Cortez, not the Pacific Ocean. As in Baja, the climate here is extremely dry and desert-like. The blazing heat of summer tends to moderate by late October. In winter, air temperatures will be pleasantly warm during the day and surprisingly cool at night. I love this weather but the sea can be distinctly chilly for swimming and snorkeling.

2. Mazatlán to Manzanillo: In my opinion, the coastal "midriff" has Mexico's finest winter weather—in the high 70s and 80s during the day, cooling to the high 50s and 60s at night. Though occasional storms may pass through during January and

February, a comfortably temperate pattern dominates from November through May. If you're looking for a jungle experience, it is worth noting that the coastal forests between Mazatlán and Puerto Vallarta are much greener and lusher than those from Puerto Vallarta to the south.

3. Ixtapa-Zihuatanejo to Tapachula: Definitely warmer and more humid than the midriff. If you're a serious beach lizard and want to spend your winter peeled down to a bathing suit or shorts, look no further. By May and June, the heat packs a wallop but the swimming is ideal.

Considering that millions of tourists flock to Mexico's resorts every year, it is remarkable that much of the Pacific coast still remains off the beaten track. Travelers who are willing to explore side roads can find relatively unspoiled villages, natural reserves and little-known beaches. With the completion of Mex 15 down the coast of Michoacán, the entire west coast is now accessible to RVs and campers. In fact, this coast shelters innumerable small winter colonies of RVers, fishermen, divers and expatriate beachcombers.

"Resort Mexico"

We often meet travelers who bitterly scorn the idea of visiting "tourist traps" such as Mazatlán, Puerto Vallarta or Acapulco. They are usually shocked to learn that we don't boycott resorts or consider them beneath the interest of hard-core Mexico lovers like ourselves. Although I might hope that bulldozers will one day reverse their course and restore the beaches of Cancún and Mazatlán to their original pristine condition, I'm not holding my breath. The secret is to pick and choose, *very carefully*, the best that these

resorts have to offer—and when you've had your fill of shrimp pizza, souvenir malls and condo touts, get out of town, *fast.*

Itinerary Suggestions

I can think of no easier itinerary than a Grand Beach Crawl along Mexico's Pacific coast. Simply start at the north end, at Puerto Peñasco, and continue south to Puerto Madero, near the Guatemalan border. Follow every side road you come to until it reaches a beach. A thorough exploration will keep you occupied for at least two or three years. This itinerary may sound a little simple, but if you give it a try, I think you'll be hooked.

Travelers descending the northwest coast of Mexico by car or bus will find that Highway 15 follows a narrow lowland corridor, closely bounded on the east by the deeply eroded Sierra Madre. Although this was once a grueling ordeal of speeding trucks and killer potholes, Mex 15 is now quite good, with many stretches of divided highway and high speed tollways. Because it is relatively flat, with few mountain curves, this drive is reassuringly tame and easy.

Mazatlán: Reaching the Pacific coast from eastern and central Mexico isn't quite so simple. The early Spanish explorers didn't name these mountains the "Mother Range" for nothing. Only a few paved highways cross the Sierra Madre: the northernmost and also most challenging is Highway 40 from Durango to Mazatlán, a brake-scorching series of hairpin curves, switchbacks and steep grades that most drivers prefer to avoid. I've done this route in vans, but only confident drivers with excellent brakes should attempt Highway 40 in large RV rigs. Get an early start and plan on spending most of the day behind the wheel. If you're taking the bus, sit near the front and consider taking Dramamine.

Puerto Vallarta to Manzanillo: Most travelers from central and eastern Mexico cross the Sierra Madre to the Pacific coast via Guadalajara. You have three major route options from "Guad": to Barra de Navidad, Tepic or Colima. In fact, for a wonderful loop itinerary that begins and ends in Guadalajara, try this: Guadalajara–Tepic–Puerto Vallarta–Barra de Navidad–Manzanillo–Colima–Guadalajara. Better yet, extend the beach portion even further south: from Manzanillo–Tecoman–Playa Azul–go east on Mex 37 to Uruapan–Pátzcuaro–Morelia–and back to Guadalajara (or Mexico City). This trip can easily be made by bus and takes in some of Mexico's best beaches and Spanish colonial highlands.

• **Michoacán:** The final link in Mexico's long awaited completion of the Pacific coast highway was the rugged stretch between Tecomán and Playa Azul (about 110 miles), in the state of Michoacán. There is still relatively little traffic here and very limited tourist facilities. Don't expect to find much other than mountains, canyons, small *ranchos* and mile after mile of undiscovered beaches.

In addition to spectacular views and roller coaster curves, the mountainous western slope of Michoacán is known for its marijuana and opium plantations. From this area southward, all the way through Guerrero and into Oaxaca, expect to find highway checkpoints, with soldiers and federal agents looking for drugs and firearms.

You may also hear that this is "bandit country." Although we've found the people of this coast to be generally friendly and hospitable, they can be shy and even wary of strangers. Historically, these people have often been in conflict with the government, big landowners and repressive law enforcement agencies. My advice, in a nutshell, is to avoid drunks and drinking scenes, stay away from drugs, be civil to the soldiers and move along quickly should things feel weird.

One additional point: You may be offered small, tempting treasures along this coast. It is strictly prohibited to buy or possess genuine artifacts and archaeological pieces in Mexico. Protect yourself from serious trouble by politely refusing such offers.

• **Ixtapa-Zihuatanejo:** Ixtapa is a high-rise beach resort that caters almost exclusively to well-heeled tourists. The nearby town of Zihuatanejo is much less expensive and far more attractive. Zihuatanejo has a good selection of budget and moderately priced hotels, restaurants, shopping and nightlife. "Zihua," or "Zee," also has the best swimming beaches, diving and shopping.

After negotiating the rugged coast of Michoacán, the drive from Zihuatanejo to Acapulco, Guerrero (150 miles, expect police checkpoints) seems downright straight and level, with only occasional hills. There is good beach access, but most of the coastline is exposed to the full force of the Pacific. Swimming can be very hazardous. We're more attracted to several extensive lagoon and estuary systems, with excellent birding, boating and fishing.

• **Acapulco:** This is Mexico's oldest beach resort. I'm no fan of crowds but I enjoy an occasional dose of Acapulco's old section, with its odorous public market, moldering cheap hotels and bustling seafood restaurants. Tourist resort it may be, but for a writer in a seedy, tropical frame of mind, Acapulco offers local color and character to spare.

Warning: Swimming at Pie de la Cuesta is definitely not recommended. Many people have drowned or been seriously injured by this beach's notoriously powerful waves. Even strong swimmers can be viciously battered by crashing surf. No matter how tempting the sea may look, especially after a couple of margaritas, don't take the plunge.

Highway 200 from Acapulco to Puerto Escondido follows the Costa Chica (the "Little Coast") for about 250 miles, past tropical lagoons and soaring mountains, with rare glimpses of empty beaches. You'll find lush vegetation, small villages, unmarked side roads and very few tourist services. This is a straightforward trip with the usual Army checkpoints. Adventurous travelers will enjoy endless possibilities for exploring the real, sometimes "nitty gritty" side of Mexico.

• **Puerto Escondido, Oaxaca:** In the late Sixties and early Seventies, this classic "sleepy Mexican fishing village" became known as an end-of-the-road refuge for wave-crazed surfers and longhaired travelers. Considering the quality of its beaches, it is hardly surprising that Puerto Escondido sprouted hotels, discos, T-shirt shops and even a small international airport. Puerto Escondido is still small enough, however, to be considered "offbeat" by most travelers.

Leaving Puerto Escondido you face a difficult choice: to continue south along the beach or turn inland, into the mountainous interior of Oaxaca.

1. If you continue south on Highway 200, you'll soon reach the turnoff to laid-back Puerto Angel and Huatulco. The heavily hyped resort of Huatulco was planned as an ecologically sensitive version of Cancún. Although the project has so far failed to live up to its banker's expectations, Huatulco's natural beauty and consistently warm climate should eventually prevail. Continuing south, you'll pass by Salina Cruz, Tehuantepec, Tuxtla Gutiérrez, Chiapas and eventually **San Cristóbal de las Casas, Chiapas**. From Salina Cruz to Tuxtla Gutiérrez is a long haul through low, humid country best known for its fierce "Tehuantepecker" winds. (This is a fast route to Chiapas and Guatemala, however, so if you decide to continue southward, turn to the Oaxaca and Chiapas itinerary, below, for more details.)

2. Turn east at Pochutla (near Puerto Angel) and take very mountainous Mex 175 into the cloud forest and highlands of the Sierra Madre, and eventually to **Oaxaca**

City. The road trip from Pochutla to Oaxaca covers just 147 miles, but it follows one of the country's slowest, most scenic highways. From humid, tropical *tierra caliente* (hot country) the highway ascends through banana and coffee plantations, past tree ferns, waterfalls and near-vertical cornfields to moss-draped cloud forests of pine and oak at about 10,000 feet. The highlands are also the home of magic mushrooms and several interesting but reclusive Indian groups. Since making an unforgettable two-week trek through these mountains, we call them "Poor Man's Nepal." Other than a few seasonal washouts, the road is paved but also quite narrow. The mountainous portion—about seventy-five miles—has so many tight curves, steep grades and switchbacks that I allow a full day to reach Oaxaca City.

3. Your third option is to save a lot of time and avoid car sickness by **flying from Puerto Escondido to Oaxaca**.

CENTRAL MEXICO: THE COLONIAL HEARTLAND

Climate • Getting around • Accommodations • Getting there: into Central Mexico and Guadalajara • Colonial Loop Itinerary

The central highlands are classic Mexico, with prickly pear cacti, heavily laden burros, red-tiled roofs, narrow cobblestone streets and drowsy afternoon siestas. In addition to Mexico's greatest cities, cathedrals, Aztec ruins, museums, markets and crumbling *haciendas*, the colonial region encompasses hundreds of hot springs, major peaks and national parks, rivers, volcanoes, caves and other natural wonders. It also includes most of Mexico's people and endures the usual stress pains associated with rapid modernization and a growing population. Nonetheless, the majority of its inhabitants are concentrated in large cities and most of the central region still has a pleasantly rustic, rural character.

Climate
Most of the central region is above 5,000 feet elevation, with peaks soaring to more than 18,000 feet. Compared to other regions of Mexico, the weather here is moderate, stable and generally "fine." Temperatures can be quite chilly at higher elevations, of course, but I find the cool winter nights and clear, warm days to be almost ideal. In summer, this is my favorite area of Mexico for rainy-season travel and van camping.

The vast, central highland plateau lies between the rain shadows of Mexico's heavily forested eastern and western *sierras*. As a general rule, conditions are dry or even arid in winter and spring. Of course, there are exceptions to this pattern of low rainfall. For example, Guadalajara and Cuernavaca boast of a moist, semi-tropical climate that produces remarkably abundant vegetation.

Getting Around
All roads in the busy central highlands lead to the DF (Mexico City is simply called "Mexico" or "DF"—Distrito Federal) or Guadalajara. As you would expect, traffic can be heavy on the main roads, especially on weekends. Fortunately, highways are generally good, public transportation is outstanding, and distances and travel times between cities are not great.

Whether you're driving or going by bus, there's no end to possible side trips and interesting back roads. Although the itinerary we suggest can be done in as little as a couple of weeks, your best strategy will be to slow down as much as possible. Find a comfortable place and use it as a base camp for side trips and sightseeing. Even if you

have your own vehicle, rather than driving everywhere, park it in a safe place and give local buses and trains a try.

Accommodations

Accommodations are plentiful, interesting and seldom require a reservation. The rates for two- and three-star hotels are a bargain and are usually competitive with RV parks. Full-service RV parks are scattered here and there, but campers will find that the highlands are dotted with public and private parks, spas, picnic grounds and informal campgrounds.

Getting There

The central highlands cover a broad area and you can easily start our loop itinerary from several points. If you're traveling by air, flights from the U.S. and Canada are usually cheapest to Mexico City and the Pacific beach resorts. You might also use an "open jaws" ticket, landing in one city and then flying out of Mexico from another. The little-known international airport in Leon, Guanajuato, is also a convenient gateway.

From Texas, the quickest overland routes to Mexico City, Guadalajara and the state of Michoacán using federal highways are:

• **El Paso to Mexico City:** Take Mex 45 to Jimenez, then Mex 49 to Torreon and Fresnillo. At Fresnillo, Mex 49 becomes Mex 45 again—take it to Zacatecas, where it changes back to Mex 49. Follow Mex 49 to San Luis Potosi, and Mex 57 all the way to Mexico City.

• **El Paso to Guadalajara:** Follow the route above to Zacatecas, then take Mex 54 straight to Guadalajara.

• **El Paso to Morelia, Michoacán:** Again, from Zacatecas, take Mex 49 toward San Luis Potosi. About twenty-one miles east of Zacatecas, turn south on Mex 45 to Aguascalientes, Lagos de Moreno and Salamanca. At Salamanca, take Mex 43 to Morelia via Yuriria, Moroleon and Cuitzeo.

• **Eastern Texas to Mexico City:** Use Mex 57 via Monterrey. The shortcut to Guadalajara via Saltillo and Zacatecas on Mex 54 also takes you to the Pacific coast or the state of Michoacán.

The Pacific coast route **into central Mexico and Guadalajara** offers several options. (Also see the *Pacific Beaches Suggested Itinerary*, above.) From north to south, these are:

• **Tepic to Guadalajara:** The old stretch of Mex 15 has badly congested traffic and a particularly slow canyon crossing. Never attempt this drive at night; there are just too many *macho* truckers and unmarked road hazards. Fortunately, a toll road now bypasses the infamous *"Barranca del Muerto."*

• **San Patricio/Melaque to Guadalajara:** Mex 80 is the most popular route between Guadalajara and the Pacific beaches. The road is quite curvy and traffic tends to be thick and fast. We avoid this highway on weekends.

• **There are scenic, less traveled "back door" routes** from the Pacific coast via Colima and another through Playa Azul. We usually take one of these highways; traffic is lighter and gasoline is available. A modern toll road also runs from Manzanillo to Guadalajara.

If the thought of driving through Mexico City gives you the heebie-jeebies, Highway 95 from Acapulco leads to a network of secondary highways that can be used as a western bypass. This is slower and more mountainous than the highways already described, but the route is quite scenic.

Colonial Loop Itinerary

Steve emphasizes that this itinerary can easily be done by bus. Or you could start your trip by bus and then rent a car after you've adjusted to Mexico's free-for-all driving style.

Lorena suggests that if you can't tear yourself away from the beach, flying from Zihuatanejo to Mexico City saves both time and a long bus ride.

The basic itinerary takes about sixteen days at a steady but not breakneck pace. It'll be closer to sixteen weeks, however, if you can't resist the colonial loop's intriguing side trips.

We'll begin our tour with apologies to Guadalajara, Jalisco. Because we believe that the best of Mexico is found in smaller towns and villages rather than big cities, this itinerary skips Guadalajara, the country's second-largest city. If you disagree, it is easy enough to jog this itinerary toward Guadalajara. In case you do . . .

Guadalajara: In comparison to Mexico City's mega-million population, "Guad" is considerably less polluted, hectic and intimidating. Getting around town is also easier, and drivers appreciate that Guadalajara's police force isn't as predatory as the DF's.

Guadalajara and nearby Lake Chapala are home to a huge number of foreign retirees and winter residents, including the world's largest colony of "expat" Americans. The climate is excellent and the city's services are modern and reasonably efficient. Guadalajara has virtually everything you need, including first-run movies, Internet connections and plenty of huge shopping malls. If you're homesick, this is a good place to recharge your gringo batteries.

Day 1—Arrive in Mexico City: In spite of its awesome size and stinging smog, Mexico City is definitely worth two or three days of your time. The Museum of Anthropology is a must-see. I also enjoy exploring the historic zone, the city's downtown core. An intense one-day walking tour can include the Zócalo, cathedral, colonial government buildings, Diego Rivera murals, the newly excavated Templo Mayor and its attached and very impressive archaeological museum. You'll also find an abundance of shops, restaurants and curious sights. You can put if off, but my preference is to explore the DF now, in order to end the trip on a mellower note.

If you arrive by noon, however, and want to go to San Miguel de Allende posthaste, take a cab directly to the northern bus terminal, called the "Terminal del Norte." There are frequent buses, especially if you go second class. The ride to San Miguel takes about four hours.

If you rent a car at the airport ask for maps and instructions on how to find Highway 57D north.

Days 2–4—San Miguel de Allende, Guanajuato: This small town is a National Historic Site, known for its fine colonial architecture, colorful fiestas and international community of artists, writers and retirees. The living can be easy here, even for travelers on a budget.

San Miguel is a great walking town, with many restaurants, galleries and shops. The selection of furniture, pottery, jewelry and *artesanía* (folk arts and crafts) is excellent.

The surrounding countryside is semi-arid, mountainous and sparsely inhabited (elevation 6,130 feet). There is good birding and day hiking in the deep, tree-shaded canyons outside town.

The church in the nearby village of Atotonilco is the center of a penitente cult. If self-flagellation doesn't interest you, there are also several thermal spas. Father Hidalgo started the revolution for independence from Spain with his *grito*, or "cry," for freedom nearby in Dolores Hidalgo. Today, the town is perhaps even more famous for its pottery and wonderful tiles.

Days 5 and 6—San Miguel to Guanajuato: This beautifully preserved colonial silver-mining center is also the capital of the state of Guanajuato. Built in a bowl with steep mountainsides, the city is a fascinating maze of twisted alleys and narrow cobblestone streets. You never know where you are, so just walk aimlessly and enjoy the sights. Some of the streets dip underground and are actually old mine tunnels.

Don't miss the highly photogenic downtown municipal market. At the park-like grounds of the Valenciana mine you can buy crystals, mineral specimens and silver jewelry. Unless you're a hard-core horror movie fan, I'd skip Guanajuato's collection of gruesome, grimacing mummies.

Day 7—Guanajuato to Pátzcuaro, Michoacán: The forested highlands of Michoacán state include some of Mexico's most interesting towns and villages. Although the region is quite mountainous, there is an extensive system of paved highways and graded secondary roads. If you're interested in cooler weather, Tarascan Indian markets, hiking and back road exploring, this is the place.

Catch a bus to Morelia from Guanajuato in the morning and you should be in the state capital of Michoacán in time for lunch. Check out the state-run Casa de las Artesanías, downtown at Humboldt and Fray Juan de San Miguel No. 129, for a great collection of folk art at reasonable prices.

When you're ready to continue on to Pátzcuaro, it's only about an hour from here by bus.

Days 8 and 9—Pátzcuaro: Set near the shore of a beautiful lake, Pátzcuaro is a rather quiet Tarascan market town. Picturesque and inexpensive, Pátzcuaro makes an ideal base for side trips throughout Michoacán. There is good *artesanía* shopping in the market and in surrounding stalls and stores. Steve says, "Check out the *Museo de Artes Populares* (Folk Art Museum) on Calle Lerin."

At an elevation of more than 7,000 feet, Pátzcuaro is usually sunny and warm, but mornings are often frosty in January and February.

Though "touristy," the island village of **Janitzio** in Lake Pátzcuaro is worth a look. The lake village of Tocuaro is known for its mask carvers, and a little farther down the same road, at Erongarícuaro, beautifully carved and painted furniture is made at Centro de Artes Aplicadas Erongarícuaro.

Michoacán side trips: Near Pátzcuaro, there's an interesting pre-Hispanic ruin at **Tzintuzuntzan**, as well as shopping for locally made pottery and small straw figures. To the west, **Santa Clara del Cobre** is an entire village of highly skilled Indian coppersmiths.

Lake Camecuaro is small, crystal clear and unusually beautiful. Several tiny islands in the lake are covered with ancient, twisted cypress trees. Early in the morning, thick, swirling mists create an eerie, otherworldly scene.

Paracho, on Highway 37 to Uruapan, is widely known for its fine handmade guitars and inexpensive musical instruments. The village lies within a mountainous region of volcanoes and forests.

Los Azufres ("The Sulfurs") is perhaps the best known of this state's many thermal springs. Take Highway 15 east from Morelia toward Zitacuaro. Los Azufres is about eleven miles northwest of Ciudad Hidalgo. Look for signs. The road is good but quite steep. (The famous winter reserve for the annual monarch butterfly migration is nearby.)

Several small lakes dot the forested crater of a dormant volcano. This is great country for day hikes and retreats. The elevation is 9,000 feet so be prepared for cold winter nights. Some accommodations are available, but services and supplies are limited. As with most Mexican spas and parks, Los Azufres is almost empty during the week and between holidays.

Day 10—Pátzcuaro to Taxco: If you haven't yet experienced travel by second-class "chicken bus," take one from Pátzcuaro back to Morelia. If you're lucky, there might be a direct bus from Morelia to Taxco. If not, take first-class, direct buses to Toluca and Taxco. This is an all-day trip.

Morelia to Mexico City shortcut (about 170 miles): If you decide to return to Mexico City, your map may not show the scenic *ruta corta* (shortcut) from Morelia. Take Mex 126 to Maravatio and El Oro de Hidalgo. From El Oro, follow Mex 6 to Atlacomulco. It is a straight shot from Atlacomulco to Toluca on Mex 55. Continue by freeway from Toluca to Mexico City or bypass it entirely by using secondary roads west of the city.

Day 11—Taxco: Yet another ancient silver-mining town that is also a national historic monument. Don't get me wrong; although Taxco is definitely "touristy," we always enjoy wandering its steep, cobblestone streets. Shoppers, this is your mother lode for silver jewelry. Taxco is also a good place to find carved wooden Guerrero masks.

Day 12—Taxco to Zihuatanejo: Pack a good lunch; it takes most of a day to reach the beach at Zihuatanejo. You may have to change buses in Acapulco.

Days 13 and 14—Zihuatanejo: You now get your chance for some well-earned beach time. As resort towns go, Zihuatanejo is fairly laid-back. If you find any empty corners in your luggage, Steve warns that the shopping is pretty good. (See *Pacific Beaches*, above.)

Day 15—Zihuatanejo to Mexico City: Allow eight to ten hours to drive or bus to Mexico City.

Day 16—Mexico City and the Museum of Anthropology. (See *Day 1: Mexico City* at the beginning of this itinerary.)

Day 17—Home?

THE GULF COAST

The Forgotten Coast • Special places and points of interest: Jalapa, Veracruz, San Andrés Tuxtla, Lake Catemaco, Villahermosa, Mex 180, Campeche, Edzna, Uxmal

The Forgotten Coast

I call the Gulf of Mexico's long sweeping shore the "Forgotten Coast." Between the border city of Matamoros and the ancient fortresses of Campeche you'll find some 1,500 miles of mostly tourist-free Mexico, including everything from exceptional seafood, beaches, nature reserves and archaeological sites to countless overlooked towns and villages. Only two cities on the entire Gulf—Veracruz and Campeche—can be called tourist attractions and even their following is quite limited. With the exception of bird watchers, treasure divers and fishermen, this amazing arc of beaches, jungles and wetlands sees few visitors. Those who do visit the Gulf seldom stray far from Mex 180, the main highway from southern Texas to the Yucatán Peninsula.

As much as we enjoy the Gulf, it does have its drawbacks. The climate is not only quite wet, but it can also be shockingly cold in winter and steambath-hot in spring and summer. Because it is positioned directly in the path of storms from Canada and the American Midwest, the Gulf's winter weather can be schizophrenic. Delicious periods of warm calm may suddenly turn into harsh winds, chilly temperatures and heavy rains. When moisture-laden *nortes* ("northers") pile up against the nearby Sierra Madre Oriental, one begins to appreciate why this region is nicknamed "Mexico's Holland."

In comparison to the Pacific Riviera and Caribbean coasts of Mexico, the Gulf's low beaches and often slightly turbid waters take a distant third place. By the time you factor in a healthy mosquito population and the inevitable pollution from major offshore oil fields, you might wonder why there are any tourists at all along this coast.

In spite of these problems, the Gulf Coast remains a very exciting area for beach-combing, fishing, birding, camping and general do-it-yourself exploration.

Special Places and Points of Interest

Jalapa, a small city in the state of Veracruz, is one of Mexico's most important artistic and cultural centers. Higher up, on the slopes of the Sierra Madre and slightly to the east, you'll find the beautiful coffee-growing region of Coatepec.

Veracruz isn't quite a Mexican version of New Orleans, but there are enough raw oysters and wild partying and colonial history here to satisfy most visitors. Just south of Veracruz, the vast estuaries of the Alvarado Lagoon and Papaloapan River are a mecca for birders and fishermen. The seafood is also awesome. Continuing south, both **San Andrés Tuxtla** and **Lake Catemaco** are well worth a visit. In **Villahermosa** you won't want to miss the Carlos Pellicier museum of archaeology, the zoological/archaeological park and the restored colonial-era architecture downtown.

Upon reaching Villahermosa and the flatlands of Tabasco and Campeche, there is a tendency to rush headlong into the Yucatán Peninsula. In fact, with a complete disregard for sightseeing, it is possible to travel from Villahermosa to Mérida or even Cancún in one marathon day. Avoid the temptation; there is much more to see in this region than meets the eye at sixty-plus miles per hour.

My suggestion is to continue following **Mex 180**, the older, slower and still very interesting Gulf Coast highway. This is the route I followed with Steve in the early Sixties, on our first trip to Mexico together. As we discovered in a nostalgic Nineties rerun of our original itinerary, the birding, camping and beachcombing along these forgotten beaches is still as good as the food. While working off a huge seafood cocktail known as *vuelve a la vida* ("return to life"), Steve and I slogged down a beach that was ankle-deep in seashells. If you're interested in history and culture, this coastal route also shelters some of the Gulf's last traditional fishing villages.

A travel tip: The distance from Villahermosa, Tabasco, to Mérida, Yucatán, via Mex 180 is about 400 miles. The journey includes ferry crossings, so allow a full day or more to travel from Villahermosa to Campeche (280 miles). As far as we know, there are no developed facilities for RVers. Free camping is abundant—and so are the mosquitoes.

The long history of **Campeche** includes enough pirates, sieges, Indian revolts and hurricanes to fill a dozen B-grade movies. Add outstanding seafood restaurants and excellent beaches to the city's dramatic colonial architecture, and it amazes me that Campeche is still just a little too far off the beaten track to attract tourism.

After plugging Campeche so hard, I have to backtrack and suggest a Campeche bypass, an alternative route to Mérida for those interested in Mayan archaeology. North of Champoton, take Mex 188 east to the ruins of **Edzna**. After touring Edzna, you can continue on Mex 261, a good but little used secondary highway to **Uxmal** and several other noteworthy Mayan sites. Rather than taking this bypass, however, my choice would be to use Campeche as a base, visiting these ruins as side trips before continuing on to Mérida.

THE INDIAN HIGHLANDS:
OAXACA AND CHIAPAS

Archaeological sites, handicrafts and scenery • Suggested itinerary: Tlacolula market, Teotitlán del Valle, Monte Albán, Puerto Angel and Puerto Escondido, Tehuantepec, Tuxtla Gutiérrez, Sumidero Canyon, San Cristóbal de Las Casas, Palenque, Villahermosa

Archaeological Sites, Handicrafts and Scenery

Lorena and I rate the mountainous southern states of Oaxaca and Chiapas very high among our personal favorites. Dominated by the Sierra Madre and scored by countless deep canyons, the scenery in this region is truly breathtaking.

In addition to its natural attractions, the southern highlands include many of Mexico's most traditional and colorful Indian groups, plus several notable archaeological sites. This region is still well off the beaten tourist track and is loaded with bargains in accommodations, meals, transportation and handicrafts. Access is easy: the city of Oaxaca is only a few hundred miles south of Mexico City.

Lorena and I have driven this sixteen-day itinerary several times in a van. Friends who took this trip using public transportation reported no particular difficulties other than a few groggy, pre-dawn wake-ups to catch 6 a.m. buses.

The pace is steady and ambitious, but not hectic. Still, an extra five or ten days would allow generous time for relaxation, shopping and unscheduled side trips. The key to using this itinerary successfully is to adjust it liberally to match your own interests and physical energy.

One caution: This itinerary covers about a thousand miles. In relatively short order you'll travel from the semi-arid valley of Oaxaca (elevation 5,000 feet) up into cool, cloud-bound oak forests and high, mystical mushroom country. After crossing the Sierra Madre, the route descends quickly through humid coffee *fincas* and tropical banana plantations to sea level, and warm Pacific beaches. Following the beach south through *tierra caliente* (hot country) to Chiapas, you'll ascend a second time to the colonial city of San Cristóbal de Las Casas (elevation 7,000 feet), then descend once again to near sea level and the tropical rain forest jungles of Palenque.

In other words, this trip is a topographical roller coaster. Some people find such changes difficult to adjust to, especially if they are not in the best of health. If you have heart or respiratory problems, or are just plain worn out, my advice is to travel carefully. Stop or slow down if the pace gets to be too much. Fortunately, slowing down is easy on this itinerary. Cities like Oaxaca and San Cristóbal de Las Casas are difficult to leave, laid-back Puerto Angel was made for relaxation, and the Mayan ruins of Palenque can enchant and distract the most determined globe-trotter.

Once you have visited the city of Oaxaca, the most tiring segment of this journey is the drive or bus ride to Tuxtla Gutiérrez, Chiapas. The route I've described to Tuxtla takes two full days of travel, not including stopovers. It also includes the Sierra Madre, Pacific beaches and some of the best scenery in Mexico. The mountain roads are paved but narrow. Depending on their enthusiasm for switchbacks, bus travelers will find mountainous portions "wonderful" or "white-knuckle."

If you're pressed for time or can't face long hours on the highway, you have two options. You can fly over the "hump" of the Sierra Madre from Oaxaca City directly to Puerto Escondido or Huatulco (very few budget places), visit Puerto Angel and then go on to Tuxtla Gutiérrez by bus. Your second option is to take the bus from Oaxaca City directly to Tuxtla or San Cristóbal de Las Casas, following Highway 190. This bypasses the most dramatic portion of the Sierra Madre and eliminates the Pacific beaches portion of the trip.

Suggested Itinerary

Although this itinerary can be done year-round, our favorite time of year in the southern highlands is autumn (early to mid-October or later), after the rainy season. If you want to beat the crowds, I also suggest you go as soon as possible. In the next few years, travel to the Oaxaca area will increase dramatically as the Cancún-like resort complex at Huatulco is developed on the Pacific coast south of Puerto Angel. If Huatulco is as successful as Cancún, the impact on this area will be considerable.

Oaxaca is most easily reached via Mexico City. Consider adding on a one-, two- or three-day extension to either end of your trip. Although twenty million people generate a lot of traffic, noise and smog, Mexico City is a fascinating place. In my opinion, the Museum of Anthropology alone is worth a sinus headache. (See *Mexico City* in the *Central Mexico: The Colonial Heartland* itinerary, above.)

Day 1: Arrive in Mexico City and then travel on to Oaxaca, either by a one-hour air flight, by bus (all day on the second-class bus or about five hours via a toll road on the Uno "super" buses) or the train. We prefer the train; if luck is with you, it will chug into Oaxaca just in time for breakfast on the plaza.

If possible, arrive in Oaxaca on a Friday in order to visit the local *tianguis* (Indian market) on Saturday. Spend your first day or evening strolling the city's tree-shaded plaza and colonial streets. Oaxaca is made for walking and do-it-yourself street touring; I especially enjoy the quiet, older neighborhoods north and east of the plaza and the busy, congested streets around the Benito Juárez market.

Visit the tourist office for free maps and handouts. Look for posters and handbills advertising local music, folk dancing and theater performances. The Hotel Monte Albán has an exuberant and inexpensive dinner/folk-dance program almost every night.

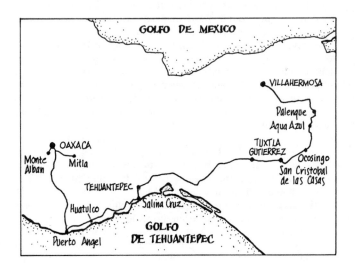

Day 2: Eat a leisurely breakfast; Oaxaca doesn't really wake up until nine or ten in the morning. Explore the markets in the morning and the Rufino Tamayo archaeological museum in the afternoon or evening. Don't miss the gold-encrusted interior of the Santo Domingo cathedral and the adjacent convent/museum. Photographers will want to catch the rich amber of late afternoon light against Santo Domingo's stone walls and nearby colonial buildings about an hour before sunset.

Day 3: If this is Sunday, take a forty-five-minute cab or bus ride or local tour to the **Zapotec Indian market at Tlacolula**. Activity peaks before noon, so arrive by 9 or 10 a.m. to beat the tour buses. The Tlacolulans come from a very long line of merchants; you'll fit in better and enjoy the market more by buying something, even if it's just a handful of peanuts, a spray of wildflowers or a small handwoven basket. Many Indians in this and other markets do not want their photographs taken or will demand payment. Paying for photographs has become the custom in many Indian communities. Be courteous and fair—or risk a tongue-lashing and a tossed tomato.

Eat a picnic lunch at the little-visited ruins of Yagul or return to Oaxaca to join Sunday afternoon activities in the plaza and nearby pedestrian streets. Avoid the temptation to see everything. Study Spanish or just sit in the shade of an Indian laurel tree. To experience the best of Mexico, learn to relax. Visit the nearby ruins at Monte Albán if you must, but I'd put it off until tomorrow.

Day 4: Make a morning trip to the Zapotec rug weaving village of **Teotitlán del Valle** and the nearby village and ruins at **Mitla**. The Frissel Museum in the village of

Mitla serves excellent, inexpensive home-cooked Zapotec/Mexican food in a wonderful setting. The museum also has cheap rooms with lots of authentic colonial "character." Don't miss the small but very interesting archaeological collection.

Return to Oaxaca for more outdoor café-sitting, street-touring, people-watching and postcard-writing. Plan to visit **Monte Albán** by 3 p.m., as the site closes at 5. In fact, if you enjoy archaeological sites or photography, visit Monte Albán at least twice while you're in Oaxaca, once in the morning and again in the late afternoon.

Day 5: Leave Oaxaca early in the morning—or indulge yourself by staying on, saving the remainder of this itinerary for a future trip. If you head west to **Puerto Angel and Puerto Escondido**, take Highway 175 via Miahuatlán. The other "highway" via Sola de Vega is slower and unpaved, but passable. Leave Oaxaca after breakfast, stop for a picnic and frequent photographs, and arrive in Puerto Angel about sunset. If you're in a hurry, fly, don't drive, especially at night.

Highway 175 ascends, descends, twists and turns, from red-dirt arroyos to moss-draped forests and misty, emerald-green jungles. If there are hotels and restaurants along the way, I haven't found them. Miahuatlán is the only town of any size, and the highway bypasses it. Strong local coffee is sometimes available at tiny cafés perched along the highway's westernmost switchbacks. Watch out for fog, rain and Indians heavily burdened with corn, coffee and firewood.

You'll meet the Pacific coast highway (Mex 200) at Pochutla. You have three choices: continue west for twenty minutes to the tiny fishing village of Puerto Angel, go north about an hour to the tourist town of Puerto Escondido, or turn south to Bahias de Huatulco, also about an hour's drive away.

Puerto Angel is small, friendly and somewhat funky around the edges. Tourist facilities and nightlife are limited. Puerto Angel is popular with aging hippies, stargazers, beachcombers, backpackers and bird watchers. Not too surprisingly, Lorena and I feel right at home. Puerto Angel is a good place to catch up on a tan and to enjoy reasonably priced seafood. We like to hire a local *panga* (skiff) to watch the sunset and to spy on rare red-billed tropic birds.

Others find Puerto Angel a little too laid-back. Those who yearn for hot showers, swimming pools and similar amenities might prefer **Puerto Escondido**. Puerto Escondido has nightlife, good beaches, shopping and lots of T-shirts. It is also famous for its surfing.

Huatulco is being touted as the next-best thing to Cancún. In my book, that's reason enough to give Huatulco a wide berth. Imagine a mega-resort carved from one of Mexico's most beautiful and once-pristine shorelines. Better yet, don't imagine it—continue on toward Tehuantepec. (A campground is available at Huatulco, but I haven't checked it out yet.)

Days 6 and 7: Enjoy the beach or hammock of your choice, swill coconut milk and *ostiones en su concha* (oysters on the half-shell). Considering the long day of travel coming on Day 8, I'd keep side trips to a minimum and dedicate myself to genuine R & R.

Day 8: Drive or bus to **Tuxtla Gutiérrez** via Salina Cruz and Tehuantepec. Make an early start to avoid driving after sunset. Compared to the *sierra* of Oaxaca, this is a long, warm and not especially scenic trip through foothills, flatlands and low mountains. **Tehuantepec** makes a good lunch stop. Visit the market (facing the plaza), but dress conservatively and be cautious with cameras; Tehuana women brook no nonsense from visitors.

Tuxtla Gutiérrez is a prosperous farming and cattle town tucked into the foothills of the Sierra Madre. Prices are generally good, but I've yet to find an interesting, inexpensive hotel. The Bonampak is reliable and has an excellent cafeteria. Though Tuxtla suffers aesthetically from faceless modernization, the area offers several noteworthy attractions. Travelers who avoid the temptation to forge on to San Cristóbal de Las Casas are usually glad they did.

Day 9: Tuxtla's unusually fine zoo displays such living treasures as a jaguar, harpy eagle, tapirs, crested guans, pit vipers, crocodiles, parrots, *tepesquintles* and many other interesting creatures, all native to Chiapas. The zoo is about fifteen minutes from the center of town, in a superb, natural jungle setting. Allow at least two hours, and don't miss the souvenir bookshop.

In town, visit the botanical gardens and the museum of anthropology. Take a cab, bus or local tour to viewpoints along the awesome **Sumidero Canyon** for views you won't soon forget.

After the zoo, our favorite activity is a trip into the Sumidero Canyon in a large outboard-powered skiff. There are frequent departures from two landings a few miles south of Tuxtla, where the highway crosses the Grijalva River. The bus to San Cristóbal will let you off at the right spot; leave your luggage at one of the small restaurants. The trip takes 1.5 to two hours. There are no rapids or white water, just mind-boggling views. Rates for the trip are set by the local boatman's *cooperativa*.

Allow two to three hours for the sinuous and very scenic drive to **San Cristóbal de Las Casas**. San Cristóbal is a small and very old colonial city set in the cool highland forests of the Sierra Madre. San Cristóbal looks, feels and even smells like Guatemala, to which it once belonged. The combination of Spanish colonial architecture, bright turquoise skies and Indians in traditional *traje* (costume) gives this town a distinctly exotic flavor. At 7,000 feet elevation, San Cristóbal can also be shockingly cold at night, especially in late autumn and winter. Pack a sweater and/or long underwear.

The cost of living is low in San Cristóbal and bargain hotels and meals are common. Shopping for both Mexican and Guatemalan Indian arts and crafts is excellent.

Days 10 and 11: Like Oaxaca, San Cristóbal should be thoroughly explored on foot, with or without a map. Start by visiting the *turismo* office under the arches on the corner of the plaza. This tourist office is one of the best in Mexico. Ask them to direct you to Mercedes Hernandez Gómez, an excellent English-speaking guide who leads educational day trips to nearby Indian communities.

Visit the local Indian market in the morning, taking care to avoid offending people with your camera. There's a long-standing rumor in San Cristóbal that a tourist was killed by Indians in a nearby village for taking photographs. "Not true," a tourism official assured me. "He was only beaten." In fact, Indian officials have posted prominent signs in several languages, warning visitors when photographs are prohibited. Respect local customs. When in doubt, ask for permission or put your camera away.

Keep an afternoon free for a conducted tour of Na Balam, a private anthropological library, research center and museum founded by Franz and Trudy Blom. Trudy Blom was one of Mexico's most active and outspoken environmentalists. Admission is by donation and there is a small book and souvenir shop. Rooms and meals are also available.

Day 12: Drive or bus to the **Mayan ruins of Palenque via Ocosingo,** a trip of about six hours. The highway is narrow and winding, with many beautiful views. Fog, mist and rain are not uncommon. The highway is almost entirely paved, other than the occasional washout or mudslide.

Ocosingo, about halfway to Palenque, has a few modest restaurants and hotels. The ruins of Toniná can be reached by hiring a local truck or hiking.

If you're driving, allow at least a couple of hours to rest, swim and bird watch along the river at Agua Azul. Hundreds of shimmering cataracts and cool, opalescent pools spill through the jungle. Bus riders must hike about two miles (downhill) into Agua Azul, hitch or luck upon a cab. Camping is allowed.

Misol Ha is smaller than Agua Azul, but no less beautiful. It is also closer to the highway.

Days 13 and 14: The small farming and tourist town of **Palenque** is several miles from the ruins. *Colectivo* service by Volkswagen van to the ruins is quick, cheap and frequent. The town has both budget and "better" hotels, as well as restaurants crowded with international vagabonds, armchair archaeologists and New Age pilgrims. A small shop near the bus station has the cheapest whole bean coffee this side of the Papaloapan. Better yet, there is a wonderful and inexpensive jungle campground, the Maya Bell, within walking distance of the ruins.

Many people consider Palenque to be Mexico's premier jungle ruin and Lost City. Rather than influence your opinion, I suggest that you go there and decide for yourself. Get to the ruins early, to beat the tour buses. Palenque covers a huge area, most of it hidden by thick moist jungle. Hire a guide to help you understand the layout and significance of the site. Later, when the tour buses arrive, strike off on a jungle trail. Picnic on a fallen temple, bathe (but don't drink) in a shaded pool, watch the treetops for monkeys and parrots—and the trail for snakes. This is it, Tarzan country! Don't worry about muddy shoes; now's the time to indulge your vine-swinging fantasies! (I'm sorry to say that because of muggers, women should avoid wandering alone though the jungle near the campground and ruins.)

Day 15: Drive or bus to **Villahermosa.** Visit the huge stone Olmec heads at the La Venta archaeological and botanical park. Walk the city's narrow pedestrian malls, talk to the "municipal parrots," eat fresh crawfish and admire the restored colonial buildings. In the evening, tour the Carlos Pellicer museum on the bank of the Grijalva River. If you missed the anthropology museum in Mexico City, the Pellicer is an excellent second choice.

Day 16: Return home or better yet, continue on to the Yucatán Peninsula.

THE YUCATÁN PENINSULA

Flatter than a tortilla • Mayan cities and ceremonial centers • Climate • Driving • Buses • Language • Suggested itinerary: Cancún, Isla Mujeres, Valladolid, Chichén Itzá, Dzitnup's cenote, Río Lagartos, Mérida, Uxmal, Kabáh, Sayil, Labná, Ticul, Mayan villages, Tulúm, Cobá • The Yucatán by bus

Flatter than a Tortilla

When Cortés was asked by his king to describe the features of New Spain, the soldier-explorer dramatically crumpled a sheet of parchment to represent the territory's awesome mountains and canyons and threw it down in front of the monarch. "There you have it!" he said, instantly creating both a legend and Mexico's first topographical map. If by some historical quirk the conquistador had detoured, however, and focused his quest for glory on the Yucatán Peninsula, his famous geography lesson could have been given with a smooth, unwrinkled sheet. In topographical terms, the peninsula is flatter than a tortilla.

The peninsula is made up of three states: Yucatán, Campeche and Quintana Roo. This Italy-sized territory is home to North America's largest indigenous Indian group, the Mayas. Thousands of pre-Columbian ceremonial sites and yet-to-be-excavated Mayan cities give the Yucatán a reputation as one of the world's richest archaeological zones. It is no exaggeration to say wherever one turns in the Yucatán, an ancient ruin is near at hand.

For the traveler, this broad, box-shaped peninsula offers a distinct contrast to the rugged topography and varied cultures of mainland Mexico. In fact, the local people think of themselves as Yucatecos first and Mexicans second. The differences between the Yucatán and Mexico aren't just superficial. Virtually everything about the peninsula, from its ruler-straight highways to its quiet, gentle people, is distinctly Yucatecan. Though Spanish is the official language, many Yucatecos, especially farmers and rural women, speak only Mayan. Even the food is different. Visitors are often surprised to find that instead of tacos and enchiladas, Yucatecan fare relies heavily on pork, venison, black beans, pickled onions, lime soup and *chile habanero*, the legendary, thermonuclear Mayan pepper that makes a *jalapeño* taste as mild as a jelly bean.

Mayan Cities and Ceremonial Centers

Until recently, the Yucatán Peninsula was isolated from both Mexico and the rest of the world. It wasn't until the Fifties and Sixties that a narrow highway finally connected this region to mainland Mexico. As late as the early Seventies, Cancún was just another beautiful sandbar on a beautiful, unknown coast.

In planning your trip, keep one important fact in mind: Cancún is no more representative of the Yucatán than Disneyland is of California. Although Cancún is one of the world's most successful planned resort cities, development has been sudden, dramatic and often highly disruptive. At the same time, however, vast areas of the peninsula remain relatively unaffected and traditionally Mayan. Tourists who venture beyond Cancún's artificial world are often amazed to find that this air-conditioned enclave is surrounded by lush jungles, extensive *milpas* (cornfields) and small, isolated villages of traditional thatch-roofed stone houses with gracefully rounded ends.

Today, millions of Mayan Indians live and work among the fallen temples and ancient cities of Cobá, Chichén Itzá, Uxmal, Dzibilchaltún, Sayil, Ek Balaam, Chunyaxche and countless others. These cities were not lonely outposts surrounded by wilderness. In fact, like New York, Wichita and San Francisco, many Mayan cities coexisted in time and were parts of a common "country."

The Yucatán's jungles still conceal dramatic evidence that Mayan cities and ceremonial centers were connected by broad stone highways, called *sacbes*. It is difficult for the modem mind to grasp, but the Mayas did more than plant corn, erect temples and worship strange gods: they also built a complex freeway system. *Sacbes* formed a meticulously planned network for commerce and communication, built by hand, without the use of the wheel or metal tools, well over a thousand years before engineers conceived of Route 66.

Climate

My favorite time of year in the Yucatán is autumn, after the summer rains have eased and before the December tourist rush begins. Contrary to many tourist brochures, the peninsula's weather is not perfect, especially during late winter and early spring. *Nortes*, cool winter "northers," will bring periodic clouds, rain and strong winds during January, February and March. Sun-worshipping tourists who expect eternal sun on Cancún's beaches tend to get very cranky after three days of windblown overcast.

Smart travelers, however, will use cool spells to their advantage by leaving the beach and going inland, to visit the normally very warm jungles and archaeological sites. Weather that is too chilly for sunbathing is usually perfect for temple-touring, day hiking, driving and sightseeing.

Lorena says, "All good trips end at the beach." This itinerary goes one better, by beginning *and* ending along the Caribbean. If the weather is cool or wet when you arrive, however, consider skipping the first few days at the beach and adding them on later, when the clouds break.

Driving

Although the peninsula's topography tends to be monotonous, there are advantages to billiard-table horizons. Travel around the Yucatán is physically less demanding and stressful than in mountainous regions such as Oaxaca and Chiapas. The Yucatán's highways aren't only flat and straight, but traffic is also light and drivers are somewhat saner.

The worst driving conditions are found on Cancún's congested, chaotic boulevards and two narrow, heavily used highways: Mex 307 from Cancún south to Tulúm and Mex 180 from Cancún to Chichén Itzá and Mérida. Both of these roads are increasingly hazardous speedways for tour buses, cabs and impatient, intoxicated tourists.

Remember: Never drive at night in Mexico and never drive while drinking or otherwise distracted.

Buses

Though most easily followed in a car, you'll save money by doing this itinerary with buses, cabs and local day tours. If you go by bus, don't hesitate to replace time-consuming side trips with more accessible ones. The caverns of Loltún, for example, are not easily reached except by car or cab. Instead of struggling to make connections, I'd spend more time exploring Uxmal or beachcombing in Celestún.

The Yucatán's bus service is good and inexpensive, but departures tend to be less frequent than in more populous areas of Mexico. First-class bus service is limited and often fully booked. On the other hand, distances between interesting places tend to be short, and second-class Mexican bus rides are seldom dull.

Buses going to and from Cancún can be very crowded, especially on weekends. On Friday and Saturday, thousands of people evacuate Cancún to visit their friends and families in the "provinces." At the same time, other thousands leave the provinces and head to Cancún, to visit their friends and families, to shop and to enjoy the beaches. The return trip on Sunday evening and Monday morning is equally hectic. The solution to finding a seat is simple: go to the bus station and join the throng. You'll enjoy the company.

Warning: Waiting beside the highway for buses will expose you to the full force of the Yucatán's powerful sun. Always carry drinking water, sun block and a broad-brimmed hat or umbrella. Believe me, you'll need them!

Language

Although Spanish and Mayan are their first languages, English is spoken by many Yucatecans, especially those who work in hotels, restaurants, shops and other tourist-related services. Mayas have told me that tourism represents their best hope of getting ahead and that learning languages, including English and French, is very important to them. It is not unusual to meet Yucatecans who are eager to practice English. An adventurous traveler can find many opportunities to teach and tutor languages, especially in smaller towns and villages.

Suggested Itinerary

To avoid crowds and save money, we suggest that you use Valladolid, Tulúm and the Uxmal area as bases for side trips. Lorena and I make every effort to avoid consecutive travel days. Changing hotels every night is not only tiring and time-consuming, it also increases your travel costs.

Although this trip is a closed loop that begins and ends in Cancún, I wouldn't hesitate to substitute Mérida or Cozumel for arrival or departure, or both. For example, if you're more interested in diving than bird watching, plan to arrive at the island of Cozumel. (Just skip Isla Mujeres entirely or visit it as a day trip.) Cozumel offers the easiest access to the Caribbean's top-notch snorkeling and scuba diving and the widest variety of diving trips. Resume the suggested itinerary on Day 4. When your trip ends, fly out of Cozumel if you need another day of diving or if you had bad weather at the beginning of your trip.

Day 1—Fly to Cancún and take airport transportation into town. Cancún is divided into two major parts, the *zona hotelera* and the *zona commercial*. The hotel zone is a narrow strip of fancy, Miami Beach–style hotels, boutiques, pseudo-Polynesian restaurants and air-conditioned shopping malls. As you may have guessed by now, this is not my favorite place in Mexico.

If Lorena and I must overnight in Cancún, we go directly to the commercial zone along Avenida Tulúm, west and slightly inland from the hotel zone. The *zona commercial* or *centro* is Cancún's version of a Mexican city. Budget hotels in this area should cost no more than $20 a night, but you'll probably have to pay double that and more. If you can't grin and bear these rates, go a couple of blocks farther west, to Avenida Yaxchilán, or to the northern part of town, in the area of Mercado 28 and Avenida López Portillo. Tell a cabbie you want "*un hotel economico.*" Your room may be small and noisy, but odds are it'll be fairly new: nothing in Cancún is old yet.

If you have no burning desire to see this sprawling Americanized resort city, take a cab or urban bus from Cancún directly to nearby Puerto Juárez, north of town. The passenger-only ferry from Puerto Juárez departs for Isla Mujeres about every sixty to ninety minutes. (To save money, don't rent a car until you leave Isla Mujeres.)

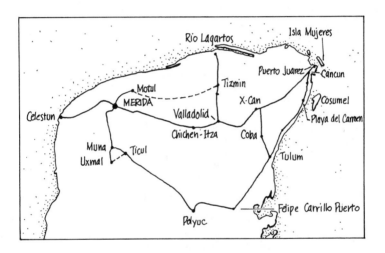

Days 2 and 3: In spite of its proximity to Cancún, **Isla Mujeres** retains the kind of contagious, off-beat charm that I associate with the "real" Mexico. The sun is warm, the beach is very close and life is slow. The streets of the village are narrow, sandy and filled with strollers. Around the plaza each night you'll find C-grade movies and carnival-style games. Shopping is good for T-shirts and sun hats, but the bakery seems to be the island's most popular shop. Isla Mujeres is the kind of place where most people wear shorts and sandals, even on Sunday.

In addition to sunbathing and people-watching at the ferry dock, major island activities include day-long snorkeling trips on small local boats, motorbike rides to a lighthouse and small Mayan temple on the island's southern tip and listening to music at night. Don't miss the tiny village market place, though you'll have to get up early. Have a taste of delicious Mayan-style pork with our old friend Nacho Be, "The King of the Tacos."

Our favorite side trip is to the **Isla Contoy** bird sanctuary, about two hours north of Isla Mujeres. Isla Contoy is a small, uninhabited island with lagoons, reefs and an (unstaffed) interpretive/research center. Displays include detailed explanations of the island's flora, fauna and sea life. An all-day trip includes a light breakfast, soft drinks and a substantial lunch of fresh grilled barracuda (caught on the trip out). Gear is provided for snorkeling, and you'll also get a close view of a large colony of seabirds, including man-o'-wars, boobies and pelicans. Take a hat and plenty of sun block.

Day 4: In the morning, cross back from the Isla to the mainland. Rent a car in Cancún or take the bus to **Valladolid**, about two hours west. Though smack on the highway between Cancún and Mérida, Valladolid is overlooked by most travelers. This small, relaxed colonial city is just awakening to its tourism potential. Valladolid is also a bargain for comfortable rooms and good food. There is only one boutique (a good one, in the hotel Misión del Marqués). The town has an unusually large *cenote* (limestone pool) close to the plaza and a fine colonial convent. Check the market for fresh cut flowers, sweet papayas and exotic, unfamiliar local fruits. I get great pleasure out of simply walking Valladolid's streets, greeting people, admiring old buildings and peeking into gardens.

Day 5: Chichén Itzá is less than an hour west of Valladolid. Rise early in order to be at the ruins by 8 or 9 a.m. In fact, to avoid crowds and heat, always visit major archaeological sites early in the morning or late in the afternoon. Bus service is good, or you can share a cab to the ruins and take a bus back.

Chichén Itzá may be the world's most heavily visited archaeological site. Its modern reception center has a bookshop, bank, ice cream parlor, cafeteria, information booth (with bus tickets and telephones), theater and small museum.

Rather than touring with your nose to a map or guidebook, hire a trained guide at the entrance. The group fee is reasonable. I didn't realize how much I was missing at archaeological sites until I began taking advantage of guide services.

Chichén Itzá has a nighttime "Sound and Light" show, but you'll have the opportunity to see a better one at Uxmal in a few days.

Picnic or lunch at the ruins or try one of Piste's many restaurant, less than a mile away, toward Mérida. If you aren't too tired, consider a visit to the cave at **Balamcanchen** on your return to Valladolid. Unfortunately, this once-secret subterranean Mayan shrine has been "improved" for tourism with melodramatic sound and light effects that I find distracting. On the plus side, kids love it. A small and very interesting botanical park surrounds the entrance to the cavern.

Tired or not, you can't miss **Dzitnup's** *cenote*, just a few miles west of Valladolid. After exploring Chichén Itzá, a swim in this limestone grotto will cool you off and fulfill your Lost World fantasies. The embroidered *huipiles* (blouses) being sold at the entrance to the *cenote* are made by local Mayan women. If you have time, visit their village, Dzitnup, just a couple of miles to the south.

Day 6: Drive or bus to **Río Lagartos**, a funky fishing village two hours to the north. (If you'd rather not overnight here, plan to return to Valladolid in late afternoon.) Río Lagartos is a bird watcher's dream, with everything from night herons and ibis to roseate spoonbills, woodstorks and white pelicans. The crowning touch, however, is a colony of thousands of American flamingos.

Note: There'll be a second chance to see flamingos at Celestún, as a side trip from Mérida.

Day 7: Travel on to **Mérida**, a three- to six-hour trip. The usual route, Mex 180 via Chichén Itzá, has heavier traffic and less interesting scenery than the lesser-known northern arterials, which pass many small, seldom-visited villages, henequen plantations and crumbling haciendas. For example, try **Valladolid–Tizmín–Temax–Motul–Mérida** or **Valladolid–Dzitas–Tunkas–Izamal–Motul–Mérida**. This latter route has some very narrow one-lane stretches with pullouts for passing. Fill your tank in Valladolid and plan to picnic along the way.

The traditional towns of **Izamal** and **Motul** offer a particularly fascinating look into the Yucatán's colonial past. In Motul, visit the *cenote* and henequen plantation by hiring an inexpensive horse-drawn carriage near the central market.

Days 8 and 9: Mérida, the "White City," is the capital of the state of Yucatán as well as the peninsula's commercial and cultural center. Tour the city on foot if you enjoy walking, or hire a horse-drawn carriage. The tourist office (on 60th Street) has good maps and a helpful staff. As Mexican cities go, Mérida is rather sedate. My favorite activity is simply to walk-and-gawk, especially in the city's sprawling food and artisan markets and surrounding streets. Across town, take a look at Paseo de Montejo, with its ritzy mansions, boutiques and multi-star hotels. On Sundays, Mérida's downtown streets and plaza are blocked to traffic. Sidewalk cafés, bake sales (rich stuff!), a flea market, street musicians and folk dancers attract local families and tourists.

Mérida has the Yucatán's best shopping. Look for hammocks, sandals, belts, henequen bags, batiks, silver jewelry, freshly baked idols, men's guayabera shirts and panama-style "jipi" palm hats. If prices aren't fixed, don't be afraid to smile and barter.

Surprisingly, Mérida has only a few museums; the largest is in the former governor's palace on the Paseo de Montejo. It can be toured in an hour or two.

If Mérida's pace is too slow for you, consider a side trip to nearby Dzibilchaltún, a large pre-classic Mayan city with a small museum, a relatively well-preserved *sacbe* and a fine *cenote*. Bird watchers and beachcombers should consider spending a night in the fishing village of Celestún, on the Gulf of Mexico about ninety minutes away. In addition to pink flamingos and many other birds, seashells are much more abundant than along the Caribbean. Celestún has one small, modest beachfront hotel (the Hotel Gutierrez), a couple of basic *casas de huéspedes*, and some of the region's finest and most economical seafood. Although Río Lagartos has a certain reckless, ramshackle appeal, many people prefer Celestún's long sand beaches.

Day 10: Sleep in or do last-minute shopping; stock up on picnic supplies. Exploring **Uxmal** and environs is much easier with a car. You can reach the ruins by bus, either as a day trip or overnight, but there's only one budget hotel, the pleasant and very friendly Rancho Uxmal, three miles from the ruins. The Rancho Uxmal also has the best prices on meals—good, solid Yucatán fare.

Hotels adjacent to the Uxmal ruins are moderately expensive, depending on the season. Of these, our hands-down favorite is the older Hacienda Uxmal. Arrive by 1 or 2 p.m. if you didn't make a room reservation from Mérida. The nearest town with hotels, all modest, is Ticul, about forty-five minutes away.

The trip to Uxmal from Mérida takes little more than an hour, but we like to visit the ex-*hacienda* **Yaxcopoil**, a remarkably well-preserved henequen and cattle estate, complete with the family furniture and antique machinery.

Uxmal marks the "ruins and relaxation" portion of this itinerary. Visit the Uxmal site the afternoon of your arrival or just kick back and save the ruins for the cool of the morning. Other than hotel bar conversation, the only nightlife in Uxmal is to stroll along the highway, listening to the jungle and admiring the stars over the Puuc Hills. Carry a flashlight and don't frighten the snakes. Spend the rest of the evening with a good book on the Maya.

Day 11: Breakfast early, then explore and photograph **Uxmal**. Hire a guide; they're all local Mayas and know the site intimately. Watch for the Uxmal woodpecker and for falcons hunting swallows among 1,000-year-old buildings. Uxmal has been called "the Athens of Mexico" and is considered one of the Yucatán's most beautiful cities.

Unfortunately, Uxmal's quiet, contemplative mood tends to dissipate faster than the morning fog when the tour buses arrive. My solution is to escape into the surrounding jungle and work up an adventurous sweat as I imagine myself exploring in the illustrious company of Stephens, Morley and Thompson. Camera, binoculars and canteen in hand, I scramble over unexcavated *montículos* (mounds, ruins) and impatiently ponder the long passage of time (until lunch). Later, slaking my thirst with a cold, fizzing mineral water, I'll share my latest discoveries and insights on Mayan civilization with Lorena, who undoubtedly spent the day sacked out in the cool shade of a pyramid, searching the clouds for bird tracks.

Day 12: Depending on your energy and interests, there are several worthy side trips in the Uxmal area. For ruins, visit the tri-cities of **Kabáh**, **Sayil** and **Labná**. These major sites have yet to be extensively excavated and only Kabáh, adorned with the face-masks of the rain god Chaac, receives many visitors. Sayil and Labná's quiet, forested settings offer shaded walking trails, peaceful views and excellent birding.

Loltún ("Stone Flower") is a huge cavern complex with evidence of ancient human use, including the bones of a mammoth, Paleolithic rock paintings, stone *metates* (corn grinders) and an unusual Olmec head. The caverns themselves are spacious and quite impressive; a guided tour takes about ninety minutes.

If you're "ruined out" by now, consider a morning visit to **Ticul**. Ticul is known for shoemaking and Mayan pottery—the same figures, plates, pipes and bowls you've seen in shops throughout the peninsula. Some of the best reproductions are found at Wilberto Gonzalez's studio on the edge of town toward Mérida, by the cemetery.

Visit Ticul's municipal market to sample fresh corn tortillas and homemade confections, then hire a *triciclo* for a leisurely tour of the town. A Mayan-powered three-wheeled bicycle "cab" costs a few dollars per person, per hour. It is polite to ask the price before making the trip. Don't be shy. To arrange a tour, just say, "*Una vuelta*" (literally "a turn" around town), or "*Una vuelta de una hora*" ("A turn of an hour"). Lorena and I do this frequently in Ticul; the cabbies are very helpful.

Any Mayan town or village is interesting, but among my favorites in this area are **Muna** (where most of the Uxmal guides live), tiny **Santa Elena** and the bustling citrus market town of **Oxkutzcab** (pronounced "oosh-kootz-cob"). There is a simple etiquette for visiting these small communities: dress conservatively (no bathing suits, shorts or revealing clothing), smile often and don't fail to greet people, even if it's just a brief "*Buenas!*" Though most people are not alarmed by cameras, take photographs with courtesy and discretion.

Many Yucatecans have asked me to pass on a request that you not give money to children. Begging is not common in the Yucatán, but it is catching on, particularly with kids. It's difficult to ignore an open hand, but generosity, especially in small towns, often backfires as crowds of children hound your every step.

Return to Uxmal for a final temple-climb or collapse under a ceiling fan for a siesta. Plan to attend the evening "Sound and Light" show. Take a sweater or a jacket; the air is often chilly by the time the performance has ended.

Day 13: Leave Uxmal in the morning and drive east to **Tulúm** via Tekax, Dzuiché, Polyuc and Felipe Carrillo Puerto. At a sane sightseeing speed (55 mph or less) the trip takes seven or eight hours, including a stop for gas and a picnic lunch. This is a straightforward drive through some of the peninsula's most empty country.

Laguna de Chicnancanab, almost midway to Tulúm, is a good picnic stop (no restaurant). There is a lake with a thatched shelter and rustic restrooms. The narrow, paved road to the lake is on your left, on the east side of the village of Dziuché.

You should have no trouble arriving in Tulúm in time for sunset. Should you get a late start, however, there are a couple of reasonably priced, reasonably comfortable hotels in Felipe Carrillo Puerto.

Bus travelers can make connections from Ticul to Felipe Carrillo Puerto, and from there to Tulúm. On the other hand, it might be more convenient to reach Tulúm by backtracking, via Mérida–Valladolid–Cobá–Tulúm or Mérida–Cancún–Tulúm.

Accommodations in the Tulúm area are best described as "romantic, offbeat and interesting." In other words, hot water is scarce but sea breezes, white sand and hammocks aren't. Typical beachfront cabanas have thatched roofs, sand floors, foam-rubber mattresses and communal bathrooms. Depending on the frills, prices range from a few bucks a night to $30 and more.

In fact, it's time to rejoice in the lack of tourist facilities. Forget about reading lamps, travel irons and swimming pools: Tulúm is your opportunity to actually live out those long-suppressed castaway fantasies on some of the Caribbean's finest white sand beaches. (I'm very sorry to add that pressure to develop a Cancún-clone in Tulúm probably spells doom for this fantasy in the not-too-distant future. In other words, enjoy it while you can.)

Day 14: The ruined, walled fortress-city of **Tulúm** occupies a strategic and scenic site on low cliffs overlooking the Caribbean. The entire city can be toured at a leisurely pace in less than two hours. Tulúm is a major target for Cancún-based tour companies, so get there early to avoid being trampled. Calm returns after 3 p.m. The low afternoon light between 4 and 5 p.m. is especially good for photographs.

There is a ramshackle souvenir arcade in the parking lot. Some shops have very steep mark-ups. To find good buys, careful comparison shopping and bartering are mandatory. My usual advice about bartering is, "When in doubt, be generous." Forget it here. This is high-volume, hand-to-hand capitalism, with no credit given or taken. Use humor, grit and determination and you may pay as little as a third or a half of the asking price.

It would take weeks to thoroughly explore the Tulúm area's many beaches, *cenotes*, jungle trails and smaller ruins. A few miles to the south, **Sian Ka'an**, one of the world's largest Biosphere Reserves, covers more than a million acres of jungles, swamp, estuaries and reefs. The reserve includes the ruins of **Chunyaxche** (on Highway 307), just now being surveyed by archaeologists.

Fifteen minutes to the north of Tulúm, toward Cancún, are the ruins and *cenotes* of **Xel-Ha**. Xel-Ha is most famous, however, for its clear, protected salt-water pools and natural, aquarium-like snorkeling park.

There's one more tempting option: do nothing more strenuous than lying on the beach or swinging in a hammock. Relax and accept that you can't see it all, at least not yet. If this trip is your annual relief from full-time employment, this is the time to take a day off. Act like a beach bum; it'll do you good.

Day 15: Cobá is a major classic period ceremonial center set in the midst of the jungle about an hour west of Tulúm. In hopes of encouraging the return of local wildlife, Cobá has been designated as an archaeological ecological park. Unlike Chichén Itzá and Uxmal, which continue to be restored and carefully groomed, most of Cobá's temples, pyramids and palaces remain in a natural state.

The site includes five lakes and dozens of *sacbes*. Paths wind through the jungle, giving sudden glimpses of huge stone stelae, fallen walls and vine-choked arches. There are birds galore, occasional snakes and frequent mosquitoes. The only "sound and light" in Cobá is that provided by nature. In fact, most of the site is so overgrown that it is difficult to grasp its size and importance in just one visit. If you enjoy ruins and jungles, visit Cobá. A guide is worthwhile.

Cobá has two hotels, the lakeside Club Med/Villa Arqueologica and the much more modest but enjoyable El Bocadito. El Bocadito, on your right as you enter the village, also has the best restaurant in town: tasty, home-cooked Mayan food at very reasonable prices. The owner, Francisco Itzá, is friendly, informative and very helpful.

Birds! Watch closely for keel-billed toucans along the highway between Tulúm and Cobá, especially during the winter.

Day 16: Return to the **airport at Cancún**. Bus travelers, take note: because cab drivers have clout, buses aren't supposed to stop at the airport exit on Highway 307. Some drivers are Good Samaritans, however, and will let you off at this interchange. Still, if you can't find a cab, it is the better part of a mile to the terminal and the sun can be very hot. Your other choice is to bus into Cancún and take a cab back to the airport. Allow at least three hours, and preferably four, to do the entire Tulúm-Cancún-airport trip. If you're driving, it takes about two hours to go from Tulúm to the airport.

The Yucatán by Bus

Both of the following itineraries can be done as loops. Take several days to a couple weeks to really enjoy the side trips. See the above itineraries for more information on the various towns on your route.

Bus Adventure #1: Cancún Bus Loop: Cancún Playa–Del Carmen–Xel-Ha–Tulúm–Cobá–Valladolid–Cancún. Don't be timid about getting off the bus when the urge strikes. The Xel-Ha stop, for example, isn't a town but a snorkeling park. You'll have to walk half a mile or so from the highway to the park, hitch a ride or flag down a (rare) cab. To resume your bus journey, simply wait alongside the highway at any point and wave down the next bus. Buses run along the Caribbean coastal highway at half-hour to two-hour intervals. (About ninety percent of the buses on the Caribbean highway won't stop; they're tour buses. Wave anyway, just in case.)

From Cobá, the bus goes to Nuevo Xcan, on the Cancún–Mérida highway, and turns west to Valladolid. I highly recommend a visit to Valladolid, an interesting and friendly colonial town. If you're pressed for time, however, and want to go directly from Cobá to Cancún, you'll probably have to get off the bus at Nuevo Xcan and transfer to the first Cancún-bound bus.

Bus Adventure #2: Cancún–Valladolid–Chichén Itzá–Mérida. As scenic drives go, the Cancún-Mérida highway will win few awards. It's an easy introductory bus trip, however, and by getting off at the suggested intermediary points, you'll find ruins, *cenotes* (limestone sinkholes), colonial buildings and very friendly people.

Spend a few days in Valladolid. Check into a hotel near the center of this old Mayan town, stroll the central plaza and side streets, eat a long lunch, take a siesta, visit the *cenote* and go to bed early. The next morning visit the market for freshly baked bread and a glass of orange juice. Ask about interesting local sights and side trips at your hotel. Check out the convent, then hike or take a cab to the *cenote* at Dzitnup. If you have time, consider taking a northbound bus to Tizimín and Río Lagartos. Visit the ruins of Chichén Itzá as a day trip or on your way to Mérida. Downtown Mérida has a number of cheap to moderately priced hotels. The Posada Toledo, a former private home with an excellent location and very helpful staff, is especially pleasant. Return to Cancún on the bus or take the train back to Valladolid and the bus from there.

THE RUTA MAYA

Climate • Your Mayan route • The Ruta Maya from Cancún to Belize, Guatemala and Honduras • The Ruta Maya via Mexico City • The Ruta Maya via Belize City • The Ruta Maya via Guatemala City • The Ruta Maya in Honduras: San Pedro Sula, Lake Yojoa, La Esperanza, Gracias, Celaque National Park, The Lenca, Santa Rosa de Copán, Copán Ruinas, Bay Islands • The Ruta Maya in Guatemala: Antigua, Chichicastenango, Lake Atitlán, Panajachel, Sololá, Ixil Triangle, Huehuetenango, Xela, San Francisco El Alto, Zunil, Fuentes Georginas, Nahualá • Side trips and extensions • Easter in Guatemala

First and most important, the Ruta Maya doesn't actually exist, so don't bother to look for it in your atlas, geography book or AAA road map. Like the mythical "Gringo Trail" or "tourist circuit," the "Mayan Route" is an *idea*, created and nurtured by travelers, writers and tourism experts.

As first proposed by William Garrett, former editor of *National Geographic* magazine, the Ruta Maya was to be a showcase for eco-tourism and an entirely fresh, enlightened approach to international cooperation. The project would unite important but widely scattered Mayan archaeological sites and nature preserves with a coordinated, carefully developed eco-tourism infrastructure (lodges, transport, guides and so on). The scope of the proposal was immense and included the southern Mexican states of Chiapas, Yucatán, Campeche and Quintana Roo, plus all of Belize and Guatemala, and a sizable portion of Honduras. These boundaries embrace several million contemporary Mayas, thousands of greater and lesser archaeological sites and countless jungles, forests, wetlands and wildlife habitats. Planning, ecosystem development, research and development would be done on a regional, multinational scale. A special tourist passport might even be created, eliminating red tape and tedious border crossings for Ruta Maya travelers.

The "human element" was an important part of the Ruta Maya concept. A portion of tourism profits would purchase wildlife habitat and sensitive natural areas. Money would also be channeled into projects to protect and nurture indigenous culture.

The Ruta Maya sounded great, *at least on paper*. After all, few people doubt that this huge territory is one of the world's most exciting and picturesque tourism destinations. On the other hand, this region is known more for government corruption than international cooperation. When neighboring countries are willing to wage war over soccer games and wealthy landowners routinely maintain private militias, it isn't too surprising that the Ruta Maya is still just an exciting idea, rather than a reality.

Climate

The Ruta Maya's complex range of topography and climate defies simple description and complicates trip preparation. In January you'll find teeth-chattering nighttime temperatures in the highland villages of Chiapas and Guatemala's Cuchumatanes Mountains and humid, lazy-warm weather in the lowland jungles just several hour's travel away.

• The lowlands of Guatemala, Honduras and Belize are warm virtually year-round, but temperatures frequently dip below 60 degrees F in the jungle on winter nights. Expect rain, damp fog and heavy dew if you're camping.

• The so-called dry season is seldom entirely dry. It is more accurate to call the winter months on the Ruta Maya the *drier* season. In other words, prepare for rain. I carry both a compact folding umbrella (also great for sun protection) and a lightweight rain jacket. If you'll be hiking or jungle bashing, take a full rain suit. You can also imitate the locals and use a sheet of plastic as cheap, ready-to-use raingear.

• If you're planning a wide-ranging Ruta Maya itinerary, the most agreeable time of year is November through March. This avoids both the hottest weather (mid-April through mid-June) and the wettest (mid-August through mid-October).

• Should you have an aversion to hot weather but must travel in the summer, I'd head for the cooler highlands of Guatemala, Honduras and Chiapas. The weather there above 5,000 feet is usually excellent (but do prepare for rain).

• Remember that short distances often separate dramatically different climates. Lorena and I got thoroughly drenched while canoeing Guatemala's Río Dulce in March—and found near-drought conditions just a few hours away by bus toward Guatemala City.

Your Mayan Route

Because the Mayan region can be approached from many angles, it is easy to get lost in a maze of tempting alternatives. The process is further complicated when you begin to make choices of traveling by air, car, bus, train or even freight canoes. Our advice is to relax: the beauty of the Ruta Maya is that every direction you go and every trail you choose to follow will soon lead to satisfying experiences and adventures.

To help you begin planning your Mayan Route, I've laid out several itineraries that we've used to explore the Ruta Maya. You might want to highlight these routes on a map to help clarify your possibilities. As you'll soon see, designing your own Ruta Maya itinerary is really just a wonderful game of connect-the-dots.

The Yucatán Peninsula: Although the Yucatán is certainly part of the Ruta Maya, there's so much to see and do here that we've created separate itineraries, including a well-tested 1,000-mile loop trip. (See previous *Suggested Itinerary*.)

The Ruta Maya from Cancún to Belize, Guatemala and Honduras

Cancún continues to survive my outspoken disfavor and is now one of the world's most profitable beach resorts. The best I can say for this Caribbean mega-resort is that airlines offer frequent service and competitive fares. As a gateway, Cancún is a logical jump-off point to explore the Yucatán Peninsula, though I still prefer the much more attractive city of Mérida if you can get a flight.

Fly into Cancún and go directly to the bus station. Take a direct bus to **Chetumal**, near the border with Belize, or hop a local bus to Playa del Carmen (an hour or less south of Cancún) and overnight there. From "Playa," grab the next first-class bus to Chetumal. (Any class is OK but *primera* is quicker and more comfortable.)

At the Chetumal bus terminal you'll find frequent cross-border connections to **Belize City**. (We left Playa del Carmen after breakfast and were in Belize City just after dark.)

The Ruta Maya via Mexico City

Fly to Mexico City and take a fast bus (five hours) or the slow, overnight train to Oaxaca. Spend two or three days (minimum) in Oaxaca and then fly on to **Villahermosa**, and bus to **Palenque**. After touring the ruins at Palenque head into the highlands of Chiapas by bus—via **Ocosingo**—to **San Cristóbal de Las Casas**. Continue south from San Cristóbal into **Guatemala** via the highland route (Comitán, La Mesilla, Huehuetenango, Quetzaltenango, etc.).

• An adventurous alternative is to enter **Guatemala's Petén through the "back door"**: by bus from **Palenque to Tenosique**, then by riverboat into Guatemala via **El Naranjo**, and by bus to **Flores** and **Tikal**.

The Ruta Maya via Belize City

Fly directly into Belize City. Consider a visit to the nearby Caribbean cays. If a more offbeat Ruta Maya trip interests you, skip the local cays and hop a regularly scheduled bush plane south to **Big Creek** and **Placencia**. (A cheap bus takes all day.) Enjoy Placencia's laid-back charms, then continue via the teeth-rattling "Jame's Bus" to the coastal town of **Punta Gorda**. Punta Gorda's isolation has thus far protected this fascinating region from tourist-trampling. Explore the area before continuing to Livingston, Guatemala, aboard a local freight canoe (cheap and quick).

Check out **Livingston**, then head up the **Río Dulce** by mail boat or chartered launch to Lake Izabal. At the highway bridge you can easily make bus connections to Guatemala City or Flores and Tikal. If you choose to go to Tikal, plan to layover for at least a couple of days at **Finca Ixobel, Poptún**. Rustic lodging at the Finca is a bargain, the food there is justifiably famous and the surrounding eco-sights are noteworthy.

"Close the loop" on your Ruta Maya tour by continuing from **Tikal to Belize City** via Melchor de Mencos and Cayo (San Ignacio). This final leg can be flown, but it's cheap, interesting and only moderately uncomfortable by bus.

• Yet another alternative: go by **bus from the Río Dulce bridge** to the Puerto Barrios–Guatemala City highway, stop over in **Quirigua**, then continue on to **Copán (Honduras)** and from there to the **Bay Islands**.

The Ruta Maya via Guatemala City

Fly into the capital city but don't plan to linger. "Guate" is interesting, but you'll find more worthwhile sights and experiences in all directions. When in doubt, start by exploring the northern and western highlands by bus and shuttle van. When you're ready for a dramatic change, fly or bus to Flores. Now that the highway is being paved, the infamously uncomfortable bus trip across the Petén isn't nearly as bad as it used to be, though it is long.

Visit **Tikal** and if time allows, make side trips to **Sayaxché** and the **Río de La Pasión** and/or Finca Ixobel, Poptun.

• Alternative: **from Tikal go north across Guatemala and into Mexico via the El Naranjo** bus/boat route (previously mentioned) to Palenque.

• Yet another alternative: enter the **Petén via the little-used overland route from Cobán**. For details, consult the *Real Guide* or *Henry's Hint$*.

The Ruta Maya in Honduras

Honduras is best known for its Caribbean cays, coral reefs and Bay Islands' dive resorts. For my money, however, the real excitement in Honduras is found in its tropical forests and remote highlands. In fact, for sheer "picturesqueness," this little-known country compares very favorably with both Guatemala and Costa Rica. The combination of rugged topography, cloud forests and colonial *pueblos* with narrow, cobbled streets and red-tiled roofs is especially striking. Development is limited to just a few cities, and the outlying villages have yet to be blighted by Coca-Cola billboards or slap-dash cement-and-steel buildings. As a result, there is an attractive, frozen-in-time quality to the Honduran countryside that is very appealing.

Culturally, Honduras also holds surprises. It is a good measure of just how little exposure this country has had that very few outsiders know of the Lenca Indians, an important ethnic group some believe to be the precursors of the Maya. Farmers and potters, the Lenca maintain a traditional culture in the country's rugged western mountains, in the region known as La Esperanza. To add to the temptation, these mountain villages hold outstanding examples of Spanish baroque architecture. According to an American architect who is studying the colonial era, the Lenca region is "one of the richest in colonial heritage in all of Central America."

Start your trip in **San Pedro Sula**; the airport is safer and more convenient than Tegucigalpa's. San Pedro is one of the fastest-growing cities in Central America, but

I'd skip its dubious attractions and go directly to **Lake Yojoa**, an easy trip of about fifty miles. (Honduras' extensive system of paved highways was built by foreign aid and is the envy of Central America.)

From Lake Yojoa head for **La Esperanza**, the capital of Intibuca province and the highest town in Honduras (1,485 meters). This may be Central America, but at this elevation winter nights can definitely be cool. On my first trip, I was glad to have a warm jacket and long underwear.

Hike, hitch or take local buses and cabs to visit the Lenca communities around La Esperanza. Keep an eye peeled for markets and small potteries.

Your next stop is the highland town of **Gracias**. The name "Thanks" supposedly derives from the gasp of relief given by Pedro de Alvarado when the exhausted conquistador stumbled across this rare piece of flat ground in 1527. I was glad to find a surprisingly comfortable hotel here, with "real" pillows and an almost-hot shower. Once considered the capital of Central America, Gracias is the quintessential Latin American time warp, straight from the pages of a Garcia Marquez novel. Be warned; if you've ever fantasized about hiding out in a quaint Central American village, Gracias could well be the place. . . . Visit the market, the plaza and just wander through the streets.

For more active exploration, there's a wonderful hot spring and the **Celaque National Park** is just outside of town. This is the highest mountain in Honduras, with steep trails and exuberant vegetation. If you've never visited a Neotropical cloud forest, you're in for a real treat. The combination of perennial moisture, mild temperatures and rich, volcanic soils create growing conditions that I call "Mother Nature on steroids." The variety and profusion of cloud forest flora and fauna must be seen to be believed.

One of the finest churches in the region is near Gracias, in the Lenca village of La Campa. The Lenca maintain many traditional customs, including their own traditional systems of communal ownership and justice (without a police force). If you are very lucky, you may observe the traditional *guancaso*, an ancient ceremony of friendship affirmation between villages.

Leaving Gracias, you'll descend to the warmer foothills at **Santa Rosa de Copán**, a large (at least by Honduran standards) and attractive colonial city. Hondurans told us that no visit would be complete without a visit to a local cigar factory, where some of the world's finest stogies are rolled by hand. Even though we are smoke-free travelers, they were correct; the tour was fascinating.

Leave Santa Rosa de Copán early in the day and continue on toward the Guatemalan border and the small town of Copán (commonly known as **"Copán Ruinas"**).

Alternate plan: From Santa Rosa de Copán **return to the mountain highlands**, traveling northward again toward Mt. Celaque. The *Central American Handbook* describes the town of **Belen Gualcho**, at 1,500 meters, as "perched on a mountainside, with two colonial churches, one architecturally fine with three domes and a fine colonnaded facade with twin bell towers, the other rustic." You can continue exploring this "outback" region for days—there are so many small towns and interconnecting mountain roads that I can't keep them straight.

Copán is among the most important and impressive archaeological sites in the Mayan world. A very important royal tomb has been discovered in Copán and the long-awaited, often-postponed archaeological museum is now open. This is a major museum of unusual design that I rate as a definite must-see.

The excavated and restored portion of the site is not especially large, but one can easily spend a day admiring the various stelae and temples. The village of Copán is an easy twenty-minute walk from the site. (Copán's history and its unique "hieroglyphical stairway" are described in *Incidents of Travel in Yucatán and Central America* by John L. Stephens and *Scribes, Warriors and Kings: City of Copán* by William and Barbara Fash, 1991. Check out back issues of *National Geographic* as well.)

For all of its fame, Copán is still off the beaten track. The atmosphere is casual and you'll find comfortable lodging and better-than-usual food. There is a small market place with fresh food and handicrafts and several interesting shops.

From Copán you can easily return to San Pedro Sula or cross the border into Guatemala, just a few miles away. (See the extension for *Copán, Honduras to Quirigua, Cobán and Nebaj, Guatemala* after the *Guatemalan Highland Loop*.)

Of course, there's always the beach option. It is quite easy to add a few days of decadent leisure in the **Bay Islands** of Honduras to either end of this itinerary. (Air connections can be made between San Pedro Sula and the islands.)

The Ruta Maya in Guatemala

Mile for mile, very few places in the world can compare with Guatemala in terms of dramatic beauty, varied scenery and colorful folkways. The highlands of this small country are formed by a series of towering, semi-active volcanic mountain ranges, offering a stunning backdrop for Spanish colonial cities and thousands of scattered Mayan *pueblos*. To the north, the vast jungles and river systems of the Petén hold some of Mesoamerica's most exciting archaeological sites.

In the itineraries that follow, we've combined some of the country's better-known, must-see sights with places and people that are well off the beaten track. Depending on your time and resources, you can follow our suggestions for a quick, "Best of Guatemala" trip or tie them all together to create an unforgettable exploration of the entire country.

• **Guatemala Highlands Loop:** It takes a minimum of ten days to do justice to this trip, but two to four weeks is even better. Guatemala is relatively small but even experienced travelers find it to be a very intense experience. First-time visitors almost always complain that they didn't allow enough time to thoroughly explore special places, or to enjoy occasional breaks from the excitement for rest and relaxation.

Traditional Mayan markets are one of Guatemala's high points. It isn't easy, however, to plan an itinerary that combines the best market days with the most efficient travel schedule. For that reason, we sometimes suggest that you double-back over your route to take in a special market. (See *Central America: Guatemala: Market Days in Guatemala*.)

Arrive at the Aurora Airport in **Guatemala City**. (If you arrive on a Saturday, this itinerary will fit nicely with several important market days.) Take a cab or shuttle directly to the highland city of **Antigua**, about an hour away. Antigua is quiet, cultured and *very* colonial. There are many old churches, fine homes and historic buildings, as well as a large municipal market place, plazas, parks and countless shops, galleries and cafés. With so much to see in a relatively small town, the best way to tour is on foot. (Don't worry about seeing it all in one visit; on this itinerary you'll return to Antigua again.)

From Antigua take buses or a shuttle to **Chichicastenango**. "Chichi" is a major Mayan ceremonial center and the site of a fantastic Indian market on Sundays and Thursdays. (To beat the crowds a little, arrive Wednesday afternoon and plan to spend the night.) You'll find everything here from cheap tourist gewgaws to genuine collectibles, including antique wooden masks, intricately woven textiles, amber, silver jewelry and colonial-era bric-a-brac. With Mayan healers swinging censers of billowing copal incense on the church steps and Indian vendors crowding every available inch of space, you'll feel as if you've stepped into the pages of *National Geographic*.

Once you've explored the market, continue on to **Lake Atitlán**, the dazzling "crown jewel" of the Guatemalan Highlands. The once-peaceful lake village of **Panajachel** is now both a town and a major international traveler's "scene." The food and coffee are good, the people-watching excellent and the traffic ridiculous. You'll find everything from private garden estates to "Típica Street," a sprawling street mall jammed with cafés, Mayan crafts, food vendors, travel agencies, shipping agents, cheap hostels and nightclubs.

Lake Atitlán is surrounded by volcanoes and steep, heavily forested ridges. The lake is huge and more than a dozen Mayan villages and towns are found along its shores. If you've got time, I definitely recommend taking one of the local passenger ferries and overnighting in some of the villages around the lake. At the very least, be sure to watch the sunset from one of the beach cafés.

Hop on an amazingly crowded bus and ascend the steep, twisting highway to the town of **Sololá** high on a ridge overlooking Lake Atitlán. During the Tuesday market, Sololá bustles with artisans and itinerant Mayan traders, many of them wearing their distinctive regional *traje* (traditional costume). It's a colorful, chaotic scene, but as in any crowded place it is wise to beware of pickpockets.

You'll return to Chichicastenango from Sololá and continue traveling northward on rougher gravel roads, deep into the Cuchumatanes Mountains, the highest range in Central America. You are headed for the three villages of the **Ixil Triangle**: **Nebaj**, **Chajul** and **Cotzal**. This dramatically beautiful region of scattered towns and Mayan hamlets was also the area of greatest suffering during the conflicts of the Seventies and Eighties. Although peace is returning and many villages have been resettled, the Ixil Triangle remains remote and little visited. There'll be discomforts on this leg of the trip, but once you meet the Mayan people of the Ixil, I think you'll understand why this country has such a strong, near-mystical attraction for so many travelers.

A full day is hardly enough to explore **Nebaj** and its environs, so if you can possibly afford it, allow more time. (Thursday is market day and with Mayas coming in from miles around, Nebaj is a sight to behold.) Wherever you go in this region, count on dramatic scenery and friendly people, as well as an abundance of crafts and colorful Indian *traje*. If you enjoy hiking, there's a good (steep) trail to the village of **Acul**, two to three hours away. Another worthy side trip is to a cheese factory near Acul owned by Italian immigrants. A picnic in their beautiful valley is unforgettable.

By the way, you can help the people of the Ixil to recover from their hardships by purchasing their wonderful crafts. Women will invite you into their homes to view and buy their work. In many households, weaving is the only source of much-needed cash.

The next segment of the trip is also the most difficult: Nebaj to **Huehuetenango** via **Aguacatan** ("Place of Avocados," Thursday market). The journey to Huehuetenango follows one of the country's most interesting back roads, with fine panoramic views of Mayan farms and the Sierra Cuchumatanes. Aguacatan, a prosperous garlic-farming community on the San Juan River, is known for its unique language (Aguateca) and the marvelous headdresses worn by the women.

Rejoining the Pan American Highway at "Huehue," you have three choices: 1. overnight in Huehuetenango or 2. immediately double-back toward the southwest, arriving late in the day in Quetzaltenango. (I recommend this hard-traveling option only if you're short on time or hope to visit the Tuesday market in San Francisco El Alto.) Option 3 is my favorite: spend one or two nights in Huehue and then take a bus back up into the highlands, to the Mam town of Todos Santos.

Quetzaltenango is better known to Guatemalans and savvy travelers as **Xela** (pronounced "SHAY-la"). The country's second-largest city is really just a large town—but it is also a very old town with a long, rich colonial history. Xela is a good place to catch your breath. The city also makes an excellent base for side trips.

The Friday market in **San Francisco El Alto** spills down a steep mountain side. On the highest ground you'll find a kind of informal country fair, with a wide variety of small-to-medium livestock being bartered and sold. Vendors and artisans crowd the lower levels of the market, filling the town's narrow streets and alleys as well as the entire central plaza, including stairs, porches and doorways. The place is absolutely packed but the vendors are friendly and eager to make a deal. This is a particularly good market for hand-loomed wool blankets, Momostenango rugs and lengths of skirt fabric. After you've done a couple of top-to-bottom rounds of the market, you'll definitely understand why this mountain town is known as "San Francisco the High."

Return to Xela on the afternoon bus and take a well-deserved siesta.

South of Xela there's a Saturday morning vegetable market in **Almolonga** where haggling over bushels of spinach and bales of fresh radishes approaches an art form. Adding to the drama, the local women wear an unusual twisted headdress seen nowhere else in Guatemala.

Farther to the west, there's an excellent women's weaving cooperative and an ornately decorated church in **Zunil**. It is a relatively short but quite dramatic drive from Zunil to the hot springs at **Fuentes Georginas**. On a clear day there are magnificent volcano views and excellent birding in the moist cloud forest, with a chance to spot a resplendent quetzal. There are restaurants, cabins and camping at Fuente Georginas.

Overnight again in Xela and then return to Antigua, stopping along the way to visit the Sunday market in **Nahualá**, a small Mayan community known for its highly skilled wood carvers and shamans. The people of Nahualá are very hospitable and market day in this traditional town is especially interesting. Their carvings are not only excellent, but individual artisans will invite you to visit their homes.

You'll probably be back in Antigua by late afternoon or early evening.

If you're taking a cab from Antigua to the airport in Guatemala City, allow at least an hour.

Side Trips and Extensions

• **Tikal Extension:** Tikal is the quintessential Lost City, an amazing combination of archaeological treasures, jungle and exotic wildlife in a spectacular natural setting. In a word, you'd be crazy to miss it, even if you have to again borrow money from your mother to get there.

Unless you've got more time than money, take a cheap flight from Guatemala City directly to **Flores**, a small town in the heart of the Petén jungle. You can overnight in Flores or take a shuttle van to the Tikal ruins, about ninety minutes from Flores.

As much as I enjoy Flores, I prefer to stay in a hotel or the campground at Tikal. This makes it easy to visit the park both early and late in the day, especially at sunset. At night you can hear howler monkeys, owls and a veritable chorus of tropical insects. Jaguars also prowl the surrounding jungle.

My next suggestion is a strong recommendation to use the services of an official, trained guide to tour the park. There's just too much to see here to rely on guidebooks and do-it-yourself wandering. As for time, I'd allow at least two or three days to really explore Tikal and, if possible, even a few days more.

• **Copán, Honduras, Extension:** A number of tour operators in Antigua offer reasonably priced one- and two-day trips to the ruins at Copán. This is a very tempting option, especially if you don't have time to do the trip on your own.

• **Honduras:** As you can see on a map, this trip easily fits onto the other itineraries we've described. In fact, all of these itineraries can be traveled in reverse order, depending on where you prefer to enter and exit your "personal" Ruta Maya.

• **Copán, Honduras, to Quirigua, Cobán and Nebaj, Guatemala:** Leave Copán after breakfast. The border is a short distance away and the legal formalities normally take only a few minutes. It takes a couple of hours on a scenic (gravel) road to reach the paved highway inside Guatemala. You might want to detour to **Esquipulas**, where one of Latin America's most important colonial churches has a black Christ carved in 1594.

Your goal is the Mayan archaeological site of **Quirigua**. Plan to overnight in a small hotel in the village and visit the ruins the following morning.

Quirigua was an important satellite of Copán and is connected to that city by river. First described by Stephens and Catherwood in 1840, it is best known for huge monster-zoomorphs and remarkably detailed stelae, including the tallest yet discovered (twenty-six to thirty-five feet, depending on whom you believe!). The site is surrounded by a vast banana plantation, but there is a protective buffer of tall, undisturbed jungle. The accessible portion of Quirigua is small and somewhat obsessively groomed, but it "works," especially if you enjoy the site as an outdoor gallery for stelae and monumental Mayan art.

From Quirigua the route continues eastward, a slow climb into the **Alta Verapaz** ("High True Peace"). In addition to its beauty, the Alta Verapaz is one of the most productive agricultural regions of Guatemala. Water is abundant and the volcanic topsoil is very rich. German and European immigrants settled here more than a century ago, establishing huge *fincas* for coffee, cardamom and dairy cattle.

Plan to spend two or more nights in the city of **Cobán** (forever to be confused with Copán, which you've just left). Consider an overnight stop at the Ruben Dario Reserve, better known as the *biotopo* or **"quetzal reserve."** I saw my first resplendent quetzal here, in the trees above the small hotel near the reserve's front gate. Once you've seen this bird's showy antics and extravagant plumage against a backdrop of lush cloud forest vegetation, you'll be a confirmed bird watcher!

Cobán is an attractive, prosperous city on the Cahabon River. Highlights include the Cathedral of Santo Domingo (1561) and its art treasures, the lively municipal market and a private botanical reserve with more than 60,000 orchids. From Cobán, you can visit **Tactic** ("White Peach") known for its finely woven blouses and colonial religious art. The open street market in **San Pedro Carcha** is also very interesting. This is an excellent opportunity to stock up on such hard-to-beat bargains as hundred-pound sacks of cardamom pods, raw coffee beans and uncured cowhides. On a smaller scale, look for primitive pottery and silver work.

The next leg of the trip takes you into the **Sierra Cuchumatanes** and the **Ixil Triangle**. You'll go from Cobán, through Uspantán and Cunen over a route one writer described as "one of the most beautiful, if rough, mountain roads in all Guatemala." This is a long, adventurous bus ride so be sure to stock up on picnic supplies in Cobán's market. Plan on making an early start and don't guzzle too much of Cobán's excellent coffee—rest stops are few and far between. By the time you roll into Nebaj, a cold shower and a sagging mattress will probably look pretty good.

At this point, your route follows the previously described Guatemala Highland itinerary. However, as an alternative, you might want to go westward from Nebaj to **Chichicastenango**, rather than north to Huehuetenango.

Easter in Guatemala

As if Guatemala weren't interesting enough, the country's spectacular Easter Week celebrations draw pilgrims and tourists from around the world. The crowds are intense but so is the experience. In the ten-day itinerary that follows, we've combined the most dramatic Easter events with some of Guatemala's most important, must-see attractions (see the *Guatemala Highlands itinerary* for details).

Please note that **advance reservations** must be made for hotels, rental cars and in-country flights during the Easter travel season. Some hotels are fully booked more than a year in advance, so don't delay.

Be aware, too, that important ceremonies, pilgrimages and fiestas follow a religious calendar. Be sure that your itinerary actually coincides with Good Friday and Easter.

Day 1 (Saturday)—**Guatemala City to Antigua**

Day 2 (Sunday)—**Chichicastenango to Lake Atitlán**

Day 3 (Monday)—**Lake Atitlán and Panajachel**

Day 4 (Tuesday)—**Sololá to Nahualá and Quetzaltenango (Xela)**

Day 5 (Wednesday)—**Almolonga and Zunil**. Return to Antigua via the Iximche archaeological park. Be back in **Antigua** by early evening, just in time to observe the Antigueños creating intricately designed "carpets" of flowers, pine boughs and colored sawdust on the streets in front of their homes.

Day 6 (Thursday)—Today, elaborately costumed **processions** honor various saints by marching through the cobbled streets, trampling the previous night's carpets. Churches are decorated with especially fine interior sawdust carpets. Between processions you can tour Antigua on foot, both for shopping and to admire the city's fine colonial architecture. Take an afternoon siesta, however, because there'll be a remarkable frenzy of carpet-making tonight. In anticipation of Good Friday's processions, the streets fill with people creating and admiring the carpets. This is an all-night activity, so bring a warm sweater and lots of film.

Day 7 (Good Friday, March 28)—Be on the streets at 6 a.m., joining the rest of the townspeople for a final look at the carpets. The main procession is in early morning, giving you plenty of time to observe the festivities before departing for Guatemala City in the afternoon and a flight to **Flores** and **Tikal**.

Day 8 (Saturday)—**Tikal:** See *Guatemala Highlands Loop: Tikal Extension.*

Day 9 (Sunday)—Return flight from Flores to **Guatemala City** and on to **Antigua** for the night, giving you time for last-minute shopping and city-touring.

Day 10 (Monday—Antigua to the **Guatemala City airport**.

GETTING AROUND

Buses: luxury, first- and second-class bus service, survival tips, terminals, tickets, baggage, border crossing by bus • City buses • Trains: tickets, reservations, baggage, pets, food, sleeping, general information and advice • Rental cars • Taxis • Colectivos • Navigating in Mexico City: subway • Air service • Ferries: tickets and reservations, vehicle requirements and restrictions, pets, tourist cards, car papers and customs inspections • Boats and beasts • Hitching: finding a good ride, in the boondocks, hitching survival tips, hitching alone • A ride to remember

Buses

Mexican bus service is truly remarkable, and the common expression "wherever there's a road, there's a bus" is no exaggeration. There are several hundred bus lines in Mexico and though service varies from Pullman-style, air-conditioned luxury to butt-bruising "chicken buses," they'll get you there somehow. For those few places inaccessible to even the most determined bus driver, transportation will almost certainly be available in some other form: by truck, small "bush" planes, dugout canoe or burro.

The excitement of visiting remote villages is sometimes overshadowed by the experience of the bus ride to it. The condition of the bus and the road and the general condition of the other passengers (particularly around fiesta time) make each bus ride a unique adventure.

Travelers who use buses—especially in rural areas—often find that they become totally immersed in Mexico. There is no other method, short of walking through the country, to establish such close and continual contact with the people.

The cost of traveling by bus is remarkably low. The expense of operating your car will buy an incredible number of bus tickets. Unless we're on a long van camping trip we almost always travel by bus (or train) and notice a substantial savings.

There are three major categories of bus service: *lujo* (luxury class), *primera* (first class) and *segunda* (second class).

Luxury Bus Service

Mexico's amazing bus system just keeps getting better. Competition with regional airlines and between rival bus companies has created an amazing class of luxury "superbus" with Pullman-style comforts and VIP terminal facilities that rival first-class jet travel. As bus companies scramble for a share of the market, new buses are being rolled out every month. Luxury buses are easy to identify: most are huge "stratoliner" types, with very high profiles, oversized tinted windows and lavish paint jobs. Their names are equally grand: Primera Plus Express, Serviconfort Uno, Pullman, Ejecutivo and so on.

If you've ever traveled on a classic "chicken bus," a ride on one of these new dream liners is like stepping into Mexico's future. Among the services and frills offered: assigned seats that actually recline rather than just rattle, bathrooms, fully extending leg rests, pillows, snacks and beverages, "flight" attendants, video movies, functioning reading lights and a policy of *No Fumar* (No Smoking).

Luxury buses are also equipped with speed monitors. When the driver exceeds the legal limit (about 55 mph) buzzers howl and lights flash. On longer runs, superbuses take the fastest, most direct route (often on new tollways) with very few stops. This is especially welcome if you're traveling long-distance at night. Once the last kung-fu video ends (around 10 p.m.), Lorena and I can usually get a full night's sleep.

Terminal service is also impressive and may include private waiting rooms, restrooms, baggage checking and advance reservations. Some of these buses are so new, however, that they don't yet have terminal space, especially in smaller cities. In this case, look for parked luxury buses on the street and ask the driver for directions to the terminal or temporary office.

The best news is that the price of this extra comfort and service is still a bargain: in an informal survey of competing bus lines, Steve found that luxury bus tickets ran about thirty to forty percent higher than first class.

Executive buses may not have the romance, color and camaraderie of a second-class ride, but, as Steve says, "For aging hippies, these new buses are a dream come true." (See *For More Information*; a few Mexican bus lines have bilingual websites.)

One bus line deserves special attention: *El Uno* ("The One") offers better movies, more sodas and a special row of single seats on one side of the bus for passengers who definitely don't want a seatmate.

Luxury service does have a couple of drawbacks. The most notable is a near constant, dawn-to-late-evening "hit parade" of kung-fu and violent action video flicks. I've seen passengers successfully ask the driver for videos *sin violencia* (without violence), but if you prefer to read, sleep or just enjoy the scenery, a good pair of natural wax earplugs (from your local drugstore) are invaluable.

My other complaint is that luxury buses aren't "scenicruisers." In fact, with heavy drapes over most windows and a wall between the driver and passengers, you sometimes get very little view of Mexico at all.

Truck bumper graffiti: Punisher of the Highway (Road Whipper)

First-Class Bus Service

First-class service is generally equal to or better than Greyhound in the U.S. You can expect assigned seating, air conditioning, bathrooms and, for better or worse, videos.

(However, the bathrooms are sometimes *afuera del servicio*—out of service—so if this is critical, ask first or take a luxury bus.) Stops are infrequent on first-class runs and occur only at terminals, major bus stops or occasional rest and refreshment points. A ride on a first-class bus doesn't have the atmosphere of a second-class junket through countless villages, but you certainly get to your destination in a hurry.

Second-Class Bus Service

Second-class buses vary from relatively new and comfortable on main routes between large urban centers to positively decrepit and back-breaking (rural areas and back roads). Once a bus becomes too funky for first-class passengers to tolerate, it is sent into second-class service. (From there the only place for it to go is into the junkyard or over a cliff.)

A second-class bus often looks just like first class and will even cover the same routes, but second-class buses stop for anyone and everyone. Some people say that they prefer to ride second class because of the white-knuckle speeds that the first-class buses attain and maintain for such long stretches. In reality, second-class buses are no slower than first class over the same roads. To make up for time lost loading passengers and their amazing luggage, the second-class driver will do anything to keep his average speed ridiculously high.

This means he'll pass on curves and hills, race "chicken" fashion to beat other vehicles to narrow bridges (they don't call these "chicken buses" just because they carry poultry!) and generally make a complete fool of himself.

As the ancient wrecks are gradually replaced, some of the color and excitement has gone out of second-class bus travel. Enough still remains, however, to satisfy most tourists when they ride one of these mobile adventures.

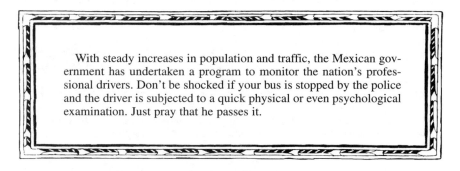

With steady increases in population and traffic, the Mexican government has undertaken a program to monitor the nation's professional drivers. Don't be shocked if your bus is stopped by the police and the driver is subjected to a quick physical or even psychological examination. Just pray that he passes it.

I once rode a first-class bus through a mountainous area because I assumed that it would be safer than second class. This involved some inconvenience because the service was not as frequent as second class. I was sufficiently impressed by the narrow road and steep mountains, however, to prepare myself in a nearby cantina through the hours before departure.

As an added precaution, I bought a small traveling bottle to use as a sleeping potion; the bus left at midnight and I certainly didn't relish the idea of having to watch the highway all night.

I discovered as soon as I boarded that I had made a critical mistake when buying my ticket by not specifically asking for a rear seat (though the swaying motion is much worse in the back). Instead I found myself behind the driver.

An hour after takeoff, we entered the mountains and I opened the bottle. The driver, nattily attired in a crisp white shirt, black tie and official-looking cap, seemed to think of himself as an airline pilot rather than a mere bus herder. As the assistant driver watched with obvious respect, the pilot went through a complicated series of "in-flight" systems checks. Had the bus suddenly lifted from the road and shot gracefully into the sky, it appeared that the driver would have been fully prepared and not at all surprised.

From my nervous vantage point, I followed his little training lecture with more interest than the real student. Neither driver nor assistant seemed to notice that most of the maneuvers involved in demonstrating brakes, engine revs and complicated shifts were taking place along blood-chilling stretches of narrow mountain road.

We would accelerate to breakneck speed and then the driver would suddenly remember another detail: the fire extinguisher under his seat or the nifty map case next to his left foot. With one hand on the wheel and paying no attention at all to the road, he would give a quick demonstration of each new item, then turn back to the chore of driving just as we crossed the road or were about to run over a cow.

He drove purely by instinct, pushing the bus to the limit on every curve, passing trucks and then cutting them off so close that the face of the driver behind us seemed to be just another passenger in the rear seat.

For the final demonstration, he began to flick his headlights from one intensity to another, at times blinding oncoming drivers with bolts of light from special high beams, then suddenly dropping to fog lights, then back to normal intensity. By then I was on the edge of my seat, feeling a deep gut fear of what I knew had to be coming as the finale, the ultimate test of his driving abilities.

He chose a long curve skirting a high rock cliff for the closing act, casually flipping off all the lights after a final demonstration of maximum illumination that had lighted the area in front of the bus as if for a night football game. The plunge into utter darkness surprised even the driver. Not the slightest feeble ray of moonlight could be seen. It was as if the projector light had gone out and the film stopped: the driver frozen at the wheel, unable to reach the switch in time to make the curve but unable to see the curve without the lights; the assistant staring into the windshield, as black as the Grim Reaper's cape, and the passengers suddenly instinctively aware of danger, a tense audience to the driver's dilemma.

As the front tires hit the ditch, the assistant, a pimply-faced kid of about sixteen, leaped to the light switch and flipped it on. At the same instant, the driver turned the wheel desperately and we slid for several heart-pounding seconds down the side of the highway, scant inches from the rock cliff.

Truck bumper graffiti: Free and Clean; They Criticize Me From Jealousy; Flavor of Death

Once we'd straightened out, the driver settled comfortably into his seat and turned to his white-faced companion saying casually, "That's the way it's done, son."

The combined sighs of relief from sixty passengers sounded like a communal "Amen!" I emptied my bottle.

All bus drivers aren't maniacs or fatalists. One in particular stands out in my mind as extremely level-headed and reasonable. He was in charge of an old American-made bus and the sign over the aisle read in English: "Your Operator—Safe, Courteous, Reliable—Jesús Cristo." A small ID-type photo of Christ attached to the sign left no doubts as to who was really in the driver's seat.

Among the qualifications of an authentic Mexico traveler is the ability to swap outrageous bus adventures with others. I suggest a light breakfast followed by a second-class bus ride across any major mountain range. . . .

Once the initial shock of being crammed into a rusty tin box with fifty other people, plus a variety of market goods and domestic animals wears off, you'll enjoy a feeling of warm camaraderie and anticipation.

As the bus lumbers out of the terminal, you smilingly agree to a woman's request to hold her wide-eyed baby while she whips up a few tacos from ingredients extracted from a greasy piece of newspaper. When she's managed to assemble lunch, she takes the baby back and offers you a rag for the mess on your lap.

Beads of sweat are breaking out on your upper lip, but the window is frozen shut by years of rust. You take a deep breath or two and find a taco under your nose. You've been invited to eat.

You want to decline the invitation, but from the thrusting motions she is making with the taco, it is clear that it would be grossly impolite to refuse. No matter, it turns out to be your favorite: steamed goat head with lots of chili pepper. The air you suck in through tightly pursed lips sounds like ripping cloth and you attempt to cover your embarrassment at reacting to the pepper by staring out the window.

Through tear-filled eyes, you gaze over a 1,000-foot precipice, but the taco, stuck halfway down your throat, blocks a scream of fear.

The lurching of the bus is considerable, very similar to that of a boat foundering on a storm-tossed sea. The ringing in your ears almost drowns out the voice behind the hand that is holding a crude pottery mug under your nose. You look up, eyes filled with a plea for mercy, but the smiling face insists. You tip the mug back, determined to do a chug-a-lug and have done with it. It is *pulque*, the fermented sap of the maguey plant, and it is distinctly slimy. It hits your stomach like warm mustard water.

Your apparently experienced manner of tossing down the pulque brings admiring remarks from other people jammed in nearby. They appreciate the fact that you're trying to be sociable, and to show this appreciation, they contribute little delicacies they're bringing home from market. A piece of deep-fried pig skin, a cactus fruit, some incredibly sour berries and two old tortillas with something brown smeared on them are offered up for your enjoyment.

You are just about to go under when the bus lurches to a stop. Everyone piles out to see what's gone wrong and you gratefully stagger into the fresh mountain air.

A front tire has blown, the second flat of the trip, and there doesn't seem to be another spare. After a quick look at the other tires, the driver decides to remove one of the rear duals and put it on the front. As he does this, his assistants, a motley collection of boys about eight years old, fill the leaking radiator with water from a nearby ditch. They're using one beer bottle and a leaky oil can so they have to make several trips.

When the repairs are finished, everyone crowds back into the bus and in the confusion you lose your seat. You're grateful, however, because you can now assume a position in the aisle near the front door. The body of the bus is so low that you have to stand with your neck slightly bent. Every really bad bump gets you a crack on the back of your skull. At least there is air to breath—since half of the windshield and the entire door are missing.

When you've settled into a more or less tolerable slouch, you begin to take a new interest in the driver and the road ahead. Before entering the mountains, the road had been reasonable. Now, however, with occasional boulders to dodge, half-filled washouts and vertical drops of hundreds of feet just scant inches from the edge of the road, you wonder seriously if the bus will make it.

Truck bumper graffiti: God Allows My Return

The driver is shifting like a madman; something is wrong with the clutch and he's having trouble on the steeper grades. You notice anxiously that the brake pedal goes very close to the floor when he throws his weight on it. You wonder then about the motto painted on the front bumper, the one you and your friends had laughed about before you left: "Guide Me God, For I Am Blind."

It's anyone's guess just how much is getting through those opaque sunglasses and the heavily decorated windshield to the driver's eyes. The garlands of plastic flowers, intertwined with blinking Christmas tree lights, have sagged so low that he has to lean forward to peer over them on particularly tight corners.

A large crucifix is mounted between the two front windshields and each point of the cross lights up to correspond with a particular gear. As he shifts, you follow the lights: white . . . green . . . red . . . red . . . green . . . white. The ceiling is plastered with an unlikely assortment of faded pictures. The Virgin Mary peers from between an old Marilyn Monroe magazine photo and a rather obscene playing card.

In addition, a variety of dangling objects, evidently amulets and charms, swing in crazily distracting patterns in front of the driver, occasionally whacking him on the forehead. Between shifts he idly fondles the gear shift knob, a blindly staring baby doll head that winks conspiratorially at each bump. Before you can determine the significance of this macabre object, the bus arrives at your destination and you gratefully jump off.

Because second-class bus rides that last more than a few minutes invariably become social affairs, it's nice to have something to offer people who offer something to you. This can be nothing more than a piece of candy, chewing gum or a turn with a newspaper.

It is not customary to offer your seat to anyone standing unless they are ill or very old. This conflicts with what most of us had drummed into our heads as children, but standing for hours in a bouncing hot bus can do a great deal of attitude changing. In most cases, you'll find that after you've offered a lady your seat, she takes it gratefully and then gets off within the next mile. You then continue standing as some guy elbows past you and drops into the vacant spot with a big sigh of relief.

If you don't feel like giving up your seat, it is polite to offer to hold something for people who are standing. Children seem to be the most common bundle, though you may be given a chicken or a bag of groceries.

Should the cozy atmosphere get to be too much for your stomach, ask the driver or his accomplice for permission to ride on the roof or rear bumper. The roof is not only much safer than the bumper, but offers a better view with less chance of fume poisoning. The only time I've ever driven a fast car in Mexico, I was passed by a second-class bus traveling at over 80 mph. This wasn't unusual, nor were the three young men on the rear bumper. The one reading a comic book, however, without holding on, seemed abnormally blasé.

After you've ridden a few genuine second-class buses, you'll understand why Mexicans refer to them as *matasanos* (health killers) and *doctorsanos* (sarcastically: doctor health). It should be kept in mind, however, that on a statistical basis—miles per accident or something like that—Mexican buses have an excellent survivor record.

Bus Survival Tips

• On buses without assigned seating don't hang back when the mob charges or you'll end up standing. Go over the top like a Marine after the Congressional Medal of Honor; that's the way it's done.

• If your assigned seat is taken and the person occupying it doesn't understand your polite request to find the correct seat, just take another. In a short time someone will ask you to move. Keep smiling and shrugging and the driver will soon straighten it all out or leave you where you are.

• When the driver slides behind the wheel and puts the bus in gear, relax: he's a professional with a large loving family and a strong desire to retire in one piece. If you backseat drive you'll soon be reduced to a slobbering wreck. Stick your nose against the window or inside a book, chat with your seatmate, drink a soda or nap; you'll be there before you know it. This took me a long time to accept but it's true—even was on the awful bus ride when the lady next to me started saying the rosary. Or that night when I looked up over the driver's shoulder and saw another bus coming at us head-on at high speed, six feet away. My scream didn't even wake the others. It took me several minutes of deep breathing to realize I'd been frightened by the reflection of our own bus in the windshield.

• If you have to get off to take a leak or to be sick, don't hesitate to tell the driver or his helper. Just say, "*Tengo que bajar, por favor*" ("I have to get off, please"), and point significantly at your stomach. They may grumble but they'd rather stop than mop.

• Fix the bus number in your mind and if necessary write it on the back of your hand. This is vital in large terminals, as the bus may pull out for refueling and then return for passengers in another loading bay.

• When the bus stops in a terminal, the driver will yell out how long you have before it leaves again. If you don't understand rapid Spanish you may be afraid to leave the bus in order to avoid being left behind. This happened to me on my first trip and I was thoroughly sick of the bus after several hundred miles of confinement to a hard seat.

In general, expect at least twenty-five minutes for meal stops, fifteen-minute stops in terminals and five minutes or more elsewhere. On back roads, the stop may be long enough for the driver to take a bath, shave, have a good lunch with a few beers and do a little gossiping. If the announced twenty-five minutes comes and he's ripping into a piece of fried beefsteak, you can bet you've got more time.

When the driver calls out "*Quince minutos,*" don't expect to come back in twenty minutes and find the bus there. It probably will be, since the driver often stays longer than he says, but if the bus is gone, it's your problem, not his.

• During long rest stops the driver may tell everyone to get off so that the bus can be locked up. On all stops it's best to leave something in your seat—a book or hat—as new passengers may not have been assigned a specific seat and will go for yours. Valuables, needless to say, should be carried with you if the bus is left open.

• Be nice to the driver and his assistant, smile at them and say "*Buenos días.*" If they notice you they'll take extra care not to leave you behind. Some but not all drivers take a head count before leaving a rest stop. If the bus starts to pull out and your friend isn't aboard, call out, "*¡Falta uno!*" ("One lacking!") and they'll wait.

• When traveling with others, make a contingency plan in case you become separated. This is an unlikely stroke of bad luck, but it doesn't hurt to take precautions. If you or a friend miss the bus, go immediately to the ticket counter and tell them what happened. They'll get you on another as fast as possible, but don't be surprised if you're charged for another ticket.

• Take first class on long hauls; it costs just slightly more than second class and will make fewer stops and detours.

• If you're in a hurry and in a small town, take a second-class bus to a larger town and then catch a first class.

• At night sit on the right side of the bus and you'll avoid the glare of oncoming headlights. During the day I always select a seat that won't get the glare and heat of the afternoon sun. Heading south, for example, I sit on the left (east) side and going north on the right. Mexicans generally avoid exposing themselves to wind even if the wind is a blistering 90 degrees. (See *¡Viva Mexico!: Superstitions.*) You may be asked to keep your window closed and if so, the shaded side of the bus will be much cooler.

• Carry drinking water and snacks. Buses leave the terminal with amazing regularity. On main routes, you'll rarely have to wait more than an hour. In fact, it is quite common to make connections so quickly that you don't have time to find a place to eat.

Whenever a bus slows down, someone will be there selling cake, tacos, sandwiches, pop, beer and fruit. Vendors will often board the bus and sell their wares between stops.

Most of this food is edible and some is downright delicious, but it is wise to be very cautious of meat and greasy delicacies while bus riding. Almost every problem we've had with diarrhea or upset stomach occurred after eating something greasy. Needless to say, being sick on a bus is not easy. I always carry a handy supply of emergency medicines, at the very minimum some type of pills or liquid to prevent uncontrollable diarrhea (see *Staying Healthy*).

In addition to regular vendors, bus passengers are the favorite targets for a variety of enterprising hucksters offering everything from Salvation to Kleenex. They often work in cooperation with the driver, who allows them aboard during regular stops or picks them up along the way, giving them a long enough ride to reel off their pitch.

The best are groups of musicians; they pile onto the bus with beat-up guitars, accordions and flutes and bang out a few discordant tunes as a hat or tin can is passed for donations. Unfortunately their routine is now being imitated by groups of aggressive young men who play insipid Gospel songs and then make a plea for donations to aid the poor. Since they're usually dressed better than most of the passengers, they often get a chilly reception.

Deaf mutes selling miniature key chain screwdrivers and sign language cards are also common. They have it down to a profitable science: they prefer buses that are making five-minute stops as most of the passengers stay aboard. The deaf mute hustles down the aisle, dropping the item for sale in each person's hand or lap. The card invariably translates as "Give generously." Once he's reached the rear of the bus he starts back, collecting donations. If you don't want a miniature screwdriver or are suffering from donor burnout, hand it back or put it on the seat beside you.

In addition to musicians and mutes you'll see people selling books on medicinal herbs (some are good). Others may give short impassioned speeches, recite epic poems or gasp out a heart-rending tale of woe that ends with the inevitable open palm.

You may be offered merchandise rather than an appeal for charity. Regional variations can be very interesting: homemade molasses in tequila bottles, honey, bottles of *rompope* (like alcoholic eggnog), bags of trimmed sugar cane, live iguanas and armadillos, birds, beadwork, guitars, Huichol Indian God's Eyes and other irresistibles. It's a far cry from the Greyhound and "Please do not speak to the operator while the coach is in motion."

Bus Terminals

The confusing variety of independent bus terminals is gradually being simplified as towns of medium size and larger create a single central bus terminal, appropriately

---

All Buses Lead to Mexico City

Like a compass, four huge terminals and several minor ones control bus traffic to and from Mexico City. You'll need to take a cab or the Metro (subway) from one terminal to another.

Terminal Central del Norte, Avenida de Los Cien Metros, #4907: This is the big one; anyone arriving from or heading north of the capital will use this terminal. The most southerly cities served by the northern terminal are Manzanillo on the Pacific Coast and Poza Rica on the Gulf of Mexico.

Terminal Central del Sur, Avenida Taxqueña 1320: Service to Cuernavaca, Taxco, Acapulco, Zihuatanejo and vicinity.

Estación TAPO: Calzada Ignacio Zaragoza. Serves eastern and southeast Mexico, including Oaxaca.

Terminal del Poniente: Río Tacubaya 102. The station for western Mexico.

called the *Central de Autobuses*. However, in some towns, each bus line has its own station or there may even be more than one large terminal. Oaxaca is a good example—it has one terminal for first-class and luxury buses and another terminal for second class. Queretaro has a huge combined terminal for first *and* second class and another (fortunately close by) terminal just for luxury buses.

Central bus terminals are also something of a misnomer, since many of them are located on the edge of town and require a taxi to reach.

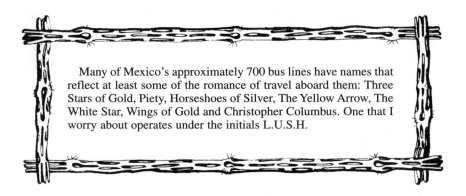

Many of Mexico's approximately 700 bus lines have names that reflect at least some of the romance of travel aboard them: Three Stars of Gold, Piety, Horseshoes of Silver, The Yellow Arrow, The White Star, Wings of Gold and Christopher Columbus. One that I worry about operates under the initials L.U.S.H.

If your Spanish is weak or your destination unpronounceable, write down the name of the place you want to go or say "*A* Oaxaca," "*A* Morelia," etc. (The "A" means "to" and is pronounced as in "Ahh, hell!") A bus driver, passenger, shoeshine boy or ticket agent will then tell you the name of the bus line you want.

Should you discover that your bus leaves from another terminal, probably on the other side of town, taking a cab is a worthwhile splurge. Wandering aimlessly in search of a bus station, particularly in the middle of the night, is a futile effort. Bus terminals seem to delight in being obscure and hard to locate.

Repeat the name of the bus line to yourself as you walk slowly to the street and to the cab. Repeat out loud the name of the bus station as the cabbie opens the door to let you in. Keep repeating it to yourself until you actually arrive, because the cabbie may forget it if he starts chatting with other passengers.

If you cannot afford a cab, follow the same procedure, but with passersby, as you wander for hours through town.

Mexico's newest bus terminals are remarkably efficient and up to date. They offer a variety of services: snack bars, restaurants, bank, post office, telegraph, newsstands, souvenir shops, fax and long-distance telephone and so on. Information booths, some staffed by English-speaking attendants, will be prominently located in the main lobbies.

Inside the bus terminal you'll find booths selling fixed-rate taxi tickets (see *Taxis*, below). There might also be a booth selling *andenes* tickets (admission to platform). To limit access, some terminals require this additional ticket to the passenger boarding areas, even if you already have a bus ticket. These tickets are very cheap. In most terminals, however, your bus ticket will serve for admission. It all depends on the whim of the management.

In larger terminals you will be told which *andenes* (platform or departure slot) your bus will leave from. If it isn't marked on your ticket or ticket envelope and you've forgotten the number, just ask any employee, from floorsweeper to bus driver. Most people go out of their way to give travelers a helping hand.

Arrivals and departures will be announced in echoing and unintelligible Spanish that

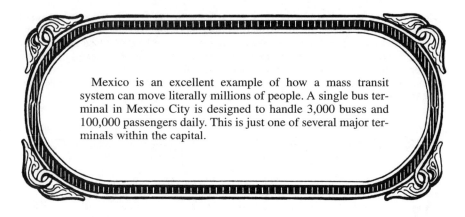

Mexico is an excellent example of how a mass transit system can move literally millions of people. A single bus terminal in Mexico City is designed to handle 3,000 buses and 100,000 passengers daily. This is just one of several major terminals within the capital.

is best ignored. Your ticket has the vital bus number and departure time, and it is more reliable than your translation of loudspeaker announcements.

At night in larger terminals you'll often see worn-out travelers sleeping on chairs, benches and the floor. If you choose to sleep, arrange your baggage securely or check it at the ticket or baggage office.

Tickets

Depending on the frills, the cost of a luxury-class seat is anywhere from forty to 100 percent more than an "ordinary" first-class ticket. In turn, a first-class bus ticket is often just a little more than second class. The greatest difference between first and second class is that first-class lines mainly operate between terminals, and have assigned seating. Second-class buses stop almost anywhere and accept all passengers, from pigs to drunks. They stop so often that it seems the bus does nothing but begin to accelerate and then immediately start braking again. (A few lines now have big, modern second-class buses which run only between large cities and stop only at terminals and *parada* [bus stop] signs, located at frequent intervals on these routes.)

Tickets for luxury- and first-class buses are purchased at the terminal and assure you of a seat (*asiento* or *silla*). During the holiday seasons, especially Christmas and Easter, it is wise to make reservations. Everyone wants to travel at these times, and you can easily be stuck for days waiting for a seat. Travel agents normally won't handle bus tickets, but some do book luxury-class tickets.

When you can't get first class or luxury, try the second-class lines. You may have to stand, but you'll almost certainly get on.

Buy your second-class ticket in the terminal or just get on the bus and wait for the *ayudante* (often a young kid) to collect fares. This is generally done after the bus gets under way. Tickets are good only for the date of issue stamped on them and, unless they are numbered, do not guarantee a seat. Be at the terminal at least half an hour before departure time if you want to be sure of getting a seat; otherwise you may be left behind or have to sit on the roof with the pigs.

You may be offered the chance to select your own seat number at the ticket counter. The diagram is similar to those used at airlines.

I always choose a seat in the teens, thirteen to nineteen, give or take a seat. This puts you in the first half of the bus, handy for quick rushes to the front door at rest stops, but far enough back to avoid having to watch traffic. When riding on buses equipped with bathrooms (almost all first class and some second class), avoid the last few seats. The strong odor and slamming door will distract you from the scenery.

Your first-class and luxury ticket will show the number of the bus, the hour of departure and your destination. Check them closely; if you or the ticketing agent makes an error it should be cleared up immediately or they'll assume you've just changed your mind about when you want to leave and are trying to pull a fast one. The departure time is marked *Salida* or *Hora*, the departure bay is *Andene*, and the bus number is under *Camíon* or *Autobus*. The *destino* may be printed right on the ticket or stamped or scribbled across it.

On a long trip, you can buy a ticket all the way through to your final destination, but you may have to wait in the terminal for connections. If you do not have a "through" ticket, you can avoid waiting by finding another bus line.

Stop-overs are usually not allowed. If you'll be stopping, buy a series of tickets: city A to city B, then B to the next stop or final destination.

Mexican Student Card discounts can be substantial. (See *Speaking Spanish: Spanish Language Schools*.) Your ticket is also your claim to insurance in the event of an accident. (This is true of almost all modes of public transportation.) From the stories we've heard, collecting this so-called insurance is evidently more difficult than winning the lottery.

If you lose your ticket, you may have to buy another, so be careful.

Tickets cannot be exchanged or refunded, though if you plead and whine, they may relent and let you trade. If you've got a ticket that you can't use, the only reliable solution is to sell it.

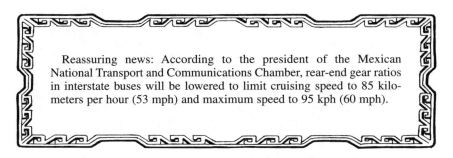

Reassuring news: According to the president of the Mexican National Transport and Communications Chamber, rear-end gear ratios in interstate buses will be lowered to limit cruising speed to 85 kilometers per hour (53 mph) and maximum speed to 95 kph (60 mph).

The first time I found myself in this situation I lurked around the doorway of the terminal hissing "Guadalajara? *¡Oiga amigo!* Won't you buy a ticket to Guadalajara?" My furtive approach sent prospective customers hustling away as fast as their legs and luggage would allow them. As the moment of departure approached, I dropped the "Psst! Hey!" routine and went right to the ticket counter, buttonholing waiting passengers. The ticket agent groaned and rolled his eyes, but did me the favor of directing two Guadalajara-bound people my way. They looked puzzled at having to buy tickets from a bearded gringo, but smiled when I gave them a small discount.

Baggage

On first-class and long-haul second-class buses, baggage can be checked through to the final destination. You should be given a claim stub and if you aren't, ask for one. Baggage handlers on a few lines tend to be sloppy about checking claim stubs, but on most they are efficient and dependable.

Some second-class lines expect passengers to take care of loading and unloading their luggage. This can be preferable to having a twelve-year-old kid slam it into the cargo compartment and bury it beneath a crate of overripe tomatoes. When loading your own, beware of spilled oil or grease. I once took my suitcase out of a second-class bus and found it soaked with motor oil. Complaining is a waste of time and air.

The standard baggage allowance is twenty-five kilos (fifty-five pounds), but unless you're carrying something extra bulky, they'll rarely hold you to the limit. I once traveled with five enormous baskets loaded with handicrafts, a full-sized backpack and a portable typewriter. It took a major conference between the bus driver, ticket agent, baggage handler and myself, but I got that nightmarish quantity aboard for a very reasonable "adjustment" fee. You might be told to purchase an extra passenger ticket for excess baggage, or pay an excess baggage fee at the ticket counter.

Hand-carried luggage can be taken aboard, but if it won't fit on the overhead rack the driver has the right to insist that it go below: either between your feet or in the cargo hold. If you really object to this, the alternative is to buy your luggage a seat of its own (which is frowned upon) or to offer a tip to let it ride on the steps or in the aisle. On second-class buses, especially older ones, baggage is put anywhere and everywhere, and size and weight are rarely problems. If your baggage requires special handling or extra muscle, you may be prodded for a tip by the driver's helper. This is a standard practice, though tourists often aren't asked to pay.

On buses that are loaded with *campesinos* coming to or from market, you'll probably observe lively bartering between the driver, his *ayudante* and the goods-laden passengers. The discussions over baggage charges can get quite animated. On one bus I rode, it took longer to hassle over fares and tips than it did to drive to our destination. The people who had baggage on top of the bus were especially hard hit; the *ayudante* would literally dangle things from the roof over the heads of the passengers, threatening to keep their stuff aboard if they didn't pay what he asked. The driver was helpfully gunning the engine at the same time.

Always label your baggage, including an extra label inside just in case it is lost or misplaced. When traveling long distances I keep my camera and valuable small personal items in a bag or box between my feet. On short rides I carry valuables on my lap or in the rack directly over my head. Rip-offs are not common, but it's easier to take a few simple precautions than to chance a loss.

Here's an important tip: place your suitcase or pack inside a tough garbage sack before you stow it beneath an older bus to protect it from dirty stowage bins.

Upon arrival you will usually take your baggage right from the bus, although some terminals do have *Andenes de Equipaje* (baggage claim platforms).

Big terminals will have porters; a few have do-it-yourself baggage carts (*carretillas*). When I'm overloaded, I always use a porter; it's far better than straining a muscle or losing track of something.

Baggage can be left at the ticket counter in small terminals or in storerooms in larger terminals. Look for signs that say *Guarda Equipaje*. Some charge a small fee, others don't. If it's the storage room for the bus line you're using, your ticket should be sufficient, though a tip isn't a bad idea. Ask if there's a time limit if you expect to be gone for a day or more. I've found that even in larger terminals the ticket agents will usually let me dump my luggage on them for a few hours without bothering with claim stubs or payment.

If by any chance your baggage is lost, don't panic. Remain calm and polite; the outraged customer routine rarely gets better results. If it seems appropriate, the polite offer of a tip (don't act as though you're bribing) can give some underpaid and overworked baggage handler sudden interest in digging through a dark storage room.

Border Crossing by Bus

At many if not all of the larger American border towns, it is quite easy to cross into Mexico by bus. Simply go to the Greyhound depot and they'll probably have frequent bus service into the neighboring Mexican city. Better yet, this bus will usually go to the *central de camiones* (main bus terminal). I often cross from El Paso to Ciudad Juárez by bus. The service is not only fast and efficient, it is also a real bargain. (For details on how such a crossing can be made, see *The Best of Mexico: Copper Canyon Itinerary: Copper Canyon by Bus*.)

First-class bus tickets for destinations inside Mexico can also be purchased in the U.S. through Greyhound and its Mexican affiliates.

There are several advantages to this: first, a ticket between the U.S. and Mexico includes the border crossing (but you'll first change to a Mexican bus). This saves a substantial cab fare.

At the station in Mexico, you'll be transferred to another bus. If you're unfamiliar with Mexico's huge bus stations, you'll probably find them slightly mind-boggling at first. Unlike cramped, slightly depressing American depots, they are more like air terminals, spacious and full of activity.

With an advance ticket in hand, you can relax and enjoy the scene: beggars, taco stands, tear-filled partings and reunions, and other wide-eyed tourists madly thumbing phrase books for the correct pronunciation of "Please direct me to the ticket agent offering connections to Ixtznitlapoapan."

When returning to the U.S., I'd probably buy a ticket to the first town on the American side of the border. Once again, this takes care of the crossing. Because Mexican ticket agents may not be aware of special fare offers in the U.S., however, wait until you've crossed into the States to buy a continuing ticket.

City Buses

City buses are just as hard to figure out here as in any part of the world. A city bus usually has *Servicio Urbano* written on it somewhere. The destination is often painted on the windshield with whitewash, but it could also be the destination of yesterday's route that the driver didn't bother to clean off. Trial and error and asking for help are the best ways to use city buses.

The cost makes them economical enough to be worth the effort. If you're hitching, you might want to ride one through town.

Buses in big cities stop only at *Parada* signs in the downtown area, but on side streets, get on whatever you can and don't hesitate to board one that is stopped at a traffic light.

These buses are often crowded, so crowded that you'll lose track of where you are or be trapped inside and unable to force your way to the door. That's the way it goes; at least you'll see parts of the city that you might have missed otherwise.

You may have to show your ticket to an occasional inspector. If you've thrown it away, he will sell you another.

As on any type of bus, the city transit bus will not stop unless you ring the buzzer over the door, speak to the driver or beat on the roof with your fist. You may have to say "*¡Baja! ¡Baja!* ("Down!"), *¡Por favor!*" or "*¡Aquí, Por favor!*" If you just yell "Stop!" in Spanish or English, it often pisses them off and they won't.

Get off through the back door if you can; the driver may not let you out the front unless it's too crowded to do otherwise.

Trains

Mexican buses are comfortable and convenient, but they don't have the easy-going style of a train, rattling through the mountains, stopping at what seems to be every other *pueblo*. The lazy traveler lounges in a seat or bed, reading a book or just staring out of the window, wondering how long it will take the beer vendor to make another round. Some young gringo on his way to Tierra del Fuego is strumming a guitar, a yawning businessman from Mexico City reads the sports section of *Excelsior*, while his wife, daughters, mother and two older sisters delve into abundantly provisioned hampers. *El portero* pokes under the seats with his broom, then discreetly sweeps the trash overboard from between the cars.

TRAIN MAP

11. Mazatlán
12. Monterrey
13. Matamoro
14. Nuevo Laredo
15. Chihuahua
16. Cuidad Juárez
17. Nogales
18. Mexicali
19. Tijuana
20. La Paz
21. Los Mochis

1. Mexico City
2. Puebla
3. Veracruz
4. Oaxaca
5. Acapulco
6. Manzanillo
7 Guadalajara
8 Tampico
9. Mérida
10. Tapachula

Passenger trains are generally made up of older cars retired from service in the U.S. The staffs also seem to have stopped the clock about thirty years back; they wear traditional railroad uniforms and are very fussy about their jobs and responsibilities. The average train consists of the *maquinista* (engineer), the *fogonero* (fireman), *conductor* (the overall boss), three *garroteros* (conductor's signalmen-helpers), one at the front, middle and rear of the train, one *portero* per car and the *auditor*, in charge of checking and selling tickets aboard the train. If there's a dining car, it has about ten cooks and waiters (*cocineros* and *meseros*).

The sad news is that the condition of Mexico's extensive passenger train system seems to be heading slowly but steadily downhill. Many so-called "first-class" trains no longer have Pullman berths or dining cars. Passengers sleep sitting up and dine from picnic baskets or treats offered by itinerant vendors.

Nonetheless, for train buffs, incurable romantics and unhurried travelers, the fact that trains are old-fashioned, don't pass each other on curves and depend more on nostalgia than speed to attract passengers makes them an excellent way to experience Mexico.

Trains often follow routes beyond the reach of highways and roads. Some stop at villages that are otherwise accessible only on foot. The countryside along the track is likely to be unspoiled, without the usual sprawl of gas stations, cafés and tire repair shops one constantly sees alongside the highway.

Despite stories that Mexican trains are inevitably hours off schedule, you will find them reasonably punctual. Delays do occur, but not often.

Tickets

First-class train travel is inexpensive and costs about the same as a ticket on a first-class bus. On some shorter routes, train travel times compare favorably with those for buses. Longer trips are another story, however, and a train will lag far behind a bus, especially if there are mountain ranges to be crossed.

The comfort of train travel is largely dependent on how much you're willing to pay. Second class is very cheap and very uncomfortable: poorly padded seats (if any padding at all), ancient cars that are crowded, dirty, noisy and hot or cold according to the weather outside. They are generally picturesque, like most uncomfortable situations when viewed from a slight distance.

Young travelers are often attracted to second class, both for the savings and for the atmosphere. In most cases they usually regret not going first class; the price difference is small and if you need excitement you can always visit the second-class cars. The bathrooms in second class are rough, to say the least.

Regular first-class accommodations can be unpredictable, especially in southern Mexico. Some first-class cars are quite nice, but others lack heat and air conditioning, and have stiff, uncomfortable seats. One car I rode in had *Primera Clase* painted over a still legible *Segunda Clase*. The only difference was the degree of crowding.

First-class seats are assigned, though this isn't enforced if the car isn't full. These cars will have restrooms (men's and women's) and on most trains they are kept reasonably clean (carry toilet paper). Drinking water and paper cups are also provided. (Nonetheless, we always carry a supply of drinking water.) Air conditioning and heating may or may not be in operation. One trip we made started with the temperature so high that passengers had to ride between the cars until the wind cooled our car down. And on another trip, in wintertime, Lorena and I sat wrapped in sleeping bags, watching less well-equipped passengers slowly turn blue.

Tickets in smaller stations may not be sold until the train arrives or shortly before. This can lead to crowding and confusion at the ticket window, but if you decide to board the train without a ticket, you'll have to pay the auditor an additional twenty-five percent above the regular fare.

If tickets are sold out and you're desperate, ask a porter if there isn't some way to get aboard. We've done this and although it took a few extra dollars, a friendly porter conjured up two first-class tickets for us. A friend calls this "Mexican witchcraft."

Round-trip tickets cost double one-way and are valid for only thirty days.

There are no special deals for groups, although students holding current Mexican Student Cards (see *Speaking Spanish: Spanish Language Schools*) can get a fifty percent discount during three vacation seasons (*ciclo especial de vacaciones*). These are:

15 to 31 December
15 to 30 May
1 July to 31 August

The student discount is for seats only, not beds.

Children under five are free; over five and under twelve, half fare; over twelve, full price.

Refunds on tickets are given only under the following conditions: if the trip is interrupted or canceled by fault of the railroad company itself; if the passenger cancels twenty-four hours in advance of departure; or if the passenger cancels three hours in advance of departure when the ticket is bought on the same day. In all cases write a nice letter explaining the circumstances in English or Spanish to: Jefe, Departamento de Tráfico de Pasajeros, Gran Estación Central de Buenavista, Av. Insurgentes Norte, México 3, DF. He can also be approached personally. Most railroad officials speak English.

Mexico by Train

Mexico by Train: tel: 800-321-1699 (U.S. and Canada); 210-661-9535 (San Antonio, Texas)

Information and reservations: Direct your letters to **Departamento de Tráfico de Pasajeros, Ferrocarriles Nacionales de México** (and use the address given below).

Trains departing from Mexico City to other points and from Monterrey, Veracruz, Chihuahua and Uruapan or Guadalajara to Mexico City: Señor Larraquival, Estación Central de Buenavista, Insurgentes Norte, 06358, Mexico, DF, Mexico (tel: 011-52-5-47-86-55)

From Nuevo Laredo: P.O. Box 595, Laredo, TX 78042

From Matamoros: Calle Hidalgo entre 9 y 10 s/n, Colonia Centro, Matamoros, Tamaulipas, México

From Piedras Negras: Calle Zaragoza y Boulevard, Piedras Negras, Coahuila, México

From Ciudad Juárez: P.O. Box 2200, El Paso, TX 79951

From Nogales: Calle Internacional No. 10, Nogales, Sonora, México

From Mexicali: P.O. Box 182, Mexicali, Baja California Norte, México

From Chihuahua to Los Mochis and return (the Copper Canyon run): Apdo Postal 46, Chihuahua, Chihuahua, México

(Veteran train traveler and writer Gary Poole kindly contributed to this list.)

If you get into a dispute over a ticket or are confused, pay what is asked, get a receipt (*recibo*) and write or speak to the people in the office mentioned above.

Exchanges of tickets come under the same rules as for refunds.

If you lose your ticket, tough luck; buy another.

Reservations

Whenever possible buy your tickets in advance. This will save standing in line or not getting aboard at all. Train travel is popular and trains are sometimes full. During the Christmas and Easter holidays, if you don't have a reservation you'd better forget it entirely.

The railroads advise tourists to make reservations by mail, one or two months in advance. Send them a letter (in English if you wish) giving all details, including number of children and their ages, etc. They will write back and tell you how much it will cost. You then send a cashier's check or certified check payable to National Railways of Mexico. No other form of payment can be used. They'll either send you the tickets or tell you where they can be picked up.

Railway offices will also send information on schedules and fares in English upon request.

Baggage

Adults are allowed 110 pounds each, children fifty-five pounds. We've often taken more and gotten away with it. It pays to hire a porter if you've got more baggage than can be easily carried in two hands. He'll find your seat and help you stow your stuff.

When you're coming into Mexico, baggage will be inspected by Mexican Customs officials at the train depot, as the passengers are being boarded. Tourists are usually hustled right through, but if you have something unusual in your luggage you may be questioned about it. A porter makes a good middleman.

Baggage cannot be checked on some trains. First-class cars, however, have extra space behind the last row of seats and most have an additional cubby hole or two for excess baggage.

If you're riding second class keep a sharp eye on your baggage. I've heard of a few cases where departing passengers took more than their share. Quick thieves may also hop into second class during stops. The first-class cars are watched by the conductor and porters, so the danger of rip-offs is much less.

Larger stations have baggage rooms (*Guarda Equipaje*). There is a small fee charged for each twenty-four hours. Baggage can be left for longer periods (weeks), but this is a private enterprise, not a service of the railway company; they take no responsibility. Don't lose your claim ticket!

Pets

Dogs and cats must ride in the baggage cars. If they aren't in a cage, box or other container they should have a collar and leash. The fee is small but the railroad takes no responsibility for the conditions under which the pet travels or its condition when it arrives. They recommend giving the baggage handlers aboard the train a good tip. Pets can also be shipped express. Birds must travel in cages.

Food

Dining cars are a thing of the past. Pack a big lunch, with plenty of drinks or pure water (we don't trust train water). Conductors may offer lunchmeat sandwiches and box lunches at relatively high prices. This prepared food isn't well refrigerated, so I'd avoid it after midday, especially in the hot country.

Fruit is sold at almost every stop, as well as the usual tacos, enchiladas, *gorditas*, chicken, rice, candy, sodas and miscellaneous junk food. Some of this food is safe and delicious but I definitely advise caution. (When in doubt, get a steaming hot tamale—food that is literally steaming is usually safe to eat.)

If you're traveling south, stop in a supermarket at the border and stock up on cheese, nuts, bread, vegetables, canned juices, crackers, condiments and magazines. Cold beer and sodas are sold on the train.

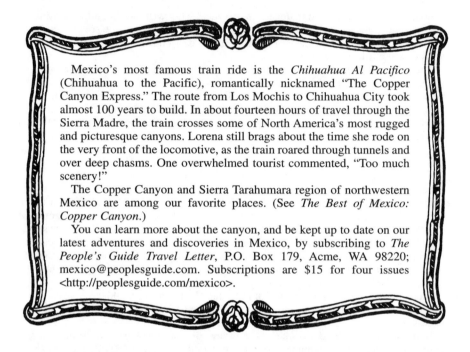

Mexico's most famous train ride is the *Chihuahua Al Pacifico* (Chihuahua to the Pacific), romantically nicknamed "The Copper Canyon Express." The route from Los Mochis to Chihuahua City took almost 100 years to build. In about fourteen hours of travel through the Sierra Madre, the train crosses some of North America's most rugged and picturesque canyons. Lorena still brags about the time she rode on the very front of the locomotive, as the train roared through tunnels and over deep chasms. One overwhelmed tourist commented, "Too much scenery!"

The Copper Canyon and Sierra Tarahumara region of northwestern Mexico are among our favorite places. (See *The Best of Mexico: Copper Canyon*.)

You can learn more about the canyon, and be kept up to date on our latest adventures and discoveries in Mexico, by subscribing to *The People's Guide Travel Letter*, P.O. Box 179, Acme, WA 98220; mexico@peoplesguide.com. Subscriptions are $15 for four issues <http://peoplesguide.com/mexico>.

Travelers heading out of Mexico City's Buenavista station can buy a box lunch there (standard fare: two ham sandwiches, one hard-boiled egg, one banana, one orange and a piece of cake). A better picnic, however, is available by shopping at the supermarket half a block from the station. Go out the front doors to the old railroad engine planted near the boulevard. From there you can see the sign of a huge supermarket/department store across the street. It has an excellent selection of cheeses and other picnic ingredients, as well as bottled water, juice and soda pop.

Beer, soft drinks, canned juices and candies are sold on the train by men carrying buckets and boxes. Their prices are not a bargain, but it is convenient. In the morning they will bring around hot, sweet coffee, calling out "*¡Café!*" It is usually stronger than hell.

Sleeping
To the dismay of train travelers, sleeping cars are rare. If you're lucky and the train isn't crowded it is possible to flop across two seats. In spite of her height, Lorena somehow manages to make this look comfortable. I'm less flexible and have to be content with sitting upright. In case you forgot my suggestion to bring an inflatable pillow, you might be able to rent a small pillow (*cojin*) at night from the porter. Pillows definitely reduce neck strain and head-knocking against the window.

Sleeping in second class is difficult to impossible. The lights are left on all night and there's usually an assortment of wailing children, loud drunks or bragging soldiers to contend with. Second-class passengers who attempt to sneak into the first-class cars for a quick nap are inevitably caught and sent back by the conductor. Pretending to be asleep is no defense; they have almost infallible memories and won't hesitate to shake you awake to check your ticket.

General Information and Advice

• Stops are frequent and vary in length from seconds to hours. The best way to determine how long you'll be at a station is to observe the other passengers: if they flock to the food vendors, it's usually a long stop. Be careful of being left behind. The conductor may know how long they'll be there, but then again, he may not. On some routes, trains are shuffled around at stops and it's easy to get confused and lose track of your particular car. Note its number carefully.

• It will be cold at night on northern routes in wintertime. Have a jacket, blanket or sleeping bag handy.

• Dollars are not normally accepted aboard the train and if they are, the rate of exchange won't be good. Change enough money into pesos to last the entire ride.

• Have toilet paper handy; there won't be any in second class and it sometimes runs out in first class.

• If you're getting off at an intermediate point, be sure to get your things ready well ahead of time. Even though the porter may promise to wake you up, don't count on it.

Lorena and I were once sound asleep in a *camarín*, engulfed, as usual, in our excess baggage, when the porter yelled that we had about three minutes to get dressed, sorted out and off the train. He and the conductor formed a baggage brigade and shortly after waking from deep dreams, we found ourselves standing knee-deep in boxes, packs and bags on a dark, deserted platform, still buttoning up our clothes.

• The *federales* and Army sometimes search cars and baggage en route (the Army always travels by train). A friend was riding second class in southern Mexico, having a nice conversation with the man seated next to him, when he noticed the fellow becoming increasingly agitated and nervous. "Would you do me a favor?" the man suddenly asked, forcing the window next to him wide open. My friend said "Yes," not understanding what was happening. The man looked around the car a few times, obviously frightened, then whispered, "Throw those boxes out the window!" He pointed to three large cartons lashed with twine sitting in the aisle.

My friend hesitated, but before he could ask any questions, the man dove headfirst through the window. There was a thud, followed by a short cry. When my friend stuck his head out the window, he saw the man lying motionless alongside the track, rapidly moving into the distance. He turned his head in the other direction and saw a group of *federales* signaling the train. Realizing that he was now stuck with whatever was in the boxes, he quickly dumped them out of the window. The other passengers watched without comment and when the cops searched the car, obviously looking for someone in particular, no one said a word.

Rental Cars

Car rental agencies can be found in Mexico City and towns of any size. Look for familiar names: Hertz, Avis de Mexico, Budget Rent-A-Car and others, Combi Rent SA, Auto Rent and so on. Most rental agencies have someone around who speaks English.

Rates are government controlled, but special offers and requirements vary from one company to another. In general, however, you'll find that renting a car is much more expensive than in the U.S. To rent a car, you'll also have to be twenty-five years old, have a valid driver's license and passport (or tourist card) and a major credit card. Check the rental agency's requirements versus their rates before deciding. Those with low prices may not accept credit cards.

For reasons I have never understood, it is often cheaper to rent a car in advance, through a travel agent or American rental agency, rather than waiting until you arrive in Mexico. Rental cars can be driven one way, but the additional charge is exorbitant.

Before renting a car, make a rough estimate of how much driving you'll be doing and what the basic charges will be. You may well find that it's cheaper to hire a cab for shorter trips and to fly for longer jaunts. Cars are considered a luxury in Mexico, not a necessity.

Taxis

Alternatives to Rental Cars

When buses aren't available, travelers can avoid the high cost of a rental car by using taxis. Hourly and daily rates for cabs often meet—or even beat—the total price (gas, parking, insurance) of a rental car. Don't discount the convenience of having a hired driver, either. Until you've locked bumpers with rush-hour traffic in Guadalajara or Mazatlán, you might not fully appreciate the challenge of driving in Mexico. In my opinion, there's no better way to cope with highway-induced stress than by using cabs.

In Small Towns

A town or village of any consequence will have at least one cab, even though it may be a wreck of a car or pickup truck with broken seats and no fenders.

Because the cost and maintenance of owning even an old car (or renting a newer one) are far beyond the means of most Mexicans, taxis are more commonly used than in the U.S.. If a Sunday outing, picnic, wedding, birthday party or shopping errand requires the use of a *coche*, it will be hired, along with the driver. What seems at first to be an extravagance is actually the opposite: rather than use private cars casually, Mexicans use buses, trains and cabs. Tourists would often save by doing the same. The cost of insurance for a private vehicle, for example, will hire a taxi for a good many miles.

Taxi rates are determined by distance and bargaining. Some cabs post their rates per kilometer or per hour in the window.

In rural areas private car owners or licensed cabbies will make irregular runs between towns, charging by the head and amount of baggage. They'll often wait until they've got a full load before leaving. If the driver sets a flat price, the passengers may beat the bushes for other riders to share the expenses, sometimes bringing the price down as low as a bus ticket.

In Larger Towns and Cities

A cab is available when the *libre* (free) flag on the meter is horizontal, though I'd try to flag down any cab that doesn't have a passenger.

Fares: If the cab has a working meter, insist that it be used. Metered fares are always the best deal, unless you're hiring the cab by the hour.

If the meter isn't working, agree to the fare before getting into the cab. Many hotels post official cab fares. Desk clerks can also give you an idea of what you should pay. Overcharging by cabbies is easily avoided by following these simple precautions.

Hourly and daily rates are available for many cabs. Such rates may be fixed or subject to haggling. Ask for the *precio por hora* or *por día* (by the hour or by the day). When done by the day, ask how many hours the driver considers a day to be; it might be only three or four. If your Spanish is weak, enlist a desk clerk to help you make the deal.

In Mexico City, and occasionally elsewhere, a ten percent nighttime surcharge is added to cab fares between 11 p.m. and 7 a.m. (See *Safety: Safety Alert*.)

Turismo Cabs: In Mexico City and some resorts you'll see *turismo* cabs, usually big American cars with an ominous black hood over the meter. The hood means they'll take both you and your budget for a ride. On the plus side, most *turismo* drivers speak English and can double as sightseeing guides.

Radio call cabs: Listed in the phone book under *Sitios*. (These cabs also have SITIO marked on the side.) They use meters, but charge an extra fee for the call service on top of what they charge for the ride. If a cruising *Sitio* cab picks you up in the street, you may also be charged extra, even though you didn't use the radio call service.

Tips: Tips are not required unless a cabbie has performed a special service—such as getting bus tickets or taking you to his favorite taco stand. On the other hand, cab drivers aren't getting rich. We usually give a ten percent *propina*.

In the event of a hassle over the fare, note the cab's number and report the incident as soon as possible to the tourist bureau. As a last resort, call a cop.

Knife blade inscription: He Will Tell You Who Your Father Is

At Bus Stations
Most bus terminals offer pre-paid taxi tickets in the lobby. Look for a booth with a sign saying *"Boletos de Taxi."* In Mexico City, for example, ticket sellers display a large city map showing concentric rings or *zonas*. Point to your destination or tell the ticket person which zone you're going to. You'll be sold a cab ticket good for any address within that zone. Take your ticket to one of the drivers outside. The trip is now completely paid for, though again, a tip is always appreciated.

In smaller bus stations there may be signs announcing what should be paid for a taxi ride to specific destinations.

At Airports
Airports usually offer two types of cab service: *colectivo* and the more expensive *especial*. Tickets for both are sold at a booth in the main concourse or outside, at the taxi loading zone. *Colectivos* charge per person, and will leave when the car or van is full. Passengers are dropped off in the order their hotels are reached. "Special" cabs charge substantially more, but you're hiring exclusive use of the car. By sharing the cost, the price of a "special" cab will still be reasonable.

At Train Stations
Train passengers are often hustled by cab drivers as they leave the station. Better deals can usually be found with cabs on the street.

Border Crossing by Cab
In border towns, some Mexican cab drivers are licensed to drive into the U.S. They'll charge a flat rate, subject to a certain amount of haggling.

Delays at the border caused by heavy traffic are part of the cabbie's normal work and are reflected in his stiff fare. On the other hand, if you've got Lorena's usual load of boxes, bags and baskets, he may expect more money if there's a long inspection, or if something about you or your luggage sets off alarms and causes an unusual delay at U.S. Customs.

Cross-border rates are posted in some bus and train stations along the border. If the cab driver won't honor them, keep looking.

Colectivos

One of the most useful forms of Mexican public transportation is the *colectivo*, a hybrid-cross between a bus or van and a cab (often called a *combi* if a VW van is used). The *combi* or *colectivo* is a van, mini-bus or other vehicle stuffed with seats. *Colectivos* run regular routes, much like buses. Their fares are more than a bus, but only about a tenth of what a cab charges for the same ride. The *colectivo* will often have a route number or their destination will be whitewashed on the windshield.

In Mexico City, most *colectivos* are mini-buses painted a light forest green. If you ride a long distance, you'll be charged double fare. Pay when you get off.

Though *colectivos* prefer to stop at designated spots, they can sometimes be flagged down. *Colectivos* are cheap, convenient, crowded and fun to use.

Navigating in Mexico City

Mexico City is literally the crossroads of the country and anyone traveling south of the capital will almost certainly have to pass through it. Just how complicated that will be depends not only on where you're going or coming from, but by what means you arrive and how much you're willing to pay for connections. If this sounds confusing—just wait until you're actually there. The population of Mexico City by the year 2020 is predicted to reach 35 to 40 million. It feels as though most of these people are already in town, just waiting to be counted.

The size and complexity of the city make it impossible to explain all the ins and outs of getting from one point to another. If you're carrying luggage, taxis are the most convenient. We use cabs for traveling to and from the airport, bus stations and hotels. For sightseeing within the city, take advantage of buses and the Metro (subway). (See *Safety: Safety Alert.*)

Subway (*Metro*)

The Metro in Mexico City is a fast and fun way to get around. Using the color codes, symbols and maps found in stations and cars, you can more or less figure out where you are and where you are going.

A ticket is ridiculously cheap and the Metro stations alone are worth the price. Many have interesting displays, including archaeological treasures from the excavation of the subway tunnels. At rush hour the downtown subways are incredibly crowded. The pushing, shoving and groping are so bad that fenced walkways are available to protect women and children during rush hours. The Metro closes at midnight; after that you'll have to rely on an occasional bus or cab. It opens again at 6 a.m.

Air Service

Air service within Mexico is good, but it costs many times the price of a first-class bus or train ticket. In the past, you could save money by waiting until you had crossed the border into Mexico before catching a plane. This is no longer true. The "border exclusion zone" agreement has closed this loophole.

Mexican planes traveling to or from the U.S. must conform to U.S. standards. Mexican airlines are very proud of their safety record.

Small planes are widely used to haul freight and passengers into isolated areas. Many of these seat-of-your-pants airlines also operate regular or sort-of-regular flights between large cities and tourist towns. Their prices are usually quite reasonable.

• **Terminals:** Travelers arriving for the first time by air will find terminal facilities are typically small, overcrowded and poorly organized. With the possible exception of Mexico City, virtually every terminal I've used, from Mazatlán to Cancun, seems to be in a perpetual state of expansion and construction. Seating is limited and restroom facilities are marginal to grim. (In comparison, Mexico's spacious bus terminals are veritable models of convenience and efficiency.)

During the day, airports offer basic survival services. You'll be able to rent a car, call home and change money, buy a magazine, have a snack and a drink or pick up a souvenir "Life's a Beach" T-shirt. However, because most flights arrive and depart Mexico during daylight hours, this leads to lapses in airport services. Once the last scheduled flight of the day has arrived or departed, the airport quickly becomes a ghost town. If your flight comes in an hour or two late, don't expect to find rental car agents, food service or much more than a sleepy cab driver.

• **Mexican Immigration and Customs** (*Migración* and *Aduana*) procedures for air travelers are simple and straightforward, with no "monkey business" or bribes. You may be confused, but they aren't. Relax, "go with the flow," and you'll find the process smooth and painless.

Mexican airports have red and green "traffic" lights in the custom inspection area. Incoming travelers push a button. If the red signal flashes, their luggage will be inspected. Green means no inspection. These lights are said to be randomly controlled.

• **Baggage:** Tag everything, inside and out. Use durable baggage tags and print your name, address and final destination in a bold, clear hand. Use permanent ink.

Baggage off-loading is slow but sure; wait patiently at the carousel and it'll arrive sooner or later. Baggage handlers are typically helpful and trustworthy. Give at least 50 cents a bag (with a $1 minimum) for their time.

• **Exit tax:** Mexico's unpopular airport exit tax is now included in the price of your airplane ticket. It is no longer necessary to tuck away money to get out of the country, *unless you buy your return air ticket inside Mexico.*

Ferries

Have you ever had the desire to take a sea cruise but couldn't afford the price? If so, consider a passage on one of Mexico's large car/passenger ferries. These ships travel between ports on the Baja California Peninsula and mainland Mexico. Made in Europe, they are fast, comfortable and equipped with a cafeteria and bar.

There are three routes from the Baja Peninsula to western Mexico: La Paz to Mazatlán, La Paz to Topolobampo, and Santa Rosalia to Guaymas. **Note:** There is no service between Cabo San Lucas and Puerto Vallarta.

Schedules may vary slightly depending on the tides, weather and amount of traffic, but the ferries are otherwise quite reliable.

• **Gulf of Mexico and Caribbean:** In spite of rumors and premature announcements that car and passenger ferry service would be established between the Yucatán Peninsula and Florida, this has yet to happen. Other than the ferries in the Sea of Cortez and along some highways, there are no regularly scheduled ferries that I know of in Mexico.

After years of benign neglect under government control, Baja's ferries are now owned and operated by SEMATUR, a private corporation. By all accounts, the *transbordadores* (ferries) are in good shape, with frequent sailings and reasonable service. Though the price of tickets for foot passengers and vehicles has increased several-fold, these trips are a bargain (unless you are towing a trailer). Your only alternative—driving around the Sea of Cortez instead of cutting across it—can take several days. (Under average conditions, the crossing between La Paz and Mazatlán is about 18 hours.)

Tickets and Reservations

Though desirable, advance reservations are not required unless you'll be traveling during peak holiday traffic at Christmas and Easter. Reservations are a must, however, if you require a bed or cabin rather than a reclining seat in the salon.

Without an advance reservation, you'll normally have to wait no more than a day or two (. . . or three or four) to get aboard. Still, the safest policy is to go to the *oficina de transbordadores* (ferry office) in the nearest port and make a reservation.

Reservations can also be made by calling ferry offices in Mexico. When they answer, ask "Do you speak English, please?" until someone who does comes to the phone. Be patient and you'll probably get along just fine.

Before you call, make a note of the exact, overall length of your vehicle (and trailer), including bumper extensions. The height isn't important unless the vehicle is unusually tall.

Phone reservations are a great idea—on paper. Unfortunately, I've heard occasional reports of phone reservations that mysteriously disappeared in the shuffle. Frankly, I'm not surprised; in Mexico, there's just no substitute for conducting business face to face. To avoid disappointment, try to confirm your reservation by visiting the ferry office a day or two before you sail.

Ferry Reservation Offices

SEMATUR: 011-525-286-1267 or 5-553-7957
La Paz: 011-52-112-53833 and 54666; fax: 112-56588
Pichilingue (La Paz): 011-52-112-29485
Mazatlán: 011-52-69-817020 and 817021; fax: 69-817023
Topolobampo: 011-52-686-20035 and 20141; fax: 686-24435
Santa Rosalia: 011-52-115-20014 and 20013
Guaymas: 011-52-622-23390; fax: 622-23393; tickets: 622-22324
Mexico, DF: 011-52-555-37957
Ferry information within Mexico: 91-800-696-96
More info: <http://mexico-travel.com/>

Passengers have a choice of four classes of accommodations (except on the routes to Guaymas and Topolobampo, where only the first two classes are available). These are *Salón, Turista, Cabina* and *Especial.*

Salón class is a bus-type reclining seat. *Salón* compartments are large, with lots of walking room (except at night when many passengers spread out for a nap on the deck) and plenty of windows. *Turista* consists of cubicles with bunk beds and washbasins. *Cabina* is a tiny cabin with two single beds and a bath. *Especial* is an even larger "suite," with four beds, shower, toilet and a writing table.

If you are traveling alone and take a cabin, you may have the room to yourself for the price of a single ticket. However, if the ferry is crowded, you will be given a roommate of the same sex. The price of a berth in any category includes your passage.

Infants travel free and children 11 years and younger are half-fare.

Salón class tickets are sold on a first-come, first-served basis, but anyone desiring a bed or traveling with a vehicle should try to make reservations in advance. This is especially advisable during the holidays, when most of the ferries are completely filled.

Vehicle Requirements and Restrictions

Baja ferries can carry just about any vehicle, including semi trucks and passenger buses. The fare is based on length, though extra-large vehicles may also be charged for height and weight. Motorcycles pay a flat fee.

Your vehicle will be measured before boarding. If you have extended the length by adding a spare tire to the front bumper or other piece of equipment, it might well put you into the next size category. When in doubt, remove any extensions if you can.

A charge is made for each vehicle, including those carried or towed by others. A dune buggy or motorcycle, for example, will be counted separately.

Once aboard you will absolutely not be allowed inside your car until the trip is over. This means you'll want to have your camera, toothbrush, picnic basket and other personal stuff ready in advance.

Pets

Pets must stay in the vehicle and no care is provided. Don't feed your pet too heavily before boarding unless it has exceptional powers of self-control. Allow adequate ventilation; the cargo compartments are tightly sealed during the crossing and get very stuffy. Give your pet plenty to drink in a stable container—if it tips over, that's it.

Tourist Cards, Car Papers and Customs Inspections

When crossing from Baja to the mainland of Mexico you must have both a tourist card and a car import permit. The latter is available in the *Aduana* office in La Paz. (For more details, see *The Best of Mexico* and *Red Tape and the Law*). **Note:** As of this writing, tourist vehicles embarking from Santa Rosalia must first have their red tape processed in La Paz. Go figure!

When leaving Baja by ferry, all passengers and vehicles are subject to inspection by Mexican Customs. This may take place either before boarding or as you disembark. Foreign tourists are almost always given the briefest treatment; it's the Mexican tourists who are carefully looked over. Since La Paz is a free port, it is a popular shopping place for mainlanders. Goods purchased by them in Baja are dutiable. In recent years, however, drug smuggling via Baja has led to an increase in searches of gringos and their cars. Dope-sniffing dogs are sometimes used, both in Baja and on the mainland.

Boats and Beasts

Small boats aren't commonly used by tourists for travel within Mexico, though many Mexicans depend on them for transportation. It is very difficult to get accurate information about boat service. The canoe someone told you about may have gone to the bottom by the time you get there or will be loaned out to a relative.

In spite of a lack of schedules, regular boat service (and by boat I mean anything that will float, from dugout canoes to modern fiberglass *pangas* with big outboards) does exist on many rivers, lagoons and coastal areas. All it takes is determination, patience and a desire to see parts of Mexico that are rarely visited by tourists. It is just about our favorite mode of travel.

One other type of transportation deserves mention—animal back. Many people would like to make long treks in search of Adventure. If it's done by *bestia* ("beast," as the people call them, from horses to burros), the real adventure may be surviving the agony of sore muscles and a blistered butt.

One problem of long trips by *bestia*, or even by foot, is that they are often made into areas considered slightly taboo by the government. In Yucatán, local authorities would not allow us to visit an area of the coast because they suspected we might be buying or looking for artifacts.

In other areas, dope might be suspected as the reason for your trip. Even if you aren't a dealer in artifacts or opium, without legitimate credentials as an archaeologist or permission from the government, you may be discouraged from making the trip.

If you go ahead with arrangements for this type of travel, get someone, preferably the owner of the animals, to go with you as a guide. He probably won't rent them to you alone if you don't know how to handle and care for the animals.

Hitching

Hitching rides is socially acceptable in Mexico. Don't think that you'll be the only person with your thumb out; there are many Mexicans, from laborers to students, doing it too. Truck drivers and middle- and upper-class Mexicans will give hitchers a lift. Their curiosity will quickly overcome any shyness they may feel toward a foreigner, especially if your appearance or equipment is distinctive.

I once asked a Mexican friend what he really thought of *turistas* who hitched around the country with just a few dollars. He paused for a few moments and then said, "Well, they don't contribute anything to the economy, but . . . well . . . you have to admit that they travel *con valor Mexicano* (with Mexican courage)." This rather grudging respect is common.

Many of the people who pick you up will offer to buy you a meal, put you up for the night or show you something of interest. Remember that when Mexicans make such an offer, they mean it and it's difficult to refuse without giving offense. The best payment you can give for a favor is a polite "thanks" or another favor in return: wash the windshield or tell a funny story.

Hitching involves almost total immersion in Mexico. For the person with a poor knowledge of Spanish or not experienced in hitching or traveling, this can be traumatic. It is important, therefore, to break into things gradually and to *know when to stop.*

We once met a guy traveling on almost nothing, eating quite well and having a very good time. His technique was to take whatever came along, whether it was a ride to a town he'd never heard of or an offer of a free dinner. Rather than freeloading, he made an effort to be useful to anyone who befriended him. He taught campers how to hang their hammocks, picked coconuts or helped them on marketing trips. The meals and rides he received in return were given gratefully and people soon began to pass him on from one friend to another as a sort of *mayordomo*. He never stayed long with one group and his visit was never an imposition.

Finding a Good Ride
There are a few tricks that can make hitching much easier: if you've been dropped off at the edge of a town that has to be crossed, it's often more convenient to take an *urbano* (city bus) rather than wait for a ride that is going through. Pemex stations are excellent places to pick up a ride and the management rarely objects if you wander around asking drivers for *un ride* or *aventón*.

Trailer parks are good places to get rides with gringos, but keep in mind that the most conservative people in Mexico are not Mexicans, they're other tourists. Gringos can be buttered up by offering to translate for them or by making it quite clear that you want a ride only for a certain time or distance. Anyone who has had the common experience of getting stuck with a hitchhiker tends to be leery when approached by another.

If you or your gear are exceptionally scroungy, your chances of a ride will diminish.

Friends who have tried hitching with such things as surfboards, large musical instruments, wheelchairs, goats and monkeys found them to be liabilities.

Hitching rides on cargo trucks is usually easy, but women are technically prohibited from riding in many company trucks. The management of these firms assumes that the female hitchhiker will be unable to restrain herself and will distract the driver's attention with panting and pawing. Don't be upset, therefore, if the driver asks a woman hitcher to get out of the truck or to hide when reaching a town or trucker's checkpoint.

Children almost always make hitching easier. We met a family in Guatemala who had been hitching together for two years. They found it a wonderful way to travel and also quite economical. There were five of them, including an infant. "We don't get many rides in small Volkswagens," the mother said, "but there's nothing like several hours in the back of a truck to keep the family spirit high."

Although hitching on main roads is generally quite easy, traveling by thumb into more remote and less populated areas can involve waiting or walking. You should definitely be prepared to do some waiting if you don't have enough money for bus fare or are one of those people who absolutely refuse to pay for a ride.

In the Boondocks

When hitching in areas with very infrequent bus service or none at all (rare), you may be asked to pay for your rides. This is common practice; any tourist who has driven into the boondocks has undoubtedly been approached by people who not only expect a lift but expect to reimburse the driver for it.

The owners of flatbeds and pickup trucks are accustomed to filling extra space with paying bodies. If you flag or thumb down a ride on one of these, ask the driver what it's going to cost; it may be surprisingly high, though a bargain in comparison to no ride at all. Drivers are forced to charge a fare based on expenses rather than a large volume of passengers. In almost every case the price will be fair.

Anyone interested in penetrating deep into the back country without backpacking will find these trucks to be a perfect, if sometimes hair-raising, means of transportation.

Hitching Survival Tips

Riding in the back of a truck over unimproved dirt roads can be exhausting. This means that when it's hot, you'll want something to drink. You can carry sodas or beer, but water is easier to stretch out and a canteen is more practical to refill and carry in a pack. Nothing is worse than having half of a grape soda soak your clothing.

If your hat doesn't have a chin strap (called *barbiquetes*), lash it to your head with a bandanna or piece of twine. Your head may feel cool from the breeze as the truck is moving, but the sun will still be roasting your nose and forehead.

While a hat is the most convenient way to block the sun, I met a hitchhiker who found an umbrella quite useful for protection both from the heat and aggressive dogs. (Mexican dogs are trained by experience; bend over as if you're looking for a good throwing stone and they'll back off.)

Several hours in the heat can be quite dangerous: if you don't have a hat, put something, even your undershorts, over the top of your head. Should a ride appear just as you're vomiting from too much heat or crawling into the bushes to collapse, you'll be out of luck.

Hitchhikers will find that an emergency stash of food will be invaluable for long waits or long rides without stops. Bananas are good, but I inevitably squash mine inside my day pack. Nuts, chia seeds, dried fruit (though it's expensive in Mexico), cheese, oranges, chocolate and granola are good for moments of low morale, sickness or ordinary hunger when nothing else is available.

When traveling through the high deserts or mountains, be adequately prepared for a night in the open. Most people on foot will have a sleeping bag, but if you don't, a warm *sarape*, jacket or sweater is advisable.

Protection from rain is essential. A poncho, garbage bag or piece of plastic large enough to cover both you and your possessions will save you a great deal of discomfort and the hassle of drying things.

Because you'll be spending a certain amount of time in the open, bottles of bug repellent and sunscreen should be taken.

One disadvantage of hitchhiking is that it is very inconvenient to be ill. If you do get sick, don't hesitate to take a bus to the next town or the first cheap hotel and hole up until you're well enough to travel again.

Anyone hitching in Mexico should be aware of the hazards of driving there. When you're standing on the edge of the road, always keep a close eye on traffic. Mexican drivers don't consider the shoulder of the road to be a safe zone for pedestrians; it's just another foot or two used for passing on the right or three abreast. If you aren't ready to jump out of the way, you may get a ride on a fender.

Keep knives and *machetes* out of sight or packed in such a manner that they don't appear as if you're ready for action. Open knives might upset people who give you rides. The police will confiscate even small penknives. A *machete* on the belt might be acceptable in the back country, but unless you're trying to go completely native, keep it out of sight. The natural distrust that some *campesinos* feel toward strangers, including both Mexicans and foreigners, will only be heightened if they see that you are armed.

Hitcher's Survival Kit

Hat with chin strap	Poncho
Canteen, water	Jacket or *sarape*
Emergency food	Day pack
Insect repellent	Plastic sheet, rope or twine
Sunscreen	Patience

Your luggage often suffers damage from rough truck trips. We always make an effort to put our backpacks in a secure spot, away from any slopping kerosene barrels or puddles of motor oil. Most cargo trucks are well coated with the dirt, grease and grime of past trips. The responsibility to avoid getting it on you and your gear is entirely your own. I'll never forget a five-hour trip in the back of a stake truck which was carrying four leaking barrels of kerosene, an overweight pig with diarrhea, and two loose truck tires and rims. On the first bump my leg was smashed against the sideboards by a shifting tire and on the second bump the pig squirted on Lorena's pack.

We now carry a small square of plastic to cover our packs with and a length of rope or heavy twine to lash them down. Be especially careful of other passengers who like to flop down on a backpack and may break the frame or contents.

Hitchhikers should be very careful about forgetting or losing gear while traveling. When you are awakened in the middle of the night at a dark intersection and the driver says, "This is where you get off," it is easy to absentmindedly leave behind a camera, hat or handbag. For this reason we always keep our loose odds and ends under control by carrying them in a shopping bag or day pack. A day pack that can be securely closed is best; I've found that when mine is left unzipped it can easily dump out smaller objects like flashlights, eyeglasses and notebooks.

If you're riding with someone who looks like they might forget you when you've gone into a restroom or behind a bush, carry valuable possessions with you at all times. This doesn't mean that you have to remove your luggage at every stop (if you're that worried, find another ride or hold your water). Just keep your camera, money, papers and other hard-to-bear-loss-of articles close at hand, whether it's for a brief rest stop, a meal or quick shopping trip.

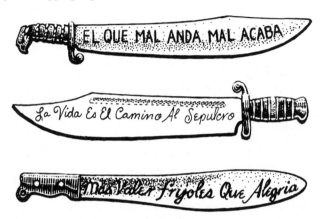

Knife blade inscriptions: He Who Acts Bad Ends Bad; Life Is the Road to the Tomb;
Beans Are Worth More Than Happiness

Hitching Alone

While hitching alone, particularly if you're a woman, take the same precautions about accepting rides as you would anywhere. Remember that it's easier to refuse a ride than to talk your way out of any situation that may develop after you're in the car.

We've met quite a few women traveling alone in Mexico and none of them felt that it was dangerous. They did say, however, that constant attention from men became very tiring. (See *¡Viva Mexico!: Machismo.*) Women may prefer hitching rides with other tourists, usually quite easy to do.

For anyone who is alone and a bit nervous, traveling with a large dog can be a great help to morale. Of the several people we've talked to who hitched with dogs, none felt that it cut down significantly on the number of rides they were given. A woman traveling with a large well-trained dog should be able to handle any situation with a few growls. Dogs, however, are complications themselves. (See *Red Tape and the Law: Pets.*)

The biggest disadvantage of traveling by thumb is that not all drivers are models of skill and self-control. Don't hesitate to bail out when things get strange or scary.

A Ride to Remember

Lorena and I were once riding in the back of a new pickup truck on a curve-filled highway. Before we'd gone a mile my heart was in my throat and my knuckles were white from clutching at the side rails.

"It must be just an illusion of speed," I said to Lorena, trying to convince myself that the wild lurching and the howl of the tires was as natural as a Sunday drive. "I'm probably scared because we haven't been in a truck for so long. When was the last time we rode in a truck?"

She gave me a long look.

Didn't she realize that after a few months without riding in a motor vehicle one lost one's perspective? A sharp curve appeared a short distance ahead. The driver went at full speed, then began braking madly in the middle of the curve.

"I think that last time was the day before yesterday. When you went to town for food, remember?" She grabbed for her hat, fending off an old man who had lost his footing and was lurching back and forth, arms flailing for a handhold. He flopped to a safe landing over a bulging sack of corn. "Very windy," he said, tipping his hat politely to Lorena as she worked her boot from beneath the small of his back.

I clambered over other passengers and cargo to the cab of the truck, determined to check our speed.

"Hey," I yelled back to Lorena, "It's really not so bad after all. We're only doing 90 to 100 kilometers an hour. That's fast but not so dangerous." I took another peek through the rear window; a curve was coming up and we were slowing to 70. I was just about to turn and work my way back when I noticed a small "MPH" beneath the speedometer needle.

MPH! I felt the blood drain from my face and go roaring through my ears and down to my feet. Seventy into a curve! One hundred on the straightaway!

"Let me off! Let me off!" I screamed, pounding the roof of the cab with my fists. I got a glimpse of the driver's startled face turned toward the rear of the truck.

He obligingly slammed on the brakes, pitching most of the passengers to their faces as we slid to a halt. I grabbed my pack and tossed it onto the side of the road, madly clawing at the grain sacks and miscellaneous boxes that had shifted over Lorena's gear. The other passengers watched in bemused silence as we leaped out.

"*Perdóneme*," the old man finally said, sweeping his eyes over the dense jungle that surrounded us, "but where are you going?"

I caught enough breath to gasp, "Camping . . . take pictures . . . pretty birds . . . *adiós, qué le vaya bien!*"

He looked at us incredulously. "Here?" he asked.

"Sure," I answered. "It's a perfect place."The driver gunned the engine.

"What do we owe you?" I called. He looked at me in the rear-view mirror, shook his head impatiently and then slammed the truck into gear. It lurched forward, spraying us with dust and gravel. The old man grabbed for his hat with one hand, waving farewell with the other. The exhaust had not yet cleared when we heard the protesting squeals of tires and brakes on the next curve.

DRIVING

*Why drive in Mexico • Why not drive • Hazards • Road conditions • City driving •
Night driving • Traffic signs • Toll roads • Cops • Surviving Mexico City • Steve's
bypass operation • Police roadblocks and highway checkpoints • Parking • Finding
your way • Green Angels and breakdowns • Ferries • Gas stations • Rip-offs •
Preparing your car: servicing and spare parts • Buying a car • Living in your vehicle • Do-it-yourself camper • Car repairs: a typical repair shop, finding a mechanic,
in the garage, body work and upholstery • Travels with Woody and Sonny*

Earlier in this book I described my first trip to Mexico in the early Sixties as "a tire-
burning, transcontinental marathon." Countless miles and many tire changes later, driving is still our favorite way to explore Mexico. We've headed south in everything
from Steve's pristine '65 Volvo to an aging but incredibly tough GMC school bus.
Over the years we've logged tens of thousands of miles in vans—mostly VW but also
Ford, Chevy and Dodge; various pickup trucks; and a number of station wagons and
family sedans. Steve and his family have driven from Oregon to Guatemala more times
than they can count, while Lorena and I have worn grooves in highways from Baja to
Belize. In all of this driving in Mexico and Central America, none of us has suffered a
serious accident or even a major fender-bender.

For some people, however, the thought of driving in Mexico is about as appealing
as skateboarding through rush hour traffic. Others have heard disquieting rumors
about complex red tape and bribe-hungry cops and put aside their car keys in favor of
a bus ticket.

Why Drive in Mexico?

In our opinion the answer is easy: the convenience and independence offered by having your own vehicle far outweighs the disadvantages. Public transportation will take
you just about anywhere in Mexico, but if you have a yen to really get out and explore,
driving is the way to go. Mexico has tens of thousands of miles of secondary roads and
countless unpublicized, off-the-beaten-track attractions. Quiet little hotels, locals-only
restaurants, eco-sanctuaries and hidden beaches are just some of the rewards that can

be found by driving your own car. Of course you can also hire cabs for relaxed Sunday drives or take a bus into the country for a picnic, but it's hardly the same.

As convenient and cheap as bus travel may be, it also tends to steer you onto an urban trip. As certified tree-huggers, bird watchers and swamp rats, Lorena and I can take only so many picturesque colonial cities and crowded markets before we require a refreshing dose of nature. With our own vehicle, we can enjoy the best of both worlds.

Traveling with children and pets is much easier in the family car. Other advantages include spreading transportation costs among three or more people, and the possibility of extended camping trips. If you're tempted by Mexico's amazing crafts—and who isn't?—Lorena has proven that three tons of pottery, weavings and wood carvings can be packed into a remarkably small space.

Why *Not* Drive?

The greatest obstacle to driving isn't crazy traffic or unscrupulous cops, but the distances, time and cost of driving your car to Mexico. I call this the "forth-and-back factor." If you live as far north as we do, just getting to the border eats up a serious chunk of your time and gas money.

Unless you're a night owl driver with a lead foot and serious bladder control, it is difficult to log more than five hundred miles a day, even on American freeways. Once you get into Mexico, where driving at night is definitely not recommended, your average daily mileage (and your speed) should drop considerably. Add in the usual delays for sightseeing, photographs, fruit stands, fresh tortillas, road repairs and jaywalking burros, and we'll make two or three hundred miles in a typical day.

Before we get into an in-depth discussion of what you need to know before driving in Mexico, here's a quick and hopefully reassuring overview:

• **Crossing the border:** It's a lot easier than you might think. After making some stupendous public relations blunders, the Mexican government has finally created a more-or-less straightforward permit process for tourist vehicles. (See *Red Tape and the Law: Car Permits* for all the necessary details.)

• **Road conditions:** Probably better than you expect and improving by the day. New freeways, divided highways and upgraded secondary highways have taken a lot of the bumps and hazards out of driving. Gripes about the high cost of Mexican tollways have to be balanced against their convenience, safety and superior condition. It will soon be possible to traverse Mexico in several directions on four-lanes and better.

• **Costs:** Depending on where you're from, Mexican gasoline will cost slightly more or slightly less than you're already paying.

• **Unleaded gasoline:** Plentiful and widely available. Leaded gas has been phased out.

• **Traffic:** It definitely keeps you on your toes. Drivers are either fast and furious or very, very s...l...o...w, and you'll often see both, at the same time and in the same lane. Mexican traffic isn't quite at the level of a free-for-all, but you can expect three-abreast passing, spectacular lane changes and similar hijinks around any corner. If you're from Los Angeles, you might feel right at home.

Sound too hectic for you? In fact, once you get used to Mexican traffic, you'll be surprised how easy and even logical it can be. Although I'm a very conservative driver at home, I appreciate the fact that Mexican drivers take nothing for granted. For example, everyone knows from experience that stop signs are primarily for decoration. Like most things in Mexico, the right-of-way at bridges, crosswalks, train crossings and intersections is always open to negotiation. Can I realistically expect a hurtling truck overloaded with ripe bananas to stop just because my miserable little VW Bug got to the intersection a few seconds earlier?

• **Parking:** It's a pain, but not a major one. Parking is generally scarce, especially on the narrow, congested streets typical of most Mexican cities. Parking lots are available but be patient: finding one where and when you need it isn't always easy.

• **Rip-offs:** As at home, car prowling is on the rise in Mexico. Our Mexican friends who live in cities never leave valuables in plain view and most of them use steering wheel locks. In town, we prefer to park inside the patio or grounds of a hotel, or in a well guarded lot. Any vehicle left on a city street overnight is subject to having its mirrors, wipers and antennas picked off.

• **Seatbelts** are required in Mexico.

Hazards

Driving in Mexico, as in all other parts of the world, is a constant battle for survival. Roadside crosses and shrines mark the fatal confrontations and commemorate the losers.

Many common driving hazards and annoyances found in the U.S. are also in Mexico, though usually in a slightly altered form.

In the U.S., the omnipresent teenager hunched birdlike behind the wheel of his 400-hp candy-colored, air-foiled Supercar, passes you dangerously close at 140 mph as he calmly munches a DoubleBurger and squeezes an annoying pimple.

In Mexico he's still the same basic teenager, apparently oblivious to other traffic and mesmerized by the blaring radio and the dangling ornaments that festoon mirrors and knobs. But there is one difference: he's behind the wheel of a hurtling semi-truckload of sugarcane. And he's passing you on a blind mountain curve. You glance over, afraid to imagine what is about to happen. He grins, flashes a peace sign and cuts you off as he swerves to miss an oncoming bus.

One of the greatest challenges you'll face when driving in Mexico is the amazing number and variety of common road hazards, from the ever-present slow trucks and speeding buses to homemade wooden pushcarts loaded with logs, steered down precipitous mountain grades by grinning old men.

Tiny motorbikes with heavy loads (firewood, kitchen sinks, baby goats, beer cases, children) teetering dangerously on the sagging back fender appear as you roar over the crest of a hill. On country roads, relaxing farm hands can be seen lying in the road, taking a little sun after a hard day's work.

And everywhere, from the coastal lowlands to the highest mountains, a constant traffic of dumb beasts—cows, pigs, horses, children and burros—parades alongside and in front of you. Nerves strain as you attempt to anticipate their next few steps, your foot poised over the brake pedal.

Low-flying buzzards are a very real hazard, as are piles of drying corn, beans and chili peppers placed on the hot pavement by enterprising farmers who prefer the smooth road surface to the dusty shoulder.

As you fly around a curve and find yourself unexpectedly in the middle of a small village, it seems that everyone suddenly leaps up and crosses the street, forcing you to brake madly. Pigs that haven't moved from gooey wallows for a week lurch frantically to their feet and stumble in front of the car, followed by reckless children beating them with twigs.

These are relatively minor hazards that you'll soon become used to. For really serious trouble, nothing compares to other drivers.

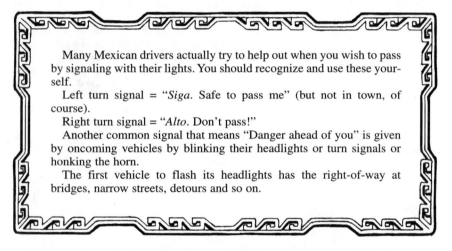

Many Mexican drivers actually try to help out when you wish to pass by signaling with their lights. You should recognize and use these yourself.

Left turn signal = "*Siga*. Safe to pass me" (but not in town, of course).

Right turn signal = "*Alto*. Don't pass!"

Another common signal that means "Danger ahead of you" is given by oncoming vehicles by blinking their headlights or turn signals or honking the horn.

The first vehicle to flash its headlights has the right-of-way at bridges, narrow streets, detours and so on.

"They may be wild but they're damn good!" is a comment you might hear, especially about Mexican truck drivers. If *good driving* involves *good sense*, however, they must surely be among the worst. Many truckers would be disqualified from a destruction derby on grounds of excessive zeal and disregard for human life.

The good news is that the average Mexican *chofer* (driver) is definitely getting better. Drivers are more courteous and less likely to indulge in macho grandstanding while behind the wheel of the family car. Bus drivers have also gotten the message about safety and many of them could give lessons to American drivers.

Still, it is dangerously easy for tourists to fall into the same driving habits they see demonstrated by others. When you're breathing fumes behind a slow diesel truck in a steep mountain pass, the temptation to pass on a blind curve can be very strong. At this point, you should seriously consider what the consequences are if you don't make it.

The secret to safe driving in Mexico is to be continually alert and patient.

A second-class bus passes you at 70, belching smoke and looking for all the world like an Express to Hell. As soon as he's around you he spots an old lady with a chicken standing on the shoulder of the road, and slams on the brakes. You madly pump your brakes, but are forced by your speed to go around him. The race is on. Thirty seconds later he passes you again. In a few more minutes you pass him while he loads more bodies and inevitably he passes you within a mile. This can go on for hours.

• **Smerge:** At some point you'll probably come across stretches of highway or city boulevards that aren't marked off into separate lanes. This is your opportunity to join in an exciting Mexican game I call "Smerge"—a skillful blending of speed, intimidation and merging to establish who has the right-of-way. This game is so popular, in fact, that some drivers play it even where lanes are clearly marked.

Let's say that you're driving innocently across Sonora on a two-lane highway, mindful of the buses that appear out of nowhere and roar past at high speeds. Suddenly you're behind two large trucks. One of the trucks has broken down and is being towed to the shop. A tow bar wasn't available so the enterprising drivers got together and felled a tree. It is now lashed from the rear bumper of the front truck to the front bumper of the second. It's not too safe, but they're only doing 60 miles per hour.

You move to pass this unlikely combination. When you're just about even with the first truck, the bark of a bus horn raises the hair on the back of your neck. You look nervously into the rear-view mirror, but all you can see is the word "ANID" in huge chrome letters. That's DINA, the company that made the bus.

The driver honks insistently and begins to edge around you. Five seconds later you're the middle vehicle of "three-abreast." It's time to play Smerge: ease very cautiously to the right—just enough to let the bus get by without forcing you into the trucks—and apply your foot ever so gently to the brake pedal. Now drop back about a quarter of a mile behind the trucks and let your pulse rate return to normal.

• **Pedestrians:** Mexican pedestrians are notorious for forcing cars to avoid hitting them. It is not uncommon to have people step nonchalantly in front of your car and then appear startled when you come to a screeching stop a few inches from them. The average back-country Mexican, with no driving experience, cannot appreciate the difficulty of stopping a fast-moving vehicle. Having to travel on foot, they tend to think of roads as footpaths.

• **Road improvements** involve a whole new group of hazards: the repairs themselves. Piles of dirt, gravel and sand neatly line the highway for mile after mile. A two-lane road turns into a one-lane or a one-and-a-half-lane ordeal as you are forced off the road time after time by trucks and buses. Some neat piles have waited so long to be used that they've dissolved and weathered into lumps. These are often marked with regular road signs portraying piles of dirt.

If road repair hasn't progressed to the point of using the dirt piles, you may see large rocks, often whitewashed, placed hazardously in the roadway, apparently marking future work areas. Surveying crews mark the roads with rocks, as do paving crews, chuckhole fillers and truck drivers who've parked to eat a watermelon.

A single white rock or tree branch on the roadway can mean anything awaits you on the other side of the hill, from a full-scale road crew with graders and dozers to a broken-down pickup truck with a dismantled engine. A plastic bag, a stick with a rag tied to the top, a row of beer bottles—any of these can be an important warning signal. Always be prepared to stop!

Sections of road being attacked by full-scale repair crews can be frustrating areas to drive through. It seems that trucks and buses never move over enough to allow you to pass easily. Strange, unintelligible hand signals and flag-waving from irate traffic directors may have you tearing out your hair with rage. As traffic behind you impatiently leans on the horn to speed you up, the repair crews frantically motion you to slow down.

The secret to driving through this maze is simple: go slow and keep calm.

• **Mexican flag signals** are a complete mystery, to them and to us. A waving flag *usually* means "keep moving"; a stationary flag *usually* means "stop." If the flagman uses his hand(s) with the palm(s) down, pumping up and down as if giving someone artificial resuscitation, it means "slow down."

If he waves you back and you stop and then he keeps waving you back so that you back up and stop, only to have him wave you impatiently even farther back, it means "come ahead." One of the most confusing and most common gestures you'll run into throughout Mexico is the waving motion that would seem to mean "go back" but instead means the exact opposite.

Confusion can become quite hysterical. You back up as you suppose you should until bumper to bumper with a semi truck. You motion him "back" (actually forward) until he gets pissed off and inches forward. You interrupt a mutual exchange of insults and horn blarings with the truck driver long enough to check the flagman. Sure enough, he's still motioning you back, but by now frantically and assisted by half the road gang.

Someone finally runs to your car and shrieks unintelligible instructions and points— ahead! You put it in gear, shake your fist at the truck driver, and go triumphantly forward. The flagman, hoping to encourage you, begins to wave you "back."

• **Right-of-way:** If an oncoming vehicle refuses to yield the right-of-way and you know that it can, or should, it's much easier to give in quickly than to become involved in an ugly confrontation that you'll probably lose anyway.

What happens if worse comes to worst and you are involved in an accident? Stay calm and turn to *Red Tape and the Law: Accidents.*

Road Conditions

Driving on secondary roads requires alertness and caution. The same hazards found on main highways are compounded by poorer road surfaces, which rarely slow down the other drivers.

• You should be aware of weather conditions. During the rainy season (May to September in most areas) the back roads can go to pieces in hours. Dirt roads literally melt before your eyes and become rushing streams. If this happens before you get back to the pavement, you'll be stranded until things drain. At the beginning of the rainy season or after unseasonal showers, paved roads will be slick with accumulated oil.

• Mudslides and falling boulders are common in the mountains, even on main highways. Fog often reduces visibility in mountain passes and is common in some lowland areas, especially early in the morning. Driving in fog in Mexico is the ultimate combination of hazards.

Truck bumper graffiti: Only God Knows Where I'm Going; Savage Wind; What's the Value of Hurry?

• If you are exploring remote mountain areas and aren't driving a four-wheel-drive vehicle or something of equal capability, it is advisable to check the condition of steep grades closely before attempting them. This is true going uphill and downhill.

• We and many others have had the experience of barely getting up a hill we casually drove down. On the other angle, we once slid *back down* a road that we attempted to go up without checking the grade or surface. The van refused to stop, even with the brakes locked and large rocks under the back tires. The loose surface of the road gave way beneath the car's weight and we slid a considerable distance before stopping. A drop of several hundred feet on our immediate right added drama to the situation.

• Some very common year-round conditions are real hazards, usually because they appear so rapidly. A broad, paved two-lane highway suddenly narrows to a single-lane bridge and you're faced with the uninviting prospect of playing chicken with an oncoming bus.

The Rules of the Road say that **the first vehicle to flash its headlights has the right-of-way** in such situations. But when you've given the signal and the other driver is still barreling along, you know that the real rules of the road are determined by size, speed and recklessness.

• Sudden chuckholes in an otherwise good road are common on the main trucking routes, particularly on the coast where roadbeds are often soft and deteriorate rapidly in the rainy season. Bad holes are sometimes marked. But the markers (usually a large boulder or pole) are hazards themselves.

Road conditions are particularly treacherous in areas where sugar cane is grown. A friend who hit an unexpected series of deep chuckholes says he now keeps in mind that sugar can lead to cavities in the road. Heavy truck traffic during the cane harvests raises hell with highway surfaces. These trucks, always overloaded, are hazards in themselves. Most are very slow and suffering from overuse. Watch out for them.

• Most Mexican roads do not have shoulders, especially those built more than a few years ago. The edge of the pavement drops six to twelve inches and may be very uneven. New roads, however, may have hazardous low curbs which prevent a safe, fast emergency exit.

• In areas where seasonal rains wash out small bridges and chunks of roadway, the pavement may suddenly end, turning to a short section of dirt and rocks that will rattle your teeth and nerves. If the washout is a yearly occurrence, as many are, the road will be graded to form a *vado* (dip), allowing the high water to pass over the roadway without destroying it completely. *Vados* may be dirt or surfaced with cobblestones, pavement or cement.

Some *vados*, especially along Baja's Transpeninsular Highway, are marked with depth indicator poles. The idea is that you'll note the depth of the water and base a decision to cross or to wait on the size of your vehicle. When in doubt, wait! I know of cases where small cars (especially a good tight VW Bug) were swept away.

• Often a village will tire of high-speed traffic racing through town and erect one or more sets of speed bumps (*topes*, *tumulos*, *vibradores* or *boyas*) to slow things down. If the *topes* aren't marked, you may hit them fast and hard. Watch for them closely.

A friend who deliberately ignored *topes* and delighted in hitting them at a fair speed learned his lesson one day when the impact caused the front bumper to fall off. As if that wasn't enough, the bumper was caught under the car and wreaked additional havoc.

City Driving

First of all, the posted speed limits on open highways are rarely enforced, but this is not true in towns and cities. Always obey the city speed limit carefully, even though it may seem ridiculously slow. Diligent city *transitos* (traffic cops) will definitely be watching.

• Driving in town can be nerve-wracking, though the speeds involved are usually less than those on the open highway. While you're desperately craning your neck to spot road signs, you must also watch for other cars, pedestrians, cops and legless beggars skateboarding through traffic. In town, drivers may ignore traffic lights completely or slow down only slightly for them; they'll drive three abreast in streets clearly marked as two-lane; and there seems to be no control over right-of-way at cross streets.

• How do you navigate in a situation like this? The best procedure is to *drive slowly* and keep your eyes on the road ahead. Let the guy behind you worry about what you're going to do, because the driver ahead of you is the most dangerous (and he's not paying attention to you, either). Unexpected stops for double-parked cars, jaywalkers and slow carts are common.

Don't let other drivers sweep you up in their lemming-like enthusiasm for speed and reckless lane-changing. When you get in a good lane, stay there until you're certain that you have to turn or move over.

At cross streets and intersections not controlled by traffic lights or police, assume that you *don't* have the right-of-way. This doesn't mean that you have to stop, just decrease your speed a bit and look in all directions. Even if you have the right-of-way, it may not be recognized by your opponents.

If an intersection is regulated by a cop, the position of his body will determine right-of-way. Facing you or with his back to you means "Stop!"; when he is sideways to you, it means "Go!"

The free-wheeling *glorieta* (traffic circle) is quickly disappearing in Mexico, much to the delight of tourists. Automatic signals now control traffic in most *glorietas* and planners have actually painted yellow lines in these former bumper-tag arenas. A few authentic *glorietas* still exist, however, and you would be wise to prepare yourself for this confusing, nerve-straining driving experience.

The classic Mexican *glorieta* is essentially a circular "free zone" established around a grotesque statue or fountain. Several streets feed into the traffic pattern that is wheeling around the circle. When you spot a street that you'd like to exit to, you merely shoot through traffic and are on your way. Unless, however, you ignore the cars speeding around you and nail one as you try to break out of orbit.

Should you get confused in a *glorieta*, grab the inner lane and maintain an orbiting pattern until you've figured out what the hell is going on. Observe the traffic whirlpooling around you; eventually you'll get the hang of it. When you do, and when your heart rate returns to near normal—*make your move*. The nice feature of the traffic circle is that it allows you to make a few reconnaissance loops if you aren't sure which street to take.

• **City bypasses:** If city driving sounds like too much of a headache, relax and take the outlying bypass (*libramiento*).

Night Driving

Anyone with any sense who has driven more than a few days in Mexico will tell you that driving at night is definitely not recommended.

Stories of cows and horses in the road don't seem to justify the intensity of the warnings, however, so you may be inclined to say, "I'll try it for myself." And you probably should. But remember, the basis of the entire "don't drive at night" warning is that all of the daytime hazards will still be there at night, but now they'll be much harder to see. (Because of the heat retained by asphalt roads, livestock and wild beasts are drawn to them at night for warmth.)

Unless you have good night vision, quick reflexes and an important appointment, leave night driving to those who do.

Mexicans sometimes deliberately drive at night without lights. The logic behind this, or so I've been told, is that they can see better without the glare of headlights. They can see, for example, the lights of oncoming cars, especially over hills and around mountain curves. This doesn't work quite so well, however, if two oncoming vehicles are both driving without lights.

Night driving on the outskirts of cities and even villages is especially hazardous due to the concentration of vehicles, foot traffic and miscellaneous livestock.

If that doesn't convince you not to drive at night, remember that most highway robberies occur after dark.

Traffic Signs

• **Traffic control signs**, such as speed limit signs, stop signs and yield right-of-way signs, are open to liberal interpretation by the driver.

Once you've mastered the decimal system and realize that a kilometer per hour is just six-tenths of a mile per hour, you'll be perplexed by Mexico's low speed limits. No one seems to take these signs seriously, and speeds are determined strictly by the driver and the limits of the vehicle. Eighty kilometers per hour (50 mph) is the usual speed limit for a good two-lane highway where the average truck is doing 70 mph and cars are going just as fast or faster. The best toll highways have top speed limits of 110 kph (about 70 mph), and secondary roads often have speed limits as low as 25 to 35 kph (15 to 20 mph).

There is a campaign in Mexico to get drivers to slow down to 95 kph (60 mph). It's called *95 Y VIVE!* It remains to be seen if "95 and live!" will overcome the "Floorboard it and pray!" attitude by which some people seem to drive.

• **Stop signs** (*ALTO*) will appear in the most unlikely places and may be completely ignored by traffic. Stop signs which appear to have no logical reason for being where they are can usually be taken to mean "caution." For the driver conditioned to the much more rigid traffic laws of the U.S., casually running a stop sign can be a traumatic experience. If this is the case, it is best to obey all signs, at least until the feelings of guilt have subsided.

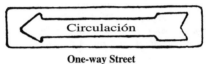

One-way Street

• **Yield-right-of-way signs**, *ceda el paso*, should read "someone yield . . ." because you're mistaken if you think that a fast-moving semi truck is going to let a little VW and a tiny sign stop him.

Remember that the laws of the highway are made by the drivers and there's no one to complain to if you feel that you've been wronged.

• **Traffic arrows:** These are commonly posted on buildings to indicate traffic flow and right-of-way. They are legally equivalent to traffic lights, though some drivers take them casually. General rules for traffic arrows are:

A red arrow facing you means *stop* (you don't have the right-of way). A green arrow is *go* (you do have the right-of-way).

The direction in which the arrow points is the direction in which traffic may flow.

A two-headed arrow means *two-way traffic*.

The designations *Tránsito* and *Circulación* (both mean "traffic") and *Preferencia* (through traffic) written on a traffic arrow also determine right-of-way. These designations, in combination with red, green and double arrows, are confusing and other drivers interpret them to their own advantage. Until you're accustomed to driving in Mexico, it is best to assume that you must stop or slow down at all dubious intersections.

Toll Roads

Modern, multi-lane toll highways are now common in the more populous and prosperous central and northern regions of Mexico. Some tollways are government operated, but many *cuotas* are privately owned. (*Autopista* is the correct term but the nickname *cuotas*, "tolls," is more commonly used.) Publicity in the U.S. and Canada about the high cost of Mexican tollways has undoubtedly contributed to the decline of tourist traffic and particularly of visiting RVers. Charges are steep enough on some privately operated *cuotas* that even well-heeled drivers may think twice before leaving the *libre* (free road) behind.

Having often prayed for better highways in Mexico, I feel that the advantages of tollways are often worth the price. These include decreased wear and tear on your nerves and vehicle, greater safety, shorter distances and much quicker driving times from point

A to point B. Tollways usually have light traffic (most Mexicans are unwilling or unable to put out the extra money) and are almost free of freight trucks. In fact, should you decide to save money by taking the free highway, you'll soon realize just how many trucks there are in Mexico.

If your budget just won't cover tolls, there's usually an alternative. Steve points out, "When I can't stand to pay another toll, I'll turn off onto the old roads. For better or worse, you're immediately back in the 'good old days,' surrounded by trucks, smoking buses and old *carcachas* (beaters)."

One toll Steve is always glad to pay is for the mountainous highway from Puebla to Oaxaca. The trip is four hours as opposed to ten or more on the old, poorly maintained Highway 190. As a bonus, the scenery on the tollway is great.

Toll rates are generally determined by the number of axles on your vehicle and trailer. Tolls vary considerably from place to place, however, as some highways are privately financed, others are state owned and still others (usually the cheaper ones) are federally administered.

Your toll ticket usually includes insurance, so tuck it away carefully.

Warning: Many of the most heavily traveled highways leading in and out of Mexico City pass through areas that are plagued by fog. If you see a flashing sign (most tollbooths have them) that says *MANEJE DESPACIO NEBLINA* ("Drive slow, fog"), take it seriously. Be on your toes for other drivers who do not heed the warnings.

Cops

One of the greatest driving "hazards" on highways in the United States is the all-too-familiar flashing red light in the rear-view mirror and the icy smile of a seven-foot cop as he slips fresh carbon paper into his ticket book. Mexico, however, seems to rely principally on the Law of Averages and the Grim Reaper to control drivers on its highways.

You will rarely see a police car on the highway that is there for the purpose of enforcing traffic laws. When not escorting dignitaries, highway patrolmen are almost always found parked beneath large shade trees, reading comic books or gossiping with ice cream vendors.

Although speeding is acceptable on most highways, it is not considered proper in town. Watch your speed closely for both legal and personal safety. City traffic police, in contrast to the highway patrol, are annoyingly efficient.

Mexico City and its surrounding "megapolis" (the Distrito Federal and state of Mexico) are the worst: predatory traffic cops are notorious for stopping both local and out-of-town cars for the sole purpose of putting the "bite" (*mordida*) on drivers. This situation is literally out of control, so you'll have to rely on luck and our own hard-learned tips to avoid paying bribes.

ROAD SIGNS

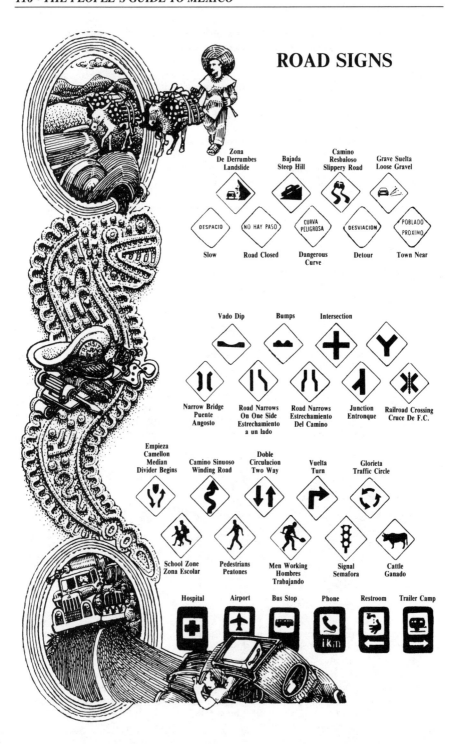

Zona De Derrumbes Landslide

Bajada Steep Hill

Camino Resbaloso Slippery Road

Grave Suelta Loose Gravel

DESPACIO — Slow

NO HAY PASO — Road Closed

CURVA PELIGROSA — Dangerous Curve

DESVIACION — Detour

POBLADO PROXIMO — Town Near

Vado Dip

Bumps

Intersection

Narrow Bridge Puente Angosto

Road Narrows On One Side Estrechamiento a un lado

Road Narrows Estrechamiento Del Camino

Junction Entronque

Railroad Crossing Cruce De F.C.

Empieza Camellon Median Divider Begins

Camino Sinuoso Winding Road

Doble Circulacion Two Way

Vuelta Turn

Glorieta Traffic Circle

School Zone Zona Escolar

Pedestrians Peatones

Men Working Hombres Trabajando

Signal Semafora

Cattle Ganado

Hospital

Airport

Bus Stop

Phone

Restroom

Trailer Camp

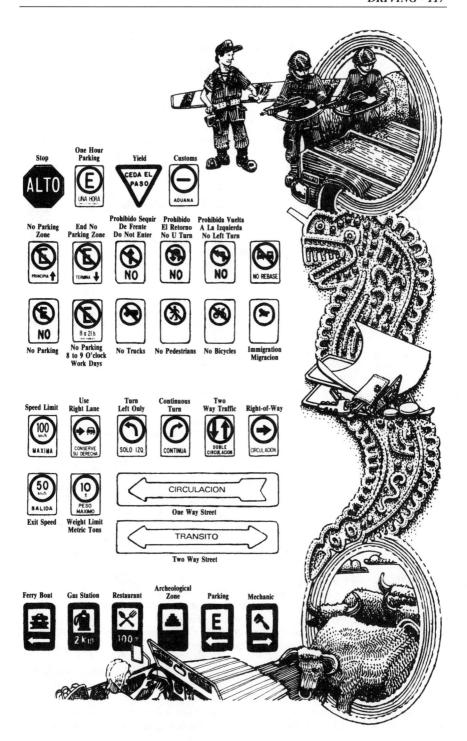

Stop

One Hour Parking

Yield

Customs

No Parking Zone

End No Parking Zone

Prohibido Sequir De Frente
Do Not Enter

Prohibido El Retorno
No U Turn

Prohibida Vuelta A La Izquierda
No Left Turn

No Parking

No Parking 8 to 9 O'clock Work Days

No Trucks

No Pedestrians

No Bicycles

Immigration Migracion

Speed Limit

Use Right Lane

Turn Left Only

Continuous Turn

Two Way Traffic

Right-of-Way

Exit Speed

Weight Limit Metric Tons

CIRCULACION

One Way Street

TRANSITO

Two Way Street

Ferry Boat

Gas Station

Restaurant

Archeological Zone

Parking

Mechanic

When you are stopped by city police for a minor violation, you can expect to receive a routine lecture and perhaps a fine. Either the lecture or fine, or both, may occur on the spot or at the station.

When the thought of facing the cops frightens you, there is an alternative. If you've been signaled to stop by a cop on foot, usually by tweeting a whistle, waving, yelling or pounding on your car with a nightstick, simply keep going. "Haul ass," as the saying goes. It's a solution that may land you in hot water if you don't pull it off, but we have tried it ourselves on occasion and it can work.

If the thought of "resisting arrest" appalls you even more than a possible fine, the next best method is to play very dumb. Unless you speak Spanish better than 99 percent of the tourists, you won't have much trouble erecting barriers to communication.

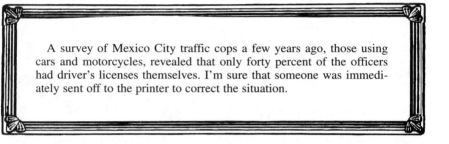

A survey of Mexico City traffic cops a few years ago, those using cars and motorcycles, revealed that only forty percent of the officers had driver's licenses themselves. I'm sure that someone was immediately sent off to the printer to correct the situation.

If you absolutely refuse to understand even the most obvious words, right down to the cognates (*policía*, *pistola*, etc.), the cop will often give up in disgust and let you off with a sneer and a wave of the hand.

If he happens to speak English, as is sometimes the case in larger cities, don't make a complete ass of yourself by speaking Pig Latin or imitation German. He'll look at your driver's license or license plate and figure out what is going on.

In Mexico City, English-speaking cops may wear a piece of red cloth on their shoulders—then again, they may not.

• **How to beat the bribes:** Fear is the favorite weapon of those who extort bribes. Mexican cops can put on a great show, but keep in mind that tourists rarely see a judge, much less a jail cell, for anything short of criminal mayhem or serious accidents. We often hear of drivers who fork over outrageous sums—$50, $100 or even more—simply because some uniformed bozo frowns at them and threatens to toss them into an airless dungeon.

Before we go into detail, here are some quick tips that we strongly recommend should you be stopped by the police:

• **Guilty or entirely innocent, always remain calm and polite.** You can let your frustration show but acting scornful, rude or belligerent usually backfires.

• **Show the cop that you are confident, patient and self-assured.** His resolve will gradually erode if you refuse to be angered or intimidated.

• **Refuse to hand over your passport, driver's license or original car papers.** Show copies or insist on being taken to the *comandancia*.

The best overall strategy, safer than running away and more dignified than affecting deafness, was given to me by a friend who advised, "Place the burden of communication on the other person."

With a cop, do this by asking for an explanation of whatever he's doing: removing the license plates, rattling his handcuffs or writing a ticket. The motive behind this isn't necessarily to wear down his patience but to make certain that you know what is happening. Don't let a cop snow you with a torrent of Spanish and then walk away with a fat "fine" if you have no idea of what it was for. When you have to pay, at least get your money's worth and a short Spanish lesson. You may discover, as I once did, that he just wanted to ask if you knew his brother in Los Angeles.

A tactic that has saved me on several occasions is to calmly take out pen and paper and note down the cop's badge and vehicle license numbers. Ask politely but firmly for his name and *grado* (rank). "So that I can explain everything to the judge." The first time I ran this bluff on a *patrulla* (patrolman) who stopped me arbitrarily, he insisted on giving me a "courtesy" escort out of town.

If you are innocent or the infraction is genuine but minor, the "Take me to your leader" ploy can be very effective. If you insist, *"Vamos a la comandancia."* ("Let's go to the police station"), you'll probably discover that he doesn't actually want to take you in, since this means turning over a greater share of the "fine" to his bosses. More important, the last thing the station officers want is an irate tourist interrupting a pleasant afternoon of soap operas.

Facing down a crooked cop in a foreign country isn't easy. Being scary is part of a cop's job and Mexican cops are particularly adept at scowling ominously. This can be very intimidating. If you've done nothing wrong, however, they don't have a leg to stand on—and they know it. Call the bluff!

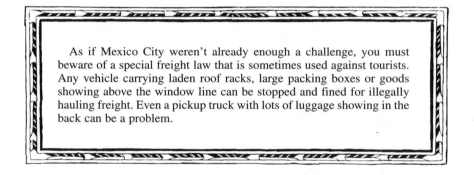

As if Mexico City weren't already enough a challenge, you must beware of a special freight law that is sometimes used against tourists. Any vehicle carrying laden roof racks, large packing boxes or goods showing above the window line can be stopped and fined for illegally hauling freight. Even a pickup truck with lots of luggage showing in the back can be a problem.

Surviving Mexico City

Unfortunately, virtually all of the country's major highways lead to Mexico City. You have two choices: bypass the city to the east or west (see *Steve's Bypass Operation*, below) or take the bull by the horns and drive straight through on the freeway. The freeway is fairly well marked, so if you don't stray and are driving an unremarkable vehicle on a day when your license number is permitted, you probably have at least a 50-50 chance of making it through without being stopped by a cop.

Steve's Bypass Operation

Can't face Mexico City's cops and congestion? Try Steve's Bypass Operation.

I know, it's a big detour, but by following these step-by-step directions you can save yourself a major headache. (Lay out a map as we do this and highlight your bypass route with a bright marking pen.) Here goes . . .

• From Querétaro, northwest of Mexico City, take Highway 57 to San Juan del Río.

• Just after you pass San Juan del Río (before the next toll gate), turn off on Highway 45 toward Pachuca. (Follow the signs for Puebla; it's well marked.)

• Once you hit Highway 85, turn right, continuing toward Pachuca.

• Bypassing Pachuca on the south, follow signs for Ciudad Sahagún.

• Continue south past Zempoala until you reach Calpulalpan and the junction with Highway 136.

You did it! Continue on toward Tlaxcala and Apizaco. Your way is now clear to Veracruz, Tlaxcala-Puebla or Oaxaca.

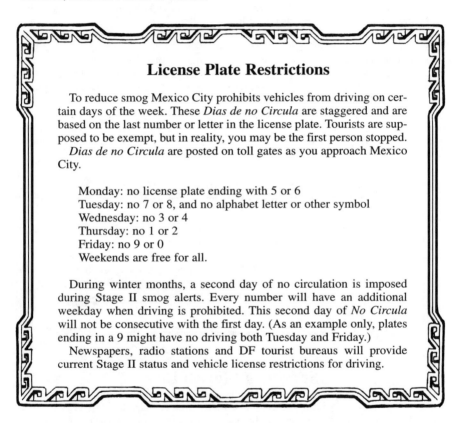

License Plate Restrictions

To reduce smog Mexico City prohibits vehicles from driving on certain days of the week. These *Dias de no Circula* are staggered and are based on the last number or letter in the license plate. Tourists are supposed to be exempt, but in reality, you may be the first person stopped.

Dias de no Circula are posted on toll gates as you approach Mexico City.

Monday: no license plate ending with 5 or 6
Tuesday: no 7 or 8, and no alphabet letter or other symbol
Wednesday: no 3 or 4
Thursday: no 1 or 2
Friday: no 9 or 0
Weekends are free for all.

During winter months, a second day of no circulation is imposed during Stage II smog alerts. Every number will have an additional weekday when driving is prohibited. This second day of *No Circula* will not be consecutive with the first day. (As an example only, plates ending in a 9 might have no driving both Tuesday and Friday.)

Newspapers, radio stations and DF tourist bureaus will provide current Stage II status and vehicle license restrictions for driving.

Police Roadblocks and Highway Checkpoints

Checkpoints (*reten*) for guns, drugs and contraband are back in operation throughout all of Mexico. You'll see a mix of law enforcement, including soldiers, plainclothes state *judiciales* and surly, all-in-black federal drug agents. Some temporary checkpoints will pop up anywhere on a major highway and others are more or less permanent. My experience with them has been that they usually pass me through quickly, perhaps with a cursory question or two: "Where are you going?" or "How many guns and kilos of cocaine are you carrying?"

The cops and soldiers at checkpoints tend to be brisk but polite, especially with white, Anglo-Saxon tourists. (Mexican-Americans can expect a closer inspection and a chillier "welcome.")

Take these checkpoints seriously. Steve's friend made the mistake of "running" a *reten*. She didn't see anyone paying attention, so she just drove through slowly without stopping. A short while later she was pulled over by a truck load of irate *judiciales* with drawn machine guns. They let her go after she convinced them it was a mistake and that she did not have a load of dope or guns.

Parking

Driving in larger cities often takes an unacceptable toll on nerves and fenders. I much prefer to park and use cabs, buses or shoe leather to get around. If you're not staying in a hotel that offers parking, look for signs that say *Estacionamiento*.

A parking lot may be as fancy as anything you'd see in the U.S., with uniformed attendants and underground parking. Or it may be as basic as an empty dirt lot guarded by scruffy kids. Whatever it looks like, a parking lot is usually safe as long as someone is on duty. After that, especially late at night, it's just another parking space. Never leave your car unlocked, even if the attendant swears the place is absolutely secure.

Rip-offs of parked vehicles usually occur at night or on side streets in large cities (and on some main streets, too). The best protection against thieves is not to leave valuables in the car. When this isn't practical, keep them well out of sight.

Car mirrors, hubcaps, gas caps and radio antennas are the first to fall prey to casual rip-offs. Take them off, secure with tamper-proof screws or carry spares.

Uniformed "play cops" or "rent-a-cops" and sometimes even real cops often supervise parking on certain city streets. These men wear quasi-official uniforms. (I've seen several wearing old Boy Scout stuff and surplus U.S. Army.) Each has his own small territory. If one of these men assists you with finding a parking space, a tip is customary. It's the way they make a living. They will also guard your car.

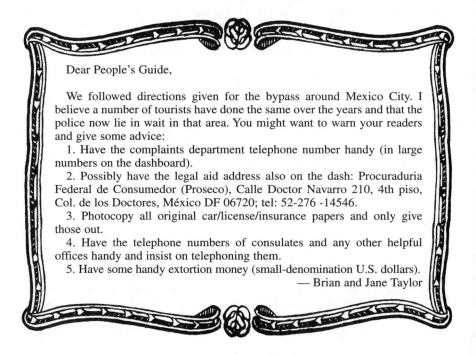

Dear People's Guide,

We followed directions given for the bypass around Mexico City. I believe a number of tourists have done the same over the years and that the police now lie in wait in that area. You might want to warn your readers and give some advice:

1. Have the complaints department telephone number handy (in large numbers on the dashboard).

2. Possibly have the legal aid address also on the dash: Procuraduria Federal de Consumedor (Proseco), Calle Doctor Navarro 210, 4th piso, Col. de los Doctores, México DF 06720; tel: 52-276 -14546.

3. Photocopy all original car/license/insurance papers and only give those out.

4. Have the telephone numbers of consulates and any other helpful offices handy and insist on telephoning them.

5. Have some handy extortion money (small-denomination U.S. dollars).
— Brian and Jane Taylor

As you're parking, a play cop or shoeshine boy may begin rapping his fist on a rear fender of your car. This rhythmic "tap-tap, tap-tap, tap-tap," will continue as long as it's safe for you to keep backing up. A sudden hard single tap means "Stop!"

The reassuring call of "*¡Pasa! ¡pasa!*" or "*¡Dalé! ¡dalé!*" ("Go ahead! Go ahead!") that often accompanies the fender slapping has led to parking attendants being nick-named *pasapasas*.

Should you leave your vehicle unattended and return to find a rent-a-cop or enter-prising kid who claims to have guarded it for you unasked, give them something for the favor. The "I didn't ask you so I don't have to pay" routine is completely unjusti-fiable when compared to the small sum it takes to satisfy them.

Kids, usually boys between the ages of three and eighteen, may approach in a howling mob, all making offers, warnings and pleading for guard duty. Pick a strong, aggressive one, capable of at least shouting for help should it be needed. Fix his face or clothing in your mind to avoid conflicts when you return. "They looked the same so I paid them all" is a frequent complaint when trying to recall which kid actually did the job.

Illegal Parking

If your car is in an illegal zone or overparked, don't be surprised to see a cop with screwdriver in hand removing your license plate. This ingenious substitute for the so-often-ignored paper parking ticket is a common method of enforcement.

Should you return to your car and find the plate missing, wait before rushing off in search of the police station until you've given the cop who removed it time enough to find you. This shouldn't be long because he'll probably be lurking nearby waiting for you. He might chew you out and make a few feeble motions toward the police station, but these can be quickly stopped by the display of money, usually not very much. If he expresses total outrage at such petty bribery, it's best to up the ante or drop the matter and go along. (This however, would be very unusual; in fact, quite remarkable.)

The legal procedure of recovering the plates involves locating the police station and paying a fine. You will then receive your license plate as a "receipt."

There are devious ways to avoid having your plate removed. One is to fix it to the car in a more or less permanent fashion. This can be done with non-removable screws or by judicious welding. If your state issued you two plates, remove one of them and carry it inside the car. It can be displayed in the rear window if you wish.

Finding Your Way

The Mexican government has made an effort to take some of the surprises out of driving through an admirable program that includes traffic lights and road signs. Until recently, most directional signs were cryptic, hand-lettered, phonetically spelled and hard to spot.

One could spend hours wandering through large cities with no idea where the main road was or sit perplexed at a crossroads until forced to flip a coin. Things are changing and now you'll be aided throughout your trip with a variety of handy international road signs.

It's off the main road where doubts still arise. It is advisable to ask for directions often, if for no other reason than to confirm that you're really going where you think you are. If you are traveling to a town some distance away—ten miles, for example— ask directions to intermediate points if you know their names. In rural areas, it's not uncommon for people to be ignorant of towns several miles away. Try to keep your questions within the range of their normal travel, usually just a few hours' walk.

When a choice is possible I prefer to ask men rather than women, both for directions and information. First of all, men tend to travel far more than women (some never leave the vicinity of their villages) and are therefore more likely to be accurate about local geography. *Campesinas* (country women) are often timid of strangers and unexpected questions may well fluster them. It is not uncommon to see a look of real fear on a woman's face when confronted by a gringo spouting fractured Spanish.

When approaching anyone for information, don't just leap into the questions, but give them a chance to size you up by leading off with a friendly, polite greeting.

Children are handy guides, mainly because they are so attracted to any passing traffic (especially tourists) that they usually know where it comes from and by which way it leaves. When you're faced with a choice between two roads and all of the kids are shrieking and pointing at one in particular, you'll be better off taking it rather than following your own intuition. The roads sometimes follow strange paths around obstacles that you can't possibly anticipate—fallen trees, washouts, landslides or a new house.

Asking for more detailed directions (i.e., "Where is the road to San X?") can be quite frustrating. Simplify the questions, thus simplifying the answers you'll get. Use hand signals; country people often wave their arms for a few explicit seconds when others would spend five minutes on detailed explanations.

When you think you're on the right road and headed in the right direction, simply point ahead and look at the person questioningly. If he smiles and nods his head, you're OK. If he scowls, frowns, laughs or shakes his head sadly, it is time for a more detailed question. Point in the general direction you think is correct and say, "*¿A San X?*" ("To San X?"). This should take care of it; he'll either say "*Sí*" or point in another direction.

Beware of irrelevant questions such as "How far is it to . . . ?" Answers will be purely subjective, varying from "very close" to "very far," and will rarely be based on driving experience. A truck driver will say "three hours" and that means that if you get in his truck you'll be there in approximately three hours, which may include lunch and a *siesta* or just three hours of solid kidney-jolting driving. A man carrying a heavy bundle of firewood may say "two days," and you'll know that he could get there in two days with his load.

You may be tricky and ask the actual distance to the next point but five miles over a terrible road can easily become hours of travel, often not much faster than walking. And if you've asked anyone but a fellow motorist, you may get the distance by footpath, invariable shorter and more direct.

As if this isn't enough, you must be very careful in your choice of words to denote "road." The common translation for "road" that you've probably learned in high school is *camino*. But outside of the city, *camino* means "path" and is used almost exclusively for any type of trail or path that is not traveled by cars. Cars travel on the *carretera*, the "highway," even though this highway may be nothing more than a rutted, rock-filled driver's nightmare.

The final frustration to finding your way is that usually no two answers are the same or even similar. Villages often have two (or more) names and the distance given may have been in leagues. *Leguas* (leagues) are a common unit of measure in back areas, particularly among *campesinos*. A *legua* corresponds roughly to an hour's walk. This varies with the individual, the terrain and the load on one's back. Three to five kilometers (1.8 to three miles) is a rough average measure of a *legua*.

Should you ask a direction by saying, "Is this the road to La Victoria?" and the person doesn't know, he might well say, "*Sí*" rather than worry you or himself any further. This reaction may be, as some say, an effort to please you, but I believe it's based on something vaguer and not so sentimental.

First of all, if you're in the back country, you have undoubtedly blown his mind by asking him anything at all. He probably doesn't completely understand the question or your strange accent, so to get rid of you he answers in a more or less positive manner. He might assume that although he's never heard of the place, it must be close or why else would you be looking for it?

Contrary to tourist-bureau propaganda, not all of the picturesque Indians in Mexico enjoy being gawked at, photographed and generally treated as subjects of an anthropological field trip, with everyone waiting expectantly for them to do something "ethnic." Ask one of these people directions to his village and he'll possibly think to himself, "*¡Madre de Dios!* Another afternoon of quiet ritual drinking about to be ruined by these *turistas* with cameras!"

He smilingly directs you to another village, not the one you want but it'll probably do.

Green Angels and Breakdowns

On major highways, particularly those frequently traveled by tourists, you'll see green government-operated pickup trucks whose purpose is to aid stranded or injured motorists. The driver and his assistant are trained in auto repair, first aid and English.

They'll help you out in any way possible, including supplying directions or gasoline. There's no charge for Green Angel service, but you will have to pay for any parts, oil or gas that they provide.

If you see a Green Angel truck and *then* your car craps out (always the way it happens), don't worry; they should be by again soon. Each truck tries to cover its route four times daily; that is, two round trips, one in the morning and one in the afternoon.

Never leave your car unattended if it breaks down on a highway. Unattended cars are good targets for thieves, vandals and the police, since any empty vehicle is considered abandoned, even if the hood is up or a tire flat. If there is no Green Angel service where you are and no friend to stay with the car, wait for another motorist (or even a pedestrian) to come along.

Ask them to get you a *mecánico* (mechanic), *grúa* or *remolque* (tow). If there is no other way than to go yourself, try your best to hire a guard. Offer a fair amount, enough to maintain their interest, and most any kid, or adult for that matter, will gladly watch the car until you return. Think of it as very cheap, short-term insurance.

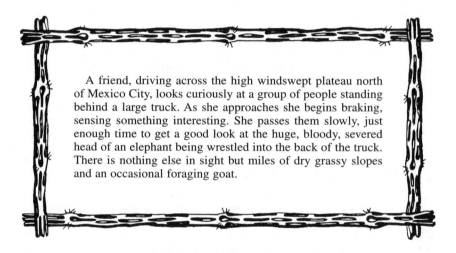

A friend, driving across the high windswept plateau north of Mexico City, looks curiously at a group of people standing behind a large truck. As she approaches she begins braking, sensing something interesting. She passes them slowly, just enough time to get a good look at the huge, bloody, severed head of an elephant being wrestled into the back of the truck. There is nothing else in sight but miles of dry grassy slopes and an occasional foraging goat.

Ferries

Although most ferries are being replaced by bridges or bypassed by new roads, many still operate, particularly in tropical areas. Ferries rarely run at night, even if they are large, and the first trip of the day is around dawn. You might like to plan around this and avoid spending a night on the landing—usually a good place for bugs. During the holiday seasons, you can expect a long wait for ferries on roads between large towns or between any beach and the main road.

Ferries that are being used to replace washed-out bridges or to cross small rivers run on very loose schedules. They often operate only when they have a full load, or if they carry just one vehicle at a time, they'll take you across whenever they get around to it.

Some ferries are free of charge but more aren't, and the fees may seem exorbitant, especially to cross a river that you could almost drive through.

Foot passengers pay less or nothing at all, depending on how inconspicuous they make themselves. The passengers of any and all vehicles, from cars to buses, have to get out while loading and unloading. If the ferry runs aground, you'll probably have to help push it free. (For long-distance ferries see *Getting Around: Ferries*.)

Gas Stations

Selection of a *gasolinera* (gas station) is quite easy. Pemex (a government monopoly) stations are the only ones to choose from. Although new Pemex stations are opening all the time, the best rule to follow is never pass one up if you can't make it to the next town.

Pemex stations are generally located at the edge of towns. Some large towns have a station on each side and possibly one in the middle for good measure. Stations are also located at important crossroads between cities and at points where major roads branch. However, you won't find the familiar American scene of competing gas stations on all four corners of a intersection. Other stations will occur at irregular and unexpected intervals, making it necessary to watch the gas gauge when traveling away from main highways.

Very few Pemex stations stay open all night; even those located in large cities often close before midnight. On main trucking routes, however, there are some large all-night stations.

Government regulation of the petroleum industry guarantees supplies and, considering Mexico's oil reserves, any shortage of fuel is highly unlikely. Individual stations do run out, however, so don't be shocked if you're told that one or more pumps are dry. (Shortages can be a real problem in Baja, however, especially when large numbers of gas-guzzling RVs pass through a town.) In small towns and in the country a gas station may have just one pump of *Nova* and nothing else, not even oil.

• **Mexican gasoline is sold in two unleaded grades:** unleaded *Premium*, in the red pump, is over 90 octane; *Magna Sin* is the green pump (87 octane, equivalent to regular unleaded in the U.S.). *Magna Sin* (*sin* means "without" lead), may be rated as "high test," but I call it "*Magna-sin-poder*" ("Magna-without-power"). Jokes aside, if your engine knocks painfully, try a mixture of *Magna Sin* and *Premium*. Unleaded *Nova* in the blue pump, which was contemptuously known by many drivers as "*No-va*" ("doesn't go"), has been phased out.

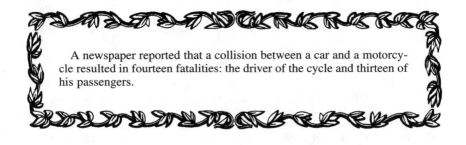

A newspaper reported that a collision between a car and a motorcycle resulted in fourteen fatalities: the driver of the cycle and thirteen of his passengers.

Opinions vary widely on the advisability of blending gasolines. If you prefer to use octane-boosting gasoline additives, ask for "*Aditivo para gasolina*" in gas stations and auto parts stores.

The prices of both oil and gasoline are controlled by the government and vary just slightly, usually a few cents more per liter in remote areas. As a general rule, Mexican gasoline prices are close to what you're paying in the U.S.

• **Diesel is widely available** and roughly one-third cheaper than gasoline. *Diesel Sin* is desulfured diesel fuel. According to our readers, however, diesel from small stations is often contaminated by dirt or water. Change your fuel filters often. Parts for high-tech diesel engines are very scarce in Mexico.

• **Engine performance is affected by altitude**. If you're making a significant change, either up or down, and will be doing a lot of driving at a new altitude, it might be wise to have the timing adjusted accordingly.

• **Water in the gas** is not uncommon in hot coastal areas, where the high humidity can condense into problems for your carburetor. Alcohol additives should be used occasionally; they blend with the water and allow it to burn. I prefer to avoid the expensive commercial additives and use drinking alcohol instead (see *Booze and Cantinas*). A liter or so every once in a while is a vague enough guideline.

An in-line filter will trap both water and dirt. Check it often for clogging and carry at least one spare. (See *Preparing Your Car*, later in this chapter.)

• **Running out:** I've run out of gas enough times to have developed a healthy respect for a spare gas can. If you have to ask for the use of a gas can from a Pemex station, be prepared to be turned down; very few of them have gas cans on hand. In a major station near Mexico City I was offered a large plastic detergent container, complete with a half-inch of hardened soap. It took me an hour to get the soap out and the suds nearly engulfed the station. After all this I was asked to pay a very hefty deposit.

Mexican motorists are very good about stopping to give a stranded tourist a helping hand. For that reason you can usually save yourself the hassle of hitching to a gas station, if you can produce a siphon hose and ask the favor of a slight drain from someone's tank.

• **Gas Can Alert!:** Annoyed by drivers who "tank up" several spare cans with cheaper U.S. fuel, the government now prohibits tourists from entering Mexico with extra gas. You can still bring the cans—but you'll have to fill them in Mexico.

• **Motor oil:** Pemex stations offer three types of oil: *Mexlub*, *Brillo* and *Premium*. Pemex oils come in familiar SAE grades of 20, 30 and 40, but 20W may be difficult to find. In general, Mexicans prefer 40W oil. Oil is sold in auto parts shops, garages and some large Pemex stations. If you buy oil in a garage, they will often change it for you as a bonus.

When you order a can of oil, always check the SAE weight before you or the attendant dumps it in. The attendants often grab the first can of oil in sight. A young kid did

Truck bumper graffiti: The King; Speedy Eagle; All for Nothing

this to us after we'd ordered a can of 30W and all he could find was 50W. He said it was "more or less the same," but we insisted on 30W, which he eventually found.

Gas and oil additives, car wax, fuses and all the other little goodies so commonly found in gas stations in the U.S. are sold only in the larger and shinier Pemex stations. Small stations may have nothing more than one grade of gas, a haphazard selection of oil and a broken tire pump. Auto parts stores and large supermarkets are the best sources of oil and automotive odds and ends. Road maps are usually not available.

• **Grease jobs**, routine lubrication, oil changes, tire repairs, car and motor cleaning and minor repairs are done at average-sized Pemex stations. The quality of the work and the price will vary from station to station. (See *Car Repairs* and *Preparing Your Car*, later in this chapter.)

• **Air and water** are available in almost every station, though it is best to *ask about the water before drinking it*. (See *Mexico A to Z: Water*.)

Because air gauges may be calibrated in kilograms instead of pounds (*libras*), it is best to have your own tire gauge and to check the tire pressure yourself. Standard tables used to convert kilograms to pounds *cannot be used for air pressures*.

• **Restrooms** in Pemex stations vary from as bright and clean as an operating room to as dark and funky as a sewer, which they often lack. As a general rule in Mexico, public bathrooms rarely have toilet paper. A wad of napkins or *papel sanitario* should be your constant traveling companion. (Some Mega Pemex stations even have public showers.)

Note: It is customary in Mexico to dispose of used tissue in a waste can, *not in the toilet*. To avoid plumbing disasters, never put toilet paper in the toilet.

• The **restaurants** that often adjoin gas stations vary as much as the restrooms, from pseudo–Howard Johnson's to stomach-knotting. If there are two restaurants near a gas station, the one farthest away is almost always independent of the station and more reasonable in price and quality.

Lorena and I were driving down a deserted highway when we noticed a police car parked in the road in front of us. As we slowed down four cops jumped out of the car and began to flag us down, indicating that we should pull off the pavement.

"I sure don't like the looks of this," I said to Lorena, rolling down my window as one of them came running over. He looked very hot and impatient.

"Where are you going?" he demanded, standing beside the car with hands on his

Truck bumper graffiti: Bird Without Direction

hips. The cop kept glancing over at the others as if for support. They acknowledged his glares by drifting around our car, looking in the windows and staring at the license plates. It didn't feel like a search, but it didn't feel very comfortable, either.

"We're going to . . . ," I answered. "Why?"

He ignored my question. "Do you have enough gas?" he asked, throwing me off guard.

"Of course," I said, now thoroughly confused. "Why?"

He continued to ignore me, turning to the others with a shout of "Get the hose!"

A cop hustled back to the patrol car and dug around in the trunk for a few moments, taking out a short length of pink plastic hose and a small galvanized bucket. I got out of the car and began to protest.

"*Señor,* wait a moment!" I said, "*¡No es posible!*" I started to protest again, trying to explain that it was impossible to siphon from this particular tank due to a dent we'd picked up in Baja.

"Don't worry, *amigo,*" he interrupted. "We'll leave you enough to get to the next *gasolinera.* We'll pay you, of course, for the gas."

The guy with the siphon hose was ordered to his knees and quickly began the job of sucking up the gas. He gave several tries but couldn't quite manage to maintain a steady flow. The gas would start to run and then trickle down to nothing.

"SUCK ON IT, you idiot!" the first cop roared, slapping his holster impatiently. The other two exchanged wary glances. I wondered how long they'd been stuck out here and whose fault it had been. I began to enjoy myself.

The man on the hose finally wobbled to his feet and ran off to the ditch, falling to his knees and retching up raw gasoline.

Without being told, another took his place. When the bucket held two or three cupfuls he followed the first to the ditch, pitching forward onto hands and knees, his back heaving up and down as he gagged convulsively. The third cop went down to the hose like a man kneeling before the chopping block. He didn't bother to join his companions but vomited instead into the bucket, spoiling what pitiful little gasoline they'd managed to accumulate.

Without a word the first cop pulled the hose from the filler neck, threw it into the dirt and stomped back to the patrol car. He climbed into the front seat, slammed the door and sat staring off into the distance. We waited a few moments, then started the car and pulled slowly away. I took a quick look in the rear-view mirror; three of Mexico's finest lay sprawled on the ground, puking, a fourth trying to fight off a fit of apoplexy. It had been an interesting interlude.

Rip-Offs

Anyone who has heard anything at all about driving in Mexico has heard stories of rip-offs in gas stations. Mexican gas station attendants are not as dishonest or conniving as most tourists believe. I'm sorry to say that many of these stories are true, however, especially in big-city gas stations and on popular highways. Whenever possible, I advise you to fill up in rural areas and smaller, neighborhood gas stations. Even there, Pemex attendants may make an occasional error. The people who work in gas stations are not generally renowned for their mathematical wizardry, so don't jump down some fourteen-year-old's throat because he shorts you a few cents.

The type of station that commonly cheats tourists is almost always easy to spot. The routine usually goes like this: as you pull in, a mob of kids surrounds your car, elbowing away old men selling yesterday's tamales and soggy sandwiches. The kids try to get you to agree to a wash job or a window-cleaning.

Before you can force your way out of the car, you hear the pump dinging away. By the time you've got the brats from under the hood or prevented them from greasing the windshield with their dirty rags, the gas tank is full. Or at least they say it is. Sometimes it really is full; more gas, in fact, than you have ever seen crammed into it before, perhaps as much as ten gallons over capacity.

The first precaution is: roll up your windows before leaving the vehicle. (If you head for the washroom, lock the car.) At the pump, observe the attendant and make sure that he rings it back to all zeros. If he leaves several liters from the previous purchase, he's going to try to soak you for it. It is this ploy that results in tanks that have apparently had more gas pumped into them than they can hold.

If this happens, just calmly point out that the tank isn't that large (*"No cabe"*—"It doesn't fit.") If this isn't enough, ask to see *el dueño* (the manager) or take down the number of the station and the reading on the pump. The attendant assumes that you're going to complain officially (which you can do with success—to both the Pemex company and the Mexican Tourist Bureau), and he will almost always rectify his "mistake." Don't get violent or nasty until he's had time to pretend it was all an error.

A very handy way to avoid this type of cheating is to put a reminder of the tank's capacity in liters on top of the gas cap or near the filler neck. This can be done with labeling tape or paint. *Capacidad 40 litros* (capacity 40 liters) is a very straightforward way of letting people know that *you* know what's going on.

Another ploy in this type of station is charging the normal price for a can of oil and then only pretending to put it in or not actually emptying the entire can into the crankcase. To avoid this, do it yourself. You should anyway, since even honest attendants often read dipsticks incorrectly and tell you that you need a liter of oil when you don't.

Similarly, attendants frequently forget to replace the gas cap, so check it at the same time. A locking gas cap will save you many a filched or forgotten cap. Put the key on a ring with the ignition key. This means that the cap can be opened only after you've stopped the engine, and it gives you time to check the pump. The engine cannot be restarted until the attendant hands back both keys.

Shortchanging happens on occasion, but may be done so subtly that you'll never be quite sure if it was tried intentionally or not.

The sneakiest method is for the attendant to count your change back very rapidly, then suddenly stop counting short of the correct amount. In many instances, the person receiving the change assumes the final count is correct and pockets the change with no suspicion of what's happening. When the customer does notice that the change stopped too soon, the attendant just pauses as if checking the count mentally and then forks over the rest.

Another method, not nearly so cool, is to wait you out hoping that, rather than search or ask for the person who owes you the change, you will give up in disgust and leave. This is usually tried by a younger attendant in stations where large groups of people make him hard to recognize.

When you aren't given enough change say, *"Me falta"* ("I'm short"). If you know how much you're short, give the amount, *"Me falta ___."*

The solution to any type of dishonest money-changing is to have the correct change or so close to it that it won't bother you if they get away with a two- or three-cent "tip."

Once you're familiar with the capacity of your tank, I strongly recommend that you order gas by the amount you wish to spend, rather than saying, "Fill 'er up." This not only saves time but also virtually eliminates the chance of being shortchanged. When you order gas in this way, show the attendant the money, but don't hand it over until the pump has stopped and you've got all of your gas.

Sometimes you will be assaulted by a screaming horde of ragged kids who want to wash the windshield. I have rarely seen them do anything but smear more dirt or even oil from their filthy rags on a window they were supposedly cleaning. Their intentions are good; they just do a lousy job.

The best way to avoid being cheated is to stay on top of the numbers. Those of us who are easily stampeded when trying to convert pesos-per-liter into dollars-per-gallon will rejoice at **Codo's Conversion**. This relatively simple formula was suggested by David Eidell, an engineer and skilled number cruncher who is aptly nicknamed "El Codo" (Cheapskate). Using a small calculator, David shows us how to quickly convert our metric gas purchases into familiar dollar-per-gallon amounts. Here's how it works:

1. Turn on your calculator and enter the price of a liter of gasoline (shown on the pump).

2. Multiply the price by 4.

3. Multiply this result by 94.64 percent and . . .

4. Divide the result of Step 3 by the current peso/dollar exchange rate to get the price, in dollars, of one gallon of gasoline.

Here's an example:

1. The price of gas is 3.0 pesos per liter.

2. 3 x 4 = 12

3. 12 x .9464 (94.64%) = 11.356

4. 11.356 ÷ 8.0 (8 pesos to $1) = $1.42.

By the way, this same formula will also convert propane prices to dollars-per-gallon. When calculating propane by weight, however, allow two kilos per gallon.

Whether it's window washing, tire repair or a lube job, always determine the price before agreeing to have anything done or the charge may be rather astounding.

Tip: If a gas station or cop tries to rip you off, flag down the next Green Angel you see and make an official complaint. Green Angel crews tell us that if more tourists would make official complaints, they might be able to do something about abuses by gas stations and crooked cops.

We had been driving for several hours through the jungle, alternately marveling at the scenery and the unexpected bonus of a brand new two-lane blacktop road. What showed on our map as unimproved dirt was actually one of the best stretches of highway we'd yet found.

"Do you realize that there's not even any traffic?" Steve said, putting the van into a near slide as he cut a sharp corner. I could hear Lorena cursing in the back as she tried to stop the avalanche of books, clothing and miscellaneous pottery that Steve's racing maneuver had loosened from the overloaded cabinets.

"Take a look at those Tarzan vines!" Steve continued, sticking his head and most of his upper body out of the side window. He was in his full tourist/driver position, glancing at the road ahead for occasional course corrections while maintaining a running commentary on the passing sights. If I failed to exclaim over the beauty of a large tree we'd narrowly missed colliding with, he'd repeat, "Did you see that tree? Did you see that tree?" until I admitted that I had, that I found it not only beautiful and amazing but perhaps even spectacular. This same routine was applied to large leafy plants, streamers of moss, unusual boulders and any form of wildlife larger than a grasshopper. Requests that he give at least equal attention to the road were useless, for like Mexican truck drivers he fully believed that the Great *Chofer* in the Sky was lending a helping hand.

"Look out!"

Steve's head snapped down, his hands clawing at the steering wheel as a huge bull lumbered across the road directly in front of us. My foot pumped at an imaginary brake as the van swerved wildly around the unfazed animal. I was still trying to catch my breath when Steve slouched back in his seat and said, "Beautiful cattle around here, don't you think?"

I gave him a hard look; he was picking idly at some colored bits of tape stuck on the steering wheel, the remnants of his homemade wrap job. Lorena and I had agreed that pink and yellow crisscrossed tape looked wonderful, just like a Mexican semi in "full dress." The problem was that the cheap adhesive-backed tape he'd used soon wore through and driving was like grappling with flypaper.

"Yeah," I answered. "A bull would have made a great hood ornament. If this van had a hood, that is." His eyes narrowed; on a previous trip he'd lashed the sun-bleached skulls of a large sea turtle and a long-horned cow to the bumper and draped a small but vicious set of shark jaws over the rear-view mirror. He glanced wistfully into the mirror; the bull was safely off the road and into the bushes. One of those ears would have looked nice flapping from the radio antenna . . .

"Hey, Carl," Steve said, turning his body to face me, his left thumb hooked into the steering wheel, eyes focused vaguely over my head, "Remember the old *Pato de Paz*?"

"Hey, watch the road . . . !" I yelled, trying to shake off the feeling that we were about to become another roadside shrine. "Why don't you let me drive for a while?" I added, knowing this would bring him back to earth if nothing else would. It seemed to work; he turned his head for a few seconds, then slowly let his eyes drift back toward me.

"Yeah, the good old Peace Duck," he sighed. "I should never have let those creeps at the border touch her."

He went off into a long monologue, reminiscing about past trips as though narrating a mental slide show.

". . . and then we stopped for lunch, remember? I had the best refried beans there. You had a chicken *torta* and a Pacifico. Remember?"

"No."

"Yeah, you do. That was the place with the parrot in the bathroom. His name was Lorenzo. Remember now?"

"No."

"Are you serious? It was just down the highway from where we ran over that giant black and green snake, remember?"

"No."

"Aw, come on. Lorena had scrambled eggs with Oaxaca cheese in them. That was the day after I changed the oil in the van. It took an extra quart and I adjusted the valves. Number three was tight. Now you *have* to remember!"

"I don't."

"You gotta be puttin' me on." He ran a hand through his hair, straining for more details. "We were listening to that Johnny Cash tape, the one with 'Ring of Fire.' I had on a blue shirt and . . ."

"Oh hell!" I interrupted. "What possible difference does it make if I remember or not?" Steve turned to me with a look of complete astonishment. "Why, well . . . because . . . what if you wanted to stop and see Lorenzo some day? How would you know where to go?"

"Steve," I sighed, turning to stare into the jungle. "I don't even remember the parrot in the first place so how could I . . ." Oh, what was the use? We tore around another sharp curve.

"Well, you must remember what we had for dinner that night. I had a piece of bar-becued . . . DID YOU SEE THAT?!"

He jammed the brake pedal to the floor, interrupting himself with a shout and the shriek of tires burning against pavement. I braced against the windshield as the van shuddered to a stop.

"That was *unbelievable!*" he said, sticking his head out the window and slamming the gearshift into reverse. Before Lorena or I could register the proper degree of curiosity at whatever had prompted our nerve-fraying stop, we were backing down the highway at 30 miles per hour.

"There it is!" Steve cried, standing on the brake pedal again, throwing us violently back against the seats. He pointed into the jungle and I strained to see this latest marvel.

"See it? See it?!" he asked, banging his head on the edge of the window sill. I looked harder: jungle, trees, bushes, not a rhino or gorilla or giant condor in sight.

"See what?" Lorena and I asked in unison, squinting now to sharpen our vision. It might be a rare miniature deer or purple-spotted tree frog.

"Right there!" Steve cried. "Right in front of you! Are you *blind*?"

In the back country, you may encounter people who think that you are public transportation. A Mexican may mistake a distant gringo van for a regular bus and try to flag it down, assuming it to be one of the small vans that operate as second-class buses in many parts of the country.

We often give rides to these people and they invariably offer to pay, even after they find out that we're not operating a bus line. People carrying loads of food to market may offer to pay in goods. We've taken a bunch of onions or a piece of fruit rather than cash.

Whether you accept payment or not, don't brush the offer away too casually or you'll offend the person offering. When the offer is made quite firmly, accept it. If they're just hitchhiking and not seriously eager to pay, you'll be able to tell by their attitude.

"I give up," I said, knowing he'd have us sitting there for an hour if that's what it took to make identification. He looked aggrieved; what was it about us that we could not remember what we had for lunch last year, or perceive these fantastic natural wonders that literally surrounded us? He gave an enormous sigh of defeat and disgust.

"The vine! The Tarzan vine!" he yelled, tracing its length with his fingers, following the greyish twisted form from treetop to ground level.

"Oh! I see it," I said. "You mean that thick vine over there all tangled up with those other thick vines. The one that looks like the thick vines we saw a couple of miles back?"

Steve didn't say a word; he just put the van into forward and pressed the gas pedal to the floor. Pearls before swine! A genuine Tarzan vine, one capable of swinging an entire family and no one around to appreciate it but Steve.

The deeper Steve delved into memories of past trips, the less he was aware of the present one. Our speed began to drop, mile by mile, until the van was barely moving. I looked nervously behind us, watching for fast-moving buses or trucks. The lack of traffic was a real godsend.

"I picked up this crippled hitchhiker just this side of Tuxtla and . . ." The monologue continued, dipping here and there into various memorable trips and experiences, most of them very familiar to both Lorena and me. Those we hadn't been involved in ourselves had been told and re-told over the years.

." . . had a huge dog, a mean S.O.B. that could sing, well, howl actually, 'Jingle Bells.' Offered me a half interest . . ."

I yawned. The van began to buck and lurch as our speed fell to about 15 miles an hour.

"You're lugging it down!" I said, not missing the chance to get one on him. When I drove he watched every move, as though I were an astronaut training on a lunar lander.

". . . the fat guy with the .45 had a carved jade mask you couldn't believe . . ." Steve's hand slipped to the gearshift and he dropped it into second. "No, I'm not" he said, breaking his account of tomb robbers.

"You aren't now but you were before," I said.

"Was what?" he countered.

"Lugging it down!" I yelled.

"I'm not lugging it down," he answered, putting the gas pedal to the floor and winding the engine up to a scream. I groaned and turned to stare into the jungle. The van immediately slowed as the travelogue resumed.

". . . about 25 cents between us and I said, 'Take a chance, you never know' and so he put it on number 7 and . . . picked up a turtle-poaching boat just this side of . . . she said, 'Where'd you get that hat' and I said . . . maybe a broken leg, but it was only a sprain so the driver . . . couple of gigantic bats, vampires I'm sure . . ."

"Hey, look out!" I said as we came around a tight curve. Steve's eyes turned to the road and his foot moved to the brake pedal. A group of workmen blocked the highway, standing around two battered dump trucks loaded with broken pieces of cement. One of the men flagged us down.

"We got just beyond the outer reef when . . ." Steve continued his story, waving irritably at the flagman. The van kept moving. Either he hadn't really noticed the signal to stop or just didn't care. The flagman gestured frantically and then waved us on with a "What the hell?" motion.

". . . got a little choppy and the captain said . . ."

The road ended in a massive washout. Steve stopped the van.

". . . the damned oil line broke and sprayed hot oil on the supercharger . . ."

A huge concrete bridge lay twisted and broken in front of us, surrounded by mountains of splintered trees and debris. It looked quite new, as new as the highway, but was obviously beyond repair. The flagman came jogging up from behind us.

". . . ate this thing that looked like a peach but . . ."

The flagman was next to Steve's window, motioning at him insistently. Steve brushed him off with a quick smile.

." . . couldn't believe the taste, man, it was fantastic!"

The flagman said something to Steve and pointed at the bridge.

"*Sí, sí,*" Steve muttered absentmindedly, rolling his eyes at me as if to say, "Catch the jerk with the flag, would ya?"

". . . lit the incense and the candles and took this poor chicken . . ."

The flagman's head was turning quickly from us to the bridge and then back again. He opened his mouth, paused, then was gone.

". . . the fog rolled in and you could still smell the hot lava . . ."

I glanced out the rear window and then toward the bridge. Where had everybody gone?

"Hey," Lorena said, looking out of her window and toward the ground, "There are legs and feet sticking out from under the van."

". . . the damnedest thing you ever saw, feathers and bones . . ." I stuck my head out of the window. There were several pairs of boots and *huarache*-shod feet on my side, too. How did they get there? What were they doing, sleeping?

". . . girl started chanting these weird words kind of like . . ."

"Hey, Steve!" I interrupted, "There's a bunch of people under the van!"

He stopped in mid-sentence, turning to me with an angry scowl. "Can't I just tell this *one story* without you guys breaking in all the time? Is that too much to ask?" I started to answer but he cut me off, eyes glazing over as he sorted through his memory for the thread of the story.

". . . oh yeah, it was just after midnight but still hot . . ."

"Something's going on here!" I yelled, reaching for the door handle. "The flagman must . . ."

KA. . . WHAM! . . . WHAM! . . . WHAM! . . . WHAM!

I stopped, stunned by the tremendous blasts. The bridge in front of us quivered . . . KA . . . WHAM! . . . WHAM! . . . WHAM! . . . twisted upward . . . WHAM! . . . WHAM! . . . then seemed to lift itself slowly from the streambed. . . KA. . . WHAM! . . . WHAM! . . . as clouds of dust shimmered around it and chunks of cement . . . KA . . . WHAM! . . . WHAM! . . . WHAM! . . . tumbled high overhead like huge softballs lofted into center field . . . and. . .

"OH, NO!" Steve screamed, eyes bulging, as the van rocked against the terrific concussions. Twenty quick explosions, then suddenly a series of five, a ripple burst, then five more, thirty, forty, fifty!

"LOOK OUT!" he cried, cramming himself between the front seat and the steering column. The softballs were coming down now, shattered meteorites of jagged cement, some the size of grapefruit, others even larger, thudding into the ground around us like a mortar barrage. A hailstorm of smaller pieces rattled against the top of the van.

The explosions continued, WHAM! WHAM! WHAM! WHAM!, completely obscuring the bridge in clouds of dirt and smoke. We held our arms over our heads, eyes tightly closed, waiting for the inevitable impact. There was no chance of running, we could only pray that the van's thin roof and overhead rack would take the main force as the cement tore through.

And then a sudden silence, punctuated by the thump of a last volley of fragments. My ears rang with the aftershock. The bridge was gone, transformed into a long mound of blasted concrete and steel rods.

Steve worked his way back up onto the seat, his face white and sweating.

"You OK?" I croaked, looking in the back of the van for Lorena.

"Fine," a voice said. She had somehow managed to crawl into the long cupboard beneath the bed. A few hours earlier she'd sworn it wouldn't hold another thing and Steve had been forced to put his extra shoes on the roof.

The flagman's grinning face was suddenly at Steve's window.

"Did you enjoy it?" he asked pleasantly.

Steve gave him the Black Death stare.

"What do you mean, enjoy it?" he snarled, flexing his hands on the steering wheel as though they were around the fellow's neck.

"I asked if you had parked in the danger zone on purpose," the flagman said, "and you said that you had. You said, '*Sí, sí!*'"

Others were crawling from beneath the van, laughing and dusting off their clothing. They looked at us as if we were completely insane.

Steve rubbed his face with the heels of his hands, muttering low curses. The flagman grinned nervously, backing away with a final, "You can wait for an hour, if you want, and there will be more to watch." He didn't wait to hear Steve's colorful reply but turned instead and began walking back to his post.

We sat for a few minutes in a heavy silence. Steve finally reached for the gear shift and put it in low, edging the van carefully down the rough, temporary road bypassing the fallen bridge. We came to the edge of a shallow stream.

"You know, this kind of reminds me of a place in Perú," Steve began. "I'd just got back from a trip up towards . . ."

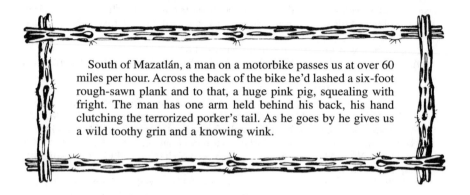

South of Mazatlán, a man on a motorbike passes us at over 60 miles per hour. Across the back of the bike he'd lashed a six-foot rough-sawn plank and to that, a huge pink pig, squealing with fright. The man has one arm held behind his back, his hand clutching the terrorized porker's tail. As he goes by he gives us a wild toothy grin and a knowing wink.

PREPARING YOUR CAR

Many people leave for Mexico with no preparation at all, just as if they were driving to the corner store for a quart of milk or a six-pack. If you're going to keep to the main roads and avoid punishing your car too much, you'll be OK. Mexico, after all, is a modern country. People who load up several spare tires and extra gas cans and paint "Mexico City or bust!" on the trunk just aren't with it.

First of all, take care of obvious repairs and servicing. It's easy to ignore a slight leak in the radiator when you're driving short distances around home. On the road, however, when you travel hundreds of miles a day, stopping every fifty miles to dip water out of a ditch to cool an overheated engine will be a major inconvenience.

For any car and for any trip, no matter how long it will be or where it will take you, I suggest the following basic precautions.

Servicing and Spare Parts

Get a complete tune-up and lubrication. Also, start your trip with the best possible tires. Tires cost more in Mexico than in the U.S., but the quality seems good. If your vehicle or trailer has odd-sized tires, you'll be lucky to locate replacements. Avoid 16.5-inch tires! Although Steve found 16.5-inch tires at an import tire store in Guadalajara, these are no longer made in Mexico. Large split-rims, such as bus tires, are common.

Check:
- tires
- brakes
- battery
- cooling system
  (clean air-cooled engines)
- steering, front end and suspension
- horn—you'll need it
- headlights
- windshield wipers

• A slight fender-bender accident will lead to much more trouble and expense than any safety precautions might cost you. Install, if possible, driving lights and driving mirrors.
• Labor is cheap in Mexico but parts and batteries are not.

Spares:
> tire
> fan belt (be sure it's the right size)
> motor oil
> oil filter (odd sizes are hard to find)
> in-line gas filter
> fuses
> flare or reflector
> repair manual (or jot down settings for plugs, points and valves)

Tools:
> large, medium and small standard screwdrivers
> medium Phillips screwdriver
> Vise-Grip pliers, regular pliers
> open-end wrenches, ten-inch Crescent wrench
> jack and lug wrench
> tire pressure gauge
> electrical tape and wire
> baling wire

• Driving conditions and roads can be tough in rural areas. If you're the type of person who doesn't care where you go or where you end up, more preparations for your car are advisable.
> **Tires:** use good ones. Back roads are murder on cheap tires. Mexico is the land of the slow leak.
> **Oil:** enough to fill the crankcase.
> **Gas:** a one-gallon can is sufficient. Never pass up an opportunity to top off your tank when driving in the boondocks.
> **Water:** for drinking and filling the radiator.
> **Tire patch kit:** include an aerosol can of tubeless tire inflater, for those awful multiple flats in the middle of nowhere.
> **Twelve-volt tire pump** that plugs into cigarette lighter. Indispensable! Someone else will need it if you don't.
> **Jumper cables:** a good set with a long reach.
> **Set of plugs, points, and condenser and feeler gauge** for setting them and the valves, or spare electronic ignition module.
> **Iron pipe or crowbar:** for breaking loose jammed lug nuts, prying bent bumpers or beating on the hood of your car out of frustration.
> **Folding shovel:** to dig out of sand and muck.
> **Chain or heavy rope:** for towing or being towed.
> **Small gifts:** to offer people who help you out.
> **Books:** to pass the time—hours or days, depending on how far off the main road you managed to get—while waiting for help or parts.

If you are the owner of a Kaiser, Edsel, Ferrari or other such offbeat, weird or very expensive car, you might be wondering what lies ahead. Since you are probably experiencing difficulty finding parts and reliable service for your car in the U.S., you are correct in assuming that the situation won't be any better in Mexico.

The following types of vehicles can be more than the normal hassle if you need parts or major servicing: anything old, long out of production or of a limited production and distribution; most foreign cars of any type; high-performance cars and motorcycles; and American luxury cars.

You may have problems finding parts for English cars, including Land Rovers, as well as Volvos, Saabs and Toyotas. Service and parts for Mexican-manufactured foreign cars such as Nissan (Datsun), Mercedes and Renault, however, are relatively easy to find.

There's no guarantee, however. For example, Mexican Nissans and many other cars made in Mexico or imported there have different engines and parts than those in the U.S.. Models also differ—a 1994 Nissan may include 1990 parts. On the plus side, there are now so many vehicles in Mexico that parts can eventually be found somewhere.

Volkswagens are manufactured in Mexico and very popular. You should have no trouble finding service and parts in almost all areas of the country. Standard American cars, such as Ford, Chevrolet and Dodge are also common, though parts for very old and very new models may be difficult to locate outside of the larger cities or northern border zone.

Don't get discouraged. The one thing that can save you and your '39 Mercury is the unlimited ingenuity of the Mexican mechanic. Given enough time and motivation—usually money but sometimes just the challenge—he will figure something out.

Almost anything can be found in Mexico City if one looks long and hard enough, and, if worse comes to worst, the part can always be ordered from your car's mother country.

Buying a Car

When buying a car you should carefully consider operating expenses, ease and availability of service, and cost of repairs and parts. Repairs to large vehicles inevitably involve large bills, especially if parts are difficult to locate, which will be the case with many off-brand delivery vans and old buses.

Check tires closely, especially on a school bus or delivery van. If it hasn't been driven recently, the tires are probably worse than they look and will go to pieces or wear quickly when you suddenly start doing hundreds of miles a day on them.

Look at a map and figure approximately how many miles you'll be traveling, *at a minimum*. Compute gas consumption and you'll have a good idea of how far you can go for your money. It cost us at least twice as much to operate a pickup truck as it did our VW van. This can mean the difference between a short trip and a long trip if your money is limited.

Many of the newer-model U.S. compact vans have large engines and are designed for freeway speeds (at least they are capable of them). However, transmissions that are geared too high to crawl up steep grades or over-powered vehicles with poor traction often run into trouble on back roads. This applies not only to towing a trailer but also to the fancy eight-cylinder "sport van" that easily does 120 mph on the freeway but won't gear down to 5 mph to hump over a large rock.

For general touring and exploring, I prefer larger American vans or pickups with campers, and VW Westfalias (with water-cooled engines). In terms of comfort, strength and reliability, these vehicles beat compact "sport" vans and older VWs hands-down. Parts and repairs for middle-aged American engines are widely available.

Fuel economy is another consideration. As Steve said, "When I filled the tank of my Dodge van in Guatemala and it cost $70 U.S., I thought a VW Bug might be a good idea after all."

In fact, for exploring Mexico's highways and back country, we have found that a van is hard to beat. With a VW, however, careful maintenance and regular servicing are absolutely mandatory, especially on older models. This is not so difficult that you can't do it yourself. VW agencies and unauthorized VW mechanics are very common. (A copy of *How to Keep Your Volkswagen Alive* is indispensable—see *For More Information*.)

Living in Your Vehicle

Selecting a vehicle that will be practical for both traveling and living requires careful thought and common sense. This applies not only to the person considering a new factory camper, but also to those with vague doubts about the practicality of taking their vintage school bus on a long trip.

What you'd like to do and where you'd like to go are the most important factors when examining the potential of a vehicle. Living arrangements can always be improvised, but if you can't drive your car or trailer to the places you'd like to see, your trip will be very frustrating.

Town driving, parking, narrow back roads and mountain curves can be mental and physical nightmares if you're driving an extra-large vehicle. The vast majority of people who go to Mexico towing large trailers, in school buses or in self-contained motor homes, are forced by the sheer physical size and difficulty of operating their vehicles to stick to the main roads.

Of the many people we've talked to who were living in such vehicles, most had the same complaints. Once they had found a good place to stay, they invariably began to feel confined by their living arrangements and began to spend a good deal of their time outside. Marketing trips or attempts at local sightseeing were always major efforts.

Some friends equipped a school bus with all the comforts of home, drove to Mexico and parked for three months near a beautiful beach. Within a week of their arrival they had moved into a palm hut and their bus sat unused for most of their stay. The wife made the most perceptive comment I've ever heard about traveling with such an elaborate set-up. "I don't like riding in buses," she said, "even when it's our own. For the money we've invested in gas and maintenance, we could have flown round-trip and rented a palatial house here."

On the other hand, another friend drives his large school bus to the same spot every winter, parks and then uses a motorcycle to run around. He has enough propane to operate a stove and lantern for months, plus stocks of staple foods. He uses the cycle for fresh food and water runs, trips to town for mail and general sightseeing. He starts the bus up every few days but it doesn't move again until he's ready to head for home.

Most factory camper set-ups are designed for showroom impact and mass appeal, not for long hard traveling and constant use. Appliances, parts and fittings such as stoves, water pumps, concealed water tanks, door hinges, interior lights and wiring can be almost impossible to repair or replace when and where they fail.

Factory campers aren't the only ones that lure you into believing that you're buying an efficient, durable and practical living arrangement. Many of the best-looking home conversions have been done by people who've never spent more than a weekend at a time living in their vehicle.

A nice big over-stuffed Salvation Army chair in the back of a milk van has great appeal as you're tooling around town enjoying a latté from your home-sized espresso machine, but when you're careening down a steep mountain road, you soon regret the extra weight and the imminent possibility that you'll be crushed by your furnishings.

When selecting a used vehicle that has been converted into a camper, the initial cost, if unusually low, may be a smokescreen to cover much-needed and costly repairs. The smoke may be thickened by beautiful cabinet work or ingenious living quarters. Ignore superficial improvements and concentrate on examining it critically for mechanical defects.

Do-It-Yourself Camper

Any living improvements, whether incorporated into a large bus or small van, should be kept simple. Some arrangements I've seen would boggle the mind of an Oriental puzzle maker. Complicated folding beds, seats and interlocking components require not only the most exact and careful construction but also a good deal of patience and dexterity to use.

When you consider the size of an average compact van, it's rather amazing that people can travel and live in them for years at a time without going berserk. The reason more people don't go insane is that they soon begin to live *around* their vehicle, rather than *inside* it. This is the key to the design of a really usable and enjoyable living arrangement in any small space.

Everything possible should be easy to remove and to use outside the vehicle. When we are traveling in a van, the interior is designed so that within minutes we can remove our food and dish cupboard, stove and icebox. This is all we need, in addition to a few folding stools and a hammock or two, to establish a comfortable camp or move into a hut or unfurnished house.

Removable units should be as lightweight as possible without being flimsy, and be able to withstand rough travel and handling without going to pieces. If building good cabinets is beyond your abilities, look for ready-made dressers, boxes, cupboards and chests in used furniture and junk stores.

Storage boxes and cabinets should be kept to a minimum. If you find yourself with an empty corner and are tempted to put some sort of storage container there, don't—unless you *really* need it. The more empty space remaining after the essential things have been built in, the less confining your vehicle will seem. Remember that while in use the interior will be much more cluttered with clothing, fresh food, baskets, books and other junk than it is when neatly packed for departure.

If you've built boxes or are using apple crates for storage of miscellaneous odds and ends, you'll be able to empty a good deal of space quickly, both for cleaning and for comfort. By piling everything neatly outside, the interior can be quickly converted into a comfortable and roomy lounging area. A little leg room feels good after driving all day.

Built-in water tanks aren't worth the expense or trouble. When a hose for filling them is not available (often the case in Mexico), you'll have to do the bucket brigade trip, so you might as well start with portable jugs. Two five-gallon cans should be a sufficient supply of fresh water for two or three people for a considerable length of time.

A sturdy ice chest that can be easily removed for use outside is much more convenient than a permanently built-in one.

Don't forget to lash, bolt or otherwise tie down all components until you are ready to take them out—or an emergency stop may send your furnishings flying.

To avoid dreading every night that you have to spend in your vehicle and to insure that you won't break down at the slightest excuse and spend money on a hotel, make the bed as comfortable as possible. This is very important. A comfortable bed will keep you from being bitchy in the morning and dead tired by noon.

The best material for a traveling mattress is a two- to four-inch foam rubber pad. It should be covered to protect it from getting dirty and rancid.

When bugs or rain force you to close yourself in, you'll want as much fresh air as you can get. If your vehicle is short on windows, install a few more. Those that open will provide air to breath, in addition to light and a better view. Overhead ventilators of the type used on house trailers are a good source of air.

Some type of bug screening is essential. Rig drapes or curtains of mosquito netting over side and back doors. They should be long enough to prevent mosquitoes from crawling underneath and loose enough so that you won't punch a hole in them with a foot or elbow.

Some people prefer a rectangular canopy of mosquito netting rigged over the bed. This allows all doors and windows to be opened but without having to screen them too. The canopy arrangement, however, forces you to stay in bed when the mosquitoes are out. (This is not always an inconvenience, but rather a good justification for reading, sleeping, etc.)

In many places where we've camped, bugs weren't a problem *most of the time*, but when they decided on an attack it was merciless and all-out. This may happen during the day as well as night. A screened refuge can mean the difference between evacuating a nice campsite or holing up for a short time.

Unless you're an exhibitionist, you should have curtains on all windows or you'll be playing to standing-room-only audiences when camped in most areas of the country. This is especially true if you spend the night in a town, schoolyard, soccer field or other public place.

When you are sleeping by a highway, the lights of passing trucks can keep you awake with their near-lighthouse intensity. Dark curtains are especially good for blocking out unwanted headlights (and daylight too, if you enjoy an occasional siesta).

Curtains also protect your possessions from greedy appraisal by would-be thieves when you are not inside.

Small folding tables attached to the back and side doors of the van are much more useful than a single large table that has to be used inside. A door shelf of some sort allows you to move the stove and cooking outside.

Some counter or table surface should be easily accessible while cooking, either inside or outside. Using the stove outside may become a hassle instead of a convenience if you have to climb in and out to cut vegetables or to set down a hot pan.

All folding tables should be very sturdily supported when in use. I will never forget the full-scale Chinese dinner Steve so lovingly prepared under the most unbelievable hardships. After hours of delicious anticipation, he gave the chow mein a final masterful stir. The stove, dinner and table crashed upside down on his foot. Screams and obscenities rang in our ears for weeks afterwards.

Interior lights are important for reading and cooking. Lights from junked cars are inexpensive and quite easy to install.

Tiny inverters that change 12 volts to 110 AC allow you to use super-efficient compact fluorescent light bulbs, small fans and even laptop computers. In combination with a solar panel and a deep-cycle RV battery, this is the perfect nomadic electrical system. (Available from Backwoods Solar; see *For More Information*.)

A roof rack will help keep the inside clutter to a minimum and is an excellent way to carry all the junk you'll accumulate during the trip. At night, you can store things on top, preferably covered, that otherwise would be underfoot or sitting on the ground. This will keep them dry and out of the reach of stray dogs or curious kids.

CAR REPAIRS

Not many of us are qualified or equipped to repair every possible breakdown we might have while traveling. Whether you need a routine oil change for your new Ford or a complete overhaul for your aging VW, you'll want to select a mechanic and a repair shop with care.

Our experience with breakdowns is extensive. We've had problems with many types of vehicles and have formed definite opinions about Mexican mechanics.

In general they are good, and often even better than the average mechanic in the U.S. Sloppy work, cheating on parts and padding bills—common problems the world over—also occur in Mexico. However, there are precautions that can be easily taken to avoid such things. (As some consolation, if you do get burned, it should cost less than in the U.S.)

A Typical Repair Shop

In Mexico, the challenge of finding a reliable garage is compounded by the new language and customs. One of the most difficult things to accept is that the best garage may look like a hobo hut in the middle of a junk yard. Appearances don't count as far as the average Mexican mechanic is concerned. You'll have to learn to accept the absence of fancy hydraulic jacks, power tools and crisp coveralls.

A typical Mexican *taller* (garage or shop) is incredibly filthy, littered with junk and parts, dark, smelly and filled with ragged kids casually smoking cigarettes as they wash strange metal objects in cans of gasoline.

In the middle of all this, reposes a brand new Detroit automobile, its engine strewn across several square feet of oily tarpaulin. A nervous, retired couple from Sun City are anxiously biting their fingernails as a twelve-year-old boy prepares to ride away with their crankshaft lashed to a rickety bicycle. He may be gone for days.

Whenever the most minor part is needed, another grease-stained boy emerges from the dark shop and pedals furiously off to some mysterious supply point. Even tools will be sent for.

The *maestro* (head mechanic, "master") notices that his clients are nervous, so he orders three of the youngest boys to wash the car. It's a minor service that will cost them nothing, but diverts their attention for an hour or so.

The elderly couple moan quietly as the boys swarm over the recently waxed automobile, wiping grease and dirt on the shiny new paint. One of the boys makes a particular effort to grease the windshield.

Before they can decide what to do about this well-intentioned "wash job," speeding bicycles converge on the garage. Parts wrapped in newspaper appear from beneath tattered shirts. The *maestro* produces an old pair of Vise-Grip pliers and attacks the dismantled engine. Gasoline is slopped carelessly and in great quantities over dirty parts. Oil is poured from dubious cans without labels.

Within a few frantic hours, the couple is happily on the road again, puzzling over the illegible bill and the sentimental farewells of the *maestro* and his staff.

Finding a Mechanic

The best way to find a reliable *mecánico* (mechanic) is to ask around. Very few Mexicans do their own repair work and most have a favorite garage. Often they will take you there or send someone to guide you.

Try to find a gringo who lives in the area to help you out. If this fails, approach a cab driver—they know everyone—or look for someone driving a vehicle similar to yours. If this fails to produce results or if your Spanish isn't up to it, you'll have to go looking yourself. Fortunately, mechanics tend to set up shop beside the highway, or in neighborhoods near large tire dealers and auto parts stores. In smaller towns, the local mechanic can be tucked away on any side street or literally under a shade tree. Again, don't be put off by his rustic work space or rudimentary tools.

During your search you might happen upon the authorized dealer or agency for your car. The clean shiny showroom, organized parts department and official coveralls would seem to indicate an efficient and reliable shop. This is not always the case. Some of the larger authorized garages are actually *worse* than an average backyard mechanic.

When a mechanic accumulates enough experience at the agency and a few spare pesos, he immediately begins thinking of his own garage. His wages at an agency are very low. With a few basic tools and room to park a car, he can open his own business. This explains why the agency may have just one qualified mechanic. Should he be off duty or busy with another job, your problem will be referred to someone with less experience.

In addition, everything costs more at the agency, from labor to parts, and usually takes longer to complete than in the independent shop. (If your car is very new, however, or has sophisticated electronics, you may require the dealer's services.) Backyard mechanics rarely charge overtime and they'll work long, hard hours to finish the job. If parts must be ordered from far away, the *maestro* will often send someone by bus to get them.

We once decided to have a brake job done on our VW van in the U.S. before leaving for Mexico. An appointment had to be made seven days in advance. The van was in the garage for three full days. The bill was staggering.

Two years later the same job was done in a garage in Mexico. It took five hours and cost a fraction of what we'd paid at home. In another memorable breakdown where parts weren't available, a Good Samaritan mechanic removed the clutch from his family car and installed it in ours.

In the Garage

There are certain precautions and procedures that should be observed when taking your car to any garage.

• **Don't be timid!** Always ask for an estimate before the job is started. "*¿Más o menos, cuánto va a costar?*" ("More or less, how much will it cost?") When there's a lot of work to be done, request a written *presupuesto* (estimate).

If the shop is small and the work to be done is extensive, you may be asked to pay for the parts in advance. This is common and acceptable since most small-time garages operate on almost no overhead.

• **Should parts be required, most shade tree mechanics will try to rebuild your faulty part or they'll buy a reconditioned part rather than a new one.**

We were once given a bill for a tune-up that amounted to less than the cost of new spark plugs. Steve naturally asked how they had managed that one. The *maestro* proudly said that in order to save us money he had replaced our old plugs with "good used ones." We checked and found that four used plugs of three different brands had been installed.

Always ask for a *nota* or *recibo* (receipt) for parts purchased in advance or used in the job. There's no need to be gruff or overly defensive; this, too, is standard procedure.

• **Once the work begins, *stay with the car*.** You don't have to sit in it while it's on the grease rack, but just lurk around, in obvious attendance. Because labor charges and wages are so low, the assistant mechanics tend to take things easy. If the car owner or a representative is present, the *maestro* will feel more obligation to do the job himself rather than delegate it to a young apprentice.

Let the *maestro* know that you're in a hurry and he'll probably let other jobs slide— those with the owner absent—until he's finished with yours.

Should you have to leave your car unsupervised, remove anything that is of irreplaceable value or especially tempting. The *maestro* will ask for the key in case the car has to be moved.

• **An almost unavoidable problem is that mechanics will attempt any job,** whether they have the necessary tools and qualifications to do it properly or not. Don't hesitate to lend a hand or offer advice if you feel that it's needed.

• **When the job has been completed, give the car a thorough going over before starting up and driving away.** Check the oil and gas cap. Mechanics will siphon whatever gasoline they need for washing parts out of your tank, but it shouldn't take more than a gallon. This is standard practice.

Kids are often given such minor jobs as putting in the oil. If the last truck he worked on held 15 liters, he might just assume that your car does too.

Take the car for a test drive. This is expected and the *maestro* will probably want to go along to see that you are satisfied and aren't going to leave without paying.

• **Before paying, ask for a *nota* or *recibo*** and don't hesitate to question any vague or unusual entries.

The vaguest entry of all is usually the number of man-hours worked. This is rarely unfair. In fact, many *maestros* don't bother to charge for labor other than their own or that of top assistants.

• **If your car craps out after you've paid for a repair job, don't hesitate to return to the shop.** Do it calmly. We've rarely had any but the most apologetic and gracious treatment when asking that a job be made good.

Body Work and Upholstery

Body work, painting and upholstery are all relatively inexpensive. Before handing your car over for extensive cosmetic work, it's best to get estimates from two or more shops. The range in prices can be considerable.

If you intend to have your car painted in Mexico, buy both the primer and paint in the U.S. Be there to witness that your paint is used rather than a substitute. We once had our van painted a shocking blue after ordering that it be done in a soft brown. When we pointed out to the *maestro* that it wasn't quite the color we'd expected, he just shrugged and said, "I got such a better price on blue." As we were about to pull out of the shop, I happened to look at the right side of the van. "There's no paint over here!" I yelled. The *maestro*, as imperturbable as a Zen Master, laughed and said, "It was parked so close to the wall I must have forgotten."

Note: Good tools are expensive in Mexico and most mechanics would give their eye teeth for a set of quality sockets or wrenches. Many gringos have found that trading tools for repair jobs saves them money and at the same time does the *mecánico* a big favor.

Note: For VW van owners, Mexican-made VW vans have 1960s vintage engines. Parts for more modern engines may be very difficult to find.

Travels with Woody and Sonny

We were camped north of Mazatlán, enjoying the surf and conducting a full-scale van cleanup after driving almost nonstop from the Pacific Northwest. Suddenly a contingent of local police and Army troops dropped in for an afternoon visit. They circulated among the campers, casually checking tourist cards and occasionally giving a car or backpack a brief search.

We had been following their approach rather apprehensively when a voice from the van parked next to us, drawled, "Well, yeaup. Uh huh. Looks like it's 'bout time to move on down the line."

A few seconds later a figure eased out of the side doors, stretching and yawning. It was Woody, an exuberant hip-hillbilly who had pulled in next to us the evening before. Woody ran a long bony hand through his scraggly brown hair, squinting into the bright sun. As he hitched sagging Army-surplus trousers over his narrow hips, his partner, lounging inside, put another country classic into their powerful tape deck. Mother

Maybelle's quavering voice blared out to one and all. A group of California surfers camped a few hundred feet away shook their heads in disgust. Sonny remained hidden, his nose undoubtedly buried between the pages of the thick pocket book he'd been reading since they'd arrived. Both of them seemed oblivious to the ear-splitting noise of the recorder.

Woody gave another huge yawn, then suddenly bent forward, jamming his right hand into the sand beneath his bare feet. "A CLAM SHELL!" he crowed, holding it up for us all to wonder and marvel at. The shell was quickly slipped into his pocket, sagging heavily with similar treasures. He cast a sneaky look toward Sonny. They may have been buddies since childhood but Woody was taking no chances; let him find his own!

"Did you say you were moving?" Steve shouted, a look of disappointment on his face. He'd spent half the night with them drinking warm Pacificos and reviewing their extensive collection of country-and-western tapes at maximum volume. After many days of being subjected to recorded concerts of surfing songs from nearby gringo vans, Woody and Sonny's arrival had been Steve's salvation. He saw them as a cultural oasis in a teenybopper wasteland.

"Yeaup!" Woody called back, scuffing the sand in hopes of another rare find. "Me and Sonny need a little more elbow room. Too much competition 'round here. All the good shells are picked over." A tiny blond-headed boy ran by, excitedly clutching half of a broken sand dollar to his chest. Woody scowled.

"Where are you headed?" Lorena asked.

"Yeah," Steve added. "We've been thinking of moving on, too." He gave us quick looks.

Lorena and I just shrugged; why not? We had no particular affection for either the Mexican Army or surfing music.

"Me and Sonny heard about a real good beach south of here a ways," he said. "Lots of nice shells."

"Just exactly where . . ."

"Oh, maybe a hundred miles from here," Woody answered vaguely, "give or take . . ."

When pressed for more definite information, he pointed to a group of people who had just returned from the beach and could give me the details. After checking the directions with them, I returned to find Steve and Lorena hastily breaking up camp.

"I've got the name of that beach," I said. "It sounds good to me."

"Great! Let's get the hell out of here as fast as we can," Steve urged.

"Looks like they're handling the heat pretty well," Lorena said, motioning toward Woody and Sonny. A crowd of slightly bewildered soldiers was gathered around their van, trying to interrogate our new friends over the mind-numbing din of the tape deck.

"You essmoke *marijuana*?" one of them shouted at Woody, ignoring the gifts of clam shells being pressed upon him. Woody gave the soldier a blank look, then turned to Sonny.

"Hey!" he yelled. "This turkey wants to know if you want to smoke some of that mary-wanna. Neat, huh?"

Sonny shook his head. He brushed this thick dark hair from his eyes and jammed his hands obstinately into the back pockets of his tattered Bermuda shorts. "Not me!" he snarled, glaring suspiciously at the soldier.

"*¡No, GRA-CI-US!*" Woody said, grabbing the man by the shoulder and pushing him toward the open doors of the van. "Have some of this here tee-quila, old buddy! It's a little rough but it does the job!" Woody thrust the bottle into the soldier's hands. He looked at it for a few seconds and then began to unscrew the cap. Loud rebel yells pierced the air as Woody and Sonny urged him on, celebrating each swallow with a high-pitched "Aieee! Aieee! Aieee!"

"You boys are all right!" Sonny laughed, passing the bottle to the next soldier with a wide toothy grin. As he raised the bottle to his lips, Sonny gave him a neighborly slap on the back, cracking the soldier's front teeth against the glass. "Here, bud, lemme put those things inside so you won't get sand in 'em!" Before they could protest Sonny grabbed their carbines and submachine guns and tossed them casually into the back of the van.

"Beats that mary-wanna, doesn't it?" Woody laughed, handing the near-empty tequila bottle to a stunned sergeant.

Steve grunted unhappily. "What are we going to do if Woody tells them where we're going?" he said. "At the rate they're guzzling that booze they may even decide to go with us!"

Fortunately, the soldiers soon tired of the overwhelming level of music. When the last swallows of tequila had been downed, they reached for their weapons. "Ya'll come back, ya hear?" Woody said, giving the sergeant another overly hearty slap on the shoulder. As the patrol wandered rather unsteadily toward the next group of campers, Woody flashed us a huge grin and a two-fingered peace sign.

An orderly repacking of the van was impossible; Steve kept one eye on the soldiers as he pitched our belongings into the open doors, urging us to hurry. Lorena looked at the chaotic mess and groaned.

"Ain't y'all ready yet?" Woody yelled, leaping into the driver's seat of his van and motioning Delly, his somewhat moth-eaten terrier, onto his lap.

Lorena got into the back of the van, offering to restore some semblance of order as we drove.

"How 'bout going ahead?" Woody added, "Soon's it gets dark I have trouble seeing what's up front!"

To illustrate his point, he turned on a single dim headlight and grinned through the dirt- and bug-spattered windshield.

Steve decided that a brief strategy session was in order. After conferring with Woody for several minutes, he slid wearily behind the wheel. "He says would we please signal when we stop or slow down, because he only has one brake and can't stop too well. And if he has a flat," Steve continued, "would we please wait for him at the turnoff."

I thought grimly of the tubes protruding from two of Woody's tires that we laughed so hilariously over early in the afternoon. In the rush to leave he had volunteered to carry our precious stove and food box, and we had been only too eager to accept.

All went well until dark. Steve beat on the horn, blinking the headlights to frighten horses and cattle from the road, while lightly tapping the brakes to signal Woody that danger lay ahead.

But when our slow progress became unbearable, Woody would pass us recklessly, often on blind curves. After leading for a few seconds he would allow us to overtake him, then jerk into the left-hand lane and drop back.

After a few of these passes, Steve became a total nervous wreck.

"Gaaaahh!" he sputtered, and suddenly swerved into the opposing lane.

"He almost got us that time!" I peered out the back window and saw the feeble candle-flicker of Woody's single headlight a few scant inches from our rear end.

We drove on nervously, Steve and I with noses pressed to the windshield, peering into the darkness for unlighted trucks and livestock. The only conversation was an occasional position report from the back seat.

"He's about fifty feet back and gaining," Lorena said. Steve gunned the motor.

"OK, about a quarter of a mile," she reported a few minutes later, causing a general relaxing of tense muscles and white knuckles.

After an hour or more of relatively uneventful travel, the turnoff to the beach appeared. Steve made a dramatic sliding turn.

Two or three miles later we gave a collective moan, "Oh, no! Woody and Sonny!" They weren't behind us.

Steve turned the van around and drove back as quickly as possible to the main road. We hung on as the van crashed into potholes and bounced over ruts.

"I hate to say this," I muttered, "but I forgot to tell them where the turnoff was. Woody doesn't even know the name of the place, much less how to get there."

"What?" Steve shouted angrily. "Are you serious? They don't know?"

"Afraid not," I answered. "And from what we've seen of the way Woody drives, the only thing we can do is wait at the crossroads until he decides to start backtracking."

"*The stove*," Steve moaned, pounding the steering wheel in frustration. "I let him take my stove."

We sat at the crossroads for half an hour, then decided to continue south. Perhaps they'd had a serious breakdown or accident and we could overtake them.

After hours of driving and no sign of the van, not even a shredded tire on the side of the road, we decided to give up and wait for Woody to find us. Conversation ended with Lorena's prediction that we'd probably be there all night. Groaning miserably, we made ourselves as comfortable as possible and tried to sleep.

"Hey! Hey! Wake up!" I jerked up from a back-breaking slouch across the front seats. Woody and Sonny were standing in front of our van.

"How come you didn't tell us you was stopping for the night?" Woody griped indignantly.

"We didn't just stop for the night!" I snarled back. "In fact, we've been trying to catch up to tell you the turn is back behind us. At least a hundred miles!"

"That's what I told ya, Grunt," Sonny said sarcastically, using Woody's endearing nickname.

"What the hell?" Woody said, suddenly cheerful again. "Let's get going. We can be at the beach in time for sunrise. Get some good shells."

I recklessly volunteered to ride with Woody in order to guide him to the turnoff.

Steve looked at me sadly but didn't argue; he was too concerned with getting to the beach and safely into a hammock.

I jumped into the seat beside Woody. Delly immediately began to wash my face affectionately.

"Git down! Git down, you mutt!" Woody laughed, engaging the clutch with a tremendous lurch.

"Hold on there, Grunt! Hold on, dang ya!" But Sonny was unable to reach a pot of coffee boiling unnoticed on the stove behind Woody's seat. With a crash and a cloud of steam, it landed on a pile of assorted junk.

"Sheeeyit!" Sonny cursed, rolling over on his strange couch-like bed in the back of the van and ignoring the dripping mess.

As we raced down the highway, Woody thumped enthusiastically on the horn in time to country-and-western music blaring from speakers suspended throughout the van. Sonny lit several candles perched precariously in holders glued to various parts of the interior and retreated into his book.

"What are you reading?" I yelled, hoping Woody might take the hint and turn the volume down on the tape. My head was reeling with gas fumes that seemed to be coming in through the floor and the thump! thump! of an electric bass.

"*Russian Revolution*," Sonny answered.

"Hang on!" Woody warned, hands and feet moving in a blur as he shifted madly and somehow steered through a group of wild-eyed horses.

A fat candle, still burning, landed on Sonny's chest. He flicked it onto a pile of books and clothing next to his couch. The candle snuffed itself out but Sonny didn't notice.

I looked back into the dimly lit rear area of the van. Psychedelic wallpaper, huge paper flowers, strings of beads, beer signs, flickering candles and a gallery of Grand Ole Opry stars plastered the inside. The furnishings could have been lifted from Snuffy Smith's living room.

The ceiling, a strangely textured, gory red-orange, caught my attention.

"Corduroy!" Woody yelled over the music, obviously pleased by my interest. "Sprayed it with Day-Glo and then fiberglassed it all over. Made quite a mess 'til I got her all finished up."

I re-examined the interior and realized that everything—ceiling, walls, doors and cabinets—was covered with a thick coat of fiberglass resin.

I turned my head away; it was just a little too much. The texture of the door next to me caught my attention. It appeared to be nothing less than a man's long-sleeved cowboy shirt fiberglassed to the door panel.

"Needs a few more coats," Woody said, noticing my stare. "Buttons fell off in Texas and the cloth is so hard that I can't seem to get 'em back on. Check this out," he said, "your friend and mine, E. Tubbs!"

I leaned over his shoulder and looked into the faces of several popular country music stars. Photos had been cut from fan magazines and glued over the instruments. Ernest Tubbs peered up at me from the speedometer, obviously the position of honor in this weird little Country Music Hall of Fame.

The decor continued over the rest of the dashboard: a nearly half-inch layer of rippled and sagging fiberglass resin covered a choice selection of beer-bottle labels, playing cards and photos of lesser country music stars.

"You ain't seen nothin! Watch this," Woody said, twisting together two wires that dangled beneath the dash. To his great delight a dim red light diffused through the photographs pasted over the instruments. Before I could comment on this latest marvel, he jerked the wires apart. A shower of gravel rattled under the van as we swerved onto the dangerously narrow shoulder of the highway.

"Gettin' pretty hot," he said casually. "That's how I blew out the headlights. Hey, Sonny!" he yelled. "Show him the rest!"

Without lowering his book Sonny stuck his hand into a hole in the side panel. The ceiling suddenly glowed with the flickering lights of a string of Christmas-tree bulbs. Some even bubbled.

"Neat, huh?" Woody asked, his face creased by a huge smile.

"I've never seen anything quite like it, Woody," I answered sincerely, wondering what else he might have in store. Steve's comment that our new acquaintances were "out of their heads, country style" seemed to be something of an understatement.

The next surprise came in the form of a slowly plodding cow that refused to yield the right-of-way. As we skidded and slid from one side of the road to another, I marveled at Woody's ability to keep the van under control, but always it seemed on the very edge of disaster.

"Damn you, Grunt," Sonny said quietly from somewhere amidst a heap of fallen books, cookware, candles and bedding, "Gawd damn you!"

Woody chuckled, then yelled over his shoulder, "It's about time you got out of that rack! We haven't seen your scrawny neck all day!"

As Sonny attempted to restore some order to the disaster area in the rear, Woody gleefully outlined the difficulties of driving a van that had one brake, one headlight and no steering.

"No steering!" I gasped, taking a new and intense interest in the curves and abrupt shoulders of the road.

"Well," he drawled, "not exactly what you'd call '*no* steering' but just *partial*. See this?" he said, demonstrating what seemed to be an impossible amount of free play in the steering wheel.

"Happened up north in Yaqui country. Me and Sonny got lost at night out in the desert and before we knew it we'd smacked us into a big cactus. Screwed up something underneath."

Sonny chuckled from the back, amused at the thought of having no steering.

"How did you hit a cactus?" I asked. "Run off the road?"

"Oh, no, we weren't on any road! We had us a load of drunk Yaqui Indians in the back and we decided to take 'em home, cross country."

"Don't worry yourself about it, Carl," Woody said, evidently noticing my drawn expression and clenched fists. "Why, it's been like this for two months and it's still going, ain't it?"

My comments were cut short by the appearance of the sign for the turnoff. Several tense moments passed as Woody deftly negotiated a flying left turn into the deeply pocked road.

"Not quite as smooth as the main stem!" he shouted, his voice barely audible over an incredible metallic crashing and banging as he attempted to maintain our previous speed. "Have to slow her down a bit, got a lot weight up there," Woody finally conceded, dropping the speed a few miles an hour.

The weight he referred to was one of the more incredible "improvements" to his van: two rectangular steel water tanks, each with a capacity of 45 gallons, mounted precariously on either side of the roof.

Woody had been told by well-meaning friends that drinking water was unavailable in Mexico. He had left his home in North Carolina carrying enough fresh water for a three-month trip.

"Hope Steve doesn't get too far ahead of us," Woody said, futilely attempting to avoid a bone-crunching series of deep holes that sent us crashing against the ceiling. I waited for the inevitable sound of a multiple blowout or broken axle.

As we hopped from rut to rut, he morbidly ticked off the remainder of the van's varied ailments, from ragged tires to burnt valves. He expected, he said, a major breakdown any minute.

"Hope she lasts a spell longer, though," Woody added thoughtfully. "Me and Sonny are down to about thirty bucks and we gotta make it home on that. Can't afford any sort of trouble."

Before I could share any gloomy predictions, we spotted Steve in the road ahead, warning us to stop by waving a flashlight.

"Whoooeee!" Woody howled. "Here we are!" A few minutes later, after doing a series of deep knee bends and push-ups, he rummaged beneath the sagging driver's seat and pulled out a battered three-cell flashlight. The lens was badly cracked and the case had been swathed in black electrical tape. "Not much, but it'll do." he chuckled, aiming the light toward me. It glowed like a cat's eye.

"Let's go get some shells!" Woody called, pointing the flashlight at the long dark expanse of beach. The surf was tinged with a faint pinkish glow from the east; sunrise was at least an hour away. Delly leaped and barked excitely, then threw himself onto the damp sand for a few refreshing rolls.

"What'sa matter! Feelin' a little tuckered out?"

Steve answered Woody with an exhausted wave of his hand. His head sank slowly down onto his arms, crisscrossed over the steering wheel. I staggered over to our van and began dragging my sleeping bag from the debris in the back. Lorena was collapsed across the bed, obviously well into a state of deep meditation.

Woody shook his head. "Well, golleeeee!" he sighed. "Guess I'll just have to get 'em all for myself! Come on, mutt!" He smacked his hand against the flashlight a few times to increase its output.

"Well, T for Texas!" Woody sang, moving off into the darkness, "and T for Tenne . . . THERE'S ONE! . . . and T for Tennesseeee! THERE'S ANOTHER! Golleeeee!"

It took Woody ten days, and often part of the nights, to fill the rooftop water tanks on his van with a tire-squashing quantity of seashells, driftwood and miscellaneous beach treasures.

"Man, the Customs people at the border are going to love that smell," I warned him. Woody just shrugged. "That's their problem, not mine."

"Y'all be careful now, ya hear?" Woody shouted, forcing the van into first gear. Sonny was lost somewhere in the rear, still an inch or so from the end of his book. We sadly waved goodbye to the "country-and-western freaks." Although they had two flat tires within half a mile of leaving the beach and less than $25, Woody and Sonny departed as cheerful and undaunted as ever.

ACCOMMODATIONS

Hotels: rates, negotiating the price of a room, cheap and comfortable, check it out first, small town hotels, super-cheap rooms, the "no-tell" motel, better safe than sorry • Renting a place: life in a Mexican town • House hunting: types of houses, what to look for • Wood-fired water heaters • Living with Mexicans • Hired help • Mary of the Light

Hotels

How do you go about choosing a hotel that is both economical and comfortable?

We've found that outward appearance is the quickest and most dependable way. If a hotel looks old (and this doesn't mean that it has to be a moldering ruin), it will probably be inexpensive or a good bargain. An older hotel is not necessarily located in a run-down area of town. There are innumerable nice old hotels located in any city, often right on the plaza and next door to newer places that cater to wealthy Mexicans and tourists.

Some colonial-style hotels that have been recently renovated may look deceptively fancy, but keep in mind that flourishes which went into the construction 200 years ago probably won't affect today's prices. Look at the windows of the rooms from the outside; if they are about ten feet tall you can bet that the ceilings inside are high. Very high ceilings are a sign of old-fashioned construction. Unless a major chain has done a total refurbishment, older hotels seldom charge more than three-star rates.

Many tourists try to economize by looking for places that fit their idea of a sleazy cheap hotel in the U.S. This type of hotel actually costs more because it does look like an American hotel.

Older hotels have other advantages besides economy. First and most important, you're in Mexico to experience the country and its people. What better way to capture the flavor of Old Mexico than to sleep in a huge, high-ceilinged room furnished with massive mahogany artifacts, genuine handmade tiles in the bathroom (though perhaps faded and cracked), a squeaking overhead fan, wrought iron grillwork on the windows and an octogenarian at the front desk? This is what traveling is all about.

Large groups and families can take advantage of the Mexican custom of putting everyone into one room; it not only saves a considerable amount of money but also makes every moment a social event. Newer hotels have reduced room space to an absolute minimum, but older hotels will almost always have a few rooms designed to accommodate parents, children, grandparents and their guests.

Many hotels include a café, restaurant and bar. The prices in these will vary considerably, but as a general rule the best bargains, and often the best food and service, will be in older, less expensive hotels. Many of these hotels cater to long-term guests and budget-conscious local businesspeople. They are always the last to raise prices.

Older hotels almost always offer more personal service than their flashier competitors. If you just have to have a piece of laundry done on short notice, the desk clerk is more likely to have the time and personal interest to find an unoccupied maid or laundress to help you out.

Employees in smaller and older hotels will usually be happy to help you unravel bus schedules, make phone calls in Spanish, direct you to the local sights and generally assist in whatever way they can. The manager of one hotel helped me plan a two-day eating itinerary designed to include the best regional dishes. When I told her that my money was limited, she said, "I'll tell you about the places that we take our friends to, not the tourist spots."

The most dramatic example of personal attention that I have experienced occurred when I was traveling solo in northern Mexico. I suddenly fell very ill while visiting a small town deep in the Sierra Madre. My one-night stop soon became a week, fighting off a fever in a hotel room. The family who ran the place brought me tea, soups and little delicacies from the kitchen (no charge) and did their best to keep me content and alive. When I took a turn for the worse, they insisted on bringing me home for closer care. I spent another week with them, treated like ailing royalty, and when I'd recovered I left with great regret.

Hotel Rates

Virtually every hotel in Mexico is inspected by the government and assigned a rating of five stars or less, with a corresponding room rate. Because this is Mexico, however, and not well-ordered Switzerland, there's often considerable latitude between hotels of equal rating and equal price. This is especially true when comparing resort and tourist hotels with hotels in the country's interior, which usually offer equivalent comforts for less money, and hotels in our preferred range of three stars or less.

Beginning with top dollar, four- and five-star beach hotels offer their guests luxury and pampering, as well as careful insulation from Mexico's grittier realities. Prices run as low as $75 a night (four-star, off-season), but climb quickly to $150 to $350 (beachfront) and then soar into realms we have yet to explore.

Three-star hotels, as well as better two-star places, tend to be comfortable, clean and unpretentious. They will vary wildly in style from quaint colonial to impersonal cinderblock. A two-star room might have copious hot water and a narrow mattress whereas the three-star hotel next door offers a decent bed but an erratic shower. Room rates vary from about $20 to $40, double occupancy.

One-star rooms are among our favorites, if only because there is a delicious air of surprise around everything. Will there be hot water tonight? What if the lights go out again? How many roosters can be crowded onto the roof of Room 6? All this entertainment, plus a pillow you could chop wood on, for $10 or less.

The authorized rate for your room will be posted on a small sign somewhere in the room. Because of competition between hotels, however, as well as devaluations in the peso and red tape loopholes, I've rarely seen an authorized rate that matched our bill. You might pay something less than the official rate or you might pay something more; it seems to be a coin toss.

The rate sheet also tells you the check-out time: *Su cuarto se vence a . . . .* and then the hour, usually 2 p.m. but sometimes noon. Failure to check out in time means you are legally obligated to pay for another night.

During holiday seasons, special room rates may be charged, especially in beach resorts. Out of respect for the law of supply and demand, the government authorizes dramatic increases in hotel rates during Christmas, Easter and summer school vacations. These legal, temporary increases often confuse tourists, who mistakenly believe they only have to pay the rate posted behind their room door on a yellowing sheet of paper.

The Price of a Room Is Open for Negotiation

Even the most experienced travelers may not realize that room rates are often open to negotiation. Although there is an authorized top limit to the price of a hotel room, there is no official bottom. We got a dramatic introduction to hotel bartering when another traveler suggested that we stay in a very nice jungle lodge near Palenque. "Can't afford it," I answered automatically. "We'll camp at the Maya Bell." When we learned that the lodge was virtually empty, however, and begging for guests, Lorena decided to check it out as a possible end-of-trip splurge. Her encounter with the manager was a classic example of "nothing ventured, nothing gained."

Lorena (smiling brightly): "Hello, how much is a double room?"

Manager (hesitating just slightly): "We have a special price on private cabins for $55." (*I felt my scalp tingle. We'll take it!*)

Lorena (frowning and shrugging): "Oh . . . well, would there be something even more economical?"

Manager (fussing and pondering): "Hmmm . . . we may have *something* in back that I could offer you for . . . $40. But I'll have to check." (*Don't bother, I wanted to say, we'll take it!*)

Lorena (giving me The Eye): "Thank you, but please don't bother. We hoped for something less expensive."

Manager (sighing): "Such as . . . ?" (*. . . A damp tent at the Maya Bell Campground again? Was she serious?*)

Lorena (smiling and edging away): "It isn't important. Perhaps on another trip."

The manager followed us through the door. (*You mean we really won't take it? I was crushed.*)

As we passed through the garden, he "remembered" a $30 room that bottomed out at $25 when we reached the lodge's conspicuously empty parking lot.

Lorena gave us a serene smile. "That's nice, but we'd like to look at the room first."

Bartering for a room isn't quite like haggling over a wood carving or a handmade blanket. The counter-offer is best made in the form of indecision: "Well . . . I don't know . . . that sounds a little expensive . . ." or the classic "Don't you have a smaller room? Something cheaper?" Don't rush; it may take the desk clerk five minutes or more to recall that there's an alternative to the Bridal Suite.

In "better" hotels I ask for the "commercial" rate or for a cheaper room without a television. In most cases, I'll get a discount on a regular room, with television. You might also ask for the student rate, the "professional" rate or an even vaguer "discount rate." One of my favorites is the woman who told the manager, "I'm a teacher. Would there be a special rate?" There was, and as the hotel was almost empty, the "educator's rate" was a bargain.

Bartering is usually easier in large hotels and in resorts during the off-season, when rooms often go begging. In hotels with a wide variety of room sizes and types, there will be a correspondingly greater range in individual room rates. For example, there may be an upper floor with small simple rooms, with or without baths. In smaller places, barter with care—the cheapest price might get you a damp broom closet or some other truly grim alternative to a regular room. Always check the room out before accepting it, no matter how generous the discount.

If the price doesn't drop far enough, don't hesitate to ask for a recommendation to a cheaper hotel. This is not only the ultimate bartering maneuver, it's also a good way to get directions. Mexicans are very casual in this regard and desk clerks will usually offer advice quite freely.

Longer stays make a good bartering point. I'll give it a one- or two-night trial, however, before suggesting to the manager that a discount on a longer stay would be very tempting. My ears are still ringing from the "perfect" motel room in Mazatlán that turned out to share a thin wall with a body shop specializing in midnight bus repairs.

Cheap and Comfortable

Finding a good inexpensive room sometimes takes a lot of legwork, but there are clues besides the appearance of the hotel that should help. Asking is always the best way to find anything.

Inexpensive rooms can be found near bus and train stations. Ask a bus driver, a ticket agent or at the information booth; you may well find a hotel within easy walking distance and avoid the additional expense of a cab. Your heavy luggage can be checked in the baggage room until you've located a place to stay. (See *Getting Around*.)

Cab drivers are classic sources of information and many have friends and relatives in the hotel business. In hopes of earning a "finder's fee," a cabbie might try to steer you to a certain hotel. I always insist, "*algo económico y cómodo*" ("something economical and comfortable") and I've never been seriously disappointed by their choice.

Arriving late one afternoon in Mexico City, I jumped into a cab at the airport and gave the driver the name of my favorite cheap hotel. Rocketing into traffic, he scowled into the mirror and shook his head disapprovingly. "I know a much better hotel," the cabbie said. "Clean, good price, very safe. That one . . ." he sniffed disdainfully. "Heavy damage from earthquakes, old . . . if I'm not mistaken, it is being torn down right now."

"Really?" I said, feigning astonishment. "I wasn't aware of that."

"No," said the cabbie. "They try to keep these things quiet. Bad for tourism. That's why I suggest this other hotel. Honest, and very good prices. Now that I think about it, the place you mention did close several months ago. Hundreds of years old, right? Well, hardly a surprise when it collapsed."

"That's incredible!" I lied. "Because my mother stayed there last week. In fact, she's waiting for me right now. I hope she's OK!"

I offered the driver my most fiendish Jack Nicholson grin and settled back for the ride.

If you want a really cheap hotel, ask in the market; the local merchants usually know the best bargains. Hotels around the market cater to a large influx of people at least once a week and these people, usually small-time merchants, aren't about to pay more than they have to.

If you're looking for a basic room, ask well-traveled-looking gringos for leads. The backpacking set often congregate in one hotel and it's bound to be inexpensive. Asking also gives you a chance to find something that isn't advertised—such as a room in someone's home.

When leaving a hotel that I've enjoyed, I always ask for a recommendation in the town I'm headed for. If someone on the staff doesn't know of a good hotel, they'll often find a guest who does. This can save a great deal of searching.

Check It Out First

After you've spotted a likely looking hotel and have asked the price, look at the room before agreeing to take it. Quality does not necessarily vary according to cost. Of two hotels with identical rates, one might offer comfortable beds, a fan, a beautiful patio and free inside parking; while in the other you get a broken bedspring in your side, exhaust fumes pouring in through a missing windowpane and a toilet that overflows on your feet.

Most cheap hotels now have hot water. However, if *agua caliente* doesn't appear when you first check the room, the hot water is probably rationed to specific hours—usually early morning and in the evening. Very basic hotels produce hot water upon request (or demand), though you'll usually have to wait while someone stokes up a wood-fueled water heater.

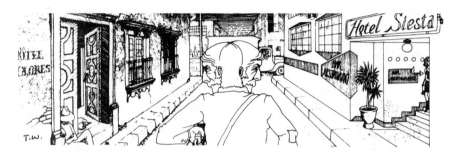

• Ask for a room facing the back or in the center of the hotel if noise bothers your sleep. The din of early morning traffic, particularly near the market, can be incredible.

• If you have a car, you'll feel less uptight by selecting a hotel that has its own parking lot or can direct you to one nearby. You might like to inspect the parking lot before agreeing to take the room. Some hotels park cars right inside the patio, which is safe; others may have a vacant lot nearby that wouldn't be any safer than the street unless there's a *velador* (night watchman).

• In hot areas ask for a room with a fan (*ventilador* or *abanico*) and check to see if it works. Keep in mind that a room on the west side of a cement block hotel may become a solar oven in late afternoon.

• If the weather is warm or wet, there will probably be mosquitoes. Some hotels offer mosquito nets over the bed, but to be sure, carry your own or a supply of repellent.

Hotels in the Yucatán and other hot parts of the country may offer a special rate to guests who bring their own hammocks rather than using beds. Hooks are fixed in the walls to hang them (the hammocks) from. Groups of people can rent one large room and fill it with hammocks—crowded but very cheap.

• Most hotels lock their front doors after a certain hour. In small towns, bedtime can be surprisingly early. Night watchmen in small hotels usually sleep on duty. If the *velador* is sleeping off a drunk, you might find it difficult to rouse someone. In the "good old days," strict, old-fashioned hotel owners would expect their guests to provide a respectable excuse for breaking curfew or risk finding another hotel.

I once told a landlady in a small town that I planned to go out and have a few drinks at the local *cantina*. She marched me to another room, pounded on the door and handed me over to a visiting priest for a stern lecture. He recognized my plight and we shared brandy in the privacy of his room.

Small Town Hotels

In the smallest towns selecting a hotel is usually just a choice of one or two. Take it or leave it. This might sound grim, but I've found that these places almost inevitably provide rich material for entertaining stories and memories. The gigantic rooster tethered outside our window, loudly protesting its captivity every thirty seconds; the insane elderly aunt locked in a spare room who demanded Coca-Cola twenty-four hours a day; the landlord's barking dog, stunned into temporary silence by an occasional fire-cracker lobbed from the front desk; a boardinghouse television tuned to incomprehensible quiz shows until midnight; being rousted at 5:00 a.m. by a desk clerk who invited me to visit his avocado orchard and watch him blow up a boulder with dynamite; blocking the door against a drunk who insisted on kissing me goodnight; opening the wrong door and finding a sheer four-story drop, and so on—an adventure or an anecdote awaiting every night.

If a town is so small that it doesn't have a hotel at all, go to someone official—the mayor, priest or schoolteacher—and ask for a place to stay. You may sleep in the jail (hopefully with a key to your cell), or get floor space in a church or public building, or you may be rewarded with a cot in a municipal guest house. In one town we slept in the armory, a cell-like room filled with ancient furniture and antique weapons, which had to be locked at night (with us in it) to protect the guns from thieves.

Whatever you find will be interesting. Expect to perform in some small way as payment for this hospitality. This might involve answering hundreds of questions about yourself and where you're from, showing off your possessions, eating gifts of food with great gusto, drinking the local booze and perhaps being subjected to a "concert" on the mayor's Victrola.

Super-Cheap Rooms

Super-cheap rooms are almost always found near the market place. They tend toward the very basic; perhaps just a wooden frame for a bed and a rough straw-filled sack that symbolizes a mattress. The communal bathroom may be quite funky, with magazines or other types of shiny paper instead of regular toilet paper. One hotel had old bank ledgers in the bathroom and I spent many interesting minutes checking out withdrawals and deposits.

The cheapest hotels and boardinghouses may double as bathhouses. In these places a bath is an additional charge, sometimes even for guests.

Casas de huéspedes and *pensiones* (boarding houses) will rent rooms for one night, though they specialize in long-term guests. No matter how low the price of a room may be, and some are quite cheap, ask if it includes meals. Tourists are sometimes confused by the low prices in these places and miss getting meals that they have paid for.

A *casa de huéspedes* may be very pleasant or then again it may be a flophouse. They are always economical and worth investigating if you are trying to save money.

The best bargain may be no hotel at all. Houses, apartments, bungalows and furnished rooms are usually cheaper than equivalent accommodations in a regular hotel, especially for two or more people. (See *Renting a Place*, later in this chapter.)

Along the coasts you can sometimes sleep in restaurants, especially if you eat there before you ask for lodging. You might do as I once did and sleep on a table or if there's room, hang your hammock on the porch. You'll be awakened very early to get your gear together before the breakfast customers arrive. Many travelers "adopt" a restaurant, eating there and using it as a boardinghouse. You should offer something in payment, but usually buying meals will be sufficient. We slept in one beachfront restaurant for over a month and it was one of our most enjoyable experiences in Mexico. When you are broke or bored, help out with the basic chores and you'll probably get free or bargain meals in return.

The "No-Tell" Motel

You see them on the outskirts of virtually every Mexican city and fair-sized town: unassuming motels surrounded by high walls, with narrow security entrances and individual, curtained garages. Unsuspecting travelers might also be puzzled by the low overnight occupancy rate and porno movies on the television. These aren't bordellos but Mexico's version of the "hot sheet" hotel, a safe, out-of-town trysting place for local lovers.

Ironically, these "no-tell" motels are often your best bet for a quiet, convenient, inexpensive room. Due to the nature of the business, most guests don't stay all night—so rooms are available when more respectable establishments are full. As Steve warns, however, "Some of these places won't accept families."

A Hotel Survival Kit

Hotel services and accommodations vary so much in Mexico, especially for those who stay in less expensive places, that it's best to anticipate possible shortages. When I'm traveling from one hotel to another, I always carry my "survival kit" in my day pack or in a small sack in my suitcase. It consists, more or less, of the following:

- **Flashlight:** for power failures and midnight trips to the bathroom.
- **Bug dope:** cheap hotels rarely have screens or mosquito nets.
- **Soap:** I always drop those tiny hotel bars down the drain.
- **Towel:** a small one, just in case. I sometimes pack an extra cotton T-shirt for a towel. It also doubles as a clean pillowcase and in emergencies can be worn as a shirt.
- **Toilet paper:** always carry toilet paper.
- **Heating coil:** this is a little device that plugs into the wall and heats up a cup of water for tea, instant coffee or bouillon. I wake up very early, before most cafés open, and the heating coil saves me from coffee withdrawal.
- **Tea, instant coffee, bouillon, Postum, etc.:** saves money if you make it yourself. Nice for times when you can't or don't want to leave your room.
- **Cups:** cheap hotels rarely provide drinking glasses or cups.
- **Water:** a liter of water is a must, so buy your own. Don't expect purified water in cheap hotels.
- A small high-intensity **reading lamp** with a long cord or a 100-watt bulb to replace the hotel's low-light bulb.
- **Good book:** for bad nights.

A final suggestion: If you're desperate for a room and can stand the excitement, go to the red-light district and stay in a brothel. The management may balk at renting a room without "services," but if you're with a woman (or are one) they'll usually relent and let you in. The posted rates are for the room.

Or it could happen that you unsuspectingly choose a cheap place and find out that it's a brothel or a "no-tell" motel. This may not matter, but if you're in a group (and our group once included my mother, to the manager's dismay), keep it in mind.

The dangers of staying in a brothel, especially for a single woman, are pretty obvious. When you're worried about the respectability of a hotel, ask someone if it is *"familiar."* This means, politely, "family hotel, not a brothel." Many hotels have this word prominently posted to ease customers' minds.

We once stayed in a hotel that featured a giant tortoise that roamed through the corridors all night, shuffling and scratching its claws against the tiled floor. The door to our room was missing and the beast spent an hour or two under the bed, butting its head against one of the brass bed legs. This same hotel was arranged around an overgrown patio, with all rooms opening onto a balcony without railings. One faulty step and the unfortunate guest could plunge into statues and decaying lawn furniture several floors below.

While preparing for bed in another hotel of this caliber, we noticed that there was an upside-down bucket in each corner of the room. Too tired to investigate, we went to bed. In the middle of the night we were awakened by strange sounds: squeaks, scratchings and other rodent-like noises that seemed to come from the buckets. Rather than risk uncovering some horror and completely ruining our rest, we compromised by hiding under the blankets. By morning the awful sounds had increased and we decided something would have to be done.

Steve solved the problem by tying a long string to the handle of one of the buckets and trailing it out the door into the corridor. We all gathered outside and he jerked the string, tipping the bucket onto its side. A mass of tiny yellow bodies ran peeping and squealing into the middle of the room. The buckets were homemade chicken incubators. We spent the next half-hour rounding up the newly hatched chicks and returning them to their nest. The manager explained later that our room was the warmest in the hotel and was used to hatch eggs, whether it was rented or not.

Better Safe Than . . .

There are disadvantages to super-cheap rooms and these include not only cardboard-thin walls and the occasional bedbug, but also a lack of privacy and even rip-offs. For the cautious traveler I heartily recommend the following precautions:

• **Keep small valuables on your person at all times.** I take my money to bed with me and unless there's another person in the room, I also take my money into the shower when bathing or using the toilet. One of the classic rip-offs in cheap hotels (and this is worldwide) happens while the unsuspecting victim is in the bathroom. When the shower is turned on, the door opens and within seconds, wallet, money, camera and other goodies disappear. "I can't believe it! I was only in there for five lousy minutes!" That's also all the time it takes for two strong men to move a refrigerator from a kitchen to a moving van.

• **When you're going out for a stroll, leave larger valuables at the desk,** even if the clerk protests that it's not necessary.

• **At night, or when sleeping, make sure the door is securely locked.** In most really cheap hotels with flimsy or improvised doors, this is difficult if not impossible. We sometimes carry small padlocks, but even this is a poor defense against a hard blow or a well-wielded screwdriver.

• **If you're a light sleeper, rig an "alarm"** that will signal if the door is moved. I usually have a few empty soda bottles on hand and arrange them to topple over with an ear-splitting racket when the door is opened. I know this works because when I wake in the middle of the night and stumble out to the bathroom, I always crash into the bottles myself.

• **If you sleep or worry heavily, move the entire bed to block the door.** It it's too heavy, find something else—table, bureau, chairs, etc.

• **Women traveling alone should be particularly careful when selecting a cheap**

room. Many women have told us that saving money on a room was sometimes offset by hassles from other lodgers or desk clerks looking for one-night romance.

Because the cheapest hotels are usually located in less than elegant neighborhoods, women should exercise caution when walking alone at night. (See *Safety* and *¡Viva Mexico!: Machismo.*)

When a man and woman travel together but always sleep in separate beds, it doesn't hurt to give the impression of being a couple. It not only avoids offending straight-laced people who may refuse or balk at letting two people share a room, but also cools down those on the prowl. This is especially true in small towns where tourists' eccentricities are unfamiliar.

Precautions such as these are rarely necessary, but I consider them to be like health care: it never seems important until things have gone wrong. Precautions are not paranoia; they're *good common sense.*

It was the end of a day of long, tiring travel, the type of day that you desperately hoped would not end in a Memorable Experience. We had decided, against our better judgment, common sense and other weak notions, to stay in a hotel as a "break" from camping. We reasoned that the cost wouldn't be bad if we looked for something slightly scroungy, a hotel of the type soon to be a vacant lot.

Steve sagged over the steering wheel as we entered town, his eyes slightly glassy.

"There's a good one," he said gloomily, pointing to a pseudo-American motel, not quite concealing his true feeling about those soft, expensive gringo beds.

"How about that one?" Lorena suggested, turning to look at a darkening ruin of a large building, obscured by weeds and fast-growing vines. "It looks like a Hilton to me," she added, referring to the joke we'd picked up from a hitchhiker who often stayed in abandoned or unfinished buildings that he called "Hiltons."

Our fatigue and foul humor were not at all eased by the traffic which literally jammed the streets. The blare of irate horns made argument impossible. Steve stuck his head out of the window in order to back into a side street, the only avenue of escape. I watched disbelievingly as a mob of kids approached us, lobbing balloons filled with water at the stalled cars.

"Look!" I yelled, and Steve turned his head to receive a fat balloon square in the face. It burst quietly, soaking him with water that smelled more than slightly of stale urine.

"You gawdamn *pendejo*!!!" he shrieked, losing what little was left of his composure. The kid who had thrown the balloon laughed uproariously and his accomplices added their apologies by launching a general attack. Balloons burst over every square inch of the van, showering us with water through open windows.

"We aren't the only ones," I said. "Look at that poor guy." The driver of the car in front of us was mopping large quantities of water from his dashboard while his wife dried their screaming baby.

"God, must be some kind of weird fiesta," Steve groaned, for by now it was obvious that the water fight was of city-wide proportions. The streets were flooded gutter deep.

As traffic crawled toward the plaza, the bombardment continued without mercy; the sight of a gringo vehicle inspired even greater and more desperate feats of daring. We soon found ourselves trapped under a waterfall of balloons and emptying buckets.

"There! There!" I yelled, pointing to a hotel that had the look of a badly neglected flophouse.

We squelched to a stop directly in front of the entrance.

"How do you propose to get in?" Steve asked sarcastically, pointing toward the eager horde of water-ballooners anticipating our next move.

"I'll open my door like I'm making a run for it and then you duck into the hotel while they attack me."

Steve looked rather dubious, but agreed to my proposal.

"Go!" I yelled, pretending to jump from my side of the van. A wave of kids launched an immediate attack, but I slammed the door before the water hit. Steve leaped to the hotel entrance, followed by a few late balloons. The manager anticipated our predicament and opened the front door just as Steve was about to break it down. A few minutes later, Steve's face appeared at an upper window and he motioned us to come up.

"What about the birds?" Lorena asked me, looking at our parrots, Arturo and Farout. "One of those balloons could really hurt them."

We pondered this additional problem for a few moments and then the sight of a slightly reeling attacker inspired me to a solution.

"We'll negotiate," I said, reaching under the seat for a bottle of tequila we'd been saving for just such a memorable occasion.

I opened my window just far enough to extend the bottle into sight of the group dedicated to drowning us. One of them immediately rushed over.

"*Oye, amigo*," I said, "if you'll let us take our parrots into the hotel without soaking them, I'll invite you all to a drink."

After consulting his friends, the pact was sealed with a round of healthy slugs from the bottle. We quickly gathered a few things together and raced safely into the lobby. The manager, dripping slightly, directed us to the room in which Steve was hiding.

The parking lot was in the center of the hotel and we would have to drive through the large front doors of the lobby and into the patio. "Oh yes! Certainly!" the manager said. "But do it quickly or they'll flood the lobby."

"Take this, it's your 'Safe Passage,'" I said, handing Steve the bottle of tequila. He looked at it skeptically, then chugged an enormous swallow.

While Lorena and I watched from the balcony of our room, he made his peace with the mob. At a signal from Steve, the huge double doors swung open and the van raced into the lobby, barely missing an end table. The balloon squad could not resist the temptation and a hail of missiles followed. A rather sour-looking bellboy caught the force of the attack.

"The manager told me this is the annual Water Fiesta," Steve said, returning from his mission looking slightly soggy.

"How are we ever going to get out for dinner?" Lorena asked. Confusion in the streets had reached panic proportions, with hundreds of people madly throwing buckets of water at each other. The cop directing traffic at the next corner stood stoically under a continual shower of water balloons, turning occasionally to glare at traffic as water dripped from his nose, obviously enjoying the entire scene. Fire hoses had been connected and pumped thousands of gallons into the surrounding traffic and passersby. A tank truck, stalled in the middle of the street, gushed forth great fountains of water from various valves and pipes as lines of dripping people waited to fill their buckets, balloons and washtubs.

Luckily the manager appeared as we were debating whether to eat or not and offered to arrange our entry into a nearby restaurant; tonight their doors opened only by appointment.

We stepped out of the hotel door with the air of dignity that quells riots and calms rabid mobs. The crowd on the street looked at us expectantly, waiting for some noble word. I turned to Steve and Lorena to say, "This is how it's done," but my words were drowned in a fusillade of balloons and a cascade of water falling from the balcony of the hotel. I looked up and thought I saw the face of the manager behind a large washtub.

"Bastards!" Steve muttered, running for safety.

The door of the restaurant opened magically in front of us and we burst into a room crowded with soaked and chattering diners. The waiter bolted the door securely before taking us to a table. I noticed that several groups seemed to have finished eating and were merely waiting for the tide to change before leaving.

We ate dinner in relative peace, though wavelets of water lapped under the door and screams and laughter from the street confirmed that the insanity was not abating. We asked for the bill and then sat back to relax for a few moments before braving the return trip. I absently noticed that another group had left without being escorted out by the waiter.

"Yaaahhh!" With a scream of triumph, the mob burst through the front door, now unlatched. Water sprayed everywhere as balloons burst on heads bowed reverently over food and tubs emptied into diners' laps.

"No!" someone screamed as one of the crowd grabbed a tablecloth and whisked the plates and tacos into a crashing heap. Tables were swept clean, chairs overturned, water flowed, waiters cringed and we ran.

Back in the hotel, dripping but safe, we listened politely while the manager apologized profusely for the entire fiesta and Mexico. As we slogged off to bed his "*perdóns*" and "*lo siento muchos*" rose above the sound of falling water and bursting balloons.

"At least we have a nice room," I said, surveying the cave we had been given for the night. The beds were cots, scrounged from some unsuccessful revolutionary camp, and the blankets looked as if they had covered untold numbers of obscene acts. The ceiling, far above our heads, gave off a light snow of plaster and paint, dislodged, I imagined, by bats unable to sleep because of the clamor in the street below.

Bam! "*¡Señor!*" Bam! "*¡Señor!*" We leaped out of bed just as the manager burst into the room, lugging a huge washtub and followed by the entire staff of the hotel, all carrying containers of water.

"Excuse me, please!" he said. "I have a little matter to take care of." They were all drunk and soaked to the skin.

Before we could ask what was happening, a bucket brigade had been established between the bathroom and the balcony. Curses and screams from the street below affirmed that the counterattack was taking its toll.

I looked at Steve and Lorena and then at the scene in the room. A bellboy was drinking our tequila while the desk clerk and maid delivered tubs of water to the railing and then dumped them in cascades onto the crowd below.

"Shall we?" I asked, reaching for an empty bucket.

RENTING A HOUSE

We'd been traveling in Mexico for several months, following our usual routine of camping out, with occasional periods in hotels or trailer parks, when we came upon the long-sought-after Perfect Spot. Almost perfect, that is, but there was no place to camp and no nearby convenient, inexpensive hotel. An old farmer kindly agreed to let us park in his alfalfa field for a night but could give no suggestions for a better long-term site. We looked over the small valley, crisscrossed by neat stone fences and carefully tended vegetable gardens, bordered on one side by forested hills and on the other by a clear stream and thought, "There's got to be a way!"

The old man was sympathetic but explained that there just wasn't room in their valley for camping. Every inch of flat or fertile ground was planted in a food or cash crop.

"The only way to live here," he said, plucking a green stem of alfalfa and chewing it idly, "is in a house." His eyes followed a billowing mass of clouds hanging over the foothills.

"A house?" Lorena said doubtfully, as though she were a gypsy suddenly faced with a twenty-year lease.

"*Sí, una casita*," he continued. "Like that little house of mine just over there on the edge of the trees."

We looked at each other for a few moments and then at the van. If we could live in that thing for months on end . . .

"How much?" Steve asked.

Ten minutes later we were residents, having agreed to rent for a month. The price was low enough that even if we got the itch to move on before the rent was up, we wouldn't really be losing anything. We shook hands with our new landlord and got a brief rundown on the village a quarter of a mile away—where to buy food and supplies, who sold the best moonshine and other domestic facts of life.

The difference between being members of the community, though only temporary, and just passing tourists was remarkable. Steve quickly struck up a friendship in the market and had long conversations on the merits of the Pacific versus Gulf Coast mango. Lorena met the landlord's wife and was soon learning to make tortillas. I had a favorite stool in Mi Oficina, the town's only *cantina*, a perfect spot to pick up odd bits of information and the subtleties of Spanish. People greeted us on the street from their fields, inquiring after our health; the local dogs quit barking at me; Lorena traded *Kaliman* comic books with the children's literary society and low-level gossip with their mothers and older sisters.

Our acceptance by the people was gratifying and for the first time in our travels, we felt that we were really getting beneath the surface. Our understanding and appreciation of how the people thought and lived increased by the day. We also noticed something else: we were relaxed and rested, thoroughly enjoying a slower pace.

Many tourists don't consider a trip to be a success unless they log a great number of miles and take in the better-known sights and attractions. Art Buchwald described this rapid tourism as "The Three-Minute Louvre." The museum's record for viewing the *Winged Victory*, *Mona Lisa* and *Venus de Milo* was won by the Japanese, Buchwald said, because of their superior track shoes.

This is two-dimensional travel: impersonal, tiring, unsatisfying and expensive.

Life in a Mexican Town

In smaller towns the arrival of a new neighbor is always an event of great interest. They'll want to know where you're from, what you're doing and why, where you're headed next, what work you do, how many kids you have and so on, right into the details of your health and sex life. This can get tiring, especially if your Spanish is shaky, but it has its rewards.

In one small *pueblo* we barely had time to hang our hammocks before the neighbors began arriving with gifts of food. "This is like the Welcome Wagon," Lorena laughed, accepting yet another fifteen pounds of squash from a blushing woman. By the time we'd bade the last of our new friends good-night, we had enough fruit and vegetables to open a stall in the market. We soon learned that the neighbors were literally in competition to see which could give us something even tastier than the others.

A few nights later we came back from an evening stroll to find an anxious group of children on our doorstep. "Where have you been?" one of them cried. "We're having a wedding fiesta and everyone is waiting for you!" We were hustled to a nearby house and greeted as if we were the bride and groom.

Participating in the daily routine of the people around you can be extremely interesting. Rather than just talking you'll often find yourself actually doing something with someone. Your neighbors might be a little startled when you offer to help with the corn harvest, but they'll soon get over the shock. There's nothing like shared work to make you one of the family.

While we were living in a beach town I overheard a conversation between several tourists, complaining that the cost of hiring a boat for fishing was beginning to add up to more than they could afford. The man they'd been hiring for several days turned out to be our neighbor. Whenever I wanted to go fishing, which was often, all I had to do was show up at his house early in the morning, ready to go. He refused any payment, even for gas and oil, but did let me help paint his boat and clean fish.

Another neighbor in the same town offered us the use of a rich irrigated garden patch after I spent a day helping him spread rock salt on a tobacco field. He also gave us an open invitation to pick fruit and avocados from his orchard.

Whenever something exciting comes up, you'll probably be told of it and invited to participate. A neighbor once stopped by to ask if I wanted to go fishing in a nearby river. I accepted and we set off, enlisting a few more people along the way. When we were half a mile out of the village and no one had yet produced any fishing equipment, I asked my friend how they intended to fish. He gave me a sly grin and began to unbutton his shirt. "Special Mexican bait," he said revealing several sticks of dynamite stuck inside the waistband of his pants.

On other occasions I've gone hunting for jaguars, deer, rabbits and treasure (all with notable lack of success) and visited illegal *mezcal* stills, uncatalogued ruins, hidden waterfalls and other local sights that the tourist rarely has the opportunity to see.

Lorena has learned about medicinal herbs, folk remedies, tortilla-making, cooking and gardening.

Many practical and valuable skills can be picked up, either on a casual basis or by working as an apprentice. I know gringos who have worked with sandal-makers, weavers, potters, jewelers, blacksmiths, cabinetmakers, bricklayers, commercial fisherman, divers and even mule skinners. Many of these trades and their techniques have succumbed to automation and technology in the U.S., but are practiced in Mexico as they have been for generations. You'll learn very basic and time-tested skills along with a lot of Spanish. Don't be shy about expressing an interest in what someone is doing; this is just about the best possible way to break the ice and, at the same time, give yourself something interesting to do.

Renting a place for a couple of weeks or more doesn't mean that you're stuck; in fact it can mean the opposite and give you much more freedom. We use a house or room as a center for side trips, a place where we can leave the bulk of our luggage while we explore by car, bus or on foot. Side trips can be anything from an afternoon stroll in the country to a few days visiting a nearby city. When you get back you've got a place to rest and relax, without the strain of constant packing and unpacking and searching for a good hotel room.

Another consideration is cost: unless you don't care about money, you'll want to keep expenses within reason. Compare the daily cost of restaurant meals and hotels to the cost of renting a house, room or apartment and cooking for yourself; you may well discover you can afford to rent a fairly fancy place and still save.

House Hunting

Although there are rental agencies (*Agencia de Renta*) and real estate agents (*Agencia de Bienes Raices*) in larger cities and tourist towns, most house hunting turns into something of a snipe hunt. There is no great surplus of dwellings and you'll find relatively few newspaper ads for housing. Like most information in Mexico, the friend-and-family grapevine seems to be efficient enough to satisfy most landlords.

The easiest way to find a vacancy is to ask a resident gringo for advice. If you want a nice house, ask a nicer-looking gringo; if you'll settle for something simple and modest, such as a humble hut, ask people (like us) who look as though they live in one.

If no resident foreigners are available, you'll have to look for yourself. Find an agreeable neighborhood and begin searching for vacancies.

If you are lucky, you may see signs advertising a house or apartment for rent. The key words on such a sign will be *Se Alquila* or *Se Renta* (for rent). Houses that are for sale (*Se Vende*) are often for rent if you inquire.

After you locate a beautiful house with a *Se Renta* sign in the window, ask someone in the neighborhood where the owner lives. Should luck be with you, the neighbor will know the owners and where they can be found. Our experience, however, has been that tracking down the *dueño de la casa* is usually even more difficult than finding the house.

You must be patient and persistent. When you've finally got your hands on your prospective landlord, you may find that the house for rent is not the one with the sign. It was put up on a friend's house, one that was in a better location and therefore easier to spot.

Small stores, supermarkets, drugstores and *cantinas* are centers of local information. In small villages or outlying neighborhoods the local *tiendas* (grocery stores) are especially helpful in locating landlords.

Because the search may become long and difficult, you will be tempted to give up or to take the first thing that comes along. Avoid either alternative if you can; a patient search usually uncovers wonderful surprises. And you get an interesting tour of Mexican homes.

Types of Houses

Available houses fall into four categories. The first category is usually rented to rich Mexicans, tourists and foreign residents. **These houses have furniture, modern appliances and conveniences, reliable plumbing and the highest rents.** By U.S. standards, however, they can still be a bargain. (In towns with a large tourist trade or gringo retirement community, rents will be higher than average but good deals can still be found.)

The second category includes **a variety of dwellings, from little two-room cinderblock cottages to defunct *haciendas*.** The old places often have more rooms than you know what to do with, huge overgrown gardens with fruit trees, pools for fish, stables and servants' quarters. In general, they cost about the same to rent as a much smaller but newer house of pseudomotel design.

Older houses may have some disadvantages: an occasional leak in the roof or falling tile, drafty rooms, erratic plumbing and ghosts guarding the inevitable buried treasure from the Revolution. As you might expect, life in one of these relics is much more interesting than in a modern house.

The average bargain-basement rental rarely includes furniture or appliances. Most have electricity but no light bulbs and few electrical outlets. Gas lines for a propane stove or water heater may be installed, but often the previous tenants will have removed the gas tanks, stove and heater. When Mexican families move, they do a complete job of it and when they get to their new home, they don't expect to find much more than a starkly empty house. Furnishings and appliances are not left behind but treated as lifetime possessions.

Very inexpensive furniture can be purchased in and around the market place and occasionally from wandering vendors. Chairs, tables, cupboards and beds of unfinished pine are reasonably priced and can be re-sold to the neighbors or given away when you leave. Some landlords will give credit toward the rent for furniture and other improvements. By using bricks, boards, wooden crates (also sold in the market), mats and your imagination, you can furnish the barest house quite adequately for very little money.

If you're traveling with your own vehicle, it is easy to carry a few basic furnishings and utensils. You may not have much more than a stool to sit on and a fruit crate for a table, but it's better than nothing. (See *Packing Up* and *Driving: Do-It-Yourself Camper* for suggestions on things to bring from home to make life easier.)

The Mexican custom of packing up the entire family for a Christmas or Easter vacation at the beach has created a third category of accommodations: **rental houses and apartments designed for families and large groups**. These are generally known as *bungalos* and *cabañas*.Because most are fully equipped, from linen to kitchen utensils, they can be ideal for the foreign tourist. This is especially true for people with children, who don't want to be cooped up with them in a hotel room or forced to rent two rooms to get a little privacy.

Bungalows are usually available by the day as well as by the week and month. They are almost always cheaper than an equivalent hotel room, not counting the savings that can come from doing your own cooking. Maid and laundry service will probably be optional, but it's best to ask to avoid paying twice. An extra charge may be made for additional beds, linen and kitchen utensils if you require them.

Large bungalows can be shared by several people and the cost per person will drop rapidly to the bargain level. If you have any doubt about the number of people allowed, ask before making any agreement. Some owners will set a limit, others couldn't care less if the tenants are stacked in the rooms like cordwood.

Most bungalows are booked in advance for the Christmas season (mid-December to about January 7) and around Easter Week (*Semana Santa*), so don't expect to find one then without a search. Rents also tend to inflate during these traditional beach holidays.

The fourth category includes what most people call **hovels, shacks and shanties**. After a few months of camping, they look like mansions. They may be below suburbia standards, but hopefully by the time you want to rent an adobe hut, you'll be beyond such unrealistic judgments. A simple house or hut of local materials (boards, bricks, rocks, sticks, fronds) is inexpensive to rent. Monthly rates range from very little to nothing; a particularly friendly landlord might allow you to use a house for free.

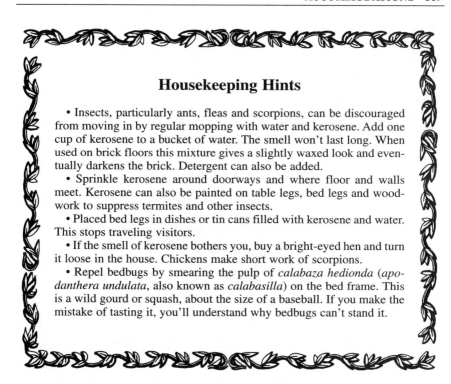

Housekeeping Hints

• Insects, particularly ants, fleas and scorpions, can be discouraged from moving in by regular mopping with water and kerosene. Add one cup of kerosene to a bucket of water. The smell won't last long. When used on brick floors this mixture gives a slightly waxed look and eventually darkens the brick. Detergent can also be added.

• Sprinkle kerosene around doorways and where floor and walls meet. Kerosene can also be painted on table legs, bed legs and woodwork to suppress termites and other insects.

• Placed bed legs in dishes or tin cans filled with kerosene and water. This stops traveling visitors.

• If the smell of kerosene bothers you, buy a bright-eyed hen and turn it loose in the house. Chickens make short work of scorpions.

• Repel bedbugs by smearing the pulp of *calabaza hedionda* (*apodanthera undulata*, also known as *calabasilla*) on the bed frame. This is a wild gourd or squash, about the size of a baseball. If you make the mistake of tasting it, you'll understand why bedbugs can't stand it.

A basic hut will have a dirt floor, few if any windows, a crude adobe stove and fleas. (See *Housekeeping Hints*, above.) Water will have to be carried from a communal faucet or well. Sanitary facilities will be the most basic and may be positively unhealthy. Garbage is usually thrown out back and picked up by dogs, pigs and the wind. Privacy is also minimal; children and animals will wander in and out when they are bored and want to see what you're up to. Neighbors will drop in at all hours, especially if you're doing something odd, like cooking, reading, writing or painting. All of these factors make your life very interesting, especially if your neighbors are friends—almost always the case.

It is not uncommon, particularly along the Pacific coast, for a family to build a small hut or room in the back yard (or on a nearby lot) especially for renters. One town we stayed in had carried this to the degree that a family without a gringo was like a family without a pet cat or dog.

"How's your gringo*?*"
"Oh, fine. Yesterday he cut his foot on the beach. How's yours?"
"Fine, too. She got a letter from her mother. Money, I think."
"It's about time, I'd say. Did you hear about Eugenia's?"
"No, what happened?"
"He won't eat meat! Can you believe it?"
"*¡No me digas!* Is he sick?"
"Who knows? He certainly eats enough of her sweet tamales!"
"Some people! *Pues*, Cona says her gringa won't eat sugar."
"*¡Ay! ¡Impossible!* That one I don't believe!"
"Well, *¿quién sabe?* With these gringos anything can happen!"

We heard this sort of banter all around town.

Renting a place in this village was as easy as stopping the first little kid you saw on the street and saying, "*Quiero un cuarto*" ("I want a room"). It would hardly take more than an hour or two to find what we wanted.

What to Look For

• **Check the roof** of your prospective home. Can you see through it? During the rainy season, you'll want a tight roof. Be wary of houses located in a low spot if rain is imminent. The saying that "shit flows downhill" is quite true.

• **Check the walls** for indications of a waterline; we once had to leave a house early because dark stains near the floor turned out to be a high water mark.

I was sitting in front of an adobe house we'd just rented, admiring the huge black clouds that had been piling up steadily, hour by hour. My daydreams were interrupted when an old man approached. He was staggering under a load of crude homemade bamboo crucifixes adorned with beautiful wildflowers. Without a word he handed me three of the crosses and pointed to the darkening sky. The look on his face was ominous.

"What do I do with these?" I asked, holding the crosses rather nervously.

He leaned toward me confidentially and said, "When the rain comes, burn one inside the house." He paused and looked at the hut. "It will prevent the roof from caving in." I looked up at the sagging beams and heavy tiles, then back to the old man. He chuckled knowingly and said, "Here, better take three more." When he'd gone I burned two in each room, though the rains were a week away.

• **Faulty or inoperative wiring**, broken windows, missing door latches, leaky faucets and all such minor discrepancies fall into the category of "nonessential details" for most landlords. They may make sincere vows to repair things or replace them, but don't be so foolish as to count on it. They feel that when you rent the house, you are accepting it as it is, not as you want them to make it later.

• **Establish exactly what you are renting** before agreeing to anything. Does the deal include the right to pick fruit and vegetables from the garden? Some landlords reserve the right to plant the land surrounding the house. Can you use the outbuildings? Should you neglect to ask, you might find that one of the buildings or even one of the rooms of the house is rented out to someone else. The landlord might reserve some rooms for use as granaries or for tool storage. This probably won't seem unreasonable—until he drives a bunch of pack mules through the patio every Sunday at 4:00 a.m. to load up corn for market.

• **Determine who pays the utilities.** Water is generally free but electricity is normally paid for by the tenant. Some landlords prefer to charge a flat rate for electricity, almost always reasonable, in order to avoid the paperwork involved in changing the name on the bills at the electric company's office. Because the electric bills are almost invariably out of date or not paid up, it is wise to ask the landlord to handle this for you.

• **Bartering over the rent is common.** It is wise to look at more than one or two places in the same area to get some idea of what the going rate seems to be.

• **The less you pay for a house, the less hassle you're likely to have with the landlord.** Along with expensive houses, you will often get such things as damage deposits, rent in advance, lease requirements and snoopy landlords. This most often happens when the landlord has had some experience with foreigners. If the house you're renting isn't worth more than a few month's rent, the landlord probably won't give a damn about anything. Fortunately, the most nosy and uptight landlord is positively relaxed and unconcerned in comparison to those in the U.S.

• When everything has been agreed to and the money handed over, **you will usually be given a dated receipt** (*recibo*). If not, ask for one, as a reminder to both you and your landlord of when the next rent is due. A receipt is especially valuable if the transaction is being handled by an agent for the owner of the house. An agent may not be above adding a little something to the rent for himself. If the owners show up, you can avoid disagreements by having a receipt.

(Interested in buying a house? See *Live and Retire in Mexico*.)

Wood-Fired Water Heaters

If you rent a cheap place or live in modest circumstances with a Mexican family, you're likely to meet a classic Mexican appliance, the wood-fired water heater. Gas stoves and water heaters are widely used in Mexico, but many people still use the basic wood-fueled ones. They are cheap to buy and install and cost little to operate.

The water heater is made up of a tall metal firebox, cylindrical in shape, surrounded by a coiled water pipe. It is simple, durable and foolproof. Or so it seems at first glance. But as with all foolproof devices, it takes the proper kind of fool to make it work.

The best fuel is small pieces of dry hardwood. Corncobs are also good and make excellent kindling for wood when soaked in kerosene. *Carbón* (charcoal) can be used but it burns too slowly to give best results. (For sources of fuel, see *Mexico A to Z: Fuels*.)

The idea is to build as hot and roaring a fire as possible. When the overflow pipe spouts off, it's time to strip and jump into the shower. Adjust the water for the minimum flow; most heaters have a small capacity and by the time you're ready for a rinse, it might be quite cold.

Problems arise when the fuel is not dry enough or the draft is fouled by gusts of wind, excessive smoke, sooting up of the exhaust pipe and so forth. Be patient; these heaters all look alike but most have individual characteristics that make them seem almost alive. Anyone who has passed through the trials and tribulations of learning to operate a wood or coal cookstove will understand.

Some travelers buy water heaters for use in remote cabins, houses without electricity and as backups to gas and electric heaters. Take precautions to avoid a freeze-up in cold climates. A cold snap in Oregon ruined Steve's beyond repair.

My own battles with Mexican heaters have been long and bitter. The worst took place with a heater that absolutely refused to produce anything but choking clouds of smoke from every opening and crack. I tried everything from dangerous amounts of kerosene to hours of fanning and got nothing for my efforts but watering eyes and clouds of pollution.

On the seventh morning my frustrations rose to the boiling point, though the shower water still ran ice cold. I shredded old newspaper, magazines and added oven-dried corncobs and slivers of *ocote* (pitch pine). I cracked every twig of firewood to insure that it was dry and arranged it in approved Scout fashion over the tinder. Then came a liberal slosh of kerosene. I stood by the small firebox door with a fan in each hand, inhaling deeply, prepared to add my own breath to the draft, even if it drove me to my knees.

I struck a match and touched it to the newspaper. Flame shot up, igniting the cobs, then the pitch pine and then the . . . smoke began billowing out the firebox door in great choking clouds. I fanned furiously, trying to protect my eyes from the oily, stinging smoke. It spread throughout the patio; I could hear Lorena muttering as she closed all windows and doors, trying to keep the awful smell from the house. I fanned even harder, my lungs burning painfully as I went down to my knees for an occasional emergency breath of air. It was no use; I was just creating more and more smoke, rising now in a column over the roof.

I dropped the fans and ran for the nearest exit: the stairway to the roof. Choking and spitting out the awful taste of scorched cobs and kerosene, I burst up out of the smoke and stood, chest heaving. Across the alleyway our neighbor was crouched in front of one of several small cages, talking to a fighting cock. It was part of his evening and morning ritual, haranguing his team of chickens into a state of lethal aggression.

"What are you doing, having a barbecue?" he called, giving me a friendly wave.

"Heating water!" I snapped, swabbing my eyes with a sooty handkerchief.

"I can tell you, *amigo*, that you'll have to wait for that." His voice was knowing and sympathetic. I swallowed my irritation and decided to ask for his advice; I must be making a basic error in the operation of the heater.

"What do you mean?" I asked, "Wait for what?"

He leaned over to whisper into a cock's ear, probably a threat about chicken enchiladas if he didn't win his next fight, "You see," he said, "that heater will only work properly when there is no wind. It's always been that way. Wait for the wind to calm and then heat your water."

"Well, OK, thanks," I said, suddenly aware that the wind was indeed quite strong. Come to think of it, the wind had been fairly steady for days.

"When does the wind stop?" I asked, hoping it wouldn't just be in the middle of the night.

He slipped the bird back into its cage, straightening up with a laugh. "Oh, it usually ends in May but sometimes not until June."

I headed back downstairs. More newspaper, more corncobs, kerosene . . . it was not yet March.

Warning: When using kerosene in a heater, don't slop it onto hot coals. The kerosene will instantly vaporize and form a very explosive gas. If the fire dies down but is still hot, dip a newspaper roll into the kerosene, light the end and put it into the firebox.

Never use gasoline. The trapped vapor inside a water heater can turn it into a bomb.

Living with Mexicans

Although some landlords will rent out houses for short periods, most prefer that you stay at least a month. If your time is short, consider renting a room in someone's home.

Mexicans are, by average American standards, very casual about taking someone in for a week, a month or even longer. Unannounced visitors, either friends or relatives, are put up without great fuss, though it may mean six kids to a bed instead of three or four. This custom makes it relatively easy for them to understand why a gringo would like a place to stay; hotels are used only as a special treat of last resort.

A young Mexican sitting next to me on a bus once asked what cities I had visited on my trip. I mentioned several and his eyes widened. "You must have a very big *familia, señor*," he said, "to be able to visit so many places." When I explained that I had no relatives at all in Mexico and stayed in hotels, he looked doubly surprised and exclaimed, "*¡Caráy!* It must be very lonely for you to travel like that!"

He was hoping that a cousin would move to Acapulco so he might go there for a visit. When I suggested that he go on his own, he just laughed.

Living in a Mexican home is a standard part of what language schools call "total immersion." The immersion can sometimes be so complete that you have to come up for air. Unless you're very reserved or a militant loner, you'll be treated as part of the household and not just a paying lodger.

This can create problems, especially if that family has traditional concepts of morality and conduct. Single boarders will probably find themselves tippling in the outhouse. If the situation becomes tense, consider finding a more relaxed place to live; another family might be completely casual about everything.

The main problem we've experienced when living with a Mexican family is that they are over-solicitous and concerned about our well-being. Anyone not at least 50 percent overweight is considered to be in imminent danger of death from malnutrition.

"Please!" the lady of the house cries, approaching the table with yet another bowl of *sopa de arroz*. "You've got to keep up your strength! You read so much!" This isn't Woody Allen doing a Jewish Mother routine; it's the landlady who forces you to eat five meals a day and worries that the neighbors might think she's starving you.

You'll undoubtedly be introduced to new customs and superstitions. Whatever you do, don't sneer, laugh or otherwise indicate disrespect for their beliefs, however bizarre they might seem. I once made the mistake of taking a shower after eating a huge afternoon meal. I'd barely gotten soaped up when there was a frantic pounding on the bathroom door. "Carlos! Carlos! What are you doing?" a voice cried. I turned off the water and called out, "Taking a bath. Why?" The voice begged me to reconsider, so I quickly rinsed, dried off and dressed, afraid that I'd done something to offend them or had used up the last of the household water.

When I emerged from the bathroom the landlord and his family apologized for bothering me, but I evidently didn't know that bathing after eating was certain death. It was only their quick intervention that had saved me from a heart attack. There are many superstitions of this type that you should be prepared to deal with. (See *¡Viva Mexico!: Superstitions*.)

Always ask what the price of your room will be and if it includes one or more meals and laundry service. The price is usually quite fair but it is customary to ask, and good sense besides. Inquire also about any particular rules of the house: no smoking, drinking, radios, late visitors and so on.

Living with a family cuts down on personal privacy, but the experience is well worth minor inconveniences. There are side benefits, too, that are difficult to place a value on: you really learn about daily life in Mexico; you eat foods that aren't served in most restaurants; you pick up Spanish, if only through contact and osmosis; and you make meaningful friendships with people who would otherwise be just another face.

When it's time to move on, consider asking for an introduction or recommendation to a family in another place. The more contacts you establish, the more you'll save on both time and money. And, of course, you'll be dealing with people who will be predisposed to help you out.

Hired Help

As soon as you've moved into a house, someone will come to the door offering to be your maid, cook, gardener, washerwoman or general helper. When faced with camping and doing all the chores yourself, the temptation is great to hire a replacement. Because the wages for even full-time help are very low, the temptation often becomes irresistible.

There are occasionally problems, however, involved in hiring someone to do housework or washing. Unless they have worked for foreigners before and thoroughly understand their idiosyncrasies, things will be done according to their ways, not yours. Most problems we've had were the result of over-enthusiasm. You want the house quickly swept so you can relax and do some writing, but before you know it, buckets of cold water are flying through the air, furniture is being hauled outside and you have to retreat to the back yard.

Determining what is fair pay can be difficult for those not accustomed to the Mexican system. Basically, it goes like this: (legal minimum) salaries are for eight hours a day, six days a week. Most people who work part time or for a few weeks at a time get less than the minimum, depending on the bargain that is made with their employer. Meals and a place to sleep can legally count for not more than one-half of a salary, but often they're figured as more than this. When Mexicans are hiring household help they drive a very hard bargain. I've never heard of a maid or gardener who preferred working with Mexicans instead of foreigners.

Unless your house or family is large, you probably won't need more than a few days of help each week. However, most of the people who apply to tourists for jobs are eager to expand their duties—and wages.

Even though you insist that the woman come and wash your clothes just twice a month, she miraculously appears every day on one pretext or another. Before you know what's happening, she's working half-time. Should you value your privacy highly or be a marginal poverty case yourself, this can pose a problem that is difficult to solve.

Happily, the minor problems involved with hiring help rarely outweigh the advantages. An intelligent cleaning woman can teach you more Spanish in a week than most formal courses do and she doesn't expect extra pay for tutoring services. You'll get instruction in cooking, how to buy food, where the best bargains are and countless other bits of domestic information very helpful to the ignorant and uninitiated. Many details in this book were supplied by such people.

A few hints about where to buy firewood or which store sells the cheapest beer can easily save you a good portion of the wages paid.

Unless the person you hire is really a loser, you'll certainly become great friends. The only problem you'll have then is leaving; there always seem to be great amounts of weeping involved, not to mention final parties, hangovers and the mutual exchange of useless gifts.

Mary of the Light

Lorena and I had been loafing on the west coast of Mexico, catching up on hammock time after a long damp winter in the Pacific Northwest. With summer approaching we decided to move to a higher altitude, to a climate more conducive to writing than the oppressive heat of the beaches. Early one afternoon we caught a second-class bus, relieved to know that by sundown we would be back among the cool pines and oaks of the mountains. We had no exact destination in mind, preferring to rely on intuition and luck.

A few hours later the bus was winding its way up the side of a long narrow valley heavily planted with sugar cane. The air had thinned noticeably. I was anxiously waiting for the first glimpse of evergreen forests when my stomach made some sudden and very unpleasant noises.

"Hey, Lorena," I said, clutching a cramp as beads of sweat popped onto my forehead. "Remember that hot-dog I just couldn't pass up outside the bus station?" She turned with a curious stare, comprehension dawning as she noticed my hand massaging the front of my shirt.

"You mean . . . ?"

"Yeah," I groaned. "I gotta get off right away or there's going to be a very embarrassing scene."

Lorena immediately began gathering up her "extras": a knapsack, a string bag filled with yarn, a yarn bag filled with fruit, a cloth bag stuffed with notebooks and pens, a hat, a small cardboard box of shells and stones and a fat green coconut.

The other passengers watched with interest as we worked our way to the front of the wildly swaying bus with repeated, "*Con permisos*." One old man bowed back courteously as I doubled over with a cramp, his dark face breaking into a grin at what he took to be my excessively formal farewell.

"We want to get off at the next *pueblo*," I gasped to the driver's helper, a ten-year-old boy who stared at us blankly over the top of an *Hermelinda* comic book. He barely had time to relay this message to the man at the wheel before we reached the crest of a ridge and bumped into a small town.

"Where are we?" I asked as we braked to a stop in front of a tiny open plaza. "*Funerales Lopez, Servicio Día y Noche*" was cast into the backs of four cracked cement benches, facing outward from a forlorn wooden bandstand and two very dry pine trees. At least we were out of the hot banana country.

"Where are you going?" the driver countered, his hand resting on the door lever.

"*Here*," I said. "What is the name of this place?"

"How can you go here when you don't know where you are?" he answered suspiciously, the door held tightly closed. I felt a slight buzzing in my ears and mopped my forehead with a shirtsleeve.

"Because . . . because . . ." I took a deep breath, willing my guts to hold off anything drastic for just a few more minutes. "Because . . . my mother lives here!" I blurted. "I'm going to visit my mother!"

The door banged open as the driver muttered sarcastically, "Then go ask your mother where you are!"

The bus had hardly pulled away before we were surrounded by a horde of children asking eager questions about our backpacks, our birthplaces, our hometown and its proximity to Washington, D.C., and the North Pole.

"Where are you coming from?"

"Where are you going?"

"What is your work?"

"Do you have a camera?"

"Hey! Wait a minute!" I yelled, trying to fend off an industrious youngster who was either polishing my left hiking boot or stealing the shoelace. "Where is a place to eat?" I knew that my best chance of finding a tolerable toilet fast would be in the nearest *comedor*.

"Over there! Over there!" several voices cried as the children began jumping up and down, little hands clutching at our gear, vying for the privilege of helping us across the street. Lorena began laughing as she handed her odds and ends to the kids. Only a few of them were taller than her waist. A small girl hissed urgently and Lorena bent down so that her reddish-blond hair could be stroked for good luck.

We moved *en masse* to the doorway that they pointed to and entered a dark cool room, crowded with oilcloth-covered tables. I explained my urgent need to one of the larger children. While Lorena draped her bags over the back of a chair, I was rushed to the rear by my sympathetic retainers. "*¡Baño!*" I explained to the startled gray-haired lady stirring a large earthen pot of beans as we hurried through the kitchen and into the patio.

Two small boys stood guard in front of the bathroom's flour-sack-covered doorway. Behind it I drifted gratefully into a Zen-like state of diarrhea detachment, my mind barely registering the low babble of speculation and laughter outside.

Fifteen minutes later, after washing my face and hands in a bucket of refreshing cold water brought to me by a blushing little girl, I wobbled back to the dining room.

"Feel better?" Lorena asked sympathetically, while slurping from a large pottery mug. "Try some of this; it'll fix you up," she said, offering me the cup.

"What is it?" I asked, edging away. Her traveling medicine bag included combinations of powders and leaves capable of gagging Don Juan.

"Why don't you just try it?" she urged, smacking her lips encouragingly.

"What's in it?" I stalled. "Anything weird?"

"Do you want to feel better or not?" Lorena demanded, increasing my suspicion.

"Well . . . I don't know . . ," I said, my resistance weakening at the twinges of another cramp.

"It's just goldenseal, a little cinnamon, some cayenne pepper, a pinch of garlic powder and a squeeze of lime juice," she said, as casually as if it were Constant Comment.

Before I had time to reject this ghastly potion, the lady I'd surprised in the kitchen bustled into the room bearing a similar steaming mug.

"*Té de perro, joven*," she smiled, setting the cup of "dog tea," a classic Mexican stomach remedy, on the table in front of me. I sniffed it warily; Lorena might have convinced her to add a little something extra, just for the sake of my health. The tea was bitter but good and its warmth soon relaxed my tense muscles. The combination of bus trip and diarrhea had been exhausting. I began to drift off, calling upon my Navy training to allow myself to doze sitting up, eyes open wide, my face making occasional twitches, falsely signaling mental activity. In the background I vaguely heard Lorena and the lady discussing our plans, lifestyles, families and finances. My eyes closed slowly . . .

"Carl? Hey, Carl!"

I snapped awake, my hand jerking convulsively, spilling the dregs of tea across my lap.

"Yeah? What? What is it?" I yawned, realizing that we were alone, actually completely alone, not an adult or kid in sight.

"I rented a house," Lorena said, her voice charged with excitement, "from the *señora* here. It's really cheap and she says that it has a good view of the valley."

I considered this news quietly, staring out at the deserted street. "Well, why not?" This looked like as good a place as any. If nothing else, the children were friendly. I yawned, easing down into the chair and stretching my legs. Somewhere in the distance a radio blared and dogs barked lazily. The air was fresh and clean; smelling vaguely of pine needles and cooked beans.

Our first view of the house Lorena had rented was something of a disappointment.

"I've seen worse," I lied, wondering if the sagging roof was holding up the crumbling adobe walls or vice versa. I surveyed the few remaining patches of whitewash, obviously applied before the Revolution, the rotting roof beams and the cracked ties. I could see three small cell-like windows, barred with weathered sticks.

It was a scene of quaint and picturesque neglect. Picturesque, that is, to a passing artist and not a new tenant.

"At least we won't have to buy a padlock," Lorena said pushing aside the curtain of burlap sacks covering the front doorway.

"Or light bulbs," I said, pointing to the kerosene lamp and candle stubs set in niches in the thick walls.

"What about the furniture and the decor?" Lorena laughed, testing a midget-sized pine chair. Her chin just about reached the level of the tabletop, barely large enough to hold a checkerboard.

There was another elf-sized table, two crudely hewn wooden stools, a few empty crates and a stove, a massive affair of adobe bricks and hardened mud. "I'd call it Late Cortéz," I said, crossing the small living room and moving into the even smaller kitchen.

"Everything is *so small*," Lorena sighed, easing her backpack onto the single narrow canvas cot that we would cling to like mountain-climbers in the nights ahead. "But at least she wasn't exaggerating about the view."

I turned to look. The boundary of our front yard was a nearly vertical drop of almost three thousand feet to the next village.

While we sat there, soaking up the sun and tossing pebbles over the edge, I privately wondered what we'd gotten ourselves into. Suddenly a boiling mass of thick clouds appeared at the foot of the valley, swelling and surging upward until we were engulfed in an eerie golden fog. The temperature dropped immediately and we hurried into the house to pull jackets from the bottom of our packs.

"That's what I'd call a $10 sunset," I said. "I just wish it had come a couple hours later." It was four in the afternoon.

That night we again sat on the edge of the cliff, watching the dim twinkle of lights below and listening to the music from the village loudspeaker echoing upward, like passengers observing the earth from a silent dirigible. When I later asked a neighbor for the quickest route down, he laughed and said, "By parachute."

The waves of interest created by our arrival eventually subsided and within a week we were tentatively accepted as members of the community. Our status floated somewhere between that of a schoolteacher and the village idiot. When it became common knowledge that I spent the mornings writing, several people began greeting me as "*Profe*," short for "*Profesor*." Others, who might have seen us flinging a Frisbee with the kids or flying homemade kites, treated us with the cautious respect reserved for the non-criminally insane.

The quiet routine we established ended abruptly on the morning of our eighth day. I had just finished writing and was about to begin the usual argument with Lorena over who had to wash dishes, when a woman's voice called a cheery, "*¡Buenos días!*" from the front doorway.

"*¡Pase usted!*" Lorena called back, expecting to see another of the neighbors.

The curtain was pushed aside and a small middle-aged woman marched into the room. "I am *María de la Luz*," she announced brightly. "And I have come to do your housework." Lorena and I looked at each other, startled, as "Mary of the Light" disappeared into the kitchen.

"Did you see her face?" I finally asked.

Lorena nodded, stunned. There was no light in one of María's eyes, it was lost in the milky blindness of vast cataracts. A tingle ran up the back of my neck. The blankness of that eyeball, in contrast to her lively smile, had somehow seemed menacing.

"Did you ask her to come?" I said.

"Never seen her before in my life!" Lorena answered, astonished.

I didn't know what to say, but judging from the sounds that came from the kitchen, María was wasting no time asserting her employment. I got up from my chair and took a deep breath, squaring my shoulders; the woman would have to be shown the door!

"I'll take care of this," I said, moving toward the kitchen. I barely avoided colliding with María as she bustled into the room, wiping her hands on the front of her full-length apron.

"Where is the soap?" she demanded, fixing me with that lopsided blind stare, a numbing psychic laser beam that left me stammering. "Er . . . it's on the shelf . . . by the stove."

"It should be by the bucket," she answered, turning her back and returning to the kitchen.

"You handled that really well," Lorena chided.

"Well, what do you want me to do?" I yelled. "Drag her out by her braids and throw her off the cliff?" I moved warily to the kitchen doorway, determined to clear up this misunderstanding without further delay.

"Ah . . . er, María?" I said. "We're sorry but we don't want you to . . ." Her sarcastic bark cut off my dismissal speech.

"*Señor,*" she laughed. "Everyone in the *pueblo* says that you, a man, wash your own clothing and cook and even . . ." she hesitated, peering at me uncertainly with her blank eye. The impropriety of my next offense was almost too terrible to mention aloud, ". . . and even *sweep the floor!*"

I blushed.

"*Señor,*" she continued. "That is not *la costumbre* here!"

Guilty of violating local custom by helping with the housework! How could I explain that if I even suggested Lorena do all of the chores, I would violate our custom and she would leave on the next bus, without me?

"*Pues . . .*" I conceded. "If it's *la costumbre* . . . but how much will it cost to have you work? We don't have much money." I added this hurriedly, certain that our emaciated budget would make the decadent practice of having a "domestic" unthinkable.

María's stare fixed on me for several long moments. She then announced a salary so fantastically low that I all but rubbed my hands together with glee. Visions of never having to touch a dishrag or mop again brought a flush to my face, erasing guilty thoughts of exploitation of the working class.

"*¡Cosa hecha!*" I cried. "It's a deal!"

"Of course," she answered, smiling indulgently as she turned back to the bucket of dishes.

During those first idyllic days, writing, hiking or just loafing on one of the funeral parlor's uncomfortable benches in the plaza, trading gossip with the kids, I had formed an image of village life that went something like this: early in the rosy predawn chill the jolly woodcutters and farmers tumbled from their cozy cornhusk mattresses to eat a simple but nourishing breakfast of beans and tortillas before tramping off into the surrounding mountains, whistling along the pine needle–covered slopes to their picturesquely steep woodlots and fields. There they engaged in honest labor until late afternoon, when they returned, still whistling, to a simple but nourishing supper of beans and tortillas and a quiet evening around the blazing hearth, relating folk tales and earthy wisdom to their attentive and well-mannered broods.

When not busy preparing simple but nourishing meals of bean and tortillas, the womenfolk were scrubbing brightly colored hand-loomed clothing and arranging it picturesquely along the banks of burbling mountain streams. Children laughed and gamboled on the grassy hillsides nearby as their older brothers and sisters tended flocks of prancing goats.

María changed all this with daily reports as lurid as the Evening News.

"That *pinche* ox Celestino borrowed the axe of Juanito and broke the handle and now the old *cabrón* says . . . that when Lupe got home his old lady was drunk on *ponche* and burned the tortillas again, that *tonta* . . . and let me tell you how Rosamunda went into Iguala to visit her sister and came back *embarasada* and . . ."

"Wait a minute," I said. "What was she embarrassed about?"

María looked at me blankly for a few seconds, then gave an ear-splitting shriek of laughter, "*Embarasada*, you fool!" She formed her hands over her belly and began clomping around the kitchen as though in the last stage of grotesque pregnancy. "No wonder you have no children!" she added, wiping a tear from her blind eye. "Don't you know how to . . ."

"OK! OK!" I said, edging toward the door.

"Wait!" she cried casting a lopsided glance at the window for eavesdroppers. "You know what those dirty little *esquincles*, those brats next door, did to Pedro's chickens yesterday?"

"No, no, that's enough!" I protested, holding up my hands and backing out of the room. "I have to work now. You can tell me later, after dinner."

"*¡Joven!*"

María's shout brought me crashing to my feet, jostling the table. My half-filled coffee cup slopped across a stack of notes. I raced into the kitchen, expecting to find her cornered by some lethal serpent or rabid hound. To my surprise, however, she was only standing in front of our small brass backpacking stove, hands on hips, her face set in an angry scowl.

"How can I cook you a meal with this . . ." María hesitated, at a rare loss for words, ". . . this piece of gringo garbage?"

This was the last straw! I'd taken her through the operating procedures a hundred times, patiently demonstrating the various steps required to light the stove. Hell, I'd even heard her brag to the neighbors, describing it as "*moderna*" and "*preciosa*."

"I've told you many times, María," I retorted angrily, "that this stove is very simple."

Her bad eye rolled upward as she twisted her shoulders in a classic Mexican "Don't kid me" shrug.

"All you have to do," I continued, ignoring her deep self-pitying sighs, "is to put this thing on here and twist this." I opened the air valve, raising my eyebrows at her.

She sighed heavily and nodded.

"Oh, yeah," I said, reaching for the cleaning tool, "I forgot to tell you that you have to put this little wire in here and do this." I worked it up and down a few times. "Then you just put some of this alcohol in here, twist this back . . . no, wait, light the alcohol first, then twist this back. *¿Está bien?*"

She nodded silently.

"OK, then after thirty to forty seconds open that and pump this." I couldn't resist adding, "It may take longer at this altitude because the fire isn't as hot."

"Fire isn't as hot here?" María snorted. "I didn't know that!"

I chose to ignore her tone of voice. "When this is hot, *muy caliente* you can adjust the fire by opening this. *¿Entiendes?* It's very simple."

She threw her hands into the air. "When Doña Lorena returns I will go for firewood," she said turning her back on me and reaching for a banana.

I ground my teeth. "Doña Lorena!" Here I was just *joven*, young man, while Lorena was the equivalent of "Lady Lorena." And this business of waiting for Lorena to return before María could leave the house, as though I were under protective custody—it was too much. I stormed out and headed for the village.

"*¡Ay, qué milagro!*" Don Antonio cried as I stepped through the door of his shop. His deep brown face was creased by a wide grin and as usual his hand automatically went to his chin, stroking the scraggly white whiskers he was cultivating in my honor. "What a miracle!" was Don Antonio's standard greeting to me, though we saw each other at least once a day.

It was to Don Antonio's that I escaped each afternoon, to sit on a fat grain sack among the pickaxes, machetes, broad-bladed hoes and stacks of empty five-gallon cans. I would sip warm Cokes laced with moonshine *mezcal* as we discussed the state of the world. He had patiently explained the politics and poverty of the local turpentine industry, and I in turn helped him to understand that Holland and Canada were separate countries and not parts of the United States. In spite of his age Don Antonio was a quick student. Our tattered Exxon road map of the United States was now tacked prominently behind the zinc-topped counter, sandwiched between a rusting tin Faros cigarette sign and a faded and flyspeckled calendar for the year 1959. He used the map to conduct impromptu geography lessons for his younger customers.

"You're early today." He smiled, dusting a bottle of Coca-Cola with a shirt-sleeve and wrenching off the cap with his front teeth. I winced, another part of the daily ritual, and accepted the bottle "*¿Con piquete?*" He asked, hooking a thumb toward the small wooden cask of moonshine that hung from the wall.

"*No, gracias,*" I said. "I'll wait until later for the stinger." I took a sip and added, "I can't work today. There's too much noise in the house."

He nodded sympathetically. Don Antonio invited your confidence and respected it; few decisions of any importance were made in the village without first seeking his opinion.

"Perhaps you should get rid of the noise?" he suggested, his voice completely neutral. María's antics were well known to him; our daily conversations often centered on her past and present exploits, sending us both into choking fits of laughter. Don Antonio had known her for more than forty years and whenever I was telling a new "María story," I felt that he was reading my mind. His words of caution and advice had been invaluable.

"I can't send her away," I answered. "You know how poor she is."

He nodded. In a village where poverty was endured with heroic stoicism, María's plight might one day become legend.

"I asked her what she had for breakfast this morning and she said 'Beans, six.'" Don Antonio roared with laughter, his forehead touching the countertop as he beat it with his right fist.

While he waited on a man interested in a dozen nails, I worked on the Coke and pondered what to do about María. I glanced at my watch: almost one o'clock, time for *comida*.

"*Con permiso*," I called, laying a few coins on the counter, "but I have to eat." Don Antonio waved, an amused grin on his face. He knew that I did not dare be late. Even if María had "forgotten" to prepare the afternoon meal, as she often did, I was still expected to appear.

"What are we eating?" I called as I entered the house, praying it wouldn't be one of her eye-watering specialties. María's love of chilies was beyond belief; she snacked on them like peanuts.

"*¡Menudo!*" She answered cheerily, sweeping into the living room with a large steaming earthen *olla*. The bowl was placed on the table with the reverence of a sacrificial offering.

"María," I groaned. "We told you that we don't like to eat meat, remember?" She stared at me coldly. "Lorena never eats meat," I continued, knowing that whatever the Doña wanted the Doña would get. "And even if I wanted meat I would not want *menudo*." I tried to smile, to soften the blow a bit, but the thought of a bowl of hot tripe brought a shudder instead.

She snatched the *olla* away, giving me a withering glare with her blind eye that said "Pearls before swine!" and marched back to the kitchen.

Lorena returned five minutes later, just as I was beginning my meal of barely warmed beans and stiff tortillas. I explained the lunch situation and she rushed off to soothe María's feelings. I soon heard laughter and the sound of pans being rattled. Lorena came back bearing a plate covered with piping hot *quesadillas*, a fresh single serving of salad and an attractively sliced avocado.

I labored grimly over my beans as Lorena laughingly told me how good old María had accidentally made *menudo*, thinking it was my favorite dish. Her extreme mental anguish had been assuaged somewhat when Lorena told her to take the stuff home.

"These are delicious," she added, munching on a *quesadilla*, "Like to try a bite?" I tore savagely at my day-old tortilla . . .

"Where are you going?"

"Out."

"Where?"

"In the mountains."

"What for?"

"To relax."

"Why? You can relax here."

"I need some air."

"When will you be back?"

"Soon."

"How soon? Don't forget dinner."

"I won't. What are we having?"

"Your favorite. *Pozole*."

"Oh, wonderful."

"What's wrong? Don't you like *pozole*?"

"Yes, María, I love it. If we didn't have it every day I think I'd die."

"Well, then, get going, you need some air."

"Yes, María, thank you. *Hasta luego*."

"*Hasta luego, joven*. Be careful, don't get lost. Or drunk."

I had been working for three weeks on a handwritten manuscript, making good progress in spite of María's repeated warnings about certain blindness from eyestrain. I finally shut her up one morning after she predicted that I would go insane from an "attack of brain pressure." I looked up at her, bugged out my eyes, and wheezed: "But María, my love, I went insane years ago!" A maniacal giggle sent her scurrying to Doña Lorena for protection.

Despite her morbid warnings María secretly approved of my writing. More than once I was approached by people who asked when I would be finished chronicling the life and times of María de la Luz.

And then my manuscript disappeared.

"What's wrong with him?" María asked, edging past Lorena with a shopping bag of yet more *pozole* ingredients.

"He lost his papers," she answered.

"I DIDN'T LOSE THEM!" I shouted. "They were STOLEN! Robbed! *¡ROBADO! ¡ROBADO!*" I flopped onto the cot, grinding my fists into my forehead. The ultimate nightmare come true! Who could have possibly wanted those pages? Who in the village could even read them! It was senseless, absolutely senseless. Hell, they didn't even use paper around here for . . . oh no! Anything but that!

I was struck by the awful image of an Indian casually tearing the yellow legal pages into quarters, squatting behind a bush with his pants around his ankles, puzzling at the funny scribbles. I moaned.

"Oh, *those* papers!" María laughed, digging into the deep pockets of her apron. "I have them here. I just borrowed them for a few hours. *¡No te preocupes, joven!*"

"Don't preoccupy myself?" I cried, leaping from the bed and snatching the pages from her hand. I tore away the piece of grass that bound the tightly rolled sheets and riffled through them quickly. They were all there.

"Are you *loca*?" I stormed. "Don't you understand what this . . . this . . ." I gasped for breath as María watched with a knowing smile: only a matter of time now; I was throwing a classic "brain pressure fit." Such a lovely ceremony they'd have, carrying me to the local *panteón* in my whitewashed pine box, spilling over with plastic gardenias. Doña Lorena would look so nice, her blond hair over black.

"Why?" I asked, trying to calm myself, "Why did you take them? What did you do with them? *You can't even read!*" She puffed up like a game hen, turning as usual to Lorena: "*Señora*," she said, "I took the papers to show to my friends. To prove that the *joven* was writing the story of my life. The didn't believe me before. Now they do." She gave me a triumphant grin; my secret project had been revealed to all.

"*¡Bueno!*" she said, fluffing her apron busily, "Isn't it time for you to begin work?" María gave Lorena a motherly pat on the arm, "Come, *señora*, it is the hour for us to take a cup of your delicious tea."

"*¡Kaaalimaaaaan!*"

I shot up from the table, the noise striking like a cold dental probe on a tender nerve. I kicked the chair away, pulling wildly at the crude door I'd fashioned from raw pine boards, my final line of defense against María's constant warnings, questions and sly suggestions about her assumed biography.

"*¡KALIMAN! ¡HOMBRE INCREDIBLE!*"

I threw the door aside, determined to put a fine end to this ultimate irritation. The radio crackled:

"*Kaliman approaches the Forbidden City in the company of little Solin . . .*"

"Yeah, maybe so," I thought, edging across the living room. "But this time he's had the course."

"*Go with patience and serenity, Solin, for only the coward dies twice!*"

I flattened myself against the wall and reached for the curtain María had rigged over the kitchen doorway. Kaliman's platitudes boomed out into the house over a background of hissing and popping static. It was a complete mystery to me how María could coax such volume from her cracked and patched transistor radio, let alone how she understood the distorted words. She often worked with the radio held inches from her ear.

"*KALIMAN ATTACKS!*"

I threw the curtain back and leaped into the kitchen, raising my hand to snatch the radio and hurl it out the window. Let Kaliman entertain the people at the bottom of the cliff!

"*The coward dies by his own hand! Take that you . . .*"

"Oh, Carl! What are you doing?" Lorena asked, looking up from the radio she held in her lap. María gave me a wicked grin, winking her bad eye deliberately.

"Would you like to listen to the program with us?" Lorena continued. "Kaliman has just approached the Forbidden City and . . ."

"I'm going to miss this place, but I have to admit that I'm getting a little bored," Lorena said one evening as we sat on the edge of our front yard tossing pebbles into the pine trees below.

We'd hiked almost the entire network of trails surrounding the village. I knew María's jokes well enough to anticipate the lurid punch lines, and conversations at Don Antonio's were as predictable as the price of turpentine.

"When María saw me looking at the map this morning, she just about flipped," I said.

Lorena sighed; leaving was going to be difficult. María seemed convinced that we had come to the village for good and had begun to say things like, "When you buy your *parcela* of land . . ." and "I think your new house should have a fireplace." It was useless to try to explain that we'd come to the village on a whim and would leave on another. In María's world, life was as regular as sunrise and sunset, with very few surprises in between.

"I gave a good reason for our leaving," I said. "I told her I wanted to write about witches and magic herbs and that we were going somewhere to look for them."

"What did she say to that?"

"Not much," I answered. "She just gave me a funny look and then left. Said she'd see us tomorrow. Come to think of it she looked sort of horrified."

We both laughed; I'd finally gotten one over on her!

María disappeared. When she didn't show up the day after I'd told her we would be leaving, we assumed she wasn't feeling well or was busy at home. The next day, however, we began to worry.

"We've got to leave by tomorrow," I said. "But if she hasn't shown up, we can get one of the kids to take us to her house." Lorena agreed, though I could tell she was ready to begin the search immediately.

I woke early the next morning, shifting carefully for a more comfortable position on the "Ledge," as we'd come to call our narrow bed. A noise from the kitchen caught my attention. I heard the blowtorch roar of the backpacking stove and the rattle of the tea kettle. María?

"Hey, Lorena," I yawned. "Time to get up. I think we'll be able to catch the morning bus after all. María is in the kitchen." I eased out of bed and began pulling on my clothes, relieved that this final complication was now resolved. Our backpacks were almost ready; we could just eat breakfast and be on our way. A cup of coffee, first, that's what I really needed.

"María," I said, pushing aside the kitchen curtain. "Is the coffee . . . ?" I stopped, recoiling from the sickening odor that filled the kitchen. María stood over a small pot, stirring it with . . . a turkey feather? Her mouth was set in a hard line, her nose seemed to be trying to crawl away of its own accord, struggling to escape the obnoxious steam that poured upward.

"What are you doing?" I cried, fanning the air before me and trying to catch a glimpse of the pot's contents. Something caught my eye. Turning to the pine table I saw a pair of scraggly dead birds, their pitiful feet tied together with bright yellow yarn, surrounded by leaves, roots and dried bark. A large basket of assorted mushrooms, some a vile pulpy red, sat on the chair. I looked up, just in time to catch María's dark eye fixed on mine. The lid of her blind eye closed slowly in a sly, calculated wink.

"*Joven*," she croaked, and I immediately caught the theatrical tone, the exaggerated old-crone whine, "I have many things to show you." She lifted the pot from the stove with one of her asbestos hands and poured the scalding liquid into a pottery mug. "Drink this!" she commanded, "and it will protect you from *El Mal Ojo!*"

I gave a tentative laugh. "The Evil Eye?" Was this for real? She pushed the cup toward me, ignoring the boiling-hot tea that splashed over her fingers.

"What is all this?" I stalled, waving my hands at the strange display on the table and chair. Was it my imagination or did she pull her head down into her shoulders and bend into a witch-like crouch?

"There are certain secrets I possess," she answered cryptically, fingering a small cloth bag that hung at her throat.

"What's that?" I asked, moving in for a better look. She immediately stuffed the bag inside the front of her dress. "I will explain," she repeated, "but now you must drink this." I took one more whiff of that awful tea and retreated to the other room.

"Lorena," I said, reaching for my boots, "I think you'd better have a little talk with María before she tries to change herself into a crow." I went to the front door. "I have to say goodbye to Don Antonio. Watch out for that thing she's got in there, it'd kill a werewolf with one sniff." She looked up from the bed, puzzled. As I walked by the tiny kitchen window I heard a stifled cackle.

"That about does it," I said, giving the kitchen a final once-over in case we'd forgotten something. María's unidentified herbs and mushrooms were now scattered in the trees below the house, along with the unfortunate birds. She had taken her unmasking as a phony witch quite well, laughing openly as she described to Lorena how she'd gathered everything she could find that looked even vaguely poisonous or weird. "But I was very afraid," she said, "that *joven* would actually drink that . . ."

The awful brew had been her undoing. When Lorena had gone into the kitchen she'd called María's bluff by not only accepting a cup, but by actually raising it to her lips for a drink. Rather than see the Doña poisoned, María had grabbed it away and dumped it onto the floor. A confession of quackery was not far behind. "The *joven* said he wanted to write about a witch so I thought . . ."

"Well, here we go," I said, raising my pack and slipping my arms through the shoulder straps. María hurried to help Lorena, clucking disapproval at the weight of her pack. She gave me a look that said, "Brute! How can you make the poor thing carry *this*?"

We parted in front of the house, shaking hands in the Indian fashion, a gentle mutual stroke that somehow conveys so much more than a *gringo* knuckle-buster. In spite of her great pretensions as our *mayordoma*, María was too shy to accompany us to the bus stop. She issued her final warnings and instructions from the yard.

"Don't sit by open windows on the bus, you'll get a bad wind and die."

"Go to the market when you get to Guadalajara and buy thicker eyeglasses."

"Drink lots of *atole;* you're too skinny."

She stopped for breath, searching her memory for another bit of folk wisdom. "Remember, a closed mouth catches no flies!" We started down the trail, waving back to her. "*¡Señora!*" she called, her voice breaking, "*Señora*, don't forget to . . . forget to . . ." María gulped, tears pouring down her cheeks, "Don't forget to listen to KALIMAN!"

We stumbled down the tree-covered ridge, following the red dirt path to the tiny plaza. Don Antonio waved and called from the doorway of his store. Somewhere in the distance a radio blared and dogs barked lazily. The air smelled vaguely of pine needles and cooked beans.

CAMPING

*Camping with children • RV motor homes and trailers: RV caravans • Van, pickup
and car campers • Rent-a-car camping • Privacy: learn to adapt • Where to camp •
Is it safe? • Where to be careful • Where not to camp • Exploring: Mosquitoes,
coconuts and shade trees • Camping and kitchen gear • A traveling kitchen • Food
from home • Odds and ends • Camping skills: building a thatched hut, sharpening a
machete, hanging a hammock*

Every good camping trip to Mexico begins with a daydream. It may be nothing more
than a vague desire to feel warm beach sand between your toes or a detailed, life-
long plan to follow jungle trails in search of a Lost City. Whether you'll be traveling
in a fully equipped motor home, a dented VW van, or by backpack and public buses,
you'll undoubtedly meet many like-minded people along the way. Foreign travel is
a great equalizer, and it is common to find people from all walks of life in the same
campground.

In a casual census of one small RV park in the Yucatán, we met an ex-crop duster
pilot, a retired Army noncom, college students, a carpenter, commercial salmon
fishermen, housewives, an antique dealer, a CPA and a realtor. We also met a French
longshoreman, a Danish bus driver and a commercial artist from Mexico City. Mix
these diverse personalities, languages and backgrounds together in an exotic location and it's no wonder that every day spent camping in Mexico is a memorable
experience.

In addition to the remarkable hospitality of its people, campers find an almost irresistible attraction in Mexico's natural beauty. There are over 6,000 miles of coastline,
most of it open and undeveloped, plus countless square miles of jungle, mountains,
deserts and forests. *Norteamericanos* who tire of "reservations only" campgrounds at
home will find plenty of opportunities to get away from the crowds and to actually
explore a country that sees relatively few campers.

There is no such thing as a "typical Mexican campground." Facilities range from
American-style RV parks with satellite dishes, immaculate tiled bathrooms, hot showers, community rooms and laundromat, to open cow pastures with a malodorous outhouse. Those who prefer independent camping can explore the innumerable side roads,
empty beaches, trails, jungle rivers and remote canyons of Mexico.

Camping with Children

Children find camping in Mexico a true delight. I wouldn't hesitate to take a child camping or even backpacking. Mexicans are literally crazy about kids. Friends who camp with children, from toddlers to teenagers, are almost unanimous in urging others to take their kids south rather than leaving them at home. Some kids make better campers than their parents, happily ignoring minor discomforts and taking pleasure in simple camp chores.

RV Motor Homes and Trailers

Although we've noted a decline in the number of independent van and car campers since the Seventies, Mexico's attractive prices, warm climate and hospitality are now tempting many retired American and Canadian RVers to cross the border. These RV retirees tend to be much more adventurous than their contemporaries back home. One couple in a campground near San Miguel de Allende complained that traveling in the U.S. was "too crowded, too expensive and too predictable." They decided to find a little excitement by knocking around Mexico in a small motor home, learning Spanish on the street and generally having the time of their lives.

Other RVers are more conservative. It isn't unusual to find entire RV parks filled with winter or even year-round residents. Typical "residential campers" will drive to Mexico in October or November, park their rig in a comfortable space and then stay put until spring. Resident campers often develop close friendships with local Mexicans and can be gold mines of information for other campers. Though this style of "camping" may not seem exciting to some, others find it both satisfying and quite economical.

RVers who prefer more active travel follow an unofficial circuit of trailer parks, spas and campgrounds. Although Mexico has many opportunities for easy, safe and free camping, RVers usually feel more comfortable in an established park with hookups. Mexico's campground circuit is extensive, but it doesn't begin to match the number of facilities available north of the border.

"I guess you could call us hopelessly middle class," one woman said to me. We stood on a grassy campsite near the edge of a rather rundown *parque de traylers*. She and her husband had been coming here for years; their van was parked to take advantage of a fine view of the Pacific Ocean. A cool breeze ruffled the tarp they'd erected over a set of folding chairs and a card table. They had hammocks, a barbecue pit and even a badminton net. This was it, their home for six months of the year. I looked around their camp again, thinking of people at home fighting winter weather, frustrated at rising prices and decreasing incomes, struggling to enjoy their free time or retirement.

"Hopelessly middle class?" I took another bite of her delicious fresh mango pie. "I don't think I heard you quite right."

A retired gringo described his lifestyle to me like this: "I've got my little boat (a twelve-foot aluminum runabout), my outboard and my fishing poles. I drive around Mexico, looking for good water. When I see some, I stop. I hardly ever fish the same place for more than a week. I've been doing this for years now and still haven't seen it all. Probably never will." He had an encyclopedic knowledge of Mexican fishing spots, but getting it out of him would have taken bamboo splinters and truth serum. "Down Michoacán way," was about as close as he'd come to divulging information. (See *Red Tape and the Law: Fishing Licenses*.)

RV Caravans
Professionally guided RV caravans have been popular in Mexico for many years. Several companies offer full-service caravanning, including insurance, wagon masters,

mechanics, organized sightseeing, shopping tours and rousing campfire songfests. Caravans are usually accompanied by Green Angels, special tourist assistance patrol trucks provided by the Mexican government.

Many RVers use caravan travel as an introduction to Mexico. Several caravan veterans have told us that the experience they gained on a caravan gave them the confidence to return to Mexico on their own. Others enjoy not having to worry about logistics, repairs and security.

One of the main disadvantages of caravanning is the inevitable clannishness that such regimented travel can produce. Meeting Mexicans is especially difficult in a tightly organized caravan with schedules that don't allow spontaneous side trips and explorations. Caravans also have a tendency to consume everything in their path, especially ice cubes, gasoline, cold drinks and fresh bread. "They're like army ants!" one angry independent camper complained after a caravan of over one hundred RV rigs made a shopping blitz through a nearby town.

Other campers, myself included, try to look on the positive side. Caravanners often stock up at home on food, hardware and other unavailable goodies. I know gringos who "work the rigs," trading everything from books and seashells to Mexican trinkets for treats from home. Caravans inevitably include vacationing handyman types who jump at the opportunity to help a fellow traveler with a problem. On the Caribbean coast, Steve and I have both been given considerable assistance by the members of an RV caravan when our vans had broken down.

Van, Pickup and Car Campers

Vans, pickup campers, delivery trucks and converted school buses make up the next largest group of recreational vehicles found in Mexico, though most of their owners seem to shy away from the term "RV." Some van campers look down their noses at RVs and motor homes, just as the owners of classic, wooden sailboats tend to sneer at the fiberglass "Tupperware Fleet." As history recycles itself, however, more and more ex-VW van drivers are beginning to kick the tires on used motor homes, daydreaming about that perfect camping spot at the end of a long Mexican beach.

In my opinion, the biggest advantage of a van or pickup camper in Mexico is maneuverability. In spite of great feats of highway building, the better part of Mexico—in terms of both area and adventure—is still off the beaten path. If you stick close to the pavement, whether it's on Baja's 850-mile-long Transpeninsular Highway or Mexico's endless two-lane arterials, there's no limit (other than courage) to the size of rig you can drive. Lorena and I just happen to be addicted to narrow streets, cul-de-sacs, dead ends, side trips, back roads and vague, dotted lines on heavily creased maps.

Rent-A-Car Camping

One of the most economical and versatile "RVs" we've ever used was nothing other than a Mexican rental car. Using a rental car as an improvised RV is a quick and efficient way to explore Mexico, especially if your time is limited.

We often meet tourists who are camping from rental cars. Their most frequent complaint: "I wish we'd planned to do this from the start and come prepared; it's great!" A bird-watching couple in the Yucatán told me, "For the price of a hotel room in Cancún, we can rent a car, explore to our heart's content, eat in restaurants whenever we want and still save money." Their camping gear consisted of hammocks, mosquito nets, blankets and a cheap styrofoam ice chest, all purchased in Mexico. "We don't camp out every night," they added, "but compared to what the other tourists are doing, this is a real adventure." In Chiapas, we met a group of American bicyclists who shared the cost of renting a VW van as a support wagon for a combination camping/hotel tour.

On the Pacific coast and Baja, campgrounds are more abundant and rental car camping is even more common, especially with travelers from the northeastern U.S., Canada and Europe.

Although rental cars are not a bargain in Mexico, the price looks much more attractive when compared to the unavoidable costs of taking your own vehicle. To many people, time is even more valuable than money. If you've got two weeks of vacation and an urge to explore offbeat Caribbean beaches and Mayan ruins, rental car camping is your obvious choice.

What Will It Cost?

After writing our first book on camping in Mexico, Lorena and I treated ourselves to six months of low-budget bliss by camping on one of Mexico's finest beaches. Our total costs for this half-year idyll amounted to less than one month's expenses at home. Our major outlay, in fact, went for labor and materials to build a very comfortable palm frond house. The balance was spent on food, ice and miscellaneous supplies, plus gasoline for an outboard motor and frequent short side trips in the van.

In general, campers will find that prices in Mexico for seasonal produce, bulk staples, dry goods and basic services are lower than in the U.S. and Canada. Some things will be very cheap. In order to preserve "social stability" the Mexican government subsidizes many must-have staples, including tortillas, bread, bus tickets, propane and sugar. Consumer goods, imported foods and luxury items, however, can cost as much as they do at home or even more. For example, gasoline usually costs slightly more per gallon in Mexico than it does in California. Meat and chicken often cost more than in the U.S., even though the average Mexican earns just a few dollars a day.

In estimating your own costs, start with unavoidable expenses such as gas, oil and insurance. Insurance runs a minimum of about $3.50 a day, depending on the value of your vehicle and the extent of the coverage.

If you live more than a day or two from the border, and hope to travel for a month or more, it's easy to put 4,000 to 5,000 miles on the odometer. At roughly $1.50 a gallon for gas, you can see that driving to and from Mexico in an RV gas-guzzler is going to cost at least several hundred dollars for fuel, plus insurance, tolls, tires and incidental repairs. That's a lot of bus tickets and cab rides.

The key to low-cost camping is to imitate Mexicans: avoid pricey tourist resorts and buy only what you need for the next few days. Buy fresh, locally grown meat and produce, rather than packaged, imported or out-of-season foods. Go easy on liquor, nightlife, souvenirs and toys. In other words, live simply and modestly.

Steve's partner Tina Rosa advises that, "Days of rest cost less and days spent sightseeing and driving around cost more."

Campers who are willing to "free camp," either on their own, with a Mexican family or in one of the country's many *balnearios* (spas) and rustic, community campgrounds, will note a considerable savings. Catch a fish now and then, barter a pair of pliers for a lifetime supply of papayas and cancel that subscription to the *Wall Street Journal*. In short order your living expenses will plunge to near-Mexican levels. I frequently meet backpack vagabonds and shoestring-budget van campers who get by on amazingly small budgets.

One (thin) young Californian lived in a campground in Chiapas by selling homemade confections to fellow campers. I know others who earn a few discreet pesos through car repair, massage, haircutting, jewelry making and other odd and inventive little jobs. Kathy, a resourceful camper from Louisiana, stuffs the cupboards of her travel trailer with garage sale bargains, from good used clothing to small household electrical appliances. Once she reaches her favorite camping area in Mexico she begins visiting—and bartering—with Mexican friends.

"Wheeling and dealing doesn't bring in much," Kathy explains. "At least not in terms of dollars and cents and pesos. But," she quickly adds, "it's sure a lot of fun and helps pay for the tortillas."

Some of my best trips to Mexico have been spur-of-the-moment, with only a token thought for planning and preparation. For example, I once spent a week in Chihuahua's Copper Canyon with nothing but a couple of changes of clothes, a sleeping bag, camera and a few personal items hurriedly stuffed into my backpack. Though I might have wished for more gear, I certainly had enough to cover my basic needs and to support a very enjoyable budget camping trip.

My favorite example of casual trip planning was related to me by a fellow I nicknamed Robinson Crusoe. He was strolling idly down a street in San Francisco when a chalkboard notice in the window of a travel agency caught his eye. It advertised a super-cheap round-trip fare to the Pacific coast of Mexico, an offer he literally couldn't refuse. As he was self-employed and accustomed to poverty, he wasn't afraid to blow most of his remaining money on the ticket. There was just one catch: the last flight available left in eight hours.

"I bought my ticket and ran like a maniac for the nearest discount store," he said. "It took about an hour to buy bug dope, a frying pan, water jugs and a cheap sleeping bag. I didn't have any spare clothes with me, either, so I took a cab to the Goodwill and got a suitcase and a whole wardrobe. I climbed on the plane wearing an Al Capone–style suit. It felt kind of ridiculous, but when I got to Mexico I traded the suit to a cab driver for a ride to the beach."

That's where I met him one morning, while I was beachcombing and surfcasting for a breakfast fish. He'd been on the beach for ten days, hiking back and forth to a nearby village for food and water, conserving his money as carefully as possible. "One catch on that discount fare," he explained, "was that I had to stay three weeks."

When he left, he traded his hobo camping outfit for another ride to the airport. For what most tourists spend on a long weekend he enjoyed a three-week vacation on a Mexican beach.

Privacy

Camping in Mexico is different in many ways from camping in the U.S. and Canada. In the back country, many Mexicans live all of their lives on a scale that we would consider "camping." Chopping firewood, hauling water, hunting, fishing, gathering herbs, wild fruits and vegetables, and sleeping on mats or hard cots are all part of the normal daily routine.

These back-country Mexicans find it difficult to understand why rich people—and *we are definitely rich* by their standards—deliberately regress from luxury to "roughing it."

Camping is therefore a rather unusual activity, something to be curious about. This curiosity makes "getting away from it all" almost impossible. The farther you go from cities and tourist areas, the more interesting you become to the local people. Your arrival in a remote area will not go unnoticed—the inhabitable areas of the country are all inhabited. People—curious, questioning, staring—are everywhere. You're mistaken if you think that all of those interesting natives are just going to stand there like natural formations while you point and take pictures. You'll find, instead, that the interest is mutual. They'll soon be out-staring you and even taking *your* picture.

Unless you camp in trailer parks and organized campgrounds, your camping trip will turn into a "people" trip. There are ways, fortunately, to increase your privacy without hiding inside a tent or camping on the edge of an active volcano.

Children are the worst intruders. To avoid them, camp a long way from the nearest village or ranch. This certainly won't eliminate their visiting, but it will keep the smaller and less adventurous away. Large kids are notoriously difficult to avoid and if they have to walk five hot, dusty miles to see you (which they will do), they'll probably make a day of it.

Avoid camping near trails, usually the major travel routes for local people.

Don't camp near obviously popular swimming holes. Half-used bars of soap, discarded scrubbers and picnic garbage near an inviting pool of water are sure indications that weekends and evenings will find it full of people.

After you've chosen a campsite, you can expect visitors within hours. On the coast and in the lower mountain areas, people are generally more open with strangers than the Indians of the high mountains.

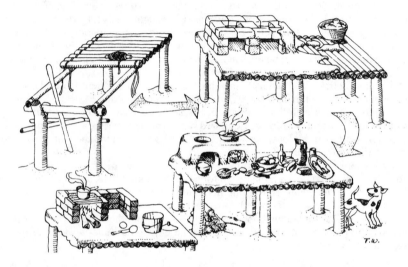

You can expect your visitors to stare. Silent staring can be unnerving (to say the least), especially if you're alone or don't speak Spanish. Paranoia may have you packing up and heading to a city if you don't understand—and try to accept—the reasons for this mute intrusion.

Natural curiosity is obviously part of the reason that people want to stare at you. You look funny. Your clothes are strange. Your car and all of your possessions are wonderful to look at and you talk and act like no normal person in the village. Curiosity itself isn't difficult to understand, but the open staring, pointing and excited talking over everything you unpack or do can be infuriating, and for some, quite frightening.

Why do they do it? How can they be so blatant and unembarrassed? The answer is that they have no feeling of "each man's house being his castle" and no concept of being rude or impolite merely because they are observing what you are doing in your house, i.e., car or tent.

You will probably notice that this open curiosity doesn't normally reach the point where visitors will walk uninvited into your camp or actually handle your things. When you want someone to "come in" you'll usually have to invite them (women are especially shy). It's as if invisible boundaries mark off the area of your camp from the general community.

This attitude can best be understood by visiting one of your curious visitor's homes. Communal activity isn't restricted to work in the fields. The same people who sat twenty feet from your car for hours on end will crowd around the house you're visiting, hanging on every word of conversation between you and your hosts.

You'll inevitably have people around camp at mealtimes. When the food supply or budget is limited, sharing a meal with ten or fifteen others could lead to a food crisis in your camp. Though we often invite Mexican visitors to eat, they almost always politely refuse or accept only a token bite as a gesture of appreciation. (It's the other tourists who eat you out of house and home.)

I personally find it difficult to eat in front of a staring crowd. Remember, however, that your guests do not feel embarrassed by eating in front of others. This, too, is just another aspect of village life.

Learn to Adapt

Maintaining normal activities (eating, reading, writing, lying around in your underwear) can be difficult with a group of people looking on but it can be done. Present a rather unexciting appearance and don't do anything hilarious or unexpected. Your visitors will eventually drift away or at least relax the intensity of their stares. Keep high-interest items such as radios, tape recorders, cameras, fishing and diving gear and tools out of sight. This will reduce their interest once the visitors have recovered from the initial shock of your presence. If you decide, however, to do a tune-up on the car, you'll undoubtedly have them on the edge of their seats—if not right in the engine compartment with you—for the entire fascinating procedure, no matter how long it may take.

Once you've accepted the fact that there are going to be people around, you can take advantage of their curiosity to satisfy your own curiosity about them. I've found that there's no better way to get into an area than to select some likely looking person and suggest that I'd like to do something: go fishing, hunting, exploring, collect water or gather firewood. The response is almost automatically enthusiastic. This quickly changes the relationship from frustrated curiosity about you to a desire to demonstrate something that they can do, whether it's climb a coco palm or lead you to an interesting ruin.

By doing this, you'll soon have real friends among your guests. Rather than feeling a slight sense of dread at their visits, you'll begin to look forward to them.

We once camped in a very remote spot on the Pacific coast where food was extremely scarce. There were several of us, all big eaters, and the nearest market was three hours away over a barely passable road. We hiked to a few small villages nearby, but there wasn't even an onion for sale. We had just about given up and were reluctantly planning to move on (the area was incredibly beautiful, which made leaving all the more difficult) when, as usual, visitors began wandering into camp.

The first, a surly-looking cowboy with a rifle casually held in one hand, rode his horse to within a few feet of our group and then just sat there, staring at us for several minutes. Our friends thought this was the prelude to a bandit raid.

I finally said, "*Buenas tardes,*" and wandered over near him. He answered my greeting with a curt word or two and offered me a large bundle wrapped in a spotless white cloth. I hesitated, but he thrust it at me insistently and muttered, "Open it."

Inside was a large pile of homemade tortillas, a few eggs, onions and a couple of rather limp tomatoes. Before I could ask if it was a gift or for sale, the cowboy said, "From my wife," and rode away. His visit was the first of many by him and other local people. Their gifts of food continued steadily for the entire month we were there and, in fact, made it possible for us to stay.

Being offered gifts of food is quite common, particularly when you're camped in an area where the local people themselves don't have very much. Their sense of sharing can be very touching. If there is any doubt in your mind whether something offered is for sale or a gift quietly ask, "*¿Cuánto le debo?*" ("What do I owe you?") or just say questioningly "*¿Regalo?*" ("Gift?"). You'll almost always get a response indicating that it is a gift. We always accept whatever is offered to avoid offending anyone. When you are given a piece of odorous fried fish, a few half-rotten bananas or some other unappetizing little treasure, accept and then carefully tuck it away somewhere, as if you're reserving it for a tasty midnight snack.

When you wish to give someone a gift in return, remember that it really is the idea that counts, not the value or quantity of what you're offering. A very poor Mexican friend came to our camp almost daily for several weeks, always bringing some type of food: tortillas, fruit, a few vegetables or an especially huge fresh fish caught just for us. Since previous offers of money had seemed to offend him, I would give him an orange, a fishhook or some equally small present in return. His thanks, made with great emotion and sincerity ("God will pay you, friend," was his favorite), would have been quite sufficient if I'd given him a gift worth hundreds of dollars.

Where to Camp

Camping in Mexico is easier after you accept the fact that almost anyplace can be a campsite, if only for a short time. Here are some common choices:

• **Wide spots:** It's the end of a hot day and you have mild diarrhea. You haven't eaten enough and would like to cook a good dinner, but you've fought off hunger with a few hits of cheap tequila. Suddenly you feel the crushing hand of exhaustion descending on your mind and body. Your companions are getting grumpy because they spotted a good place to stop forty miles back but you casually said, "I feel like I could drive all night."

The smartest and most logical thing to do under these circumstances is to find a wide spot—any place wide enough to get safely off the highway—and to forget about plugging along until something better shows up. It probably never would anyway, so you might as well stop before you're totally done in.

Use common sense when choosing a wide spot. The busier a highway is, the better the odds that some passing jerk may decide to check you out. For obvious reasons of safety, try to park out of sight. In general, we feel safer camped on a side road or in the boondocks than close to busy highways and cities. Use wide spots as temporary rest stops, not for regular camping.

• **Side roads:** These all lead to that mythical Perfect Camping Spot, or at least they would seem to. Of the hundreds of side roads that we've followed, most led to sand traps, mud holes, ranches and towns. Unlike secondary roads in the U.S., which seem to go everywhere—and nowhere in particular—Mexican side roads almost without exception lead to a group of houses or a village. If you park your car so that it blocks the road, even though you'll swear it's a long-abandoned trail, you can almost count on being blasted out of bed by someone leaning impatiently on the horn of a bus or truck.

• **Schoolyards and soccer fields:** You may be driven by desperation to stop near a town or village. The edge of a schoolyard has the advantages of being reasonably level and away from noisy *cantinas* and drunks. The big disadvantage, however, is that schoolyards, playfields and soccer fields are frequented by packs of children and there are very few bushes to squat behind. Don't park in front of the goalposts of a soccer field or you might block (as we did) an early morning game.

• **Dumps:** I personally prefer dumps over most other desperation campsites. Unlike dumps in the U.S., full of rotting food and rats, Mexican dumps are usually dry and relatively pest-free. This is undoubtedly because few Mexicans throw away food. Dumps are usually just flat areas close to the road and easily spotted by swirling heaps of plastic bags. Not AAA approved but very convenient.

• **Gas stations:** You can try this but it doesn't always work: buy some gas and then ask the attendant if you can park behind the station for the night. Noisy, bright and smelly but better than nothing.

• **Cemeteries:** Don't drive right into the cemetery, but don't make yourself conspicuous by attempting to hide. Park openly near an entrance and you won't arouse suspicions of grave robbery. I enjoy an early morning tour of the graves and have never met with any resentment or hostility from caretakers or visitors. Cemeteries are quiet, peaceful places with very few curious children hanging around, especially after dark.

• **Police stations:** Some people seem to think the police (being public "servants") should know of good camping places, so they make a point of going to the station to ask where they can park. The usual answers seem to be 1. a motel, 2. a parking lot or 3. nowhere, get out of town. But there is a sneaky way to avoid actually going to the station while still enjoying its protection. (I don't recommend this if you look very freaky.) Find the police station and then park on the street, just around the corner. The logic to this is that criminals and drunks won't be lurking so close to the cops. I prefer the cemetery or a good dump.

• **Streets:** When you have to park on a city street, do it very near the plaza in a small town or on a side street in the business district of a larger town or city. If anyone asks what you're doing, give them a simple honest answer: sleeping (*durmiendo*). If the police roust you, the offer of a modest "donation" to their Benevolent Fund can work wonders.

• **Bridges:** At one or both ends of many bridges, you should see the remains of a road leading to an older bridge or ferry landing. These roads are often quite indistinct, particularly at night. They are good camping places, especially as many lead right to the water's edge.

• **Quarries and dirt pits:** Found along many highways, especially if they are new or recently repaired. Be very careful when driving into one of these places; some are soft, others have huge pits and trenches that you could easily plunge into at night. If it has been raining, send someone ahead to check the firmness of the ground. But don't forget that a human foot may not make a dent where a heavy car would sink.

Friends of ours almost lost their van when the wife walked ahead into an old excavation, on what looked and felt like wet grass. It turned out to be a bog, covered with a very thick layer of floating weeds. It took a passing team of oxen and a large gang of *campesinos* to save the van from sinking.

• **The desert:** Many unfortunate travelers reach the desperation point and say, "Hell, let's just pull off into the desert!" And there they remain, stuck in sand or dust, until help comes along.

The desert is occasionally made of gravel, but more often of something softer. In winter, when rain is extremely rare, the ground dries out to be quite hard in some spots—and quite soft and dusty in others. During the rainy season it may be surprisingly soft, even after a light sprinkle.

Always check the ground directly in line with where you're moving the vehicle before leaving the road. Once off the road, don't get carried away and race a quarter of a mile onto the desert just because the ground is solid; it may suddenly change to a sand trap.

Among the worst hazards of off-the-road driving in the desert are cactus spines and thorns. They are all over the ground and will play hell with your tires.

• **Motels:** Many tourists prefer to camp on the grounds of a motel rather than at dumps or under bridges. Some motels offer various conveniences for campers, just as trailer parks do. The price should be much cheaper than actually taking a room.

• **Trailer parks:** Common on the tourist circuits but few and far between elsewhere. If you prefer to camp in trailer parks, try to learn their exact location ahead of time. Tourist literature (both from the U.S. and Mexican tourism offices) may help, but the most reliable method is to ask other travelers. Some trailer parks are that in name only and have no real facilities; others have everything from hot water to neatly trimmed lawns. Many trailer parks charge an unhealthy rate, but they're still cheaper than a motel room if you need a night of "civilization."

• **National parks:** Camping facilities within parks, reserves and national monuments are very rare. Most are closed at night and camping is not allowed. If you are told that you can't camp, it is occasionally possible to make a "special arrangement." This means you pay the guard or caretaker and agree to leave early in the morning.

• ***Balnearios*:** Spas may include camping facilities of some kind or if not, they'll usually be open to the suggestion. *Balnearios* have bathrooms and showers, picnic tables, and best of all, swimming pools—often with thermal water. *Balnearios* are found all over Mexico and especially in the central region.

Is It Safe?

Camping in Mexico is very safe but it can, and very probably will, make you slightly nervous until you've become acquainted with the country and with new night sounds and activities. You don't expect a burro train of firewood to pass by at 3 a.m., so when it does it'll probably startle you. It's not easy to be completely relaxed when you don't fully understand what everyone else is doing and why.

Once you get over your initial nervousness, you'll find that the people of rural Mexico are basically very honest, hardworking, proud and willing to give visitors more than a fair chance to prove themselves worthy of trust and friendship. Among this nation of Scout-like folks, however, there are the inevitable drunks, petty thieves and miscellaneous scoundrels who can so easily give an entire area a bad name.

Paul Theroux wrote, "travel writing is a funny thing . . . the worst trips make the best reading." What better way to get someone's attention, either in a book or sitting around the living room swapping tales, than with some awful horror story?

The popular gringo image of a mustachioed *bandido* brandishing a rifle in one hand and a smoking pistol in the other, however, went out with silent movies and the decline of the narrow-gauge steam locomotive. Today, the word *bandido* means "thief, criminal, perverse person." Forget the picturesque wide-brimmed hat and crossed *bandoliers* of ammunition, they're as rare as war-painted Indians firing arrows into a circle of motor homes in Yellowstone.

Take reasonable precautions while you are camped and chances are you'll never have a problem. Be especially careful, however, while in the larger cities. (Ironically, we've heard of more campers being robbed on their way to Mexico than south of the border. Professional rip-off artists in the U.S. know that a loaded motor home or van makes a fat target.)

Most rip-offs take place on the beach (or in cities) and are often the direct result of a camper's own laziness and lack of even normal vigilance. It is very common to see excited campers fling their valuables to the sand and run into the surf, only to return ten minutes later to find they've been robbed. Let's face it, the temptation is incredible when a thief or poor person is presented with a golden opportunity to snag a camera or a wallet. If you must leave things, ask someone (in a store, restaurant or another camper) to keep an eye on your stuff.

Backpackers should keep their gear neatly stowed at all times. We like to keep our things out of sight as much as possible, without being obviously paranoid. "Don't touch that!" is no way to deal with a curious visitor. Rural people are very open about handling your things, though they'll often make polite hints before looking at something. Sleeping bags, stoves, lanterns, tools, and kitchen gear interest them a great deal. Oblige their curiosity but don't leave valuables lying around carelessly lest you tempt someone beyond reason.

A friend had the wits scared out of him on his first night in Mexico. He parked his van on the edge of a recently harvested cornfield, well away from the nearest highway. He woke in the middle of the night to the sound of gunshots and shouts, some quite close. Before he could gather his wits and flee, a very excited *campesino* farmer appeared, yelling something about rabbits. Once our friend had regained his composure, he realized the farmer only wanted to know if he'd be interested in buying a freshly killed *conejo* (rabbit). He'd camped in a popular hunting area.

There are many strange things, at least strange to the complete newcomer to Mexico, that can turn a perfectly normal day into a bad experience. Learn to accept the unknown gracefully. Don't be scared off by your own imagination; once your fears have been explained you'll be glad you didn't overreact.

Camping alone in Mexico is a lot easier for men than for women. I wish it weren't true, but machismo can ruin camping for single women and even for groups of women. The relentless attention of Mexican men can be unnerving, irritating and potentially dangerous.

Where to Be Careful

Steve says, "In nearly forty years I have never had a major problem while camping in Mexico. That's more than I can say for other aspects of my life! Rather than fret, take common-sense precautions to relax your mind and minimize risk. Here are a couple of guidelines our family always follow."

• **Don't camp in places where you've heard that there have been problems.** Some beaches have a reputation for petty rip-offs of property and a few have a reputation for occasional armed stickups. Keep your ears open, talk to other campers and pay heed to what you hear. The rumors often aren't entirely true or are wildly exaggerated, or the problem may have been ten years ago, but it pays to listen and act prudently.

• **There really is strength in numbers.** When in doubt, you will probably feel safer camping with others. Again, talk to local people and other campers and see what it feels like before you set up camp.

Michoacán and Guerrero Coast: Avoid lonely coastal stretches in the states of Guerrero and Michoacán. This is an active region for *narcos* and *traficantes* (dope growers and dealers). Several people have reported wild, unpleasant adventures while camping there.

Dope-growing areas: Sinaloa is widely known as the drug capital of Mexico. Avoid camping in this infamous dope-growing area, especially along Highway 15 between Los Mochis and Mazatlán and Highway 40 between Mazatlán and Durango.

When heading into remote areas, ask for advice. Tourist information offices, cops, schoolteachers, truck drivers and others will gladly warn you if there is the potential for trouble. Conflicts between drug smugglers and the authorities rarely involve tourists, but it pays to be cautious.

Where *Not* to Camp

Note: The following suggestions about places *not to camp* are included to help you sleep better and not because they involve any real threat to your safety. If you camp in one of these places, as we often have, you will be quite secure.

Hills: Because of the incredible number of large trucks and buses on the highways at night, most without mufflers, a hill is a lousy place to get any sleep. We once camped in a place even worse than a hill—a tiny valley between two hills. The little valley, so peaceful in the early afternoon, was just one-eighth of a mile long and represented over twenty shift points for the trucks and buses, which passed at the rate of one every thirty seconds. Each shift brought forth a great diesel blast and awful rasping of gears.

Markets: If you find yourself forced to camp in town, don't park near the market, even if it appears to be deserted and quiet. In the very early morning all of the trucks that kept the people camped on hills awake will roar into town and head for the market place. If the sound doesn't ruin your sleep, exhaust fumes will.

Archaeological sites: These used to be favored campsites but because of looting and vandalism, very few archaeological sites are now open to camping. In fact, most sites close at 5 p.m. and you run the risk of being arrested if you are caught on the grounds after closing.

One of our most unsettling experiences took place while camped on a lonely beach on the Gulf of Mexico. We were sleeping in the sand around the remnants of a campfire when we all simultaneously awoke at the sound of approaching hoofbeats. As they grew louder, we raised ourselves from our beds and waited apprehensively for the attack.

Suddenly we were surrounded by several armed men on horseback, silhouetted dramatically against the moonlit sky. Rifles were slung casually over their saddles. They seemed barely able to keep their prancing horses from trampling us.

Steve called out shakily, "*¡Buenas noches!*" but there was no reply. After a minute or two of blood-chilling scrutiny, one of them grunted and they road away, yelling and whooping into the night. Badly shaken, we stoked the fire and spent a restless night wondering what else might happen.

The next morning the horsemen reappeared and with a great commotion of yells and laughter gave us a large fish. They were sorry, they said, to have disturbed our sleep the night before, but they'd spotted our camp while returning from a hunting trip and wanted to see if we were OK. They had been worried that the tide would wash us away.

Exploring

When you're looking for a place to camp for more than one night, and eventually even the hardest-traveling people do, you'll want something better than a wide spot in the road or a dump. What's the best method for locating a good campsite? There's only one sure way: *explore*.

Your guidebooks may rave about fabulous diving or sparkling rivers but when you get to the place they've recommended, you might find an ugly hotel or cold rain. Because of extremely variable weather, bug and building conditions, the only way to be sure that a place is good for camping is to go there and look at it yourself.

Don't let others scare you off or delude you. A very common problem when asking people for advice, either old friends or someone you've met on the road, is that few of them can describe a place objectively and accurately. Their well-intentioned advice frequently turns out to be a case of four blind men describing an elephant. I've heard some of the best camping areas in Mexico described as "full of cops," "bug-infested," "absolutely no food or water" or "really nothing much to see there."

Should you meet another traveler who seems reliable, frame your questions about a particular spot around your particular interests. When I ask someone about skin-diving conditions, I ask specific questions: whether or not they have done any diving there themselves, if there are local fishermen (always a good indication of fish being available) and if the water is clear and easily accessible. One person might recall each detail of a reef while another who spent two months in the same place will say vaguely that "the beach was nice" or "the people were friendly."

Once you've found the area you'd like to camp in, the decision of just exactly where comes up. The more people there are in your group the more difficult this final selection can be. With Steve and Lorena along it invariably went something like this, a complicated three-way battle of wits:

"I vote that we stop here," Steve says as we reach the outskirts of a small fishing village. "Doesn't seem to be much point in going on." He adds cleverly, "The road is getting too soft; we may be stuck."

He neglects to add that we've just driven several hours on an identical road and could easily keep traveling if *he* wanted to.

"Don't you think we're just a little close to town?" I ask sarcastically, pointing to several nearby huts. Steve is obviously worried about just four things: stop, eat, drink, meet people.

Each of us is willing to sacrifice the wishes of the others to satisfy our own requirements. The problem becomes one of convincing the others that this would be a Good Thing.

"Let's just keep going for a few more minutes," Lorena says. "We may even come to a river."

She has just played her most powerful card, the mythological River we've pursued for years, where the clothes wash themselves and the water is whatever temperature you wish. We all know this is a pipe dream but we can't resist. I give us another five miles of driving just on this one ploy alone.

"There! There!" I yell enthusiastically, pointing to a group of jagged rock pinnacles outside the surf line. "Good diving!" I am almost in tears at the thought of fish and oysters waiting there patiently for the harvest. Both Steve and Lorena moan their disagreement.

"We're five miles from the nearest food," Steve complains, momentarily forgetting that we are supposed to be living on the fruits of our own labor and ingenuity.

"It's awfully windy here," Lorena says. "Don't you think we ought to look for a spot with some shade?"

I might admit that the barren windswept beach is a bit bleak and sunburnt but the thought of those oyster-covered rocks causes me to stand firm. "What do you want, anyway?" I sneer. "Palm trees? Grass to lie on? A burbling brook?"

"That's it!" she cries. "That's exactly what I want and I'm sure we'll find it if we just go a little bit farther."

Steve and I now groan in unison; this is going to be a tough one.

Mosquitoes, Coconuts and Shade Trees

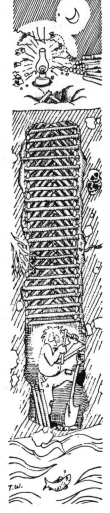

Everyone wants both a beautiful and comfortable campsite. Unfortunately the most comfortable places are not always the most aesthetically pleasing. You may find yourself—and your group—torn between camping in a grove of trees, with lots of shade and places to hang hammocks, or on the beach with beautiful sunsets and the sound of the surf. I advise you to choose in favor of the most comfortable location. You'll find that you will be able to enjoy everything much more: sleeping, the weather, the food and the view. If you have to stake your sleeping bag down to keep from sliding over a cliff, the fabulous sunrises and sunsets will soon begin to pale in comparison to a good night's sleep.

Camping on the beach means camping in sand. Sand can drive you crazy. It will soon be in your hair, food, clothes, crotch, books and toothbrush. In addition to the sand, there's the salt mist from the spray and from the wind blowing over the sea. This mist soon has everything either damp or feeling slightly greasy and salty. Avoid this by camping back from the beach if possible. You'll be amazed at how much easier and more enjoyable your camp life will be.

Camping away from the beach often means, however, that you lose cooling breezes that moderate the temperature and act as a barrier against mosquitoes. Trees and brush are favorite mosquito haunts, even on cool windy days. We've found that some beaches were made unlivable by mosquitoes unless we camped right on the edge of the water. What little wind there was kept the bugs from harassing us.

If mosquitoes bother you, avoiding them is the most important thing you can do for your comfort and peace of mind. This is a good example of finding the proper balance between you and Mother Nature.

A good camping place requires access to food and water. Long hikes for a few tomatoes and a canteen of water tend to get longer and less desirable as the days go by, even though the campsite itself is a perfect Garden of Eden.

Since you're going to save money by living on fresh rather than canned foods, you'll want to be able to buy at least such basic things as eggs, tomatoes, onions, beans, bananas, oranges and cooking oil. If there are no stores nearby, ask local people if they will sell you fruits, vegetables and eggs from their own homes. In isolated areas, it may take you a week or more to establish good contacts. Allow for this by carrying sufficient food and water to carry you through.

No matter where you camp, if you have a car, park with the assumption that it won't start when you decide to leave and that you will need a push. Assume that the battery will be dead, either from too many hours of bedtime reading or too many tapes played on the stereo or that it will just be "one of those things." In many cases, it's best to play it safe by parking near a road and establishing the camp away from the car.

Protection from the sun is very important. If you can't build a sunshade, you'll have to look for some sort of natural protection. Finding a shady spot involves locating a large tree or overhanging cliff. First of all, if you've found an overhanging cliff, examine the possibility that it may quit hanging one day and start falling, either in pieces or all at once. It's better to look for a tree, and on the coast this almost always means a coconut palm.

When I first went to Mexico, I spent a lot of time sleeping and lounging under coconut palms, not considering the obvious danger until a coconut fell one night, narrowly missing my head but knocking some sense into it. On calm nights when there isn't the slightest breeze to disturb them, you'll hear coco palms dropping their heavy nuts. The thudding impact will give you an idea of what they can do to your head or the roof of your car. Fronds that are brown and obviously dead also have the disturbing habit of falling when there's no wind. One missed us by inches on a quiet afternoon, splattering into the middle of our kitchen, destroying our lunch and a great deal of pottery.

Another potentially dangerous tree, the *Manzanillo*, is found on the Pacific coast. It is large, offers excellent shade and bears a distinctive fruit that resembles a small green apple. The fruit and the sap of the *Manzanillo* are poisonous. If you break off one of these "apples" you'll notice a milky white fluid exuding from both the stem and the fruit. This fluid will raise blisters on your skin and on your tongue if you taste it (as I did). This tree occasionally drips its poisonous sap onto the ground. Woe to anyone underneath.

In places where palm huts (*palapas*, *ramadas*) are built for Christmas and Easter, traditional times for Mexicans to visit the beach, you can often just move into an empty one during the off-season and nothing will be said. It is always best to ask someone, however. You may be told to move out or more likely, to pay rent.

Abandoned houses are uncommon, but you may occasionally find one that can be used as a camp. When asking permission to use an old house or hut, it helps to suggest to the owner that you plan to improve it a little. The people that we've asked for permission to live in old houses have been very casual; unless you burn or tear down the building, they usually don't pay any attention to what you do with it.

Camping and Kitchen Gear

Camping in Mexico does not require special equipment. Unless your plans include jungle bashing or serious desert exploration, your gear can probably be found right at home or in any decent outdoor shop or mail order catalog. I do recommend, however, that you test any recently purchased equipment before you leave, not after. One of the advantages of familiar used gear is that you'll already know its limitations and weaknesses and can prepare for them. The tendency to splurge on novelty gear and new stuff just for your "special" trip should be resisted.

Camping equipment (including Coleman stoves) is sold throughout Mexico in sporting goods stores, Sam's Club and WalMart. From what we've seen, however, prices and selection are not very good.

Sleeping bags: An astonishing number of people take Arctic sleeping bags to Mexico. Unless you'll be sleeping directly under the stars in the mountains or in northern Mexico in wintertime, a summer-weight bag is all you'll need. Using a good compressor stuff sack, I can squeeze my ultralight down bag into a very small space.

In warm or hot weather a light blanket, cotton sheet or hostel-style "sleepsack" (rudely known as a "fartsack") will keep the mosquitoes off your chest without roasting you and give sufficient protection from dew and early morning breezes.

If you find that your sheet or bag isn't warm enough, just go to the beach. You'll soon find someone selling their down-filled superbag for a bargain price.

Backpacks: Avoid packs with rigid frames. A frame won't survive being tossed from the top of a bus or out the back of a chili-pepper truck. The bag should be strong, water resistant and not too large. It is an axiom of packing, from knapsacks to motor homes, that every available space will be filled, even if you have to take something totally useless.

Backpacks are made to be carried on your back. They don't fit well into the overhead storage bins on buses and airplanes or in the trunk of a typical small Mexican taxi. Unless you're a serious hiker, a travel bag that also converts to a backpack is the best choice. (I prefer bags made by Eagle Creek.) We also use duffel bags for camping. They are easily lashed to burros and don't take up much space when empty.

A medium-sized day pack carried inside your suitcase will usually be adequate for short hikes. A day pack works well as a shopping bag, lunch and book bag, or extra souvenir storage.

By the way, be sure to take a couple of strong garbage sacks to protect your pack from the grease and oil found in many bus luggage compartments.

Tents: If you're camping with a vehicle, any sturdy "family" tent will probably do, especially for a short trip. Your tent should be easy to erect in sand, able to withstand a brisk wind, well ventilated and bug-proof. With good ventilation and bug screens you'll be able to lie naked on top of your Arctic sleeping bag without being eaten alive.

We like Eureka brand tents for Mexico. They are strong, attractive, easy to assemble and very reasonably priced. I've found that for jungle camping, a tent with a full rain fly and plenty of ventilation is essential.

Sleeping pads: Air mattress, Ensolite pad or self-inflating? The sleeping conditions you'll find on the road in Mexico are varied (and I have slept, literally, on the road). In the end, we've settled on self-inflating mattresses from Therm-a-Rest. Remarkably tough and surprisingly comfortable, this nifty mattress rolls, folds and squashes down into a truly compact bundle. I regularly use my Therm-a-Rest to soften the lumps and hard edges when bunking in cheap hotels or Spartan ranchos.

Cooking kits: If you must have one, get a good kit; cheap ones fall to pieces before your eyes and in the middle of a meal. Teflon-coated cookware does not withstand washing with sand.

Cheap tin, aluminum and plastic plates, cups, utensils and cooking pots are widely available in Mexico and quite adequate.

Stoves and lamps: Unless you're a fruitarian and prepare meals with a paring knife, you'll need a good stove. And while supper is cooking, a lamp will make reading this book and studying your map much easier than by the flickering light of a candle.

Stoves and lamps should be sturdy, easily operated and cleaned, and most important, easy to supply with fuel.

The most practical fuel in Mexico is propane. It can be found almost anywhere and is very inexpensive. Propane is clean burning—essential if you're cooking inside a van and don't want to look like a chimney sweep after every meal. Propane stoves and lamps are easier to maintain than other types and cheaper to repair when they do fail. Standard fittings for American-made equipment are available at most propane stations.

Warning: If you use a stove or lantern inside a vehicle or tent, be sure to provide generous outside ventilation. Don't kill yourself: open a window!

If your present gas stove and lamp use disposable fuel cartridges, buy a hose and conversion fitting to connect them to a regular small propane tank. Throw-away propane cylinders are rare in Mexico.

Mexican white gas is expensive and difficult to locate. (See *Mexico A to Z: Fuels.*) The manufacturer warns against it, but like many campers, we sometimes have to burn Premium unleaded in our stoves and lamps. This gasoline stinks and gives a yellowish, dirty flame, but it does work. (I use a Coleman Peak 1 multi-fuel stove.) Premium gasoline is very hard on the generator, however, so carry one or more spare generators (this is a vital stove/lamp part). Generators are easy to sell to other campers if you don't need them yourself.

Kerosene is very cheap in Mexico (and almost all of Latin America), but *petroleo* isn't always easy to locate. Kerosene stoves and lamps sold in Mexico are not designed for travelers' hard use and constant knocks. Parts for Aladdin lamps are not available. Alcohol is probably a better choice; it is sold in every drugstore and isn't as messy as kerosene.

A Traveling Kitchen

Our nomadic way of life requires us to carry most of what we need for easy, enjoyable living. Whether we're traveling by van, bus or hitchhiking, we prefer to do as much of our own cooking as possible. This saves money, increases our independence, cuts down on indigestion and gives us a more stable diet.

Cooking isn't as easy on the road as it is at home. Eating well while traveling is very important and your cooking equipment should be selected with great care. By assembling your kitchen long in advance, you'll be sure to have utensils that you know and understand. You should like your cooking equipment and it should cooperate and fit together.

Be aware that the following list reflects our own style of cooking and traveling, and our personal eccentricities, from Lorena's fairly strict vegetarianism to my love for all things edible. We prepare for everything from renting a house for six months to camping on the beach. When outfitting your own traveling kitchen, use this rule of thumb: *when in doubt, don't take it.* If you find that you've left something vital behind, virtually everything on this list can be found in Mexico.

Bring from home:

plates	food mill
bowls	whisk
cups	small funnel
forks	measuring spoons
spoons	measuring cup
table knives	small strainer
pressure cooker	combination-type can-opener
large skillet or Dutch oven	cutting board
small skillet	pot holders
large kettle	coffee pot
medium saucepans (two)	tea bob
butcher knife	vacuum bottle
paring knife	old towels
spatula	cup hooks
unbreakable juice container	liquid soap
assorted unbreakable food containers with lids	dishpan or bucket
unbreakable egg containers	fire grate
scouring pads	folding barbecue grill
aluminum foil	blender
wax paper	electric fry pan
Baggies	toaster
paper plates	electric mixer
potato peeler	extension cord
grater	plastic water jugs

Buy in Mexico:

bean and potato masher	fire fan
orange juice squeezer	shopping bag
lime squeezer	baskets (for food storage)
casserole dish	unglazed bean pot
salad bowl	*comal*
wooden spoons and stirring paddles	tortilla press
mortar and pestle (for grinding bulk spices and making sauces)	

Discussion

Pressure cooker: A pressure cooker saves time and fuel. Consider how you'd feel about cooking brown rice (forty-five minutes) after ten hours of driving. A pressure cooker will do it in a fraction of that time. Beef stew takes just fifteen minutes and even Mexican beef will come out tender.

Food mill: A food mill turns those wonderful fresh fruits and Mexican vegetables into juices, stews, soups, purees and sauces.

Juice container: Buying fresh juices *para llevar* (to go) is quite common. A wide-mouth vacuum jar or plastic container is easiest to fill and clean.

Egg containers: Eggs are sold loose or in flimsy plastic bags. You'll probably follow our example and crack two eggs per dozen before they're used. The nifty collapsible wire egg baskets sold in Mexico aren't suitable for rough roads and casual handling, so buy unbreakable plastic cartons before you leave.

Aluminum foil, paper plates, etc.: These are things that you should learn to do without by the time they're used up, but are nice to have until they're gone. A large package of cheap paper plates (not plastic!) is equal to a mountain of regular dirty plates and quite a bit of dishwater. Available in Mexico, but you might as well have a stock on hand.

Old towels: People love to give away old towels and they have a multitude of uses, from washing the windshield to blowing your nose.

Cup hooks: For hanging things from posts and beams, especially while camped in sand, and for houses and huts not equipped with shelves.

Liquid soap: Easier to handle than powdered soap and gives better results in salt water. Biodegradable liquid soaps are sold in health-food stores, outdoor equipment shops and some supermarkets in the U.S. Steve notes that he still hasn't found high quality liquid soap in Mexico.

Dishpan or bucket: For washing dishes, clothes, yourself, the car; boiling lobsters; mixing adobe; etc. An aluminum bucket is very light and can be used to cook in. Galvanized buckets leach dangerous substances and should not be used for food.

Fire grate: The type with folding legs almost makes cooking over an open fire easy. Longer grates are best; a short one is awkward over a large fire.

Folding barbecue grill: Essential for grilling fish and meat over open fires. Available in Mexico, but the heavier, long-handled types sold in the U.S. are worth the extra money. To clean the grill after use, scorch off any excess fat and then beat it against a tree or car bumper.

Blender, fry pan, electric mixer, etc.: If you camp in trailer parks or want to rent a house, a few lightweight electric appliances are very handy. They also make wonderful gifts or trade goods. Take a good extension cord along.

Juice squeezer: Although juice squeezers can sometimes be found in junk stores in the U.S., they are much more common in Mexico.

Comal: These round, flat, pottery or metal pans are used for cooking tortillas. The metal type makes a good griddle for campfire cooking—fish, hotcakes, toast, etc. A *comal* is also handy for roasting chilies and tomatoes before peeling, and for reheating tortillas.

Food from Home

What do you do when you're preparing your favorite dish, *Hin Nu Hwe*, in the middle of the highlands of Chiapas and there is not a spot of anchovy paste to be found? If special foods and condiments are an irreplaceable part of your diet, the answer is that you'd better have a good supply from home.

Although we've located almost all the items below during our travels in Mexico, none were common and many were very expensive. (See *Markets and Stores* and *Our Favorite Mexican Recipes* for more ideas.) Natural food stores (*tienda naturista*) are found in most Mexican cities of any size. Although not as well stocked as their counterparts in the U.S., you should find brown rice, vitamins and many common natural food items. Home-baked whole wheat bread, honey, cookies, granola and fresh yogurt are usually available.

Dried baking yeast	Live yeast is sold by some *panaderías* (bakeries) and health-food stores in larger cities.
Brewer's yeast	Available in some drugstores and health-food stores but expensive and not very tasty.
Brown rice	You can easily sell or give away any extra you might have to people who didn't read this.
Dried fruit	Most are imported from California and expensive.
Herbs	Special herbs, such as goldenseal and ginseng, are available only in a few places, if at all.

Mung beans, alfalfa	Mung beans are seldom available and Mexican alfalfa seeds are almost always chemically treated for planting and should not be eaten. Lentils can be sprouted and they are common.
Pet food	Steve says, "Good dog food costs like sin. Try WalMart, Sam's Club or other big discount stores."
Toasted sesame oil	Not available, though regular *aceite de ajonjolí* is common and good.
Sourdough starter	Not available. Mexicans prefer sweet bread but may be pleasantly amazed by sourdough.
Soy sauce	Available but of mediocre quality.
Spices	Bottled spices are expensive in Mexico but you can refill your containers there with inexpensive fresh bulk spices as you find them. Bring ginger root if you use it.
Teas	Good, "proper" black tea and Chinese green teas are rare. Herb teas are sold everywhere.
Vitamins	Not available at discount prices but otherwise easy to locate. One of the few pharmaceutical products that is not considerably cheaper than in the U.S.

Odds and Ends

After hauling unbelievable amounts of junk and nonessential weight to and from Mexico and Central America, we offer these sincere words of advice: don't take anything that you aren't willing to give away, lose, sell cheap, carry in and out of Customs, explain the function of innumerable times, and pack and unpack continually.

If you're now thinking to yourself "Well, hell! *Nothing* I have can pass that test!" you are on your way to traveling light.

In the fall of 1969, as we began the slow trip from Seattle to the Mexican border, we frequently heard comments like the following whenever we stopped for gas or to visit friends.

"Moving out, huh?"

"What have you got in there, anyway?"

"Going homesteading?"

"Hey, you got a low tire."

After looks of amazement when they heard that we were headed for Mexico, there would be an inevitable, "Do you think you'll make it?"

When one wise gas station attendant asked, "Do you really need all of that stuff?" I immediately leaped to our defense, pointing out to him that in order to have a truly excellent trip it was necessary to anticipate *everything*.

"That's what the boat is for," I elaborated. "We decided we couldn't really enjoy diving and fishing without a boat."

"Well, what's that other crap?" he asked. "Don't all look like a boat to me."

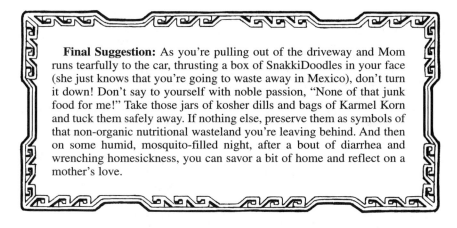

Final Suggestion: As you're pulling out of the driveway and Mom runs tearfully to the car, thrusting a box of SnakkiDoodles in your face (she just knows that you're going to waste away in Mexico), don't turn it down! Don't say to yourself with noble passion, "None of that junk food for me!" Take those jars of kosher dills and bags of Karmel Korn and tuck them safely away. If nothing else, preserve them as symbols of that non-organic nutritional wasteland you're leaving behind. And then on some humid, mosquito-filled night, after a bout of diarrhea and wrenching homesickness, you can savor a bit of home and reflect on a mother's love.

I surveyed the top of our VW van, swathed in tarps and crisscrossed with a profusion of rope, bulging three feet over the roof rack.

"No, of course not," I agreed. "That lump there," and I pointed to a corner of old rug showing beneath a tarp, "is the outboard motor."

"Outboard! What do you need a motor for?"

"The boat we have is inflatable," I explained patiently. "But we decided that with all this diving gear plus our weight, too, we'd need a motor to move it." I went on to explain that after buying the motor, we realized we'd need even more fishing and diving equipment to take full advantage of the boat. "So that bump," I indicated, "is the spearguns and fishing-pole package and that sea bag is full of diving gear."

He looked at the huge mound in disbelief. "What are those boxes?"

"Oh, yeah!" I coughed to cover a slight embarrassment. "The grey one has the extra food and the yellow case is full of spices. Those green things are stoves."

"Stoves?" he asked, barely concealing a growing sneer of amusement.

"Well, you see," I began lamely, "Steve felt that two stoves were necessary. He gets nervous without at least four burners to cook on."

"Oh, of course!" he agreed. "I can really see his point!" and with a final "Good luck!" he hurried back to pumping gas.

I stood by the car as Steve checked the tires for the hundredth time, wondering if we really were going to make it. I hadn't had time to point out the rest of the essentials we were going to be so glad we brought: "Let's see, there's still the tent, two gas cans, tackle boxes, water jugs and extra clothes on the roof." I peered into the back window: "Books (about 175), paint set, jewelry-making kit, air mattresses, typewriter, two gasoline lamps, more food and clothes, blankets, two turkeys (cooked, courtesy of Lorena's mother). . . ." I gave up and decided to cut down on weight by fixing a turkey sandwich.

Everything, except one stove, 150 books and the typewriter—profitably traded for a large Mayan drum—returned with us to Seattle several months later. The engine in the van, however, suffered a fatal stroke and remained in Mexico.

We now keep our odds and ends to a closely supervised minimum. We miss some of it, but we don't miss the hassles involved with overloading.

If you are the fortunate person whose imagination can leap ahead to the havoc and chaos that may result from unrestrained and indiscriminate gathering of junk, you'll be able to use the following list properly: as a list of *possible things to select from*, not as a blanket suggestion to take it all. Think ahead carefully to what you intend to do on your trip. If you want to skin-dive, take only the basic equipment; chances are you'll find much to divert you from your original plans. *Don't let your trip be planned by your possessions.*

boat
bicycle or motorbike
diving gear
fishing equipment
art supplies
photographic film (take plenty,
    if you use an unusual type)
whisk broom
*wash basin
    first aid kit (see *Staying Healthy*)
Sun Shower or water can with sprinkler
    head (for shower, see *A To Z Bathing*.)
hammer
nails
crowbar
hand drill and bits
*sharpening stone
*rope
light tarp
electrical wire

Elmer's glue
Liquid Wrench
rust-preventive oil (WD-40)
knapsack
canteen
maps
*mirror
saws (hand saw, firewood saw,
    hacksaw)
hatchet
chisel
folding shovel
*machete
*twine
baling wire
solder, flux
propane torch
epoxy glue
electrical tape
assorted nuts, bolts, screws

*Items marked with an asterisk are easily found in Mexico. Most of the things on this list can be bought in Mexico, but in general they're cheaper or easier to find in the U.S.

Discussion

Diving and fishing gear: Mexican sporting goods stores now have fishing, camping and diving gear.

Many tourists sell their diving gear for one reason or another. Hotels where younger travelers hang out are good places to find bargains.

Scuba gear can be rented in tourist towns and the same shops will offer diving tours. I've never taken a tour, but I've looked at their gear and it seemed to be of good quality. Dive tour and rental shops will be the only consistent sources for air.

Mexican fishing equipment runs heavily to the basic hook, line and sinker, with perhaps an oversized swivel and a feather jig for the real aficionado. Rods and reels are expensive. Lures are sold but almost entirely for heavy gear and big fish. A wire leader kit is good to have, especially if you prefer braided wire over single strand, the Mexican standard.

Hammer, saws, folding shovel, machete, etc.: These tools will not only be invaluable for camp construction projects but also useful for repairing your car, digging it out of sand and mires, setting up a tent, hanging hammocks, cutting firewood and making adobe.

Regular hand saws are best for building things, but a folding woodcutting saw is handy for firewood. Hacksaws are indispensable for jury-rigged repairs on cars and lawn furniture.

A sharp, three-sided file is a valuable tool for repairs and sharpening knives and machetes.

Electrical wire, solder, propane torch, tape, anti-rust oil, glue, etc.: With these miscellaneous items you can, and will very likely have to, perform miracles of improvisation and repair. They will be invaluable for lashing your car back together if it tends to loosen up on poor roads. (See *Driving: Preparing Your Car.*)

People in isolated areas believe that gringos can fix anything. You can often help them out by providing basic tools and parts that few of them can afford. In one day I was asked to repair a watch, solder two radios and analyze a couple of strange rocks. The watch and rocks were beyond me, but I fixed the radios by heating a nail with a propane torch and using it as a soldering iron. The solder was scraped from the seam of a milk can.

In payment for this simple job, we were given coconuts, tortillas, a sack of tomatoes and a large fish. We were also treated to several hours of blaring static-filled rock and roll music by the pleased owners of the radios.

A propane torch (non-refillable cylinder type) will last a long time if used sparingly. Rust-preventive oil is very important for lubricating metal that has been exposed to salt water and salt spray.

Whisk broom: For cleaning the car before crossing borders or between your toes before going to bed.

Mirror: Combing your hair or shaving in the rear-view mirror of your car can be a drag. Get a small mirror that will hang on a nail. If you don't have a close friend along, you may also need a mirror to check your rear end for ticks. Don't laugh . . .

Camping Skills

One of the most enjoyable aspects of camping is the opportunity to play games normally restricted to children: building crude shelters, digging in the sand, fishing and beachcombing, lashing sticks together and so on. For me and many others, camping in Mexico is a childhood dream come true.

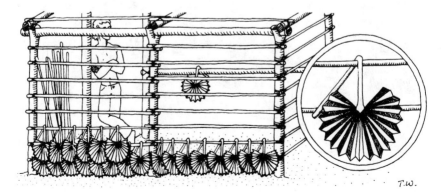

Palmetto leaf hut

Building a *palapa*

Building a Thatched Hut

A *palapa* (hut, also *ramada*, *choza* or *jacal*) is basically a shelter made of sticks and palm fronds (also called *palapas*). They are very common on all the coasts of Mexico. Although many *palapas* are torn down when not in use to prevent the theft or natural loss of the poles, you may find one already built.

Building a hut that will be waterproof and long-lasting is not simple. A *palapa* of your own construction will be adequate as a sun and wind shelter, but if you're hoping to live in it for several months, it's quite easy and inexpensive to have a really good one built for you. A good hut-builder can finish a small one in four or five days. In most cases the only tool he'll use will be his machete—even for digging the holes—and all of the materials will be gathered in the surrounding coconut groves or jungle.

If you are building the *palapa* yourself, you should determine its size; spectators and their endless suggestions are to be ignored completely. When they become persistent, go swimming until the heat changes their attitudes.

Begin by finding four sturdy poles about eight feet long and forked on one end. (You'll probably have to buy or beachcomb these materials. Never cut trees, fronds or firewood in Mexico without permission.) Shorter poles can be used but eight feet will give about a six-foot headroom inside. Dig four holes, two or more feet deep, and place the poles. If sand keeps filling the holes, use water to moisten and firm it up as you dig. The easiest shape to use for a *palapa* is a square. It is even easier if the distance between the poles is the length of your palm fronds. It takes a lot of fronds to cover both roof and walls so keep the size within reason. *Petates*, mats, can also be used if fronds are scarce.

When the corner posts are in place, find at least four more poles for the roof rafters. These do not have to be forked, but they must be sturdy enough to support the weight of the frond roof; usually considerable. Place the four rafters between the upright corner posts and lash them together. Additional rafters spanning the roof area will be a substantial help in supporting fronds that are small or broken.

A tin can oven

Next, locate some coconut palm fronds. **Warning!** If you are building a hut from fallen fronds or from materials scrounged from another hut, watch for snakes and scorpions! They like to sit in piles of fronds, leaves and coconut husks and will often be in the walls and roofs of old huts. Move heaps of fallen fronds with a stick and don't thrust your hands or feet into these piles. Never carry an old frond or piece of dry firewood on top of your head. A scorpion may pop out and nail you on the nose. When cutting fresh fronds, check first to see if there might be a snake resting his weary bones on top.

The worst hassle of gathering fronds isn't scorpions or snakes, but ticks. Check yourself carefully, including your clothing, after rooting around in the coconut groves or bushes. (See *Staying Healthy: Bites and Stings*.)

Dry rather than green fronds are best for building as they are lighter and much easier to split. Don't try to split them from the large end. Slip the blade of a machete into the thin end and use it to keep the split even and to avoid breaking the frond off short.

Begin roofing by laying the half-fronds (whole ones aren't as neat or efficient) at a 90-degree angle to the roof rafters, overlapping them as closely as you can afford to. The center rib of the frond should be up. In this way each rib acts as a weight for the leaves of the frond beneath it, preventing your *palapa* from looking like a wild head of hair. Alternate large and small ends of the fronds to keep the weight evenly distributed. It is not necessary to lash the fronds down as you do the roofing. However, it's best to determine the direction of the prevailing wind (if there is one) and to begin roofing at the side away from the wind. When it blows hard, the resistance will be less and the weight of the fronds alone should keep them from blowing away.

During the rainy season, sheets of thin plastic (*plástico*), available in the market and hardware stores, laid under the roof and behind the walls (preferably before placing the fronds) will give reasonably good protection from water.

To make walls, just lash frond halves between the corner posts, starting at the ground. Your *palapa* will look very neat and trim if you overlap the fronds with the loose leafy side facing inward. This works fine for three of the walls, but if you'd like a fourth to be covered too, you'll have to allow for a doorway.

A doorway and window can be made by adding just two more poles to the framework. This can be done after finishing the roof and three walls.

Plant another upright pole (it doesn't have to be forked but should at least be lashed to the roof rafter) about two-and-a-half feet from either corner post. This is the doorway. The remaining wall space can be completely covered with fronds or a long window can be left in the wall by lashing another pole, horizontally, between the door post and the other corner post. (If this crossbar is about waist-high, it can also be used as the main support for a table or counter, inside and outside the *palapa*.) Lash fronds beneath the crossbar from the ground up.

Sharpening a Machete

The usual temptation for the tourist is to buy the biggest, heaviest, nastiest-looking blade he can find. This is a real mistake; those without long experience of handling a machete often injure themselves seriously with these wicked knives. Unusually long machetes and those with unique shapes are designed for specific uses—cutting sugar cane, husking coconuts, clearing brush and so on. The tourist who buys one of these special-use machetes is greatly increasing his chances for an unfortunate accident. For general camp use—cutting poles, firewood, opening coconuts—the most practical type of machete is short with a broad blade, and not *razor*-sharp. Machetes, especially long ones, have the nasty habit of ricocheting when you least expect it. A very sharp blade is not essential for the occasional use it will be put to while camping.

New machetes are as dull as butter knives. By far the easiest way to sharpen them is to have it done by a metal shop or wandering knife sharpener. He can put a good edge on it in just a few minutes.

To do it yourself, you will need a file.

Brace the machete against something solid with the edge of the blade toward you. Holding the file at a low angle to the blade, run it in long even strokes from the handle to the tip. Do this three or four times and then turn the machete over. Now repeat the same number of strokes, running the file from the tip toward the handle. You should always be filing toward the blade, a slightly risky motion but necessary for a good clean edge. By keeping the strokes even in pressure and number on each side, you'll avoid a lopsided or wavy edge.

Once you've got the edge to the point where it might just cut something, you are ready for the sharpening stone. I use a regular machete stone, the type sold in every market and hardware store. (See illustration.)

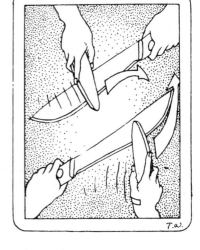

Pour a shot of cooking oil or water on the stone and drip the excess onto the blade. Smear it around on both. Hold the machete as you did while filing and repeat the same motions with the stone. Always keep the stone at a very low angle to the blade. The machete will be sharp when your arms are too tired to lift.

Work the machete over with the stone every time you use it and it will never degenerate to the point where it must be refiled. When the blade gets black from oxidation, slice a lime in half and rub it vigorously over the metal. Before the juice dries, wipe it off with a rag.

Hanging a Hammock

The procedure for properly hanging a hammock is simple, but even a simple mistake will destroy the entire purpose—to have a comfortable bed.

The method used to attach the ropes to the ends of the hammock is important. Special S-shaped iron hooks are available, but if you don't have them, use a short piece of wood (see illustration). The ropes can be tied directly to the hammock ends, but the knots soon become too tight to untie and may chafe through the end of the hammock after long use.

The hammock should be tied so that it hangs symmetrically; that is, both ends should be the same distance from the ground and tied with equal lengths of rope. The middle of the hammock should be lower than the ends, but not so low that your chin touches your knees when you lie in it. The worst mistake is to hang a hammock too low. It takes only a few scrapes against the ground to weaken or break the strings, even on a new hammock.

Once the hammock is hanging properly, you shouldn't pile in and lie any old way you want. There is a proper position for the body. Lie at a thirty- to forty-five-degree angle to the long axis of the hammock. This prevents the hammock from sagging and stretching and gives your body the type of support needed for comfortable sleeping. Don't let your friends violate this rule, either, or you'll soon find that your hammock will stretch and won't be as comfortable as it should be.

Sleeping in a hammock, particularly outdoors, is wonderful. Lie with a blanket underneath you, especially if there's a breeze. Mosquitoes enjoy a rear attack, but a blanket will stop them.

Getting into the hammock and keeping covered up with a blanket at the same time can be a real trick. First of all, put a blanket cape-like over your back, allowing enough length so that your feet will be covered when you get in. Clutching another

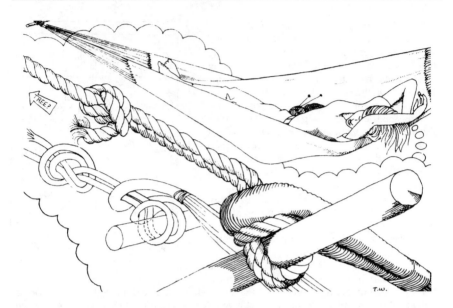

blanket to your chest like a parachute, back slowly into the hammock until it's safe to fall backwards. If you haven't opened the hammock far enough you will do a neat back flip—to the great delight of anyone nearby. Once inside, form the blankets into a cocoon. If another person is getting in, the procedure is the same except that the second person just drops in next to the first without being wrapped in a blanket.

Before doubling or coupling in a hammock, check it to insure that the ropes and whatever it's tied to will take the strain. If you're in a crude *palapa* (at least one built from my instructions) this is especially important. The posts, if not properly placed, will be pulled together by your weight and could knock you silly.

PACKING UP

Clothing • Travel-light packing suggestions • The hidden pocket • Health information and insurance • Useful travel accessories • Odds and ends, gift and trade goods

Watching friends prepare for a trip can be more enjoyable than traveling itself. It usually goes like this: "Hey, look at this nifty little heating coil; it's not that expensive!"

"What's it for?"

"Heating coffee and tea in hotel rooms. Neat! I think I'll get one!"

"Do you have a cup?"

"No, but here's one over here. Oh yeah, I better buy some tea bags. And some instant coffee."

"How about hot chocolate?"

"Good idea!"

"And bouillon cubes for quick soups?"

"Definitely!"

"You'll need a spoon, won't you?"

"Of course. In fact, I'd better get two. Never know when I'll be having company."

"Then you'll need another cup. And how about bowls?"

"Glad you thought of it! Maybe some of that instant pudding . . . dried milk and granola . . . a bit of honey . . ."

This type of chain-reaction planning and buying not only destroys your budget, but leads to suitcases and backpacks weighing in at the twisted hernia range. For those traveling with a vehicle the temptation to take one more thing is especially great: how many cars and vans have you seen on the highway that looked like refugees from the collapse of the American Dream, loaded to the top and then some with "just the essentials"?

When preparing for your trip to Mexico, keep in mind that you aren't going there as a colonist but as a temporary visitor. Your interests and the length of your trip certainly influence what you'll need, but in general it won't require more than you'd take to visit the next state or to go camping in Yosemite.

Clothing

Your clothes should be practical. When you drool mango juice over your white pants, you'll wish they were a darker, camouflaging color. Flimsy clothing will fall to pieces if washed on rocks very often.

Unless you're going to live high on the hog in Mexico's resorts, you won't need to dress up. As in many warmer countries, it is considered proper to wear light, casual clothing. The *guayabera* shirt from Yucatán is suitable in place of a sport coat or jacket. Mexican politicians always seem to wear them, along with highly reflective sunglasses.

You'll be correctly dressed almost all the time if your clothes are neat, clean and relatively conservative. Unusual, innovative or bizarre clothing should be left at home if you are sensitive about stares. Pants on women are now common, but bare shoulders and skirts above the knee still draw attention in small towns and Indian villages. Women travelers get by just fine with pants and a casual dress or two. Shorts are inappropriate for men or women anywhere but at the beach.

Weather is an important consideration. (See *Traveling in Mexico: Geography and Climate*.) Nights will be cold at higher altitudes and in northern areas during the winter. A jacket or sweater and warm footwear are desirable. Sandals will do at the beach, but you'll also want shoes with good traction for slippery cobblestones. A long-sleeved shirt will not only keep you warm when necessary, but also protect your arms from sunburn and mosquito bites.

Travel-Light Packing Suggestions

Suggested Packing List for Women and Men

❑ Strong, comfortable running or walking shoes, with non-skid soles
❑ Several pairs of socks—we prefer cotton
❑ Two pairs of pants (denim is too heavy)
❑ Women: dress or skirt (easily washed and packed)
❑ Two shirts or blouses (long- or short-sleeved but modest)
❑ Sweater, lightweight
❑ Jacket (lightweight) or windbreaker
❑ Rain jacket or compact umbrella (rainy season)
❑ T-shirt or two (widely available in Mexico, if needed)
❑ Sleepwear (long T-shirt)
❑ Lounging outfit (I use light sweatpants)
❑ Shorts (for the beach only)
❑ Swimsuit (be aware that in Mexico a thong still attracts throngs)
❑ Day pack, small and lightweight
❑ Munchies, tea bags or special condiments you can't live without
❑ Zip-Loc bags (several sizes)
❑ Flashlight, small (a must)
❑ Small keychain-style compass (very helpful with a guidebook)
❑ Notebook, pen, map
❑ Sun protection—hat, sunglasses, sun-block ointment
❑ Suntan (a few ten- to fifteen-minute pre-trip tanning parlor sessions help prevent sunburns)
❑ Mini travel alarm
❑ Camera and film
❑ Hidden pocket (see following section) or money belt

❑ Traveler's checks, ATM card
❑ Glasses or contacts (bring prescription)
❑ Small towel and/or beach towel
❑ Soap, bath and laundry (small bars or refillable container)
❑ Stretch clothesline
❑ Small sewing kit
❑ Medicines, vitamins and supplements in original bottles or with prescriptions
❑ Pictures of your home, family, countryside or postcards or picture books

Optional
❑ Comfortable sandals or shower shoes
❑ Inexpensive penknife
❑ Earplugs (if Mexico's noisy streets might disturb your sleep)
❑ Blockbuster novel, small travel game
❑ Walkman (with headphones, favorite cassette)
❑ Surge protector (if you use electrical devices)

Do not bring: Jewelry, large sums of cash, fancy knives. (Steve says he's lost several knives over the years at police and Army highway checkpoints.)

Mexicans carry an umbrella or large square of thin plastic in their pockets for afternoon showers during the rainy season. It is very compact, cheap and has a variety of uses.

If you need resort wear and can't find it in Minnesota, you can have clothing made to order (*hecha a la medida*) or buy it ready-made in Mexico. Handmade clothes aren't wash-and-wear, although many types are presentable without ironing. Some garments (an all-cotton Oaxaca shirt, for example) might be a dense ball of wrinkles after washing. Most inexpensive handmade clothing also shrinks considerably, so buy large. Speaking of large—if you're wide and/or tall, it will be difficult to impossible to buy ready-made clothing and shoes. Steve often buys underwear, socks and the like in Mexican department stores or even in supermarkets. He says that Levis made in Mexico appear to be the same as those purchased in the U.S. but they cost less. The only problem is finding clothing as ample as he is.

Used clothing from the U.S. can be found in many markets. Some of it still has price tags and stickers from the Goodwill and Salvation Army. If you're lucky you may find a bargain from an exclusive shop or designer.

When a piece of clothing becomes too worn, too dirty or just too much hassle, give it away or hang it on a bush. Someone will find it and certainly use it.

Mexican shoe sizes seem to stop at about size nine. Custom-made sandals cost less than factory-made ones of equal quality. A friend says that children's shoes are an excellent bargain in Mexico. Shoe sizes are the length of the foot in centimeters.

Hat sizes are the circumference of the head in centimeters.

The Hidden Pocket

"Hey, has anyone seen my (traveler's checks, tourist card, passport, driver's license or other important paper)?" is a question all too frequently heard while traveling. The slight note of anxiety in the person's voice quickly turns to panic when everyone nearby casually answers, "Nope!" Nothing quite matches the gut-numbing feeling that comes from being unexpectedly penniless, without a shred of identification and thousands of miles from home.

The steps that some people take to avoid this unpleasant situation are seldom more

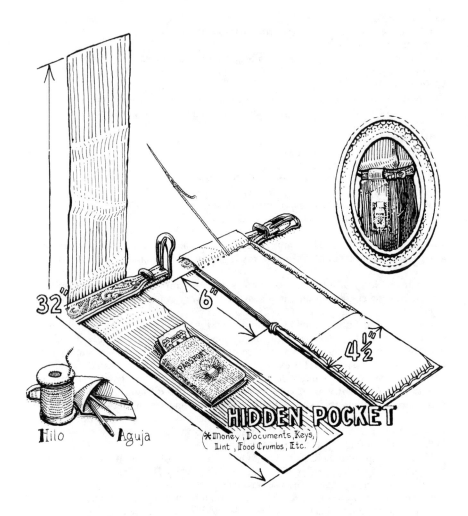

32"

6"

4½"

Hilo   Aguja

HIDDEN POCKET

*Money, Documents, Keys, Lint, Food Crumbs, Etc.

secure than an ordinary wallet or purse: pouches that hang around the neck (these bang against your chest and chafe until the string breaks), secret compartments in luggage (not much good if the suitcase is misplaced) and so forth.

Our solution to this problem was inspired by Papillon, a French convict-turned-writer. He wrote that prisoners on Devil's Island hid jewels and large bank notes in small stainless-steel cylinders. These cylinders, called "chargers," were hidden inside a person's . . . well, it's enough to say that it was very difficult to detect and to separate a man from.

The hidden pocket (see illustration), is much easier to use (and more comfortable) than a charger, far safer than a pouch or wallet, and more convenient than money belts or hidden compartments. It will easily hold a passport, traveler's checks and even small lumpy objects, if necessary. The greatest advantage, other than security, is that once you begin using the pocket, you soon lose that nagging background fear of being separated from your valuables. At night it's a simple matter to take the pocket to bed with you. Never leave it with your clothing when sleeping, showering or sunbathing; that's the first place a thief will look.

A belt, cord or stout string inserted through the top "loop" of the pocket allows it to be worn hanging from the waist, though placed inside your pants, shorts or skirt. In a very short time the pocket and its contents will mold against your hip and be almost indistinguishable from the natural curve of your body and clothing. Variations are also possible: with elastic straps at top and bottom, the pocket can be worn on your leg like a knife sheath; pins or sewn-on ties will attach it to the inside of a shirt or dress. The important thing is that it be usable on all of your clothing. This not only saves the hassle of making permanent hidden pockets in every pair of pants or skirt, but increases your awareness of where your valuables are at every minute. You should be as aware of your money and documents as you are of car keys and eyeglasses.

If you're carrying more money, papers or valuables than one pocket will conveniently hold, another pocket can be worn on the other side.

In the many years we've used the pocket we've never lost anything from them (knock on wood). Once you've become accustomed to it, you'll probably find that a wallet isn't necessary at all. I always carry whatever cash I need for immediate use in a buttoned shirt pocket and spare change in my pants pocket.

Sewing instructions: The pocket should be made of a durable but lightweight material. Plain dark colors will be the least noticeable on your belt. It is important to have something safe, sturdy and inconspicuous rather than fancily made.

The material can be cut in a long strip, 6 inches by 32 inches or in a rectangle 12 inches by 16 inches.

If you start with the 32-inch strip, first fold it double to 6 inches by 16 inches. Leave 2 inches at the top for the belt loop. Now sew down one side, across the bottom and back up for about 6 inches. The remaining gap is for inserting your passport and money. Leave an opening large enough to easily insert and remove valuables but not so large that they might work their way out.

If you want to have the stitching hidden on the inside, turn the pocket inside out; now sew another seam 2 inches below the top to form the belt loop.

If your fabric is squarish (12 inches by 16 inches), fold it in half to 6 inches by 16 inches. Now sew across the top and bottom and 6 inches up one side. Turn it inside out and sew the belt loop seam 2 inches below the top. Slice the fabric at the closed end of the belt loop.

Remember: The pocket goes inside your clothing, not outside.

Ready-made money belts large enough to hold a passport are sold by outdoor and specialty shops and AAA offices. An excellent, inexpensive version is available by mail from Europe Through the Back Door, P.O. Box C-2009, Edmonds, WA 98020, tel: 425-771-8303; fax: 425-771-0833; website: <http://www.ricksteves.com>.

Health Information and Insurance

Should you be involved in a serious accident or illness while traveling, a few simple preparations will make medical treatment quicker and more effective. A very brief medical record can be compiled on half a sheet of paper and kept with your passport or identification. *Be sure that it is legible.* Emergency information can also be engraved on bracelets and medallions. These are available from drugstores, jewelry shops and MedicAlert Foundation, a nonprofit organization at 2323 Colorado Avenue, Turlock, CA 95382; tel: 800-825-3785, fax: 209-669-2495; <www.medicalert.org>.

Your medical emergency information should include any allergies or hypersensitivities and the names of all medications you are currently using; your blood type; chronic ailments; immunization history; eyeglasses prescription; type of health insurance and policy number; the name, address and phone number of your physician (arrange to have collect calls accepted in your name in case of emergency); your social security number, religion and dietary restrictions.

If you have health insurance, check with your agent to see if coverage includes Mexico. Most policies do, though you may have to pay any bills and present receipts after returning home to recover the money. Medicare *does not* cover you outside of the U.S.

Useful Travel Accessories

Camera and film	Day pack and/or belt pouch
Shortwave radio	Inflatable pillow
Earplugs	Hot water bottle
Reading light	Mini mess kit

Discussion

Camera and film: Unless you're a hard-core photo-snapper, don't buy an expensive camera just for your trip. Many people think that a fancy 35 mm camera is as essential as a bathing suit or sunglasses and though they may use it only rarely, they've still got to have one around their neck. An albatross would be cheaper.

There are far too many good cameras available to discuss specific models here, but if a simple record of your trip is what you want, keep your camera simple. Leave light meters, filters, lenses, tripods and other paraphernalia for the professional or avid amateur. You'll save in initial cost, upkeep (such as the replacement or repair when you drop it in the Gulf of Mexico) and ease of operation.

Lorena's all-time favorite is a compact, Olympus point-and-shoot. The camera is always in her fanny pack, inconspicuous and comfortably close at hand.

If you carry a full-featured 35 mm camera, protect the lens with a UV (ultraviolet) or skylight filter. Polarizing and glare filters are very handy for beaches, bright water and clouds. Carry lens paper and a camel's hair brush.

Standard print film is widely available in Mexico at reasonable prices, but slide film can be difficult to find. You can legally take twelve rolls of film to Mexico, but they'll rarely object if you have more, especially if you remove the original wrapper.

If you use a Polaroid, I'd bring sufficient film from home, though you may find it in resorts and major cities. Quick photo processing is now common. Lorena likes to take pictures of people we meet and give the photos to them as presents.

Note: Replace the batteries in your camera and flash with fresh ones before leaving home. The common battery sizes in Mexico are D, C and AA. Small nicad batteries, AAA, and other special camera or video-cam batteries are sold in photo shops, malls and large drugstores.

Change film out of the direct rays of the sun and never leave your camera sitting in the sun for more than a few minutes, especially inside a closed car. Heat will ruin the film and may melt plastic camera parts. When traveling on rough roads, protect the camera from vibration by holding it in your lap or on a cushion of some sort. I wrap mine in a towel.

Shortwave radio: From Carl's journal: "This would almost be like a Sunday at home—windy, rainy and cool—if it weren't for the fact that I'm alone in a small hotel in a Honduran mountain village. I'm also in bed at 3 p.m., bundled up in a jacket and warm pants, listening to shortwave and eating over-ripe bananas. In spite of really enjoying Honduras, I'm also feeling a little homesick. . . ."

Total immersion in a foreign country is fine, but the time usually comes when most of us crave a familiar dose of English-language news, commentary and music. I began using a shortwave (world band) radio on long solo trips into Mexico's Sierra Madre, Central America and other out-of-the-way places where books (and the lights to read them by) were seldom available. Rather than carry a hefty world band guidebook, I surf shortwave as I travel and make notes on the best stations and their schedules. I soon have an excellent list of programs from sources as diverse as Radio Netherlands (in-depth news and great rock and roll), the BBC and CBC, *Voice of America* and the *Christian Science Monitor*. Shortwave is also an excellent way to tune up your Spanish, as many powerful stations broadcast in several languages. Radio stations in larger Mexican cities usually offer at least a couple of hours a day of English-language programming.

At just 3.75 by 6.5 inches, my Sony nine-band radio (model ICF-SW15) is slightly smaller than a paperback novel and fits nicely inside a thick hiking sock. The internal speaker isn't much so I also use a set of cheap, ultralight headphones. I've found that a compact, reel-type antenna from Radio Shack can greatly expand my listening reach.

One of the most important features on my radio is a power button lock. Whenever I absentmindedly pack the radio without locking the power button to "off," the radio inevitably manages to turn itself on. The next time I sit down to enjoy "As It Happens" or the BBC Saturday evening theatre, I discover that my batteries are near death and useless.

A good source for shortwave radios is C. Crane Company, tel: 707-725-9000; fax 707-725-9000; orders only: 800-522-8863, email: ccraneco@aol.com; website: <http://www.ccrane.com>. It offers an excellent catalog of world band and AM/FM radios, antennas and consumer telecom equipment. You'll find good prices, money-back guarantees, and recommendations on "best made" and "best for the money" radios. Check the pocket-sized Sangean 789A ten-band radio for $49.95 and the $10.95 Portable Antenna.

Earplugs: Round-the-clock roosters, bellowing burros and honking buses, church bells pealing and metal doors clanging, fireworks, fiestas, pre-dawn *mariachis* and ear-splitting loudspeakers: let's face it, Mexico is noisy! Rather than grouse or lose sleep, buy good earplugs at a large drugstore. I carry two sets of natural wax earplugs; they are much more comfortable than foam plugs and well worth the extra cost.

Reading light: Regardless of what you pay for a hotel room in Latin America, you'll be darned lucky to get a decent desk lamp or reading light. In at least nine out of ten rooms we've stayed in, the room is lighted by a dim, dusty ceiling bulb or wall fixture somewhere beyond the foot of the bed. Unless you're blessed with the night vision of an owl, reading in bed will be a definite strain.

Battery-powered headlamps make good reading lights, but the ones I've tried often create disturbing reflections in my eyeglasses. I prefer a clip-on style mini book light. If serious reading or studying is in your plan, a compact halogen desk light (with spare bulb) and a twenty-foot lamp cord are very worthwhile.

Day pack and/or belt pouch: The usefulness of these items is obvious; I just want to warn you, however: do not carry your passport, money, tourist card or other valuable papers in your day pack or external pouch. Use a money belt or hidden pocket! One moment of absentmindedness or one brief encounter with a fast thief—and you could find yourself peso-less and panic-stricken.

Inflatable pillow: One of the most useful travel accessories I own is a 12 inch by 15 inch inflatable pillow from Basic Designs. I squeeze the air out of the pillow and carry it as a liner-pad inside my day pack. My pillow has many uses: in planes, buses and dugout canoes, on stone benches at archaeological sites or to cushion the bumps while hitching rides in the back of trucks. Wrapped in a T-shirt or jacket for additional comfort, this pillow often replaces the lumpy cement bags favored by cheap hotels. Though not Coast Guard approved, an inflatable pillow offers some hope as a life preserver in the event of shipwreck or tidal waves.

Hot water bottle: Believe it or not, Mexico and Central America can be quite chilly, especially in winter. If you're as cold-blooded as Lorena, a hot water bottle can bring comfort to the draftiest hotel rooms and the coldest beds. I carry one on winter treks in the northern Sierra Madre. If I don't need my hot water bottle to thaw out my sleeping bag, there's usually someone around with a sore back who begs to borrow it.

Mini mess kit: Yours should include the following.

Insulated cup with lid	Lexan spoon, fork, knife
Plastic bowl with lid	Assorted Zip-Loc bags
Coil-type immersion heate	Coffee/tea "sock"
Water bottle or canteen	Water filter (optional)

Lorena and I enjoy frequent bedside and tailgate picnics while traveling. Preparing simple, do-it-yourself meals not only saves money and time, but if you're like us, you'll eventually tire of overly rich restaurant fare. In the morning, I use the immersion heater (available at travel accessory and department stores) to prepare tea or coffee. Later in the day, we might boil water for soup or prepare instant ramen noodles (both are very common in Mexico and Central America).

A spill-proof plastic container with a locking lid—the type used for leftovers—makes an excellent all-purpose traveling bowl. It can also be used to take out an order of rice or refried beans from a market *fonda* (food stall).

If you're really serious about traveling light, you might want to eat your meals from Zip-Loc bags instead of a bowl. We use Zip-Locs for crackers and tortillas, sliced fruit, vegetables and even tossed salads (a damp piece of paper or cloth inside the bag helps keep the salad fresh). Restaurant salad bars and supermarket delis are great places to assemble a "Zip-Loc lunch" when you're facing a long bus ride.

Tableware made of strong, lightweight Lexan—a fancy, high-tech plastic—is available from the usual camping and outdoor supply sources.

A canteen is virtually indispensable . . . but a leak-proof canteen is virtually impossible to find. Fortunately, purified water is now sold throughout Mexico and Central America in surprisingly durable plastic bottles. Convenient sizes of less than a pint to half-liters, liters and gallons are available. I've carried these bottles on extensive bus and burro trips and have rarely sprung a leak.

Portable water purifiers seem like a good idea until you actually get to Mexico and find out how easy it is to buy bottled purified water. Unless you'll be living for extended periods in remote villages, you probably won't need your own water purification equipment. Considering the weight, bulk and cost of a water purifier, I prefer to buy bottled water and carry a small, backup dropper-bottle of Microdyne, a common Mexican water purification chemical. (For a much more detailed discussion of purified water, see *Mexico A to Z: Water.*)

I admit it; I'm hopelessly addicted to "sock coffee" and "sock tea." To satisfy my habit I boil a cup of water at least twice a day (using an immersion heater), then dunk and steep a tiny tapered cotton "sock" stuffed with freshly ground Oaxaca coffee or a delicious herbal tea. As Thoreau said, "The man is richest whose pleasures are the cheapest." *¡Qué rico!*

Reusable cotton coffee and tea filters are available from the Coffee Sock Company, P.O. Box 10023, Eugene, OR 97440.

Odds and Ends

Playing cards	Volleyball, soccer ball
Checkers set	Picture book, postcards
Frisbee	English instruction book

Playing cards and checkers set: If you enjoy cultivating the friendship of people who might visit your camp or home, a deck of cards or game of checkers is a great way to establish communication. The Mexican checkers game is considerably more difficult than ours, though the board is identical.

Frisbee or soccer ball: When you stop in the middle of some remote village and a huge crowd forms around your car, staring into windows and upsetting the more nervous members of your group, it is time for a diversion. A Frisbee or soccer ball will keep a lot of kids busy who were previously standing on the car hood driving your dog into fits. If you can afford it, bring extra Frisbees or balls to give away; they will be greatly appreciated. Give them to the schoolteacher, priest or village official to avoid jealousy.

Picture book and postcards: A picture answers a thousand questions about your home country. In the same day, two *campesinos* (country people) asked me, "Do the waves look the same in California as they do here?" *Campesinos* love postcards showing prize farm animals.

English instruction book: If you enjoy casual teaching, or if you meet a person who really wants to learn English, an instruction book is good to have.

Gifts and Trade Goods

Blankets	Picture postcards
Toy	Seeds
Tools	Guitar strings
Flashlights	Playing cards
Ballpoint pens	

When someone helps dig your car out of a sand trap or gives you Spanish lessons and refuses payment, it's nice to offer something in return. Many poorer Mexicans still operate on a bartering and trading economy rather than cash. The person who refuses to accept money, either out of pride or generosity, will usually be delighted with a simple gift. (I do not suggest, however, that you play Santa Claus and hand out gifts randomly.)

Blankets, clothing, cosmetics, toys, pens, pencils and paper are always appreciated. We usually stuff a sea bag with this stuff and then give it to someone to distribute for us—a teacher, priest or someone who knows who needs it. Warm clothing and blankets are especially needed by the poor. The poorest children may not have any toys at all. A simple, durable doll or rubber ball will become a treasure.

Hammers, pliers, chisels, screwdrivers, saws, scissors, adjustable wrenches, files and hacksaws make excellent gifts or trade goods for small repair jobs. Most Mexican mechanics gladly exchange labor for tools.

Seeds, both vegetable and flowers, are perfect traveler's gifts; they're light, inexpensive (buy at end of season) and greatly appreciated. Take practical rather than exotic vegetable seeds or the produce may go to waste; rural Mexicans have very traditional eating habits and are reluctant to try new things.

Have you forgotten anything? Be sure to read *Red Tape and the Law.*

MEXICO: A TO Z

AA and 12-Step meetings • Addresses • Banks and money: exchanging money; banks; casa de cambio; money changers; credit cards; debit cards and ATMs; traveler's checks; money hints • Bank and legal holidays • Bathrooms • Bathing: a traveling shower, public baths • Business hours • Consulates and embassies • Electricity • Email • Fuels • Laundry: washing clothes while camping • Post office and mail: letters and packages sent to Mexico, receiving letters in Mexico, packages • Taxes • Telegraph service • Telephones and fax service • Time and zones • Tipping • Tourist information • Vegetables: purifying • Volunteer and aid groups • Water and ice: reasonable precautions, purify it, finding pure water, ice

AA and 12-Step Meetings

The following is adapted from an article written by "Mexico Mike" Nelson in his book *Live Better South of the Border*. Mike maintains an excellent list of Alcoholics Anonymous meetings in Mexico on his web page and in Sanborn's Travelog. In Mike's own words:

"This material on AA is *not* copyrighted and you are free to share it with others. That's the idea, isn't it?

"You'll find AA throughout Mexico, even in small towns. AA is very visible but as in the U.S., meetings move or change. Look for the AA symbol inside a triangle and a circle, usually on a blue background jutting out from buildings.

"There are two different types of AA in Mexico. One is regular AA and the other is *"Grupo de 24 Horas."* These "24 Hour Groups" are more like institutional settings and the message here is of the hard-core, "put the plug in the jug" type.

"Meetings are usually at 8 or 8:30 p.m. in Spanish. Even if you don't speak Spanish, you will be welcome and often asked to speak. Remember, you are always welcome at a Spanish-speaking meeting, even if you don't speak the language. As an AA, you speak a universal language. Go ahead. It will do you good.

"Meetings (*reunión* or *sesión*) last an hour and a half. There are often refreshments and AA birthdays are celebrated, except you might get tamales instead of cake, or both. Have a ball.

"You'll be pleasantly surprised to find English-speaking meetings in most towns with a large gringo presence. Just in case you forgot your International Directory, a list of all the ones I know about, arranged by geographic sections of the country, is on my web page <http://www.Mexicomike.com>. If a meeting is no longer where I said it was, check the nearest English-language newspaper. If not, just find a Spanish meeting and ask. (Your help in getting new information on meetings is appreciated—you know how these groups move around.)

"NA [Narcotics Addicts Anonymous] has a sizable presence in the larger towns. Al-Anon is almost everywhere. OA [Overeaters Anonymous] and other programs are less likely to be encountered outside major cities. You'll also find Al-Anon and NA, though NA is not as "popular." You'll always be welcome at an AA meeting.

"If you have an AA medallion or ring and wear it in Mexico, you'll be surprised at the people you'll meet. Well, that's all the sobriety wisdom I have for now. I hope it helps at least one person. The main thing is to remember that you are not alone in Mexico. You can have a great trip and not lose your program."

Addresses

Thanks to Spanish colonists, most towns are arranged in a logical grid of streets (*calle, calzada, paseo*) and avenues (*avenida*) radiating from the central plaza (also *parque central* or *zócalo*, and less commonly, the *jardín*, garden). Avenues run north-south and streets go east-west. Both may be known by a name or number, so don't be surprised if your map doesn't match local directions. Addresses may include abbreviations: Nte. (*Norte*, north), Sur (South), Ote. (*Oriente*, east), Pte. (*Poniente*, west), esq. (*esquina*, corner), Col. (*Colonia*, colony or neighborhood).

The ground floor of a building—what we call the "first floor"—is the PB (*Planta Baja*). In Mexico, Piso 1 (*primer piso*) is actually the second floor. Try to think of it as the "first floor above the street." In Guatemala, towns are divided into *zonas* (zones). This is important to note as street numbers repeat within each zone.

Banks and Money

Banks, ATMs and private money exchanging shops (*casa de cambio*) are common and easy to locate. Two of the largest banks are *Banamex* (*Banco Nacional de México*) and *Bancomer* (*Banco de Comercio*). To avoid frequent trips to the bank, we use credit cards and an ATM card whenever possible. We also carry "walking around money," both cash and $100-denomination traveler's checks, in a money belt or a hidden pocket (see *Packing Up*).

Exchanging Money
Cashing traveler's checks and exchanging dollars into pesos is usually easy. (By the way, forget about the *mercado negro*; there is no black market.) In addition to banks, you can exchange money at exchange shops (*casa de cambio*), hotels, restaurants and stores. Though rates vary slightly from one bank to another, the bank exchange rate is almost always better than any other. One exception is the attractive rate tourist shops sometimes offer with a purchase to draw in customers. Attention Canadians! You'll find that U.S. currency and traveler's checks are usually the easiest to exchange.

Banks
If you fly into Mexico City, the airport bank is easy to use, nearly always open and often gives the best rate in the entire country. Exchange enough dollars to last for at least a few days. (Don't expect such rates at other airports.)

Normal Mexican banking hours are 9 a.m. to 1:30 or 2:30 p.m., Monday through Friday (and rarely on Saturday morning). Some banks are now extending their hours from 4:30 to 8 p.m. However, the hours for money exchange services are much more limited: usually from 10:30 a.m. (when the day's exchange rate has been established) until noon. Occasionally, a bank will set a limit on how many dollars can be traded for pesos, or they may use up all of their pesos and suspend exchange services for the day. For this reason, try to avoid running out of pesos entirely.

A typical *tipo de cambo* (rate of exchange) notice in a bank looks like this (of course, the figure 10.27 is strictly hypothetical).

> *Tipo de cambio:*   10.27
> *Venta:*   10.905
> *Compra:*   10.27

The *venta* (sell) figure is the number of pesos you must pay to buy one dollar. This figure will interest you only when you leave Mexico and want to exchange your excess pesos for dollars.

The *compra* (buy) figure is the number of pesos the bank offers you for each dollar you exchange. If you exchange $100 at a rate of 10.27 pesos per dollar, you'll get 100 x 10.27 or 1,027 pesos.

Most banks give a slightly better rate of exchange for traveler's checks than for United States currency. It is easy to cash a traveler's check, though you must sometimes wait in one or more lines. A bank officer's initial is usually required; just go up to any employee, show your checks and you'll be directed to the proper desk or window. In some banks you'll be given a slip of paper saying *Caja* (teller) and a number. If not, go to the *Cambios* or *Cheques* window. A slight charge may be made for cashing your check.

Casa de Cambio

A money exchange shop (*casa de cambio*) is a legal and convenient alternative to exchanging money in a bank. Lorena once spent an hour cashing a traveler's check in a major Mexico City bank. A few days later, an identical transaction took five minutes at a *casa de cambio*. You'll get a slightly lower exchange rate at a *casa de cambio*, but the quick service and longer hours are usually worth it.

Money Changers

Freelance money changers (sometimes called *turcos*, Turks) may approach you on the street offering to trade pesos for dollars at surprisingly good rates. In fact, these fast-talking, eager-to-please men work on minuscule commissions, earning a few tenths of a percent off each dollar they exchange. Most are honest, but others aren't above running a "quick change" routine on gullible tourists.

Warning: If the rate they offer is better than the bank rate, pass it up; the offer is simply too good to be true. If you use their services, do your own calculations. Count your money slowly and carefully. Never allow yourself to be hurried, distracted or confused, whether it's in a bank or on the street corner.

Credit Cards, Debit Cards and ATMs

Hotels, restaurants, airlines, shops and supermarkets commonly accept a well-known American *tarjeta de crédito* (credit card) such as Visa, MasterCard or American Express. In fact, renting a car can be difficult to impossible without a credit card as security.

Many large banks give cash advances on major credit cards (and you usually get a better exchange rate than with dollars or traveler's checks). Go to the customer service desk and show your credit card; they'll take it from there. Some banks give advances up to the limit of your line of credit; others set lower limits, such as $200 a day.

A passport is your best ID, but a driver's license and tourist card will also be accepted. You'll have to wait while they verify your card via computer. When the card clears, you'll be given a slip of paper to take to a teller. Advances are paid in pesos.

Major banks now have cash machines that accept credit cards, ATM cards and debit cards. If you "draw" directly from your bank account with the ATM or debit card, you'll save credit card charges and interest, and get the best peso/dollar exchange rate. However, you'll probably pay a bank charge for the withdrawal.

We've found that "plastic" often saves time and gives better value than cash or traveler's checks. For example, if you pay a hotel bill in Mexico today, it won't be charged against your U.S. account for at least a week or two, and sometimes much longer. During this grace period, the peso may devalue against the dollar. When your credit card statement arrives, you'll find that your account was charged at this later rate of exchange, not at the *tipo de cambio* on the day you used the card in Mexico. Some businesses add a surcharge, however, for credit card payments. This is most common, as usual, in fancier hotels and restaurants.

Traveler's Checks

Advertisements may lead you to believe that traveler's checks are as easy to use as real money, when in truth they are not. To minimize difficulties, buy only the most well-known brands of American checks (American Express and Bank of America). We buy a few $20 checks to cash in stores and $100 checks for banks and *casas de cambio*. Forget personal checks; they are virtually impossible to cash or spend in Mexico.

Although banks may give a slightly better rate for traveler's checks than for U.S. cash, other businesses tend to charge a fee to cash a traveler's check. Because of counterfeits, frauds, thefts and lack of confidence, Mexicans sometimes balk at cashing large traveler's checks. Once you get off the beaten track (and you don't have to go very far), cashing traveler's checks is very difficult unless you go to a bank.

Leave a copy of your traveler's check numbers at home and carry another copy with you. If this seems like a bother, which it is, just consider: when lost or stolen, the checks are no better than cash if you can't reclaim them.

After cashing a check, strike its number off your list. If you have to reclaim a lost check you'll want to know exactly which one it was. Reclaiming a check in Mexico can be difficult or even impossible if you: 1. don't know the exact number or have the carbon copy recording the purchase, or 2. are trying to reclaim a check from a company that is not well known. (Even with the check number, this second hang-up may prevent a refund before you return home.)

Though not required for travel to Mexico, a valid passport is without doubt the best identification for any banking transaction. Keep in mind that crooks also take vacations. Mexicans who have been stung by bad credit cards won't accept any ID but a passport. The official look of a passport will often sway a hesitant gas station attendant or store owner in your favor.

If you don't have a passport or can't get one, you'll need a picture ID (a driver's license is best) to use with your tourist card for identification.

Sign the check clearly. Mexicans prefer a signature that has a final flourish, but don't overdo it.

Money Hints

• **Hoard your small bills and change.** Carry plenty of cash in denominations of five, ten and twenty pesos as "walking money" for cabs, tips, meals and small purchases. People often throw their hands up in dismay at the mere sight of a large note. Make a point of breaking larger bills (100, 200 and 500 pesos) in gas stations, restaurants, shops and hotels. For reasons I've never understood, banks are often short on small bills.

• **Carry some U.S. cash, preferably smaller bills** such as fives, tens and twenties. Mexicans are often leery of U.S. fifties and hundreds because of possible counterfeits. American dollar bills are great for tips, but U.S. coins are difficult or even impossible to exchange.

• **Don't carry large sums, especially cash.** Leave your extra cash in the hotel's safe-deposit box. Carry only what you need for one or two days. Reclaim your valuables from the desk during normal working hours, not at 4 a.m. or midnight.

• **Don't put all your pesos in one basket.** I hide a modest sum of emergency money in my luggage and notebook.

• **If the peso devalues** while you're in Mexico, don't get nervous. Banks may close for a few days while they sort things out, but it won't be long before it's "business as usual." The good news is that you'll get a better exchange rate after a devaluation.

• **Deliberate shortchanging is uncommon** (except in busy gas stations), but mistakes do occur. If you are shortchanged, smile and say, "*Falta*" or "*Me falta*" ("I'm short . . ."). Count the money carefully in front of the other person. Don't get angry; it's not worth the blood pressure.

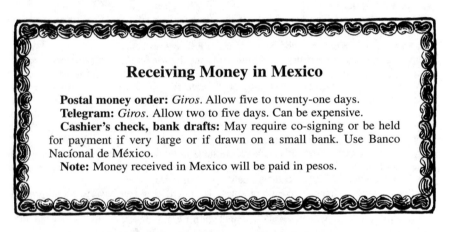

Receiving Money in Mexico

Postal money order: *Giros*. Allow five to twenty-one days.
Telegram: *Giros*. Allow two to five days. Can be expensive.
Cashier's check, bank drafts: May require co-signing or be held for payment if very large or if drawn on a small bank. Use Banco Nacíonal de México.
Note: Money received in Mexico will be paid in pesos.

Bank and Legal Holidays

Be aware that most, but usually not all, private businesses close on major religious holidays.

January 1: New Year's Day
February 5: Constitution Day
March 21: Benito Juárez's Birthday
Good Thursday and Good Friday are official holidays, though many public
    employees skip out for the entire Easter week.
May 1: Labor Day
May 5: Cinco de Mayo
September 1: Presidential address to the nation
September 16: Independence Day
October 12: Día de la Raza
November 20: Revolution Day
December 12: Feast of the Virgin of Guadalupe
December 25: Christmas (many restaurants close)

For more details on major holidays and celebrations, see *¡Viva Mexico!: Celebrations and Fiestas: Holiday Calendar*.

Bathing

Bathing can be difficult while camping. Rivers and lakes never seem to show up at the right moment, especially when you enjoy a good wash before going to bed. One answer to this problem is the portable "Sun Shower," a very strong plastic water bag with a small attached sprayhead. Fill this compact shower bag with water and lay it out in the sun for an hour or two. *¡Caramba!* Before you know it, the water in the Sun Shower is hot (be careful; the Mexican sun can heat your shower to a scalding temperature). Sun Showers come in various sizes—look for one at an outdoor store.

A Traveling Shower

A good imitation of a Sun Shower can be improvised from a cheap plastic water jug. Just remove the cap and insert a large cork fitted with a sprinkler head (the type used for watering flowers). This isn't going to be the kind of shower you loll around in, but it will get you clean.

Fill the jug whenever you stop at a gas station. The water will be surprisingly warm within a few hours when lashed to the roof of your car, stored in the trunk or placed in the sun.

To take a shower, have someone stand on the car roof and slowly spray the water over you. Use the "Navy shower" technique: enough water to get wet, enough soap to get clean and then enough water to rinse.

Public Baths

Baños Públicos can be found near the market place, in some gas stations, trailer parks and dirty factory districts. For a very reasonable charge, you get a long steam bath or both a steam bath and shower. Steam baths are called *Baños de Vapor*. If the sign just says *Regador* or *Baños de Regador*, it's a shower bath. Soap and (very small) towels are extra; you can bring your own if you wish.

Couples can sometimes bathe together, but larger groups cause a scandal.

If you're also looking for a room, many bath houses double as super-cheap hotels. The bed and room may be extremely basic, but you're at least assured of keeping clean.

Bathrooms

To be blunt, the average *baño publico* (public restroom, also *excusado*, *sanitario*, *servicio*) in a busy restaurant, bar or other public place won't pass a white-glove inspection.

• **Don't put paper into the toilet!** Low water pressure and narrow, twisted plumbing are chronic problems in Mexico. As a result, the toilet might well plug up if you discard paper into it. You'll realize your mistake, of course, when it overflows onto your new *huaraches*. As a reminder, most Mexican bathrooms have a basket, bucket or other container close to the stool to discard paper and sanitary napkins.

Breaking a lifetime toilet-training habit isn't easy. Fortunately, the plumbing in most resort hotels will handle toilet paper (only). If there's a basket or other receptacle close at hand, however, it's better to play it safe rather than discard paper into the toilet, especially if you want to keep your sandals dry.

• **Carry toilet tissue.** Supplies of toilet paper (*papel de baño* or *papel sanitario*) are definitely hit-or-miss in public restrooms. If an attendant is on hand, the modest price of admission includes an immodestly small square of flimsy tissue or just a scrap of newsprint. Even tourist businesses don't always succeed in keeping their bathrooms stocked with tissue. Savvy travelers always carry a supply of soft paper (go ahead; use a few pages of this book).

• **Unless you're a customer, private businesses may be reluctant to let you use their bathroom.** Buy a soda or smile desperately and say, "*¡Por favor, es urgente!*" ("Please, it's urgent!").

• **Why don't public toilets have seats?** Answer: toilet seats of flimsy plastic are so easily broken that rather than install one, many facilities provide a bare throne. If there is a seat, be careful, especially if you are large. Poorly made toilet seats can slip and pinch painfully.

Business Hours

Government and public offices are open from 8 a.m. to 3 p.m. (0800 to 1500). Try to be in the office no later than 10 or 11 a.m. or your business may not be completed that day.

Private businesses open between 8:30 and 10 a.m. Most don't close until 7 or 8 p.m., though they will take a two-hour siesta, usually from 1 or 2 p.m. to 3 or 4 p.m. In northern Mexico, many businesses operate on a gringo-like 9-to-5 schedule, but retail shops close later, at 7 or 8 p.m.

Most privately employed Mexicans work a half or even full day on Saturday. Many service-related businesses close for the weekend on Saturday afternoon.

Consulates and Embassies

Canadian Embassy in Mexico City: Schiller 529, Colonia Polanco, México DF, CP 11560, México

American Embassy in Mexico: Paseo de la Reforma 305, Colonia Cuauhtémoc, México DF, CP 06500, México

This information is adapted from lists provided by the National Commission for Democracy in Mexico (website: http://kafka.uvic.ea/~vipirg/SISIS/links/mexcons.html) and the Consul General of Mexico in New York.

Mexican Consulates and Embassy in Canada

Montreal: Consul General Celso Humberto Delgado, 200 Rue Mansfield, Suite 1015, Montreal, P.Q., Canada H3A 2Z7; tel: 514-288-2502; fax: 514-288-8287

Ottawa: Her Excellency Sandra Fuentes-Berain, Ambassador of México, 45 O'Connor Street, Suite 1500, Ottawa, Ontario, Canada K1P 1A4; fax: 613-235-9123; email: nstn0281@fox.nstn.ca; website: <http://www.DocuWeb.ca/Mexico>

Toronto: Consul General Ramon Gonzalez, 199 Bay Street, Suite 4440, Commerce Court West, Toronto, Ont. Canada M5L 1E9; tel: 416-368-2875; fax: 416-368-3478; website: <http://www.quicklink.com/mexico/toronto/consulado.htm>

Vancouver: Consul General Gabriel Rosales Vega, 810-1130 W. Pender St., Vancouver, BC, Canada V6E 4A4; tel: 604-684-3547; fax: 604-684-2485

Mexican Consulates in the U.S.

Arizona: Consul General Roberto Rodriguez, 486 Grand Avenue and Terminal Street, Nogales, AZ 85621; tel: 520-287-2521; fax: 520-287-3175

Consul General Luis Cabrera Cuaron, 1990 W. Camel Back Road, Suite 110, Phoenix, AZ; tel: 612-242-7398; fax: 612-242-2957

Consul General Marco Antonio Garcia Blanco, 553 S. Stone Avenue, Tucson, AZ 85701; tel: 520-822-5595; fax: 520-822-8959

California: Consul General Ecce Iei Mendoza Machado, 331 W. Second Street, Calexico, CA 92231; tel: 619-357-3863; fax: 619-357-6284

Consul General Guillermo Ramos, 830 Van Ness Avenue, Fresno, CA 93721; tel: 209-233-4219; fax: 209-233-5638

Consul General Jose Angel Pescador, 2401 W. 6th Street, Los Angeles, CA 90057; tel: 213-351-6800; fax: 213-389-6864

Consul General Luz Elena Bueno Zirion, Transportation Center, 201 E. 4th Street, Rom 209, Oxnard, CA 93030; tel: 805-484-4684; fax: 805-385-3527

Consul General Carolina Zaragoza 716 J. St., 1010 8th Street, Sacramento, CA 95827; tel: 916-393-0404; fax: 916-363-0625; email: edomcuri@quiknet.com; website: <http://www.quiknet.com/mexico/spanish.html>

Consul General Rosa Curto Perez, 532 North D. Street, San Bernardion, CA 92401; tel: 909-889-9836 or 889-9837; fax: 909-889-8285

Consul General Luis Herrera-Lasso, 1549 India Street, San Diego, CA 92101; tel: 619-231-9741; fax: 619-231-4802

Consul General Cesar Lajud, 870 Market Street, Suite 528, San Francisco, CA 94102; tel: 415-392-6576; fax: 415-392-3233; email: conmxsf@quicklink.com; website: <http://quicklink.com/consulmex-SF>

Consul General Sergio Casanueva, 380 N. First Street, Suite 102, San Jose, CA 95112; tel: 408-294-1954; fax: 408-294-4506

Consul General Ma. Maricela Quijano, 282 N. Broadway Street, Santa Ana, CA 92701; tel: 714-835-3069; fax: 714-835-3472

Colorado: Consul General Carlos Barros, 48 Steele Street, Denver, CO 80206; tel: 303-331-1871; fax: 303-331-0169; email: mexico@vaultbbs.com; website: <http://www.vaultbbs.com/%7EMexico>

Florida: Consul General Luis Ortiz Monasterios Castellanos, 1200 N.W. 78th Avenue, Suite 200, Miami, FL 33126; tel: 305-716-4977; fax: 305-593-2758

Consul General Martin Torres, 823 East Colonial Drive, Orlando, FL 32803; tel: 407-894-0514; fax: 407-895-6140

Georgia: Consul General Teodoro Maus, 3220 Peachtree Road N.E., Atlanta, GA 30305; tel: 404-266-1913; fax: 404-266-2309

Illinois: Consul General Leonardo French, 300 North Michigan Avenue, 2nd Floor, Chicago, IL 60601; tel: 312-855-0056; fax: 312-855-9257

Louisiana: Consul General Agustin Garcia Lopez, World Trade Center Building, 2 Canal Street, Suite 840, New Orleans, LA 70130; tel: 504-522-3698; fax: 504-525-2332

Massachusetts: Consul General Martha Ortiz, 20 Park Plaza, 5th Floor, Suite 506, Boston, MA 02116; tel: 617-426-8782; fax: 617-695-1957

Michigan: Consul General Miguel Angel Reyes, 600 Renaissance Center, Suite 1510, Detroit, MI 48243; tel: 313-567-7709; fax: 313-567-6543

New Mexico: Consul General Carlos Gonzalez, 400 Gold SW, Suite 100, Albuquerque NM 87102; tel: 505-247-2139; 800-926-2898; fax: 505-842-9490

New York: Consul General Jorge Pinto Mazal, 8 East 41st Street, New York, NY 10017; tel: 212-689-0465; fax: 212-545-8197; email: conmxny@quicklink.com; website (Spanish): http://www.quicklink.com/mexico>; website (English): http://www.quicklink.com/mexico/ingles/ing.htm>

Oregon: Consul General Gustavo Maza, 1234 South West Morrison, Portland, OR 97205; tel: 503-274-1442; fax: 503-274-1540

Pennsylvania: Consul General Manuel Lombera Lopez Collada, 111 South Independence Mall East, Bourse Building, Suite 1010, Philadelphia, PA 19106; tel: 215-625-4897; fax: 215-923-7281

Texas: Consul General Robert Gamboa, 200 East 6th Street, Suite 200, Austin, TX 78701; tel: 512-478-9031; fax: 512-478-8008

Consul General Juan Carlos Cue Vega, 724 Elizabeth, Brownsville, TX 78520; tel: 210-542-2051; fax: 210-542-7267

Consul General Armando Beteta, 800 North Shoreline Boulevard, Suite 410N, Corpus Christi, TX 78401; tel: 512-882-3375; fax: 512-882-9324

Consul General Julian Adem Diaz, 8855 Stemmons Freeway, Dallas, TX 75247; tel: 214-630-7341; fax: 214-630-3511

Consul General Mario Najera, 300 East Losoya, Del Rio, TX 78840; tel: 210-775-2352; fax: 210-774-6497

Consul General Javier Aguilar Rangel, 140 Adams Street, Eagle Pass, TX 78852; tel: 210-773-9255; fax: 210-773-9397

Consul General, 910 E. San Antonio Street, El Paso, TX 79901; tel: 915-533-3645; fax: 915-532-7163

Consul General Manuel Perez Cardenas, 3015 Richmond, Suite 100, Houston, TX 77098; tel: 713-524-2300; fax: 713-523-6244

Consul General Luis Humberto Ramirez R., 1612 Farragut Street, Laredo, TX 78040; tel: 210-723-6369; fax: 210-723-1741

Consul General Sr. Ortiz Rosas, 600 South Broadway Avenue, McAllen, TX 78501; tel: 210-686-0243; fax: 210-686-4901

Consul General Ismael Orozco, Jose Luis Suarez, 511 W. Ohio, Suite 121, Midland, TX 79701; tel: 915-687-2334; fax: 915-687-3952

Consul General Carlos Manuel Sada, 127 Navarro Street, San Antonio, TX 78205; tel: 210-227-1085; fax: 210-227-1718

Utah: Consul General Araceli Perez Charles, 458 E. 200 South, Salt Lake City, UT 84111; tel: 801-521-8502 or 521-8503; fax: 801-521-0534

Washington: Consul General Hugo Abel Castro, 2132 Third Avenue, Seattle, WA 98121; tel: 206-441-0552; fax: 206-448-4771

Electricity

Mexico's power is more or less the same as in the U.S. By this, I mean that the 110-volt AC current you expect from a wall outlet may occasionally "sag" to 40 or 50 volts—or spike much higher, frying your travel iron or laptop computer. Brownouts and surges in *la luz* (power, "the light") are common in smaller towns and cheap hotels.

Email

The high cost of international phone calls makes electronic mail a very attractive option for keeping in touch with home. You'll find *correo electrónico* service is available at many telephone *casetas* (see *Telephones and Fax Service*, later in this chapter). If you don't already have email at home, consider opening a free account through Yahoo, Juno or one of the other large, commercial providers on the World Wide Web. (See *For More Information: Cyber Cafes and Traveler's Email Services*.)

Fax Service

See *Telephones and Fax Service*, below.

Fuels

Propane and LPG: Propane stations are located on the outskirts of almost every town. Most are open from morning to night, seven days a week. Look for signs proclaiming *Gas, L.P.*, etc. Propane is simply called *gas*.

Standard refillable LP tanks purchased in the U.S. can be filled in Mexico. Because the weight systems are different, however, it's advisable to convert the capacity of your tank to kilograms before having it filled. Divide the capacity in pounds by 2.2 (pounds per kilogram) or multiply the capacity in gallons by two (two kilos per gallon). Mark this figure prominently on the tank (for example, on a five-gallon cylinder: *Capacidad 10 kg*).

Some attendants accurately calculate capacities but others just guess. If you're filling a small tank, even a minor error can result in a blown valve. When this happened to us we had to replace the valve ourselves since we couldn't prove that it was the attendant's fault.

Gas is available in remote areas, but many small towns do not offer refilling service. However, you can pay a deposit on a large tank, called a *tambor*, use it while you're in the area and then turn it in when you move on. Don't fail to get a receipt (*recibo*) for the deposit or you might be stuck with the tank.

Bottled gas can be delivered to your house or even to your campsite if you make arrangements with the nearest dealer. When signaled, most bulk trucks also stop and fill L.P.G.-powered vehicles on the spot.

White gas (*gasolina blanca*) is never easy to locate and when you do, it is relatively expensive. The best consistent source of *gasolina blanca* is found in the authorized government outlets of the Pemex company, called *Expendio de Pemex*. *Expendios* are little hole-in-the-wall stores found in obscure parts of town. They are usually closed, and when they are open they are usually out of white gas.

Drugstores sometimes stock white gas. They will measure it out, almost drop by drop, into your container. Other occasional sources are hardware stores, *tlapalerías* (paint stores), general stores and tire vulcanizing shops. These are very occasional sources.

In the absence of anything better, you might be tempted to follow our example and use unleaded gasoline as a substitute for white gas. Unleaded gasoline does work in some camp stoves and lanterns but it burns yellow and smelly. Gasoline is also very hard on the stove's generator.

Kerosene (*petroleo*) is cheap but it isn't as easy to find as you might expect. *Petroleo* can usually be purchased in small stores or from government pumps near the market. In areas where the sale of *petroleo* is tightly controlled by the government (for some reason), you must buy it at authorized *Expendios* or under the counter. Kerosene bootlegging might sound silly, but it is a large operation. When you want some and can't find it, you'll really appreciate the little old lady

who has a drum of *petroleo* in her back room. By asking discreetly, "*¿No hay petroleo?*" ("Isn't there any kerosene?") you should eventually locate a source.

Expendios also sell **wicks** for kerosene lamps (*mechas*) and sometimes they have **mantles** for gas lamps. Mantles are called *camisas* ("shirts") or *mechas*. They are inexpensive, so when you find them, buy several extras to give to people who couldn't locate their own.

Charcoal, firewood: One of the most common (and controversial) cooking fuels is *carbón*. *Carbón* is charcoal, unpressed, and still in the shape of twigs and branches. It makes such an excellent fuel that entire forests are converted into charcoal. *Carbón* is sold in and around the market, in small stores or by individuals who make it themselves and pack it into town. When used for barbecuing, *carbón* should not be ignited with gasoline, oil or *petroleo* as they taint the food with obnoxious fumes and soot.

Charcoal briquettes are sold in bags in supermarkets.

Firewood (*leña*) is sold throughout the country. The price varies considerably with the time of year and availability. A burro load is called a *carga*.

Stores that sell *carbón* often sell firewood, either by the piece (*por pedazo*), the handful (*por mano*, two or three sticks) or the burro load (*carga*).

In areas where considerable quantities of wood are used during the winter for fireplaces, *leña* is available in *toneladas* (tons). Never pay in advance or accept firewood before it has been unloaded and you've had a chance to appraise the quality and quantity. Wet hardwoods such as mesquite must be dried for months before they are suitable for burning. Vendors love to unload a ton of green wood, complete with fresh leaves, on unsuspecting gringos.

Always bargain; the price varies, depending on who is selling, who is buying and what type of wood you want. (Don't cut your own; sawing firewood and cutting trees without a permit is illegal.)

Ocote (pitch pine) is sold in the market in small bundles. It is excellent for starting fires and can even be used as sooty candles.

Laundry

Laundromats are common, but *lavanderias* aren't cheap and they are not self-service. Folding of clothes and soap are included in the price, but ironing is optional. Service also varies from while-you-wait to *mañana* or beyond. If you have a train to catch, make certain the attendant understands your schedule. Hotels usually offer laundry service or will direct you to a laundry or washerwoman. Trailer parks may have genuine do-it-yourself machines.

When you have time, it is usually possible to find a woman to handwash your clothes to unprecedented states of cleanliness. As Steve notes, however, intense scrubbing and the lavish use of bleach and harsh detergents also cause faster wear of your clothing. "My underwear comes back from a washerwoman 'whiter than white' but with dead elastic from all the bleach."

Don't hand over your clothes until you establish when you'll get them back. Two days—one to wash and one to dry—is usually more than enough time.

Some women charge a flat rate for a bundle of clothes and others will ask for a "fair payment." In general, however, you'll be charged by the piece. I call this the "Shirt Standard." For example, a shirt, pair of pants or towel counts as *una pieza* (one piece). Underwear counts two for one (*dos por uno*), so twenty-four pairs of panties is equal to a dozen shirts. Socks count four for one (forty-eight per dozen price) and bedsheets go the other way, one for four (three per dozen price). The charge for a dozen pieces will vary, but in general a "load" costs as much or even more as in a laundromat.

You also pay for the soap and bleach. If you're buying it, ask if she prefers powdered soap or bars (*jabón en polvo* or *barra*). She may want some of each, according to the types of clothing she'll be washing.

A mobile washing machine can be made from any large closed container with an opening big enough to stuff clothing through. A plastic trash can with a tight fitting lid, milk can, metal ammunition box or any other reasonably watertight container will do.

The only other thing needed is a vehicle, preferably a car or van; carrying a load of wet clothes on the back of a motorcycle is difficult.

The basic idea is to create washing machine action by the natural bouncing of the car as you drive. If you have a van or bus with a roof rack, the "washing machine" can be lashed above without worrying about suds and water should it leak. In the trunk of a car, the machine should be packed away from anything that might be ruined if the contents are suddenly coughed up on a bad *tope* (speed bump).

Stuff a few items of clothing into the machine (avoid overloading), cover with water and add soap. Secure the container well and forget about it until you stop for the evening. The clothes should be washed reasonably well. You might like to time the rinsing with a stop at a gas station or village communal faucet.

A very crafty way of washing clothes without using your own car is to ask someone camped nearby if they would mind taking your washing machine with them when they make a side trip. They might think it strange but it beats washing by hand.

If you don't have a car, combine dirty clothing, soap and water in tightly sealed garbage bags. (The risks of a puncture are fairly great, so double up the bags.) To heat the water, just leave the bag out in the sun for an hour or two. Slosh and massage the bags from time to time and *voila*! your clothes are (sort of) clean!

Washing Clothes While Camping

Like it or not, we usually have to handwash our own clothes while camping. If nothing else, long hours spent hunched over a wet rock have inspired us to pare down our so-called wardrobes to the very minimum. The technique we use is not the traditional wash done by Mexican women. Instead of rubbing the clothes against themselves, we scrub them with a heavy bristle brush. I've tried the other method, but just can't do it as well as with the brush.

Lay an article of wet clothing on a clean rock, board, tarp or reed mat. A rock works fine, but it may cause minor damage to parts of clothing that are scrubbed against bumps and sharp edges. A tarp or mat is best since it's flatter and larger than most rocks and can be moved about. Sprinkle a little powdered soap or liquid detergent on the clothing, flip a handful of water over the soap and start scrubbing. It doesn't take much soap, but it does require a lot of arm work. This method is tedious but practical. It will encourage you to have fewer clothes and will also keep your fingernails clean.

Post Office and Mail

Locating the post office (*el correo*) in a large town is usually just a matter of touring around the plaza and asking a few questions.

Post office hours are 9 a.m. to 1 p.m. and 3 to 6 p.m. on weekdays and 8 a.m. to 12 noon on Saturdays. If the branch office does a brisk business, it may be open during siesta. (The main office in Mexico City is open until late at night and on weekends.) Package and money order services are generally offered only on weekdays and during peak hours.

In small towns, the post office may be located in the corner of a *tienda* or dry goods store, and its hours are subject to liberal adjustment. Should the store owner get sick or go away on business, the mail will probably be unavailable for a time. In one case, the postmistress in the village where we were living went on a drunk and was fired from her post. Unfortunately, it took more than a week to find a replacement for her. The post office was closed, of course, during that time. As a final stroke of bad luck (at least for us, since we were eagerly awaiting mail), the ex-postmistress hid what mail was on hand in an attempt to regain her job through blackmail. After a week of pleas and threats, the police finally managed to convince her to return the mail.

Postal service varies between remarkably quick and efficient to exasperatingly slow and inept. (In one village we camped near, the postmistress was illiterate; she relied on neighbors to decipher addresses and to complete postal forms.) The length of time it takes for your mail to be delivered to you in Mexico or to arrive in the U.S. from Mexico is directly dependent on two factors: location of the post office in Mexico and the type of postage used. This is also true of mail sent from one place to another within the country. If you are in a large city that has direct air service to the U.S. or Mexico City, you might receive letters from the United States within seven days, but two weeks is more like it. In a small town, don't expect letters to arrive in less than ten to twenty days.

Letters and Packages

Use airmail from Mexico if you want your letter to arrive during your lifetime. Surface mail is all but subterranean. Letters sent to Mexico from the United States should be marked Airmail or *Correo Aereo* or just *Aereo*. Without these words Mexican postal workers won't handle it as airmail.

Stamped, airmail envelopes (*sobres aereos*) and postcards (*tarjetas aereos*) are (sometimes) sold at the post office. If available, airgrams (*aereogramas*) include special handling in the purchase price.

A registered (*registrada*) or certified (*certificada*) letter costs about twice as much as airmail. Be sure to get a *recibo* (receipt). **Note:** The declared value on a registered letter is not covered by insurance. You must pay an additional fee for *seguro* to cover any loss.

Postal money orders (*giros*) are paid in pesos, even when purchased in the U.S. with dollars or other currency.

Sending packages and gifts to Mexico can be more of a burden than a benefit to the person receiving them. Although eyeglasses, medicines, used clothing and books are supposedly allowed in duty-free, don't hold your breath. Books are rarely held for custom charges, but anything else probably will be. Toys are a favorite target for high duty. These charges are arbitrary and often unreasonable.

Note: When mailing to Mexico, always put the postal code (*Codigo Postal*, abbreviated CP) before the city, not after. Because Mexico uses five-digit postal codes—the same as U.S. zip codes—letters to Mexico often get mistakenly sent to the U.S. city with the same zip code. To prevent this, you have to hide the Mexican postal code by putting it between the city and the state (see example below).

Receiving Letters in Mexico

Your probable address will be *Lista de Correos* (General Delivery). *Lista de Correos* is often more convenient and reliable than other methods of receiving mail (American Express, consulates, hotels, etc.) because post offices are located in every town. Using General Delivery is especially valuable when you have no firm schedule or route.

Your complete address will look like this:

Richard Smith
Lista de Correos
Oaxaca, 68000, Oaxaca (city, postal code and state)
Mexico

Tell your family and friends to print your name and address clearly, as the post office people often have trouble deciphering unfamiliar names. When the *Lista* is posted (which should be daily but often isn't) interpret it liberally. I know when I see *MRcarl* on the *Lista* that it's probably for me.

If the *Lista* is not posted, go to the clerk and ask, *"¿Está la lista de hoy?"* ("Is today's list here?"). Should he say *"¡Sí!"* tell him your name (better yet, write it down) and he'll look through the letters.

In the more efficient post offices just note the number next to your name and the date of the *Lista*. Give both to the clerk and he'll give you your mail. He may ask for identification. Don't expect to be able to pick up mail for friends or even relatives. Some obliging types will give you another person's mail if you show both your identification and the identification of the person whose mail you want. Other clerks may ask for a letter of authority, a *carta poder*. Forms are available at the post office for a legal *carta poder* (you must buy special stamps to affix to this form letter). They will often accept a handwritten letter as well. It should say something like: *Administrador, Oficina de Correos* (name of town and state): *Favor de entregar mi correspondencia* (or *cartas*) *a* (name of person picking up mail). *Gracias.* Add your name and the date. The neater and more official it looks, the better.

All mail, including registered letters, telegrams and packages addressed to *Lista de Correos* will be posted on the daily list. Mail sent *Post Restante* will be treated as General Delivery, but not posted on the *Lista*. The addressee will have to inquire for mail. *Post Restante* is convenient for fugitives.

Mail is held for ten to fourteen days when addressed to *Lista de Correos* or *Post Restante* and then returned to the sender if not claimed. Anticipate this when advising people of your address to avoid arriving somewhere after your correspondence has started the return trip.

You can also write "hold for arrival" (*"Favor retener, paga almacenaje"*), but expect to pay a fee for each additional day the mail is held.

Packages are held longer, but there is also a small daily storage fee.

Private mail services are common in larger towns and resident gringo communities. Some of these offer excellent service, but I'd ask around before entrusting a small business with anything of serious value. (DHL and major courier companies are fast and reliable but expensive.)

Unless you can arrange your route and schedule very tightly, you'll eventually have to have mail forwarded from one post office to another. This can be done by filling out a small white change of address card in the post office (*Tarjeta de Cambio de Dirección*). This card can be left at the post office as a forwarding address or sent back to retrieve mail left behind or expected at a previous post office. Address the card to: *Administrador, Oficina de Correos, town, state, Mexico.* Remember that the *delivery time for the card itself* will determine whether or not your mail meets you. Sending it back may take a week or more, and by the time it reaches your previous post office, your mail may have been returned.

The abbreviation for U.S.-bound mail is either EE.UU. or E.U.A., though U.S.A. is also understood.

Packages

The delivery time for packages mailed to and from Mexico varies from quick to legendary. Most people—including us—report that packages sent to the U.S. arrive in about three weeks, but others tell of receiving packages a year after they were airmailed.

Packages can be sent first class (air), second and third class (books, magazines, periodicals) or fifth class. Most people use fifth class to send large packages, up to twenty kilos. The maximum weight for first class is two kilos. Whenever possible, mail packages from larger post offices.

Another choice is MexPost, an express delivery service similar to overnight mail in the U.S. MexPost guarantees delivery to any address in the U.S.A. within seventy-two hours if the post office you send from is within a day's drive of a major Mexican airport.

Because the cost of mailing a package by air can be shocking, have it weighed before telling the clerk that you want postage for it. When he licks the backs of a square foot of stamps and you realize that the contents aren't worth a fraction of their cost, well, too bad. (Special rates for unsealed envelopes and packages are less than regular postage, but I wouldn't risk it.)

Check with the local post office before you wrap up a package. In general, packages must be in a wrapped box, tied with string. If the clerk thinks you should have tape, wire or convenient rope handles on the package too, you'll have to comply. Most offices accept packages in sturdy, well-made baskets with lids if they are securely wired or tied shut. (The basket itself makes an attractive gift.) Large envelopes can often be used for smaller items, especially clothing. You never know, however, so always check in advance.

Shops that sell school supplies and wrapping paper often wrap packages to postal specifications. Tourist shops may offer the same service, either free or for a small charge. Look for signs saying *"Se envuelve paquetes"* ("packages wrapped") or ask, *"¿Puede envolver un paquete por favor?"* ("Can you wrap a package, please?").

Film and magnetic recording tapes should be labeled prominently in English to avoid their being exposed to X-rays at U.S. Customs. Write: FILM! *Please do not X-ray*, and hope for the best. Sometimes they'll X-ray it anyway. If you're worried, large camera shops and airport gift stores in the U.S. sell X-ray proof film bags.

Never send someone at home a package of dope. Many packages are inspected by U.S. Customs and your gift may be followed by narcs.

The Christmas Rush

Mexican postal authorities have devised the most ingenious scheme to cope with mass mailings of Christmas gifts and cards: they go on vacation and don't worry about it. During the Christmas season (December 16 to January 6), Easter Week and the last two weeks of May, don't count on mail service to be anything but reluctant. During a World Soccer Cup, the employees in one post office refused to give service until breaks between televised games.

All packages mailed out of Mexico must have a Customs declaration card attached (available at the post office) listing the contents and their value.

Packages with a value of less than $100 U.S. can be sent duty-free to the U.S. if they are bona fide gifts. Write "Unsolicited Gift Under $100" on the outside of the package.

You can send any number of these unsolicited $100 gifts, but no more than one per day to any one person in the U.S. **Note:** You cannot send a "gift" to yourself or to anyone traveling with you. (The value of mailed gifts does not subtract from your duty-free limit when you return to the U.S.)

Taxes

There is a national value-added sales tax called IVA (pronounced ee-vah) of fifteen percent. IVA is paid by everyone, residents and visitors alike. This tax applies to most items but to take out the sting, it will often be "buried" in the total cost of restaurant bills, store purchases and excursions.

Tax is also added to the price of airline tickets within Mexico for travel commencing in Mexico (ten percent for domestic travel and 2.5 percent for international travel). Prepaid tickets may include these taxes. Ask the airlines for details.

Telegraph Service

The telegraph office is sometimes near the post office, but it may be hidden behind a small *Telégrafos* sign in an obscure part of town. Working hours are similar to the post office, although the telegraph office is sometimes open later.

There are three types of telegrams: *urgente* (urgent), *ordinario* (ordinary, regular) and *carta nocturna* or *carta de noche* (night letter).

An *urgente* telegram will be sent immediately, an *ordinario* the same day and a *nocturna* that day or the next, arriving just a little later than the *ordinario*.

Telegrams sent from one town to another inside Mexico are very cheap.

Service is good and though there are mistakes, especially in the spelling of English words, most errors are minor.

International telegrams can be received at the *Telégrafos* office, the post office, a hotel or a private home. If you want to receive your telegram at the post office, it should be addressed just as a letter: *Lista de Correos*, etc. To receive it at the telegraph office it should be addressed with your name, *Lista de Telégrafos*, city, state and Mexico.

Money can be wired to Mexico in U.S. currency. It will be converted at the current rate of exchange and paid at the telegraph office in pesos. A passport or tourist card is needed for identification when you receive money by wire. This type of telegram is called a *giro*.

Telephones and Fax Service

A private phone is still considered a luxury in most Mexican homes.

Although local calls are quite reasonable, long distance (both international and within Mexico) is very expensive. A sizable tax is added to international calls, nearly doubling their cost. To avoid this tax, make arrangements to have collect calls accepted or use a calling card. Some hotels will place calls for you, but I'd ask about the surcharge first. (Usually steep.)

The day rate is the most expensive rate: from 7 a.m. to 7 p.m., Monday through Saturday and on Sunday, from 5 p.m. until midnight. The cheapest rate, Monday through Saturday, is 11 p.m. to 7 a.m. and on Sunday, from midnight to 7 a.m.

Card phones: Telmex, the national phone company, offers ultramodern "debit card" telephones with Spanish-language viewer screens to prompt the caller about the number

USEFUL PHONE NUMBERS

Direct dialing to the U.S. and Canada is easy but expensive. Rates for calls to the U.S. from Mexico via 95-800 prefixes are the same, regardless of the time of day or day of the week. The following numbers can be used on both private and pay phones.

Lada 09: English-speaking international operator. Collect calls, calling card calls (cards other than AT&T are sometimes difficult to use with the international operator. See 95-800+ below), and calls charged to a third number.

02: Long-distance calls within Mexico, operator assisted (collect, person-to-person, etc.)

91: Station-to-station direct dialing within Mexico. Dial 91 + Mexican area code + number.

92: Person-to-person within Mexico, either direct or collect. There will be a service charge even if the call isn't completed.

95: Station-to-station direct dialing to the U.S. and Canada. Dial 95 + area code + number. For a U.S. operator in the states (when calling collect or using your calling card): 95-800 + (AT&T) 462-4240; (Sprint) 877-8000; (MCI) 674-7000.

96: Direct dialing person-to-person, or person-to-person collect to the U.S. and Canada. Dial 96 + area code + number.

98: Worldwide station-to-station via satellite. Dial 98 + country code + area code + number.

99: International collect and person-to-person.

011-52: To call Mexico from the U.S.: 011-52 + area code + number.

---

dialed and the time remaining on the card as it is being used. The prepaid cards are cleverly sold in nearby stores, in denominations of twenty, fifty and one hundred pesos. Card phones are cheaper than the *caseta de larga distancia* (see below). All services (station-to-station, person-to-person, collect and Mexican third party) are available. Calls to the U.S. typically cost $1 per minute.

Try to avoid those bright blue "Call U.S.A. Collect or Credit Card" telephones. These "coinless bandits" offer convenient, crystal clear connections to a U.S. operator, but their cost is astonishing. Eight dollars per minute for a standard station-to-station call is long-distance robbery. (Thanks to David "El Codo" Eidell for this update.)

Ladatel phones: Pay phones called *Ladatel* accept coins, and they usually (but not always) accept MasterCard or Visa credit cards. *Ladatel* phones are the best way to dial 95-800+ numbers to reach a U.S. operator. (See 95-800+ below.) You can also dial **01 on *Ladatel* to reach AT&T operators.

Credit card and collect calls: For collect and calling card calls, use *Ladatel* or a private phone to direct dial an operator in the U.S. (See box for details.) It's convenient and you'll avoid the Mexican phone tax. A typical call is about $1 a minute from northern Mexico, and $2 a minute from central and southern Mexico. U.S. operators can also connect you to directory assistance for a fee of several dollars.

Long-distance phone offices: Privately operated long-distance phone and fax services—commonly called *casetas*—can be found in restaurants, cafés and bus stations. This is very convenient because such places are often open late at night. While you're waiting for your call, you can guzzle a soda and eat a ham and cheese *torta*. Look for a blue and white sign saying *Servicio de Larga Distancia*. Many hang out a picture of a phone to aid tourists and the illiterate.

Most phone offices, main or branch, can handle a call or fax to the U.S. and Canada with no trouble. However, the person placing the call for you may not have experience with foreign names, addresses or telephone numbers. It is important, therefore, to write out very clearly all the information needed to place the call and to attempt to help should any problems develop. If all else fails, ask to be connected with the *Operador Internacional*, who will speak English and can clear up any confusion.

There are two types of long-distance calls: *A quien contesta* (station-to-station, literally whoever answers) and *persona a persona*. These calls can be made collect (*por cobrar*), paid on the spot (*pago aquí*, "I'll pay here") or with a calling card.

Calling cards are accepted at some phone offices but not at others. Ask them "*¿Acepta tarjeta de crédito?*" If they do, write the card number on the same piece of paper as the phone number and other information. You might not have to show the card itself; it depends on the attitude of the employee in the office and the credibility of your excuse if you don't have the card.

The procedure of placing a call is quite simple. Let's assume that you are calling home for one of the usual reasons (homesick, broke or suddenly got married). The call will be station-to-station and, of course, collect.

Take a piece of paper and write:

> *Por cobrar* (collect)
> *A quien contesta* (station-to-station)
> City
> State
> Country
> Area code and number
> *De* your name (from . . .)

Whether your call is accepted or not, there is often a service charge for making the attempt. This is also true with calling card calls.

Connections to the U.S. are usually made in a reasonable length of time. If the voice at the other end sounds like Donald Duck, tell the operator at your end, "*No puedo oir*" ("I can't hear"). They'll probably try another connection.

Fax Service

To save money, you can't beat a fax (or email). Go to a long-distance *caseta* and ask, "*¿Se puede mandar un fax?*" ("Can one send a fax?"). When receiving a fax in a *caseta*, instruct your correspondent at the other end to write your name in bold letters at the head of the fax: *Atencion* Douglas Havens.

If you're trying to send a fax to Mexico and you keep getting a live Spanish-speaking person, ask for a fax tone: "*¿Puede darme un tono de fax, por favor?*"

I've found that modest tips often improve the attentiveness of the person receiving and sending faxes for me.

Time and Zones

Mexico runs on the **twenty-four-hour clock**, sometimes known in the U.S. as "military time." This is measured from 0001 *horas* (one minute past midnight) to 2400 *horas* (*medianoche*, midnight). Note that this twenty-four-hour clock is used for written time but not for "spoken" time. For example, 7:00 p.m. is written as 1900 but spoken as *siete de la noche* ("seven at night"). In the morning, 0700 hours is spoken as *siete de la mañana*.

A time tip: 1200 hours is noon. After 1200 hours, just add the hour to 1200 and you'll get the correct afternoon or evening time. Example: 1200 + 4:00 = 1600 hours (4 p.m.); 1200 + 10 = 2200 hours (10 p.m.).

Mexico has three **time zones**: Pacific Standard (Baja California Norte); Mountain (Baja Sur, Sonora, Sinaloa), and Central for the rest of the country. Daylight savings time is observed and is called *tiempo de verano* (summer time).

Tipping

The people who serve you in Mexico are lucky if they earn the minimum wage. Salaries simply do not keep up with inflation. We tip fifteen percent in restaurants and at least fifty cents per night for the chambermaid. Fifty cents a bag for porters is reasonable. Though it isn't the custom, we give cabbies ten percent of the fare. Mexicans constantly tell me that *propinas* (tips) from tourists make up the difference between hardship wages and "getting by." As one man told me, "We survive on our wages, but we live on our tips."

Tourist Information

Local, state and federal tourist offices inside Mexico (generally called *oficina de turismo*) vary wildly in quality. The best offer genuinely useful advice and good resources. So few tourism "professionals" are actually travelers themselves, however, that most offices dispense nothing but brochures and a few locally produced maps. Some of this information is useful, but for the real stuff—such as road reports, red-tape updates, hot tips on hotels and other firsthand travel advice—I prefer the Internet's discussion groups and newsletters on Mexican travel. (See *For More Information*.)

Mexican Government Tourist Offices in the U.S. and Canada

New York: 212-755-7261; fax: 212-753-2874
Chicago: 312-565-2778; fax: 312-609-0808

Houston: 713-880-5153; fax: 713-880-8742
Los Angeles: 310-203-8191; fax: 213-203-8316
Coral Gables: 305-443-9160; fax: 305-443-1186
Washington, D.C.: 202-728-1750; fax: 202-659-9881
Toronto, Canada: 2 Bloor Street West, #1801, Toronto, Ont., M4W 3E2, Canada, 416-925-0704; fax: 416-925-6061
Montreal, Canada: 1 Place Ville Marie, #2409, Montreal, QC, H3B 3M9, Canada, 514-871-1052
Tourism Mexico Entry Information Service: Call SECTUR (800-44-MEXICO, 800-446-3942) for the latest red-tape requirements. For additional information use their Fax Me Mexico service at 541-385-9282, and start with their menu index. Website: <http://mexico-travel.com/>

In Mexico: Complaints, Emergencies and Information: We've had mixed results when calling these numbers but they're always worth a try.
Twenty-four-Hour Hotline (based in Mexico City): For emergencies and tourist information in English and Spanish, call 915-250-6217 or 254-1954. Also: 915-250-0123 or 250-0151.
SACTEL: To register complaints about Mexican border officials, call 91-800-00-148.

Vegetables: Purifying

Yodo isn't the name of a witch doctor, but the word for iodine. Ask for *yodo para lavar verduras* (iodine for washing vegetables) in a drugstore. Mixing *yodo* in a pan or plastic bag filled with water will sterilize your fresh foods without leaving an aftertaste.

Soak the food for at least ten to thirty minutes and then air-dry.

Household bleach can be used to purify vegetables and water. Just be certain it's bleach and not some other cleanser. Water purifying tablets, *hidro-clonazone*, take longer to dissolve and are not as reliable as liquid bleach and iodine. (For exact doses and more details on water purification, see *Water: Purify It!*.

Always carry two containers of *yodo* or pills. When one is used up or misplaced, you'll have the other and won't feel tempted to overlook the sterilizing of the food "just this once."

When the use of *yodo* has become a habit, you should notice a marked decrease in trips to the toilet.

Microdyn is a purifying agent sold in Mexican pharmacies and some grocery stores. There is some controversy over its effects on your liver and kidneys if used over a long period. (Microdyn is a preparation of colloidal silver.) Microdyn has the advantage of being cheap and almost entirely tasteless.

Volunteer and Aid Groups

Piña Palmera is an organization at Zipolite (on the coast of Oaxaca) that provides shelter, meals, training and support for people with physical disabilities. It was severely damaged by Hurricane Pauline. It is being rebuilt with donations.

Checks and money orders to support their work can be sent to: Slade Child Foundation, L'Enfant Plaza, P.O. Box 44246, Washington, D.C. 20026. Make the check out to "Slade Child Foundation, for Piña Palmera." Your entire donation will go to Piña Palmera. Their website is at: <http://www.eden.com/~tomzap/pina.html>; email: pinapalmera@laneta.apc.org. (Suggested by Stan Gotlieb, "Letters From Mexico," at <http://www.mexconnect.com/letters_from_mexico/lettersindex.html>.)

Water and Ice

Mexicans are well aware that tourists don't trust the water. Hotels with their own purification systems post "Pure Water" signs in the rooms and stickers on the bathroom mirror. If the hotel's drinking water is delivered from a purification plant, there'll be a full carafe on the nightstand. (If you're still not sure about the hotel's water, or just want to double-check that it is purified, by all means ask the manager or desk clerk.)

Over the years we've developed a practical approach to drinking water that has protected us from dysentery, typhoid fever, cholera or any of the other dread diseases said to come from the tap. Our system is based on common sense, the necessities of traveling and a certain amount of innate fatalism, along with regular doses of enzymes, acidophilus and Pepto Bismol. (See *Staying Healthy: Remedies and Cures: Diarrhea and Dysentery*.)

Reasonable Precautions

Our first precaution is to avoid tap water. Even if you're like W.C. Fields and prefer to avoid water entirely because fish "frolic" in it, you won't go thirsty. Mexico is literally the land of liquid refreshment and some kind of beverage is always close at hand. In addition to bottled *agua purificada* (purified water), you'll find a wide selection of soft drinks, *limonada* (fresh limeade), mineral water and delicious natural fruit juices. (See *Restaurants and Typical Food*.)

Purify It!

Our second precaution is to purify our drinking water rather than spend a great deal of time worrying about it. This can be done by three methods: filtering (small hand-held water filters are sold at outdoor shops in the U.S.), boiling or treating the water chemically, with *yodo* (iodine) or water purification tablets or liquid bleach.

Bill Drake, a sharp-eyed reader from Nevada City, California, pointed out that in three different books, I gave three slightly different recommendations for purifying drinking water. My excuse is that the "experts" I've consulted can't seem to agree on a consistent, definitive set of rules for purifying water. To set the record straight on water purification, however, I now use a respected source: the Travel Clinic at the Seattle-King County Department of Public Health. The following combines their recommendations with our personal experience.

Note: Portable water filters remove giardia and bacteria, but they usually don't filter out viruses. To completely purify water of disease-causing organisms, the following methods are the most effective (choose one).

• **Use a water filter.** Gravity-fed and pump-style filters may remove viruses if they are used properly. However, you will probably have to pump the water slowly or filter it twice. To be effective, the filter element has to be regularly cleaned or replaced.

• **Treat the water with tincture of iodine.** If the water is clear, add five drops of iodine per quart and allow it to stand for thirty minutes. If the water is cloudy, add ten drops of iodine per quart and let it stand for sixty minutes. For simplicity and reliability, iodine is probably the most preferred method to purify water.

(Follow the manufacturer's instructions for other iodine products, including crystals and tablets.)

• **Our preferred method is to use both methods:** treat the water with iodine or bleach, let it sit and then pump this water through a filter to remove the chemical taste.

• **Boil water vigorously** for one minute (three minutes at 20,000 feet).

• **Treat the water with liquid chlorine.** Because Halazone (chlorine) tablets may soon disintegrate after opening the bottle, they aren't as reliable as liquid chlorine.

• **Liquid bleach** or "laundry" bleach can be used only if it contains sodium hypoclorite and no other active ingredients. Check the label closely. (Mexican bleach bottles usually include water purifying instructions in Spanish.) The dosage for four to six percent chlorine (typical laundry bleach) is two drops to one quart of clear water and four drops for one quart of cloudy water.

Chlorine acts quickly, but I let my treated water stand for a while, if only to allow the chemical to dissipate. The awful taste of chlorine can be masked with lime juice, vitamin C powder, citrus juice or a dash of vinegar. Cheers!

• **To sanitize water containers and dishes**, mix two tablespoons of bleach in a gallon of lukewarm water and soak for fifteen minutes.

• **To remove taste and odors** from cookware and canteens, add five tablespoons of *vinagre* (vinegar) to a quart of water.

(See *Vegetables: Purifying*, later in this chapter.)

Finding Pure Water

There are many sources of pure drinking water. One-gallon jugs and 1.5-liter plastic bottles of purified water (*agua purificada*) are commonly sold in supermarkets, liquor stores, *farmacias* and neighborhood *tiendas*. Pure water is also available in large glass or plastic bottles of about five gallons capacity (a one-time deposit is required). Your empty *garrafón* can be exchanged for a full one at the water plant or from itinerant water vendors. Water vendors have regular delivery routes, carrying the bottles in trucks, carts or specially built bicycles. If you're living in a house, you can have bottled water delivered whenever you wish.

Handle your *garrafón* carefully. Those made of plastic fracture rather easily and they always check for cracks when you turn your bottle in.

Small hand pumps and spigots for the *garrafón* are sold in hardware stores and large supermarkets. Metal "pouring stands" that allow the heavy bottle to be tipped without dropping it or drenching your feet are sold at some water plants.

If you prefer not to carry a *garrafón* of water, the water plant or delivery trucks will fill your own containers for you.

City water systems connected to water purification plants are becoming more common. A sign saying *Agua Potable* is usually posted on the outskirts of the town or village. Some cities, however, have potable water only in certain sections, so there's still a certain amount of doubt about the particular *pila* (faucet) you're using.

Gas stations have water, but it falls into the category of "dubious." You can ask if the water is good to drink ("*¿Es bueno para tomar?*"), but because of the risk of contamination from spilled gasoline, we don't drink any gas station water.

Hotels, motels and trailer parks will usually allow you (though sometimes for a slight charge) to fill your containers from their taps. They always say that the water is safe. I feel that this standard answer may well be prejudiced by the fact that they don't want to scare off tourists.

Ice plants (*fábrica de hielo*), of course, have water and many of them have genuine purified water. The general practice seems to be that they won't charge for water unless it really is purified.

Breweries and soda bottling plants sometimes offer free purified water from an outside tap on the side of the building.

Wells, particularly in small towns, are common sources of water. Anyone can use the town *pozo*, but you must bring your own bucket and often your own rope, too. Be careful to avoid stirring up sediment with your *cubo* (bucket) or you'll also stir up resentment among the people waiting in line behind you. Well water should be treated with suspicion; a dirty bucket alone can contaminate a pure well. A private well has a better chance of being pure than the communal type, as the owner takes a very personal interest in keeping it clean and salable.

Many people have private wells or rainwater cisterns. This is particularly common in areas such as Yucatán where water is scarce or tastes strongly of minerals or salt. Good-tasting water is referred to as *agua dulce* (sweet water). It always has to be paid for, though the charge is low.

Rivers, lakes, creeks, ponds and mud puddles are not safe sources of water, no matter how clean they may look. Even though the water is crystal clear, cold and burbling musically through a shady glen, don't dip your lips into it. Somewhere, far out of sight, a farmer is plowing a field that adjoins that little creek and he's using chemicals or manure for fertilizer. The rain will wash contaminants into the creek or the sun and wind will dry out the manure and blow it into the water. Always purify water from these sources.

Finally, if you must drink dubious water, take three seconds to chant "Pure! Pure! Pure!" It's effective but not infallible.

Ice

Many tourists make a flat rule of never using ice (*hielo*) in drinks. We go by the same rules that we apply to water (never eat an ice cube made from a mud puddle).

In resorts, virtually all ice is purified. In fact, ice cube makers are usually part of the water purification system in hotels, restaurants and privately operated plants. In such a warm country, ice cubes are a big business.

Ice cubes (*cubitos de hielo*) are sold in ice plants, *supermercados*, gas stations, liquor stores, RV parks and many roadside stores. Ice cubes sold in plastic bags are almost always made with purified water.

Block ice, however, is purified only in the most modern plants. In other words, when in doubt, ask, "*¿Es purificado?*"

Block ice is sold at ice plants (*fábrica de hielo*) in most towns. For some reason, the *fábrica* is never easy to locate. One of the best ways to find it or the water plant, since they're often in the same building, is to look for a large puddle in the street or on the sidewalk. If it isn't raining, this water is a good indication that the ice plant is nearby.

If it isn't obvious, ask, "*¿Donde está la fábrica de hielo, por favor?*" ("Where is the ice plant, please?")

A full block of ice, large enough to skate on, is a *marqueta*. One-eighth of a block, an *octavo*, will fill the average ice chest. The price for an *octavo* will be much higher in remote areas where ice is trucked in or made in backyard factories.

An ice pick is a *picahielo*.

STAYING HEALTHY

Precautions: moderation, health precautions • Got sick anyway • Curandera or doctor? Farmacia or first aid?: locating a curandera, buying herbs, farmacias, doctors and hospitals, dentists, optometrists and eyeglasses • Remedies and cures: health and first aid kit; AIDS; altitude illness; birth control pills and hormones; bites and stings; bleeding; burns; cholera; colds, coughs and sore throat; cramps, aches and pains; diarrhea and dysentery; earaches; falling down; fever; hangover; heat prostration and sunstroke; hepatitis A; infections and wounds; intestinal parasites; malaria; nausea; nervousness and tension; rashes; seasickness; shock; sprains; sunburn • Secrets of the Maya revealed!

"Take my advice, dear; never eat anything ugly or wrinkled."
—overheard in a Cancún restaurant

First of all, let me assure you that you don't have to get sick in Mexico! Thanks to our self-sacrificing research and painful experience with scorpion stings, severe sunburn, sprains and stomach-wrenching diarrhea, we know what it takes to stay healthy. Follow the advice offered here and you'll have an excellent chance of coming home even healthier than you left.

It is sad but true that gringos sometimes get sick while traveling in Mexico. In fairness, Mexicans may also become ill when visiting the United States. Some people even experience health problems traveling inside their own country. In other words, travel may broaden the mind, but it also tends to upset our stomach.

Why? The short answer is that our body's naturally occurring bacteria are adapted to our present location. Unfortunately, these bacteria don't travel well and when we move far away from home, they can't handle it. Once we arrive in Mexico (or Paris, Missoula, Tokyo, etc.), our body must re-adapt to other, new bacteria. Until we've completed this adjustment, we not only don't feel as healthy as usual, but we have a tendency to become irritable and to blame our queasiness on the local enchiladas and ice cubes. Unfortunately, this process of adaptation seems to span most of the average traveler's vacation time.

In addition to homesick bacteria (known medically as "traveler's diarrhea"), travel also subjects us to stressful changes in climate, altitude and daily routines. Throw in the anxiety of last-minute travel preparations, white-knuckle cab rides and long nights in short, lumpy hotel beds, and it's a wonder the traveler survives at all.

The first step in staying healthy is to recognize that most health problems you'll encounter in Mexico come from three sources: food, beverages (especially water) and Acts of Nature (sunburn, bug bites, tripping over cobblestones, etc.).

Not surprisingly, food and beverages are the biggest offenders. Next to overeating, the most likely cause of diarrhea suffered by both Mexicans and tourists (once they've adjusted to their location) is improper food handling and accidental contamination. No matter how fancy the restaurant or delicious the aroma, if the cook's hands, knives or dishes are dirty, the food will not be clean.

A very poor Mexican family once invited me to eat dinner with them. I accepted, knowing quite well that they had no real concept of sanitation. Water was scarce and the entire family was very dirty. To my surprise, and perhaps in honor of having a guest present, they used a whole bucket of water to wash with. The sad thing, however, was that they washed only their faces and then *after dinner* rather than before.

Always attempt to reduce the chances of infection. I say *reduce* because for the most part it is impossible to completely eliminate the opportunities to eat or drink something that is contaminated.

My invitation to dinner was also an invitation to a stomach-scouring case of diarrhea. I knew this when I accepted, but felt that the possibility of becoming ill meant less to me than offending friends who couldn't help being a health hazard.

This is one of the risks involved in leaving home. If the risk is too much for you, you'll have to restrict the range of your traveling and experiences. You should not, however, carry a "come what may" attitude to extremes.

Precautions

"Your cautious friends and family will probably force you to prepare for your adventurous journey by filling yourself full of typhoid serum . . . quinine to dose the malaria they are sure you will acquire, and flannel bellybands to protect you from cholera. . . ."

—Leone and Alice Moats, *Off to Mexico* (1935)

Smart travelers are aware of their bodies. "Shall I have just one more taco and another beer?" "Do I dare lie out on the beach until noon or should I go in now?" "Am I too tired to tour the ruins and still get back by dinnertime?" Each of these situations requires a decision, one that can mean the difference between a good night's sleep and indigestion, a tan or a burn and a relaxed day versus a marathon.

Since most of our vacations are all-too-short, such decisions become very important. Yes, you can buy a fistful of anti-acid tablets at the local *farmacia* or smother your back with sunburn ointment, but why suffer the discomfort and inconvenience? It's much smarter, both for your health and pleasure, to know when to stop and what to avoid. Rather than load up on medicines and remedies, think of prevention as your best protection against health problems.

Moderation

At the risk of sounding like your conscience, I must tell you that overindulging is the leading cause of tourist's stomach complaints. Every day, visitors ladle chili sauce over mounds of cream-drenched enchiladas, wash it down with a few cold *cervezas* and a heavy dessert—and then gripe about the food when their stomach rebels.

On a tour of highland colonial cities, Lorena and I decided to treat our group to a buffet dinner and folkloric dance show. When I inquired about the menu, the manager proudly described a banquet of traditional dishes that included *nopal* cactus leaves stuffed with sirloin, tamales stuffed with chicken and avocados stuffed with fresh shrimp. An entire roast pig stuffed with herbed rice would eventually be followed by pastries stuffed with thick cream and tropical fruit.

My anticipation turned to alarm. Clearly, the specialty of the house was more than just "stuffed." In terms of calories and cholesterol, the buffet made a holiday smorgasbord sound like a frozen Weight Watcher's entree.

As a precaution, I gave our group a stirring pre-dinner harangue on the tremendous health benefits of eating in moderation, not overdoing it, etc., etc. Later, however, as we feasted . . .

"Carl, what's that dessert you're eating?" Harvey asked.

I swallowed carefully. "This one?" I answered. "I'm not sure but I think it's mountain apricots in some kind of guava and honey sauce. It's good," I added, "but awfully rich."

"No," he persisted, "I mean that dark, cake-like stuff, next to those fried tarts. On the edge of your other plate," Harvey added dryly. "Behind that large portion of flan. . . ."

It is possible, of course, to be served food that is tainted or slightly "off" wherever you go. However, food, water and ice are easy scapegoats for those of us who don't always know when to quit.

The manager of a Puerto Vallarta hotel and I were strolling by the pool one morning, studying recent trends in swimming suit design, when we passed a group of guests sprawled on recliner lounges, with dark sunglasses and distinctly queasy expressions on their faces.

"*¡Buenos días!*" Sergio boomed cheerily. "Did you enjoy the fiesta last night?"

They flinched, then answered in a feeble chorus.

"Too much! Great! What a blast!"

"That's wonderful!" Sergio cried. "But aren't you having breakfast? How about a big plate of scrambled eggs with chorizo sausage? Or some refried beans with hot sauce?"

They groaned in unison. "Maybe later," one of them gasped, shielding his eyes with a forearm. Sergio laughed heartily and led me into the restaurant.

"Those folks tried to drink up all my tequila again last night," he chuckled. "Hey, Sergio!" he mimicked, "there's something wrong with this ice! Every time I drink six or seven margaritas I get a stomachache!" There was a note of exasperation in his laughter.

As we took a table, a waiter quickly placed a heaping basket of hot pastries between us. As usual, Sergio beat me to the croissant.

"Carl, tell me something," he said, reaching for the butter. "If I go to the States and eat and drink everything in sight, and then I get sick, what should I do? Complain about the food?"

"There's a better way," I said, savoring my orange juice. "Just blame it on the weather."

"You will receive all kinds of advice about eating only tinned foods, avoiding lettuce, and drinking nothing but bottled water. Most of it is nonsense."
—Leone and Alice Moats, *Off to Mexico* (1935)

Health Precautions

• **Relax! Take siestas:** Your trip should refresh you, not wear you to a frazzle. Do whatever is necessary to relax and truly enjoy yourself, including just lying on your back staring at the sky for days at a time.

• **Don't over do it:** "Twenty archaeological sites, twelve museums, six *folklorico* performances and . . . oh yeah . . . two leg cramps, a backache, scorched nose and fourteen blisters." Take naps and frequent unscheduled stops. Don't be afraid to turn in while others are forcing themselves to carry on.

• **Adjust to the altitude:** It takes me a full week to adjust from living near sea level to a change of 7,000 feet (the elevation of Mexico City and much of the central plateau). Going the other way, from high to low, takes less time, but still must be considered. Go very easy on exercise, alcohol, drugs of all types and life in general until you've adjusted.

• **Avoid sunburn:** An extra fifteen minutes of hot sun can cause many days of discomfort.

• **Don't wander around with bare feet:** Except for beaches, bare feet are not safe. Avoid the hazards of broken glass, rusty metal, infections from animal and human feces (very common), and hookworm. Do as the Mexicans, and at least wear sandals.

• **Wash your hands often:** Mother was right, washing up before meals is actually good for your health. As you travel, your hands make constant contact with foreign objects, from doorknobs and hand rails to souvenirs and coins. Washing several times a day will help protect you from colds, flu and other hand-to-mouth illnesses.

• **Easy does it on alcohol:** Some people get over-exuberant and spend their vacation hoisting beer bottles and cocktail glasses. When combined with driving, ruin-hopping, shopping and deep-sea fishing, too much drinking can leave you completely exhausted.

• **Eat moderately:** Avoid both overeating and eating too little. A vacation isn't the time for strict dieting or fasting. *Avoid greasy foods:* If you're a marginal vegetarian you'll learn, as I have, that not eating meat in Mexico cuts down dramatically on stomach problems. If those pork ribs are dripping with grease, pass them by.

• **Avoid raw dairy products or cook them well.** To pasteurize raw (or suspicious) milk, bring it to a boil, then cool for two hours.

• **Street foods**, especially *fritangas* (tacos and other fried treats), are both tempting and tricky. Vendors may try their best, but studies clearly show that hygienic conditions are very poor in most sidewalk food stands. Meat dishes are commonly held at low temperatures, encouraging microbes.

Be careful with uncooked vegetables in street food. Traditional warnings to avoid all fruits and vegetables that aren't peeled or cooked are simply out of date. Though well intentioned, such advice exaggerates health risks and frightens travelers. This doesn't mean, however, that some precautions aren't in order.

When in doubt, imitate Mexicans: drench raw vegetables with lime juice and sprinkle them with chili pepper. Raw fruits and vegetables can also be purified with bleach or iodine solutions. (See *A to Z: Vegetables: Purifying.*) Peeling fruit and vegetables is always a good idea—if it's done with a clean knife.

• **Drink purified water:** Purified water is widely available in half-liter to one-gallon plastic bottles. You can also purify water yourself. (See *A to Z: Water: Purify It!*.) My solution to the "What if it's not purified?" dilemma is to drink plain mineral water, sodas and fruit juices. Yes, you can brush your teeth in Coca-Cola.

• **Use Pepto Bismol as a diarrhea preventative:** See *Remedies and Cures: Diarrhea*, below.

At first glance, these precautions might seem to rule out everything you enjoy eating. This should not be true—as long as you use discretion when breaking the "rules."

Got Sick Anyway . . .

What happens when your careful precautions let you down, as they sometimes do? It's time to decide what, *if anything*, needs to be done. Most people overreact to temporary discomfort or illness, and travelers are certainly no exception. "I've got a headache, dear, please run down to the drugstore and get me some morphine." Even a conservative person reaches almost automatically for the ever-present aspirin bottle.

First and most important, when you realize you're sick, *don't panic*. I once met a young guy who gave up plans to stay in Mexico for several months just because of a case of diarrhea. He couldn't speak Spanish and was afraid to go to a doctor by himself.

This might sound extreme if you're reading this at home, but when you're alone in a foreign country, sick and unable to communicate, it's an entirely different situation.

Curandera or Doctor? *Farmacia* or First Aid?

Most common ailments suffered by travelers won't require professional medical attention. Assuming you haven't fallen off the balcony of your hotel room and broken your neck, review this chapter carefully before you hit the panic button. Can the problem be alleviated or cured by simple rest? If so, go right to bed. If not, it's time to decide between a visit to your first aid kit, a doctor, a pharmacy or a *curandera* (healer).

There is a Mexican saying, "When a rich man is ill, he goes to a doctor; when he's desperate, he goes to a *curandera*. When a poor man is ill, he goes to a *curandera*, and when he's desperate, to a doctor."

Curanderas (healers), *brujas* (witches) and *espiritualistas* (spiritualists) might not outnumber licensed doctors and nurses in Mexico, but they are still common. This doesn't mean, however, that you'll be consulting someone in a bat-filled cave. Many Mexicans, especially *campesinos* and Indians, use their extensive knowledge of medicinal plants and home remedies as confidently as gringos take Tums for indigestion. Medicinal plants and natural remedies are available everywhere, from the market place to sidewalk vendors and even in the pharmacy.

To appreciate the typical Mexican's relationship with natural medicine you must first accept that it is a real system. In some cases, such as the use of plants or substances that are proven sources of therapeutic agents, it is easy to see their value. *Epazote* (wormseed) is a powerful preventative and cure for intestinal parasites. The Mexican plant, *cabeza de negro*, was found to contain the hormone progesterone, which led to the development of birth control pills. *Toloache* (known in the U.S. as locoweed) contains scopolamine, a common ingredient in sleeping pills. This list is extensive and grows as large pharmaceutical firms continue exploration and research.

Unfortunately, skeptics use bizarre practices and humorous superstitions to discount all natural healing. We have Mexican friends who sincerely believe that eating watermelon while angry will cause a heart attack (I tried it and got a stomachache). These same people have a wide knowledge of useful medicinal plants and are adept at healing massage. The contrast seems incongruous. In practice, their system makes little distinction, if any, between superstition and "reality." The wise person will take the best and leave the remainder for entertaining anecdotes. (See *¡Viva Mexico!: Superstitions*.)

Our approach to health care is to take manufactured medicines only as a last resort. This doesn't mean waiting until you're on death's doorstep, but giving other alternatives a good try before escalating the treatment. This same attitude also applies to natural healing; start with simple and easy treatments before resorting to anything more powerful.

Locating a *Curandera*

How do you locate a healer or a witch? The best way is to ask someone, *"¿Hay una persona que sabe curar?"* ("Is there someone who knows how to cure?"). *Curanderas* rarely hang out a shingle, though their practice is entirely reputable. Ask at a pharmacy, neighborhood *tienda* or an herb stall in the market. Health food shops and vegetarian restaurants are also good sources of information.

(Naturopaths, homeopaths and chiropractors are relatively common; look in the Yellow Pages.)

Buying Herbs

One of the most familiar and interesting sidewalk attractions in Mexico is the traveling herb salesman. Neatly wrapped parcels labeled "Blood," "Kidneys," "Nervousness" or "Sexual Weakness" make up just a small part of these natural pharmacies. Among the display, usually lined up against the wall of a building, you may see more esoteric items: dead hummingbirds (a powerful love amulet), sand dollars and deer antlers (good luck), crudely printed prayers with pictures of a particular saint (*oraciones*, used to invoke luck, health, wealth, etc.), lodestones (*piedra imán*, for luck), assorted seeds (used individually or in mixtures as charms), insects, chameleons, special candles, sea shells, dried snake meat and other things less easily identified but essential to the practice of witchcraft.

Other vendors specialize in one remedy for common ailments: intestinal parasites (displaying disgusting jars of pickled worms), lack of appetite (greatly feared), venereal disease, kidney disorders (attributed to many ailments) and the common cold. Some sell ready-mixed packages of herbs, others hawk what can only be described as "snake oil." What the vendors all have in common is an incredible ability to maintain a loud and insistent spiel, warning of the dangers of whatever they're selling the cure to. Most rely on vast lung power, but others have portable loudspeakers and can warn passersby a block away of some dire ailment stalking them at that very moment.

I particularly enjoy browsing through the books that are also offered. These are very cheap editions, including reprints of old treatises on magic and witchcraft. The graphics are usually worth the price. The text itself is difficult to check in advance as few have the pages separated; the customer must do that later, with a sharp knife or razor. My favorite, a book on witchcraft by Doctor Papus (which includes some easily memorized chants) has the warning "Do Not Open This Book For Simple Curiosity!" printed over a paper seal. Who could resist?

Almost every market place has at least one herb stall and larger markets will have several. Many herbs and plants are displayed, usually unlabeled, and others are kept under the counter. It used to be possible, for example, to buy peyote in some places, but it is now illegal and vendors rarely admit they have it. Because of strong beliefs in witchcraft and black magic, some vendors are reluctant to chat with foreigners. If your interest goes beyond some simple stomach remedy, you may have to find an intermediary or a more relaxed vendor to get the information and ingredients you want.

A much easier source of information on herbal medicine is from a regular storefront distributor. These shops are found in larger cities. Traveling sidewalk vendors often operate out of a central store and these people are easy to talk to, to say the least.

When buying herbs and plants, ask how they are prepared and the dosage. The most common method is in teas, but it is important to know the proper amounts, as some can be dangerous. *Epazote*, for example, is not recommended in large doses for pregnant women.

Farmacias

A Mexican pharmacy is not quite like a typical drugstore in the U.S. Many medicines such as antibiotics are dispensed without a *receta* (prescription), though a prescription may be legally required.

Although many *farmacias* are owned and operated by licensed physicians, diagnoses are often made on the spot by pharmacists and their assistants. This is a very convenient system, but even doctors make mistakes, and it can be assumed that a pharmacist isn't infallible either. Unless your problem is obvious—a bad case of diarrhea, upset stomach, headache or a wound—the pharmacist is usually not adequately trained to give the most reliable opinion. If you prefer to see a doctor, the pharmacist will refer you to one.

Pills can be purchased one at a time and liquid medicines by the dose or measure. In addition to medicines taken orally, the *farmacia* offers instant *inyecciones* (injections). You pay for the medicine and throwaway syringe, plus a small fee for sticking it in. Mexicans take do-it-yourself medicine one step further. To the delight of hypochondriacs, towns of any size have walk-in *laboratorios* where X-rays and inexpensive *análisis* of blood, urine, stools and so on are done upon request.

Pill-pushing in Mexico (and the Third World in general) is a major industry. Uneducated people take antibiotics for almost every complaint. A neighbor says, "My little Juanita took just two of those *pastillas* and got better." Then, when Pablo sprains his ankle or gets a gut ache from eating green mangos, his mother will also go to the *farmacia* for pills or an injection.

Inyecciones are synonymous with effective treatment. Whether it's a megadose of vitamin B for a hangover or tetracycline for the sniffles, most pharmacists are eager to help out.

When filling a prescription, be very careful that you get exactly what the doctor ordered. If they don't have it, go to another pharmacy or return to the doctor and ask for advice. Substitutions should be made by the doctor, not the pharmacist.

I was once sold a package of pills that were "identical" to what the doctor prescribed. For some reason I felt suspicious and opened the box. Inside were six of the largest pills I'd ever seen, so large, in fact, that I'd have to cut them into pieces to get them down.

"How can I possibly take these?" I asked.

The pharmacist shrugged and said, "With a large glass of water." A few seconds later he suddenly laughed and said, "Those are vaginal suppositories. I made a mistake." He replaced them with pills of more reasonable size. Still laughing, he said, "That's very odd. I did the same thing last week. For a dog."

Drug prices are government controlled. The maximum price is marked on the package (*Precio máximo al público $ . . .*). Discount drugstores, *farmacias de descuento*, charge less than the maximum price. **Boticas** look just like a pharmacy, but they deal mainly in aspirin, cosmetics and love potions. They are **farmacias de segunda clase** (second class) while an actual pharmacy is **primera clase** (first class).

After regular closing hours, every town will have at least one pharmacy that is open all night. This is called *la farmacia de la guardia* or *de la vigilancia* (on guard, on duty). If the doors are closed, knock; there'll be someone dozing inside. For the address of the *guardia*, ask a cop or cab driver.

Doctors and Hospitals

It is quite easy to find a doctor in Mexico; just inquire at any pharmacy or stop someone on the street. "*¿Dónde hay un doctor, por favor?*" ("Where is there a doctor, please?")

The U.S. and British embassies (and I assume the Canadian, also) have lists of "approved" English-speaking doctors. The majority of Mexican doctors, approved or not, speak at least enough English to figure out your problem. Many have studied in the U.S. and Europe.

Mexican doctors make house calls and most have an open door policy on office visits. The average fee for consultation is a fraction of what is charged in the U.S.

Hospitals are quite plentiful, though most of those in smaller cities are government operated. These hospitals are commonly called *"El Seguro Social"* (The Social Security). This is from the full name, *Instituto Mexicano de Seguro Social, IMSS*. The *IMSS* is known by cynics as *"Importa Madre Su Salud,"* a very rude wisecrack that loosely translates as "your health is of no damned importance." In spite of this nickname, in our experience, *IMSS* clinics do give good service, at little or no charge.

In the largest cities, all types of hospitals and clinics can be found and their health care is excellent.

Dentists

A *dentista* (jokingly called *sacamuellas*, "toothpullers") is as easy to find as a doctor. Once again, just ask at any pharmacy. Dental care is inexpensive. Dentists often oblige tourists by doing their work immediately and without appointment. Many people plan their vacations around major dental repair. I prefer to wait until tears of pain blur my vision before resigning myself to a dental chair.

The best dentists tend to set up shop in the largest cities. Their equipment and techniques are the most modern, and appointments are often necessary. In Guadalajara and other gringo colonies, dentists advertise their services in English-language publications.

Optometrists and Eyeglasses

Optometristas are found in all the larger cities. In smaller towns, you may find an *oculista*, a person trained to fit people for eyeglasses. Examinations are usually free and most optometrists also sell frames, lenses, contact lenses and sunglasses. Lenses are less expensive than in the U.S., but most frames are not.

My experience with Mexican oculists has been good, though I recommend one who gives a thorough sit-down *examen de la vista* rather than an over-the-counter exam.

The quickest service is by optometrists who have lens-grinding facilities right at hand. In some shops you can have an examination and fitting and walk out two hours later, a *"cuatro ojos"* ("four eyes"). Be aware, however, that your eyeglasses may arrive "on Mexican time." I've had my bifocal prescription filled several times in Mexico and it was often later than promised. A deposit of about 50 percent is usually expected.

Tell them that you want your lens *blanco* (clear) or you will very likely get tinted ones. Mexicans have a fetish about sunglasses and wear them even at night. Plain glass lenses cost less than plastic—the reverse of the situation in the U.S.

Remedies and Cures

A health and first aid kit is well worth having, especially in remote areas. Keep it reasonable; some people lug around enough splints, bandages and emergency medicines to make a paramedic jealous. The aid kit described here is more than adequate for the average trip and should serve you well while camping and exploring. The principle behind the kit includes prevention as well as first aid.

Anyone venturing far off the beaten path is advised to carry—and read in advance—a good first aid manual. Our favorite, **Where There Is No Doctor**, is available in both Spanish and English. (See *For More Information* and *Vocabulary* in the *Appendices* for Spanish translations of health-related terms.)

Health and First Aid Kit

For purifying food and water: 1 ounce of *Yodo*, Microdyne or water purifying pills.

For diarrhea and nausea: Pepto Bismol, Immodium AD, enzymes and probiotics (acidophilus and bifidus), garlic capsules, herbal teas such as dog tea (*té de perro*), mint (*menta, yerba buena*), camomile (*manzanilla*).

For cuts and wounds, infections: Gauze (*gasa*), Band-Aids (*curitas, vendas*), adhesive tape (*cinta adhesiva*), scissors, antiseptic soap (*jabón*), alcohol or hydrogen peroxide, penicillin (*pentrexyl*), triple antibiotic cream.

For sun and wind: Sun block, aloe vera gel or burn ointment, lip balm.

For *gripe*, flu and colds, fever: Limes (*limones*), garlic (*ajo*), goldenseal and echinacea tincture or capsules, Yin Chiao, Cyclone Cider, Alfa CF, Comtrex (for allergies), herbal lozenges (with zinc), Nutrabiotic, aspirin (*aspirina*), thermometer.

Insect repellents and stings: Green Ban herbal repellent and Cutter's (or one with DEET), pennyroyal oil, Sting Eze, baking soda.

Miscellaneous: Cornstarch or talcum (*maizena*), pain pills, several cloves or clove oil (*clavos de olor, aceite de clavo*), moleskin, salt tablets (*pastillas de sal*), tweezers (fine point) (*pinzas*), needle (*aguja*).

Homeopathic tablets and supplements: Sepia, Arnica Montana, Ruta Grava, Rescue Remedy; Super Blue Green Algae; vitamins A, B, C, and E (*vitamina A, B, C, y E*); calcium (*calcio*); book or mind-occupier, massage.

Some items on this list require a doctor's prescription in the U.S., but everything mentioned should be available over the counter in Mexico. When you return home don't forget to declare medicines purchased in Mexico at U.S. Customs. If you don't, they might well seize the medicines and fine you. Most Customs agents will allow small amounts of prescription drugs even without a prescription, if they are properly declared.

Comments

• **Vitamin C:** Effervescent tablets are called *comprimidos efervescentes vitamina C*.

• **Limes:** This is one "medicine" that tastes good. A Mexican folk medicine book lists 172 ailments cured by taking *jugo* or *zumo de limón* (lime juice). Squeezing lime juice over food enhances flavor and reduces the chance that unpleasant bacteria will reach your stomach. Lime juice will supposedly purify water, but just to be sure I add enough to make limeade. Water treated with lime juice makes terrible coffee.

Lime juice can be used (carefully, in moderation) to clean wounds and soothe insect bites, to remove rust from metal and to polish tarnished fishing lures.

• **Garlic:** The medicinal value of *ajo* is now widely accepted. Garlic protects against intestinal parasites, disinfects wounds, discourages mosquitoes and soothes insect bites. If you can't stand to chew raw garlic like candy, as Lorena does, chop the cloves up and slosh them down with juice or mineral water, or mash it with an avocado and lime juice. If this is too strong for you, deodorized garlic tablets are sold in health food stores in the U.S. and Mexico.

• **Echinacea** is an excellent tonic for the immune system.

• **Goldenseal** (*Hydrastis canadensis*) is used for everything from infections to colds. Lorena wouldn't be without it. It's available in powder in some parts of Mexico, but it's much easier and more reliable to bring a supply from a health food store at home.

• **Nutrabiotic** is a very potent grapefruit seed extract used for skin infections. This stuff made short work of a persistent fungus Lorena picked up on a jungle canoe trip in Guatemala.

• **Homeopathic Sepia** is good for cramps (especially legs); try **Arnica Montana** for overexerted muscles and strains, **Ruta Grav** for tendinitis and **Rescue Remedy** for shock.

• **Super Blue Green Algae:** This high-energy food supplement and all-around immune system tonic has given us better health, as well as increased physical energy and mental stamina. In addition, the enzymes and probiotics (acidophilus and bifidus) strengthen the digestive system and protect us from stomach upsets. If you'd like more information on "SBG Algae," call Lorena at 800-927-2527, extension 03726 (voicemail).

• **Book or mind-occupier:** It sounds like a soap opera, but if you're among "The Sick and The Restless" you might be tempted to continue moving when you should be resting. Keep a good book in reserve, a game or something to occupy your mind. Lorena knits; I'll read, daydream or study Spanish. Rest now and you'll go a lot farther later.

• **Massage:** Traveling often brings out aches and pains, either from long hours in a bus seat or too much body surfing, or muscular tension caused by a stomachache. If there isn't someone around to give you a *masage* or *soba* (massage), do it yourself. Massaging your own feet, hands, arms, neck and legs can do wonders, especially before and after a hot shower. *Aceite de ajonjolí* (sesame oil for cooking) makes a good massage oil, especially when scented with herbs. Coconut oil (*aceite do coco*) also works well but is greasier. Ask for it in the *farmacia*.

AIDS • Altitude discomfort • Birth control and hormones • Bites and stings • Bleeding • Burns • Cholera • Colds, coughs and sore throat • Cramps, aches and pains • Cuts: See Infections and Wounds *• Cultural Shock: See* Shock *• Diarrhea, dysentery and food poisoning • Earaches • Falling down • Fever • Food poisoning: See* Diarrhea *• Gripe and flu: See* Colds *• Hangover • Heat prostration and sunstroke • Hepatitis • Infections and wounds • Insomnia: See* Nervousness and Tension *• Intestinal parasites (worms) • Malaria • Nausea • Nervousness and Tension • Rashes • Seasickness • Shock, physical and cultural • Sprains • Sunburn • Sunstroke: See* Heat Prostration

AIDS

Whether it's the hormone rush brought on by all that sun and bare skin at the beach or a moonlight-and-margarita romance, tourists can be alarmingly casual about sex. Unfortunately, you can't escape the risk of AIDS simply by leaving home. On the contrary, AIDS is moving around the world at a truly frightening rate.

In addition to problems of money and education, the spread of AIDS in Latin America is complicated by the region's culture. Though rarely acknowledged in public, bisexual relations among men are more common than anyone will admit. In an unusually frank discussion of *SIDA* (AIDS) in Mexico, the magazine *Proceso* warned that casual "macho" sex—between men and with prostitutes—puts many unsuspecting women in grave danger.

The risks for those who find themselves being charmed and courted by another traveler or local lover are also great. Please, don't take the chance. (If this AIDS warning doesn't cool you down, be sure to bring a good supply of condoms from home. The quality of Mexican condoms is uncertain.)

Altitude Illness and Discomfort

Common symptoms are headache, slight nausea, poor appetite, mental confusion (I simply could not spell "mountain" above 12,000 feet), poor memory, weakness, yawning, chills, shortness of breath (especially while sleeping) and fatigue. The best cure is to take it easy on everything, from sightseeing to booze. Rest, eat lightly (even if you're not hungry), drink lots of liquids and don't charge up pyramids like an Olympic contender.

Birth Control Pills and Hormones

Birth control pills (*pastillas contraceptivas*) were invented in Mexico—and are dispensed without a prescription. Brand names are different from those in the U.S.; you might prefer to bring a supply from home.

Condoms (*condón, contraceptivas*) are sold in *famacias*. One brand is ominously known as *Buena Suerte* (Good Luck!). Foam spermicides (*espuma contraceptiva*) are also common. Diaphragms are available in Mexico City; if you use one, consider taking an extra. If it is lost or damaged you will have to see a doctor to order another one or resort to *Buena Suerte*.

Premerin (artificial estrogen) is available in *farmacias*, but Lorena has been unable to find progesterone. If you need natural estrogen and progesterone, bring them from home.

Bites and Stings

Wash all bites and stings frequently with soap and water and/or fresh lime juice to prevent infections.

Ants, bees, wasps, hornets, mosquitoes: If a stinger is left behind, usually the case with honeybees, it should be carefully removed by scraping, not pulling.

Slice a lime in half and press it against the sting. Some people recommend heating the lime and sprinkling it with salt. Baking soda mixed with just enough water to form a paste will quickly reduce pain. When tromping through the jungle, I carry a supply of baking soda in a 35 mm film can.

Aloe vera gel and crushed garlic relieve itching, but Lorena's first choice is Sting Eze (available at outdoor shops and drugstores), a very effective chemical potion. Cortico-steroid ointments also ease itching and swelling. Ask for *pomada para piquetes* (salve for bites) or by brand name, Synalar or Fusalar.

Most anything containing ammonia will give quick relief. I've used Windex and it really helps. A strong (10 percent) solution of household ammonia in water is very effective. Mexican folk remedies that work: crush the head of a match (or use ashes), mix with saliva and apply to the sting. Also wet tea bags, tobacco, crushed parsley or equal parts of camphor and chloral hydrate.

Bug-in-your-ear: Pour a small amount of oil (not motor oil) into your ear to smother the intruder. Pouring tequila in your ear also produces dramatic results.

Chiggers: To reduce itching and to smother the chiggers, apply a mixture of 25 percent camphor and 5 percent phenol in mineral oil. A salve of one part sulfur (*azufre*) to ten parts of Vaseline, lard or shortening is also good.

Horse flies: Horse flies love to bite when your skin is wet or damp; by staying dry you'll attract fewer of them. Wear more clothes when *tabanos* are about. Pennyroyal oil is an effective repellent. Treat as an insect bite.

Fleas: Often a problem in small villages and crowded ranch houses. Eucalyptus leaves (or oil) repel fleas; put a bag of leaves in your sleeping bag and another in your backpack or shirt pocket.

Jellyfish: Urine quickly soothes the sting, as does a mild ammonia solution, Windex or other sting balms. Meat tenderizer or papaya juice also helps. Mix ashes with saliva and rub on the stings. Treat as a bee sting.

If you are stung while swimming, don't panic. To avoid becoming entangled in more stinging tentacles, move as slowly as possible until you're sure that you're not swimming right into the jellyfish. Many broken drifting tentacles retain their stingers. You might run into these fragments rather than an entire jellyfish.

Mosquitoes: The best protection against mosquitoes and mosquito-borne diseases such as malaria is clothing, not repellents. Light-colored, muted clothing attracts fewer mosquitoes. Garlic, taken internally or on the skin, is a fairly effective mosquito repellent. For an unforgettable lotion, mix a handful of crushed garlic in half a cup of oil (sesame, olive or coconut). Let this soak for a week to ten days and then strain. Add several drops of pennyroyal oil for additional protection against no-see-ums, crushed eucalyptus leaves for fleas and parsley to reduce the garlic odor. This brew is also a good balm for bites and stings.

Parsley rubbed on the skin is said to be effective against mosquitoes. Smudge fires, especially of coconut husks, help reduce their numbers.

Repellents last longer when applied to clothing. When the bugs are fierce, we treat a shirt, pair of pants and socks with repellents. Our bug clothing is kept in a plastic bag when not in use. Don't wash them until they're really ripe; most repellents are effective for weeks.

The most common Mexican insect repellents are 6-12 (*Seis-Doce*) with a relatively mild citronella base and Autan, a DEET repellent.

A mosquito netting (*pabellón*) is very effective protection. They are sold ready-made in most tropical areas. You can also buy lengths of *manta de cielo* (sometimes call *mosquitero*) and have it sewn up at a tailor shop.

No-see-um bites (*jejenes*) fade away in about ten minutes if you don't scratch them. When the itch becomes too much to bear, apply finger pressure for a few seconds and it should be relieved. Once you scratch, it'll last for days.

Scorpions: The danger of an *alacrán* sting have been greatly exaggerated. Scorpion "bites" are rarely fatal, especially to a healthy adult, though they can be quite painful. The risk is greatest if you have a serious heart or respiratory problem, are allergic to bee stings or weigh less than about thirty pounds (children under three years). Otherwise, don't worry! The pain may persist for some time, but you aren't going to croak!

Lorena, Steve and I have all been stung more than a few times. After an initial scream and a sharp, burning sensation, it's about like a bad bee or wasp sting.

Anti-alacrán (anti-scorpion) serum is sold in drugstores in areas where scorpions abound (mainly the states of Durango, Nayarit, Colima and Jalisco). More fatalities are attributed to *anti-alacrán* than to scorpions themselves. The serum can cause a severe reaction and a reaction test must be made before administering the serum. If you must have it around, ask a doctor for advice.

What if a scorpion nails you? First and most important, lie down and relax. The discomfort is aggravated by over-excitement and exertion. The symptoms can be quite unpleasant: an immediate burning pain and swelling, followed by stinging, numbness, prickling in the throat and perhaps a "thick" tongue. You may have some trouble breathing, too, especially if the scorpion was large and full of venom. There's still no need to panic.

First of all, take a massive dose of vitamin C (suck a bag of limes). Next, apply crushed garlic and several drops of lime juice to the sting. Now swallow at least half a dozen large (chopped) cloves of garlic. Finally, cut the scorpion in half and tape or tie the fleshy side of the head to the wound. The assumption is that the scorpion has some natural anti-venom in its body. *¿Quién sabe?* By the way, this treatment is used by a Mexican physician who treats scorpion stings almost every day. It seemed to help us a great deal, though the lime juice made my throat and stomach burn.

Pack the sting area with ice if you have it. Cooling slows the action of the venom.

If the pain is truly unbearable, aspirin can be taken, but **no opiates or morphine derivatives** (no codeine, Darvon, Demerol or paregoric). Some doctors advise doses of antihistamines; if you have some on hand take a reasonable dose, not a handful. An antihistamine reduces the swelling and makes breathing easier.

Don't eat anything, especially dairy products, or smoke or drink alcohol for at least twenty-four hours. Fruit juices are OK. If the bite doesn't hurt after a few hours, a light meal can probably be taken without ill effects.

The severity of a scorpion sting varies from very minor to quite painful. If you feel that you're seriously ill, go to a *farmacia*, hospital or Red Cross station. In areas where scorpion stings are common, nearly every village will have the antivenin and someone (often a nurse) knows how to do the reaction test.

Scorpions hang out in and under brush, rocks, old coconuts, mattresses and blankets, rotten wood and driftwood and anything damp or dark. When you're in scorpion areas, shake out your blankets before going to bed and check your shoes, socks and pants before you put them on.

Sea urchin spines: The spines are next to impossible to dig out, so don't even try. Mexican divers apply lots of lime juice; it dissolves the spine and cleanses the wound. Treat as a puncture wound.

Snakebites: Mexico has an amazing variety of snakes, some of them amazingly poisonous. Fortunately, very few tourists even see a poisonous snake, much less have the misfortune to be bitten by one. Treatment for *víbora* bites tends to be radical. If antitoxins are available they should be administered within three hours.

It is vital to keep in mind that most bites from poisonous snakes are not fatal, though they'll undoubtedly hurt like hell. Remain calm and keep still. Have someone take you to a doctor, but don't panic. Panic hastens the spread of venom—if there is any venom at all. Non-poisonous snakes also bite, so your problem may be nothing more than a simple puncture wound (see *Infections and Wounds*).

Take massive doses of vitamin C and garlic. You may also be suffering from shock as a result of the fright of being bitten (see *Shock*).

Spider bites: Sprinkle goldenseal powder on a spider bite. Lorena finds this very effective for bites on the lip that don't heal easily.

Stingrays: *Rayas* are common in shallow water. Contrary to popular belief, the stinger (actually a barbed shaft) is not poisonous, though it does produce a nasty, easily infected wound. To avoid being hit, shuffle your feet along the bottom rather than prancing through the surf like a gazelle. When you bump into a ray, it will swim away harmlessly. Should you step on its back, however, the tail arches over and jabs the stinger in your foot or ankle.

Treat as a puncture wound (see *Infections and Wounds*). A common folk cure is to gather a bunch of leaves from a low-running, green, thick-leafed plant found at the edge of the beach (known in some areas as *yerba de raya*), boil them for twenty minutes and wash the wound in the liquid.

Another folk remedy, one that sounds suspiciously like attempted suicide, is to have someone rub your entire body with rags soaked in hot water, then wrap up in warm blankets and chug-a-lug a liter of tequila.

Ticks: If you bushwhack at all, you'll probably pick up one or more ticks (*garrapatas, guinas*). In brushy, tick-infested jungle, you might be boarded by hundreds of the little buggers. Many ticks are too small to see until they're gorged with blood. To get rid of them, find a long switch and mercilessly attack your clothing. Stretch your shirt and pants out tight away from your body and whip the cloth furiously with the switch. This will remove most ticks, but you'll undoubtedly have some that hang on and burrow into our skin.

Imbedded ticks (look *everywhere*, from your butt to inside your ears) are removed by a steady, gentle tugging on the tick's body. Unfortunately, the head often separates and remains beneath the skin. To avoid this, coat the body of the tick with cooking oil, kerosene, fingernail polish, Vaseline or any substance that suffocates it and allows complete removal. Touching a hot match or cigarette to the tick will shrivel the body and may make it difficult to remove. Wash the tick wound carefully with soap and clean water.

Tarantulas: Tarantula bites are not poisonous but they do infect easily. Treat as a wound: wash thoroughly and bandage.

Vampire bats: If you can't sleep inside a tent, mosquito net or enclosed space, at least stuff cloves of garlic between your toes to ward off *vampiros*.

Bleeding
Bleeding can almost always be stopped by applying pressure directly over the wound (lean on it, even if it takes an hour!) and by elevating the wounded part as high as possible.

Burns
Immediately put the burn in cold water to stop the burning. Burns should be cleaned gently with warm water and soap. Cover the burn with a sterile, fine-meshed, absorbent gauze to keep it clean.

Lorena keeps a vitamin E capsule handy and immediately squirts a few drops of the oil on burns. Swallow the rest of the capsule. Any light oil would probably help, but never use butter or any other salted grease.

A compress of cool water or ice greatly relieves the pain of a burn. The gel from the aloe vera plant (*sabila*, very common in Mexico) is also very effective for pain and promotes healing, as is the juice of any succulent cactus. Wet tea bags (black tea) are said to give relief when used as a poultice. Grated or mashed raw potatoes or onions also work quite well. Sprinkle *tepezcohuite* on burns and it seals the skin. (See *Infections and Wounds*.)

Maintain treatment until the burn does not hurt, taking care to keep it clean until it has healed. Don't pop blisters!

If the burn is serious, drink lots of fluids (see *Diarrhea* for special cocktail; also see *Sunburns*.).

Cholera
Immunizations against cholera are available but their effectiveness is not very good. If you follow our advice on healthy food and water, the odds of getting cholera are extremely low. Should you experience uncontrollable diarrhea and vomiting, however, see a doctor. It's probably just a bad case of *turista* or food poisoning, but don't take chances. In otherwise healthy adults, cholera usually isn't fatal, just intensely miserable. Cholera causes extreme dehydration, so take *lots* of liquids. (See *Diarrhea* for suggestions on dealing with dehydration.) Again, your best protection is to take sensible, constant precautions by avoiding potentially contaminated food and water.

Colds, Coughs and Sore Throat

Gripe is a Mexican term that covers everything from mild colds to the most miserable flu. *Gripe* responds poorly to treatment and most people resign themselves to a few days of bedrest and aspirin.

Gripe is tough but Lorena's treatment has a good rate of success. At the first sign of distress, take 2,000 to 5,000 units of vitamin C, echinacea tincture and immune strengtheners such as goldenseal or Cat's Claw & Chuchuasa. She also uses Cyclone Cider: apple vinegar with garlic, cayenne, horseradish root, ginger, etc. Two hours later, take more vitamin C with Yin Chiao, a Chinese herbal "disinfectant." If the *gripe* persists, alternate doses of vitamin C with tinctures or Yin Chiao every two hours.

If you prefer not to use an alcohol tincture, some tinctures have a glycerin or vinegar base. Or take four tablets of echinacea and herbs, or four capsules (00, double-ought) of goldenseal powder and two capsules (00) of cayenne powder.

Mexicans drink lots of tea for *gripe:* sage (*salvia*), cinnamon (*canela*), bay leaves (*laurel*), mint (*yerba buena* and *menta*) and camomile (*manzanilla*), either one at a time or all together.

Cramps, Aches and Pains

Stomach cramps (*calambres*) often accompany severe cases of diarrhea and indigestion. These and other cramps, such as the notorious "chicken bus backache" and menstrual cramps, may be relieved by calcium supplements. (Calcium improves pain tolerance and should probably be taken for any injury.) Be aware that eating dairy products can actually aggravate calcium deficiencies. Lorena now uses homeopathic Sepia, especially for leg cramps. Camomile tea, rest, hot baths and massage do wonders.

Calcio is sold in drugstores or you can just dissolve an eggshell overnight in lime juice. Add to water and drink.

Diarrhea and Dysentery

Powdered scorpions, chia and Seven-Up, chamomile and "dog tea," acidophilus, papaya seeds, dried apricot pits: when it comes to upset stomachs, nausea, diarrhea and *disentería*, I've tried most everything. As a firm believer in the value of medicinal plants and folk remedies, I'm sorry to announce that a dose of bismuth solution (such as Pepto Bismol) seems to beat them all. In fact, our experience clearly shows that taking the pink stuff in moderate doses before, during and even after traveling can dramatically reduce stomach problems.

In a 1986 brochure titled *"Traveler's Advisory,"* Proctor & Gamble gave these directions for a preventative regimen of Pepto Bismol for a generic adult: "Start taking two tablets four times a day (with meals and at bedtime) one day before you leave. Continue that dosage while traveling and for two days after your return home, for up to twenty-one days." (Proctor & Gamble no longer gives dosage recommendations for traveler's diarrhea. Instead, the company suggests that you consult your physician.)

Though it is effective, I'm no fan of bismuth's cloying pink taste and I don't like to pour it repeatedly into my stomach. I now take about half of an adult's dosage (one tablespoon three to four times a day). I start my bismuth program a few days before leaving home and continue taking it once or twice a day for about a week. If my stomach shows no sign of rebellion in that time, I go to "standby" and keep the bismuth close at hand in the event of sudden turmoil. (Lorena only takes Pepto Bismol when she gets that queasy, "shouldn't-have-eaten-that" feeling, instead relying on food enzymes and probiotics.)

Warning: Read the bismuth instructions carefully. Pepto Bismol also contains aspirin and must be used with appropriate caution. If you experience headaches, stomach cramps or other side effects, refrain from using bismuth solutions or tablets. Don't

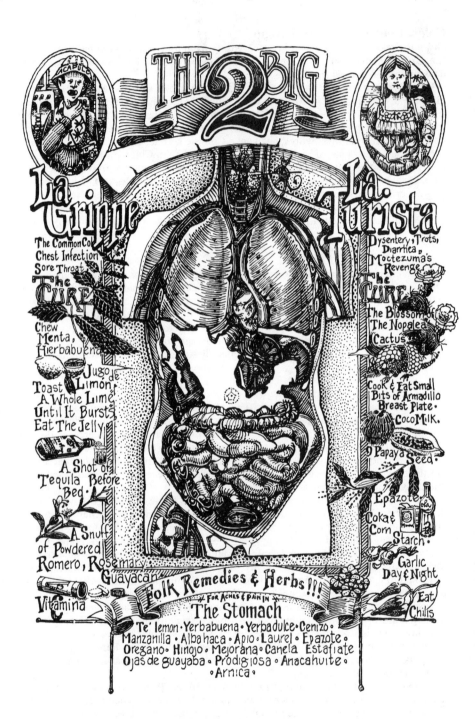

be frightened if your tongue (and stool) turn black; this isn't the Black Death, the "pink stuff" is to blame.

Pepto Bismol liquid is widely available in Mexican *farmacias* (pharmacies), but chewable tablets aren't as common. For some reason, Mexican Pepto tastes slightly different from that sold in the U.S.

"Traveler's diarrhea": Because doctors recognize that diarrhea can be a "natural" reaction to travel rather than just an illness, their approach to treatment now includes remedies that sound suspiciously like those used by natural healers.

First of all, don't resort to antibiotics or "liquid cork." The body needs to flush out, not plug up. Lomotil, Kaopectate and other classic diarrhea medicines will only prolong the problem and may even aggravate it, by forcing the body to delay healing. Rest and give yourself a few days to recover.

A sudden bout of diarrhea is often more severe than a person expects: cramps, nausea, vomiting, chills and fever as high as 103 degrees F. It lasts from one to three days and may end suddenly, leaving you weak but happy.

Avoid coffee, black tea, alcohol, chilies, black pepper, raw fruit, and anything greasy, spicy or extremely hot or cold. Papaya contains digestive enzymes that soothe the stomach. Many Mexicans eat three papaya seeds a day to prevent diarrhea and nine a day for nine days to cure it.

The greatest danger with diarrhea is dehydration, especially in children. The following drink is recommended by the U.S. Centers for Disease Control. It can be used as a preventative aid as well as for relief from diarrhea.

Anti-diarrhea cocktail: Put eight ounces of fruit juice in a glass and add half a teaspoon of honey (or sugar) and a pinch of salt. In another glass, mix eight ounces of water (can use mineral or carbonated) and one quarter teaspoon of baking soda. Drink them down, alternating sips from one glass to the other. An adult should take several doses a day, and a child at least four. (If you can't find these ingredients, mix soft drinks and water with Alka-Seltzer.)

For all internal ailments drink plenty of liquids. The Mexican classic is dog tea, *té de perro*. It really works. Add a handful of dog tea or another herb to one liter of boiling water. Let it stand (not boiling) for up to thirty minutes. Drink a glass whenever you're thirsty. It's good with lime juice. *Té de manzanilla* is also popular and if you can get them, *tuna de cardón* (cactus fruits). Eat four a day until you've recovered. Coconut milk is good, though eating too much of the oily meat will increase the problem. One teaspoon of chia seeds in a large glass of water, juice or soft drink will soothe your stomach and plug you up. We also use echinacea and goldenseal in a tincture, or take one or two 00 capsules, three times daily.

If diarrhea persists beyond four days, you'd better see a doctor. When you take antibiotics, follow them up with live yogurt. Most supermarket yogurt has been heated, which kills the beneficial acidophilus and probiotics. A more reliable way to restore healthy bacteria in your digestive trace is to bring capsules from home containing acidophilus, or acidophilus and bifidus. (Taken regularly, these help strengthen the digestive system and make it less likely that you'll get diarrhea in the first place.)

Gotta go? Can't wait! When I'm traveling by public transportation, I carry just enough Immodium AD to stop diarrhea. Pick it up in the U.S.; as far as I know,

Immodium AD is not yet available in Mexico. Avoid Lomotil; it can have dangerous side effects.

Disentería is used in Mexico to describe both dysentery and diarrhea. This leads many gringos to erroneously believe they're suffering from amoebic dysentery when in fact it's either traveler's diarrhea or food poisoning.

Don't assume, just because the symptoms are severe, that you've got a case of dysentery. Dysentery should be diagnosed by a doctor, not by some sympathetic traveler in the next room. The treatment should be done under a doctor's supervision.

Amoebic dysentery is caused by a parasite. Diarrhea can be caused by many factors, including bacteria, stomach irritations, food poisoning, too much alcohol, overheating and stress. When I had amoebas my main symptoms were headache, depression and sore muscles—not diarrhea.

Food poisoning, either mild or severe, is not uncommon in Mexico. The symptoms are similar to diarrhea, but usually come on much faster and are more severe. Food poisoning also tends to end quickly; a common variety lasts only about twelve hours. Use the same treatments for food poisoning as for diarrhea. You'll probably have no choice but to rest.

Earaches on the Airplane

If you have problems with your ears on the plane (and it still happens despite pressurized cabins), chew gum on the way up as well as on the way down. If your ears still won't pop, try holding your nose (Lorena also has to push her first finger and thumb against the top of her sinuses about one inch below the eyes), blow gently *and* swallow at the same time. Lorena also takes an antihistamine one hour before the flight if she has a cold or if the earache on the last flight was severe.

Falling Down

Falling down is a very real hazard, especially on cobblestones and steep, Aztec temples. I spent six months with my left wrist in a brace after a confrontation with a slippery beach rock in Tulum. Wear well-fitted shoes or sandals that give positive traction. Carry a small flashlight after dark. When climbing temples, don't be embarrassed to use your hands and knees—I do. "Gringo traps" abound in Mexico, from unexpected holes in sidewalks to head-knocker shop awnings. Expect the unexpected underfoot, overhead, from ahead or behind. *Let the pedestrian beware* is the motto.

Fever

A *fiebre* can be expected with cases of diarrhea and sometimes with *gripe*. If the body temperature goes above 102 degrees F (see *Appendices* for conversion to Centigrade), take aspirin and uncover. Fevers above 104 degrees F can be cooled by bathing the person with wet cloths and placing damp cloths on the chest and forehead. Alcohol or aloe vera gel rubs also help.

Fever caused by sunstroke can go very high. It should be checked with a rectal thermometer. If the rectal temperature is over 106 degrees F, the victim should be immersed in an ice water bath or wrapped in a soaking wet blanket. The skin should be massaged vigorously until the body temperature falls. The rectal temperature should be checked every ten minutes and the person removed from the ice water before it falls below 102 degrees F.

If you're traveling alone and come down with a bad fever, ask someone to keep an eye on you. I've always found people to be very sympathetic; hotel employees will gladly bring you tea and drinks.

A Mexican fever remedy common in desert areas is to toast a leaf of aloe vera, then slice it open, coat with cooking oil and sprinkle with a few petals of *rosa de castille* (optional). Place against the soles of the feet, wrap and leave overnight. Teas of lime juice, hibiscus (*jamaica*, very common), borage (*boraja*), parsley and alfalfa are also used.

Hangover

An all-too-common Mexican remedy for *la cruda* is to continue drinking. For a safer cure than a hair-of-the-dog, try dog tea (*té de perro*). A large glistening bowl of spicy intestine stew (*menudo*) is also traditional, as is a cocktail of raw eggs, orange juice and hot sauce. Survivors of these treatments might resort to massive injections of vitamin B. I've seen people return from the grave after a quick pick-me-up like this. In fact, some were able to celebrate their recovery with another drink.

Heat Prostration and Sunstroke

Heat and sunburn can affect us in unexpected ways. Headache, dizziness, nausea, fatigue, irritability, swollen feet and ankles, and diarrhea may sound like penalties for a particularly wild fiesta, but these are also common symptoms of too much heat and sunburn.

Heat prostration and sunstroke (also called heatstroke) are caused by excessive physical exertion in heat and prolonged exposure to the sun. However, the symptoms and treatments are distinctly different for each.

• **Heat prostration** is relatively common and can come on very quickly. Take it easy when it's hot; wear light, loose, well-ventilated clothing (heavier clothing is advisable in deserts) and a broad-brimmed hat. Drink lots of fluids and eat high-energy foods. Increase your intake of salt in hot, dry areas.

Symptoms: The skin is ashen, cold and clammy; sweating may be heavy; pulse less than 100 and no significant increase in body temperature. Other symptoms are headache, dizziness, weakness, vertigo, dim or blurred vision, irritability and mild muscular cramps. In other words, you feel really rotten.

At the first sign of heat prostration (a headache usually), I take two salt tablets, guzzle a quart or more of water and get out of the sun. (There is controversy about the efficacy of salt tablets, but we've found them useful.) This usually does the trick.

The treatment for heat prostration is very simple; loosen your clothing and lie down in a reclining position (feet *higher* than the head) in a cool, shaded place. Cool water may be taken.

• **Sunstroke** is less common but much more serious than heat prostration. Sunstroke is often brought on by very hot weather when even the nights are unpleasantly warm. The measures taken to avoid it are similar to those used for heat prostration.

However, the symptoms of sunstroke are in many ways almost opposite to those of heat prostration. The attack may be sudden or preceded by complaints of weakness, headache, vertigo and nausea. A reduction or even cessation of sweating may occur several hours before the attack. The victim is flushed, with hot, dry skin. Cramps or twitching may occur and the victim appears anxious and listless. The pupils are contracted early, but dilate (open) later. The pulse may be 160 or more, respiration rate 20 or 30 per minute and body temperature 105 to 106 degrees F (see *Fever* in this chapter right now!). Have the victim lie down with the feet *lower* than the head. *It's time to find a doctor!* Don't wait; just do what you can to lower the fever on your way to the hospital.

Sunstroke is serious and the symptoms are obvious, so don't wait around until the situation becomes critical—rush to a doctor or to a place where adequate measures (ice, fast transportation, etc.) can be taken if necessary.

Beat the Heat

• **Wear loose, light-colored clothing.** When appropriate (at the beach), wear shorts and sandals without socks.

• **Use a hat.**

• **Drink lots of water** and non-alcoholic liquids, even when you don't feel particularly thirsty.

• **Rest frequently.** Give your body time to cool off several times a day. If you're walking, sightseeing or window shopping, rest often in the shade. Take cool showers or splash water over your face, hands and arms often.

• **Limit your exposure to the full sun to half an hour a day**, even if you are fully clothed. The effects of heat are cumulative. You can only take so much before it knocks you down.

Heat continues to affect you after dark. If you're feeling queasy or weak in the knees, avoid too much exertion at night. On warm evenings, dancing is like running a midday marathon.

Should you suffer from too much heat, you may experience brightly flushed skin, profuse sweating and dizziness or even cold, clammy skin and a cessation of sweating. *Cool down as quickly as possible.* When our friend Jean got red in the face and cranky while visiting the ruins of Chichén Itzá, I immediately led her into the shade and slowly poured a bottle of cold mineral water over her head. She splashed a second bottle over her face and arms, and drank a third one for good measure. Jean was back on her feet within an hour, but she took it easy for the next couple of days.

Hepatitis A

Hepatitis A is a highly communicable disease spread by saliva, food and drink (hepatitis B is spread via blood or sexual contact). Injections of gamma globulin are no longer recommended for protection against hepatitis A. However, a very effective vaccine is available.

The symptoms of hepatitis A are jaundice (the whites of the eyes and eventually the skin look yellowish), loss of appetite, fatigue (are you sleeping fourteen hours?), aches and pains, nausea and brownish urine. If you have the disease or have come into contact with someone who does, take extra care to avoid passing it on. Make every effort to keep separate eating utensils (boil those used by the sick person or use paper plates and cups) and, if possible, use a separate bathroom. Keep your hands clean! (The danger of passing along the infection ends when the signs of jaundice have passed.)

The treatment is simple but slow: a good diet (lots of fresh fruits and vegetables), B vitamins and plenty of rest. Avoid alcohol and tobacco entirely. Don't push yourself too soon or you'll have a relapse. Hospitalization is required only in severe cases. Because drugs are sold so freely in Mexico, many hepatitis sufferers mistakenly take lots of antibiotics.

Infections and Wounds

The most minor cut or scrape can lead to serious trouble if ignored, especially in the tropics, where casual scratching of mosquito bites often leads to open sores and infections.

Puncture wounds are very prone to infection. Bacteria may literally be injected into the flesh and there's usually no great flow of blood to rinse them out again. They should be cleaned as thoroughly as possible and, if necessary, enlarged (time to bite the bullet). Although you might prefer to delay the operation until it appears essential (such as the appearance of pus and swelling), a puncture wound can infect rapidly if not properly cleaned. If infection does set in (red with pus and swelling), it may be necessary to enlarge the wound and clean it again.

To both prevent and heal infections, clean wounds, insect bites and infections often. It is far easier to prevent infections with soap and water than to cure them. If the wound is deep or too painful to scrub, flush it well with soapy water and then hydrogen peroxide. The foaming action of the peroxide removes particles of dirt and grime. If possible, soak the wound in a bucket of warm water. Add a teaspoon of soap. Apply hot compresses for twenty minutes, four times daily, to improve circulation in the wounded area.

Washing a wound with lime juice (it stings!) or alcohol helps prevent infection. The use of lime juice on wounds and infections speeds up healing by killing weak tissue, but don't overdo it. Reapply if the area around the wound begins to redden.

A compress of crushed garlic also helps prevent infection. Cover the wound and surrounding skin with some type of cooking or massage oil, then apply crushed garlic (a couple of cloves on a small wound). If the garlic causes burning, remove, wash and reapply, using more oil. Cover the garlic with a bandage. The wound should be cleaned two or three times a day and a fresh garlic poultice applied. Goldenseal powder can also be sprinkled on infections.

Steve and his family swear by the healing power of *tepezcohuite*. This powdered tree bark (*Mimosa tenuiflora poiret* or *árbol del piel*) from Chiapas is sold by street vendors, *boticas* and health food shops. Sprinkle *tepezcohuite* on abrasions, cuts and burns. It will soothe and seal the skin, and stop bleeding. "Amazing stuff!"

Persistent infections, such as itching sores, are common in tropical areas. The common practice of using antibiotic salves is seldom as effective as careful and continual washing with soap and water. Clean the sores thoroughly at least three times a day and keep them dry; don't go swimming. Lime juice can also applied several times a day until it no longer stings.

Blood poisoning can develop very quickly but it is quickly controlled with antibiotics. A friend had a noticeable red line along one arm just thirty hours after poking a large cactus spine into his thumb. A typical treatment is 250 milligrams of penicillin four times a day for five days. (Stop taking it if you experience any allergic reaction.) If the red line is gone before you've finished the penicillin tablets, continue to take them until they're finished. If you fail to complete the treatment, the infection can reappear.

Warning: Blood poisoning can be fatal. Self-medication is sometimes necessary but your best strategy, especially if the red line grows, is to see a doctor as soon as possible.

Minor urinary infections, typified by a sensation of having to urinate but can't, or a burning sensation, are relieved by drinking large quantities of *té de jamaica* (hibiscus). Pour one liter of boiling water over a handful of dry flowers and steep, or soak the flowers in cold water for several hours. If the symptoms seem worse, try *boldo* or eucalyptus leaf tea. Cranberry juice (available in some large supermarkets), herbal teas or even plain water will also help. Avoid coffee, black tea and booze.

Vaginal infections are common for women who are unable to bathe regularly, usually the case when camping or traveling in remote areas.

If the symptoms are mild (burning sensation, itching), a douche one to three times daily should be sufficient. Add one or two tablespoons of vinegar or lime juice to a liter of purified water. It is best to avoid intercourse until the infection is cleared up.

Do not use antibiotics unless you are unable to stop the infection with other treatments. If antibiotics are used, be sure to complete the full treatment to avoid a recurrence. If you must resort to antibiotics and are having intercourse, your partner should follow the same treatment.

Yeast infections (itching, burning and sometimes a whitish discharge) should be treated with a yogurt douche or the lime or vinegar mixture. Another remedy is to carefully peel a clove of garlic (don't cut or nick the garlic) and tie it in a gauze strip with a tail for easy removal. Insert the garlic high in the vagina for 24 hours. Repeat daily as necessary. Boric acid, in capsules, is also effective. Insert one capsule high in the vagina each morning and evening.

Warning: Antibiotics actually cause yeast infections and should not be used in an attempt to treat them.

Intestinal Parasites (Worms)

I have a real aversion to intestinal worms, a common problem in Latin American countries. To avoid them, as I have so far, eat lots of garlic (swallow a few chopped cloves at least once a day as if they were aspirin), lime juice and drink *epazote* tea. (Pregnant women should not drink *epazote* tea.) A healthy digestive track helps keep intestinal parasites from getting a foothold. We also take acidophilus and other probiotics (see *Health and First Aid Kit*). Papaya seeds are also effective: take three a day to prevent worms and nine a day for nine days to eliminate them. Other common preventatives are to eat *pepitas* (squash seeds) in generous quantities and thin-skinned avocados—skin and pulp, but not the seed.

Epazote

Malaria

Malaria exists below about 3,000 feet in elevation in parts of Mexico, but it is more prevalent in Belize and lowland Guatemala. This brief discussion doesn't mean malaria should be shrugged off, especially if you'll be camping, jungle-bashing or bushwhacking. However, your best protection against malaria is simply to avoid being bitten by disease-carrying mosquitoes. This can't be emphasized enough. When mosquitoes are present (usually at dusk and dawn), we wear long-sleeved shirts, trousers and socks. We go out of our way to avoid mosquito bites—even if it means looking unfashionable and sweating like a pack of wild boars. As much as I hate the stuff, we sometimes use potent mosquito repellents that contain the ingredient DEET.

Anti-malarial medications are available, but they're too powerful to be taken casually. For much more on malaria prevention and other travel health topics, consult the excellent book **Staying Healthy in Asia, Africa and Latin America** by Dirk Schroeder. (See *For More Information: Health.*)

Nausea

A cup of *té de perro* (dog tea) or *té de manzanilla* (camomile) will relieve that queasy feeling in your stomach after a trip through the meat stalls in the market. Add cinnamon if you have it. Chewing ginger root or eating soda crackers also helps, and if that doesn't do the trick, Alka-Seltzer is widely available.

Nervousness and Tension

Tranquilizers such as Valium and Librium may be sold without a prescription, though a prescription is legally required. A better alternative, however, is to eat a natural tranquilizer such as the delicious, slightly narcotic *zapote borracho* ("drunken" *zapote*, also *zapote negro*) or a *zapote blanco*. A tea of *zapote* leaves is also said to be calming. Teas made from mint, rue (*ruda*), valerian (*valeriana*), orange leaves, linden (*flor de tila*), lemon plant (*té de limón*) and camomile are also effective *calmantes*. Sidewalk herb vendors sell packages of mixed teas for *nervios* and *insomnio*. I've used them and they work.

Calcium and B vitamins (nutritional or brewer's yeast) are also effective. Calcium (with magnesium and zinc) is good for insomnia. (Natural sources are tortillas, sesame seeds, greens and sprouts.)

Rashes

Rashes caused by sweating frequently bother travelers unaccustomed to constant warm, humid air. Although talcum powder (*talco*) is sold in pharmacies and *boticas*, cornstarch (*maizena*) is even more common and much cheaper. Buy a small box and transfer the contents to something leak-proof. Dust it on the rash every few hours. Aloe vera gel quickly soothes rashes and promotes healing. Wear loose clothing.

Seasickness
I feel your pain: as an apprentice marine biologist in Alaska I was seasick for five months and lost almost forty pounds. While praying for calm seas, I suggest you stare at the horizon and breathe deeply. Don't look down at the water, don't go below decks and don't hide your head in your arms; it'll just get worse. Bathe your face in cool water. After puking, eat dry crackers and drink lots of water to avoid dehydration. Motion sickness pills (*pastillas para mareo*) will (hopefully) cause drowsiness.

Shock
There are two types of shock: physical and mental. When you try to flag down a cab in Escarcega and it runs you over, you'll suffer the first variety. To treat **physical shock**, have the patient sit down with their head between their knees. In severe cases—a faint rapid pulse, fast breathing, dry tongue and sweating—have the victim lie down. Elevate the feet about twelve inches. Cover, but don't allow overheating. Small amounts of liquids can be given in mild cases, but none is allowed when the shock is severe.

Mental shock, better known to travelers as "culture shock," isn't something to laugh off lightly. Culture shock is the result of a fast and almost total change in environment, exactly the situation most of us experience when we visit Mexico. The symptoms may be complicated by physical exhaustion or other travel-related ailments such as diarrhea, sunburn or hangover. The usual signs of culture shock are: vague feelings of paranoia and weirdness, irritability, loss of appetite, crying jags, a sudden compulsive desire to go to Yosemite National Park instead of Puebla and a sense of isolation from what is happening around you.

The treatment must begin at once. For mild cases, read selected articles to the victim from American magazines or newspapers, particularly *Time, Newsweek* and *Reader's Digest*. Evoke memories of Safeway and McDonald's while guiding the patient to a comfortable bench in the plaza. Daydream aloud about exotic islands and tropical sunsets, while speculating on traffic jams and winter snow depths at home.

Severe cases of culture shock should be isolated, preferably on a beach. Beaches can cure even terminal shock, but beware of setbacks caused by trips to town.

If you're traveling alone, immediately seek the company of other well-seasoned travelers. Under no circumstances should you indulge in the mutual exchange of "horror stories" about diarrhea, scorpions, bus wrecks or *federales*. Visits to traumatically American-style hotels, restaurants and trailer parks can cure some cases, but may lead to disastrous and irreversible addiction. In the most severe cases of culture shock, a well-adjusted friend can administer careful doses of peanut butter, Campbell's tomato soup and white *Bimbo* bread.

Letters from home can bring an instant cure. It may be necessary for concerned friends to fabricate gloomy correspondence with appropriate news items ("All of your friends have left for Mexico," ". . . and then the water pipes froze and burst" and so on).

Sprains
Keep the sprain as still as possible. Wrap it well to give firm support. Within the first twenty-four hours after the injury, apply ice once an hour for ten to fifteen minutes or soak it in cold water to reduce swelling and pain. Afterwards, soak in hot water several times a day. I also use ibuprofen to reduce pain and swelling.

Sunburn
• **Limit your exposure** to the sun to fifteen to twenty-five minutes a day until your skin begins to tan. Avoid the harshest rays, between 11 a.m. and 3 p.m.

• **Use sun block liberally and frequently.** If you perspire heavily (and in the hot sun, who doesn't?) or swim, use a good waterproof block. Reapply it often, just to be safe.

• **Apply sun block to your lips, ears, balding head and the tops of your bare feet.** Bring plenty of sun block from home and apply it repeatedly from dawn to dusk. I once sunburned my feet so badly that I couldn't wear sandals or shoes for two weeks. Protect the backs of your knees as well.

• **Keep a hat, dark glasses and clothing close at hand.**

• **Don't forget to drink plenty of non-alcoholic fluids.**

• **Think of sunburn as "solar radiation sickness"** and you'll understand why it can cause severe headaches, nausea and even diarrhea.

• **If you're taking antibiotics, avoid sunbathing entirely** or you may have a serious reaction.

Your first wonderful day at the beach may be the last you'll spend outdoors for weeks. Your initial exposure to bright sun shouldn't exceed fifteen or twenty minutes, even if your skin is naturally dark. People with red or blond hair should take even less sun. Around sand, water or snow, decrease your exposure times even more. Clouds are not sun filters and many tourists suffer very serious burns on overcast days.

When you're in doubt about how much sun you've taken and how much more you can stand—get into the shade. Put on light clothing, but if it's loosely woven you will probably get a sunburn right through the material.

To test your skin for burning, press one or two fingers firmly over the exposed area and hold down for several seconds. Now quickly release the pressure. A pale spot will mark the finger impression. If the spot is still distinct after you've said, "I've got a sunburn," you're right, you do. Use this test all over your body; some parts burn much faster than others. Remember: burning retards tanning.

Serious sunburns may be accompanied by heat prostration or sunstroke. Until the worst reaction is over, it is necessary to stay completely out of the sun—not too difficult as a few feeble rays will feel like the touch of a blowtorch.

If you've been burned, use liberal amounts of aloe vera gel (Lorena's favorite). It has an amazing ability to both relieve pain and prevent blistering. Compresses of grated or crushed raw potatoes or onions are very effective. Fresh or canned milk also helps, but it must be applied frequently. Vinegar can also be used.

Peeling of badly sunburned skin can lead to infection. If blisters appear, *leave them alone*. Without the protection of skin and natural fluids, the sensitive skin underneath will dry and crack, hurting like hell.

Avoid lotions that contain more than a trace of alcohol. Pure coconut oil (*aceite de coco*) is inexpensive in Mexico and a good post-sun skin conditioner

Note: Please don't buy Mexican turtle oil. Sea turtles are protected by law, but illegal turtle products purchased by tourists definitely contribute to poaching. Turtle products cannot be imported into the U.S.

Secrets of the Maya Revealed!

The usual early morning vocal battle between the village dogs and roosters had just erupted as I sagged wearily into my dew-moistened hammock.

"Lorena! Steve!" I called weakly. "Wake up! I'm dying." The only response from the hammocks slung nearby was a low, "Hummmmm?"

"I said, I'm dying, goddamit! The least you could do is wake up and look!" Lorena's head poked from beneath a blanket.

"Still got diarrhea?" she asked sleepily.

"Have I got it?" I moaned. "Hell, yes! I've been sitting in the bushes all night!"

I was about to launch into a detailed description of my ailments when a familiar voice called, "*¡Ola! ¡Carlitos!*" It was Nacho, an old friend who fed us during our visits in exchange for odd jobs around his tiny restaurant. I had agreed the night before to help him prepare *cochinita pibil* (baked pig). The first step, unfortunately, was to dig a deep pit in the loose sand. I looked over at him standing patiently with a shovel in one hand and a cup of coffee for me in the other, and gave an involuntary groan.

"Carlitos?" he said anxiously. "What is it? Are you sick?"

"I will soon be over there, Nacho." I waved feebly at the cemetery behind his restaurant, twisting my face into an appropriate grimace of agony.

He laughed uproariously and called to Steve and Lorena, "I told you that one day Carlos would never be able to leave this beautiful place." As they chuckled over this bit of humor, I suddenly clutched my stomach and rushed into the nearby bushes.

A few minutes later, white-faced and shaking, I slipped tenderly back into the hammock. Nacho looked at me with genuine concern and said, "You look *terrible*. I'm going to get *la abuela* to help you."

"What was that?" Lorena asked, sitting upright and turning toward me with an eager look on her face. "What did Nacho say?"

"He's going to get the grandmother," I said. "At least, someone seems concerned about what happens to me."

I knew that Lorena's sudden interest came from the aura of mystery that surrounded Nacho's aged mother, a person we had seen off and on during our many visits, but only as a dark wrinkled face in the tiny kitchen behind the restaurant. It was said that she had not left the immediate area in over seven years. Because Nacho delighted in nighttime tales of strange Mayan lore, we more than suspected the grandmother of *brujería* (witchcraft). Lorena had been waiting for an opportunity such as this to break into the old woman's isolation.

Nacho soon returned, followed not only by his mother but also by the rest of the family, from his wife and children to various nieces and in-laws. Ribald comments over my condition came by the dozen.

"*¡Oye, Carlos!* How many times last night?"

"*¡Caray!* You made a new path into the woods!"

"That's what you get for drinking Tonio's rum!"

The grandmother shushed them impatiently and stared deeply into my eyes. Nacho whispered into her ear. "Shall we give him the *chiles*?" She shook her old head slowly and uttered the first words we'd heard her say in a surprisingly strong, clear voice. "No, this is bad. He needs *El Alacrán!*"

"The Scorpion?" I thought. "For God's sake, isn't this carrying things a little too far? Who is this lady anyway? What does she know?"

As I started to object, Nacho laid his hand soothingly on my shoulder and said, "Don't worry, *amigo*. It's a dead scorpion and dry as dust!"

I laughed nervously, but was interrupted by grandmother's abrupt command: "You have to eat it!"

The children chattered with excitement, "Carlos is going to eat *el alacrán!*"

Nacho broke up the entire group by adding, "With *chile* sauce."

"Quiet!" grandmother ordered sharply, motioning one of the young girls to her side. I watched anxiously as she slipped the girl a coin and muttered something in her ear.

"What was that?" I asked, amazed at the speed with which the girl had dashed off toward the village.

"¿Mamá?" Nacho said. "What is it?"

She shrugged her shoulders casually and said, "It's nothing, just el polvito."

I looked sullenly at Lorena and Steve. "Now, that's it!" I said quietly in English. "She just sent off for the 'little powder' and I'm not up for that one."

Lorena fairly danced with glee; this was the real thing, an authentic Mayan secret remedy!

While the family followed Grandma respectfully back to their morning chores, I continued my protests. "Look, you guys. I honestly don't think this is going to help me out any. That scorpion sounds bad enough, but I really don't like the idea of taking 'little powders.' Maybe it's something dangerous."

"Oh, Carl," Lorena exclaimed, "think of what a great chance this is! This may be a whole new thing for the book, a really natural cure for diarrhea!"

"I think I'd rather stick with Lomotil," I muttered, "and try Granny's potions on somebody else."

Steve interrupted to say, "Well, you're too late now. You'll have to take their cure so you don't hurt anyone's feelings. Besides, it's a hell of a long ways to the nearest drugstore."

Before I could protest further, Nacho called, "Come here, Carlitos. It's almost ready."

I trudged slowly through the sand to the single large table that comprised the restaurant's furniture. Granny was carefully grinding a large brown scorpion in her stone molcajete. The ground scorpion was then mixed with a white powder, presumably el polvito.

"Which do you want?" Nacho asked, opening the lid of the beer cooler.

"What?" I said.

"Which do you want?" he repeated. "We've got Coca, Sidral, grape or orange."

"Why?" I stammered, by now completely confused.

"For the cure, Carlitos," he explained patiently. "You have to drink it with a bottle of pop."

I looked at Lorena; her faith in Mayan remedies had just dropped several degrees. Steve was smirking over a bottle of warm Coke, enjoying the scene intensely.

"Grape," I croaked, my throat suddenly dry and chalky.

With great ceremony, Nacho wiped the bottle clean and popped off the top with his teeth. Grandmother drank off the top few inches with a faint grin and then sifted the mixture of powders into the purplish liquid. Foam immediately formed and she thrust the bottle at me quickly, ordering, "Drink it fast! All of it!"

I choked down bubbly sweet mouthfuls as fast as possible, feeling the gritty scorpion stick between my teeth. As the last gulp disappeared, a loud roar of approval came from the crowd around me.

"You're cured!" Nacho laughed, slapping me on the shoulder, "and only we know what it was that did it!"

I was about to ask what he meant when a sudden cramp sent me scurrying back into the bushes. Happy shouts followed:

"Not again! There he goes!"

"Give him another scorpion!"

"Watch where you step!"

Several hours later Nacho approached the hammock. "How goes it, Carlitos?" he asked. "Bad, Nacho," I answered. "That cure didn't do it."

"Yes," he said sadly, "we didn't think it would."

"What do you mean?" I asked intently. "Why not?"

"They were out of the powder we wanted, so grandmother gave you sugar instead. She thought it might help. Too bad, though," he mused. "The other stuff is really strong."

"What other stuff?" I asked.

"Oh, Carlitos, you know," Nacho said casually. "Alka-Seltzer."

SAFETY

Is Mexico safe? • *The accidental tourist* • *Drinking and drugs* • *Valuables and rip-offs* • *Swimming and lifeguards* • *Parasailing* • *Revolutions and guerrillas* • *Safety alert*

Mexico is a very foreign country. On a scale of "foreignness" from 1 to 10, I rate Tacoma as a 1 (very familiar), Canada a 2, Texas a 3 and Mexico a solid 10. In spite of its proximity to the U.S., Mexico often seems as different to us as Ecuador or China.

"Like Mexico, there are not two," is a popular expression of pride in the country's unique personality. In other words, Mexico is not the United States, but a distinct and different country, with its own language, foods and customs. This can be overwhelming at times, especially for the person who expects Mexico to be some kind of predictable theme-park filled with *mariachi* music and tequila sunrises.

Is Mexico Safe?

• **"Will I be safe in Mexico?"** After giving a Mexico travel seminar and slide show in Seattle, I was approached by an excited, silver-haired grandmother who pressed my hand and exclaimed, "Oh, thank you! I'm so relieved! My husband's friends swore that if we went to Mexico we wouldn't have a chance!" She recounted a chilling list of horror stories, premeditated crimes and bandit antics that her well-meaning friends claimed await anyone foolish enough to step south of the border.

"It sounded just too awful to be true!" she concluded. "But then again, I wanted to hear your opinion before we bought tickets to Acapulco."

I didn't know whether to laugh or to cry.

Even such anxious queries as "Can I avoid diarrhea?" (yes, see *Staying Healthy*) and "Where's your favorite beach?" (a closely guarded secret) take a back seat to the question, "Is Mexico safe?" Having lived and traveled in Mexico for most of the past twenty years, we answer this question with an emphatic *yes*!

• **OK, if Mexico is safe, why are some people so nervous?** In a word, bad news not only travels fast but it dies very slowly. We still hear nervous questions about well-publicized crimes and natural disasters that took place many years ago.

Mexicans and foreign residents often complain that in the eyes of the American and international press, "the only news about Mexico is bad news." Drug wars, bus wrecks, floods and hurricanes make good headlines and attention-grabbing sound bites. This sensational form of news coverage contributes to the mistaken impression that Mexico (or the world beyond our own borders) is a riskier place than home.

"As a matter of cold fact, there are more bandits in a city like Los Angeles in one night than in the entire Republic of Mexico in a year. But being more picturesque, every bandit in Mexico becomes an alluring drama to the Yankee newspapers."
— Harry Carr, *Old Mother Mexico* (1931)

Keep in mind that several million tourists visit Mexico every year, including students, families, tour groups, singles, retirees and honeymooners. Of these millions of annual visitors only the tiniest fraction have problems during their stay. As I said, however, Mexico is definitely different. A certain amount of nervousness is natural. Once you get used to that difference, you'll relax and be able to laugh off your old fears.

"I was lying on the beach near Zihuatanejo, getting a suntan, when all of a sudden a bunch of soldiers with machine guns went by. What was it, a revolution?"

No, it wasn't a revolution or war maneuvers; it was Mexico's way of telling tourists to relax! Military patrols on beaches are part of Mexico's *Immediate Action Program For Tourism Promotion*. This ambitious plan includes measures to improve Mexico's safety, to spruce up the country's image and to expand tourism facilities and services.

Eighteen-year-old marines toting machine guns on public beaches and Army units posted on major tourist highways are part of this reassurance program, as are increased numbers of uniformed cops and Green Angel highway patrols. More than a thousand Green Angel trucks offer tourists everything from on-the-spot car repairs and gasoline to medical assistance and directions. (See *Driving: Green Angels*.)

In our experience, tourists lead a charmed life in Mexico. In fact, statistics show that you are more likely to be the victim of violent crime while in the United States than in Mexico.

If you're like me and find cold comfort in statistics, consider what Lorena and I have heard expressed by hundreds of Mexico travelers, from backpackers and budget vagabonds to stockbrokers, secretaries, college professors, retirees, students and snowbirds escaping northern winters. Among those who spend more than a couple of weeks in Mexico or who make repeat visits, the consensus is virtually unanimous: Mexico actually *feels safer* than the U.S. (As several parents pointed out, children play freely in public parks and walk city streets without close supervision.)

Although Mexico is safe, it is by no means perfectly safe. Some tourists are the victims of crimes (committed both by Mexicans and other tourists). Others have problems that are best described as "self-inflicted." Of these, drinking, drugging and reckless driving top the list. I'll never forget the drunken American woman shouting across the hotel lobby, "I've got $2,000 and two days to blow it!" For a moment, I was tempted to "help" her out myself.

Unfortunately, scenes like this aren't that uncommon, especially in resorts. When it comes to trouble, tequila takes a far higher toll than the busiest *bandido*. I consider it a testimony to Mexico's safety that so few tourists infected with "fiesta fever" actually land in hot water.

• Solo and first-time travelers are especially vulnerable to strained nerves.
The normal stresses and minor anxieties associated with travel are often heightened by not being able to talk things out with a friend or family member. Bottling up our fears and frustrations can lead to a malady I call Traveler's Paranoia. Symptoms include a morbid fascination with airline timetables and uncontrollable fantasies of

being stranded in the middle of Mexico City without your traveler's checks. (See *Staying Healthy: Shock: Cultural*.)

 • **Women traveling alone may be the object of unwanted attention from men** (see *Machismo*). Follow the example of Mexican women: sit with other women on buses and trains; don't respond to men's comments and overtures; look for other women or tourist companions for trips to ruins, beaches and other out-of-the-way places.

Use cabs late at night rather than walking. Unfortunately, men often assume that women on lonely streets and deserted beaches are searching for companionship. Carry a keychain whistle and, if you're bothered by someone, give your whistle a mighty blast. Mexican cops use whistles to signal each other and to scare off troublemakers.

Until you feel comfortable in Mexico, don't be embarrassed to pamper yourself a little. Travelers on a tight budget should be especially careful not to subject themselves to more of Mexico than they can comfortably handle. As a rule of thumb, the cheaper a hotel room is, the more "interesting" it will be. When your sense of humor about the situation has worn as thin as the sheets, it's time for a temporary upgrade in accommodations, at least until you get your feet back on the ground.

The Accidental Tourist

In Mexico, "look before you leap" isn't just an expression, it's a survival tip. Forget about bandits; the greatest threat to your safety comes from slippery cobblestones, uneven sidewalks, knee-high curbs, head-knocking signs, eye-poking awnings, toe-stubbing thresholds, open trenches, unexpected drop-offs and discarded construction debris.

In Zihuatenajo, a busy sidewalk collapsed into a pit deeper and darker than a storm sewer. Rather than close the sidewalk, pedestrians were forced to step carefully around this unmarked hazard. In Mexico City, construction workers stretched a heavy dark wire across a busy downtown sidewalk, at ankle height. Did anyone call the cops? No, passersby simply stepped over this dangerous hurdle.

We call these unexpected pedestrian pitfalls "GRINGO traps," though they also catch Mexicans, Europeans, Japanese and anyone else who forgets to watch their step.

In a single day in Puerto Vallarta, I saw three women tourists sprawl painfully on cobblestones and uneven sidewalks. At Uxmal, a popular archaeological site in the Yucatán Peninsula, two young Mexican women near me tripped over each other while climbing the steep, narrow stairs of a pyramid. They took a horrifying, bone-breaking fall to the bottom.

In a Pacific coast resort, starry-eyed honeymooners strolling along an unlighted seawall plunged through a gap in the guardrail and brought their vacation to a painful (but not fatal) end. The message is clear: watch your step!

When tourists aren't stumbling or falling down, we're banging our heads. Though I'm of average (gringo) height, I can't count the number of times I've bashed my skull against low doorways, overhanging signs and swinging lamps. Be especially careful in souvenir malls and public markets, where low sun awnings and miscellaneous head-knockers abound.

If you hurt yourself in Mexico, who pays? In virtually every circumstance, you do. Unlike the U.S., where every injury can lead to a lawsuit, suing someone is very difficult in Mexico. Poolside mishaps in hotels, for example, are almost always considered "no fault" under the law. When you smack your forehead against a gift shop sign that hangs perilously low over the sidewalk, the law assumes you weren't keeping your eyes open.

The benefit of this custom is that private individuals and businesses aren't crippled by insurance bills and lawsuits. If you are injured in Mexico, keep copies of any medical bills you incur and try to collect on your insurance policy at home.

Drinking and Drugs

Tourists who turn their vacations into a nonstop happy hour wear out their welcome very fast. They also suffer the vast majority of accidents, arguments, misunderstandings and minor unpleasantries. Crooks find gringo party animals to be particularly easy pickings. Officials I've talked to say it's no coincidence that tipsy tourists attract muggers, scam artists and thieves.

There is an unwritten tradition that (most) Mexican cops won't arrest a drunk unless he or she weaves or staggers. If you're at all unsteady—just to be safe—take a taxi.

One of the reasons I no longer drink is that I finally made the connection between trouble and tequila. Whenever a situation gets uncomfortable, weird or alarming, don't hesitate to leave. This is especially true when drinking is involved. If you do drink while visiting Mexico, keep it very moderate.

Mexicans may wink when tourists get carried away by too much sun, sand and *cerveza* (beer), but when it comes to drugs, their tolerance is close to zero. Don't kid yourself; Mexico is no longer as loose and easy as it once was. Cops with keen noses regularly patrol resort beaches and they regularly arrest foolish tourists for smoking marijuana. U.S.-trained, English-speaking narcs and paid informants also circulate in popular discos and nightclubs.

Reflecting Mexico's conservative attitude, penalties for possession of small quantities of marijuana, cocaine and so-called recreational drugs are extremely harsh. I cannot emphasize strongly enough the dangers of mixing drugs with travel in Mexico. The smallest pinch of marijuana or cocaine can take you directly to a Mexican dungeon. (See *Red Tape and the Law: Drugs and Marijuana.*)

Valuables and Rip-Offs

• **The best protection for your valuables is to leave most of them at home**, especially expensive jewelry. Be watchful in crowded places, including in the U.S. Many people lose baggage and cameras in large American airports while traveling to and from Mexico. In an ironic twist, a Mexican friend, a tourism official herself, had her luggage stolen by a well-dressed, fast-moving American woman in the lobby of a hotel in Acapulco.

• **Keep your valuables in the hotel safe.** Hotel rooms are not security vaults. Don't take chances with your extra money, expensive jewelry and other valuables. This simple precaution can't be overstressed. Hotel *cajas de seguridad* (safe-deposit boxes) are your best protection against theft and accidental loss.

• **Wear a money belt or hidden pocket.** If you don't have a money belt or hidden pocket (see *Mexico A to Z: Hidden Pocket* for instructions on making your own), safety-pin a sock inside your pants or shirt and stuff it with your valuables. Money belts and thin leather wallets that can be worn inside your clothing can be found in Mexican luggage and leather-goods shops.

"Better safe than sorry" doesn't sound like a cliché when you consider the consequences of losing your money and identification. If I don't like the looks of the hotel's security boxes (or the desk clerk), I keep my money belt close at hand, twenty-four hours a day. This includes taking my money belt into the bathroom while showering or using the toilet, especially in rooms that don't have double locks on the door.

"Today in Mexico one may occasionally be held up on the road, just as one may be held up in Wyoming or Vermont, but brigandage as a lucrative career for young men of courage has been suppressed."

— Charles Flandrau, **Viva Mexico** (1908)

• **Take reasonable precautions against muggers.** The same precautions you observe at home or when visiting an American city will protect you in Mexico. Most muggings and petty crimes occur late at night. Main thoroughfares and busy streets are usually lighted until 10 p.m. or later, but lighting isn't dependable on side streets, parks, alleys, shopping arcades and beaches. When in doubt, walk in groups on darker streets or take a taxi.

If you are an unescorted woman, you will attract unwanted attention. Always use cabs after 9 p.m.

Resort beaches may or may not be patrolled by the police at night. Where they aren't patrolled, beaches have a way of attracting "night people," from down-on-their-luck *campesinos* (countryfolk) looking for a warm bed of sand to strollers, drunks, lovers and skinny-dippers. Needless to say, these innocent "fish" may attract a few sharks. Because of this, I'm sorry to say that romantic, midnight walks on dark deserted beaches are not wise.

In the daytime be alert for pickpockets in crowded places. Pickpockets, purse snatchers, baggage "nappers" and other rip-off artists tend to work crowds. The richest pickings are at airports, bus stations, subways, banks, hotel lobbies, churches, public events, crowded markets and street celebrations.

I make a simple rule never to carry more in my pockets than I'm willing to lose; the rest of my valuables are either in a hotel security box or inside my money belt.

Avoid carrying valuables in purses, belt pouches and shoulder bags. Expensive bags are obvious targets, but thieves aren't above slitting a dusty day pack to get at the contents.

When I'm on the subway or in a city crowd, I carry my day pack or shoulder bag on my chest, with one arm draped across it. This simple precaution should be enough to protect your bag and to advise potential thieves that you're on guard.

Be equally cautious on resort beaches. Unless you're planning to haggle for souvenirs, take only a little pocket money. Beach thieves have sharper eyes than a *zopilote* (vulture). Hiding your watch, money and passport under a towel or burying them in the sand is the oldest trick in the book—and an invitation to get ripped off.

• **Keep track of your personal belongings.** When Lorena and I lead tours or travel with friends, we continually pick up our companions' stray cameras, passports, purses and room keys. Tourists routinely walk away from their suitcases, leave their credit cards at souvenir shops and their only shoes at the beach, and can't recall which *lavandería* (laundry) they left their clothes in.

Absentmindedness isn't limited to possessions. Cab drivers are regularly confronted by panicked tourists who have absolutely no recollection of what city they're in, much less the name of their hotel.

If something "goes missing," make a thorough search of your luggage and hotel room before you report it as lost or stolen. The notion that thievery is common in Mexico is definitely exaggerated. In many cases, tourists themselves are to blame.

A fellow we traveled with in eastern Mexico left his binoculars hanging on a chair in the restaurant of a small hotel. By the time he realized his mistake we were hundreds of miles away and couldn't go back. When I returned to the hotel two years later, the owner's first words were, "I have the binoculars your friend forgot."

"You should have sold them," I teased. "I would have."

"I couldn't do that," he said, clearly shocked. "*¡No son míos!*" ("They aren't mine!")

As a postscript, the fellow who lost and regained the binoculars returned to travel with us again. This time he left a very expensive Nikon camera in the washroom of a museum. In this case, however, the camera had vanished by the time we returned for it.

• **Stay safe in Mexico City:** The "Big Enchilada" is safer than New York City and Los Angeles, but petty thieves and pickpockets are on the increase. Stick to well-traveled tourist zones (don't venture into distant barrios), wear a money belt, and keep five or ten dollars' worth of pesos stuffed into a pocket. If you are mugged, hand this money over quickly, without argument. Mexican muggers seldom terrorize or attack their victims, especially if they don't put up a fight.

Swimming and Lifeguards

"If I ever have trouble in the water," a young tourist asked me nervously, "what should I yell in Spanish?"

"HELLLLLPPP!!" I demonstrated, adding, "the translation speaks for itself."

Tourism officials are quick to brag that Mexico has 6,000 miles of ocean coastline and too many swimming pools to count. Very little is said, however, about an almost complete absence of lifeguards, rescue boats and other safeguards for swimmers. On busy public beaches and even in hotel pools, it's swim at your own risk.

Unless you're a strong, practiced swimmer, be very careful when swimming in the ocean. Depending on the tides and weather, some of Mexico's most popular beaches have crunching surf and strong, unpredictable currents. Conditions change very quickly and even experienced swimmers can be taken unawares.

If body surfing is on your list of must-experience vacation thrills, go carefully. I can testify from painful personal experience that there's more to this sport than merely throwing yourself in front of a wave.

Against my advice, a friend challenged a powerful, fast-breaking surf near Manzanillo one afternoon. After being pounded and scraped across the bottom, he crawled from the sea with a bloody head and a badly sprained shoulder. It took an hour to excavate the sand from his ears. To add to his problems, he couldn't straighten up enough to drive his rental car. Later, he confessed that it took him a month to recover.

It is no coincidence that many beachfront hotels offer one or more swimming pools as an alternative to ocean swimming. Don't take risks. If there's any doubt, use the pool.

Parasailing

Compared to safe sports like mountain climbing, bungee jumping and hang gliding, parasailing is probably even more dangerous than it looks. Dunkings, collisions with beachfront hotels, tangled ropes and tow boats that break down or run out of gas are just some of the risks parasailors run.

Any temptation I had to try parasailing came to an end one awful afternoon, when I watched a middle-aged gringa drop out of the sky onto a palm tree. As someone observed, other than multiple fractures, abrasions and mild hysteria, she was "lucky."

Less than an hour later, the same boat's crew goofed again. Following a close shave with a hotel balcony, a young man was nearly skewered on a sailboat mast. He plunged into the sea screaming obscenities. After nearly drowning in the tangled, sunken parachute, the hapless tourist was dragged to shore, choking and spitting. Without a blush, the boat's crew insisted on full payment for the ride. The tourist's outraged bellow stopped a volleyball game half a mile away. It took several people to pry his hands off the parasail captain's throat.

There is no insurance on parasail rides and no guarantee that the equipment is safe or the operators well trained. Although most tourists don't have problems, the risks are real. My advice is to skip parasailing and keep your feet planted firmly on the beach.

Revolutions and Guerrillas

We've experienced a variety of coups, uprisings and crises during our travels in Mexico and Latin America. In general, travelers are more likely to be inconvenienced than actually at risk: businesses might be shuttered for a few days, strategic highways will be temporarily closed and public transportation curtailed. It can be hard to cash traveler's checks or make phone calls, and fresh yogurt could be scarce at your favorite café.

My advice when traveling into unsettled areas is simple: take U.S. State Department Travel Advisories with a large grain of salt—they are extremely conservative. Carry your passport and tourist card at all times, as well as extra cash in local currency and U.S. dollars, in a money belt hidden beneath your clothing. Keep a flashlight close at hand. No matter how tempting don't photograph armed people unless invited to.

To be extra safe in troubled areas, stay in after 8 p.m. Avoid parades, political rallies, demonstrations and protest marches. Take a room in the back of the hotel. Keep snacks, drinks and a fat novel handy: when in doubt—don't go out.

Fireworks are part of virtually every fiesta, but if you're nervous you'll probably mistake them for gunfire. To avoid the potential embarrassment of diving under a table, quickly tie your shoes or examine your toes.

Safety Alert

Year by year, the perennial question of "Is Mexico safe?" becomes more difficult to answer. Yes, I respond, Mexico is safe, but like every other country in the world, Mexico is not perfectly safe, nor is the country quite as safe as it used to be. As we all know from watching the evening news, crime is on the increase throughout the Americas—including the United States.

In Mexico, where any crime against a tourist is treated with special alarm by the foreign media, an increase in taxi robberies and street crime in Mexico City has generated dire warnings about personal safety. Tourism officials plead that the D.F.'s problem is no worse than that in any other big city. Programs have been instituted to better protect tourists, but fear, once released, is highly contagious and difficult to eradicate.

Our advice is to use the same streetwise precautions and common sense when visiting Mexico City that you follow in New York, Seattle, or Atlanta. To be doubly safe, and to increase your own peace of mind, avoid hailing cabs on the street—ask your hotel's desk clerk to call a cab, or take one from the lineup at a sitio (cab stand).

The most common targets of street criminals are well-dressed business people and the obviously affluent tourist or local resident. Avoid wearing any jewelry in public; don't carry fancy bags; and make your ATM withdrawals during busy hours. Most important, if you should be confronted by a thief, don't run and don't resist: hand over the loot with a minimum of fuss. Remember, it's not prudent to walk on deserted beaches at night, especially for women. Don't drive at night!

RED TAPE AND THE LAW

Tourists cards: validation, multiple-entry tourist cards, tourist card extension, lost tourist cards, student visas, immunization • Car permits: bonding your car, driving to Guatemala or Belize • Yachts and private aircraft • Pets • Guns and hunting • Fishing licenses • Official documents and checkpoints • Car insurance • Accidents • Mexican Customs inspections: border hassles, bribery, bribes • Tourists and Mexican law: what are my rights as a tourist? do tourists need to worry about cops? drugs and marijuana

Tourist Cards

There is just one thing that really makes going to Mexico different from crossing the border between neighboring U.S. states: a tourist card.

A tourist card is your permission from the Mexican government to visit Mexico. It is available free of charge at the border, at Mexican consulates, at Mexican Government Tourism Department Delegation offices (in large U.S. cities), at travel agencies or from the airline office or airport if you are flying. American and Canadian citizens will be issued a tourist card upon presentation of proof of citizenship. This can be an original birth certificate (a hospital copy is not accepted), a passport or a notarized affidavit of citizenship. Voter registration cards are no long valid for identification. Naturalized citizens must have a passport or naturalization papers.

If you don't have a passport, you will also need a photo ID. A driver's license can be used as a photo ID, but not as proof of citizenship.

The parents' written notarized consent is required if a minor (under 18) is going to Mexico alone or with another person, even if that person is the other parent. For example, a father must have the mother's consent to take any child under 18 into Mexico. In addition, if a minor travels with one parent and the other parent is deceased, or if the child has only one legal parent, a notarized statement must be given as proof.

These rules are strictly enforced, especially for tourists traveling by air.

Children under fifteen may be included on their parent's tourist card. Although this eliminates some paperwork, the child will not be allowed to leave Mexico without the parent or the parent without the child. It's easier and more flexible to fill out a separate tourist card for everyone in the family.

Validation

Validation of the tourist card is very important. This is done inside Mexico, at or just inside the border, or in the airport when you land. The length of your stay is determined at this point.

Tourist cards are dated ninety days from the day of issue. You must begin using the card by this date.

The length of time you may remain in Mexico is written or typed in the space preceded by the words in Spanish, English and French: "Authorized To Remain In Mexico (number of days) Days From Date of Entry."

Tourist cards issued by airlines and tourist agencies may already have thirty, sixty or ninety days in the space preceded by the words "Authorized To Remain In Mexico." In any case, always ask for more time than you think you'll need. Most tourists are given the maximum of 180 days, but some say, "Oh, just give me a thirty-day card. I'll only be here a few weeks." Then, when they've found their dream spot and would like to spend an extra month, their short tourist cards force them to return or to ask for an extension (see *Tourist Card Extension*, below).

The best way to convince a skeptical official that you should be given the amount of time you want in Mexico is to be very polite and as respectable-looking as possible. Forget about bribes and concentrate instead on charm. You'll have to take what you get or turn around and enter Mexico at another border point.

Important tourist card precautions: Once your tourist card has been validated you will be given the blue copy. Don't lose it! Your tourist card must be returned to Mexican Immigration upon departure. Also, write down your tourist card number and

keep this number separate from your travel documents—jot it down in the back of this book. If your tourist card is lost, having the original number will help greatly. Last, but definitely not least: unless you enjoy tangles of red tape, always give "tourist" or "pleasure" as your reason for visiting Mexico, not "business" or "student." These latter categories require heartbreaking amounts of additional paperwork.

Multiple-Entry Tourist Cards

Multiple-entry tourist cards valid for 180 days are available. If you'll be traveling back and forth to Mexico, ask for one of these. When you drive into Mexico, you usually get both a multiple-entry tourist card and car permit.

Tourist Card Extension

Extending your tourist card is possible, but you must apply for an extension *before your present card expires*. To stay longer than 180 days, you'll have to leave the country, if only for a few hours, and re-enter all over again. This is technically *prohibido* but commonly done.

To extend your tourist card, visit an office of *Migración* (Immigration) or *Turismo* (Tourism). They'll tell you what to do next. Be patient and polite; in our experience, it takes one to three days to get an extension. Be prepared to show credit cards or other proof of solvency (money) or you may be out of luck. It all depends on the mood of the official you talk to and your gift of gab.

If you remain in Mexico with an expired tourist card, you are liable for a fine. Though risky, some tourists simply leave Mexico without turning over their expired tourist cards. Inspections at the border of overland tourists are often lax. If you're flying home, however, expect a much closer scrutiny.

Special Chiapas Alert: To discourage visits from potential Zapatista supporters, tourists entering Chiapas from Guatemala are given just fifteen days in Mexico at the Comitan border crossing. We later had our fifteen-day visas extended in Oaxaca, but it was a hassle. Travelers in Chiapas also report that visas are sometimes canceled on the spot at Army checkpoints in and around Zapatista communities.

Lost Tourist Cards

Can't find your tourist card or car papers? Again, go to the nearest *Oficina de Turismo* (government tourist office) or *Migración*. In case of theft, a written report from the nearest police department will often speed things up.

Student Visas

A renewable, one-year Non-Immigrant Student Visa is available for those who intend to study in Mexico without leaving the country for more than 180 days a year. The requirements include proof of solvency, a good conduct letter from your local police, extra photos, etc. Not even school and immigration officials advise going through this red tape if you can get by using a regular tourist card. Further details and requirements are available at Mexican Consulates (see *For More Information*).

Immunizations

There are no mandatory vaccinations or shots needed for traveling in Mexico, but do-it-yourself explorers should probably have a recent tetanus shot.

Car Permits: A Step By Step Explanation

There's been a lot of hoopla about the red tape involved in driving a vehicle into Mexico. In fact, the process isn't half as difficult as rumor makes it out to be. As usual when dealing with any bureaucracy, be patient and good-humored. The entire process rarely delays us more than thirty minutes to an hour.

If you are taking a motor vehicle, trailer or boat into Mexico for more than seventy-two hours or are traveling beyond the "border zone" (about twelve miles south of the border), you'll need a vehicle permit in addition to your tourist card. Vehicle and boat importation permits are issued at the border when you cross into Mexico or at a special highway checkpoint when you leave the border zone.

Vehicles used in Baja and northwestern Sonora are exempt from this requirement, but boats still need permits. You'll also need a vehicle permit if you cross on the ferry from Baja to mainland Mexico. (See *The Best of Mexico: Baja California.*)

To take a vehicle into Mexico today, you will complete the following steps:

1. Produce a valid driver's license and proof of citizenship (see *Tourist Cards*, at the beginning of this chapter).

2. Present the vehicle's title, in your name (no borrowed cars). What if you aren't the legal title holder? Get a certified copy of the title and a notarized affidavit from the bank or other lien holder, giving you permission to take the vehicle into Mexico.

3. Have current license plates on the vehicle that will not expire while you are in Mexico.

4. Pay a bonding fee of about $12 with a major credit card—MasterCard, Visa, American Express or Diners Club only. The name on the credit card must match the applicant's name on the vehicle title, driver's license and personal identification. If you don't have a credit card, see *Bonding Your Car*, below.

5. Sign an affidavit vowing you will not sell your vehicle in Mexico, nor allow anyone (other than your spouse or children) to drive the vehicle unless you are in it. If you violate this pledge, the vehicle can be seized.

Bonding Your Car

Since 1991, Mexico has required drivers to get bonded vehicle permits (except for the states of Baja and Sonora). This bond is held in trust by the Mexican Army Bank (*Banjercito*) for the Mexican Treasury Department, better known as *Hacienda*. The purpose of the bond is simple: it discourages tourists from selling or abandoning their vehicles in Mexico.

As I've said, posting a bond is simple if you have a major credit card. If you aren't the lucky owner of a Big Four credit card, however, there are alternatives other than taking the bus.

• **Use a debit card:** A debit card is essentially a plastic check that draws directly from your bank account. Even though a debit card is not a credit card, it looks like one and can be used to pay the vehicle bonding fee.

• **Use a secured credit card:** Some banks offer special secured accounts for customers who can't qualify for a regular credit card or debit card. The cardholder makes a minimum cash deposit ($200 is common) which can't be touched. The "secured" Visa card can then be used up to the credit limit—which is equal to the cash deposit. You make a minimum monthly payment or pay off the entire balance, just like a normal Visa account. This is a neat way to get a major credit card but there's one caution: it can take weeks to set this all up, so don't delay; call your bank immediately.

Once you've got the new card, prepay at least $12 before you leave home. This way, the credit card balance will remain at zero when Banjercito charges their $12 bonding fee to your account. Assuming you don't use the card for other purchases, no payments will be due while you're in Mexico.

• **Post a cash deposit:** If you carry cash instead of plastic, a refundable deposit can be made with Banjercito. Based on a sliding scale, you can expect to put up at least $500 in cash for twenty-year-old passenger cars and pickup trucks, and about $3,000 cash for vehicles worth $20,000. Trailers and other towed units are not assessed for bonding.

When you leave Mexico, you'll have to take the bonded vehicle back to the same Banjercito used for entry. Your cash deposit will be returned in U.S. dollars (twenty-four hours a day).

• **Post a collateralized bond:** Non-refundable vehicle bonds are very similar to the bond you posted to get your worthless brother-in-law out of jail. The average traveler will pay $125 to several hundred dollars for such a bond, depending on the value of the vehicle and the agency used. As collateral, you will sign over the title to your vehicle to the bonding company until you return, which can be no more than 180 days.

Mexican bond agents can be found in border cities and around the office of Banjercito (the office which actually registers the bond). Pick an agent who will accept the vehicle title as collateral. Some agents require a cash deposit and an original birth certificate, not a copy. If the agent isn't there when you return, it's much easier to replace a vehicle title than a cash deposit of several hundred dollars.

To verify the latest entry requirements, contact **Tourism Mexico Entry Information Service:** 800-44-MEXICO (800-446-3942) for the latest red-tape requirements. For additional information use their "Fax Me Mexico" service (541-385-9282) and start with their menu index. Website: <http://mexico-travel.com/>.

Reliable updates on entry requirements are also available from the staff of **Sanborn's Insurance** (call 210-686-3601, in McAllen, Texas, during working hours). Sanborn's and AAA also issue tourist cards and immigration and Customs forms, and help their customers with the red tape for driving into Mexico.

Vehicle permit sticker: Once the car permit is issued, an official decal will be affixed to your windshield. At one time, a discreet tip prevented having the decal placed directly in the passenger's line of sight. Times are supposedly changing, but it doesn't hurt to be prepared.

Although a windshield filled with old tourist stickers is the mark of a veteran traveler, such a collection can also attract unwanted attention from immigration officials and cops. We always scrape off expired tourist stickers before re-entering Mexico.

Important notes about multiple entries: Your Mexican vehicle permit is valid for multiple entries during a maximum period of 180 days. Therefore, don't turn in your papers when you leave if you plan to return to Mexico within the time left on your papers. Hang onto the permit and avoid the hassle of getting a new one. However, if you leave and re-enter Mexico with a multiple-entry document, be sure that your papers don't expire inside Mexico. Once the permit expires, the vehicle can be confiscated.

Don't forget to return your car papers to Banjercito before you cross the border into the U.S. You must stop at the Banjercito office (usually next to the *Aduana*— Customs) and turn in your car permit. An *Aduana* official will scrape the sticker off your car window. Neglect to do this and you'll risk a substantial fine. In fact, you may not be allowed back into Mexico.

Impounding your car: If you must leave Mexico without your car or if something happens that prevents you from taking the vehicle out of Mexico before the permit expires, it can be temporarily impounded at a large airport or with a Customs office (*Oficina Federal de Hacienda*). A storage fee may be charged.

Boats, trailers, motorcycles and towed cars: A monthly fee and a registration fee based on weight are charged for sport boats taken into Mexico. Depending on the official who issues your papers, this fee may be applied to car-top boats or it may not. Boats over twenty-two feet in length must be bonded.

Boats, trailers and towed vehicles are usually treated separately, though they may be included on your car permit if the official at the border decides that would be easier. In other words, your motorbike might have its own papers or your boat, bike, trailer and hang glider might all be lumped together as accessories. The more toys you take into Mexico the more patient you must be with the inevitable red tape. Tourists who fly off the handle may find themselves refused entry into Mexico. As a visitor it is your responsibility to be cooperative. David Eidell sends this update on new rules for towed trailers on the Mexican mainland: "All trailers must have current license tags and be registered to the towing vehicle's owner. Travel trailers are issued a no-cost 'Twenty-Year Import' document and may remain in the country, even when the owner and towing vehicle depart."

Accessories: Your vehicle permit will also show accessories such as air conditioners, radios, tape decks, small trailers and so on. All listed accessories must leave Mexico with you and the car or you'll be liable for very stiff Customs duties. Accessories aren't always checked when you leave Mexico but you never know.

CB radios: CBers have been assigned three channels: 11 (emergencies), 13 (caravans) and 14 (general chatter). Permission from the government is required to use other channels.

Driving to Guatemala or Belize
When leaving Mexico to enter Guatemala or Belize, you may have to remind the Mexican officials that you have *multiple entrada* (multiple entry) car papers and/or tourist cards. If they attempt to collect your permit, insist (politely) that you want to hang on to it for the return trip. Once you surrender your multiple-entry documents, you'll have to go through the whole paper shuffle again (and risk getting only fifteen days or less at Chiapas border points).

Yachts and Private Aircraft

Clearance papers for yachts may be obtained at Mexican Consulate offices or from marine Customs brokers. These must be shown at ports of entry and departure. Boats under five tons are exempt from entry charges (theoretically, anyway). If you or your crew intend to go ashore you should obtain tourist cards in advance.

The basic regulations for aircraft are about the same as for cars. You must also send a written report of your flight plan to authorities of the international airport closest to where you intend to cross the border. There are other requirements and I suggest that you visit the nearest Mexican Consulate or write to Departmento de Transporte Aereo Internacional, Direccion General de Aeronautica Civil, Secretaria de Comunicaciones y Transportes, Avenida Universidad y Xola, 2 Piso, Mexico 12, DF (phone 5-19-81-83 or 5-19-76-25). Or, easier yet, write to Aircraft Owners and Pilots Association, 421 Aviation Way, Frederick, MD 21701, 301-695-2000. They also have a web page at <http://www.aopa.org>

AOPA offers a packet of comprehensive information for anyone considering flying into Mexico, including aircraft entry information, Customs guide, weather service companies, sample flight reports, a checklist for flight information, survival equipment sources, etc.

Pets

To take a dog or cat into Mexico and Guatemala, you must have a veterinarian's certificate stating that the animal is in good health and has been inoculated against rabies within the past six months. For Mexico, this certificate must be visaed (stamped) by the Mexican consul nearest your home. Although Mexicans rarely enforce these regulations at the border, Guatemalans are much stricter. (See *Guatemala: Red Tape.*)

Check with your veterinarian, the Mexican consul or a state or federal animal health official for regulations about pets of other types. You may find that you can take your pet into Mexico with no trouble but when you come back to the U.S., the poor thing will be considered "undesirable" by U.S. Customs officials. (See *Back to the U.S.A.*)

A good friend of ours who traveled with a chicken solved this problem by having her feathered companion smuggled across the border in a paper sack by a Mexican child. If you're traveling with a pig, this wouldn't be easy.

Having traveled many thousands of miles with Steve and his long-haired Guatemalan mutt Xuxa, my comments on pets will tend to be cynical. If you have a pet and are quite attached to it, I'm sure that no amount of negative advice will deter you from taking it with you. (We used to travel with two boisterous parrots.) Let my comments at least serve as warnings to help you avoid unexpected difficulties.

Pets in general do not enjoy the same exalted status in Mexico as they do in the U.S. This is particularly true of dogs. Dogs are considered by most Mexicans to be on the borderline between pests and severe inconveniences. Someone once estimated the canine population of Mexico City to be around one million. The fact that the majority of these dogs aren't owned or supported by any particular person or family, and just run free, is a good clue to the reason for their low esteem.

The threat of rabies causes both civil authorities and private individuals to carry out methodical programs of extermination among the dog population. Many tourist's pets have been inadvertently poisoned.

What does this anti-dog attitude mean for Killer, your cuddly 150-pound German shepherd? It means you'd better keep him close to you and under control. If he races into the market, knocking over food and people, you may spend hours settling damages and cooling tempers. At best, you'll rescue the beast and face a torrent of angry abuse.

Pets are not allowed in hotels or motels, almost without exception. It doesn't matter if you've tranquilized, muzzled and wrapped it in a log chain, your dog will have to find accommodations elsewhere. Pets aren't allowed on first-class buses and must travel in the baggage car on trains.

Before committing yourself to caring for a pet on a long trip, consider not only how you'll feel if it becomes a problem, but how your pet will feel. The animal may never forgive you for being dragged along on a leash, teased by kids, kept prisoner in a hot car for hours and otherwise made to feel like less than a member of the family.

Steve snaps back: "Carl is just upset because Xuxa drooled on his sleeping bag. Many RVers have dogs and if you're used to dealing with a dog, it isn't much different in Mexico than at home. We 'dog people' find it worth the trouble. Contrary to Carl's libelous wisecracks about Xuxa, we've had no major problems traveling with her in Mexico. You must also consider that a dog left with a sitter or in a kennel may be very unhappy without its owners, and vice versa. Xuxa seems quite willing to put up with the discomfort of travel to be with us."

Guns and Hunting

The Mexican government has a very definite attitude toward firearms—they don't want tourists to have them in Mexico. Not only is a hunting license expensive but the paperwork involved in taking guns to Mexico is awesome. I won't even bother to list the requirements. If you are serious about hunting in Mexico contact the Wildlife Advisory Services, P.O. Box 76132, Los Angeles, CA 90076; tel. 213-385-9311, fax 213-385-0782. They'll explain everything and help you do the paperwork.

Illegally sneaking a gun into Mexico is extremely stupid. The illegal possession of a firearm is like a reserved ticket for a prison cell. Even those Mexicans who use their guns for subsistence hunting are harassed by the authorities as laws concerning firearms become increasingly strict. Mexicans often ask tourists to bring them guns, but nothing will ruin your vacation faster than getting caught.

Fishing Licenses

The permit fee for fishing, spearfishing and seafood foraging is quite reasonable and I recommend that you get one. Although enforcement is lax, you are open to fines and/or losing your gear (including boats) if you are caught. Popular bass fishing lakes are fairly well patrolled; some wardens will sell you a license if you don't already have one.

Children under twelve do not need a license. Technically, if anyone in a boat is fishing, then everybody in that boat over the age of sixteen needs a license. Again, enforcement is very spotty. Lost licenses cannot be replaced; you must buy another.

Fishing licenses are available from *Oficina de Pesca* in Mexico (at port cities) or by mail from the Mexican Department of Fisheries, 2550 5th Avenue, Suite 101, San Diego, CA 92103; 619-233-6956. Fishing licenses are also available through the Discover Baja Travel Club, 3089 Clairemont Drive, Suite A-2, San Diego, CA 92117; 800-727-BAJA (-2252); email discovbaja@aol.com. Tackle stores and travel agents near the border often sell Mexican licenses.

Boats taken to Mexico for fishing also require a permit. The necessary information will be included with your application when you buy a fishing permit.

Official Documents and Checkpoints

Once you have your tourist card, car permit, pet papers, fishing license and insurance policy safely in hand, put them where they won't get lost, dirty or damaged. When driving, we keep our various official documents in a zippered "diplomatic pouch." Should we need them, our papers are immediately at hand and they aren't dirty, folded, torn, chewed or otherwise defiled. Government-issued documents shouldn't look like pages from a well-thumbed sex novel. An irate immigration official once told Steve that dirty smudges on his tourist card were "an insult to the Republic." The only thing that could take his outraged eyes from the card was a bank note, also well thumbed.

Having your papers ready and well organized also reduces the time you'll spend at highway checkpoints. Your tourist card and car papers may be checked anywhere in the country by local and federal police, immigration officials or the Army. Passengers on northbound buses and trains may be checked as they approach the border between Mexico and the U.S. You'll definitely be checked at the airport if you leave Mexico by plane. When driving north, you may be stopped at a checkpoint twelve to twenty miles south of the border. If things aren't in order, cross your fingers and hope for the best. Smiling and talking can sometimes work wonders, but bribes are no longer in style. Still, it never hurts to be prepared.

A hidden pocket makes a convenient, secure place to carry both money and documents, especially for those traveling by public transportation. (See *Packing Up: Hidden Pocket.*)

Car Insurance

American and Canadian car insurance is rarely valid in Mexico. (Some policies will repay you for collision damage.) Second, even though you are not required by Mexican law to have car insurance, the Uninsured Motorist (a dreaded term anywhere) is particularly vulnerable to both imprisonment and costly legal action.

When an accident occurs, all parties involved may be detained for investigation and their vehicles impounded. After the claims have been settled everyone gets to go home. Everyone, that is, but the uninsured motorist, who doesn't have enough cash to pay all the expense of the accident. An insurance policy is considered a guarantee that damages can be paid. A valid policy can keep you out of jail, even when you are at fault. However, if you don't have an insurance agent to intercede for you, you'll have to deal with the police on your own. Needless to say, the situation could become very complicated. (See *Accidents*, later in this chapter.)

By now you should be ready for a policy, and I strongly recommend that you get one. There are a number of very obvious insurance agencies on both sides of the border and they'll whip out a policy in just a few minutes. Some of these companies, such as Sears, Sanborn's and AAA are handled by Americans, if that makes you more comfortable. Insurance rates are government controlled, however, and minimum charges cannot legally vary between companies. The rates, based on a sliding scale, decrease significantly for longer policies. When you buy insurance, the agent will certainly try to sell you maximum coverage. If you're not too worried about body work, medical expenses, meteorites or unreasonable Acts of God, just get liability. Theft insurance usually covers only total loss of the vehicle. Since most thefts involve the contents or accessories, read the policy carefully before buying.

Should you buy insurance for a longer period of time than you actually spend in Mexico, you can apply for a refund. Some companies (Sanborn's for one) offer rebates if you visit Central America while your Mexican policy is in effect. Once again, you leave your coverage behind when you cross a border.

If you can't afford to buy insurance for the entire trip, at least buy a few days' worth; enough to get you to your intended destination. When you move on or head home, you can again buy a few more days of insurance. Large towns have agents who sell policies by the day or month. Look in the phone book under *Seguros*.

Does your policy cover anyone who drives your car? Check it carefully to be certain. You also won't be covered (in most policies) if you have an accident while driving another vehicle.

Towed trailers and boats must also be insured. If you have an accident while towing an uninsured boat or trailer, your entire coverage is invalid.

Sanborn's (800-222-0158), **Instant Mexican Auto Insurance** (800-345-4701, from the U.S. and Canada), **International Gateways** (800-4232646), **Oscar Padilla** (800-258-8600). Larger companies such as Sanborn's and AAA give away free guidebooks, road maps and other information with their policies.

Insurance discounts are available through the **Discover Baja** travel club. (See *For More Information.*)

Seguros del Noroeste: Their American broker is ADA-VIS Global Mexican Insurance Services, 2555 Yesteryear Lane, Fallbrook, CA 92028; tel. 800-909-4457, fax 800-909-1007, e-mail <ada-vis@tfb.com>.

Steve bought a year of basic liability from them covering all of Mexico and Baja for $58. He insured his driver's license, which means his insurance covers him for any vehicle he uses. Here's what he got: property damage to third parties, $10,000 limit per event; civil liability for bodily injury to third parties, $50,000 limit per event, $25,000 limit per person. This policy covers just one driver. If another person will also be driving, they will need their own policy.

Steve says, "I called their toll-free number, gave them a credit card and they faxed me a Binder of Insurance. They sent the policy by mail. This company also has collision coverage, fire and theft, auto, boat and trailer insurance. For $25 a year their Mexico Legal Service will provide a lawyer if you have a problem. Sure can't beat the price. I hope I don't have to find out if it is worth it!"

Accidents

First and most important, if you have insurance, show the policy to the police. This is your "Get Out of Jail Free" card. Without it, you will very likely be held until all claims have been settled.

Your insurance agent should take care of everything. In cases when liability is not easily determined or damages difficult to assess, you will be asked to remain in the area. The tourist is almost always assumed to be at fault. If you have insurance, this won't present a problem.

• **Fatal accidents**, especially those presumed to be caused by drinking or drugs, can lead to criminal charges. What happens depends to a great extent on the report of the investigating officer. If he believes your story, you'll probably get off; if he doesn't, you'll usually be charged with "accidental homicide." The sentence is three days to five years, depending on the state. Tourists are often released on bond (substantial) and allowed to flee the country.

• **Single car accidents:** Cops are adept at turning the most minor incident—such as running off the road—into a case of negligent or reckless driving. You might be fined for "damage to the roadbed" or the replacement of a tree, piece of curbing or fence. Whenever possible leave the scene before trouble arrives.

• **Leaving the scene:** This is a particularly sensitive point with tourists. The thought of "hit-and-run" leaves most of us jelly-kneed. My advice, and that given to me by law officials, is to get away from the scene of an accident as fast and unobtrusively as possible. The other person involved is probably doing the same thing.

Unless serious injury is involved, leaving the scene is not illegal, though if you're caught you may be denied bond.

Mexican cops are infamous for working all the angles. You may not think that a fender-bender accident is worth their time or trouble, but it will be, especially if you have money.

As a tourist, you are vulnerable to bullying by the police and other persons involved in an accident. Unless you remain calm and are able to communicate the facts in a convincing manner, the cops probably won't even bother to talk to you. While the other person is filling the officer's ear with tales and his pocket with pesos, your position is rapidly worsening. If you're insured, this will be a minor hassle; if you're not, it will get complicated.

• **Livestock:** If you nail one of those cows, burros or chickens that haunt Mexican highways, don't even bother to look back. You'll notice that Mexican trucks all have large "cow catchers" welded over the grill. The only time you're liable for hitting livestock is when speeding or otherwise violating the law. The only way they can accuse you is if you stop.

• **Stolen cars:** Contact your insurance agent and go immediately to the nearest police station to file a complaint. Get a certified copy of the complaint; you'll need it to leave the country if the car is not recovered. If the car is involved in an accident or crime, you are not liable, but you'll need an insurance agent or lawyer to help you recover it.

• **Car papers:** If your car is completely disabled and can't be moved out of Mexico before the permit expires, ask the *Turismo* people to help you through the bureaucratic maze. In worst cases, vehicles can be shipped to the border and then towed into the U.S. or just signed over to the Mexican government (usually done in cases of total destruction).

• **Lawyers:** When in doubt or really confused about what to do, consider seeking out a lawyer (*licenciado* or *notario*). Explain your problem and ask for a *presupuesto* (an estimate, preferably in writing) of charges. Lawyers have the advantage of knowing the ropes and how to untangle the more frustrating knots. They are especially useful for creative solutions of dubious legality.

Mexican Customs Inspections

Tourists are given a Customs inspection at the point where your car papers are issued or tourist cards validated and occasionally at "flying checkpoints" on major highways in northern Mexico.

Most Mexican Customs checkpoints and airports use a system of red and green "traffic" lights. The incoming tourist pushes a button (while holding her/his breath). If the signal flashes red your luggage will be inspected. A green light means "pass Go," no inspection. Should this system inspire you to make a rude wisecrack, you'll probably get inspected anyway.

If you're traveling with a vehicle or have a great heap of luggage you might attract a detailed inspection. Unusual amounts of new clothing and consumer goods are the main point of these searches, but if you take the precaution of removing packaging, price tags and other labeling, you shouldn't have a problem.

Bribes: in our experience, the official "no bribes" policy now in effect at the border is surprisingly effective. On the other hand, there are still exceptions to the rule. Discrepancies in your paperwork or violations of Customs regulations (too many computers, too much whiskey in the cupboard, etc.) might lead to opportunities for "dollar diplomacy."

Border Hassles
Back in the good old days, border crossings were always moments of high drama, and we always adjusted our clothing style to fit our budget. If we were well-off we just

drove on into Mexico without even combing our hair or taming our beards, but if we were broke, we stopped ahead of time and put on our "thousand-dollar suits." We bought these suits for $3 each from an old lady selling used clothing on the side of the highway near El Paso. A last-minute pressing at a dry cleaner made us look as crisp as a page out of a Sears' catalog.

I liberally slicked down my hair or gave it a slight trim with the scissors. Lorena fixed her long hair into a tight bun at the back of her head. She wore a knee-length skirt with a thin baggy sweater and carried a shiny black purse. Steve sucked in his gut and corseted it with a carefully buttoned polyester vest. Instead of counterculture dropouts, we tried to look like small town schoolteachers or mildly befuddled missionaries. The border officials loved us.

Border hassles are no longer common but to play it safe, be friendly, polite and mildly ingratiating. You will be asked your profession for entry on the tourist card. Don't blow it by saying "unemployed," but don't overdo things by claiming to be an astronaut, movie star or nuclear physicist. Teachers and businessmen are good occupations if you're not really young, and technical trades such as mechanic, secretary, electrician and plumber are always reasonable choices.

Be ready to explain why you're on a six-month vacation. Never claim to be entering Mexico for business reasons (prohibited for tourists) or for school. This requires a student visa.

When asked your ultimate destination, give a resort or large city, preferably not in Chiapas. Don't say, "Oh, I'm going to express my solidarity with Comandante Marcos of the Zapatistas!"

Be confident but never condescending toward officials. A sneering, arrogant or contemptuous attitude will foul up even the most affluent tourist or at least make the crossing long and tedious. When crossing the border with a friend, don't bother claming to be married if you aren't; they don't care.

Should the border official make a friendly overture, respond in a positive manner. If he says, "Oh, you'll like Mexico City," don't answer with "I've been there. The smog almost killed me!"

Bribery: True or False?

The "word" along the border these days is to forget about tips, gratuities, donations and other forms of *la mordida*, "the bite." It is a brave new world in Mexico and the recent breed of bureaucrats is untouchable. In fact, there has been a tremendous reduction in obvious corruption. Once the latest well-publicized cleanup was completed, however, I was invited to drop a "contribution" into a border official's lower desk drawer. I added five dollars to that day's "take," a pile of loose bank notes at least a foot deep. Steve had a similar experience at Mexico's southern border.

Like it or not, the custom of greasing palms is as old as Mexico itself (and is hardly confined to one country, as Vice President Spiro Agnew greedily demonstrated). In a culture as complex as Mexico's, purges and presidential decrees are like fireworks at a neighborhood fiesta. Once the smoke clears, everything remains much the same.

Although most travelers will never be asked to give a bribe, the possibility does exist. In delicate situations, it literally pays to be prepared. With this in mind, we offer the following advice rather than editing our remarks to conform to official promises and wishful government press releases.

Bribes

The usual response of most law-abiding citizens to the thought of bribes is, "Pay 'em off? You mean *corrupt* someone? *Bribe a government official*? Are you serious?"

Yes, over the years I've given "considerations" to everyone from post office workers who couldn't seem to remember my name to border officials who didn't like my looks.

The *mordida* is easy, relatively inexpensive, convenient and even has certain procedural rules to keep it "honest." To say that circumventing the law is immoral is to assume that the law itself is moral and right. A Mexican border official once told me that he had to show a large amount of money before being allowed into the U.S. "Is it not fair," he asked, "that I should enforce our laws on you in the same manner?"

"Yes," I replied, "but it's not reasonable. Here's a few dollars."

"How long a tourist card would you like?" he asked, reaching for his typewriter.

You don't bribe someone by stuffing a wad of bills in his pocket and saying, "Here ya go, baby, a little something for the wife and kids!" There are more subtle and respectable techniques used to feel out the other person on their attitude and price. The easiest is the, "Gee whiz, I sure wish you'd tell me what to do" angle. Other effective openers to the pay-off are: "Isn't there any way this can be worked out?" or "Will there be an extra charge?" or the national favorite, "Is there no other way of arranging the matter?" (See *Appendices: Vocabulary: Red Tape*.)

Unless the response is unmistakably negative, proceed immediately to the next step—the money. The handing over of the *mordida* is done without embarrassment on the part of either person. None of this, "Pssst! Meet me in urinal four at eight o'clock!" Instead you dip discreetly into your wallet (or your pocket if you're really prepared), extract a few dollars and hand them over. If it isn't enough, the official will shake his head. You pull out another bill and another and when the right amount has been reached, business will proceed as usual. Corrupt officials generally take "fair" amounts and manage to restrain themselves from really bilking people. Being offensive, however, will up the ante.

Handle the situation with the proper attitude; just assume that every bribe is a legal and required fee. Don't act like a naughty child or a criminal or the person being bribed will react defensively and probably raise the price. When you both pretend that a small "contribution for sodas" is legitimate, the transaction will be fast and friendly.

Tourists and Mexican Law

When the time came to write this section, I dutifully assembled and reviewed all of my notes, newspaper articles, personal experiences and unsolicited tragedies from friends and acquaintances. Together they would have made a great crime novel, a saga of almost every accident and woe to befall the person adventurous enough to leave their front yard. I was then faced with a difficult decision: leave the section out (and it represented a lot of work), water it down ("Prison offers ample opportunities for language study") or just hope that readers would take it calmly instead of freaking out and heading for Yellowstone. The answer came in the words of a friend: "A minute of paranoia is worth a year's detention."

When you're in trouble, whether it's in Seattle or Sinaloa, you're in *trouble*. Anything you can do to help yourself is valuable. Don't let this chapter scare you; the odds are very low that things will go wrong instead of right and that you'll need some hard-earned advice.

To ensure that my information was as accurate as possible, I decided, against my natural inclinations, to verify it with the police. My first interview was with a Mexican traffic cop in the process of arresting us for running a hidden stop sign.

"Is it legal to drink and drive?" I asked, hoping to deflect his attention from our minor infraction. The cop paused over the ticket book for several seconds, then said, "I drink vodka. It's relaxing." He noted our license number then added, "But if you're passing a cop and going fast—very fast—put the bottle between your legs rather than letting him see you drink."

I then arranged for a series of interviews with a judge and district attorney. To almost each of my questions the answer was the same: "It depends." In frustration, since I knew that it did indeed "depend," but couldn't offer just that explanation in a book, I said, "OK. Tell me what *really happens* instead of what is supposed to happen. "

"Will my name be mentioned?" they asked in anxious unison.

"No." I said, and from there the interviews went quite smoothly. Not too surprisingly, their information confirmed or supported my own material in almost every detail. The following questions and answers, therefore, most accurately represent an interview between myself and friends, backed up by "expert" opinion. And by the way: if you want to stay out of trouble in Mexico, statistics clearly show that tourists who run afoul of the law usually do so because of alcohol, drugs, auto accidents or "immoral" behavior.

What Are My Rights as a Tourist?

As a *turista* you enjoy almost all of the rights of a Mexican citizen, with these exceptions: tourists cannot work without special permission and you cannot vote.

Some facts about the Mexican legal system and laws (based largely on the Napoleonic Code) of interest to tourists follow.

• Laws vary from state to state, but are generally modeled on the code of the *Distrito Federal* (Federal District, equivalent to Washington, D.C.).

• Judges decide all cases, not juries.

• A person can be held for up to seventy-two hours without being charged.

• Any offense that involves drinking, drugs or minors is usually considered more severe than if it did not. If, for example, you kidnap a child and crash your car while drunk and stoned, you're in deep trouble.

• Nudity is illegal and punishable by a fine and short jail term.

• Abortion is illegal, though commonly done. There is a pro-abortion movement that is gaining strength.

• Homosexuality is not illegal. Sex acts between adults and minors, however, are illegal. Between consenting adults and/or animals, anything goes (in private).

• Prostitution is legal in many states.

• Pornography is illegal and common.
• All babies born in Mexico, regardless of the nationality of their parents, are entitled to Mexican citizenship (the birth must be registered).

Do Tourists Need to Worry About the Cops?

Millions of people visit Mexico each year and very few of them get thrown into jail or are involved in legal difficulties of any type. The best story you can hope for will be typical: ". . . so I slipped the big guy five bucks and they let us go."

Tourists who find themselves being hassled for traffic violations, public drunkenness or disputes with taxi drivers should *remain calm*. Don't shout, "By Gawd, I'm an American citizen and you can't do this . . . blah . . . blah . . . !" or you'll find yourself facing strong resentment. In almost every case the police will prefer to settle the matter quietly, on the spot, rather than have you drag in tourist bureau officials or lawyers. Be reasonable; if you're in the right but are expected to pay a small "consideration," do it and forget about it.

Note: A special word to punks, bikers, skinheads, aging hippies and miscellaneous weirdoes: it's only natural that the less you look like Dick and Jane, the more you'll be looked at by Mexican cops. If this bothers you, try a disguise.

Cops, being professionally snoopy, may decide you look more like a potential arrest than the straight tourists he sees. When he decides to approach, what happens next almost always depends on you. A calm, friendly reaction will usually put you back into the tourist, rather than dope-crazed maniac, category.

Try your best to understand where that cop's head is at. If he can read, he probably scans the tabloids once a month, enjoying lurid accounts of axe murders, rapes and *narcotraficantes*. So when you tell him you're bathing nude because, "We are all children under the sun," he thinks you're insane or covering up something even worse, something so awful he can't figure it out.

I'd say, "A dog stole my swimming suit," and apologize.

As a compromise with sun-loving European tourists who think nudity is natural rather than offensive, a few Mexican beaches are now unofficially designated as topless. In general, however, Mexicans are very uptight about public nudity. In the early Seventies, large numbers of tourists gathered in southern Mexico to observe a solar eclipse. When their sky-gazing progressed to nude sunbathing, the local authorities were incensed. In the round-up that followed, the offending tourists were obligated to atone for their sins by building a rural school. They spent several days at hard labor before being shipped home.

Drugs and Marijuana

During the Sixties and Seventies, many travelers took a relaxed, what-can-it-hurt? attitude toward drugs in Mexico. At that time, Mexico did not have a drug problem of its own. With the *policía* often shaking their heads in bemusement at the antics of tourists and small-time smugglers, law enforcement tended to be an on-the-spot *mordida*, a few days in the *bote* (can, jail) or a swift, northbound kick over the border.

In those days, popular lore about travel in Latin America included hilarious stories of Keystone Kop drug busts, white-knuckle border crossings and hair-breadth escapes. Books and articles describing the ritual use of hallucinogenic mushrooms, peyote and alcohol by native Indian healers and shamans added to the romance. Carlos Castenada's best-selling books on Yaqui sorcery put the final polish on the drug mystique apple. There were times in the mid-Seventies, in fact, when it seemed as if you couldn't climb a sacred mountain in Mexico or step around a cactus without stumbling over some spaced-out peyote pilgrim in search of Don Juan's separate reality.

As we all know, attitudes about drugs have changed considerably. Drug abuse and

A Field Guide to Mexican Cops

Preventivos: Preventives, the equivalent of a regular beat cop in the U.S. brown or blue uniforms.

Tránsito: Traffic cops, mounted or on foot, are sometimes nicknamed after the tropical fruit called *"tamarindos"*—both for their brown uniforms and often bulging profile. May be armed.

Caminos: Properly known as *caminos federales* (federal highways). This is the highway patrol. Grey pants and a light brown shirt. Armed.

Policia Judicial Federal: The unloved PJF or *federales*, also known as *jefes* (chiefs). They dress as they please, in everything from camo to all-black, or like well-to-do West Texans. Armed and arrogant.

Servicio Secreto: The SS, Secret Service. Civilian clothes and very heavily tinted sunglasses. Armed.

Policia Judicial Estatal: The highly unpopular State Judicial Police are known as PJE or just *judiciales*. Often confused with the more elite PJF, cynics call these "state bulls" *perjudiciales* , a bitter word play on *perjudicar*, "to damage, injure or wrong." Armed and dangerous; don't give them any grief.

Comisionados: The modern day *rurales*, a rag-tag militia formed by the *ejidos* (rural cooperatives). They have no police powers.

Guaruras: Bodyguards, armed and can be considered dangerous. No self-respecting politician, *latifundo* (big landowner) or *rico* (rich man) would be without at least one. They are popularly known as *nacos* (scum, thugs).

Mordelón: A derogatory term for a cop, implying that they are "big biters," i.e., takers of bribes.

Note: If a town can't afford standard uniforms, the *preventivos* and *tránsitos* may be dressed differently than described above.

drug trafficking are now considered a crisis of worldwide proportions. When we speak of drug wars, it is no exaggeration to say that Mexico is literally on the front lines.

As far as tourists are concerned, it all boils down to this simple fact: drug laws are vigorously enforced in Mexico. It is not only illegal to possess and use drugs (the usual types, from marijuana to pills and heroin) but dangerous to be around anyone who does. The Mexican police operate on the principle that it's easier to arrest everyone at the scene of a suspected crime and then sort out the guilty from the innocent later (sometimes a lot later).

Ironically, penalties for possession and trafficking are often harsher in Mexico than in the U.S. As pressure mounts for the country to clean up its act, Mexican cops and judges can take a very hard line with drug-using visitors.

An American consular officer in southern Mexico with plenty of experience confirms the trend toward harsh treatment of convicted tourists. "Please," she said, "warn people not to fool with drugs in Mexico. So many people who come down these days just don't seem to understand. Mexico is changing. Getting caught with drugs just isn't worth it."

Possession of even small amounts of "recreational" drugs like marijuana and mushrooms runs the risk of terrifying jail sentences. Forget about bribes; travelers are now being jailed for minor drug offenses that used to be settled with a "golden handshake." Corruption hasn't been eliminated, but the days are over when virtually every offense was open to "negotiation." Pressure from the U.S. will continue to harden Mexico's policy toward drugs. In a word, using drugs in Mexico is probably the most hazardous thing a traveler can do.

Some years ago, Lorena and I were driving north from Mexico City toward Texas. Suddenly, in the middle of nowhere, traffic came to a complete halt. Craning her head out the window and looking past a long line of trucks, buses and cars, Lorena said, "Looks like the cops."

After several minutes of crawl-and-stop progress, we finally came within sight of the roadblock. Long inspection tables had been set up beside the highway, complete with lights for nighttime operations. In the midst of a confusion of cars, cargo trucks and passenger buses, at least a dozen heavily armed men were searching everything from chicken crates to handbags and suitcases.

"Look," I said. "Look over there." Slightly ahead of us, beside the northbound lane, a young gringo couple stood in the sun next to a late model pickup camper. The woman's face was drawn and pale, her eyes squinted against the glare. In spite of the harsh afternoon heat she rubbed her arms as though deeply chilled. Her partner stood beside her, motionless, in an attitude of great patience: hands behind his back, eyes fixed on the horizon. He wore a rumpled blue *guayabera* shirt, khaki shorts and rubber shower thongs. I had the impression of a young couple headed home from a long vacation, inconveniently delayed by a flat tire or a tedious roadside breakdown.

On the ground in front of them, two men were trussing up a large, lumpy burlap sack. Then, as the men rose to their feet, I saw that they were *federales*. I realized, too, that the young woman wasn't just squinting, she was crying. Her partner turned to say something to her; his hands were tied behind his back with rough, common twine.

"Move ahead," Lorena croaked miserably.

A bored cop waved us to the shoulder of the road as a clapped-out, dirt-caked Ford station wagon with a missing rear window roared up behind us, swerved, and then slid to a dramatic, dust-raising stop just inches from the rear bumper of the gringo pickup. Two men got out of the station wagon. Both wore leather boots and casual, western-style clothes. They could have been ranchers—if ranchers carried .45 pistols and submachine guns. Without so much as a glance at the gringos, the driver swaggered over to the pickup, opened the door and slid behind the wheel. He started the truck's engine, revving it brutally, while his partner pried open the station wagon's badly dented rear cargo door. The *federales* with the burlap sack now took the dazed couple by an arm and steered them brusquely to the back of the Ford. With no further ado, prisoners, burlap bag and cops were all jammed into the sagging station wagon. With a casual wave to the men at the roadblock, the *federal* in the pickup truck pulled onto the highway, then made a hard U-turn. The station wagon followed. As the two vehicles passed us, heading south, I felt a delicious lunch of chicken tacos turning to a jagged block of ice in my stomach. Beside me, Lorena sighed very heavily.

Yet another cop now approached our van. "Do you have any drugs or firearms?" He asked the question matter-of-factly, in unnervingly good English.

"No," I said wearily, "I don't have anything." He looked vaguely toward the rear of the van, nodded politely at Lorena, then slapped my door good-naturedly with the back of his hand. "Have a nice trip," the cop said, waving us on. Before I could pop the clutch he was already questioning the driver behind me.

As we pulled back onto the highway, I looked into the rear-view mirror. The highway behind us seemed plugged with semi trucks and second-class buses. In my imagination, however, I clearly saw a badly overloaded Ford station wagon, trailing dust and pale blue smoke, heading deeper into Mexico than I ever care to go.

• **Set-ups:** Do Mexican cops "plant" illegal drugs on tourists and then arrest them? I've heard this rumor repeated countless times. I've also been searched countless times by Mexican cops without ever being arrested or falsely accused. Though entrapment undoubtedly happens in rare cases, it's not something to worry about. As one cynical *federal* told me, "There's enough gringos carrying drugs already. I'm busy enough as it is."

On the other hand, "sting" operations do happen in Mexico. The classic sting is to simply have someone (undercover cop, previously busted informant, etc.) sell drugs to a tourist, then move in and arrest the tourist. Obviously, such ploys are only a hazard to the person (and their unwitting companions) foolish enough to look for drugs in the first place.

• **Searches of passenger buses and private vehicles are routine** on major highways and many arterials. Unless you're intoxicated or disturbing the peace, however, it would be very unusual to be stopped and searched on the street. In fact, this has never happened to me, even in my most counterculture era.

Searches can come in any area of the country, but the most likely regions are along the Pacific coast, on highways leading directly to the U.S. border and in remote mountain ranges. The states of Chiapas, Sinaloa, Guerrero, Michoacán and Oaxaca also host perennial anti-weapon and drug operations. Marine patrols make random landings along Pacific and Caribbean beaches, combing for "square grouper" (marijuana bales), pot-puffers, turtle poachers and smugglers. Searches in campgrounds, in public places or on private property are very rare.

If you visit isolated places, you may encounter Army patrols or *judiciales*. Be polite and cooperative. If you can relax, they will too. On the other hand, never make sarcastic or flippant remarks. They may speak excellent English, but will usually pretend not to. These men are usually veterans of deadly combat with drug growers. They expect to be taken very seriously.

When a search does come, it will be unexpected and fast. We've greeted them from small planes, boats, jeeps, passenger bus and even horseback. They'll come at any hour of the day or night, either with great commotion or on their hands and knees in the bushes. Anything to get the job done.

In areas where the cops are looking for giant stashes, the search might be brief (especially if you aren't too suspicious looking or rude), but most of the time they'll go over everything, from Tampax to tire tubes. If you speak Spanish, you'll be questioned and probably told how the search is part of some operation with U.S. support, etc., etc.

Act as if everything you own is made of fine china. These searches are supposed to be conducted with respect for your belongings. One *federal* made his men dust off everything after looking at it.

The Army likes to pull "John Wayne" searches. Lorena and I were alone one day in our camp on a very remote Pacific beach, enjoying an atmosphere of total relaxation. While she drowsed in a hammock, I beachcombed and swam. After hours of this, I wandered back through the bushes toward camp, ready for a quiet drink in the shady coconut grove. I was about to cross a narrow clearing when I noticed movements in the bushes in front of me. To my amazement, five soldiers in full combat regalia, including twigs and leaves on their helmets, were crawling toward Lorena, submachine guns "at the ready."

After surveying this unlikely scene, I walked up behind one of them and said, "*¡Buenas tardes!*" They were so embarrassed that they made their dope search as brief as possible, even though one whispered to me that they'd come forty miles by bus to "get us." The motive for the Army's search wasn't to bust us with a lid—or even a kilo—but to determine if we were big dealers. Our preference for really isolated areas tends to lead us to others who enjoy isolation, mainly large-scale dope growers. They, in turn, attract a lot of heavy police activity. (Another factor against us was our VW van, at that time commonly associated throughout Mexico with American dealers.)

The Army often works in conjunction with the *federales*. You can spot a soldier by his uniform but a *federal* is most easily identified by his gun—often a light submachine gun, sawed-off shotgun or a flashy pistol. *Federales* love to drive American cars and trucks—with American plates—that they've confiscated from unfortunate smugglers. We've seen them in everything from new Ford trucks with campers to old beat-up station wagons with New York plates. They sometimes pose as Mexican-Americans on vacation.

Cops rarely search a person's clothing or body unless they are extremely suspicious or have already found something incriminating.

• **You're busted!** If you are busted, don't panic; as with snake bites, the outcome will depend largely on what you do in that first crucial hour.

If the amount is small, you may get out of it with a fast bribe. The so-called "new breed" of *federal* supposedly will not accept gratuities. My advice is a simple, "Don't count on it." If you're very lucky, however, they'll take whatever money and possessions they can get and turn you loose. The usual protocol is to offer the bribe to the officer in charge. "Could we please arrange this now? Could I pay a *multa* (fine) now?"

The amount you pay depends, of course, on how worried you are and what you can afford. Successful bribes can range anywhere from a few dollars to thousands.

If one person in a group is caught, others will probably be arrested or at least hassled. By immediately taking the blame, you can take the heat off your friends and probably keep the overall expense of the bust much lower. Since a car can be confiscated if dope is found in it, it's wise to have someone other than the owner take the blame.

The thought of going to jail alone might disturb you, but you're better off having a friend outside who can arrange your release.

You might bluff your way out of an arrest, especially if the amount of dope is very small or you're just being taken in on suspicion. Hysterics, fainting and vomiting—especially if done by women—can deflate a cop's determination.

Scream, rant, cry, beat your head against a wall, anything to convince them you're not about to go for something you're not guilty of. If the cops feel that they don't have you in a bad spot, the "indignant tourist" ploy can upset them completely. This is the only time such tactics are warranted. Don't claim to be the illegitimate nephew of the president of Mexico unless you can follow it up.

A good friend was arrested by the Army on suspicion of being a dealer. When they got him to the door of his cell, he claimed to be a U.S. senator. To prove it, he produced several impressive letters, decorated with seals and stamps, written in Spanish and introducing him "to whom it may concern." The head cop became sufficiently concerned that he decided to throw my friend an apology party, complete with sliced watermelon and cold drinks.

Before you resort to theatrics, however, play for sympathy. A friend was released by the *federales* when he told them that the shame of having her son exposed as a marijuana addict would break his mother's heart. They tore off a chunk of his kilo, gave it to him with a warning to be more discreet in the future and sent him on his way.

• **Behind bars:** If you've been arrested by the city cops, you'll have to come before a judge within three days. The Army can hold you for twenty-four hours; then they must turn you over to the *federales* who can hold you (god forbid) almost indefinitely. If you're innocent, but suspected of something awful, they'll keep you around even longer. Pre-trial procedures can take several months. In cases of minor possession, you'll probably be deported fairly quickly. Since each situation is different, it's difficult to say what a person should do if you find yourself in jail and the "wheels of justice" seem to have rolled to a stop. I would sit around for a while, especially if the charge isn't grave, and see what develops. There are cases where the cops released people because it wasn't worth hassling them. And there are cases where prisoners languish for a good long time.

Although you can accept the services of a court-appointed legal advisor (not necessarily a qualified lawyer by any means), it is best not to; he is their stooge. Contact the American Embassy in Mexico City or the nearest tourist bureau office. About the only thing they'll be willing to do is give you the name of a lawyer to hire. (See *Mexico A to Z: Consulates and Embassies.*)

Serious charges can cost thousands of dollars and take months to negotiate. Some lucky cases are finally settled by allowing the accused out on bond with the assumption that they will leave Mexico at top speed and never return.

• **Penalties:** Drug laws are federal and it is important to note that they do not apply these penalties to anyone under eighteen years of age. Minors may be held by the authorities for a time, but they'll probably be deported quickly.

These penalties are for both marijuana and *estupefacientes* (stupefiers, everything from mushrooms to heroin). The line between possession, dealing and smuggling is determined by the judge.

2 to 9 years for possession and cultivation.
3 to 12 years for transporting and dealing.
4 to 12 years for causing addiction in a minor.
6 to 15 years for smuggling across a border.
6 to 15 years for owners of any place used to manufacture, deal or use drugs.
Fines also go along with jail terms.

The sun had just disappeared behind the mountains in front of us when Lorena spotted a clearing in the thick jungle. With several taps on the brake pedal, Steve signaled our friends, Bonnie and Hayden, that we'd found a camping place. Steve eased the van gently across a shallow ditch separating the highway from several starkly empty acres of dirt and gravel.

After parking side by side at the edge of a deep hole, we climbed wearily out of our vans to survey the place we'd selected.

"Well?" Steve asked. "What about it?"

Bonnie looked dubious; while in Alaska she had heard enough of his glowing accounts of Mexico to know that this wasn't one of those so-called "paradise" spots. She and Hayden had driven thousands of miles on the strength of those stories and now that they'd joined us, here we were, spending our first night together in a gravel pit.

"Not bad, Steve," Bonnie said, surveying the desolation with hands on hips. "Not bad at all."

"This jungle is really something in the daylight," Steve said. "The country north of here is full of some pretty rough characters. A lot of interesting Indians, too," he ended lamely, looking at me for some sort of supporting anecdote to keep the conversation going.

"I'm sure it is," she said, "but right now we'd better settle for something to eat."

As I wandered away to look for firewood, I heard her ask Steve, "Which of us takes the first watch?"

Several minutes later, I was hunched over a pile of twigs in the bottom of the excavation next to our vans, trying to coax a fire out of the damp jungle wood. As the flames crept higher, casting an eerie light in the deep hole, I vaguely heard the sound of voices above me. Assuming that it was the others discussing dinner, I continued to build up the fire. After I noisily broke a large branch over my knee, a loud gruff voice barked in Spanish, "Don't move!"

I jerked up. There in the firelight stood a stocky man dressed in baggy cotton trousers, tattered denim shirt and decaying *huaraches.* "Don't move!" he repeated, tightening his grip on the submachine gun leveled at my chest.

As my knees sagged with fear, I instinctively raised my hands high over my head. Behind him other dim figures suddenly came into focus. Steve, standing off to one side of the camp, was trying to finish taking a leak while staring around the black O's of a double barrel shotgun. Several roughly dressed characters carrying a frightening assortment of weapons, from machetes to pistols, were arranging the rest of our group alongside Hayden's van.

With a vicious grin the man guarding me snarled, "Come here!" He raised the gun as if to fire and I all but leaped into his arms. With the barrel lightly touching the back of my shirt, he escorted me into the center of camp.

The others were standing silently, waiting, it seemed, for something appropriately awful to happen. The tension eased slightly when Steve appeared, closely followed by a shotgun.

"He finally finished!" the man yelled to his companions. "Lucky we gave him time to get it out before we came in!" Everyone laughed but us. The big man ended his laugh suddenly.

"What's wrong, *amigos,* you unhappy?" There was a menacing tone to his voice that clearly said, "You've got a reason to be."

He watched us for a few seconds, then after judging that we were sufficiently frightened, he barked officially, "*¡Capitán de policía federal!*"

Bonnie and Hayden looked puzzled as Steve, Lorena and I gave audible sighs of relief. The *federales* weren't fun, but bandits with automatic weapons could be positively depressing.

"Just what the hell is going on?" Bonnie snapped.

I realized then that neither of them had understood what had been said. Hayden looked at her significantly, telepathing, "Don't say anything, Bonnie, and I'll take you to France!"

"Is this some kind of a holdup?" she continued, walking boldly over to Steve and the big *federal.* The *capitán* looked at Steve knowingly, then ordered, "Tell her. You can figure out what we're here for."

"Look, Bonnie," Steve said. "These guys are federal police, probably looking for dope, and the best thing to do is to let us handle it and not piss them off. Act scared!" She looked at Lorena and me—we were certainly acting scared—then conceded by returning quietly to Hayden's side.

"Hokay?" the fat *federal* asked slowly. He looked at his men. "Let's get started!" he ordered, motioning them toward our vans. With a jerk of his head he indicated that Steve and I should stand off to one side of the camp.

"You aspeak Spanish?" he asked with exaggerated care. We both answered, "*Sí*" and the captain immediately launched into a long lecture, interrupted by frequent questions directed at one or the other of us. As we denied being drug addicts and affirmed our loyal support for Operation Cooperation, he stepped up the intensity of his questioning.

Did we understand that he was merely doing his duty?

"*¡Sí!*" we chorused.

Did we appreciate the danger of dope?

"Oh, *¡Sí!*"

Did we want our families corrupted by crime?

"Of course not!"

I looked over his shoulder. One of the lesser *federales* was trying to open my typewriter case. I caught the tail end of the last question as a finger poked my shoulder emphatically.

"¡*Sí!*," I muttered in exasperation, catching only the words "drug smuggler."

"What?" he gasped in horror, jumping back as if I'd plunged a syringe into his arm. "What did you say?"

Steve was staring at me in disbelief. "Oh, brother," I thought. "What have I done now?" The stunned *federal* was raising the shotgun in a menacing manner. "I'm confused!" I yelled. "Ask me again, *please!*" He gave me a quick, sly look, but said, "I asked if you were a drug smuggler and you said you were."

I chuckled nervously. "I thought you said, 'No, you are not a drug smuggler, are you?'" The *federal* pondered this for a moment and I hastened to add, "My Spanish is bad. I just want to say, 'No, I am not a smuggler.'"

He relaxed visibly and the shotgun once again hung at his side. My inappropriate answer had so disrupted his drug lecture that we stood there without further comment, watching the search continue in the corners and crannies of our vans.

Lorena was having a hell of a time explaining her large collection of herbal teas, all in unmarked plastic bags. Bonnie and Hayden watched with growing irritation as several pairs of hands fumbled through their neatly packed suitcases and cabinets. Bonnie examined and criticized the appearance and lineage of each *federal* in fluent French, while Hayden attempted to keep their things from falling into total disarray.

A shout of triumph burst from the inside of our van. A short wiry man leaped out holding a small flat can and rushed to where we stood. The *capitán* took the can distrustfully, twisting off the lid as if it might hold some powerful poison. He sniffed it daintily, then turned to us and said, "This is hashish. Where's the rest?"

"No," Steve said, his voice quavering slightly. "It's tobacco. Snuff. You put it in your mouth." And before the *federales* could ponder this absurd statement, Steve reached over, dipped a large hit and packed it professionally under his lower lip.

"Spit that out!" the captain roared. "That stuff's illegal!" Steve's rather idiotic grin confirmed the *federal*'s worst suspicions. "You Americans don't have any brains!" he snorted, motioning the other agents to stand behind us in case we tried to escape.

At this, I yelled desperately to Lorena, "Get the magazine!" Within seconds she was standing next to the captain, thumbing through an issue of *Esquire* to a full-page advertisement for Copenhagen snuff. He looked at it impassively for a few minutes, trying to translate the English by sheer willpower, then waved the magazine in Steve's face with a fatherly, "you should have told me" grin. At the same time, he yelled at the men searching to give it up. We were clean!

The mood changed immediately from one of armed suspicion to friendly curiosity.

What were we doing? the *capitán* asked. Didn't we know that this was a major pick-up point for opium from the northern mountains? Didn't we know that they were there specifically for the purpose of ambushing some gringos who were on their way in VW vans to get the dope? How could we be so stupid?

"We don't know anything about dope, that's why," I ventured to say.

He looked at me wisely for a second.

"You mean to say you don't even smoke marijuana?"

"Oh, no!" we chorused, for even Bonnie and Hayden knew that word of Spanish. "Oh, no! Wouldn't think of it! Gosh, no!"

The *capitán* shook his head in disbelief. "Well, if you don't," and he paused significantly, "you certainly ought to!"

"Look at you," he said, opening his arms as if to embrace us, cars and all. "You people can't tell me you don't know how to live. Travel, eat good, drink . . ." He stopped as if at a loss for words, then continued, "Hell! *Mota* is all you need!"

We smiled nervously as he motioned his men back to the jungle. When his face was just a faint warm glow in the fading firelight, the captain turned and yelled back, "Meet me at *Playa* . . . tomorrow. I'll give you some of the damned stuff!" With that and a hearty laugh, he slipped into the darkness.

¡VIVA MEXICO!

*Customs and traditions • Superstitions • Celebrations and fiestas: holiday calendar •
Festivals, fairs and circuses • Beggars and con artists • National lottery • Machismo:
tourists and machismo • Brothels • The bullfight: a typical bullfight, tickets, seasons
and fights, the bulls, bullrings, bullfight suggestions • Mexico: a brief history • What
the hell is that? • Saints' days*

I was sitting in a tiny store in the highlands of southern Mexico, sampling the horrible
local liquor as I waited for an afternoon cloudburst to clear up. Suddenly a weird, wailing cry sounded outside. Before I could rise from my bench, a boisterous mob poured
through the doorway, pushing, shoving and falling over each other.

Within seconds, fifteen to twenty men had packed themselves into the tiny room.
Choking on my drink, I saw that their drenched, muddy bodies were disguised by the
most hideous costumes and masks I'd ever seen. Several of them were dressed as
women, but their faces were distorted by tightly bound strips of inner tube, electrical
tape, foil and dirty cloth. The effect was startling and definitely not human.

Although I'd seen a good many Indian fiesta costumes, none were as outlandish and
disturbing as these. As the revelers pressed me tightly against the wall, I felt an involuntary shudder of revulsion.

With hoarse, drunken moans and animal grunts, the group made it known to the
wary woman behind the counter that they wanted liquor (I later learned that by custom
no intelligible word could be spoken). Muddy hands snatched the bottles and their
entire contents were drained in what seemed like suicidal chug-a-lugs. When the last
drink had been guzzled, the mob began to give off a low and unnervingly throaty chorus. I had finally been noticed.

Desperately pushing toward a dark corner, I felt my scalp prickle with dread.
Suddenly a grotesque bird-like apparition leaped in front of me. Transfixed by its
beady, unblinking eyes, I watched in disbelief as it raised a slender, silver-headed staff
over my head. With a sudden awful shriek the nightmare creature began striking me
sharply across the shoulders with the polished hardwood. His companions instantly set
upon me, kicking, prodding, jabbing and bouncing me around the room. Throwing up

my arms and hunching my shoulders against their blows, I charged further into the corner. Although I was certainly getting a good thrashing, I took heart in the recognition that no real effort was being made to hurt me.

When the beating suddenly stopped. I looked up cautiously. The bird figure loomed before me, restraining the mob with outstretched arms. Raising his staff once again, he cried out in clear Spanish, "Buy us a drink!"

I nodded rather shakily to the grinning proprietress, resigning myself to a wallet-flattening round. To my surprise, however, my assailants made no objection when she served them each a very small measure. Quickly tossing down the liquor, the mob rushed again for the door, grunting and brawling into the muddy street outside.

I paid my bill quickly and took the opposite direction home. A few weeks later a dignified elderly man approached me in the same store. I noticed that he carried a beautifully polished, silver-headed staff, marking him as an Indian official. With an ironic smile the old man introduced himself as the bird figure, and the leader of a traditional Mayan dance group. After explaining the significance of the ritual I'd inadvertently joined, he graciously thanked me for my "cooperation." I insisted that it had been my pleasure. He responded by offering the use of a house, rent-free, for as long as I and my friends cared to use it. I could obviously be trusted, he said, because I'd agreed to buy the dancers a round even though they could have easily drained every bottle in the place.

"But what if I'd said no?" I asked. "What if I'd refused?"

"Oh, well." The bird-man smiled enigmatically and fingered his staff. "In that case it might have been necessary to help you change your mind."

Customs and Traditions

Traveling is a learning process that takes place in a real rather than an artificial environment. Mexico is not a butterfly pinned to a piece of cork, passive and subject to the curious collector's whims, nor is it a giant amusement park constructed and controlled for the tourist's benefit. By learning to treat a country (or a town, group, etc.) as a living thing, you will soon perceive its reaction to you and what you do. Specific customs can be studied in advance, but if you are a sensitive traveler you won't need a guidebook or an anthropology text to tell you how the people feel about what you are doing.

"Culture shock" is a popular term used to describe what happens when tourists have their minds completely blown by a foreign country and culture (see *Staying Healthy: Shock*). What most tourists fail to realize is that cultural shock works both ways. Imagine, for example, the effect on a quiet Mexican village when two carloads of tourists unexpectedly drop in.

The automobiles—late, semi-luxury models—stop in front of the tiny adobe municipal building. All eyes in the plaza watch curiously as five elderly couples climb out of the cars and stand blinking in the hot sun. They are members of a large tour group and each wears an identification badge. The men wear Bermuda shorts and sandals with black socks. Their shirts are loud print shirts and their straw hats have translucent plastic visors. The women sport tight pants, new *serapes* and oversized floppy sombreros with *Recuerdo de México* emblazoned in brightly colored yarn. They are all very pale in complexion and peer myopically at everything in sight.

By now the men on the iron benches in the plaza are watching in open amazement. The tourists are having a heated conversation; one of the women keeps pointing toward an old man dozing on a bench, waving her camera and looking excited and upset. Finally she goes over to him and says quite loudly, "*¿CUANTO?*"

The old man jerks up with surprise and is again abruptly asked, "*¿CUANTO?*" He shakes his head slowly, then begins to wag his forefinger back and forth to indicate that he doesn't understand.

"What'sa matter, Phyllis," another woman calls out loudly. "Won't he let you take his picture?"

"I asked him how much he wants, but he won't answer me," Phyllis complains, ignoring the bewildered looks the old man is casting about.

"Just give him some money and take it anyway," her friend advises. By now a crowd is gathering and the tourists feel distinctly uneasy.

Phyllis steps back and nervously snaps the picture. Hurriedly, she rummages through her purse and hands the old man an American quarter. He accepts the coin disdainfully, then walks away to discuss the strange happening with friends.

As Phyllis rejoins the group near the cars, one of them says, "Let's get out of here; this place gives me the creeps. What are all these people staring at, anyway?"

As they bounce slowly out of the village, Arnold, known in the group as a real wit, says wisely, "Probably never seen a camera before."

> "*A cada quien su vida.*"
> ("To each his own life.")
> —Mexican proverb

> "To each his own; it's all unknown."
> —Bob Dylan

Should tourists unwittingly violate some local custom, it is unlikely that the irate populace will stone them to death or splash "Yanqui go home!" across the nearest wall. Establishing rapport with people is very difficult, however, if respect and appreciation for the beliefs of others is not shown. The natural gap in understanding that lies between two cultures can be bridged by an awareness that differences are not good or bad, right or wrong; they're just different.

• **Customs of dress** are probably the most often violated by those who stray very far from the well-traveled tourist track. The offenders include all groups from super-straight to ultra-hip. The best way to avoid looking out of place or offending anyone is to look as much like everyone else as you can. You don't have to conform too strictly to avoid attention, just be reasonable.

Incongruous clothing is commonly worn by tourists, even those who normally take great care with their appearance. The popular image of a red-faced American wearing a gaudy shirt, a grossly large sombrero and painful new sandals on sunburned feet is embarrassingly accurate. What many people fail to realize, however, is that a barefoot, blond-haired gringa, wearing tight jeans, a man's Oaxaca wedding shirt, a Huichol belt and a string of beads is even more ridiculous-looking to the Mexican eye (especially the Indians).

Since women generally attract more attention than men, it is not surprising that their clothing and style are also subject to closer inspection and comment. This attention can be anything from open stares, wagging fingers and occasional whistles, to leers and downright lewd comments. In extreme cases, such as an overexposure of bare skin, someone may pointedly suggest that a visitor wear something more "decent."

Although up-to-date clothing styles are seen in larger Mexican cities and resorts, they are not as common in the rest of the country. For example, it is generally considered in poor taste to go barefoot except at the beach. Mexicans have a high regard for shoes (and polish), even though they may be the mere vestiges of a pair of cheap plastic loafers. When we first traveled to Mexico, Lorena's crude *huaraches* (sandals) earned many disapproving looks in town.

Indians who wear *traje* (traditional costumes) can be especially sensitive to clothing and style, probably because their own clothing has a distinctive and almost invariable appearance. Some Indians will not wear "foreign" clothing even if it is given to them.

Lorena was once walking down a path wearing her favorite *huipil* (loose Indian blouse) without a skirt—since the *huipil* fell to her knees. Several women stopped her and began laughing hysterically at her "get-up." It seemed obvious to them that Lorena had forgotten to finish dressing before leaving the house.

What amused them more, however, was the intricate design woven into the *huipil*. These symbols indicated that Lorena was a mother with children. The women knew this wasn't true and thought it truly astounding that she would wear that pattern. From then on, Lorena reserved this *huipil* for places where the design was unknown.

The best way to offend the maximum number of people, regardless of their individual opinions about clothing styles, is to go partially or fully nude in public. A *playera* (T-shirt) and pants is usually OK on a man, but a bare chest is frowned upon except at the beach. On our first trip to Mexico, Steve removed his shirt in a busy gas station in order to wash grease off his arms. An indignant cop ordered him to put it back on. (Mexico's "dress code" is gradually relaxing, but I still prefer to wear more clothes rather than less, especially in small towns.)

Men are often seen on crowded beaches wearing nothing but a pair of baggy, semi-transparent undershorts. Though their balls may be almost in public view, they are properly attired *for the beach*.

Traditional dress codes for women in rural Mexico can be quite strict. A small boy may romp stark naked, whereas a girl, even though just a toddler, will cause a scandal if she appears with a bare butt. Women occasionally bathe in secluded spots with their breasts exposed, but they'll rarely remove their underskirts. Mixed bathing with soap is not common and is considered very daring.

Mixed nude bathing is very risky and can lead to serious trouble (see *Red Tape and the Law*). I know many cases where Mexicans tolerated open dope smoking, laughed at foolish drunken stunts and then called the cops when people swam nude.

Beards are accepted in Mexico but have never been considered fashionable. You'll see beards on student agitators, truck drivers, intellectuals, poets, tourists and the odd travel writer. Long hair on men is tolerated, but the average Mexican man still finds the sight unsettling.

• **Food and drink:** Customs and rituals for eating and drinking are most commonly seen in humble restaurants and private homes. The more purely Mexican the surroundings, the more traditional the customs.

In tiny restaurants or eating stalls, several people will be seated at one or two tables. When you wish to sit down ask, "*¿Con permiso?*" ("May I?") and one or all of the diners will say something affirmative, usually "*Andele.*" ("Go ahead.") This is strictly a formality, but it breaks the silence.

"*¡Buen provecho!*" ("Good appetite!") is used as a greeting or blessing to those already eating and as a means of excusing yourself when you're finished. The response is "*Gracias.*" (You can also say, "*¿Con permiso?*" when leaving.)

The exchange of greetings and their responses may become confusing. In some areas people say "*Gracias*" when they leave the table. Whatever is said, answer it with something: "*Gracias*" or "*andele.*"

In a traditional household five regular meals are served: first comes *desayuno*, an early morning snack of coffee and sweet breads, followed by an early lunch (*almuerzo*); then a big late lunch (*comida*, the main meal); yet another light meal (*merienda*, like a tea); and last but not least, *cena*, a late supper. Still hungry?

It is customary to wash your hands before eating.

Men and/or guests are always served first, and many times guests will eat in front of everyone else. Disconcerting, but you almost get used to it.

Food is served already dished up, usually course by course. When one plate is clean it is quickly replaced by another dish.

This custom works both ways; if you're the host, you should serve your guests everything and force second helpings, as guests will not serve themselves and will sit there for hours without eating. The traditional "finger foods" menu and heavy dependence on tortillas means that eating with the fingers is usually acceptable (unless it is soup). Overeating is encouraged. (Mexicans are finally getting over the belief that overweight people are extra-healthy.)

When booze is served, the same custom applies. The host proposes toast after toast and constantly refills your glass. Nondrinkers may find it difficult to refuse, but a profuse "*No, gracias*" is usually sufficient. Bottles of liquor are left unfinished and a party rarely ends before the booze and participants are completely exhausted.

If a meal is given at a fiesta, it usually won't be served until midnight or even later.

It would be unusual for a blessing or grace to be said before a meal.

If a fork falls to the floor it means another guest is coming.

When inviting people to dinner, drinks or any type of social gathering, it is best to name each person you expect to attend. For example, you might wish to invite a family to dinner, but when the time comes only the husband shows up.

• **"Hot" and "cold"** are classifications given to foods, beverages, home remedies and even some activities. In this context, hot and cold don't refer to temperature, but to a property or condition, much like the Asian concept of yin and yang.

It is important to maintain the proper balance of hot and cold to avoid *pasmo*, an illness caused by too much of one or the other. *Pasmo* can cause cramps to heart failure; those who believe take it quite seriously.

Some typical hot and cold situations: I was standing in front of an open fire after bathing. A Mexican friend literally dragged me away, saying the combination of a "cold" bath (though the water was hot) with a "hot" fire would cause leprosy.

On another occasion I went on a short, very dry hike with a friend. When we returned to his store I asked for a cold drink. To my amazement he refused, explaining with profuse apologies that a cold drink would kill me or severely damage my innards.

Don't be surprised if guests politely decline a cold drink or neglect it until it warms.

It hasn't been that many years since soda pop and beer were almost always served *al tiempo* (at room temperature).

Once you accept one of these beliefs, it should be easier to appreciate the more bizarre.

Water, and all things that live in it, are "cold," but ice is "hot."

Too many "cold" fruits cause dysentery.

"Hot" foods are generally safer and more nourishing than "cold."

When a Mexican friend offered Lorena a recipe for lima bean soup she said, "Whatever you do, don't forget to add cumin seeds. Lima beans are 'cold' and without the 'hot' cumin, it will give a woman a stomachache."

• **Time, invitations and obligations:** The old cliché that Mexicans are always late or don't show up at all is difficult to argue with. Oddly enough, after years of living in Mexico I not only accept this custom but I've adopted it as my own, casually making engagements that I don't expect to attend. As a general rule, Mexicans and I agree to everything, but we only comply with what suits us.

The practice of being "blunt," "honest" or "out front," so revered by Americans, is considered somewhat rude in Mexico. My *compadre* Nacho explained this when I asked why he'd accepted an invitation to a party that he absolutely dreaded attending. "In order to avoid telling them 'no,' I told them 'yes.'" When I pointed out that he shouldn't force himself to go, he just laughed and said, "Of course I'm not going, but it is worse to refuse than not to show up."

• *Mañana:* Mexicans don't like to be pinned down. Your high school Spanish teacher probably defined the word *mañana* as "morning" or "tomorrow." In Mexico, however, *mañana* isn't quite so predictable. For example, if you ask a direct question, "When will I see you again?" or "When will this be ready?" the answer is almost inevitably, *"Mañana."* Don't get your hopes up; like a desert mirage, "tomorrow" is often a false promise. As actually used, *mañana* means "in the future."

Examples of polite evasions abound: your laundry won't be ready today as promised, but will certainly be pressed and folded *mañana*; your new friend "forgot" to meet you for dinner but would love to try again *mañana*; the boy was late, the girl was already gone, the water was off, the key has been lost, the ice wasn't delivered—but not to worry—everything will be taken care of with a smile, perhaps as soon as . . . *mañana*?

My favorite definition of *mañana* was given by a Mexican friend, who explained with a perfectly straight face, "Tomorrow means 'not today.'" (As a final consolation, Mexicans are often just as irritated and inconvenienced by the *mañana* syndrome as gringos.)

Exceptions to the rule: Contrary to legend, Mexico's buses and trains are usually quite punctual, as are organized sightseeing tours. If you dawdle over coffee, don't be surprised if you're left behind.

"The mañana syndrome is . . . not a symptom of chronic inefficiency or laziness, but rather evidence of an entirely different philosophy of time. If the past is safe, the present can be improvised and the future will look after itself."
— Alan Riding, **Distant Neighbors** (1984)

• *Ocho días:* Eight days make up a week in Mexico. *Ocho días en adelante*, eight days from now, is what we would call "a week from today." The time is also given on a twenty-four-hour basis: *1900 horas* means 7 p.m. (1200 noon plus seven hours). Midnight is *2400 horas* and one minute past midnight is 0001.

• *Colas* (tails, queues, waiting lines) are contrary to the Mexican sense of right and order. *"Señora, ¡hay cola!"* ("Lady, there's a line!") is wasted breath in most cases. Use your energy instead to elbow and bluff your way to the front. About the only place that a line is observed is at the *tortillería* (tortilla factory). Old ladies with years of heavy kitchen work and hardbody biceps will make short work of crowders and bargers.

Gringos are often timid about shoving ahead or may be embarrassed to be served before others who were there first. Get over it; you can bet that one day you'll spend half an hour trying to buy a stamp as aggressive Mexicans make short work of you.

Because of out-of-control population growth, Mexico City is often called "*la ciudad de colas*" ("the city of lines").

• *¡Salud!* is both a drinking toast and a sneeze blessing. When you sneeze and hear "*¡Salud!*" the proper response is "*Gracias.*" Many people believe that a sneeze means someone is thinking ill of you.

• **Handshakes** are very important. Friends who see each other daily will shake hands when meeting and when taking their leave. Men shake hands with women, children with adults, girls with boys, shopkeepers trade handshakes with customers and family members respectfully offer their hands to relatives and elders. Handshakes, even between men, are usually very gentle. Man-to-man knuckle crushing is definitely not polite. Indians may only brush each other's hands or even kiss them lightly.

As Steve and I can attest, anyone with a beard or a pro-Cuba, Marxist-Leninist gleam in their eye should be alert for the "solidarity grip" when shaking hands with students and younger men. It can be rather embarrassing if you fumble it.

• The *abrazo*, a combination of ritualistic shoulder-slapping and hugging, is practiced between Mexican men but rarely with foreigners. Depending on the situation, the traditional comradely hug can signify mutual respect or admiration rather than affection. For example, politicians often exchange the full *abrazo*, a tricky 1-2-3 combination of handshake (with one hand clutching the other man's elbow for extra emphasis), pat-on-the-back and quick embrace. If cameras are present, add a frozen, insincere smile for emphasis.

• **Siestas:** Mexicans are both night owls and early birds; they like to stay up late and jump out of bed at dawn. By mid-afternoon, however, the sun is at its peak and most people are ready to take a break—the siesta. Those who think the custom of siestas is a vice of the lazy don't realize that most Mexicans don't go to bed until almost midnight. Nightlife rarely picks up until late evening and spending the entire night *en vela* ("in candle," awake) is common.

Originally introduced to Mexico by early Spanish colonists, this common-sense custom probably originated with the Moors of North Africa. The siesta is a time to relax or to nap after enjoying a leisurely *comida* (the largest meal). Shops and offices will close, sidewalks empty and life generally winds down in anticipation of a long evening.

• **Admiring another person's possessions** can lead to embarrassing scenes.

Because it is customary to give away the object admired, a refusal to accept, even if sincere and well intentioned, might give offense.

Lorena was reminded of this when she admired a friend's wedding ring. To her horror, the woman immediately took off the ring and gave it to her. Lorena tried to refuse, but the woman wouldn't hear of it and she eventually had to accept the gift.

• **The *paseo*** (stroll or promenade) is an ancient custom much like cruising. Instead of driving around in cars, however, everyone is on foot. A description of a typical evening's *paseo* is essential to hack travel articles: "Sharp-eyed chaperons dressed in black hover behind dark-eyed flashing beauties. . . ." The reality is often different, with dark-eyed beauties in Gap gear trading off-color insults with their male counterparts as they circle the plaza on inline skates. The lively atmosphere may be enhanced, for the guys, by an occasional nip of tequila, giving one young man the courage to call out, "Oh, my little dear, you have a body just like a dove!" When the object of this *piropo* (flirtatious remark) responds with a rude hand signal, he quickly adds, "A big butt and skinny legs!" before joining his friends in sarcastic laughter.

The *paseo* occurs almost every night of the week, with full participation on Sunday evening. This is the night to dress up, for the *catrín* (dude) to put on his best *cacles* (shoes) and do a little "panthering" among the ladies. A set of keys dangles casually from the hand or pants pocket, as though an automobile—instead of a bicycle—were parked somewhere nearby. The men and boys circle the plaza in one direction, the unattached ladies in knots of two to four and couples in the opposite. This provides constantly refreshing opportunities for eye contact, wisecracks and suggestive body movements.

Those who have budding relationships usually attach themselves to another couple as a buffer against looking too serious. If things work out, they'll be seen later pressed into the frustrating semi-privacy of a shadowy doorway.

• **The Family Sunday:** Most Mexicans work half or even full days on Saturday, which leaves only Sunday for church, *futbol* games (soccer), picnics and big family outings. Unless the family is lucky enough to have a car, these weekend jaunts will be made by bus or taxi. *Campesinos* (farmers, country people) often use farm trucks for picnics and trips to the beach. In some towns, streets are blocked off on Sunday afternoon so that strollers can enjoy open-air concerts, folk dancing, and perhaps a *kermess*, a traditional food and bake sale hosted by a local charity or civic organization.

• ***La Serenata:*** When a boy's best efforts to attract a girl at fiestas draw only blank stares and his clever *piropos* fall on deaf ears, it's time for more dramatic gestures. Sending a miniature gold religious medallion by messenger has a certain flair, but when even that fails to turn her head, it is probably time for a "crowing rooster." To put on a *"gallo"* (better known as a *serenata* or serenade), a young man will gather his musically inclined friends together or hire a band to charm the girl he loves. Regardless of what her bleary-eyed father might think, it is generally agreed that for sheer drama and romantic power, nothing matches a live *mariachi* band rattling a girl's windows at the crack of dawn with, "Awake my beloved, listen to the voice of the one who loves you!" Needless to say, offering a serenade is considered a serious advance.

• ***La Quinceniera:*** Of all the parties that a girl will attend, none equals the excitement or importance of her "coming of age" fifteenth birthday, the *quinceniera*. The ceremony (which often rivals or even eclipses the girl's wedding), begins with a special Mass attended by all of her friends and family. Dressed in a bridal-like white gown, *la quinceniera* —"the fifteenth"—is escorted to the altar by fourteen boys and fourteen girls. The priest then delivers a homily, a kind of "this is your life" sermon based on the girl's childhood, parents and upbringing. Following this service, everyone moves to a large hall or ballroom. The first dance, a waltz, is always reserved for the girl and her father. As they sweep around the floor, they are joined by the fourteen couples. If she has brothers, they eventually cut in and replace the father. Eventually, all the guests begin to dance and the fiesta really begins. Later in the evening there will be a traditional supper, after which the guest of honor—now recognized as a woman of marriageable age—will receive suitably grown-up gifts of perfume and gold jewelry.

• *Compadrazgo* is a very important system of relationships between people who may otherwise have no formal connection. It is easiest to compare *compadrazgo* with the godparent relationship in other societies, though two people may become *compadres* without involving children. Anything of importance can lead to new *compadres:*marriage, births, buying a new house, a business deal, a close friendship and so on. We have a friend who acquired a *compadre* when he managed to save up the money for a new pick-up truck.

Compadres are supposed to support each other in times of need (though they often don't). This tightens the social structure, especially in poorer communities. *Compadres* are often on quite different social and economic levels, however, and the social bond is anchored in mutual respect. A businessman, for example, who accepts an employee's invitation to be his *compadre* upon the birth of a child, is now more than just an employer, he's a shirttail relative.

You'll often hear people refer to each other as *compadre* (also *compa*) and *comadre*, or *comadre* Maria, *compadre* Pancho, etc. Once the relationship is entered into, this title replaces the person's name or is added to it. Dropping *compadre-madre* is impolite.

Compadre and *comadre* are frequently used among younger people who are actually not *compadres*, but just good friends. *Compadre* and *comadre* are used as slang to mean "friend" or "buddy."

• **Mexican women don't shave their legs.** This isn't necessarily a sign of liberation, but a holdover from times when hairy legs meant European rather than Indian blood. Class-conscious Mexicans look down upon the Indians, though they often collect their artifacts and craft works.

• *Un tesoro de la Revolución* (a treasure from the Revolution) is a very common legend, especially in rural areas. Because of looting, banditry and kidnap-for-ransom during the 1910 Revolution, many people buried their money and valuables. Some of these caches were recovered, but others were not. Treasures that remain *enterrado* (buried) may be guarded by powerful spirits.

• **Business cards** are vitally important to anyone who has a *negocio* (business), line of B.S. or just a hope and a prayer for profit. Taxi drivers have them, as well as traveling salesmen, students (in early anticipation of the degree claimed), bartenders, bureaucrats, teachers and anyone else with pretensions to a title or position. *Tarjetas* are very cheap and can be quickly printed up just around the corner. "John Doe, Dealer in Rare Earths" or "Jane Doe, Specialized Consultant" can be a nice change from "bulldozer operator" and "housewife."

Identification cards with photos are also highly valued. It seems that some organizations exist solely to provide their members with these. An evening in a *cantina* invariably requires a mutual show-and-brag ID card session.

• **Church etiquette:** Although the Catholic church no longer requires women to cover their heads when inside a church, many still do. Men take their hats off in church and devout Mexican men remove them when passing a church. A very brief prayer is given when passing a church or shrine. The more traditional Catholics, particularly in small towns and in the country, still observe meatless Fridays.

Superstitions

• *Bilis* (bile) might well be called the national ailment of Mexico. It is said to be caused by emotional upset: extreme anger, frustration, embarrassment, etc. The symptoms are as varied as the treatments, but generally appear as stomach troubles, headaches, lack of energy and loss of appetite. *Bilis* is considered to be psychosomatic by most gringos, including those addicted to Tums, Maalox and tranquilizers.

• *Vientos* (winds) and *mal aires* (bad airs) are a common cause of various ailments, though usually associated with respiratory problems, toothache, cramps and paralysis. During the night and early morning you'll see people with their heads swathed in cloths or towels as a protection against bad air.
 The worst aspect of a belief in ill winds and bad breezes is that people avoid what we consider normal ventilation. Unless the weather is quite warm, you'll probably notice that others move away from an open bus window or ask that it be closed again. Children go around bundled up to the ears as if for a snowstorm when their parents are behind the house, harvesting bananas.

• *Limpias* (cleansings) are used to cure victims of the evil eye, those with bad luck, *bilis* or an improper hot/cold balance. The patient is usually brushed with a chicken egg (preferably a ranch egg rather than a white factory egg). Herbs may also be used. Some *curanderas* break the egg into a glass of water after the cleansing and diagnose the problem by observing the action of the egg yolk and white. People will travel hundreds of miles for a good *limpia*. The practice is followed by Mexicans from all social and economic levels.
 Fortune telling may be done in conjunction with the *limpia*. The charge is usually more than for a standard cleansing.

• **Salt is bad luck.** To have *sal* usually leads to poverty, if not illness and death. Salt can be removed by a cleansing of a person or building. Protection is also provided by charms.

• All types of **charms, amulets and prayers** are commonly used for protection against illness and spiritual problems, including black magic. *Oraciones* are small printed prayers sold in herb stalls and around churches. They are used in conjunction with other charms or alone, as a chant. Each has its special powers; ask the vendor what it's for.

Lodestones (*piedra imán*) are very powerful amulets. They are not cheap. Elaborate preparations are necessary to prepare a lodestone for use and the new owner must "feed" metal filings to the stone. (Steve notes that the Mercado Sonora in Mexico City specializes in magical supplies and is extremely interesting to visit.)

Retablos are pictures painted by persons seeking relief from disease or divine intervention. They are placed at the altar of a favored saint. Many *retablos* are considered to be fine examples of folk art and are bought by collectors. Never remove a *retablo* from a church or shrine!

• *Mal ojo*, the evil eye, is caused by someone who admires another person too intensely or thinks ill of him or her. Some people can cast *mal ojo* at will, but they are (fortunately) uncommon. An otherwise normal person can inadvertently cast the Eye on another without being aware of it. Persistent illnesses are often caused by the evil eye. Consult a *curandera*.

• *Envidiá* (envy) is blamed by *campesinos* and Indians for many problems, from the death of family members and livestock to poor corn crops or failing business profits. Elaborate measures are taken against envy. Not so long ago the best cure for *envidiá* was considered to be eliminating the person causing the trouble.

• *Espanto* and *susto* (fright) are disorders caused by anger, shock, frustration or other emotional stresses. Indians are especially vulnerable to *espanto*. Death as a result of it is not uncommon. The cures are varied. Doctors are rarely consulted since people know by now that the medical profession either can't or won't do anything for it.

Loss of appetite is a common symptom of both *espanto* and *susto*. Even the average Mexican fears loss of appetite. Overeating and being overweight are generally considered signs of good health and a strong constitution.

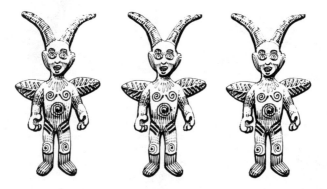

• **The Bogeyman** will be waiting for you in Mexico. He is commonly called *El Diablo* (the Devil), *El Coco* (the Head—bald) and *El Sombrerón* (also *El Sombrero*, the Big Hat). The *Sombrerón* has the rude habit of copulating with female horses and then braiding their tails. He is easily recognizable: look for a giant headless man wearing a huge hat and riding a flying white horse. A close friend who saw *El Sombrerón* late one night sneered when I suggested it might have been the bottle of tequila he'd drunk, rather than a real ghost. "The tequila just allowed me to see him," he answered. "If sober people could see him, they'd all be scared!"

La Llorona, The Weeper, is a woman dressed in long white robes. She drags around her floor-length hair, crying out "*¡Ay, mis hijos!*" ("Ay, my children!") and giving bad little girls and boys the night sweats.

Chanecos live in the forests and jungles. People follow their friendly laughter and then disappear. No one who has set after a *chaneco* has ever returned to describe them. (Survivors of a *chaneco* chase do exist, but they are hopelessly insane.)

In recent years a hybrid monster called the Chupacabra has been responsible for mischief and mayhem throughout Mexico. Authentic, almost completely believable photos of this ghastly goat-sucking beast are available on the Internet (see *For More Information*).

• **Note:** These are just a few examples of treasured Mexican superstitions; every region has its own monsters and favorite spirits. One of the most popular in the north is the ghost of Pancho Villa. Villa does everything from scaring children to healing illness and bestowing good luck. Watch for him.

Celebrations and Fiestas

"Most of the Mexican fiestas are the products of boredom. . . ."
— Herbert Cerwin, *These Are the Mexicans* (1947)

According to the Mexican Department of Tourism there are 5,000 to 6,000 *known* fiestas celebrated each year in Mexico. Observing even a fraction of them would exhaust the most dedicated party-goer.

Almost anything can spark a fiesta. It seems that when a family isn't honoring someone's birthday, Saint Day, birth, death, promotion or return from Mexico City with a private *pachanga*, they're attending a similar party at a relative's house. Neighbors celebrate their own particular patron Saint Day, as do *colonias* (neighborhoods), *pueblos* (villages), *municipios* (counties), *ejidos* (collectives), states and even regions. When the religious calendar fails to give reason for a fiesta someone will create a *Guelaguetza*, a Radish Fiesta or a Day of the *Compadre*.

Some fiestas are very predictable, others come and go according to the whim of organizers and participants. If the fiesta in San Andres is more *vivo*, alive, than one in San Pablo on the same day, the people of San Pablo will forsake their own festivities to attend the other. Weather or lack of money for a proper fireworks display may delay a fiesta. If the schedule says "honor San X on Thursday," his Saintedness may have to wait until Saturday or Sunday; after all, people have jobs.

The most important ingredient in a good fiesta is not the cost or color of the trimmings—it's the participants themselves. Fiestas were not designed to be observed but to be participated in. Leave your camera in your hotel room, toss the book explaining the hidden significance of everything into a corner and go out and join in.

Although it is late evening, crowds are just beginning to fill the small plaza. Children run in excited packs, gawking up at the tall *castillos*, elaborate wooden and bamboo structures covered with fireworks. These will be lit much later, after the people have enjoyed snacks from the many temporary food stalls offering steaming sweet tamales, sizzling tacos and strips of charcoal-broiled beef. There's cotton candy, hotcakes smeared with strawberry jam, *buñuelos*, popcorn, *churros* dusted with sugar, special sweet breads, *aguas frescas*, soft drinks and plenty of washtubs filled with ice and beer. Colored lights are hanging from the fronts of buildings; crêpe paper streams from lampposts and trees.

A sudden silence falls upon the crowd, followed by a mass sigh of pleasure. A huge *globo* rises slowly over the town, its thin cloth and paper skin flickering with the flame of a kerosene pot inside. This balloon—actually a miniature blimp—rocks crazily in the breeze, then erupts into a ball of flame as the kerosene fire touches the paper. Cries of glee follow its fiery plunge onto the roof of the elementary school. Fortunately the tiles are fire-proof; by early morning they'll be littered with expended rockets and flares.

The *globo* is followed by others, each raising the crowd's spirit until even the most staid citizens laugh with excitement. Firecrackers and small rockets explode at people's feet; a poorly aimed star shell showers sparks into the very center of the plaza, causing a moment of hilarious panic among the women operating the *kermess*, a benefit food and knickknack sale.

The interior of the church glows with the light of hundreds of devotional candles as worshippers come and go in a steady stream. In the courtyard outside, *conchero* dancers in wildly colorful costumes follow rhythms far older than the stone walls that tower above them. The monotonous strumming of armadillo-shell guitars fades beneath the sudden blare of the town loudspeaker, announcing unintelligible self-congratulations from local *políticos* on the event of this, the greatest ever celebration of who-knows-what.

Beggars hustle between the front of the church and the plaza, caught in the dilemma of whether to hit up the devout or the prosperous couples who walk arm in arm, calling greetings to their friends. A policeman hurries by, one arm on an unruly drunk's shoulder, the other squeezing steadily on a hinged "come-along" clamped like a nutcracker over the offender's wrist. In the morning he will work off his fine and hangover by cleaning up the debris of the night's festivities.

A commotion near a street corner erupts into a swirl of running bodies, clouds of confetti, glitter and friendly insults. Eggshells, loaded with everything from powdered paint to metallic flakes, fly over the crowd, exploding harmlessly on the flagstones— or directly on a well-chosen head. A polite young man about twelve years of age asks the tourist if he is having a good time. Before an answer can be given, the boy plants a loaded eggshell directly in the center of an unsuspecting chest. What choice do you have but to buy some of these wonderful eggs and join the fun?

• **Folk dancing:** The ancient myths and traditions of Mexico's many Indian cultures strongly influence the *baile folklórico* (folk dance). No fiesta is complete without dancing and the competition between dance groups is intense. Most towns have at least one folk dancing troupe and dancing is also taught at school. Among the most popular are dances performed by groups called *concheros*. The steps are simple but hypnotic as the gaily costumed dancers accompany themselves with primitive drums, rattles and guitars made from armadillo shells. In the state of Michoacán, Tarascan Indians perform *Los Viejitos*, the Dance of the Old Men.

• **Private parties:** Private fiestas and *pachangas* (blow-outs) are rarely bring-your-own-bottle or potluck. Although both these customs are being adopted by middle- and upper-class Mexicans, at most parties the hosts provide everything. Traditional Mexicans might even be miffed if a guest were to bring food or refreshments. *Machismo* says that when you invite someone to your house you make damned sure they'll be well taken care of.

In obviously poor households, however, a discreetly offered gift will almost always be accepted, especially if you say, "*Es nuestra costumbre*" ("It is our custom"). When you're going to someone's house to eat and want to take something, keep it simple: flowers or a plant, fruit, or a small bottle of tequila.

If the party is a birthday, saint's day or wedding, a gift is probably in order. What to take? For men a bottle of brandy, for women a plant or knickknack and for children a toy. Music cassettes also make good gifts, but books are rarely given unless you're certain the person likes to read.

At some parties the host or hostess offers gifts to their guests. This is called *el remojo*. A *remojo* party usually celebrates a new house, car or other major acquisition.

• *Día de santo* (saint's day) is a sort of second birthday, honoring the saint after which a baby is named. A man called Antonio, for example, would celebrate his *día de santo* on San Antonio's Day, whether or not it is his actual birthday. (See *Saints' Days* at the end of this chapter.) The barrio of San Antonio holds an annual *fiesta* on the same day, and the village of that name will, too.

"*¡Hoy es mi santo!*" ("Today is my saint!") can lead to an invitation to a *pachanga* (blow-out). A birthday may go by almost unnoticed, but a saint's day must be elebrated.

• *Mariachis:* With their silver *concha* belts and tight-fitting *charro* outfits, the *mariachi* band is both the symbol and the sound of classic Mexico. In downtown Mexico City, hundreds of *mariachi* musicians gather every evening in Garibaldi Square to offer their services. As tourists and locals stroll by, trumpets, violins and high-strung guitars called *vihuelas* duel for their attention. To the accompaniment of a heavily throbbing *guitarrón* (bass guitar), a heavily mustachioed singer tilts back his huge sombrero and wails out the opening line of a tear-jerking *ranchera* tune: "Life is worth nothing in Guanajuato . . ."

Holiday Calendar

The dates for national holidays and most major festivals are fixed, but local celebrations and religious events often vary from one year to the next. In the calendar below, a question mark after a date indicates that the date may change. Be aware, too, that Indian communities often celebrate both the eve of an important fiesta and the day itself.

January 1: New Year's Day (*Año Nuevo*) is a national holiday. Indian communities install their leaders and officials. New Year's Eve is *Nochevieja* (Old Night). Bank holiday.

January 6: Day of the Kings (*Día de los Reyes*). The traditional day of gift-giving marks the end of the Christmas season.

January 12–31 (?): Regional Fair, Leon, Guanajuato. A huge *feria* (fair) with everything from animal exhibits and food to parades and crafts.

January 17: Blessing of the Animals (*Día de San Antonio*). Pets, caged birds and even farm animals are taken to church for an official blessing.

February 2: Candlemas (*Día de Candelaria*). This nationwide celebration of plants, seeds and renewed fertility marks winter's end.

February 5: Constitution Day (*Día de la Constitución*) is a national holiday commemorating Mexico's 1917 constitution. Bank holiday.

February (?) (varies, begins the weekend before Lent): *Carnaval* is a five-day, pull-out-the-stops Mardi Gras–style extravaganza celebrated in several ports. *Carnaval* is especially frantic in Mazatlán and Veracruz, though they do their best in La Paz and Ensenada, too.

The day and night revel includes fantastic costumes, parades, fireworks and masked hijinks. Though it began as a time of release in preparation for the restrained atmosphere and fasting of Lent, the religious significance of *Carnaval* tends to get lost in the crowds and public craziness. *Carnaval* is more traditional (but no less zany) in Indian communities, with elaborately staged dances, mock battles between Good and Evil and spirited pageants.

February 24: Flag Day, nationwide. You might call it "Day of the Pols," for all of the chest-beating speeches given by politicians.

March 21: The birthday of Benito Juárez is a national holiday for a revered ex-president, "Mexico's Abe Lincoln." Bank holiday.

March 21: Spring Equinox (*Equinoccio*). Between March 19 and 23, tens of thousands crowd the Mayan ruins of Chichén Itzá to watch the Plumed Serpent's shadow ascend the Temple of Kukulkan.

March 23–30 (?): Holy Week (*Semana Santa*). Mexico's favorite holiday marks the end of Lent (*La Cuaresma*). *Semana Santa* is a time of religious pilgrimages, Passion plays and elaborate Masses. All businesses and institutions close up tight on Thursday and Friday, but everyone tries to get away for the entire week, preferably to the beach.
Holy Week begins on Palm Sunday (*Domingo de Ramos*). It continues on through Ash Wednesday (*Miércoles de Ceniza*) and Maundy Thursday (*Jueves Santo*). Good Friday (*Viernes Santo*) is devoted to re-enactments of Christ's crucifixion. (Elaborate Good Friday processions are held in Taxco and San Luis Potosi.) The Mass of Glory is celebrated on Saturday, followed by fireworks, parades and the burning of effigies of Judas. By Easter Sunday (*Domingo de Resurrección*) everyone is worn out and on their way home.
Easter in Guatemala is one of the most colorful celebrations in the world. (See *The Best of Mexico: Ruta Maya: Easter in Guatemala*.) Holy Thursday and Friday are bank holidays.

April/May: The three-week *Feria de San Marcos* in Aguascalientes begins in mid-April. The country's largest fair is a marathon celebration of bullfights, *charreadas* (rodeos), folk dancing, markets, music and *mariachis*. The main parade is April 25 (San Marcos Day).

May 1: Labor Day (*Día del Trabajo*), nationwide, with an emphasis on breast-beating speeches and union parades. Bank holiday.

May 5: *Cinco de Mayo* or *Día de la Batalla de Puebla*. The Battle of Puebla Day is a national holiday honoring the defeat of French invaders in 1862. It doesn't stir much excitement, however, unless you're in Puebla (or the U.S., where *Cinco de Mayo* has become a kind of Indo-Hispanic recognition day). Bank holiday.

May 10: Mother's Day (*Día de la Madre*) is taken very seriously by Mexico's sons, daughters and husbands.

June: The month-long **Ceramics Fair and Fiesta** in Tlaquepaque (near Guadalajara) combines a major fiesta with all manner of arts and crafts exhibitions.

June (?): Feast of Corpus Christi, nationwide. The *Voladores of Papantla* perform a dizzying, much-publicized "dance" while whirling atop a tall pole.

July (last week): The *Guelaguetza* in Oaxaca is an intensely colorful celebration of Indian dance, theater and music that attracts hordes of international travelers.

August (?): Feast of the Assumption, nationwide. In Huamantla, Tlaxcala, a parade on streets decorated with lavish, flower petal "carpets" is followed by a pulse-quickening running of the bulls. (Body armor recommended.)

August 10–18 (?): Guitar Fair, Paracho, Michoacán. Highly skilled artisans display guitars, crafts and stringed instruments.

August 11–25 (?): Copper Fair, Santa Clara del Cobre, Michoacán. All manner of handcrafted copper utensils, art, gewgaws, ornaments and decorations.

September 1: Presidential "State of the Nation" speech and national holiday.

September 14: Day of the Charros. The *charro*, or gentleman cowboy, has come to symbolize the ideal Mexican man. Impeccably attired in tight black trousers, embroidered jacket and silver-handled pistol, he is a brave and handsome patriot, a hero mounted on a high-spirited horse, proud to the point of recklessness. To demonstrate that their skills go beyond fancy dress, groups of *charros* perform daring stunts on horseback at *charreadas*, rodeo-like events that also include folk dancing, games and music. Women *charras* also participate; showing off the distinctive *china poblana* costume of long skirts, shawls and fine slippers. Although the *charreada* is not quite as rough-and-tumble as an American-style rodeo, it is an impressive spectacle that traces its origins to Mexican *vaqueros*, this continent's original cowboys.

September 15–16: Independence Day (*Día de Independencia*), nationwide. Mexicans celebrate their *independencia* from Spanish rule with special enthusiasm. Two days of drum-bashing parades, patriotic speeches, bullfights, pageants and non-stop parties are capped at 11 p.m. with a stirring re-enactment of "*El Grito*," Father Hidalgo's famous "cry" for revolution in 1810. "*Viva México!*" the public responds.
   In Mexico City and many other towns, *El Grito* triggers extravagant fireworks displays featuring *castillos*, or "castles." As the crowd surges around them, fuses are lit and huge rickety towers covered with rockets, pinwheels and starshells erupt like volcanoes in the middle of the plaza. Bank holiday.

September 22: Autumn Equinox. At Chichén Itzá the Plumed Serpent's shadow descends Kukulkan (see March 21).

October: A month-long *Fiestas de Octubre* in Guadalajara features *mariachis*, *Ballet Folklórico* productions, *charreadas*, operas, symphonies and antiques and crafts markets.

October 3–4: St. Francis Day (*Día de San Francisco*). Traditional celebrations in many Indian communities.

October 5–23 (?): The International Cervantino Festival, Guanajuato. This is now a world-class celebration, with major artists and international music, dance and theater performances. Advance tickets and hotel reservations are necessary.

October 12: Day of the Race (*Día de la Raza*). The arrival of Columbus marks the joining of Spanish and Indian blood and the creation of the Mexican "race."

November 1–2: The Days of the Dead are celebrated in cemeteries nationwide but especially in Oaxaca; Janitzio, Michoacán; and near Mexico City at Mixquic. Can you imagine holding a party in a cemetery? November 1 is All Saint's Day (*Todos los Santos*) and on November 2, *Día de los Muertos* (All Soul's Day, "Day of the Dead"), children romp around the tombs and leaning crucifixes, munching tiny sugar skulls as their parents sit near the grave of a departed loved one, eating sweet tamales, *pan de los muertos* (bread of the dead) and recalling fond memories of their *difuntos* (deceased).

A few older kids set up a game on top of grandmother's crypt; with tiny dice and nuts for markers, they play *Oca* (Goose) and other traditional *Día de los Muertos* games.

The youngest child, just four years old, arranges miniature wooden and cardboard furniture, setting the tiny table with pea-sized pottery dishes. These are from the family altar, where yesterday, on November 1, the souls of little brothers and sisters who didn't survive their first years descended to play and to "eat" the treats set out for them.

A few graves away, an older brother sips from a small bottle of tequila, also from the altar. Earlier in the day, this same bottle cheered the souls of older family *difuntos*, along with the special breads, tamales and turkey *mole* the dead must do without for the remainder of the year.

An uncle leans against a tombstone, engrossed in the newspaper. He suddenly barks out a laugh, calling the others to listen as he reads out a bawdy, satirical poem that rudely caricatures the local mayor. These articles are *calaveras* (skeletons) and anyone in the public eye might find their hidden skeletons leaping from the closet to the front page on these days. Comic skeletal figures accompany the *calaveras*, portraying the *políticos* as having squandered municipal funds on the lottery.

The Days of the Dead originated in Europe in the ninth century and were introduced by Spaniards after the Conquest. This celebration blended quite nicely with already existing Aztec beliefs concerning death and departed spirits. The result is as Mexican as *mole* sauce.

About a week before the first of November vendors set up stalls and begin selling sugar skulls, coffins, tombs, skeletons and whatever else they can fashion into grisly reminders of mortality. The skulls have names: if Uncle Pancho drove his truck off a cliff last year, you'll buy a Pancho skull for the family altar and perhaps a large sugar skeleton clutching a real bottle of his favorite tequila and a cigarette.

Kids exchange sugar skeletons with each other's names on them and happily munch candy coffins. When their parent's aren't looking they'll snatch skull-shaped cookies and other treats from the family's *ofrendas*, offerings placed on an altar decorated with the photographs, mementos and favorite foods of deceased relatives.

Loaves of bread, representing departed souls, are also sold, as well as miniatures of almost anything one can think of to please those who have but one day a year in which to again enjoy the earthly plane. These offerings all go on the family altar. On the first of November the souls of the children descend to enjoy their treats; on the second day, it's the turn of the adults. Afterwards the treats will be eaten by the family and guests.

When visiting a house during the Days of the Dead, guests bring small gifts for the altar: food, flowers (especially marigolds), candles, miniatures and, perhaps, liquor. None of these offerings is eaten until the souls have had their chance to partake.

November 20: Revolution Day (*Día de la Revolución*), nationwide bank holiday devoted to parades and patriotic speeches (Revolution of 1910). Bank holiday.

November 29–December 6 (?): Silver Fair (*Feria de la Plata*) and silver-smithing competitions in Taxco, Mexico's "silver city," plus concerts, markets, dances and fireworks.

December 12: Feast of the Virgin of Guadalupe (*Día de Nuestra Señora de Guadalupe*). Mexico's most important religious holiday is also **Flag Day** (*Día de la Bandera*), a national holiday.

No religious or historical figure is more important to Mexicans than the Virgin of Guadalupe. As the country's official "Patroness and Protectress," the Virgin's image is reproduced on everything from beach towels to gold jewelry. Her "*día de santo*" (saint's day) on December 12 is one of Mexico's principal religious festivals. Hundreds of thousands of people flock to her shrine in Mexico City, including many who walk for days or even crawl on their knees to beg special favors from the saint. In other parts of Mexico, teams of cross-country runners honor the Virgin by relaying flaming torches for long distances. Bank holiday.

December 16–January 6: The season of Christmas. *La Navidad* combines fiestas, religious pageants, special Catholic Masses and a national vacation. In fact, so many families go to the beach during the season that most of the country's serious business is put on hold.

On the first evening of Christmas, December 16, nine consecutive nights of *posadas* begin. These re-enact Joseph and Mary's search for lodging (*posada*). *Posadas* are hosted by different families every night; for most Mexicans, the preparation and excitement that surround them mark the high points of Christmas. Once the procession reaches the house and is granted permission to enter, poems are recited, refreshments are served and the children are offered a *piñata*.

Piñatas are clay pots stuffed with candy, coins and small toys, decorated with brightly colored paper to look like fanciful birds, animals or even popular cartoon characters. The *piñata* is hung from a strong cord and blindfolded children take turns making wild swings with a stick, hoping to smash it open. Someone controls the *piñata* by means of a rope, jerking it up and down to increase the crowd's excitement as the child careens wildly around the room, flailing the air. When a blow connects solidly, the *piñata* bursts, spraying its goodies onto the floor and prompting a mad scramble among the kids.

Nativity scenes are set up during the *posadas*, many of them incredibly elaborate, incorporating miniature figures that have been in the family for hundreds of years. Some families offer fruit and candy to groups of people wandering the streets to admire Nativity scenes and enjoy the evening's festivities. The children (and some adults) of the house toss treats from the roof to those below. Sometimes they get carried away: my brother was peering in a window at an elaborate Nativity scene when an entire washtub of oranges was dumped on his head from the roof above.

December 23: Festival of the Radishes (*Fiesta de los Rabanos*), Oaxaca. Any excuse for a party . . . but a fiesta for carved radishes? It's wild!

December 25: Christmas Day (*La Navidad*). As a religious holiday, celebration is the theme of *Navidad*, rather than shopping. Children receive small gifts on the *Día de los Reyes*, January 6, the Day of the Kings. Presents are traditionally delivered by the Magi (though Santa Claus is steadily increasing his territory). Bank holiday.

December 28: Innocents Day (*Día de los Inocentes*) is Mexico's version of April Fool's Day. Rather than playing practical jokes such as "You just won the lottery!" Mexicans go to elaborate ruses to borrow things. "Nice looking pen you've got there. May I look at it?" You hand it over, the treasured ballpoint that you bought at the '62 Seattle World's Fair, but instead of its being returned you hear:

> *Inocente Palomita*
> *Que te dejas enganar,*
> *En este día de los inocentes*
> *Con tú (pluma) me he de quedar.*

Which means:
> *Innocent little Dove*
> *You've allowed yourself to be tricked,*
> *On this day of the innocents*
> *Your (pen) I'm entitled to keep.*

If this bit of humor causes the person who was fooled to scream and rant, the item "borrowed" can be returned without a loss of face, since you were "entitled" to keep it but don't have to. I lost my pen to a waiter in a small restaurant this way, but retaliated later by admiring his wife's gold earring. In spite of the fact that there were many "innocents" around, she didn't expect a gringo to know the rhyme. The look of dismay on the waiter's face as his wife calmly allowed me to borrow her earring "to show to Lorena" was worth a case of pens.

On a grander scale, Steve and I were completely fooled by a 28 December newspaper headline that screamed, "Peso devalues by 100%!!!"

Festivals, Fairs and Circuses

I won't try to describe a Mexican carnival or fair; the only person who could do it justice would be a ten-year-old in from the hills for his or her first glimpse of the big city. To really appreciate the experience, especially when the outward trappings are not lavish, forget that you've seen Barnum & Bailey, Disneyland and the Rose Parade. Pretend, if only for a few minutes, that this is *it!*, that mind-blowing trip to town you've waited for all of your life.

Once you've adopted this new identity, you'll feel yourself being swept up by people around you, noticing the things they appreciate, not what tourists are told is especially colorful or quaint. Buy a greasy *quesadilla* near the merry-go-round, shoot off a firecracker, throw confetti in people's faces—just don't stand on the sidelines with your camera and expect to understand what's happening.

After you've worked yourself into a real state, be sure to visit the sideshow. Such rare treats as the Snake Woman so convince the *campesinos* that barkers continually reassure them that it's a fake.

Circuses, like fairs and carnivals, are not produced for a sophisticated audience. Consequently, they are very real and enjoyable. The elephants seem ready to fall in your lap rather than parading precisely around a distant arena, just one small act in a carefully executed program. If you've watched aerial acts in a big circus in the U.S. without really expecting anyone to fall, you'll appreciate the tension of the Mexican audience as a performer twists and twirls under the well-patched "Big Top."

Small tent shows, called *carpas*, are also great fun. Many are operated by gypsies (*hungaros*).

Beggars and Con Artists

Beggars tend to disturb and unsettle tourists. It is a popular myth that every ragged beggar goes home at night to a well-fed family and empties bulging pockets into a wall safe or the trunk of a Mercedes. This is a good justification for not giving them anything and allows you to "see through" the dirt and rags that have obviously been carefully applied to achieve the desired effect on the gullible gringo.

Because a few enterprising cripples have turned their problems into a means of support, people assume that every outstretched hand is a rip-off. Don't believe it. Most of the beggars you'll see are in bad shape, and they need a handout to eat or to get a place to sleep, not for tires for the family car. The most transparently phony beggars are small children trying to make a few pesos for a Coke and the movie.

Mexicans accept beggars as facts of life. Store owners rarely turn down an outstretched hand, though they may give only a tiny sum. Beggars may be shooed from a restaurant or food shop, but seldom leave without something to eat. Poor people, as well as the obviously affluent, will take pity on a *mendigo* (beggar, also *pordiosero*); having very little themselves, they can easily appreciate having nothing.

I always look upon whatever I give away as the installment payment on a long-term karmic insurance policy. When you don't want to give, however, don't; it is considered unlucky to offer something unless the sentiment behind the gift is genuine.

If a beggar approaches while you're eating or marketing and you dislike the idea of giving money, offer something to eat. Often your suspicions about authenticity will disappear when the food is wolfed down hungrily.

A drunken beggar really upsets most people, but they ignore the fact that poverty leads to begging and from there to drinking. If you were dirt poor and had to face the prospect of having to beg to support your family, a few shots of *mezcal* would surely make things a bit more bearable.

If you want to give, but really can't afford it, get a pocketful of small change. Peso by peso, a dollar goes a long way.

Beggars usually bless you after you've donated (or curse you if you haven't), and they may go so far as to kiss your hand, the money or food. This can be embarrassing but it's just another of those customs that you'll eventually get used to.

In tourist areas, particularly beach towns, you may run into a form of begging that is actually a con game. It often runs like this: the beggar, a child or an adult, has a "stroke" or "attack" near a group of tourists. The unsuspecting fish run to the victim's aid. Often it appears to be an epileptic fit and they naturally do all they can.

At the point of calling an ambulance or a doctor, the poor victim pulls together long enough to feebly extract a prescription from a pocket. A few croaking sounds and a final collapse impress the crowd with the severity of the illness.

At this point, the gringo may be approached by another person who has just "happened along" and who helpfully translates the prescription and explains the situation. The situation is this: the victim has something wrong (epilepsy, heart trouble, etc.) and has a prescription but no money and is asking for help.

The first time this trick was pulled on me the kid had the misfortune to collapse on a hill of stinging ants. He rolled his eyeballs, did a few very convincing convulsions and then lapsed into what a "passerby" described as a coma. The coma ended when the ants got in his ears.

If you are approached by people begging for money to buy medicine, take them to a drugstore if you can and get the druggist's help. Socialized medicine has helped a lot of people, but there are still many who, for one reason or another, are not eligible or able to get medical aid. People often hike in from isolated villages for medicine for others who are unable to move and, with a druggist's advice and a small amount of money, you could very well save someone's life.

Unfortunately, the unfilled prescription has been turned into a hustle by some people. I was approached by a woman asking for money for medicine and during her spiel I realized that I recognized her—and her routine, from the year before. "That's an old *receta*," I said. "I know you!" She snatched back the prescription and yelled indignantly, "It's not old! I've only had this one for three months!"

Finally, should you give a guy a few cents—or even a few dollars—and later see him emerge from a chauffeur-driven Rolls, lighting a Cuban *puro* with a lottery ticket as he ducks into the Ambassador Hotel to meet his mistress for dinner, don't be bitter: "*¡Dios se lo pague!*" "God will repay you!"

Child Beggars

While nothing unsettles a tourist quite like the outstretched hand of an aggressive beggar, tourists often encourage children and adults to beg by distributing treats, money and small novelties. This problem is especially common in off-the-beaten-track communities visited by tour buses and "eco-tourism" groups.

Simply put, it is not the tradition among Mexicans to give gifts to strangers. No matter how selfless the intention, unsolicited gifts of money, candy, pens, toys and clothing quickly turn children into semi-professional beggars. In the Copper Canyon I observed tourists shoveling huge quantities of gum, candy and junk food into the hands of Tarahumara children. This goes on day after day, year after year, and has horrifying implications for these children's health.

National Lottery

The *lotería* (national lottery) is a major institution and its importance can be gauged by the fact that it is second only to the Social Security tax for federal revenues from a single source. Since 65 percent of that money goes back to the public as prizes, you might reconsider buying a ticket before you brush off that little old man lurking next to your elbow.

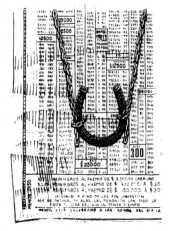

Prizes range from a few pesos to many millions, though only a lucky few hit it big. The price of a ticket capable of winning the entire first prize may cost thousands of pesos itself. Tickets are broken down into parts, consisting of twenty fractions of a whole ticket. You have to buy all the fractions to win all of the prize. Each of the fractions has the number of the whole ticket and holders of the fractions divide the prize. You can buy from one-twentieth to twenty-twentieths (a whole) of a ticket. *Sorteos*, drawings, are held three times a week. The results are published in newspapers and posted in large sheets on the front of official lottery offices. If you win, you must pay a federal tax.

I recommend that every tourist buy at least one lottery ticket; it may extend your vacation for a long time.

A sports lottery, *Pronósticos Deportivos Para La Asistencia Pública* (Sports Forecasts for the Public Welfare), PN for short, is actually a soccer pool. Tickets have to be marked with your guess at either win, lose or draw for each team and game. The ticket is then converted into a computer punch card and you are given a *talón* (ticket stub). Drawings are held once a week.

Machismo

Many wise and learned things have been written about the origins and causes of *machismo* (manliness, virility) in Mexico. Rather than attempting a detailed explanation, I will contain my comments to areas where *machismo* most directly and dramatically affects the traveler.

"What the hell are those guys trying to prove?" a gringo newly arrived in Mexico once asked me in a bar. He had just been through a few typical experiences involving the *macho* mentality: an insanely dangerous bus ride, an unpleasant scene with a drunk in a *cantina* and a look at the young men strutting around the plaza.

His question goes right to the point of *machismo*: *proving you are* macho—to the other driver on the highway, the passengers in your bus, the guy who dares not to drink with you, the women—especially to the women—and of course, to yourself.

This constant pressure to prove oneself can be very tiring. Tourists aren't the only

people to shake their heads at a display of *machismo*. Mexicans, particularly those with some education, openly speak of the need to end the vicious circle of *machismo*. Unfortunately this is about as difficult as outlawing patriotism. Although *machismo* can be dangerous, especially on the highway or in drunken quarrels, it is most often nothing more than a minor background hassle, something the experienced traveler learns to anticipate and avoid.

I had a close Mexican friend who constantly spoke of ways to eliminate *machismo*. He was a poet and political liberal, able to demolish opposing arguments in four languages, including Nahuatl. When he drank, however, he literally became everything he rejected. One night, after an attack on a tequila bottle, I pointed out to him that he was acting like a typical *macho*. He'd just blown the last of his salary on booze and the lottery, insulted a woman on the street and challenged a cab driver to a duel with tire irons.

He reacted to this accusation with angry curses and threats, pausing only long enough to lubricate his throat with gulps of tequila. When he'd finally settled down he said, "Will you loan me a hundred dollars?"

"What for?" I countered, taken aback. A moment before he'd damned my ancestors all the way back to the Neanderthals.

"You question my need for money?" he roared. "What are friends for?"

"I just wondered." I hurried to add. "I don't have much."

"Well, if you must know," he said, "I want to buy a gun. You've insulted me to the point where I have to shoot you."

I thought about this for a few seconds, realizing that he was entirely serious, if not entirely logical. "Can't you get one for less than a hundred?" I asked.

"Stop!" he howled. "Now you've gone too far! Do you think I'd shoot a friend with a cheap shitty pistol? No! I want something good!"

I refused him the loan and he threw me out, reminding me that to deny money to a friend was reason enough to end our friendship forever. And it did.

Situations such as this are not commonly encountered by tourists. A more usual form of *machismo*, one that has its humorous aspects, is bragging.

". . . if the conversation is about airplanes, and no one would believe him if he says that he has one, then he will say he has a friend who has two."
—Arturo Linares Suarez, *Como El Mexicano No Hay Dos*

Dealing with a *macho* braggart requires self-control and a fine sense of timing, for until you challenge a statement, neither of you has to prove that it is true. I once spent an afternoon in the countryside, listening to a man describe his magnificent fighting cocks. The top rooster in his team, called *El Capitán*, was capable of rendering feathered opponents unfit for use in soup. He had never been beaten and never would be! What a chicken!

"Can I see him?" I asked, opening a vast can of worms with that simple challenge to the rooster's existence.

I paid for my apparent doubt by having to hike ten miles under a blistering sun, only to find upon arrival at a remote *ranchito* that *El Capitán* had been "borrowed" for the day to improve the breed on a relative's *ranchito*, even farther into the mountains. I knew then that my friend was prepared to walk the length and breadth of Mexico, leading me toward that ever-receding mythical fowl.

Tourists and *Machismo*

Machismo frequently appears as what we might consider a childish and neurotic sense of pride. When someone offers you a cigarette, it doesn't matter that your polite refusal is based on the fact that you don't smoke. To the sensitive *macho*, any refusal, however rational, is still a refusal and therefore an insult.

I once asked a bartender how, in such a situation, it was humanly possible to avoid offense. He answered: "Take a cigarette and put it behind your ear. Tell the guy you will save it as a souvenir of your meeting."

Thus, you save face for the person who offered the cigarette since you symbolically join him in smoking. You soon learn the devious tricks of avoiding those conversations and situations that inevitably lead to some display of *machismo*.

• In a bar, don't offer or accept anything unless you really want to become involved with the other person. This is particularly true of an offer of booze.

• On the highway, *never* do anything to provoke another driver. When a truck tries to pass you on a hill, allow him to go around rather than forcing him to drop back right at the last moment. The reason for this is that he is not going to drop back, even if it kills you both.

• Irate horn honking is an invitation to do battle. ("Shave and a haircut" is very offensive in Mexico.) The true *macho* driver never allows a question of honor to go unanswered, even when he has committed some outrageous blunder. Death before dishonor!

• Be polite and never allow yourself to be goaded into displays of anger. A *macho* always stays cool on the outside. Losing your temper automatically escalates things, whether it's horn honking or a sharp response to a suggestive look.

• Don't question idle boasting.

• When dealing with other men, a *macho* wants to hear "*Sí*" and "*No*." Indecisiveness is considered weak. When dealing with women, the *macho* only understands "*No*"; everything else is taken as "Maybe."

• Don't question customs when there is no possible benefit from doing so. In the country, for example, women stay in the kitchen or sit on the edge of conversations. Accept this: you'll only embarrass everyone if you make a scene of being democratic.

"La mujer como el vidrio, siempre está en peligro." ("A woman is like glass, always in danger.")

—*Macho* saying

• Mexican men treat female relatives and friends with great courtesy, especially in public. They are also neurotically protective of them. If an acquaintance introduces you to "his" women, treat them like royalty. Exaggerated courtesy is the norm.

Barroom discussions of women inevitably lead to outbursts of *machismo*. Any conversation that involves a *macho*'s woman is potentially tricky. It's better to ask, "How is the family?" rather than "How's your wife?"

• For most Mexican women, raising a family and keeping a house aren't career options but their inevitable role in life. The expression "A woman's place is in the home" is still taken literally in traditional households. When they do leave the house, women seldom go alone. From toddlers to pre-teens, young girls are closely supervised by their mother or older sisters and brothers. As teenagers, girls are in constant company with their schoolmates, friends or family. Once she has married, a young woman's attention turns to housekeeping and babies. Her free time is spent in family activities or with close female friends.

The more rude demonstrations of *machismo* occur on the street or in casual encounters between men and women who do not know each other.

". . . the image of the mala mujer—*the bad woman, is almost always accompanied by the idea of aggressive activity. She is not passive like the 'self-denying mother,' the 'waiting sweetheart,' . . . she comes and goes, she looks for men and then leaves them. . . ."*

Octavio Paz's description from *The Labyrinth of Solitude* certainly is applied to gringas as well as Mexicans. When a *macho* sees a woman striding down the sidewalk, hair flying and breasts jiggling, an overnight bag in one hand and a guidebook in the other, he thinks *"¡Saqué la lotería, hombre!"* ("I've won the lottery, man!"). The only problem, of course, is trying to figure out how to collect.

Mexican men, from lewd old businessmen to bearded intellectuals, will go to almost any lengths to seduce a gringa. Any restrictions they might operate under with Mexican women are lifted in their relationships with foreigners.

The techniques range from loud, gross comments in public to intense, soul-searching conversations designed to disprove any taint of chauvinism in their character. If you just happen to be her escort, you'll be included in the conversations. But then, when you're on your way back from the restroom, you will get a glimpse of the crux of the discussion: a hand on her knee, an intense whispering in her ear . . .

Single women must exert great self-control and common sense when dealing with *machismo*. Any response, even negative, is taken as an opening.

Many women tell us that traveling alone doesn't scare them from the standpoint of physical danger, but that dealing with men on the make can be an almost continual hassle. The effort involved in keeping their guard up soon got many of them down. Some women quit traveling alone, others give up entirely and go home.

One of the most effective solutions to the problem is to travel with a guy, even if he's just "borrowed" for the day. This won't stop the *machos* entirely, but it definitely tones down their approaches.

Women would do well to observe how the *mexicanas* deal with men and *machismo*. Mexican women seldom leave the house alone and travel alone only when they can't find a friend, relative or neighbor to accompany them. Follow their example; sit and associate with other women whenever possible.

Mexican women avoid eye contact with strangers, especially on the street. I've often marveled at the seemingly impenetrable cocoon that surrounds them as they march to the store for a box of rice. We call this "practical invisibility." If you don't direct your attention to someone, it's less likely they'll notice you.

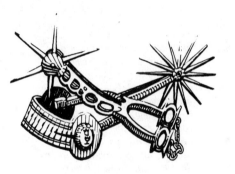

Pay attention to where you're going. When you notice a group of men ahead of you, especially at night, cross the street or go around the block to avoid a possible confrontation.

In a country where dark hair is almost universal, anything else is highly noticeable. Thanks to advertising, blonde hair has become a synonym for sex. ("The high-class blonde" is the trademark for a well-known Mexican beer.) Lorena always wears a scarf in public. When she is alone and prefers to be even more inconspicuous, she wears her hair braided and up on her head. Out of sight, out of mind.

Flamboyant clothing, bare arms and legs, or breasts showing or wiggling are considered by *machos* to mean, "I'm free and easy."

Any attitude other than aloofness is taken as flirtatious. To me, one of the most irritating backlashes of *machismo* is that casual encounters with Mexican women are usually cold and impersonal. The kind of easy bantering that goes on in an American supermarket, for example, between customers who collide their shopping carts near the lettuce just doesn't happen in Mexico. A curt, "Excuse me," is all you can expect. Being reserved and on the alert is so ingrained that Mexicans will seldom drop it, even for a few seconds. A *macho* sees an innocently friendly look or remark as an opening through which to ride his Trojan horse of compliments, exaggerations, bravado and white lies.

This doesn't mean that women travelers should be unfriendly. Remaining aloof and inconspicuous should be thought of as a defense against unwanted attention, and need not cause aggressively unpleasant behavior. Relax with other women; you will soon learn which situations can be controlled and which cannot.

In discussing *machismo*, it is difficult to leave the *macho* male with anything but the short end of the stick. Harsh judgments, however, will not change the situation. The following songs illustrate the dilemma in which the *macho* finds himself: the self-proclaimed king of a world without value. The first is what I call "The *Macho* Anthem." It is very popular in *cantinas*. Contrary to the aggressiveness of the lyrics, it is sung in a mournful, lamenting tone. The second song, also a *cantina* classic, leaves one reaching for the tequila bottle with a groan of "Why bother?"

Sigo Siendo El Rey	**I Continue to Be the King**

Yo sé bien que estoy afuera,
  pero el día en que yo me muera,
Sé que vas a llorar y llorar
  llorar y llorar
Dirís que no me quisiste,
  pero vas a estar muy triste,
Y así te vas a quedar.

I know well that I'm on the outside,
  but the day in which I die,
I know that you're going to cry,
  cry and cry, cry and cry.
You'll say that you didn't love me,
  but you're going to be very sad,
And that's how you'll remain.

Chorus:
Con dinero o sin dinero,
hago siempre lo que quiero
Y mi palabra es la ley;
No tengo trono ni reina,
ni nadie que me comprenda,
Pero sigo siendo el Rey.

With money or without money,
  I always do what I want,
And my word is the law.
I have no throne or queen,
  nor anyone who understands me,
But I continue to be the King.

Una piedra en el camino me
  enseño que mi destino,
Era rodar y rodar, rodar y rodar,
rodar y rodar.
Luego me dijo un arriero,
que no hay que llegar primero,
Sino hay que saber llegar.

A rock in the road showed me
  that my destiny
Was to roll and roll, roll and roll,
  roll and roll.
Then a mule skinner told me,
  that you don't have to arrive first,
But only have to know how to arrive.

Chorus:
Con dinero o sin dinero . . .

With money or without money . . .

No Vale Nada La Vida	**Life Is Worth Nothing**
No vale nada la vida, la vida *no vale nada.* *Comienza siempre llorando y* *así llorando se acaba;* *Por eso es que en este mundo, la* *vida no vale nada.*	Life is worth nothing, there is no value to life. It always begins with crying and so crying it ends; That is because in this world, life is worth nothing.
Bonito León, Guanajuato, *su feria con sus jugadas,* *Allí se apuesta la vida, y se* *respeta al que gana.* *Allí en mi León, Guanajuato,* *la vida no vale nada.*	Pretty Leon, Guanajuato, it's fair with its games, There one bets their life, and the winner is respected. There in my Leon, Guanajuato, life is worth nothing.
Chorus: *No vale nada la vida*	Life is worth nothing
Camino de Santa Rosa, *que pasa por tanto pueblo,* *No pases por Salamanca,* *que allí me hiere el recuerdo.* *Vete rodeando veredas, no pases* *porque me muero.*	Road from Santa Rosa, that passes through so many towns, Don't go through Salamanca, because there memory wounds me. Go around by other paths, don't go through because I'll die.
Chorus: *No vale nada la vida*	Life is worth nothing
El Cristo de la Montaña, del Cerro *del Cubilete* *Consuelo de los que sufren y* *adoración de las gentes.* *El Cristo de la Montaña, del* *Cerro del Cubilette.*	The Christ of the Mountain, of the Hill of Cubilete, Consolation of those who suffer and adoration of the people. The Christ of the Mountain, of the Hill of Cubilette.
Chorus: *No vale nada la vida*	Life is worth nothing

Brothels

Warning: The following information on brothels is included to educate you, not to encourage or condone risky sexual adventures. AIDS (*SIDA* in Spanish) and other sexually transmitted diseases are extremely serious hazards. Sex with prostitutes, and especially sex without condoms, is like playing Russian roulette with a fully loaded pistol. (See *Staying Healthy: AIDS*.)

Prostitution is an accepted and legal institution in most of Mexico. In the few states that have outlawed it, prostitution flourishes undercover at inflated prices.

Although women are not legally allowed in the average *cantina*, you'll sometimes see *putas* (prostitutes) in them. For this reason, a "respectable" woman will not enter such a *cantina*, even if the bartender turns his head. Most prostitutes, however, are found in established houses located in groups on the outskirts of town.

Brothels invariably double as nightclubs with bands and dance floors. Because the majority are operated legally, brothels are considered just another place for men to meet friends and drink. There is rarely a furtive or secretive atmosphere.

The easiest way to locate *la zona* (the zone) is to ask a cab driver to take you there. Leave your car parked in a safer area, especially if you plan to get drunk.

A typical small-town brothel is usually a rather hilarious place. (Those that cater to tourists along the border or near resorts are designed for foreign tastes and can't be considered typical.) Although the women in a border town bordello might be slightly overdone, they can't begin to approach the degree of high camp achieved by their sisters farther south.

Unless you're really horny, a visit to a brothel that caters to *campesinos* and local businessmen is funny and surrealistic rather than erotic.

Regardless of the season, Christmas decorations are often used lavishly to create that special mood designed to turn a nervous *campesino* into a snorting stud. The sensual glow of the red, blue and green bulbs gives just enough light to make the women clustered in a shadowy corner of the room appear tantalizing, muted and desirable.

T.W.

Like colorful jungle birds, they signal their potential mates with splashy purple, red, violet and crimson plumages. The real knockout women almost overwhelm the senses with hair piled high in massive "beehives" and bleached a shocking white.

Just to rub it in they will occasionally wobble to the bar on elevating high heels, then bend over to whisper confidentially into the bartender's ear. This contortion raises the ballet-type mini skirt, flashing an enormously broad and bare ass into the room.

Particularly aggressive women may approach the men themselves, but they usually wait for arrangements to be made through the bartender or pimp.

The main activities of the evening are drinking, shouting, bragging, dancing, singing and eating. Since a tiny brothel beer costs five times what it's worth, most of the profits of the house are made during preparations for the climactic act. The final splurge takes about as long as a trip to the urinal.

A visit to a brothel is expensive if you do anything more than sip a beer and watch the "action." The *macho* types seem to take particular pleasure in dropping large numbers of pesos in a few hours of intense drinking. Getting laid is incidental and, for many, a duty performed only to maintain and fulfill the *macho* image.

Although most women will haggle over prices, some brothels have them posted prominently over the bar. The bill of fare may range from "Girl, one hour and room" to "Girl, all night, room, bottle of rum and six cokes."

In general, the price for getting laid isn't much more than that for a round of drinks. Prices are subject to increase on weekends and holidays.

During the holidays, many enterprising people build temporary *cantina*-brothels on the beach. (See *Staying Healthy: AIDS*.)

The Bullfight

What is bullfighting? To the Spanish, who invented it, it's the *Fiesta Brava* (the Brave Celebration); to the Mexicans it's *Seda, Sangre y Sol* (Silk, Blood and Sun) and to most gringos it's a cruel, ritualized slaughter of innocent cattle.

Bullfighting, also known as the *corrida de toros* (running of the bulls), *lidia de toros* (fighting of bulls) and *sombra y sol* (shade and sun), is definitely not a sport. Some call it a spectacle, while others see it as theater, filled with symbolism and hidden meaning. Siquieros, one of Mexico's most popular muralists, contemptuously referred to bullfighting as "the dance of the butchers."

Whatever you call it, one thing is certain: until you've seen a bullfight you can't begin to appreciate it. This, anyway, was what I kept telling myself as I shifted uncomfortably on the hard concrete bench next to Nacho, shielding my eyes from the glare of the late afternoon sun. In the ring below, the young matador nervously maneuvered toward another attempt at a kill. The bull watched him warily, its dusty black shoulders quivering with exhaustion and scarlet rivulets of blood. This would be the sixth *estocada* (sword thrust); less than two minutes remained for the matador to make his kill or be ordered from the ring.

"Use it on yourself, you *pinche* . . . !" a voice raged from behind us.

"We'll give the bull your ear!" Another frustrated *aficionado* cried, attempting to add injury to insult by hurling an expensive cowboy boot at the flustered matador.

"Put it up your . . . !"

The matador suddenly tensed, raising the bloody curved blade with his right arm, sighting along its length for *la cruz*, the crucial entry spot above and between the beast's heaving shoulders. The bull tossed its head stubbornly, whipping long streamers of red flecked saliva through the air. Then, with a final agonized bellow, the bull's knees buckled, the huge body collapsing into the dust. The bull was dead, killed by a steady loss of blood rather than a sword thrust. The final moment of truth would have required a quick transfusion.

"*¡Cuidado compadre!*" Nacho said, ducking his head as a barrage of seat cushions, hats, shoes and scathing insults were hurled upon the hapless bullfighter.

The bullfighter walked quickly toward the exit, his colorful *traje de luces* (suit of lights) the only bright spot in his miserable existence.

A large paper cup struck the humiliated *torero* (without making a kill no one would honor him with the title matador, "killer") in the leg, soaking his immaculate white knee-high stocking.

"They're throwing beer!" I laughed, amazed at the crowd's ferocious assault. A volley of cups arched through the air, causing the bullfighter to run for shelter.

"That is not beer, *compadre*," Nacho said, his face darkening with embarrassment. I looked high into the stands below us; yes, I could see men fumbling with their pants, bending furtively over paper cups.

"A very poor fight," Nacho sighed, grimacing slightly as a half-filled bottle of José Cuervo sailed over our heads and shattered in the aisle. Fifty feet to our right the air filled with hats. "What are they doing?" I asked, amazed to see a veritable tower of sombreros piled on top of another. The majority were cheap woven straw of the type worn by *campesinos*, but mixed in were others, obviously expensive.

"It is nothing!" Nacho answered. "The benches are cement and cannot burn." As if on signal the huge mound of headgear erupted in a column of bright flame. The crowd renewed its attack with missiles and expletives.

"Come, *compadre*," Nacho said. "It will only get worse." He rose to his feet and headed for the nearest exit, shoulders slumped with disappointment. By "worse" I knew he meant the bullfights, not the crowd. It had been another washout.

A Typical Bullfight

The *corrida de toros* is not actually considered to be a fight. Rather, it is a demonstration of supreme control by the matador over himself, to dominate his natural fear; control over the bull, both to escape its deadly horns and to lead it through traditional cape passes; and control over the crowd. A good bullfighter works the audience with the skill of a nighttime talk show host. Some of the most popular fighters woo crowds (and through them, the judges) with flamboyant maneuvers. Kneeling before the bull, for example, with the matador's back to the wall, is a favorite. What most fans do not realize, however, is that the bull has no desire to collide with the wall and tends to avoid it.

The *corrida* is divided into three parts, called *tercios*. Following the preliminary formalities and the colorful parade of participants in the ring, the first bull is released.

The bull bursts from the holding pen at top speed. A few handfuls of dirt thrown on his back before he enters the ring enhance the effect of brute power as dust streams behind the animal. Cape men attract the bull's attention and work it around the ring. They take refuge behind stout barriers whenever the bull approaches, keeping the animal in motion and allowing the matador time to study its movements.

A trumpet sounds, beginning the first *tercio*, called *puyazos* (stabs). Two *picadores* enter on heavily padded horses. Their long lances will be used to weaken the bull's shoulder muscles, causing the head to sag downward. This helps to expose *la cruz*, the entry point for the killing sword thrust that will end the fight.

The less experienced *picador* goes first, thrusting his lance into the thick mass of shoulder muscle. The heavy metal point, the *puya*, is 8.5 centimeters long (three and one-third inches) with a guard to prevent deeper penetration.

After the first thrust the senior *picador* moves in, giving the bull a second and perhaps a third stab. If too many *puyazos* are given, the bull will be seriously weakened and may even die. The crowd invariably screams disapproval if more than one or two stabs are ordered by the judge. In rare cases a ferocious bull may be stabbed more than three times.

The matador watches the bull's behavior during the first *tercio*, assessing its strength. If he is inspired he will do cape passes, called *tercio de quites*, between each attack by the *picadores*.

When the horsemen retire from the ring, the trumpet signals the second *tercio*, called *banderillas*. Men on foot, and sometimes the matador himself, stab brightly decorated darts, about two and a half feet long, into the bull's shoulders. Three pairs of *banderillas* are placed, alternating from one side of the shoulders to the other. This supposedly replaces the image of a horse and rider as the enemy with that of a man on foot, and makes the bull aware of danger from all sides. This *tercio* is not considered dangerous, though it calls for some fancy footwork to avoid the animal's horns as the darts are placed. Following the fight, the *banderillas* are sold to fans or given to special friends and guests of the matador.

The last *tercio* is what most spectators are there for: cape work by the matador and the "moment of truth," the final fatal *estocada* (sword thrust).

The trumpet call sounding the third *tercio* also begins a sixteen-minute countdown. The bull must be killed within that time. *Aficionados* (fans) will be watching closely; good fighting is a thing of subtleties, not foolhardy displays of bravery or theatrical posturing. The matador's performance is judged according to four traditional criteria.

Aguantar (restraint, control) is the first—the positioning of the bull by the matador rather than vice versa. The bull will select a *querencia* (favorite spot) to defend, but the matador wants things his way. If a lady friend is in the stands he will probably use the cape to position the bull directly in front of her. Most fighters place the bull in good view of the judge and more expensive seats.

The matador is also judged by posture, called *parar*. Ideally, he will stand fully erect, feet close together, not allowing the bull to force him to move as he works it with the cape.

Mandar (command) is control of the bull through movements of the cape and matador's body. The bull becomes an enormous and very angry puppet, drawn to the matador but not allowed to intimidate him. A fighter who commands the bull's passes is said to *torear* (from *toro*, bull). If the bull takes charge, forcing the matador to follow him around in order to demonstrate his cape work, it's called *dar pases* (giving passes). The crowd derisively chants "¡*Toro!* ¡*Toro!*" to tell the judge and matador that the bull is running the show.

El temple or **templar**, style and timing, is fourth. It is based on such things as the distance between the bull and the cape during a pass, the distance between the cape and fighter (holding it at arm's length isn't good) and the distance between the bull and the man. If the *torero* holds excellent posture (*parar*), but is run over and trampled by the bull, he has—or had—lousy *templar*.

The **faena** is the killing of the bull. When the matador feels that the bull (and the crowd) are ready, he exchanges the large cape for a smaller killing cape, called a *muleta*. Removing his hat, he approaches the judge for permission to kill. The bull is dedicated, sometimes to the crowd (by holding his hat up to them). The crowd receives the honor with cheers, but will expect a good kill.

Once again, the matador positions the bull. Before it can charge, he raises the sword, sights and meets its rush with a quick cape pass and thrust.

A good *estocada* (sword thrust) will kill the bull almost instantly. If you're squeamish about gallons of hot blood, however, the gore produced will detract from "the moment of truth." A poor thrust can be very dangerous; deflected swords have punctured more than one unfortunate matador.

When the bull drops, an assistant uses a short dagger to give a *golpe de gracia*. If it's still alive and standing, another attempt is made by the matador. Twelve minutes after the beginning of the *tercio* the trumpet gives first warning, *el primer aviso*. Two minutes later, with the matador worried, the crowd angry and the bull suffering multiple stab wounds, the second warning sounds. At sixteen minutes, the matador is ordered from the ring, disgraced. The bull is lured back to the corrals by tame cattle and then slaughtered. The crowd loses what little remains of its self-control.

A good *corrida* ends with the awarding of one or more parts of the bull to the matador. One ear is good, two are great and the addition of the tail is fantastic—the crowd will be on its feet and screaming.

One fight quickly follows another and six bulls will be killed by three matadors in a typical *corrida*.

Tickets

There are two basic types of tickets: *sol* (sunny side of the ring) and *sombra* (shady side). The *sombra* seats cost substantially more; unless you're sensitive to heat and sunlight they aren't worth the extra money. I prefer the *sol* seats for another reason: that's where the average over-excitable fan sits and where the insults and crowd reactions are most colorful. With a hat and sunglasses you should be comfortable. (The tradition of *sombra y sol* is imported from Spain, where the afternoon sun is much hotter than in Mexico.)

The seats closest to the ring are called *barreras*. In small rings, the sunny side is General Admission, first-come, first-seated. In larger rings, there are various sub-categories. The more you pay, the closer to the action you get.

Ticket scalping is popular for all Mexican sporting events (and even movies). If you don't get to the ring in time, you may be approached by a *revendedor* (scalper). The mark-ups are considerable, but a real *aficionado* will pay the price.

Seasons and Fights

The main season, called the *temporada formal* or *temporada grande* is in wintertime. The off-season is summertime and is called the *temporada chica*. Fights (*corridas*) are held on Sunday afternoons, usually at four o'clock. Fights from larger cities are often televised.

Novilladas, novice fights, are held in summertime and run the risk of being rained out. The *novillero*, novice fighter, fights *novillos*, young bulls of at least 335 kilos (837 pounds). The full matador fights bulls of at least 435 kilos (957 pounds), though bulls as heavy as 800 kilos (1,760 pounds!) have been used.

A *novillero* becomes a full matador at a fight called the *alternativa*. The novice (who in spite of the term has much experience) is sponsored by a known matador. A bullfighter's prestige is very important; if the *alternativa* is bungled, the novice is disgraced and his sponsor publicly embarrassed.

Alternativas can be held in any bullring, but Mexico City's has much more class than one in the "provinces." If the event is held outside the capital, it must be reconfirmed there (or in Madrid) in another fight, called a confirmation (*confirmación de alternativa*).

A *corrida mixta* is the only time both full matadors and *novilleros* fight on the same program. The matadors go first.

The Bulls

The average Mexican fighting *toro* weighs almost half a ton. They are lighter than Spanish bulls and considered inferior to them, though six Mexican bulls from the

Mimiahuapam Ranch were sent to Madrid in 1971 and supposedly fought well.

There are about 150 *ganaderias* (cattle ranches) that raise *ganado bravo* (brave, fierce cattle). About 50,000 bulls, cows and calves live on almost 500,000 acres of land. They are carefully isolated from humans and constantly culled to eliminate weaknesses in the breed.

Bulls must be delivered to the *plaza de toros* four days before the fight (Thursday if the *corrida* is Sunday). During this time, they are weighed, graded and generally checked for defects or illness.

The worst calamity to befall a *ganaderia* is to have its bulls called *mansos* (meek). Although great care is taken to produce mean, aggressive bulls, there's no guarantee that one won't turn chicken in the ring. If the bull doesn't display the proper degree of ferocity, the judge orders it back to the corral for immediate slaughter. A *manso* is replaced by one of two alternates. If both alternates are used and a third bull comes out *manso*, instead of getting *puyazos* (stabs) it receives four pairs of black *banderillas*. These have points twice as large as normal. The fight goes on, but the *gananderia* is in disgrace and its bulls are banned for one year.

Six bulls are killed in the average *corrida*. The carcasses are usually dressed and butchered on the spot (in big cities they are sold to meat packers) and the meat is sold to the public. It ends up in the stew pots of the poor and the snack plates of local *cantinas*. Any leftover blood is also sold and eaten, usually in soup or sausages. In past times the matador received the carcass as payment for the fight.

Bullrings

There are three classes of *plaza de toros:* third class, seating fewer than 4,000 persons; second class, 4,000 to fewer than 10,000; and first class, 10,000 and above. The *Plaza Mexico*, largest in the world, seats (crams) 50,000 people and is twice as large as any in Spain.

In small towns, temporary bullrings of poles, sticks and planks will be literally lashed together during special fiestas and fairs. The fights in these improvised rings have all the excitement and uncertainty of small town rodeos in the U.S. No one quite knows what is going to happen—or to whom.

Bullfight Suggestions

• Don't worry about understanding the details of the fight until you've appreciated it as an experience. You don't have to know the names of all the players and the diameter of a baseball to watch the World Series.

• Watch three or four fights before taking photos. This will give you time to become familiar with the rituals and to plan your shots.

• Buy tickets in advance if you can or go at least an hour or two early. Take binoculars if you have them, especially if the bullring is large.

• Take something to sit on, a hat and sunglasses.

• Carry enough small change to buy whatever sodas or beer you'll want. Vendors work very fast and don't like to make change or forget to return it.

• Don't carry knives. At many bullrings male fans are given a quick search for weapons. The smallest pen knife may be confiscated; getting it back would be difficult to impossible.

• If you don't like the fight—leave. Exclamations of disgust are an insult to those who see it differently.

• Watch for pickpockets, especially in big bullrings. Try to leave handbags in your hotel or car (out of sight). Keep a firm grip on everything else, particularly during hectic crowd scenes at the end of the fights.

• Each fight is different. If one is a flop, don't lose interest; the next might make the morning papers.

"*¡Olé!*" The crowd roared, thousands of *aficionados* leaping to their feet. The third bull of the afternoon dropped into the blood-soaked dust, killed by a perfect *estocada.* Nacho mopped perspiration from his brow with a yellow bandanna as he joined in cheering the matador. An obviously well-off young rancher sailed his Stetson into the ring; his wife matched his enthusiasm by throwing down her leather purse. The matador took a long drink from the wineskin he'd caught in mid-air, then reached down to throw back the hat and bag, which quickly passed from hand to hand to their owners.

"*¡Nos tocó la suerte, compadre!*" Nacho grinned, draining his cup of Corona. Luck had indeed touched us—"and it's about time," I thought to myself, one more lousy Sunday at the bullfights and I'd take up ping pong. After many *corridas* with Nacho and his friends, I'd picked up plenty of trivia, but felt nothing more than a sense of boredom and distaste for the actual fighting.

"Today you shall see the difference," Nacho had assured me, adding an ominous "*¡Ojalá!*" ("God willing!"). From the first charge of the first bull I'd sensed a strong current of anticipation in the crowd. The matador must have felt it too. He worked the bull through an especially daring series of passes before the kill, whipping the fans into a frenzy. The judge awarded him one ear, seconded by the cheers of the spectators.

"*Vamos a ver, vamos a ver,*" Nacho muttered as the second bull burst from the pens. His hopeful "We'll see" was reflected by others seated around us. Each successful fight dramatically increased their excitement and enjoyment. But each new encounter was like a fresh hand of poker; *¡ojalá!* that it be good.

The second matador, a young man noted for theatrics, dropped to his knees in the center of the ring, facing the bull's head-on charge with outstretched arms. The crowd cheered its approval.

"*Villamelones,*"* Nacho spat disgustedly, though his eyes sparkled with pleasure. The huge animal thundered past the matador, tossed its head wildly from side to side. The rest of the fight, as if in appeasement to traditionalists like Nacho, followed a more classic pattern. With each cape pass the crowd's fervor increased; a storm of *¡olés!* erupted at the kill, once again almost perfectly executed.

The third bull was small. The placard announcing its weight brought indignant shouts of "*Becero*" (calf) from the stands. With two excellent fights under their belts the fans were now prepared to go wild with happiness—or mad with frustration.

Nacho signaled a passing beer vendor. The young man popped the caps from two bottles, pouring the cold brew into paper cups. He stowed the empty bottles in his bucket, safely away from anyone who might use them to bean an unpopular matador.

"*¡Para emocionarnos!*" ("To excite ourselves!") Nacho laughed, downing half the beer in one thirsty gulp.

In spite of its small size, the third bull had extraordinary stamina. The fight was fast and intense, the matador handling the animal with dangerously close natural passes. Now, as the team of horses was hitched to the corpse, the crowd began chanting.

"*¡Vuelta! ¡Vuel-ta! ¡Vuel-ta!*" demanding that this bull be dragged around the ring to honor its courage. The horsemen received the order from the judge and the crowd went wild. When the body had completed its circuit and the matador had displayed the two ears he'd been awarded, the *plaza* settled down in anticipation of the next bull.

"Each matador fights two bulls," Nacho explained, "and usually keeps the best for his second fight." The fourth fight was conducted in almost total silence, broken only by perfectly chorused "*¡Olés!*" as the matador worked the bull directly below us, favoring the cheaper seats with a magnificent performance. As he approached the judge for permission to kill, the tension in the hot afternoon air was almost unbearable.

Villamelon is a derogatory term for a fan who applauds a move that is not as dangerous or well executed as it may appear. Gringos who follow the fights are notorious *villamelons.*

The matador raised his hat to the crowd, dedicating the bull to them. The entire *plaza* exploded with cheers.

"*¡Ora sí!*" Nacho said excitedly ("This is it!"). The bull was worked into position and once again the *sol* (sun) seats were given the best view. Then, at the moment the sword was raised for the final killing pass, the matador suddenly turned his back on the bull, raising his hat once again to the fans. I heard Nacho suck in a great breath as we were given this unusual and dangerous second dedication. A few moments later, the bull lay dead at the matador's feet.

My ears rang with shouts and cries as hysterical fans leaped from their seats and poured over the guardrails, vaulting barricades and jumping into the bullring. A veritable blizzard of cushions, hats, shoes and clothing showered upon the proud matador. A brass band struck up a tune, barely audible beneath the cries of adulation. I took a swig from a passing brandy bottle, then another from a wineskin. I climbed onto the concrete bench to join Nacho. His hat sailed away to honor the fighter and the bull. "Throw it, *compadre!*" He urged, tapping the brim of my own sombrero. And there it went, curving into the lengthening shadow that crept across the bloody arena. "*Olé!*" we cried, "*Olé!*"

Mexico: A Brief History

Mexican history is fascinating but very confusing. Did the Aztecs take over from the Toltecs or the Maya and who did Madero really assassinate, Carranza or Obregón or either one? To make telling the bad guys from the good guys easier, just note which historical figures have city streets, dams and schools named after them—and which don't (Cortés and Porfirio Díaz, among others).

1200–500 B.C.:	The rise and decline of the Olmecs.
300–900 A.D.:	The rise and fall of the Mayas.
1000 A.D.:	Fall of the Toltecs.
1325:	Founding of Tenochtitlán (Mexico City) by the Aztecs.
1440–1469:	Reign of Emperor Moctezuma I, accompanied by much human sacrifice.
1519:	Cortés lands near Veracruz and is mistaken for the returned god Quetzalcoatl. Moctezuma II tries to buy him off, but the Spaniards join his enemies and attack.
1521:	Cortés captures the Emperor, lays siege to Tenochtitlán and Moctezuma II is killed. Cuauhtemoc takes over, surrenders and is killed. The pillage and Conquest begin. (Semi-official holiday observed on August 13.)
1521–1650:	The Conquistadores replace human sacrifice with Christianity, the Inquisition, smallpox and slavery. Five percent survive and are put to work in the newly discovered silver mines.

1650–1800:   Consolidation of Spanish control, including expansion into California, Texas and the Southwest. Jesuit order expelled. Spain gradually loses power in Europe.

1810:   September 16, Father Hidalgo utters *El Grito*,* the cry for independence. The "Father of Mexico" calls for an end to slavery and *pulque* taxes and is killed a year later. Father Morelos continues the fight. (National holiday.)

1815:   Morelos is captured and killed. (September 30, his birthday, is an unofficial holiday.)

1821:   Mexico wins independence, but General Iturbide declares himself Emperor, for which arrogance he is killed in 1824.

1824:   Guadalupe Victoria becomes the first elected president, but his term is followed by years of revolt, civil war and rapidly changing governments.

1836–48:   Texas revolts; the U.S. declares war and takes half of Mexico at one gulp. Texans will never again be trusted in Mexico. The Caste War of Yucatán erupts, but on the eve of victory the Mayas withdraw from a siege of Mérida to plant their corn crops.

1857:   A constitution is proclaimed. (National holiday on February 5.)

1859:   Benito Juárez, a full-blooded Zapotec Indian from Oaxaca, becomes president and initiates widespread liberal reforms. European forces invade the country to collect unpaid bills.

1862:   May 5. The French are defeated at Puebla, but still manage to take over the capital. Juárez escapes north, to the border (national holiday).

1864:   Maximilian, brother of the Emperor of Austria, is declared Emperor of Mexico by the French. Juárez attacks.

1867:   Mexico's last Emperor is captured and executed.

1867–1910:   General Porfirio Díaz (*Don* Porfirio) controls the presidency for thirty-five years, creating a corrupt dictatorship. Mexico's resources

---

*Some Mexicans have their own *"Grito"*: *"¡Viva México, hijos de la chingada!"*

are sold to the highest foreign bidder. Opposition is violently suppressed. Massive land grabs from the peasantry, forced labor camps, wage slavery and wholesale murder prepare the country for revolt.

1910–11: Pay close attention; this is where the real confusion begins. Madero revolts in the north and is joined by Pancho Villa. Zapata rises in the south. Díaz is exiled. Madero becomes president, but Zapata distrusts him and continues to lead peasant uprisings against the rich. (November 20 is a national holiday honoring the Revolution.)

1913: Madero is executed by Huerta in a move supported by the U.S. Ambassador (quickly recalled to Washington for his sins). Carranza rises against Huerta, as do Villa and Obregón (who all distrust each other).

1914–15: Obregón ousts the dictator Huerta. Carranza occupies Mexico City, but is forced out by Zapata and Villa, who then decide to go home instead of taking over. Obregón reoccupies the capital, and then attacks Pancho Villa and defeats him. Zapata grabs the capital while Obregón is occupied with Villa, but goes home to the state of Morelos once again and is there attacked by Obregón. (Have you got that?)

1917: Another constitution is signed. Carranza is elected President and assassinated, to be replaced by the hard-to-beat Obregón.

1919: Zapata is betrayed and murdered (presumably on Obregón's orders).

1920: Pancho Villa gives up, but is allowed freedom and later murdered (Obregón again?).

1925–30: The bloody Cristero War between Church-led peasants and the central government erupts. Obregón's sins catch up with him: he is assassinated.

1930–37: Things finally begin to settle down.

1938: President Cárdenas shocks the world by daring to nationalize the foreign-dominated oil industry. This occasion is now almost a religious holiday, especially since the discovery of vast new oil fields. The Mexican equivalent of the Boston Tea Party.

1946–52: Miguel Aleman is President and begins programs to increase national productivity.

1968: Hundreds of demonstrating students are massacred in Mexico City by the Army and professional goon squads on the eve of the Olympic Games.

1970–76: President Echeverria cripples the economy. The peso is devalued amid rumors of a military takeover.

1976–82: Portillo is elected President and institutes economic reforms. When Mexico discovers great reserves of oil and gas, the U.S. suddenly develops a craving for tortillas and new amigos.

1982–88: Falling prices pull the plug on Mexico's oil dreams as Miguel de la Madrid Hurtado inherits a crippling external debt. Inflation soars as the value of the peso tumbles.

1988–94: Economic recovery is hailed. The "Mexican Miracle" embraces techo-capitalism, mass tourism, and McDonald's hamburgers. Mexico bets its future on the North America Free Trade Agreement—and impoverished Mayan peasants in Chiapas rebel after 500 years of servitude.

1994–98: Mexico's foundations are rocked by political assassinations, billion-dollar embezzlements and revelations that "*narco-políticos*" may control the country. President Zedillo vows that the long-ruling PRI party will win again, even if they have to do it honestly.

2020: *Mexico City swells to 40 million souls and sinks beneath their weight into the ooze of Lake Texcoco, thus fulfilling the mayor's promise to solve smog and traffic problems.*

What the Hell Is *That*?

In your travels to foreign lands you will encounter many strange and exotic customs. One of the most difficult to figure out is the Mexican bureaucracy's love of initials. A radio news broadcast might go: "MMH met with PRI and DF officials at UNAM to discuss PDR activities. . . ." The confusion is mutual; Mexicans translate PPM as *Partido del Pueblo Mexicano* (Mexican People's Party) or *Partido Proletario Mexicano* or *Partido Popular Mexicano*.

E.U.M. *Estados Unidos Mexicanos*: The United States of Mexico, the Republic's official name.

EZLN *Ejército Zapatista de Liberación Nacional*: The Zapatista Army of National Liberation ruined Mexico's NAFTA celebration by revolting in Chiapas on January 1, 1994.

PRD *Partido Revolucionario Democrático*: Feisty political party founded by unhappy, left-of-center PRI members.

LIC. *Licenciado*, lawyer.

PRI *Partido Revolucionario Institutional*: The Institutional Revolutionary Party is the ruling political party and by far the largest in Mexico.

PAN *Partido Acción Nacional*: National Action Party. The minority political party; said to be controlled by right-wing conservatives.

PMT *Partido Mexicano de Trabajadores*: The Mexican Worker's Party.

PCM *Partido Comunista Mexicano*.

PARM *Partido Auténtico Revoluncionario Mexicano*: The Authentic Mexican Revolution Party.

PDM *Partido Demócrata Mexicana*.

PPS *Partido Popular Socialista*.

PPM *Partido Popular Mexicano*.

PSR *Partido Socialista Revolucionario*.

PRT *Partido Revolucionario de Trabajadores* (Workers).

PST *Partido Socialista de Trabajadores*.

POAM *Partido Obrero Agrario Mexicano*: Agrarian Worker's Party.

UGOCM *Union General de Obreros y Campesinos Mexicanos*.

CCI *Centro Campesinos Independiente*.

CTM *Confederación de Trabajadores Mexicanos*.

CROM *Confederación Regional Obrero Mexicanos*.

CNOP *Confederación Nacional de Organizaciones Populares*: PRI labor union.

CNC *Confederación Nacional Campesina*: PRI union of *campesinos* (country people).

CROC *Confederación Revolucionaria de Obreros y Campesinos*: PRI labor union syndicate.

CNEP *Comisión Nacional de Erradicar Paludismo*: The National Commission to Eradicate Malaria. This abbreviation and a number painted on a house or building indicates that it has been checked and perhaps sprayed by a *paludismo* team.

CDIA *Centro de Investigaciones Agrarias*: Center for Agrarian Investigation, whatever that means.

INI *Instituto Nacional Indigenista*: The Indigenous Office, equivalent to the Bureau of Indian Affairs.

INAH *Instituto Nacional de Antropología e Historia*.

UNAM *Universidad Nacional Autónoma de México*: The University of Mexico in Mexico City.

C.I.A. The abbreviation for "company" and not the organization that first came to your mind.

CFE *Comisión Federal de Electricidad*: Federal Commission of Electricity.

DF *Distrito Federal*: Federal District, comparable to Washington, D.C.

DDT *Departamento de Tránsito*: Department of Transit, or the pesticide.

DGN A federal liquor standard. If your tequila bottle doesn't have this, it's not *legítimo*.

GL *Gay Lussac*: GL 40° means 40 percent alcohol (80 proof).

M.N. *Moneda Nacional*: National Currency, i.e., the Mexican peso. Mexico uses this sign, $, for pesos or M.N.

ISSSTE A federal social service agency. The name is so long I couldn't find anyone who remembered what it meant. It is popularly known as "*Inútil Solicitar Sus Servicios Tardan Eternidades*." ("Useless to Ask; Your Services Delayed Eternities").

IMSS *Instituto Mexicano de Seguro Social*: Mexican Insitute of Social Security.

IMSSA A manufacturer of truck bodies.

S.A.	*Sociedad Anónima*: Equivalent to "incorporated," used by companies that sell shares of stock.
S.A. de C.V.	*Sociedad Anónima de Capital Variable*: Large companies registered to do interstate business.
SAG	*Secretaría de Agricultura y Ganado*: Secretary of Agriculture and Livestock (federal agency).
SEDUE	*Secretaría de Ecologia*: the powerful Ministry of Ecology, pronounced "Say-dewey."
SEP	*Secretaría de Educación Publica*.
SOP	*Secretaría de Obras Publicas*: Secretary of Public Works (federal agency).
SPF	*Servicio Público Federal*: A costly federal trucking license that allows the owner to operate throughout the country.
SRH	*Secretaría de Recursos Hidráulicos*: Secretary of Water Resources (federal agency).
Caseta Fiscal	Tax collection stations for commercial trucks. Many of these*casetas* serve only to line the pockets of local bigwigs.
Caseta Forestal	Inspection stations for forest products, all tightly controlled and taxed.
Censada	Census: A *Censada* sticker is placed on the door of each house that has been checked by the census taker.
Teepees	Large cement teepees seen in the countryside are government (CONA-SUPO) commodity warehouses. Yes, they do look rather odd.

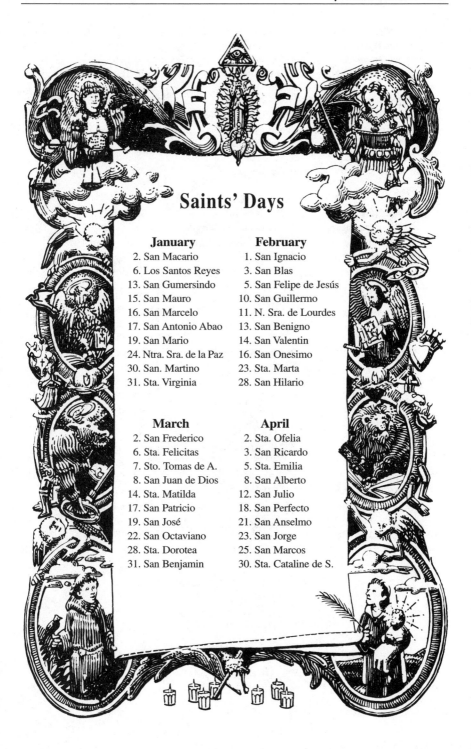

Saints' Days

January
2. San Macario
6. Los Santos Reyes
13. San Gumersindo
15. San Mauro
16. San Marcelo
17. San Antonio Abao
19. San Mario
24. Ntra. Sra. de la Paz
30. San. Martino
31. Sta. Virginia

February
1. San Ignacio
3. San Blas
5. San Felipe de Jesús
10. San Guillermo
11. N. Sra. de Lourdes
13. San Benigno
14. San Valentin
16. San Onesimo
23. Sta. Marta
28. San Hilario

March
2. San Frederico
6. Sta. Felicitas
7. Sto. Tomas de A.
8. San Juan de Dios
14. Sta. Matilda
17. San Patricio
19. San José
22. San Octaviano
28. Sta. Dorotea
31. San Benjamin

April
2. Sta. Ofelia
3. San Ricardo
5. Sta. Emilia
8. San Alberto
12. San Julio
18. San Perfecto
21. San Anselmo
23. San Jorge
25. San Marcos
30. Sta. Cataline de S.

May

1. Sta. Berta
8. San Bonifacio
9. San Gregorio N.
10. San Antonio
15. San Isidoro
20. San Bernardino
25. Corpus Christi
26. San Felipe Neri
27. Sta. Carolina
30. San Fernando

June

3. Sta. Clotilde
7. San Roberto
9. San Feliciano
15. San Modesto
17. San Gregorio
21. San Luis Gonzaga
24. San Juan Bautista
26. San Antelmo
29. San Pedro y San Pablo
30. Sta. Lucina

July

1. San Aaron
2. San Martiniano
7. San Fermin
8. Sta. Isabel
11. San Abundio
19. Sta. Rufina
24. Sta. Christina
27. San Celestino
28. San Victor
31. San Ignacio de Loyola

August

1. Sta. Esperanza
6. San Justo
9. San Roman
10. San Lorenzo
12. Sta. Clara
20. San Bernardo
25. San Luis Rey
27. San Armando
28. San Agustín
31. San Ramon N.

September

1. N. Sra. de los Remedios
4. Sta. Rosalia
8. San Sergio
10. San Nicholas de T.
19. San Genaro
21. San Mateo
25. Sta. Aurelia
27. San Cosme
29. San Miguel
30. San Jeromino

October

3. San Gerardo
4. San Francisco de Asís
5. San Placido
13. San Eduardo
15. Sta. Teresa de Jesús
17. Sta. Margarita
18. San Lucas
24. San Rafael Arc.
27. San Florencio
30. San Claudio

November

4. San Carlos B.
6. San Leonardo
7. San Ernesto
8. San Victorino
11. San Martin
13. San Diego
17. San Gregorio
23. San Clemente
25. Sta. Catalina
30. San Andres Ap.

December

1. Sta. Natalia
4. Sta. Barbara
7. San Ambrosio
13. Sta. Lucia
15. San Arturo
17. San Lázaro
18. San Ausencio
20. San Filogonio
21. Sta. Tomás Ap.
27. San Juan Ap.

BOOZE AND CANTINAS

Drinking customs: liquor stores • Vino or wine? • Beer • Tequila and mezcal • Hard liquors • Pulque • Home brews • Bars and cantinas • She who went away

Unlike present-day Mexicans, the Aztecs took a dim view of alcoholic beverages. Recognizing the destructive power of overindulgence, they restricted drinking to the ruling priest class and old people. Everyone else was automatically enrolled in what must have been the world's most unpopular chapter of AA; drunks were simply strangled or clubbed to death. A tough thing to face with a hangover.

The *conquistadores* were horrified by this savage custom. Once they had completed the subjugation of the native population (and roasted Emperor Cuauhtémoc alive) booze was made available to the survivors. The Spanish could point out both the humanity of such a reform and the economic good sense: Spain produced vast quantities of wines and spirits. The market potential of the New World was considerable.

Today, the thirsty traveler is offered cold beer at gas stations, bus depots, aboard the train, from sidewalk stands, in innumerable small stores, supermarkets and liquor stores, and even on the beach from dripping buckets lugged by enterprising vendors.

In addition to beer, there's a wide variety of imported wines and liquors, not to mention such Mexican specialties as tequila, *mezcal*, rum, brandy and Kahlua. Local concoctions fill any gaps that might remain in your thirst: *pulque, tepache, tesquino, coco locos* and many others.

No good fiesta, celebration or public rally is without liquid refreshment, though it may be sold discreetly in a temporary covered bar on a side street. Sporting events, bullfights in particular, just aren't the same without ice cold beer in paper cups and *botas* filled with everything from wine to margaritas.

When ordering alcoholic beverages, keep in mind that Mexican-made wine and spirits (*doméstico* or *nacional*) are bargains compared to imports from Europe or the United States. High import duties can easily triple the tab if you automatically order your favorite Kentucky bourbon, scotch or California wine.

Drinking Customs

Even though alcoholic drinks are widely available, Mexicans tend to frown on public drunkenness. In between fiestas and bullfights, drinking is done mostly in *cantinas*, bars and at home.

Women sometimes drink in the company of men, but only in "lady's bars" (not *cantinas*), restaurants and at private parties. It is rare to see an unescorted woman drinking except at more sophisticated bars and clubs in big cities and tourist towns. A man who occasionally ties one on is considered *macho;* a woman who does the same is a disgrace.

One of the most disturbing customs encountered in Mexico (and Guatemala) is called ritual drinking. Ritual drinking has been practiced for untold years by many Indian groups in conjunction with fiestas, religious and civil ceremonies and celebrations such as harvests, deaths and births. At these times it is not only considered proper, *but necessary*, to get rip-roaring drunk. At a wedding, for example, it may be expected that everyone drink in order for the marriage to have a successful beginning. Failure to drink would be like a gringo ceremony without a clergyman or a shower of rice.

Public officials in Indian communities are often expected to drink while performing their duties. Because terms of office run for a year, it is said that many are alcoholics by the time they've served their time.

Tourists will rarely have the opportunity to participate in this type of drinking. Those who visit Indian towns to observe a fiesta, however, should be aware of it. At times it seems that whole villages are determined to drink themselves into the ground. As one anthropologist wrote, "A fiesta's success is determined by the number of drunks jailed."

In the rest of the country, ritual drinking is more likely to come in the form of the classic Mexican *borrachera*. Unlike the Indian system, the success of a "spree" is measured by the amount of money blown, time spent intoxicated, days of work missed and the severity of the hangover. This type of drinking is considered more normal than a regular intake of several cocktails each evening. A typical man might be a model of

sobriety for six months, then suddenly jump off the wagon with a cry of, "¡*Agarrate a la borrachera!*" ("Grab onto the binge!")

A *borrachera* can be pre-meditated, such as the celebration of someone's saint day (see ¡*Viva Mexico!: Customs and Traditions*) or it may begin casually: "Let's stop somewhere on the way home and have a couple of hundred beers." This spontaneous spree is the most difficult type to avoid.

I once gave a man a lift on a lonely country road. "What can I pay you?" he asked when I let him out. We had stopped in front of a small palm-thatched store and I was thirsty. I didn't want money, so to be polite I suggested a beer. Twenty hours later I continued my trip. My passenger departed for home on a mule, safely lashed to the saddle by his three young sons. He spent more money repaying a ten-mile ride than he would have on a chartered plane.

> *Después de los celos queda la duda,*
> *Y después de la borrachera, la cruda.*
>
> After jealousy remains doubt,
> And after a *borrachera*, the hangover.

Liquor Stores

Liquor stores are called *licorerías* and *vinos y licores*. (The term *licores* includes both distilled liquors, liqueurs and apertifs.) A *Ultramarinos* store sells liquor and prepackaged snacks, a kind of Mexican deli. Liquor stores often have interesting names. My favorite is "*El Exorcisto.*"

Supermarkets sell beer, liquor and wine. They often run sales (¡*Oferta!*) which include a bottle of booze, drinking glasses, ashtrays, sodas and whatever else it takes to attract a customer.

Every town usually has one store that consistently undersells others. In one village, for example, the best buy was in the post office, which also sold the tastiest home-roasted coffee.

Cantinas sell beer and hard liquor to go at steep prices.

Vino or Wine?

On my first trip to Mexico, I strolled into a *cantina*, slouched against the bar and confidently ordered "a glass of wine." I'd read Steinbeck's *Tortilla Flats* and knew that Mexicans love a good big tumbler of wine.

"What kind?" the *cantinero* asked, raising his eyebrows at the other patrons as if to say, "Hey, catch this one!"

I hesitated. "What kind?" I didn't know brand names, but rather than show my ignorance I said, "*Blanco.* Give me a *vino blanco!*"

The bartender reached down and held up a tiny shot glass. I shook my head. I wanted a *glass* of wine, not a sniff! He noted my look of disdain and exchanged the shot glass for one just slightly larger. I groaned dramatically. Up came a tall tumbler with a colored reproduction of the Virgin of Guadalupe painted on the side. Now this was something you could get your hands around.

"¿*Todo?*" he asked, giving the other drinkers another of those annoying eyebrow signals.

"Yes, yes!" I answered. "Fill it up!" I sighed, shaking my head sadly. Evidently these folks just didn't understand thirst. Steinbeck would have been disappointed.

"There you go, *amigo!*" the bartender said, sliding the glass across the bar toward me. It was filled right up to the brim. I carefully lifted the wine to my lips. I took a big mouthful, allowing it to trickle down my throat to catch the flavor. Suddenly my lungs and chest convulsed, expelling the wine back through my nose in a searing atomized sneeze.

"Gaaaahhhh!" I cried, hacking and coughing in a desperate struggle to replace fumes with oxygen. The bartender watched impassively. I threw my sunglasses onto the bar, swabbing my eyes with a shirt sleeve, croaking and gurgling like someone drowning on their feet. "Wha . . . is . . . this?" I gasped, drumming on my chest in an effort at self-resuscitation.

"*Vino blanco*," he answered calmly, reaching for the bottle. The label was turned toward me: tequila. For the next half hour, while I gingerly nursed the remainder of the booze, the bartender helpfully explained that in Mexico, *vino* means liquor and *vino blanco*, though also the correct term for white wine, is actually the common name for any clear liquor, including, heaven forbid—pure alcohol.

To order "real" wine, ask for *vino de uva* (grape wine) and then specify *blanco* or *rojo*.

The average Mexican seldom drinks wine. Because Mexico offered excellent grape-growing conditions, the production of wine was severely limited by the early Spaniards, who feared competition with their own wines in the lucrative European market. As a result, the Mexican wine industry has never approached its potential. Even today wine is considered an upper-class drink.

Today, Mexico's domestic wines are widely available but seldom highly praised. A friend who was served a particularly harsh vintage suggested that the ban on Mexican wine-making was lifted a couple of hundred years too soon. Jokes aside, tourists should find most of Mexico's domestic wines quite acceptable.

Mexican wines tend to be sweeter than American or French wines, though sometimes they are too sour. Variations from one bottle to the next can be expected. Wine lovers usually buy several bottles when they happen upon a particularly good vintage.

Beer

Mexican *cerveza* (beer) is of excellent quality, from high-class *Bohemia* to proletarian *Victoria* (also known rudely as *Pee-toria*). Most Mexican breweries are operated under strict Germanic guidelines and their products often compare favorably to European beers. Americans who develop a taste for Mexican beer usually find it difficult to readjust to the lighter and less tasty brews back home.

By American standards, Mexican *cerveza* isn't cheap. Don't be shocked if a tall, frosty bottle of Corona costs you as much or even more in Los Cabos as it does in Denver.

Beer is sold by the *cartón* (case), *canastilla* or *seis* (six-pack), *bote* (can) and the *botella*. A standard tall bottle is a *media*. Liter-sized bottles are a good buy. Liters are "*caguamas*" ("sea turtles") in some areas and "*ballenas*" ("whales") in others. I once ordered a *caguama* in central Mexico and was treated like a nut case. The bartender finally handed me a liter of beer, advising me with great seriousness that it was a *ballena*.

The slang terms for beer than can be used (again, some are regional) to impress your friends and the bartender are *chelas*, *chupes*, *cheves*, *eladas*, *elódias* and *las frías*.

Regular and large bottles come in both returnable (*retornable*) and throwaway (*desechable*). *Cerveza de bote* (canned) is more expensive than bottled. Many Mexicans consider it classier to drink from cans.

Beer by the case is cheaper than singles or six-packs, though case prices are given only at authorized agencies (*agencia* or *deposito de cerveza*). Everyone pays the wholesale price at the agency, whether a tourist or store owner. Beer agencies are very common; a small town may have three or four. In large towns there will be many agencies and subagencies (*sub deposito*). The *sub deposito* may have a smaller selection and probably won't offer blocks of ice.

Agencies have both canned and bottled beer. A bottle deposit is required and you should ask for a *recibo* (receipt). You'll probably have to buy a full case before they'll bother to write out a receipt. This piece of paper authorizes you to sell the bottles back, without it you're stuck. Bottles are not interchangeable between companies (though they may be identical in shape). Agencies of the same brewery may balk at refunding a deposit from another town. Be patient and insistent, but if they absolutely refuse to take the bottles, it's easier to give them away than argue.

Beer bottles are generally called *envases* rather than *botellas*, though the latter is certainly understood. A common slang term for bottles is *cascos*.

Ask for a case of cold beer (*cerveza helada* or *fría*) when you buy it at the agency. Some have beer in large coolers and others will give away chunks of ice.

Delivery trucks sell beer at agency prices or just slightly higher. If you're renting a place or are camped in one spot for more than a few days, ask the driver to put you on his route. Beer trucks usually carry ice, but they prefer to sell or give it to regular customers.

Beer agencies also handle soft drinks by the case and the price is a bargain. If you're hooked on mineral water (our favorite soft drink), buy it at the agency.

When ordering a beer, specify *fría* (cold) or *al tiempo* (air temperature). Beer is automatically served cold in most bars and restaurants, but you'll still run into places where they ask how you want it.

You may also be asked, "*¿de bote?*" ("canned?") if you order a beer without specifying a brand.

Tequila and *Mezcal*

There is as much myth and misinformation floating around about these two liquors as there is about the fall of Mayan civilization. Because the English spelling of *mezcal*—mescal—is just three letters short of the psychedelic drug "mescaline," it has been attributed with broader properties than it rightly deserves. Although it's quite true that drinking a liter of *mezcal* will induce states of "non-ordinary reality," the same can be said of drinking a liter of peppermint gin. *Mezcal*, in reality, is nothing more or less than hard liquor and basically the same drink as tequila, though the taste is quite different. The rumors, however, persist.

To be an instant expert on tequila and *mezcal* you have only to memorize these few facts:

• Tequila is a type of *mezcal* and is correctly called *mezcal de tequila*, just as rye is a type of whiskey.

• True tequila is made only from *Agave tequiliana*, also known as Weber's maguey, the blue agave or *mezcal azul*.

• *Mezcal* can be made from many different types of maguey.

• Maguey and other "tequila plants" with sword-like leaves are agaves, not cacti.

The basic procedures for making both tequila and *mezcal* are similar; the main difference is the type of maguey used. *Mezcal* stills often look like something out of the Middle Ages, especially when compared to modern tequila factories.

The traditional process begins by trimming off the long spiky leaves of the maguey with a stubby iron blade called a *coa*, leaving a huge pineapple-like heart, the *piña*. The hearts are slow roasted in enormous pits, shredded in mule-powered grinders, fermented and finally distilled in handmade pottery and copper stills. Good traditional *mezcal* is not made with sugar, but where it is available, sugar is usually added to boost the alcohol content of the mash. Big-time distillers now use giant autoclaves and other machinery to process the *piñas*.

A type of fat grub that lives in maguey plants, called *gusano de maguey*, is traditionally

added to each bottle of *mezcal*. Swallowing the worm with a great flourish is the traditional way to polish off a jug of mescal. These unappetizing worms are also considered a treat when fried. I've never been able to develop a taste for them, though I've tried.

Mezcal is made both legally and illegally, wherever maguey plants are found. Traditional mescal, with it's unique, smoky bite, is as scarce as good Kentucky moonshine. The best I've tasted came from the mountains of Durango. But the most well-known and widely marketed *mezcal* is made in Oaxaca.

Most moonshine *mezcal* is unaged and clear. Commercial *mezcals*, on the other hand, are usually gold and aged, though they rarely brag for how long. Tequila that has been aged is also gold in color and will be called *añejo* or *reposado* (aged or rested). *Tequila joven* is young tequila.

Mezcal is usually less potent than tequila (38 percent or 76 proof is common), but moonshine *mezcal* may be very strong, depending on the whim of the bootlegger.

Because of the huge demand for tequila and Mexico's limited supply of agaves, some creative distillers flavor bottles of watered-down alcohol with just enough tequila to fool customers. To protect consumers, the Mexican government decreed that only the states of Jalisco, Nayarit and Tamaulipas produce the proper blue agave, and only tequilas made from agaves grown in those states can carry the letters DGN to signify that it is *legítimo* (legitimate).

In the towns of Tequila and Oaxaca, centers for tequila and *mezcal* respectively, factory outlets offer good discounts on bulk purchases. Customers are invited to sample various types and to admire an assortment of possible containers for their liquor, everything from a plain five-gallon jug to a personally embossed wooden cask with a spigot. Be careful. Dishonest dealers may pull a switch, filling your container with something cheaper than what you tasted and ordered. If you are interested in the best, visit some of the smaller outlying distilleries. Most produce such limited quantities that they don't have to bother with merchandising and sell direct to regular customers.

Hard Liquors

Brandy is considered a status drink, though domestic Mexican brandies are not expensive. There's nothing Mexicans love better than to sit around in a *cantina* with a full bottle of brandy, inviting friends and even strangers to join in. Bottles of brandy sprout up at any good party or fiesta, and big seafood bashes in restaurants are incomplete without at least one bottle of brandy.

There are a bewildering variety of liqueurs available. The best known, Kahlua, is made from coffee. *Controy* (Cointreau, also called *licor de naranjas*) is made from oranges and used in margaritas and *coco locos*. Almond liqueurs are also popular.

Aguardiente ("firewater," which it definitely is) is very common and comes in many regional forms. It is sometimes called "brandy," though the first sip immediately confirms that it has never been near a grape. *Aguardiente* is almost always made from sugar cane and is unaged. It is known variously as *habanero, charanda, refino, trago* (literally "a drink or swallow"), *aguar, comiteco, anís* (when flavored with anise), *bacanora, caña* and others.

The potency of *aguardiente* varies from about 75 proof on up. *Aguardiente* burns well and can be used in stoves. Add *aguardiente* to your car's gas tank to rid it of water.

Alcohol is the poor people's drink. On market day in most towns you'll see ragged drunks staggering down the street clutching a soft drink bottle half filled with clear "popskull."

Note: Mexico's alcoholic beverages are rated by their percentage of alcohol, not by the American system of "proof." If the label says 42 GL (Gay Lussac), that means 42 percent alcohol—the equivalent of 84 proof. Beer labels also say *bebida de moderación*—a moderate beverage.

Pulque

"Wherever pulque *can be obtained, it should be used in preference to any other drink. It is thoroughly wholesome, and has a tendency to decrease the bilious habit that in many persons is induced by an altitude of a mile above the sea level. It should be drunk . . . from a sense of duty."*

—Thomas A. Janvier, *The Mexican Guide* (1897)

Pulque is the fermented sap of the maguey plant. It tends to have a slimy texture and a tangy, nut-like flavor. *Pulque* is mildly alcoholic, about like beer, and is loaded with vitamins and minerals.

Pulque was a sacred Aztec drink, governed by the god Two Rabbit. Two Rabbit had 400 rabbit sons, and a *pulque* high was graded in rabbit-units, with total drunkenness apparently reaching 400 rabbits. I swallowed a lot of *pulque*, but rarely achieved more than fifty rabbits. In some areas poor people literally live on *pulque*.

(2½ Lt.)
CAMIÓN o MACETA

(1 Lt.)
CATRINA

(1 Lt.)
TORNILLO

(¾ Lt.)
JARRA o TORREÓN

(½ Lt.)
TRIPA

It is so nourishing, in fact, that the Mexican government has tried in vain for years to bottle *pulque* without ruining the flavor.

Although the government encourages *pulque* drinking, the soft drink and beer industries are making serious inroads and the number of *pulquerías* is steadily diminishing.

Pulquerías are renowned for their quaint atmosphere and clubbiness. Because it is customary to slop a bit of *pulque* on the sawdust floor (a drink for Two Rabbit), the atmosphere can be all but unbreathable. The club spirit makes women totally unwelcome, and strangers run a close second. Beer and soft drinks may be served, but rarely anything stronger.

Pulquerías usually have humorous and often ironic names: "The Effects of the Battle," "The White Nectar of Black Dreams," "Leave If You Can," "The Last Station" (across from a cemetery), "Blood of the Maguey," "The Great Wound," "Here I'll Remain," "Memories of the Future" and so on.

A good respectable *pulquería* will serve only pure *pulque* (*pulque dulce* is young and sweet, *pulque fuerte* is older, slightly stronger and may be sour or acid), but because of shortages some places adulterate it with water. It is best to ask a knowledgeable person for a recommendation.

Better *pulquerías* offer customers a variety of mugs to choose from, depending on the degree of thirst. Those shown are either of glass or decorated gourds (*jícaras*). Many places have given up the battle against breakage and serve *pulque* in cheap pottery mugs, named according to their capacities.

> *Detente caminante,*
> *¡Un tornillo y adelante!*
> Stop walker,
> A screw [a liter] and onward!

The process of making *pulque* is very simple, but loaded with superstition and custom. When a maguey plant is several years old it prepares to sprout. A tall pole-like flower emerges from the center of the maguey (familiar to Americans as the century plant). Before this sprout can develop, however, the center of the plant is "castrated." A deep depression is gouged from the heart and begins to fill with sap, called *agua miel* (honey water). The *agua miel* is very tasty itself.

(½ Lt.)
VIOLA

(¼ Lt.)
TORNILLO CHICO

(¼ Lt.)
VASO

The *agua miel* is drawn off (a good plant will give up to gallon a day) by siphoning with a long gourd (*acocote*; look for them in the market, they make interesting souvenirs). The man who does this is called a *tlachiquero*.

The *agua miel* is collected in vats or huge pottery urns in the fermenting house. This place, the *tinacal*, is still semi-sacred, an interesting holdover from Aztec beliefs. Women are not allowed inside and men must remove their hats. Strangers are also discouraged or prohibited, depending who is in charge. I lived next to a *tinacal* for several months and was never able to enter, though I was refused quite gracefully and eventually understood that it was not personal.

Pulque is not easy for a tourist to find. The heavy demand and limited supply makes people jealous of their *pulque*. The best way to get good pure stuff is through a Mexican friend, not from a *pulquería* or market vendor (almost always adulterated with dubious water).

(1½ Lt.)
REYNA

(1 Lt.)
CACARIZA

Home Brews

Many people can't afford store-bought spirits or just prefer their own traditional drinks. These are often regional and will be completely unknown outside a specific area; some are basic fermented drinks similar to "beers" and "jungle juices" made worldwide. Like most home brews, they tend to be an acquired taste and hard to digest.

Tepache is found throughout Mexico. A basic *tepache* recipe calls for pineapple, brown sugar and water. Variations include the addition or substitution of cooked whole barley, sugar cane (pulp or juice), squash (preferably *chilacayote*), honey, other fruits, *pulque* and god-knows-what. It is drunk while still "young," which in some cases is only one or two days old and all but premature. It tends to scour the novice drinker's stomach.

Chicha is the liquor produced by fermenting corn in sweetened water, but it may also be made from fruit. *Chicha* made from sugar cane is similar to *tepache*. The raw cane is squeezed by animal or human power in a crude wooden press called a *trapiche*.

Tesgüino or *tecuín* is a "beer" made by fermenting a sprouted corn, corn stalks or wheat. *Tuba* is the fermented sap of the coconut palm. *Balche* is a Mayan concoction of sugar cane juice and the dried bark of the Lonchocarpus tree (*palo*

(½ Lt)
CACARICITA

(⅘ Lt.)
CHIVATO o CABRÓN

(⅓ Lt.)
CHIVO

(1 Lt.)
JICARA

(½ Lt.)
JICARA

(¼ Lt.)
JICARA

de huarapo). Other bark, such as pine, can be used if you run out of Lonchocarpus. Even the Maya say that *balche* tastes rather awful. *Sotol*, a drink brewed from maguey flowers, is sacred to the Huichol Indians. *Colonche* is a fermented brew of cactus fruits (*tunas*).

> *No hay sabados sin sol*
> *Ni domingos sin borrachos.*
> There are no Saturdays without sun,
> or Sundays without drunks.

Bars and Cantinas

Mexico's resorts have a wide variety of nightspots and watering holes, from cocktail lounges and ESPN-powered sports bars to imitation English pubs, cool jazz lounges, discos and frenetic, swinging singles bars. No vacation south of the border would be complete, however, without a visit to a genuine *cantina*. *Or would it?*

Gringos who broaden their experience with a *cantina*-crawl often get more than they'd bargained for. As the saying goes, there are tourist *cantinas* and then there are . . . *cantinas*! The tourist *cantina* is usually a large, cheerful bar decorated with colorful *serapes*, sombreros and bullfight posters. These are rocking, good-time places, with fiesta-style music, well-stocked bars and restrooms that don't take your breath away.

In contrast, a real *cantina* is a place for no-frills drinking and serious male bonding. The conversation will be boisterous and the music loud and mournful. If there is a restroom, you'll want to have a strong drink or two before using it. In most *cantinas*, the urinal is nothing but a damp, malodorous trough in open view of the bar. Should there be women present, they are almost certainly prostitutes (or risk being mistaken for one).

Are *cantinas* dangerous? Usually not, especially for men who stay friendly, alert and reasonably sober. On the other hand, gringos who run into problems often do so in *cantinas*. Although some *cantinas* will tolerate a visit from female tourists, this is definitely flirting with trouble. Since no "respectable" woman would even consider entering a *cantina*, even with Clint Eastwood as her escort, the patrons will assume she is looking for some kind of adventure.

The difference between a genuine *cantina* and a bar or club is quite simple: *women are not allowed in cantinas*. If the place admits women and provides restrooms for them it is not a *cantina*. *Cantinas* are exclusively male, though it is not unusual for a woman to own one and even to work in it. If women drink in a *cantina*, they're either prostitutes or don't give a damn if they're mistaken for one.

In tourist areas a bar may present itself as a "wannabe" *cantina*, capitalizing on the word recognition. When in doubt, ask the bartender, "¿*Se admite mujeres?*" ("Do you admit women?") Some *cantinas* state the message quite clearly over the door: *No se admite mujeres, menores de edad ni uniformados* (No women, minors or uniformed persons admitted).

The appealing term "Ladies Bar" is also deceptive. In reality, this can be a signal that professional "ladies" are available inside. Unless a Ladies Bar has an obvious tourist clientele, steer clear.

Men, don't be intimidated by your first glance into a crowded *cantina*. Mexican farmers, ranchers and other hardworking types tend to look quite tough. With some exceptions, they are just the opposite and will treat the polite gringo with friendly consideration.

Consider this picture: The *cantinero* (bartender), a paternal ex-bullfighter, singer or truck driver, greets one and all with democratic cheerfulness, dispensing both drinks and wise advice. The customers, usually simple working folk, lift glasses of tequila ("a fiery potent liquor") and loudly proclaim toasts of mutual admiration. Near the picturesque swinging doors a wandering group of *mariachis* strike up a rousing, lusty folk song. The *cantinero*'s son, an honest-faced boy of about twelve, circulates among the tables, delivering plates of deliciously spicy regional snacks to the appreciative drinkers. At a corner table a group of ranch hands are engaged in a lively bilingual political discussion with a recently arrived tourist.

Now picture this same *cantina* through the eyes of the person who warns you not to expose yourself to the seamier side of Mexican life: The bartender, a disreputable thug in a torn undershirt, watches impassively as the gringo approaches the crowded bar. Without a word, he pours a drink and shoves it toward the customer, slopping booze onto his hands. The *cantina*'s metal tables are crowded with sweaty, yelling drunks who do their best to shout over the blare of the band. When the song ends, a cursing match erupts over who gets the privilege of paying for the noise. A furtive boy throws down plates of indigestible snacks designed to burn the throat and sell more beer. In a dark corner, someone is pissing into a reeking five-gallon can.

My own *cantina* experiences fall somewhere between these two descriptions. Be warned, however, that once you take the plunge and are accepted into the *macho* clubbiness that prevails in most *cantinas*, you'll find it difficult, if not impossible, to make a diplomatic exit. This is especially true if you have accepted an invitation to drink with someone.

This is all part of the *machismo* thinking process. The Big Spender who invites you to have a drink may be blowing his last pesos, but he will absolutely insist on buying the drinks until it's all gone. When his money is spent, you can both start on yours.

> *Para que el vino sepa a vino,*
> *Hay que tomarlo con un amigo.*

> In order that booze tastes like booze,
> It has to be drunk with a friend.

The only sure way to avoid offending someone who offers you a drink is to leave. I usually thank them but say firmly, "*No, gracias. Me hace daño.*" ("No, thanks. It isn't good for me.") The implication is that you can handle one or two drinks but no more. If the guy can see that you're lying—you've just knocked off a dozen beers—he'll probably be offended. Should you feel uneasy, it would be best to leave before trouble develops. Trouble is not common, but it could happen.

As long as you remain polite, *cantina* trouble rarely involves gringos. The bartender or another customer will almost invariably steer irritating or belligerent drunks away from the tourists. When fighting erupts, however, it is definitely best to make a hasty

exit. Most *campesinos* are armed with machetes. They have a disturbing tendency to use them on each other to settle their differences. Pistols and knives are preferred over fistfighting, which is considered more of an aerobic exercise than a honorable means of resolving quarrels.

The police inevitably arrive after the shooting stops, in time to arrest the survivors.

As a friend approached a neighborhood *cantina*, he saw a large man with a .45 pistol confronting a smaller unarmed man in the street. The smaller of the two was screaming obscenities at the other, accusing him of not being *macho* enough to use the gun. The curses and tension increased by the second and my friend, in anticipation of what seemed inevitable bloodshed, ducked into a nearby doorway.

Suddenly two policeman appeared. They drew their long, heavy clubs and rushed to stop the tragedy. Without a word, one of the cops stepped up behind the small unarmed man and felled him with a powerful stroke of his billy club. With the other officer's help, the unconscious body was hauled off to justice.

The big man, smiling triumphantly, jammed his pistol into his belt and returned to his beer.

When ordering single drinks always say, "*Una copita de tequila, ron, brandy,* etc." rather than simply asking for tequila, *ron* or brandy. The reason you specify *una copita* (a drink) is that many people order whole bottles to drink on the premises. A shot of tequila is sometimes called a *tequilazo* or *tequilito*.

Steve and I were once stuck for a long afternoon in the outskirts of a large city, waiting for a mechanic to perform some small miracle on our car. An almost steady procession of men entering and leaving a raucous *cantina* across the street caught our attention.

There was a noticeable decrease in the noise level as two bearded gringos walked through the swinging doors. We went directly to the bar and Steve ordered two tequilas. The bartender slid the glasses to us and demanded at least four times the going rate. The other customers visibly flinched. They might have chuckled at doubling the price, but this was too much for even gringos to pay in such a dump.

We tossed off the tequilas. Steve motioned to the *cantinero*, his nose safely buried between the pages of a comic book.

"Two more?" he asked warily, glancing around the room. There was almost complete silence, broken only by a drunken snore from somewhere under a table.

"No, *amigo,*" Steve said loudly. "It's too *rico* for us. Give me two drinks of Mexican gasoline at Mexican prices."

The *cantina* rocked with laughter. With a grin the *cantinero* poured two of the largest tequilas we'd ever seen, then charged us a fraction of the previous price.

Sangrita is a nonalcoholic tomato juice and chili concoction (plus other spices) taken as a chaser with tequila or used in cocktails.

Drinking etiquette is not as formalized as most gringos believe. The well-known lime-salt ritual which accompanies tequila guzzling has as many variations as can be managed by individual drinkers. Some lick the salt off the back of their hand, others off the lime itself and others just forget both steps and drink their tequila right out of the jug. As any experienced drinker knows, the object is not to eat salt and limes but to drink the booze.

The lime-salt combination does have a real purpose, however. The salt, if taken first and allowed to raise saliva at the back of the throat, will protect sensitive tissues from the burning of the alcohol. The lime will also do this and when taken after the drink cleanses the mouth of the awful taste of the liquor.

Mexicans believe that a drink of straight booze relieves the tension of an overstuffed stomach. "*El desempanze*" is the belly deflater. "*Lo del estribo*" (the one of the stirrup, stirrup cup) is the equivalent of "one for the road." It is important not to call this last

drink *la ultima*. Superstition says that the ultimate drink is quite literally your last drink on earth. Mexicans say "*La penultima*," the next-to-the-last.

A common toast, one that usually comes when the atmosphere is loose, is "*¡Arriba! ¡Abajo! ¡Al centro! ¡Adentro!*" ("Up! Down! To the middle! Inside!") "*Salud y pesetas*" is a common contraction of the Spanish classic: "*Salud y pesetas el tiempo para gozarlas*" ("Health and *pesetas* and the time to enjoy them!")

When you drink beer with friends, it is customary to leave the bottles on the table as a means of settling what is owed. A table crowded with empties is also considered to be cool and *macho*.

Botanas (snacks) are often served free with beer or drinks. Most of them are quite spicy.

Should you be passed over when the *botanas* are served, just ask politely, "*¿No hay botanas?*" ("Aren't there any snacks?") Many *cantineros* wrongly assume that gringo customers can't handle the chili or won't like the taste of whatever is being served. If you request a *botana*, however, you'll have to eat it or look stupid.

During a visit to "*El Higado No Existe*" ("The Liver Doesn't Exist"), Steve noticed that everyone but us was served plates of tacos. A word to the bartender quickly solved that; in fact, we were honored with napkins as an apology.

One bite of our tacos caused us to regret our sensitive feelings. The filling was cooked blood from the loser of a recent bullfight.

Musicians may offer to play for you, but always agree to the price per song before they start. They'll always barter and some raise their prices for tourists.

Don't be shocked, however, if *mariachis* charge quite a bit for a song, especially if there are more than two or three in the group. When Mexicans are partying they don't quibble over a few dollars here and there; a few songs can easily cost more than an evening's drinks.

If you don't want to pay for music, say politely but emphatically, "*No, gracias*." Don't waffle around; if you nod and mutter, "Well, I don't know," they'll blast out a quick tune and expect to be paid. Avoid potential disputes by being clear.

A jukebox is about as indispensable to the atmosphere of a good *cantina* as the bull-fight posters on the walls. My favorite song, one that never fails to bring appreciative nods from other customers is:

La Que Se Fue	**She Who Went Away**
Estoy en el rincón de una cantina,	I'm in the corner of a *cantina,*
oyendo la canción que yo pedí	listening to the song I requested
Me estan sirviendo ahorita mi tequila,	They are just now serving my *tequila,*
Ya va mi pensamiento rumbo a ti.	Now my thoughts go toward you.
Yo sé que tu recuerdo es mi desgracia	I know that your memory is my disgrace
Y vengo aquí nomas a recordar	And I come here only to remember.
Que amargas son las cosas que nos pasan	How bitter are the things that happen to us
Cuando hay una mujer que paga mal.	When there's an ungrateful woman.
¿Quien no sabe en esta vida	Who in this life doesn't know
La traición tan conocida,	The betrayal so familiar, that is
que nos deja un mal amor?	left to us by a bad love?
¿Quien no llega a la cantina,	Who doesn't come to the *cantina,*
Exigiendo su tequila y pidiendo	Ordering his *tequila* and
su canción	requesting his song?
Me estan sirviendo ya la del estribo	Now they're serving me one for the road,
Ahorita ya no sé si tento fe	Right now I don't know if I have faith
Ahorita solamente yo les pido,	Right now I only ask them,
Que toquen otra vez la que se fue.	To play again *She Who Went Away.*
Yo lo que quiero es que vuelva, que	What I wish is that she return, return
vuelva conmigo, la que se fue.	with me, she who went away.

A final reminder about drinking and driving: as I mentioned in a discussion of Mexican law and legal hassles, Mexico is an exceptionally safe place for travelers. Tourists who do get into trouble, however, often do so because of alcohol and alcohol-related traffic accidents. To put it bluntly, a traffic accident involving alcohol is a quick ticket to a Mexican jail. If you drink, hail a taxi or let a sober friend take the wheel.

SHOPPING

Shopping and souvenirs • Bartering • Imports: fortune or fantasy? • Shopping: sandals, Indian clothing, blankets and serapes, hammocks, artifacts • Steve's shopping tips: where is the best place to buy crafts? best areas for specific crafts, pottery • Parrot fever

Shopping and Souvenirs

"When confirmed shoppers die and go to heaven, they may well find themselves in Mexico."
—Steve Rogers and Tina Rosa, *The Shopper's Guide to Mexico*

"If you are intending to do much shopping in Guadalajara, it is not unusual to call a cargador to carry your money. . . . To wander around on a shopping excursion with what amounts to two or three hundred dollars in silver half-dollar pieces is no light job."
—Harry Carr, *Old Mother Mexico* (1931)

Mexico is renowned for its highly creative *artesanía* (folk art and crafts). To dedicated shoppers, the country is a dream come true of *tianguis* (Indian markets), shops, souvenir malls, boutiques, flea markets, galleries, beach vendors, sidewalk artists and hole-in-the-wall kiosks. Even the stingiest tourists find their hands twitching toward wallets and purses, rationalizing, "What the heck! It's only a couple of bucks!" This is the type of logic that leads to overloaded luggage and unbalanced budgets.

Look around before buying, even if it's just a fast stroll through several shops or one large market. How many times have I bought the Deal of a Lifetime and then found something even nicer at the next stall? Mexican vendors appreciate the diligent shopper, and you may well find them bringing out better and better things to tempt you.

Although crisscrossing the country looking for bargains and rare finds can be a great adventure, you really don't have to. Most items will be cheapest where they're made, but the best selection is usually found in large markets and shops. As money magnets, Mexico's resorts attract some of the country's finest arts and crafts. A day of resort shopping can turn up everything from three-legged ceramic drums and intricately woven baskets to laquerware furniture, fine woolen *serapes*, silver filigree jewelry and delightful wooden toys.

Shops are convenient but we prefer to buy directly from the artisan or an *artesanía* co-op whenever possible. With decades of shopping experience behind him, Steve points out that by dealing directly you get a better deal and so does the artisan. Most shops pay artists amazingly little and then mark up their work greatly. "I find the *artesanso* is almost always eager to sell to me if I'm paying more than the shop owner.

Bartering

Successful shopping isn't just a matter of driving a hard bargain. For many items, particularly small handicrafts, the price is so low to begin with that it's almost no consideration. Always buy the best quality you can afford, particularly if the price difference between it and something inferior is not great. When you see a real treasure, don't let it get away just because the seller holds out for a few extra pesos. If you go home empty-handed, that small sum will haunt you.

Remember that bartering is a deeply established tradition. When it comes to capitalism, Mexicans definitely know the ropes.

To become adept at bartering, you must take the plunge and practice. Many shy or impatient people say, "But this is Art! How can you be so crude as to haggle over it?" The answer is that haggling over prices, whether it's for a sack of potatoes or a fine wood carving, is both proper and expected; that's why the price comes down if you work at it. By not bartering, you overlook the opportunity to participate in a friendly exchange with the other person.

Like any game, bartering has a few rules. Here's the way it goes:

• **Bartering is not a battle of wits or contest of wills.** It is a polite discussion about prices that both parties hope to conclude with a fair and mutually satisfying agreement. Never use an insulting, sarcastic or argumentative tone, even in jest. If you offend the seller, there's almost no price that will make it right again; the game is over. One of the first rules of bartering is *don't take it too seriously*. Keep it light, friendly and easy-going. You'll notice beach vendors, for example, who are particularly good at enticing gringos into bartering through jokes and friendly, teasing conversation.

By the way, there's no need to worry about offending shopkeepers or taking unfair advantage of souvenir vendors. Mexicans begin haggling as children. They've been "buying cheap and selling dear" for thousands of years. I've yet to see anyone take a loss because some skillful gringo out-bartered them.

I Hate Souvenir Shopping

Tired of the same old polyester *serapes*, stamped leather purses and mass-produced souvenirs? Would you prefer more original gifts and souvenirs, many of them handmade or unusual, one-of-a-kind conversation pieces for just a fraction of the cost of both tourist-grade attic stuffers and overpriced collectibles? You can find real treasures by exploring the shelves in Mexico's supermarkets, hardware and kitchen stores, notions shops and neighborhood *tiendas* (grocery stores).

Many of the simple utensils, tools and everyday supplies used in Mexican households, ranches and homesteads make wonderful souvenirs. One of my favorites, for example, is a classic witch's broom, an inexpensive *escoba* (broom) with a whittled stick handle and a long, thick sweep. (Similar hand-made brooms sell for a very fancy price in Appalachian craft shops.)

Modernization and technology haven't yet reached Mexico's poor farmers and ranchers. In hardware stores and ironmonger's stalls you'll find ready-made collectibles like hand-forged knives and door latches, rustic iron hinges, pot hooks and pioneer-style tools and garden implements. Talk about folk art, I picked up a fearsome steel rat trap fashioned from scrap metal for a dollar in a tiny stall at the back of a public market.

Things that are common or ordinary in Mexico often make striking and unusual decorations at home. In a shop catering to small-time ranchers I found incredible buys on a dozen hand-forged horseshoes, a small wooden burro saddle, hand-braided lariats, spurs and other authentic frontier tack. You may also run across charcoal-fired clothes irons, hand-powered coffee mills, candle lanterns and cow bells made from copper pipe.

In supermarkets and kitchen shops look for souvenirs that are both decorative and useful: tortilla-warmers and dishcloths, natural bristle pot scrubbers, loufas, wooden cutting boards, enameled spoons and dishes, wooden ladles and paddles, nesting baskets, inexpensive cups and bowls, old-fashioned printed oilcloth and all types of shopping bags, from reusable plastic and cloth to handwoven natural fibers.

Food and spices also make great souvenirs. If you'd like to amaze your stay-at-home friends with truly authentic touches to a Mexican meal or fiesta, visit a *supermercado* or market and pick up: whole coffee beans, braids of garlic, bulk or locally packaged spices, whole dried or powdered chilies (try the rich but relatively mild *chile ancho*), bottled hot sauces (*habanero* is wicked!), vanilla extract, canned exotic fruits, traditional hot chocolate mixes and candies. The top-rated souvenir of a tour group we led was unusual tropical drink mixes, especially mango-flavored Tang. (All of these food items can be taken back to the U.S. but you'll still have to declare them.)

Novelty and notions shops—the Mexican equivalent of our dimestores—are great sources of inexpensive party favors, napkins, banners, printed paper tablecloths, fiesta trimmings and Mexican holiday decorations.

• **How do I get started?** Begin by browsing and comparing prices. Because a few tourists will pay the first price asked, no matter how outrageous, some vendors throw out astronomical prices in hopes of landing a fat fish. Competition is fierce, however, and it shouldn't take you long to establish a rough idea of asking-prices. You can short-cut this process even faster by asking other tourists what they paid for their blanket, T-shirt, hammock or other souvenir. Be aware, of course, that some people happily pay fifteen bucks for a $5 *sombrero*.

• **Where should I barter?** Haggling is standard operating procedure with vendors in markets, on sidewalks and beaches, in souvenir stalls, craft bazaars, open-air arcades and many small shops. My favorite place to barter, however, is at the local *mercado* (public market).

• **Where is bartering not appropriate?** Haggling is rarely practiced in regular retail shops (groceries, hardware, dry goods, shoes, etc.), department stores and supermarkets.
Precios fijos (fixed prices) are also found in hotel and museum gift shops and American-style malls. As one tourist observed, "If the store is air-conditioned, the prices are usually frozen, too." So-called "better" tourist shops and boutiques don't like to barter—but they do offer sales and many will give discounts if you politely ask for their "best price."

• **Don't barter until you're ready to buy.** Once the game begins, a vendor won't let you go easily. Also, it is unfair to waste the vendor's time by bartering for a price that you don't actually intend to pay—and then to walk away.

• **How much should I offer?** Prices vary considerably, but the mark-ups are especially high in resort markets and busy souvenir arcades, where haggling typically brings discounts of thirty to fifty percent on crafts, trinkets and clothing. Discounts can even go deeper, especially on "big ticket" purchases such as handloomed blankets, leather goods and silver jewelry.
Some beach vendors spend too much time in the sun and their prices are drastically overheated. Don't be timid about low-low offers (one-half to a third of the asking price). If the vendor runs screaming into the surf, you're probably too low. If he or she immediately smiles and accepts, you were too high—but according to the "rules," you ought to buy the item anyway.
When you don't have the foggiest idea of what an item is worth, don't make a specific offer, just keep up a gentle downward pressure by refusing to commit yourself. "I like it, but. . . ," "It seems high . . . ," "I don't think so . . . " and other vague hesitations will be clearly understood, in English or Spanish.

• **Don't haggle quickly, play it out.** If the vendor is impatient, hurried or eager to make a sale, it's usually just a clever ploy. Quick deals and fast compromises seldom work in your favor.
Most haggling involves a gradual exchange of offers and counteroffers. You'll soon develop a sixth sense when you're approaching the bottom line. This is the moment to make a final offer and then politely but firmly dig in your heels. At this point, silence is golden, so wait and see what develops. Smile, comment on the weather or stare at the ceiling. If your offer isn't accepted within a few minutes, give a fatalistic, Mexican-style shrug and a "thanks-but-no-thanks" smile. Move away slowly, giving an Academy Award performance of being disappointed but no longer interested. "Not today, *gracias*," "I'll think about it" or just, "*No, gracias*" often pushes the vendor to accept your final offer.
If their customers are sunbathing or buried up to their chins in the sand, clever beach

vendors may walk away from a sale—and then turn up again a few minutes later, ready to make a deal.

• **Haggle gently.** We enjoy bartering but there are times when we only go through the motions. I definitely don't believe in driving hard bargains for small sums when dealing directly with artisans and independent vendors. Even those annoyingly persistent beach vendors have to make a living. As one weary hammock salesman confided to me, "This is a difficult way to feed a family." When in doubt, pay the price that is fair rather than going for rock-bottom.

• **Do I have to speak Spanish?** Definitely not. In situations where only Spanish is spoken, tourists who barter with sign language, smiles and pidgin phrases sometimes strike the best bargains. I'll never forget the mild-mannered grandmother who brought a veteran blanket vendor to his knees by softly repeating in English, "That's absolutely lovely, dear, but I don't think I can quite afford it."

Lorena says, "Cheaper by the Dozen"

If you hate to shop or have a long list of friends and relatives to choose gifts for but find yourself running low on time and pesos, try "doing-the-dozens," Lorena's sure-fire, low-cost method of buying souvenirs in bulk. For the price of one tourist blanket or carved onyx chess set you can stuff a shopping bag with colorful *recuerdos* (souvenirs). Here's how it works:

As we travel and sightsee, Lorena watches shop windows and sidewalk stalls for small, distinctive souvenirs that can be purchased in bulk or by the dozen. Many of her choices can be used as decorations, party favors, jewelry or knickknacks. In Puerto Vallarta, for example, she spotted two-inch-high handpainted parrots on wire-loop perches in a boutique. After asking the price, Lorena did some comparison shopping around town, then returned to the boutique and made an offer on "*tres docenas*" (three dozen). (Doing-the-dozens is also a great way to learn the art of haggling.) After consulting with the owner, the salesgirl accepted the offer—and helpfully wrapped each parrot in a twist of paper.

Once she's gathered "a dozen of this and a dozen of that," Lorena packs her souvenirs in baskets (also for gifts). At home, she'll spread her treasures out on a bright tortilla cloth and invite friends and relatives to choose their own souvenir gifts. Some favorites: painted wooden fish and birds, tiny opal turtles, tin boxes, Christmas ornaments, Day of the Dead figurines, straw birds, jewelry of wire and beads, tiny thread dolls, hand-painted greeting cards, handmade dollhouse miniatures, woven coin purses and yarn friendship bracelets.

Do you know someone who studies or teaches Spanish? For a great gift, pick up a stack of inexpensive used comic books, illustrated *telenovelas* (soap opera comics) and assorted magazines at a small bookshop or magazine kiosk. Mexican publications make cheap study aids but they're very hard to find in the U.S.

• **Many merchants are very superstitious about the first sale of each day.** It is bad luck to have a customer walk away without buying something. For this reason, the crafty, cynical barterer will tumble out of bed at the crack of dawn to test others' willpower. Lorena once bought a shawl for what was obviously less than wholesale. The vendor took the money with a weary smile, then muttered a quick blessing (another custom for the first money taken in) over the bills and stuck them away.

Imports: Fortune or Fantasy?

I first began writing the *People's Guide to Mexico* in the late Sixties, while living on the shore of Lake Atitlán in Guatemala. Like many would-be authors, however, I soon became discouraged with long hours at the typewriter and nail-biting insecurity. To soothe my nerves and refresh my inspiration, I hiked into town one afternoon and spent a few hours chatting with a local *artesanía* (arts and crafts) trader. One thing led to another, and before I knew what happened, I'd traded my trusty Olympia portable typewriter for a huge Mayan drum.

Steve was shocked. "Are you kidding me?" he sneered. "That thing isn't worth five *quetzales*!"

Lorena was puzzled. "I thought you were writing a book?"

Early the next morning, I trudged back into town again and ransomed my typewriter for far more than it was worth. The drum went into the closet of our van, where it was forgotten for several months.

A few days later Steve had a brainstorm. "Why don't we load up the van with local arts and crafts to sell back in the States? When people see this stuff we'll be rich!"

From such naive enthusiasms lives are changed and careers are born. In our case, money belts and coin purses were also emptied. Although we eventually sold off our imported treasures (my drum went to a private museum), the experience convinced me that trading in *típica* (folk art) is almost as risky as writing or gambling.

Steve is much more stubborn. He later joined forces with weaver and writer Tina Rosa to found Amerind Arts, a homegrown business featuring unusual crafts and indigenous art from Mexico and Central America. Countless research and collecting trips led, in turn, to writing a book—*The Shopper's Guide to Mexico* (sadly the book is now out of print, but look for it in used bookstores).

Today, a tremendous number of shops in the U.S. sell Mexican and Central American imports. As a result, many enterprising people travel south with the bright idea of buying arts and crafts to resell at home. Most of them end up as the reluctant owners of seventeen *serapes*, thirty-four Oaxaca shirts and hundreds of pounds of pottery.

Our own experience and that of many friends has been that the only items which can be easily and consistently sold in the U.S. are those that can go for less than $20 (and preferably, less than $15) and still give a 300 to 500 percent profit. Unless you have a definite order or an excellent outlet, any expensive item, whether it's an incredible work of art or not, will be difficult to sell. It's easy enough to unload a 25-cent pottery cup for a dollar, but a $100 weaving, even though worth hundreds more, will be a slow mover.

The average shop—and the average consumer—prefers things that aren't too exotic. Shirts, simple skirts, blouses, sandals, small pottery items, wooden carvings, utensils, jewelry and inexpensive musical instruments will usually sell for a good profit and with reasonable ease. When buying on speculation, *never buy anything you can't afford and wouldn't like to keep.*

U.S. import regulations can also complicate your scheme to buy and resell a hundred tortoise-shell ashtrays or two bales of handwoven pot holders. Before spending the money, write to U.S. Customs, P.O. Box 7118, Washington, D.C. 20044. Ask for copies of these booklets: *U.S. Import Requirements, Customs Rulings on Imports* and

Marketing of Country of Origin and *Exporting to the United States*. For other publications relating to importing, write to the same address and ask for a catalog. It could save you a great deal of money and red tape.

Shopping

The following discussion and suggestions cover only the most obvious and irresistible things you'll find to spend your money on. For more detailed information, read *Steve's Shopping Tips*, later in this chapter. Also check your local library; many fine (and usually expensive) books have been written on all aspects of Mexican arts and crafts. By jotting down the names of specific villages, markets and artisans you can save a great deal of guesswork about where to go and what to buy. (See *Markets and Stores: Market Days*, and *For More Information*.)

Sandals
To prove that you've actually been to Mexico, every tourist should purchase at least one pair of authentic *huaraches* (sandals). A good pair, with well-nailed or sewn tire-tread soles and strong leather straps, will last for years, if not decades. *Huaraches* vary in price, depending on the intricacy of the work involved and the type of leather and sole used.

• "Hey, pick me up a pair of sandals, would you?" is a request that all too often results in someone returning home with the wrong-sized sandals for a friend. Don't rely on guesswork; take an outline drawing of both feet or measure them from heel to toe and convert this to centimeters. (See *Appendices: Conversion Tables*.)

• A non-adjustable sandal should fit snugly when new. Will you be wearing socks with your sandals? If so, wear them when you try a pair of *huaraches* on. Sandals made of leather stretch with use. The thinner the leather, the more it will stretch.

• Break in new sandals by soaking them in fresh water. (Salt rots leather.) Now wear them until they dry. Continue this process (it can take up to two weeks if the leather is thick) until the sandals shape themselves to your feet.

• Sandals with extra-thick tire-tread soles are heavy and not very flexible. I much prefer a pair with average or slightly thin soles. *Hule de orilla* (sidewall rubber) is more flexible, but wears faster than *hule de centro* (center, treaded rubber).

• Check the fastenings carefully. Some straps are wired to the sole and will chafe through faster than a looped or sewn-on strap. Cheap buckles never last long and may cut through the straps. The longest-lasting sandals are either a basket weave, semi-shoe type or have two or three wide leather straps. The latter type is open and cool.

• Sandal makers will copy your sandals for a reasonable price. Tire-tread soles can also be put on your shoes or boots, but beware, it will make them much heavier and less flexible.

Indian Clothing
The greatest problem when shopping for Indian clothing and fabrics (*ropa típica* or *indigena*) is deciding which things you can possibly do without. Comparison shopping is important, as price and quality may vary greatly from one vendor or weaver to another.

Small shops often handle old things, and these are likely to be the best examples (and the best buys) of clothing, belts, bags and ceremonial or decorative weavings.

Mark-ups on fabric goods are usually quite steep, but unless you're in the area where an article is made, vendors may stand firm on a high price. Fine Oaxaca shirts are sold to tourists in other parts of the country for as much as in the U.S.

Almost all colored fabrics are *firme* (colorfast), but they should be washed with care and in cold water (at least at first). Shrinkage is a problem; most large shirts will be reduced to the equivalent of "small" after washing.

Buttons rarely last long on most shirts, so you might prefer a pullover style instead. Don't be surprised if the seams aren't very strong; it's expected that the customer (or his wife) will go over them carefully with a needle and thread.

Blankets and *Serapes*

Unless your blanket or *serape* will be used strictly for decoration or a rug, don't buy one that feels scratchy. Many weavers use coarse, uncleaned wool, often mixed with stiff burro hair. These blankets won't get softer with use, but actually scratchier, especially after they pick up a few burrs and twigs in your travels.

The finest blankets and *serapes* and the best selections are found right where the weaving is done, often in a small factory. Roaming blanket vendors are crafty and adept barterers; many tourists pay two or three times the actual value of a blanket.

Price is determined by wool content, weight, pattern and coloring. A brightly colored, mixed wool and cotton blanket may cost one-fourth the price of an all-wool, vegetable-dyed one about the same weight. A thick narrow blanket will cost as much as a thin wide one.

The price range in *serapes* is great. It takes diligent shopping to find a really good one; the market seems glutted with those made for tourists.

Hammocks

The buying and selling of *hamacas* is a tricky business; a normally honest crafts vendor may suddenly become sly and tricky when offering a tourist a hammock. The reason, perhaps, is that hammocks themselves are complicated, with many subtle variations in construction, materials, quality and comfort. I've met innumerable tourists who swore their hammock was "the biggest and the best," when in fact it was average or less. To avoid getting something other than what you want, study the following suggestions very carefully before shopping.

• The best hammocks come from Yucatán; Mérida, the capital, has the widest selection. There are many shops offering a bewildering variety of hammocks, from cheap twine ones to fabulously comfortable (and expensive) linen models. (Good hammocks are also made in the state of Oaxaca, but they don't compare to those from Yucatán.)

• The largest hammocks, called *matrimonial* (marriage-sized), can hold two people with no crowding at all. Most tourists are so amazed at the size of an authentic single hammock that they are easily convinced it is a *matrimonial*. What's the difference? A genuine *matrimonial* will be about sixteen feet long (at least one-third of this the woven section), weigh 4.5 to 5.5 pounds and stretch out to ten to sixteen feet in width without pulling too hard. It should have a hundred or more pairs of strings at each end (these string pairs are called *brazos*).

• A medium-sized hammock, ideal for sleeping one adult or two kids, should weigh 2.5 to 3.5 pounds, with slightly smaller measurements and string count than the marriage size. **Warning:** A medium hammock is often sold as a *matrimonial*.

• The best hammocks are pure cotton. Nylon end strings are becoming common but they are inferior to natural fibers. The thinner the thread, the better. Thin thread is longer fibered, wears better and is more comfortable than thick threads. Cotton resists stretching, is more colorfast (*firme*) and just plain feels better than synthetic.

• The edges are very important. There should be ten to sixteen strings along the edge, well secured to the body of the hammock. This is critical for maintaining the shape and preventing uncomfortable sagging.

• Check the weave. The tighter it is, the more resilient and comfortable the hammock will be. A good hammock will be double- or triple-woven and the holes between the threads will be small. When one person is in a *matrimonial* the weave looks almost solid, like cloth. A *matrimonial* is said to require five miles of thread, a medium three miles. Measure it. The fewer splices the better.

• Check the end loops. They should be thick and tightly wrapped.

• A *ciguana* hammock has a beeswax coating on the threads. These feel silky and are especially resistant to dampness and mildew.

• Hammocks can be ordered custom-made. Ask for the best quality string and construction. Specify the dimensions; I once ordered a hammock and got one that was well made but much too small. Mayan Indians tend to be shorter than gringos and their hammocks are sized accordingly.

• Hammocks should be washed by hand in cold water. Store them in a mouse- and moth-proof container; my first Yucatán hammock lasted eleven years before being eaten by vicious rodents, those rotten little . . .

• **How to hang it:** Learning to hang your hammock properly is as important as learning how to buy one. See *Camping: Camping Skills* for detailed instructions.

Artifacts

Once the United States prohibited the importation of genuine artifacts, freshly baked *ídolos* (idols) became a big business in Mexico and Guatemala. Copies and reproductions have increased in quality and price. Some of the best, in fact, are made from genuine pre-Columbian molds. The clay may not have been baked a thousand years ago, but the design is certainly authentic. Many of these fine reproductions cost as much as the real thing did in the days of unrestricted artifact trading.

Genuine artifacts of small size or very common design are sometimes sold in shops. The Mexican government cracks down only when the object is of significant historical or monetary value. The penalty for possession of unauthorized artifacts is stiff. When in doubt, ask for an export permit from the seller.

Antiques are legally sold to tourists and may be imported into the U.S.

Steve's Shopping Tips

Everywhere you go in Mexico you will find folk art and handmade crafts for sale—in the streets, in the markets, in stores and galleries, and from vendors who approach when you are trying to read on the beach or drink coffee in a sidewalk café.

Where Is the Best Place to Buy Crafts?

If you're just picking up a few souvenirs or inexpensive gifts for the folks at home, it really doesn't matter where you shop. When you see a nice weaving in an airport gift shop or a one-of-a-kind Christmas crèche fashioned out of old beer cans for a reasonable price on a street corner, go ahead and buy. You may see a similar item for less money later and kick yourself for being hasty, but then again you might not. This is a case where it can be better to leap before you spend too much time looking, as we are not talking big bucks.

On the other hand, if you are shopping for expensive items or are a collector or commercial buyer, it definitely pays to do some serious comparison shopping before you make your purchase.

As a general rule when shopping for folk art and crafts, the farther you go down the "food chain" toward the actual creator of the piece you want, the better the price. Let's use a handcarved wooden ceremonial mask from Guerrero as an example. You can buy this mask in an upscale folk art shop in Seattle for $300. Or you can head for Tijuana and find a similar mask for $150. Travel all the way to Mexico City and you'll get your mask in the fancy "Pink Zone" for $100. For the price of a few subway tickets, however, you can shop in Mexico City's many craft markets: the same mask goes for $60 at the Ciudadela market.

So, you reason, why not go right to the horse's mouth, where the mask is made, and get the best possible deal? In Taxco, Guerrero, you learn that the mask is back up to $100—Taxco is a popular tourist town. Iguala is just thirty miles away, however, and thanks to your high school Spanish you eventually locate a wholesaler who goes into the hills and buys from the artisans. He offers your mask for $40. You aren't giving in yet—you rent a pack mule and go into the hills yourself. On the second or third day you track down the wood carver and buy the mask right out of his hands for just $20, a spectacular savings of $280! (not counting a few expenses).

Shopping the back country: Mexico's vast back country can be an extremely interesting place to do your shopping, but it isn't for everyone. If your Spanish is weak or nonexistent, you will need a bilingual or even a trilingual guide. Many indigenous people don't speak Spanish, and some artisans will not sell to people they don't know. Also, there are areas where strangers aren't welcome because of moonshining, marijuana, feuds or other dubious activities. If you do decide to venture far off the beaten track, do your best to find out what you might be getting into first.

Shops and galleries: Although prices are higher, there are definite advantages to buying folk art in an established shop or gallery. The owners are often very knowledgeable and will have pieces by the best artists. They will have good background information on the artist, and explain her techniques and style. Most will arrange shipping to your home, a big help if you want to buy more than you can carry. Some of the shops I deal with are willing to ship items purchased elsewhere, as long as you buy something from them.

Fonart: Fonart is not a place but a chain of stores operated by the Mexican government to promote the sale of folk art and crafts. Fonart stores are found in many cities that have an active tourist trade. Items for sale are of good quality and prices are not bad, though they seem to be getting higher of late and are often not much less than prices in private shops and galleries.

Tourist resorts: You'll find a good selection in many resorts, but the prices can be as high as a good shop in the U.S. (**Note:** Cancún has a large selection of Taxco silver at relatively reasonable prices.)

Border towns: Large border cities such as Tijuana, Ciudad Juárez and Nuevo Laredo have a surprisingly good selection of handicrafts. Prices are higher than at the source, but thanks to tough competition, they aren't as high as you would think—and usually a lot lower than tourist resorts. If your only reason to visit Mexico is to shop, you might as well just go to the nearest border city.

Best Areas for Specific Crafts

Silver: *Taxco, Guerrero*, is *the* silversmithing center of Mexico. The selection is huge and ranges from amazingly inexpensive silver rings and earrings to sterling silver table services worth thousands of dollars. Jewelry from Taxco is available in tourist centers throughout Mexico, but the widest choices and best prices are found in Taxco's more than one hundred silver shops.

Note: Sterling silver is often stamped with the number 922. This means the piece is 92.2 percent silver, which makes it "sterling." Pure, 100 percent silver is called "fine" and is sometimes stamped "1000 *fine*." Fine silver is actually too soft for most jewelry. Jewelry stamped "*alpaca*" is a nickel alloy known as "nickel silver" or "German silver." Whatever you call it, this nickel alloy jewelry contains *no silver at all*.

Hammocks: The finest hammocks in Mexico are made in the **Yucatán**. My favorite shop is in Mérida: Tejidos y Cordeles Nacionales, S.A. de C.V. at Calle 56 No. 516-B, located near the main post office in the market area. The selection is amazing and their hammocks are sold by weight, with fixed, very fair prices. Selling by weight virtually eliminates doubt about the hammock's actual size and avoids your having to count strings. If you are buying hammocks wholesale, this store is definitely your best bet.

Panama hats: The best palm hats aren't from Panama but from the small town of **Bécal**, in the state of Campeche. They are called Panama hats because this type of hat was widely used by people working on the construction of the Panama Canal. In Mérida, check out Sombrerería "El Becaleño" on Calle 65 No. 483 between 56A and 58. You will also find Panama hats in the market and numerous other shops in Mérida.

Wooden masks: Carved wooden masks depicting animals, devils, demons and various mythical beasts are a tradition in the state of **Guerrero**. They are often referred to as, you guessed it, "Guerrero masks" or more accurately, "dance masks." These masks are carved from a very light fibrous wood with a long unpronounceable name. Old masks that have been used in dances and ceremonies are collectable, expensive and hard to come by, but many newer masks are very well done and relatively inexpensive.

Guerrero masks are available throughout Mexico. Although the best prices are probably in Iguala, Guerrero, you have to search to find them there. Ask around, but frankly, it's a lot easier and not much more expensive to buy masks in Mexico City.

Rugs and blankets: Handwoven woolen rugs and traditional blankets from Teotitlán del Valle, Oaxaca, can be purchased throughout Mexico, but the best prices and selection are found in **Teotitlán del Valle**, a small Zapotec town outside of Oaxaca City. Markets and shops in Oaxaca have lots of textiles, as do many of the *tianguis* (weekly outdoor markets) in surrounding towns and villages.

Other places for rugs include **Temoaya**, near Toluca in the state of Mexico, where hand-tied Oriental-style rugs are made; the **Toluca market** itself has handwoven blankets and *serapes* from surrounding villages; **Tlaxcala**, for brightly striped Saltillo-style blankets; **San Miguel de Allende, Guanajuato**, and **Pátzcuaro, Michoacán**, both have locally woven rugs, blankets and other textiles.

Metalwork: For copper worked by hand into beautiful vases, trays, candlesticks, plates and so on, **Santa Clara del Cobre, Michoacán** (near Pátzcuaro) is definitely the place to go.

Tinware: *Hojalatería* is produced in **Oaxaca, San Miguel de Allende, Guanajuato** and **Toluca**.

Pottery

Pottery is locally made and sold all over the country. Mexican *alfarería* is often low fired, utilitarian kitchenware. This pottery is attractive and inexpensive, but lead glazes fired at low temperatures can be a health hazard, especially if the pottery is used with acidic foods. (See the box *Pottery and Lead Poisoning*, below). High-fired stoneware is safe for all uses.

Major pottery centers include **Tonalá, Jalisco**, a small town on the outskirts of Guadalajara. Pottery of every description is sold in Tonalá's large street market (Thursday and Sunday) and numerous shops and ceramic studios. Ken Edwards, a famous potter who along with Jorge Wilmot introduced stoneware pottery to Mexico, has his studio here.

Tlaquepaque, also within the "greater" Guadalajara area, is famous for art and crafts of all kinds. Tlaquepaque is the home of ceramic sculptor Sérgio Bustamente. This famous artist's work can be seen at No. 236 Avenida Independencia and in major galleries around the country.

Dolores Hildalgo, Guanajuato: This town is a center for the production of *majólica*-style ceramics and tiles as well as more utilitarian kitchenware. You will see this pottery for sale in markets all over the country.

Acatlán, Puebla: This small town is crammed with low-fired pottery of all sorts. It is known for garden patio pottery and animal-shaped fireplaces. The family of the late Herón Martinez still produces some of his most famous designs of animals, candelabra and *Arboles de la Vida* (Trees of Life).

Puebla, Puebla: *Majólica* pottery is known in Puebla as *talavera*. This is brightly colored pottery, tin-glazed and high-fired with intricate designs. *Talavera* was first introduced from Spain in the sixteenth century. You can find it for sale in downtown

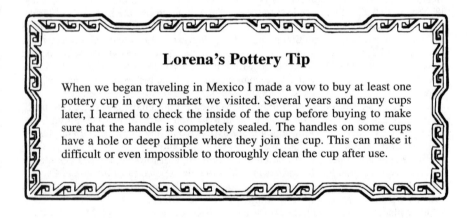

Lorena's Pottery Tip

When we began traveling in Mexico I made a vow to buy at least one pottery cup in every market we visited. Several years and many cups later, I learned to check the inside of the cup before buying to make sure that the handle is completely sealed. The handles on some cups have a hole or deep dimple where they join the cup. This can make it difficult or even impossible to thoroughly clean the cup after use.

Puebla at the El Parián craft market and in numerous shops and downtown galleries. (**Carl's note:** This pottery isn't cheap. As Steve said on our last trip through Puebla, "When I pay twenty bucks for a dinner plate, I expect it to come heaped with food.")

Several towns in the state of **Michoacán** produce some interesting ceramics: **Tzintzuntzán** has low-fired dinnerware and kitchen pottery. They use a cream-colored glaze, and many of the designs include a very attractive fish motif drawn in brown. The small town of **Capula**, near Morelia, produces a low-fired pottery with distinctive pointillist designs (formed with many tiny dots). **Ocumicho** is a small Tarascan Indian town famous for its "devil pottery"—wild and crazy sculptures of devils, demons and fantastic creatures engaged in such everyday pursuits as driving a Coca-Cola truck or romping in graphic group sex. Needless to say, Ocumicho pieces are considered very unusual. **Patambán** is another small Tarascan town (near Ocumicho) that produces a more traditional dark green, low-fired pottery. Its pottery co-op does some very beautiful stoneware. The state-run Casa de Las Artesanías in **Morelia** has a great collection of reasonably priced pottery and folk

Pottery and Lead Poisoning

The following excerpt* from *A Potter's Mexico* is included to clarify the problem of possible lead poisoning when using pottery for food and beverages. Your only other consideration when buying a piece of pottery should be how to stuff your suitcase with all those treasures without breaking the straps.

1. Acid foods and drinks should not be stored in glazed vessels.
2. The daily use of glazed pitchers and drinking vessels for acid drinks such as orange juice, lemon or limeade, or tomato juice should be avoided.
3. Glazed cooking pots should not be used to prepare such acid foods as tomatoes, or such fruits as limes, lemons, oranges or plums.
4. The Mexican *cazuela*, or stew pot, though an ideal shape for tossed salads, should not be used with dressings containing vinegar or lemon or lime juice; certainly, not on a regular basis.
5. Under no circumstances should green-colored glazed pottery be used for any drinks or moist foods. Copper, the green colorant, dramatically increases the lead release from lead glazes.

In all probability, the occasional use of Mexican glazed pottery, even for the most acid of foods and drinks, would pose no problem for the average user, though in a few rare instances it might.

—Irwin and Emily Whitaker, *A Potter's Mexico*

*Reprinted courtesy of the University of New Mexico Press, Albuquerque, New Mexico. Thanks.

art. If your time is limited, this is the place to shop for folk art (Humboldt and Fray Juan de San Miguel No. 129, downtown Morelia).

Atzompa, Oaxaca: A small town (near Oaxaca City) famous for green glazed kitchenware. Beware of the lead content. Green glaze is the worst! You will also find natural tan unglazed figurines. The family of the late Teodora Blanco still makes figurines in the style she made famous as *muñecas abordadas*, dolls "embroidered" with clay.

San Bartolo Coyotepec, Oaxaca (near Oaxaca City) was made famous by the late Doña Rosa and her distinctive black pottery. Her studio, Alfarería Doña Rosa, is operated by her family and has black pottery items for sale. There is heavy tourist traffic here, however, and you can get better deals around the downtown market in Oaxaca City.

Amatenango del Valle, Chiapas: Primitive pottery is baked in open fires in the streets and courtyards of this small town, thirty-five kilometers south of San Cristóbal de las Casas. Look for animal figures, large clay water pots and pottery fireplaces.

Parrot Fever

It was 7 a.m. and Steve was in the kitchen, blearily preparing *atole** for his newest baby. The latest arrival in our growing family was perched on the back of a wooden chair across the table from me, teetering dangerously as it screamed its fool head off for breakfast. Lorena was still in bed, refusing to lift her head from a deep pile of pillows until the morning sun thoroughly warmed the front porch. I was nursing a dull headache with a cup of strong Guatemalan coffee, trying to figure out where our latest brilliant scheme had gone wrong.

Guatemala, 1970: "Let's buy a bunch of parrots and take them back to the States. People pay hundreds of dollars for parrots that aren't half as beautiful as these in Guatemala. They're cheap and we can sell them for a fortune!"

The record is unclear on exactly who came up with this historic brainstorm, but the results are known: With no further delay or second thoughts, Steve was dispatched to the huge central market place in Guatemala City to buy some of these fabled birds.

He returned three days later, grinning like the cat that swallowed the canary. In this case, however, the "canary" was a full-grown Double Yellow Head Amazon parrot that paced Steve's shoulder like the poop deck of a pirate ship, shouting grotesque Spanish obscenities at the top of its lungs. "Poop deck" wasn't off the mark—a gruesome stain down the back of Steve's shirt was ample proof that the bird wasn't housebroken.

It was obvious from the moment he stepped through the door, however, that Steve's delight in this parrot knew no bounds. Every time it cut loose with another volley of ferocious obscenities, Steve clutched his belly and trembled with laughter.

"Carl and Lorena, I want you to meet Arturo. Isn't he neat? Man, you won't believe what I paid for him. Four dollars!"

As I approached the bird it scrambled warily around Steve's head and surveyed me suspiciously from his other shoulder. Steve winced as the parrot's long talons bit through his thin cotton T-shirt.

"He likes me," Steve said wonderingly. "He rode on my shoulder on the city bus, all the way from the market to where I'd parked the van. I don't know . . . it's almost like . . . it's almost like we knew each other at first sight. Isn't that right, Arty?" He teased the bird by pursing his thick lips into an exaggerated kiss.

Arty? On the other side of the kitchen, Lorena's eyes rolled in the first signs of panic.

"We only had one little problem, didn't we now?" Steve scolded the bird in baby talk, bobbing his head playfully. "Arty pulled a little trick on Steve, didn't you? You were being naughty, weren't you?" Steve shook his head in mock disapproval.

Misinterpreting my look of horror and disbelief, Steve released a huge laugh. Turning his head carefully away from the bird, he said in a near whisper, "I was repeating everything the parrot said on the bus. Then it turns out that he was

Atole is an ancient drink made from finely milled corn or grain. It is mixed with hot water or milk and taken as a drink or thick gruel. In Guatemala, *atole* is sometimes laced with chili peppers. You won't find it on the menus of "better" restaurants, but travelers who've been served this stuff as often as we have firmly believe that the use of *atole* contributed significantly to the Mayan Collapse.

actually teaching me to say, 'What a prick!'" Steve laughed appreciatively. "Man!" he choked, "You know how conservative some of these Guatemalans are?"

Yes, I suppose I did. On the other hand, try as I might, I couldn't quite imagine the reaction of the average Guatemalan bus commuter to the sight of an extra-large Jerry Garcia-look-a-like trading hard-core *groserias* with a bird.

Swiping away tears with the back of his hand, Steve dismissed the incident passengers with a huge snort of disdain. "I guess somebody got a little tense and said something to the driver. Can you believe it, he actually pulled over and made us get off a couple of blocks early! Cost me two cents."

Steve swiveled his head and looked the parrot right in the eye. "You think you're pretty neat, don't cha?" he cooed.

The parrot responded by snuggling up against the side of Steve's head, nibbling intimately at his earlobe. Ruffling up its brilliant green feathers as though plumping the pillows for bed, the bird gradually settled into a cozy crouch. With its eyes closed sleepily, the bird began humming a throaty, off-key lullaby. Steve beamed lovingly.

I felt the hair prickling on the back of my neck.

"Steve," I began carefully. "What do you think a bird like this is worth in the States?"

Steve blinked nervously, dismissing my question with a vague, "Who knows?" wave of the hands.

"No, really." I persisted. "Do you think we can get three or four hundred bucks for him. Maybe even five?"

Lorena, washing half a bushel of spinach over at the sink, was all ears.

"Oh, man!" Steve writhed. "Couldn't we, you know. . . ." He glanced meaningfully at the parrot, then lowered his voice to a conspiratorial whisper. "Couldn't we talk about it later?"

I looked over again at Lorena. She shrugged her shoulders helplessly and took refuge in a series of deep breathing exercises. Not prepared to give up the struggle quite this early, I followed Steve into the living room, where he readied the parrot for bed. "Bed" for Arturo was a fancy four-foot-high wire cage outfitted with everything from a tiny mirror and tin cup of fresh water to a plate of sliced fruit. A circle of bright cloth covered the floor like a miniature carpet. There was even a tiny brass bell dangling from the center of the cage.

"In case he needs me in the night," Steve joked weakly.

A week later Steve returned to Guatemala City to buy a second parrot. Lorena went along, vowing not to let Steve out of her sight.

"This time I'll buy a little one," Steve promised. "It's a lot harder to get attached to the little ones. Don't worry. Little parrots just don't have the personality of a mature bird like Arturo."

After they pulled away, I closed the garden gate and went back down the path toward the lake. It was a deliciously quiet morning and for the first time in months I had the house entirely to myself.

"Carl?" "Carl?" "CARL!!!"

Well, almost entirely to myself.

"Yeah, Arturo. What is it now?"

"¿Café?"

"¿Café?"

"¿Café?"

"Alright, alright!" I sighed, detouring toward the kitchen. "Keep your shirt on, I was going to make another pot anyway."

While the coffee water boiled, I fixed myself a couple of pieces of toast with mango jam. On second thought I buttered a third slice for Arturo. "Remember," Steve had cautioned me the night before. "He won't eat margarine. Use real butter."

When I came back onto the veranda Arturo was strutting excitedly back and forth on the arm of his favorite chair—formerly my favorite chair. The bird gave a curious yodel of contentment as I served his toast and coffee ("Cream," Steve had instructed. "And warm but not hot. But no sugar. Sugar really isn't good for him.")

The bird tore into his breakfast with characteristic gusto, occasionally tossing his head and flipping bits of buttered toast far over his shoulder. Turning to his cup ("The blue ceramic one with the jungly flower pattern; that's his favorite.") Arturo took coffee like a real stevedore, plunging his beak deep into the cup and muttering to himself as he gargled the rich brew.

As we shared our morning repast, thick fleecy clouds wreathed the distant summit of the Atitlán volcano. Once the sun had finally warmed the bricks beneath my bare feet, Arturo walked sleepily across the table and settled himself into a comfortable perch on my left knee. Yawning hugely, the bird ducked his head and fanned the feathers on his neck, imploring me to scratch his bare skin.

"What the matter, Arty?" I said. "Dandruff bothering you again?"

While Steve and Lorena shopped for parrots in Guatemala City, I planned to take advantage of the peace and quite and get some writing done. Coffee cup in hand, I went into the bedroom/office, closing the door firmly behind me. Now, I could finally focus my mind on the work at hand. I rolled a fresh sheet of paper into the Olympia portable. . . .

"*Steve?*"

"*Steve?*"

"*STEVE!!!*"

Toenails clicked impatiently across the tiles as the parrot came down from his kitchen perch and searched the house from room to room for his mentor. After several seconds of silence, I tried cautiously typing my name at the top of the page.

"Steve?" Steve!" With an excited cry the bird changed direction and headed directly toward the bedroom.

"Steve's gone and I'm busy, dammit!" I shouted. "Go outside and play with the crows!" Ignoring the babbling, unintelligible Spanish outside my door, I stretched my arms and swiveled my neck to improve the flow of creative juices. Ready at last, I stared expectantly at the blank page before me, then raised my hands to the keyboard. . . .

"*St.. st... st.... steeeeve?*"

"*St.. st... st.... steeeeve?*"

The confounded bird was actually whining!

Arturo's pleas were worthy of a soap opera, but the bedroom door remained firmly closed. Turning back to my work-in-progress, however, I couldn't help noticing that the parrot's histrionic cries were gradually beginning to change. From whining and pathetic sniveling, Arturo skillfully segued to a tone of peevish confusion—"Steve? *Steve?*"—and when even that failed to bring results, he switched to cynical, head-on barks of exasperation: "*Steve! Steve? Steve!*"

Pushing away from the typewriter, I kneeled down and put my ear next to the door. On the other side of the wood, the parrot paused for breath, muttering darkly as it searched its memory for more persuasive sounds. I didn't have long to wait. His calls for his big buddy now trembled with an imploring, infantile warble. I chewed my knuckles to avoid laughing aloud as the parrot's quavering voice dredged the low end of the emotional scale. Disappointment, disillusionment, betrayal: in the end, the crafty bird settled for a heart-rending medley of bottomless grief. I held the door firmly closed.

"*Gloria?*"

"*Gloriaaaa?*"

Anguished cries for his former mistress also proved hopeless. Though our little house reverberated with maudlin echoes of loss and dislocation, dear departed Gloria did not appear.

Arturo gradually abandoned all hope and broke into inconsolable, hiccuping sobs. Rising again to my feet, I was amazed to find that my eyes were actually beginning to sting a little.

I jerked the door open. Arturo fluttered back in surprise.

"Now what do you want?" I barked.

Looking me square in the eye, he breezily chirped, "*Steve?*" and charged past me into the bedroom. By the time I'd regained my composure, the parrot was chortling happily from the back of my chair.

Steve's first words when they returned from Guatemala City were an anxious, "Did you miss me?" It took me a few moments to realize that he wasn't talking to me, but to the parrot on my shoulder.

When Arturo yawned noncommittally, Steve's face showed a flicker of disappointment. Turning back to the van, he quickly regained his enthusiasm when he saw Lorena climbing down from the front seat. "Wait'll you see this!" Steve said, rubbing his hands excitedly.

Lorena approached us with a small lidded straw basket held gently in her hands, as though bearing some rare gift.

"Careful," she cautioned as Steve reached out and tugged at the lid. "It's still asleep."

Curious, but also slightly apprehensive, I leaned forward for a better look. Based on past experience, I half-expected to find a coiled snake or some equally startling natural wonder. As our travels through Mexico and Guatemala lengthened from months to years, our van was gradually filling with offbeat curiosities and irresistible collectibles that one or the other of us "just couldn't pass up."

"My god! What is it?" Peering up at me from a nest of damp cotton wadding was a bizarre naked creature, all eyes and beak and bare puckered skin.

"Oh, man!" I said, looking up at Steve and Lorena. "You don't mean . . . oh, man! Don't tell me this is a . . . "

"It's a parrot!" Steve cried joyously. "It's a baby parrot!" He wrung his hands with excitement. Beside him, Lorena grinned foolishly.

"Oh, no!" I said, shaking my head at her in disbelief. "You promised!"

"Hey, what can I say?" Lorena shrugged. "It only cost a dollar."

"A dollar!" Steve crowed delightedly. "Can you believe that! We bought a parrot for a dollar? A real parrot!"

"That's not a real parrot!" I protested. "It's some kind of mutant chicken. It doesn't even have feathers! My god, it's pathetic!"

We stared in fascination as the bug-eyed creature stirred uneasily in the bottom of the basket. Slowly blinking its enormous brown eyes, its beak opened in a cavernous pink yawn.

"She's hungry again!" Steve cried gleefully. Snatching the basket from Lorena's hands, he stuck his face just inches from the startled bird's. Without so much as a blush, Steve began cooing a kind of bilingual Gerber-speak. This, I recognized, was his way of introducing the creature to its new "family."

Once the saccharine formalities were completed, Steve looked up at us with shining eyes. "Okay, you guys," he said hoarsely. "Now, let's go make this baby a nice glass of *atole*." Nestling the basket protectively in his arms, he hurried off toward the kitchen.

The days slid by. In that idyllic time before parrot fever struck us, we often wandered into the kitchen as late as 8 or 9 a.m. for our first quiet cups of coffee. Now, with jungle creatures living in our midst, the morning began just before dawn, with an eye-opening chorus of shrieks, curses and crashing, traffic-like honks. To the best of his abilities—which were considerable—Arturo woke us with a vivid audio portrait of morning activity in the Guatemala City market.

"Hey, customer! Come here! Try it! Take it! Take it! Gloria? A kilo? No change! Bastard!" This tirade was accompanied by a clamorous frenzy of babbling voices, whistles, catcalls and sirens. All the performance lacked for complete sensory overload was the fragrant perfume of rotting produce and a cloud of diesel fumes.

On the chair beside Arturo, our fast-growing fledgling raised her voice in an ear-splitting echo. Steve had christened her "Far Out," for the inevitable exclamations visitors made when they saw the baby parrot cuddled in his lap, taking greedy gulps of *atole* until its soft, naked body was as swollen as a sock. "Far out! It's a baby parrot! That's really far out!"

After breakfast—more *atole* for Far Out, fruit and bread dunked in coffee for Steve and Arturo—the birds would move to chairs placed on the porch in the early morning sun. While Lorena caught up on her journal, Steve would accompany the birds on his guitar, entertaining the puzzled Mayan fishermen with an hour or two of rousing "parrot jazz."

In the meantime, I retreated to my bedroom-office to write. It was understood, of course, that I was not to be interrupted, disturbed or in any way distracted from my search for the elusive Muse. It was also a rare day when Steve didn't come quietly tapping at my door, unable to resist sharing some precious moment he'd just spent with the parrots.

"Carl, I really hate to bother you but . . . " followed by such fascinating developments as Arturo's uncanny, pitch-perfect rendition of the opening bars of "The Orange Blossom Special."

"Well . . . it was almost perfect," Steve bragged. "But he still needs to do some work on those early chord changes."

On another occasion the interruption announced Far Out's memorable attempt to scratch her head. "Carl, I really hate to bother you but this is just too much! Far Out forgets she's already standing on one leg, so when she picks up that leg to scratch with, she falls over!"

"Carl, I really hate to bother you but . . . Arturo just spoke English!"

"He did? What did he say?"

"I swear! He was sitting on a chair eating a banana and we were listening to some Merle Haggard tapes. Far Out was in the kitchen and . . . "

"OK, OK! What did he say?"

Steve looked at me and the laughter rose in his chest like huge trembling waves. With one hand clamped over his mouth, his eyes widened into dark pools of childlike wonder. When I thought he might literally explode with the glee of it all, Steve finally began spluttering. "Arturo said . . . I mean he sang, 'If I had the wings of an angel!' And then get this! It's hard to believe but he actually did some Merle Haggard riffs. I'm telling you, he sounded exactly like a steel guitar."

Steve's eyes were glazed with excitement. "But that's not the best part. When he got done, he looked over at me, and, Carl, I swear this is true, he looked over at me and he said in this weird growlly kind of voice, 'Oh, God, Steve! Oh, Lordy God!'"

Poleaxed and momentarily exhausted by the significance of what he'd heard, Steve sagged against the door frame, shaking his head in total and utter astonishment.

"That's pretty amazing, Steve, I gotta admit." A few days earlier Steve had reported with almost equal excitement that Arturo could perfectly mimic the sound of urine as it streamed into the toilet. A few days before that Arturo barked like a dog. And gobbled like a turkey. It was suspected, but as yet unconfirmed, that he could also buzz like a bee.

There was no doubt about it, the parrot's talents were both varied and amazing. On the other hand, I was not only getting a little weary of life in the Animal Kingdom, but it frequently occurred to me that the world's zoos and pet shops were overflowing with appealing, talented creatures.

It was thoughts such as these, in fact, which foolishly led me to blurt, "Steve, do you think speaking English will increase his resale value very much?"

Steve stiffened instantly. "You're not serious? You gotta be kidding, right?" He sounded as though I'd proposed a bank heist or a suicide pact.

"Well," I said. "We actually bought the birds to make some money, remember?"

With his back to the door and one hand on the knob, Steve hissed angrily. "Man, I never thought you'd sink that low. Sell Arturo? My god! I can't believe this! That's sick!"

"Sick?" I protested, pushing my chair back from the typewriter. "Hey, you're the one who's sick. You don't see me reading James Michener novels to a bird. Come to think of it, I never realized until now that parrot fever is probably some kind of a mental disease!"

"Very funny!" Steve shouted. "Carl, that's really very, very funny. Now I suppose you're gonna tell me you want to sell Far Out, too?"

"To the highest bidder," I shot back. "Money talks and Chicken Little walks!"

Steve's lips trembled. There was silence for a moment and then we both burst out laughing.

"Chicken Little walks!" Steve laughed appreciatively. "Hey, that's pretty good! You better write that one down, you may be able to use it."

"I thought that'd get to you." I grinned, tearing the paper from my typewriter and tossing it into the wastebasket. With the tension eased, Steve opened the door and started to leave. His smile suddenly dissolved.

"Just one thing," he added. "I know you like to tease about selling the parrots. But do me a favor, all right?" The bantering tone was now edged with steel. "Don't say anything like that in front of the birds, OK? You never know," Steve warned. "They just might take it wrong."

RESTAURANTS AND TYPICAL FOODS

*The joy of eating • Types of restaurants • Street food • Mexican fast-food tips •
Ordering a meal • Paying up • Tips • Vegetarians • What you'll eat: tortillas, bread,
chilies, meat, fish, seafood, potatoes, eggs and breakfast, beans, soups, sandwiches,
tacos, enchiladas, salads and snacks • Junk food, desserts and candy • Beverages:
coffee and tea, juices and fruit drinks, soft drinks*

The Joy of Eating

One of the greatest pleasures of traveling in a foreign country is encountering new
foods and eating customs. This is especially true in Mexico, where at times you'll feel
inundated with food smells, food vendors and raw food materials themselves.

Our memories of a trip often focus not on museums or a group of loud *mariachis*, but
on eating. "Do you remember that side street in Oaxaca, where we sat next to a smoky
charcoal brazier as a Mixtec Indian woman grilled *quesadillas* and tossed tortilla scraps
to the scarecrow dogs browsing at our feet?" Like Pavlov's salivating canine, my mind
responds to the word "Mexico" with mouth-watering visions of grilled lobsters swimming in garlic sauce, golden tacos stuffed with thick wedges of buttery avocado and baskets of plump, warm pastries washed down with tall glasses of fresh orange juice. Of
course there's more to Mexico than stuffing yourself—but how can I forget the first taste
of a mango milkshake or the sensory overload of fresh *chile habanero*?

There is an incredible range of food in Mexico and interesting places to eat it. The journey involves surprises; those with a love for the unknown, who dare to be adventurous,
will be richly rewarded. My motto is: When in doubt, close your eyes and chew.

The question of health naturally arises. How can you sample these savory new
dishes without encountering some indigestible, stomach-scouring bacteria? Unlike
McDonald's and Howard Johnson's, Mexican restaurants (especially the less expensive ones) are not as easily categorized by appearance. Many excellent but modest
restaurants don't have the time or staff to scrupulously wipe down each table between
groups of customers. On a typical Sunday afternoon, for example, a crowded seafood
restaurant operates in near-pandemonium, with waiters slipping on shrimp shells and
discarded limes, diners demanding more fish soup and beer and crackers, beggars

looking for a kind face or a forgotten bread roll, kids spilling sodas and crying, and a couple of hungry tourists standing hesitantly in the doorway, wondering if this is some kind of crazy private fiesta or just normal lunch time disorder.

The best criteria for judging a restaurant are the same as at home: personal experience, intuition and optimism. Clean floors and ironed tablecloths don't tell you a thing about what's going on in the kitchen. If the place is full of customers hungrily diving into their food and savory odors bring eager rumbles from your stomach, it's probably a good place to eat.

Keep in mind that *all of the food comes from the market.* A white-jacketed waiter, a Diner's Club card in the window or an impressively printed menu do not sterilize the lettuce or disinfect the dishes. Once you've adjusted to the initial sensory overload of most Mexican restaurants, you can begin to notice details. The tiny market stall serving refried beans is quite clean, though a whiff of overripe fruit from the next aisle might have first led you to believe otherwise.

"Approximately 70% of the produce consumed in the U.S. during January and February of each year is grown in Mexico and 50% of the produce sold in supermarkets between December and April is imported, much of it from south of the border."
—David Steinman
"Broccoli in January, Strawberries in November," **California Magazine**

As this article suggests, you've probably been eating "Mexican food" for years without realizing it. In other words, there's no reason to expect to get ill in Mexico, especially if you use common sense and follow the simple precautions given in this book. Dire warnings about fresh vegetables and fruit may have been valid fifty years ago, but sanitary conditions have definitely improved, especially in tourist restaurants. Visitors who avoid Mexico's excellent fresh foods or live on packaged snacks and junk food are simply being unrealistic.

Warnings that all fresh foods should be cooked or peeled before eating are usually based on the myth that human waste ("nightsoil") is used as fertilizer. This is false. For better or worse, Mexican farmers use modern chemical fertilizers, herbicides and pesticides. We wash fresh food, both at home and in Mexico, to remove chemical residues and ordinary dirt. I don't wash bananas, however, because they are very easy to peel— but if I'm going to squeeze fruit for juice, I wash it well.

Relax—Mexico's fruit and produce are of far better quality and flavor than most of what we get at home.

Types of Restaurants

• **Expensive restaurants** are most easily identified by their clientele: Mexicans wearing designer clothes and tourists shaking their heads in confusion over the *menú* or poring over maps. Credit card signs in the window also indicate large bills.

Always check the *menú* (these restaurants are the only type that consistently have one, often posted outside) before committing yourself; it may send you running to the market.

The humble appearance of many **seafood restaurants** doesn't prevent them from charging relatively high prices. Check before you casually order a lobster dinner, though even obviously expensive seafood restaurants often have side dishes (fish soup, seafood cocktails, etc.) for reasonable prices.

Mexicans love seafood. It's a touching experience to see an entire family, from grandma to tiny children, move into a restaurant for several hours of intense seafood gorging. The bill for one of these feasts would feed a village for a month. (See *Seafood*, below.)

• The next category, the **businessman's restaurant**, is very similar throughout the world: good food, quite a bit of it, at reasonable prices. These are most commonly located in cities and usually near the plaza. The service in the early afternoon may be slow, as this is their most popular hour. If you order anything other than the *comida corrida* (daily special), your meal may be delayed while the ready-made food is served. The *comida* is usually served after 1 p.m. and could be sold out as early as 3 p.m. This meal is a good bargain, even in many expensive restaurants.

In large restaurants the *comida* is posted on a sign board or inserted in the menu; in other restaurants you'll have to ask. There may be a choice of main dishes and side dishes. If so, select something from each category, i.e., main dish, side dish, dessert and beverage. Don't ask for substitutions and don't expect to get everything on the list.

I call the *lonchería* or *comedor* "the people's restaurant." It doesn't offer comfort, atmosphere or an interesting view, just a constant production of good, inexpensive, traditional food. The service may be slow, the portions unequal and the selection very limited (they may not have a printed menu), but these restaurants are the wise traveler's most frequent and reasonable choice.

• **Resort restaurants** with names like "Pancho & Lefty's" or "Aztec Steak and Lobster" appeal directly to gringo tourists. As one Mexican restaurateur diplomatically phrased it, "You have 'delicate' stomachs." To reassure customers about their food and service, many resort restaurants deliberately Americanize themselves. Inducements such as menus in English, breakfast specials, two-for-one prices, salad bars and free cocktails with dinner are intended to make tourists feel comfortable and more at home, sometimes at the risk of caricaturing their "Mexican-ness." Some restaurants even post English-speaking "greeters" near the front entrance to lure timid Americans inside. They'll also employ at least one hostess or headwaiter fluent in English to seat American guests. The prices in these culturally confused establishments tend to be high, but the food is seldom better than average.

• **Specialty restaurants** such as Chinese, Italian, European, Middle Eastern (there are many Lebanese living in Mexico) and vegetarian are found in larger cities and tourist towns. Look in the *Paginas Amarillas* (Yellow Pages) for addresses, but whenever possible ask locally for a recommendation.

I'd advise every traveler, penny pincher or not, to allow themselves at least one "blow-out" meal. Many fine restaurants serve memorable meals for surprisingly reasonable prices; once again, keep in mind that a fancy decor isn't necessarily a reflection of what's going on behind the kitchen door. The cost of a splurge will be vastly inflated by expensive cocktails and bottles of wine, especially if from imported stock. Try a Mexican cocktail, wine or beer instead. (See *Booze and Cantinas*.)

Many gringo fast-food chains are opening in Mexico. Unless you need something familiar to cure a severe case of culture shock, stick with *real food*: Mexican.

• **Older hotels** and **boarding houses** often provide good bargain meals, especially the *comida corrida*. Some boarding houses, however, will serve only their own lodgers.

• *Fondas*, the restaurants or eating stalls found in the market, are another good choice for the adventurous eater. (In some areas small restaurants are called *Fondas* even if they're outside the market place.) As you wander past the *fondas* and their rows of steaming kettles, cauldrons and giant plates heaped with rice, chicken and other goodies, don't be embarrassed to ask prices and move on until you've found just exactly what you want. It's customary to peer into the pot, ask what is cooking and what it costs, and then do the same at an adjoining stall.

Because the cooks will often collar you and insist that you sample something, this can turn into a very enjoyable pastime. Getting away after a sip or a bite is the difficult part. I have been all but dragged to a table after expressing interest in the contents of a bubbling pot.

In the *fonda* you are usually faced with a choice of several main courses. Beans, rice and soup are also available, as are tortillas, bread and beverages. If you order a main course, you'll get it and nothing else. This probably won't fill you up, so you'll order a plate of rice and tortillas and perhaps soup, too. When you first asked the price, it sounded like the bargain meal of the year. However, after adding on the cost of your other dishes and a beer, you may find that the bill mounted up considerably. It was still an economical meal, but it was certainly no cheaper than a restaurant.

The answer to eating a filling and inexpensive meal isn't a secret word to the cook that will get you an extra leg of chicken; it's the tortilla. (See *Tortillas* under *What You'll Eat*, below.)

• **Temporary or improvised restaurants** often appear on the edge of carnivals, fairs, large weekly markets and in city streets. Business is brisk in the evening, with tables and benches appearing out of nowhere to block traffic. Old ladies and little girls furiously cook up chickens, soups, tacos and all of the other good things to be found in simple restaurants.

Prices vary considerably from one temporary restaurant to another, as do the selection and quality of food, so look around before sitting down to a meal.

• **Truck stops** are among Steve's favorite dining places. "I often eat at truck stops far from a town (they may not have a sign—just look for a few semis parked outside). You usually get a good meal at a cheap price. What a truck stop may lack in variety is made up in quantity.

"Another of my favorite roadside attractions are stands selling *pollos rostizados* (roast chickens). I'll buy a whole barbecued chicken in the morning and put it directly into the ice chest for lunch or dinner.

"By the way, in my experience food in Mexican restaurants is rarely awful—unlike some meals I've been served in the U.S. Even the most humble *comedor* usually has well-prepared and tasty food."

Street Food

What Steve fondly calls "street grunting" is one of our favorite ways to eat out. It covers everything that doesn't have to be eaten while sitting at a table, truly a vast and tasty area.

Anyone who stops at a sidewalk stand and drinks an orange juice or buys a taco and then eats it while wandering through the market is indulging in street grunting. To many people this is just grabbing a snack, but when done systematically it can be the source of regular meals. This doesn't mean that you'll have to live on popcorn, orange juice and tamales. Street grunting is an entire system of eating that eliminates much of the hassle and time involved with ordering, menus, tips and other restaurant rituals.

My introduction to street food came during my first visit to Mexico in a small town in Yucatán. A Mayan friend asked me if I wanted something for lunch and I said, "*Sí.*" Without consulting me further he went to a nearby street vendor selling meat from a glass box. The sides of the box were encrusted with spattered grease and the meat inside looked absolutely disgusting. I couldn't believe that I was going to have to eat it.

My friend smilingly handed me a fat *torta* (sandwich made with a French roll) wrapped in a piece of newspaper, dripping grease and pepper juice. Before I could make an excuse, I smelled the delicious aroma of pit-roasted turkey. From that moment on, I was hooked.

Economy is a very good reason to dine on the street. The *torta* I ate on the sidewalk would have cost two or three times as much in a restaurant. If you aren't overly concerned about comfort, you can buy the various parts of a meal from vendors and then find a bench or doorstep to eat them on. When a park or plaza is handy, your meal becomes a pleasant picnic. It is considered quite normal in Mexico to eat in public.

Select street food as carefully as you'd select a restaurant. If it doesn't look good, don't eat it. Indigestion rather than diarrhea is the street grunter's most common complaint. Eating pastries, a pig meat taco, then a warm beer followed by a fried banana will have your stomach crying, "Take it back!" and leave you a quivering wreck for hours.

Once you've developed a sixth sense for sanitation, broaden your eating horizons by sampling unknown foods. The worst I've tried was fried worms, and the best a strange avocado paste served on a sweet roll. Avid street grunters should study the foods described in the *Market* chapter for more eating possibilities.

Mexican Fast-Food Tips

• Take a container to the market and have it filled with fresh juice. Juice tastes much better while traveling than a lukewarm cola. When fresh juice is not available or cannot be kept for as long as you wish, stop at a CONASUPO store or *tienda* and stock up on canned juices.

• Go to eating stalls in the market or small restaurants with a container and buy cooked rice and beans *para llevar* (to go). This precooked food will form the basis for a great number of meals, all quick to make and quite good. Ready-made *tortas* (see *Restaurants and Typical Foods: What You'll Eat*) are inexpensive, and are perfect for lunches or a quick dinner before going to bed.

Fresh bread, cheese and tortillas are available almost everywhere and are good supplements for beans, rice and eggs.

Very good quick meals can be made using *bistec de res aplanada* (flattened beefsteaks) and *carne de res molida* (ground beef). Both can be made into *tortas*, cooked with beans, rice, macaroni, spaghetti, potatoes or served with fried eggs.

Warning: It grieves me to report that studies of what bureaucrats call "ambulatory food stalls" show a high incidence of nasty bacteria. The Mexican government is trying to educate food vendors in the rites and rituals of sanitation, but it's a big job. Street grunting involves a certain amount of risk, if only from indigestion. You don't have to get sick, however, especially if you follow our well-tested recommendations in the *Health* chapter.

Ordering a Meal

One of the most difficult things about eating in Mexico is understanding exactly what you are ordering and what you're likely to get. Direct translations of menus may be misleading. The words might be correct, but often the resulting food won't be anything like you expected.

You want coffee with cream before breakfast. Your friend sees *café con leche* (coffee with milk) on the menu and says authoritatively, "That must be it. They just don't have cream."

Not being a skeptic you agree. You order and begin waiting impatiently; you want your coffee immediately and can't understand what the delay is about.

When your breakfast arrives, there's still no sign of the coffee. Finally a waiter sets a tall glass in front of you. He begins to pour hot black coffee, watching you expectantly.

When the glass is half full and he's begun to look at you rather oddly, you smile nervously and nod your head. He immediately stops pouring.

As you're reaching for the coffee the waiter grabs your wrist and quickly fills the glass to the brim with hot milk from a teapot.

"What is this?" you moan. "He's just ruined my cup of coffee!"

What happened? This is the way *café con leche* is traditionally served. The problem was the tourist's assumption that coffee with milk would come out looking like coffee with cream in Dayton, Ohio.

The coffee came during breakfast rather than immediately because that too is the custom. Very few Mexicans would think of drinking coffee on an empty stomach.

• **When ordering, speak slowly and clearly.** Never subject people serving you to a long blast of imperfect Spanish that cannot possibly be understood completely. If they don't understand everything, chances are they'll delete the vague parts and not worry about it. This means that you may get coffee and bread instead of coffee, fried fish, rice, milk and bread.

Was your request for a club sandwich rewarded with a blank stare? Repeat your order slowly, clearly and in a normal tone of voice. Still no luck? Be patient; if you raise your voice or look obviously upset, you'll probably just rattle the server or even frighten her off entirely.

Remember, it is the custom in Mexico to show great patience when two people don't understand each other. Mexicans won't sneer or laugh at your efforts to order food in Spanish. Return the favor by being considerate of their limited knowledge of English.

• **Keep it simple.** Unless the server demonstrates an obvious fluency in English, your detailed questions about the *chilaquiles* or the garbanzo soup will only confuse the issue. It also helps to keep in mind that if there's confusion over an order, you may literally eat any mistakes.

I once derailed a waiter struggling to master "Menu English" when I casually said, "I'll have that too." I was referring to the breakfast my companion had just ordered. "You . . . two?" the young man asked, obviously puzzled. "Yes. Me too." Not catching his confusion, I responded absentmindedly. "I would like that breakfast, too." "Two . . . " he repeated carefully. Sure enough, I was soon served two complete and identical breakfasts.

• **Make up your mind before ordering.** We've learned the hard way that it is risky to discuss your order in Spanish in front of the person serving you—you may get everything you read aloud or whatever sticks in the server's mind.

The quickest way to rattle a server is to change your order. This is especially risky when dining with a group. For some reason—perhaps pride—Mexican servers often rely on memory rather than writing orders down. When half a dozen hungry gringos rattle off volleys of rapid English or imperfect Spanish, changing their orders and asking questions about the chili sauce, the results can be quite interesting, "Ugh! Who ordered these corn fungus tacos? Carl? These must be yours!"

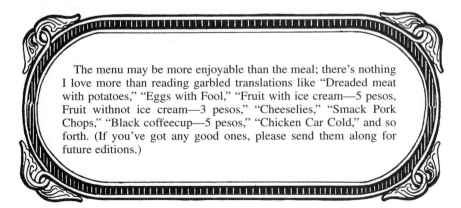

The menu may be more enjoyable than the meal; there's nothing I love more than reading garbled translations like "Dreaded meat with potatoes," "Eggs with Fool," "Fruit with ice cream—5 pesos, Fruit withnot ice cream—3 pesos," "Cheeselies," "Smack Pork Chops," "Black coffeecup—5 pesos," "Chicken Car Cold," and so forth. (If you've got any good ones, please send them along for future editions.)

• **Combine group orders.** If you're with a group, one person should give all of the orders and attempt to combine them; for example, three orders of fried fish, two coffees, one salad, etc. This is the golden rule for groups of four or more persons. When dining en masse, be especially careful about mobbing the server with orders. Since the waiter or waitress rarely writes down the orders, no matter how complex they may be it is quite common to be served one dish and then to be asked again what else it was that you wanted.

When we take a large, lively group into a restaurant, I take the further precaution of noting each person's order on a piece of paper. I then review this carefully with the server. They usually appreciate this, since mistakes have a way of reducing *propinas* (tips). Once our food arrives, the list reminds the group what they ordered. This takes care of the people who try to claim my shrimp cocktail when I know they ordered tuna salad.

• **Order what the menu offers.** Asking a Mexican kitchen to alter a recipe or to substitute noodles for beans is simply asking for trouble. In most Mexican restaurants, what-you-see (on the menu) is-what-you-get. Unless the *cocinero* (cook) is a true chef, such simple instructions, as "Please put the eggs on top of the hotcakes" can have the most surprising results.

"*On top?*" the waitress repeated disbelievingly. "On top of the hotcakes? You want me to put the . . . "

"Yes! *¡Sí!* On top!"

Ten minutes later she slid my breakfast across the table as gingerly as a land mine. The meal was exactly as I'd ordered: two perfectly fried eggs, sunny-side up, *on their own plate*, were balanced carefully on top of a thick stack of buttered hotcakes.

Eating in a Mexican restaurant, from the most lavish to the most humble, is never a cut-and-dried experience. An element of suspense lingers about everything, from the intensity of the hot sauce to what you're actually going to be served. Like a magician the cook will change your order of tacos to enchiladas, your tea to coffee and your bread to tortillas.

Steve and I once decided to splurge and order a seafood plate. We were literally drooling at the thought and waited very impatiently for over an hour. The waiter assured us repeatedly that dinner was just about ready. It came with a great clatter of bowls, plates and tableware.

"What," I howled, "do you call *this?*"

Steve stared blankly at the meal in front of him.

The waiter caught our looks of disbelief and whisked to the table, "Oh!" he said calmly. "There was no seafood, just this."

Steve gave me his "Well, after all this is Mexico" shrug and dug into a bowl of tripe soup while I attacked a boiled shoulder of goat.

• **Ask what there is.** Even if you're given a menu, it's best to ask "*¿Qúe hay?*" ("What is there?") before making any agonizing decisions. Menus, especially in small restaurants, often reflect what the owner would *like* to offer rather than what is actually available.

In a small village restaurant we learned another quirk of ordering a meal. Our mistake was asking if they had chicken instead of just asking what was available.

"Oh, yes!" the owner said, signaling to his teenage son. While they went into a whispering huddle in a corner we sipped our drinks and wondered what was up.

"*¡Momentito!*" the man called encouragingly. A few seconds later the son flashed by the open doorway on a clattering bicycle.

"Steve," I said, "Do you get the odd feeling that . . ."

"Yeah," he answered, staring sourly at the table. Half an hour later the kid was back, a squawking rooster clutched under one arm, its feet lashed with a piece of red cloth. The boy gave us a wink as he ran into the back of the restaurant.

"That was chicken you ordered, correct?" the owner asked, anxiously hovering over us in case we'd changed our minds. Steve shrugged his shoulders; why not? We'd already waited this long.

"*Sí,*" he answered.

The man turned, yelled out "*¡Sí!*" and before the word had echoed off the high ceiling, a brutal *Chop! Squawk!* and a convulsive rustling of feathers was heard from the kitchen.

I looked at Steve; something seemed to have stuck in his throat. "Well," I said, "At least we didn't order a pork chop."

If you're looking for a dining adventure, try ordering "*Lo que sea*" ("Whatever there is," often an option in small restaurants). Requesting *Lo que sea* can also speed things up considerably, as you'll usually get whatever's ready and on the stove. While living with a family that operated a modest restaurant, we ate much better by sharing their meals rather than ordering less appetizing dishes from the menu. I tried to convince them that they should throw out their menu and just serve traditional family recipes, but they thought I'd lost my mind. "Everyone *asks* for this type of meal!" the lady of the house protested. "It's not my fault if I can't cook it well. Anyway, they eat it!"

• **Don't be timid about sharing.** Portions in most resort restaurants are about twenty years behind the times; in other words, *servings are large*. Ask for a second plate and tell the waiter, "*Vamos a compartir.*" ("We're going to share.")

• **Take your time and enjoy your meal.** If you expect quick, American-style service you can expect to be frustrated. To Mexicans, restaurants aren't just pit stops in the fast lane of life, they are places to savor good food and drink, as well as social centers and unofficial community clubs. Meals are traditionally a time to relax and slow down, to chat with friends and family over a long, leisurely meal. Like a picnic in the country or an afternoon at the beach, visiting a restaurant is an event, to be prolonged rather than rushed. In such an easy-going atmosphere, quick service simply isn't needed or even appreciated.

Our friend Sergio Legarreta observes that, "Gringos are sometimes insulted by service that we Mexicans take entirely for granted."

Ramón, a popular headwaiter with over thirty years of restaurant experience on both sides of the border, pointed out another common misunderstanding. "Compared to Mexicans, Americans are very shy about asking for things," he said. "Especially if they don't speak Spanish or aren't sure if we understand English. This glass of water, for example. We don't always put it on the table because most Mexicans drink water after their meal, not before."

Ramón went on to give a definition of "good service" that neatly explains how simple differences between gringos and *mexicanos* can lead to complaints.

"In the United States," he said, "a good waiter is supposed to anticipate your every need. In Mexico, a good waiter tries, on the contrary, to fulfill your every *request*. Waiters stand around not because we are lazy, but because we are waiting to be told what you'd like us to do. Tell us what you want," Ramón concluded, "and we'll do our best to get it."

To attract a server's attention, call out "*Señor*," "*Señorita*" or "*¡Por favor!*" ("Please!"). "Excuse me?" in English will also do the trick. Though Americans may think it slightly rude, Mexicans frequently summon help with a brief hiss. It definitely is rude, however, to whistle for service or to snap your fingers.

We sat down in a typical *lonchería* for a relaxed meal. A young guy took our orders, then asked what we wanted to drink: Coke or Pepsi?

"*Coca*," I answered clearly.

"There is none," he said without smiling.

I hesitated for a second and changed my order to Pepsi.

"Warm or cold?" he asked.

"Cold," I answered.

"There are none cold." he said.

"Then give me a warm one," I answered, suddenly very weary of the whole thing.

"*Sí, señor*," he said very politely and brought me a cold Coke.

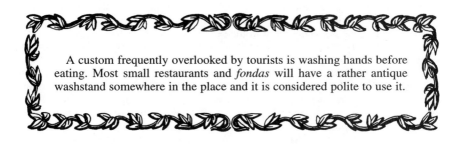

A custom frequently overlooked by tourists is washing hands before eating. Most small restaurants and *fondas* will have a rather antique washstand somewhere in the place and it is considered polite to use it.

Paying Up

• **It is the custom to present the bill only when the customer asks for it.** Servers are very careful not to rush their customers or to appear impatient if a group "camps" at a table. Lingering over coffee, ordering "just one more" dessert or treating friends to yet another last drink are all common ways to politely delay ending the meal. Asking for the bill is a clear signal that the party is over. Request the bill at least ten minutes before you are ready to leave: "*La cuenta, por favor*" ("The bill, please"). A discreet hand motion, as if signing a check, will also be understood.

We once explained to a Mexican waitress that gringo restaurants usually present their bill even before the customer has finished eating. The woman's eyes widened in horror. Throwing up her hands, she cried, "*¡Qué barbaro!*" ("How barbaric!") When I added that many American restaurants plainly prefer that customers not linger around after eating, she shook her head in frank disbelief.

"In Mexico," the waitress said proudly, "such abuses are not tolerated!"

• **It is customary for one person to pay the entire bill.** Asking for individual checks only invites confusion and delays. People who do the "I had the rice and you had the beans and you had three tortillas . . ." routine often find that in the confusion, they actually pay more than if they'd settled on one communal bill. Among Mexicans there is almost always a big show of whipping out the money and paying for everyone.

• **Pricier restaurants may add tax and service to the bill.** In "better" places, charges for *servicio* or *propinas* (tips) will be fifteen to twenty percent. Mexico's value-added tax, called IVA, runs another six to fifteen percent. Rather than confuse their tourist clientele with IVA entries, however, most businesses include the IVA tax in menu prices.

• **Look the bill over and verify the total.** Mistakes are seldom deliberate but they do occur. There's nothing wrong with taking a few moments to roughly total up the charges. Busy tourist restaurants and places with a high turnover of customers are the most obvious places to double-check *la cuenta*. In your hotel restaurant, signing for the check rather than paying in cash helps prevent padding and gives you an itemized receipt.

Were you served everything that you ordered? The most common mistake I've found on bills is a tendency to charge customers for side dishes and drinks that didn't actually reach the table. Again, this is more often due to a server's haphazard memory, rather than an attempt to pad the bill.

Small neighborhood restaurants and cafés often won't itemize a bill or the server may just quote a total figure. In most tourist places, however, the bill will be written out and itemized.

• **Don't raise the roof over billing errors.** If you call attention to an apparent error, it is the custom to be diplomatic rather than blunt, especially in public. This benefits both ways: gringos who shout first and double-check their math later look very foolish when the mistake is shown to be their own.

All it should take is a quiet word to the server or cashier. "There might be an error here," or "Please, is this correct?" are polite ways to call for another accounting. Give the other person plenty of time to do a face-saving double-check. If a mistake is found, a simple, *"No hay de que,"* ("It's nothing") or *"Muy bien,"* is the best way to close the matter.

A few years ago I heard tourists in Puerto Vallarta complain loud and hard about a mysterious five percent "tax" on their restaurant bills. In each incident the staff explained that restaurants were being encouraged to give their customers a five percent rebate as part of a nationwide program to reduce inflation. A more careful reading of the bill would have saved these folks a great deal of embarrassment. Rather than a charge, the five percent entry on the check was actually a deduction.

Tips

• **Tip the same as you would at home, ten to fifteen percent.** When using a credit card, I usually leave a tip in cash rather than adding it to my credit card bill. Though the management will pass credit card tips along to the staff, I prefer to give a more direct and personal reward for good service, especially if I'll be eating there again soon.

If you eat in one place often, generous tips can make it much easier to order, especially if you're having difficulty with the language. The distracted fifteen-year-old waitress who barely listened the day before will take a new interest in your welfare if she decides it's worth the effort.

In most of the smaller restaurants where we eat, any tip at all would be considered something of an event. The nicest tip I've seen was given by two produce truck drivers who met for lunch at a roadside café. One driver left a cantaloupe, the other a cabbage.

• **Compliment the food.** Although Mexicans tend to be as shy with compliments as they are with complaints, don't hesitate to express your appreciation for good food and service. Your compliments may bring embarrassed smiles or even puzzled looks, but this is one gringo custom that is seldom misunderstood. It doesn't have to be long or eloquent to make your point: a simple "*¡Muy rico!*" ("Very rich, tasty!") or "*¡Muy bueno!*" ("Very good!") says it all.

Vegetarians

The eating potential for vegetarians is almost unlimited. The variety and quality of fresh fruits and vegetables in the average market are excellent, as are the nuts, seeds, fresh juices and dairy products.

Unfortunately, all the wonderful food you'll see in the market doesn't look quite the same after it's been processed through a typical restaurant kitchen. Mexicans prefer well-cooked food and few vegetables are served raw or even steamed.

Fortunately (for vegetarians), the Mexican craving for meat is strongly tempered by its cost, and many dishes are almost all vegetable. This is especially true in cheaper restaurants where the so-called meat dish may not be recognized as such by either vegetarian or carnivore. Tortillas, both at home and in a restaurant, make up the bulk of a poor person's meal.

The majority of Mexicans practice what I call "reluctant vegetarianism," eating meat only when they can afford it, which is often never. Others are giving up flesh for reasons of health, and vegetarian restaurants are opening across the country. Your best bet for a genuine vegetarian meal will be in a city or tourist resort. Look in the phone book or ask for suggestions at tourist information offices and health food shops.

Vegetarian restaurants that cater to students, wage earners and travelers are moderately priced. As always, the *comida corrida* will be the best deal.

Thanks to its relatively high cost and a growing awareness of cholesterol's hazards, lard is no longer commonly used in Mexican kitchens. The main exceptions are restaurants that specialize in *comida típica* (traditional dishes) and rural households. *Campesinos* almost always have a pig or two in the backyard—and a huge "cannibal pot" nearby for rendering pork fat into lard.

Because the flavor of *manteca* (lard) is highly esteemed, however, asking a cook, "Do these beans have lard in them?" can backfire. Even if the food was actually prepared with vegetable oil or shortening, the answer might still be, "Yes, we use lard." Again, lard is considered to be *muy rico* (very rich, flavorful) and therefore *good*.

If the food is too greasy for your taste, garnish it with lime juice or chili. Lorena swears that eating chilies helps her to avoid a heavy feeling in the stomach after "pigging out."

Eating a cheap non-meat meal is quite easy; corn, beans, rice, tomatoes, onions, chilies, eggs and cheese are all commonly served. This diet is nutritious, but many travelers soon tire of it. At this point, salvation lies in the direction of the market, where juices, nuts, raw vegetables and fruits should keep the vegetarian well fed and content.

Travelers who are prepared to do their own cooking will find that it's quite easy and inexpensive to follow a vegetarian diet. Traveling in remote areas, however, often means that food of any type is limited and more expensive. High in the mountains, for example, the menu runs heavily to the Aztec staples—especially corn, beans, rice, eggs and chilies.

Because few Mexicans voluntarily give up meat, they find it amazing that anyone else would either. Lorena's best explanation, though not the most accurate, is, "It's my religion." Even hardheaded meat eaters accept that as legitimate. In restaurants we usually don't have the time or energy for long explanations and confusion reigns.

"She would like something without meat," I say to the waitress, completing my order and Steve's, ending with Lorena's since it will be a hassle.

There is a long silence. The waitress doesn't understand.

"What do you have without meat?" I repeat. "Anything?"

"Beans?" she asks, looking utterly confused.

"Don't you have anything besides beans?"

"One moment, please!" she says, rushing off to the kitchen. A few minutes later she returns triumphant.

"We have *menudo!*" she says, eyeing Lorena expectantly.

"What's *menudo?*" Lorena asks.

"Tripe," Steve says.

"Please," I beg the waitress, "that is meat. She wants something without any meat, without any meat *at all*."

"Tacos?" the girl asks, obviously beyond reach but trying to please us and end this ordeal so she can get back to her comic book.

"What kind do you have?" Lorena asks.

"Pork, chicken and sausage," she answers calmly.

"But those are meat!" I say, wishing Lorena would accept beans and forget this circus.

"One moment, please!" and she runs off to the kitchen. She returns in a few minutes, again triumphant but obviously cautious.

"*Mama* says she has tacos without meat!"

"What are they?" I ask. "Chicken?"

"No," she says proudly. "Beans!"

"Look," I say. "How about an order of chicken tacos but without any chicken or meat or *menudo* in them. Just chicken tacos without the chicken, OK?"

"*Sí, señor,* " she says politely, drifting from the table with looks of distrust. Then, when a safe distance away, she runs into the kitchen for the final time. Half an hour later she throws a plate in front of Lorena and retreats quickly.

"She did it!" Lorena says happily. "Cheese, beans, cabbage, cooked potato and chili sauce but not a bit of chicken."

When the meal is finished, we ask for the bill. The waitress computes out loud, adding it up on her fingers as she goes around the table from plate to plate. She stops at Lorena's plate—a look of panic crosses her face.

"One order of chicken tacos," she says.

"Wait!" I protest. "There was no chicken in those tacos; they can't cost as much as ours."

She stands staring at the empty plates until her mouth opens and she shrieks, half hysterically, "*¡MAMA!*"

Mama comes trucking out of the kitchen, wiping greasy hands on a newspaper, preparing to do battle with the gringo maniacs who are destroying her tranquillity and her daughter's tenuous grip on sanity.

"Something wrong?" she says sweetly. "Was the food alright?"

"Delicious!" I answer. "I just thought that chicken tacos without chicken," and I motion to Lorena's plate, "should not cost the same as chicken tacos with chicken. Right?"

"Wrong, *señor!*" she says firmly. "I only took the chicken out as a favor to the *señorita,*" and she smiles heavily towards Lorena. "They were still chicken tacos. Do I charge less if you ask me to leave out the chile?"

We stare at our plates as mother and daughter beam happily. As an after-thought the *señora* says, "And anyway, everyone knows that chicken is not meat at all! It isn't red!"

• **Stay healthy: avoid meat.** Over the years I've noticed a curious correlation between my diet and my health. Almost against my will, it gradually became obvious that delicious meals of *bistek*, *carnitas* and *barbacoa* often led to gastric distress and Pepto

Bismol. In fact, the evidence was overwhelming: the less meat I ate while in Mexico (and at home), the less I experienced diarrhea, indigestion and other health problems. As a result, I became an "almost vegetarian," eating meat only when I felt it was too awkward to refuse—or just too tempting to turn down. Though I'm not as hard-core a vegetarian as Lorena, the improvement in my overall well-being has been dramatic. In fact, I continue to reduce the amount of meat I eat, especially while traveling.

What You'll Eat

"Without a placemat and a knife and a spoon, a papaya, like a mango, can be successfully managed only while naked in a bath tub."
—Charles Flandrau, **Viva Mexico** (1908)

First-time visitors to Mexico are often boggled by the variety of dishes offered from one restaurant and region to another. If your idea of Mexican food is tacos and enchiladas, be prepared for a pleasant surprise.

One of the main reasons that true Mexican dishes are not available outside the country is the incredible amount of work and time that go into their preparation. A good *mole* sauce, for example, might take as long as a week to prepare and contain thirty ingredients or more. Special utensils and processes, such as the time-consuming and wearying grinding of corn with a *mano* and *metate* (stone hand roller and grinding stone), make it impractical to serve genuinely Mexican dishes in the U.S. In fact, most Mexican restaurants will only offer things requiring elaborate preparation on certain days of the week. Look for signs hanging in the window or on the door that say "*Hoy Mole*" ("*Mole* Today") or the name of some other special meal.

Tourists often make the mistake of ordering the same dishes time after time. This is an easy habit to fall into, especially if your Spanish is weak or your palate is having a difficult time adjusting. On my first trip to Mexico I lived almost entirely on broiled chicken and bread and it was a major effort to plow through an order of *chiles rellenos*.

You will notice that menus change from area to area. Many regional dishes and styles of cooking are quite different from each other and should be tried: look for *platos regionales* (regional dishes) or for dishes identified by the name of a city or state (*a la oaxaqueña, a la veracruzana*, and so on).

Tortillas

Tortillas have been around for thousands of years and are the Staff of Life in Mexico. Tortillas are round cooked cakes of corn or wheat flour, about as heavy as blotter paper, which is what I thought they tasted like when I first tried one. They range in diameter from a few inches across to what seems to be a few feet, but the standard size is about five inches across.

The best tortillas are made by hand, a long and laborious task that occupies many of the waking hours of legions of Mexican women. The rhythmic "pat-pat-pat" as the cakes are formed has been called Mexico's heartbeat. The traditional process involves soaking kernels of corn in lime water to form *nixtamal* (like hominy). This is ground on a stone *metate* into dough, called *masa*. The *masa* is shaped into small balls and then patted out by hand into tortillas, which are then cooked on a *comal*, a round flat earthenware or metal griddle. It seems very simple, at least until you try it yourself. (See *Our Favorite Mexican Recipes*.)

Did you know that the two apparently identical sides of a tortilla are actually quite different? One side is much thinner than the other and is called the *pancita*, the belly. When rolling a tortilla around a filling or piece of food the *pancita* faces inward and the *espalada*, the thicker "back" is on the outside. To the woman who explained this to us, it was as obvious as the difference between crust and bread.

Tortilla technology has advanced to the point of mechanized factories, churning out tortillas that taste as bland as enriched white bread. Some short cuts, however don't noticeably affect the quality of a well-made tortilla: power-operated *nixtamal* grinders and small wooden or metal presses. Among good Mexican cooks, though, anything ground by machine is considered of poorer taste and quality.

Corn tortillas commonly come in two colors: white and yellow. White tortillas are made from lighter shades of corn and are generally preferred over the yellow ones. A Mexican friend explained to me that yellow corn is associated with the poorer classes, especially Indians. Some people, myself included, prefer the yellow tortillas, much as some prefer dark whole grain breads to those made from bleached flour. It is not uncommon, when eating with poorer people to have them apologize for serving yellow tortillas. When I tell them that I prefer the darker tortillas, they usually admit that they have more vitamins and "give more sustenance."

Blue and red tortillas, called *prietas*, are made from naturally colored corn and considered a special treat. They are rarely served in restaurants. Food coloring may also be added to the *masa* for a special fiesta. There's nothing like beans and pink or green tortillas to fill you up fast.

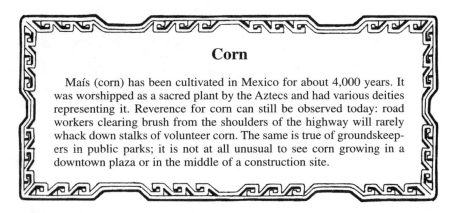

Corn

Maís (corn) has been cultivated in Mexico for about 4,000 years. It was worshipped as a sacred plant by the Aztecs and had various deities representing it. Reverence for corn can still be observed today: road workers clearing brush from the shoulders of the highway will rarely whack down stalks of volunteer corn. The same is true of groundskeepers in public parks; it is not at all unusual to see corn growing in a downtown plaza or in the middle of a construction site.

Tortillas that are only about three inches in diameter and quite thin are served on special occasions, to be eaten with tasty snacks. They are also served in the type of ostentatious restaurant that doesn't allow common tortillas to cross the threshold.

Flour tortillas, usually white but sometimes made of whole wheat, are typical of northern Mexico and are rarely seen in the south, except at altitudes where corn will not grow. Flour tortillas are now commonly sold in supermarkets, prepackaged and frozen.

Tortillas can be purchased from *tortillerías* (tortilla factories) or in and around the market from women and girls who bring them from home to sell. You can find the most appealing and then barter. They are sold individually and by the dozen. These tortillas are almost always far superior to factory-made, though watch out for women reselling factory tortillas if you want handmade.

Tortillerías must legally close for one day a week, but they try to stagger it so that a constant supply is assured.

A kilo will feed several tourists or one or two Mexicans. Fortunately, they can be purchased in smaller amounts such as a *medio* (half-kilo), *cuarto* (quarter-kilo) or by the tortilla.

In *fondas* (market eating stalls), the tortillas are generally supplied by little old ladies who go from stall to stall, insisting that the diners feel the texture of the tortillas, test them for proper warmth and buy more than they can possibly eat. Other restaurants usually include all the tortillas you can eat in the price of the meal. Don't hesitate to ask for more.

Portions served in more humble restaurants often seem very small to the tourist. When you order pork and get one thin rib, you begin to wonder how you're going to get full. The answer is tortillas. By making a Poverty Taco—slivers of meat or tiny amounts of other foods wrapped in three or four tortillas—you'll find the most meager dishes filling and satisfying.

Tortillas are not only cheap, they turn a simple bowl of beans and chilies into a very nourishing, balanced meal. Poor people often have to forgo the luxury of beans and will dine on plain tortillas and salt.

Learn to use tortillas as eating utensils. It is quite proper to tear meat apart with your fingers to make tacos. Watch other people; the techniques vary throughout the country. A really basic restaurant will offer only spoons and tortillas; forks are unnecessary.

Bread

Pan, the Spanish word for bread, usually refers to the *bolillo*, a French-style roll (called *pan francés* in Yucatán). Sliced *pan Bimbo*, a tasteless brand of white bread, is also served in some restaurants. Plain toasted bread is called *pan tostado* or *pan dorado*. *Pan dulce* (sweet bread or cake) may be served in the morning. If a basket of sweet rolls or cake is placed on the table, you will pay only for those that are eaten. (There's rarely any charge for *bolillos* or *Bimbo*, except in *fondas*.)

Butter (*mantequilla*) is seldom offered except in fancier restaurants, and even then you may get margarine (*margarina*).

Chilies

Because many tourists tend to overemphasize that they don't want anything *con chile*, many restaurants automatically hold back the delicious sauces that they customarily serve with meals. It's a shame not to give them a try. The majority of people who add chili to their food eventually become quite fond of it. (Chilies are an excellent source of vitamin C. See the *Markets* chapter, for more on chilies.)

If you want chilies or sauce, ask for chilies, *salsa* or *salsa picante* (hot sauce).

When you're given a bottle of hot sauce (some of the regionally brewed concoctions are very good) and prefer something made fresh, ask for *salsa casera*.

Mexicans firmly believe that chilies improve the appetite and aid digestion. However, experience has taught me to go easy until my body has built up a tolerance for them. Some of the milder varieties, such as the *chile poblano*, can be eaten in quantities that fool the mouth but devastate the stomach and lower regions. Don't get overconfident just because it doesn't burn at first. For a flaming mouth, the best cure is to eat salt and bread. Drinking orange juice also helps to cool the chili burn.

Pimienta negra (ground black pepper) is rarely on the table, but they will probably have it in the kitchen if you ask.

Meats

The most common meat (*carne*) dish is *bistec* (also called *bistek* or *biftec*), a general term for anything resembling a steak, even if cut from the side of a tuna. You must specify what type of *bistec* you wish: *bistec de res* (beefsteak), *bistec de puerco* (pork steak), *bistec de pescado* (fish steak), etc.

A *bistec de res* is not at all similar to a typical beefsteak in the U.S. It is thin, cooked well done and usually tough.

Steaks served with sauces of tomato, chilies and other ingredients are called *bistec de res ranchero* and *bistec de res estilo mexicano*. A steak may be named after an area of the country (*bistec tampiqueño*, *bistec norteño*, etc.), but most of these just have a variation in the sauce.

Filet mignon is sometimes offered, even in smaller places, and will be called *filete mignon* or *miñón*. Don't confuse filet mignon with *filete*, another term for ordinary *bistec*. Tenderloin is called *lomo* or *lomito*. These finer cuts rarely cost much more than regular steaks and are almost always better eating. One of the best steaks I've ever tasted was served to me in a small middle-of-nowhere town. When I saw *filet miñón* on the menu, it seemed so unlikely that I immediately had to try it. When it came, wrapped in bacon and beautifully grilled, I could hardly believe my eyes.

The other *bistecs*—pork, fish, venison and turtle—are served in forms similar to those of beef. *Bistec de venado* (venison) is very common in the Yucatán Peninsula. *Bistec de tortuga* (turtle, also *caguama*) is sold by seafood restaurants when available. Although it tastes good, eating a piece of turtle meat definitely contributes to their extinction. Mexican fishermen are killing turtles indiscriminately—and illegally—because of the demand in restaurants. *Huevos de tortuga* (turtle eggs) may also be served. I think the practice of eating turtle eggs is particularly stupid because they really don't taste very good.

"Save a Turtle; Eat a Fish."

I cut my teeth, so to speak, on *milanesa*. Thin breaded cutlets of beef, pork and veal (*milanesa de res*, *puerco* and *ternero*, respectively) are usually much more tender than a plain fried steak and are equivalent to an American "chicken-fried steak."

Stuff a French-style roll (*bolillo*) with a batter-fried steak and you've got a *torta de milanesa*, a tasty cure for a hamburger craving. Even if this popular *torta* is not on the menu, they'll usually whip one up.

Carne asada is grilled meat, usually a beefsteak, though once again it may be pork, goat (*cabrito*), venison or turtle. Meat prepared *asada* is often tough but flavorful. When grilled over charcoal, it is called *al carbón*.

Chuletas de puerco (pork chops) taste better than pork chops in the U.S. *Chuletas de puerco ahumadas* (smoked pork chops) are very delicious.

Carne de chango (monkey meat) fools many tourists and travel writers who believe they are dining on some endangered primate. The meat is actually cured ham. The best "monkey meat" is cured in a kind of tropical fruit jam and then smoked. It's outrageous.

Guisados are meat stews of various types, cooked with or without other ingredients (chilies, vegetables, etc.) and served either wet or dry, hot or cold. The meat is usually much more tender than a *bistec*.

Caldo de olla and *puchero* are stews that might be compared to a New England Boiled Dinner, if you aren't from New England.

Salpicón de venado (or *de res, puerco* or *tortuga*) is cold cooked meat mixed with chilies. A variation of this, usually made with ground beef, raw or cooked, is called *picadillo*. The first time I blithely gorged down a dish of *salpicón de venado*, I almost fainted from lack of breath. This was long after I considered myself quite immune to such embarrassing scenes as pouring sugar or jugs of water into my mouth to quell the flames. My downfall in this case was the dreaded *chile habanero* from the Yucatán. It's known to the Maya as the "crying tongue" chili and should be considered dangerous.

Carne adobada, adobo and *cecina* are meats cured with chilies and other spices. *Cecina* may be dried quite hard and then fried before serving, usually in a sauce. These dishes can be tough on a tender stomach.

Carne machaca is cured and dried meat, usually beef, shredded and served in sauces and with eggs.

Albóndigas are very tasty meatballs.

Carnes en alambres, sometimes called *carne en brochete* (shish-ka-bob), is usually made of beef or lamb (*carnero*).

Barbacoa (barbecued meat) is not prepared as in the U.S. The meat is placed in a container, covered with *maguey* or banana leaves, then buried beneath a slow fire or with hot stones. (Our version of barbecue is more similar to *carne asado* or *al carbón*).

Cochinita pibil (barbecued pig) is a specialty of Yucatán. The meat is coated with a sauce of oranges and spices before it is interred in the *pib* (pit). This gives the *pibil* meat a delicious and distinctive flavor. Turkeys and deer (*pavo* and *venado*) are also cooked *pibil*-style.

Birria (*carnero* in some areas) is goat or mutton barbecued Mexican-style. Most stands serving it will display the skull (usually with horns) to let the customers know that the meat isn't pork.

Carnitas are made by rendering a pig, from tail to snout, in a huge, oil-filled cauldron. After a batch of *carnitas* has been prepared, it is arranged in a pile with all of the skin, intestines, ears and odds and ends heaped over the lean meat. Ask for *carne maciza* (lean meat) and the vendor will root through the stuff (avert your eyes if you must) and extract a delicious loin or shoulder. You can also ask for *pura carne* (pure meat) or *carne sin grasa* (meat without fat) to get lean meat.

If you don't care what you get, ask for *surtido* and you'll be given a selection of everything from ears to ribs. It all costs the same.

The meat is prepared with great care and is cooked at a high temperature, usually just hours before it is sold. By avoiding large pieces of fat, meat that is obviously old or a particularly dirty stand, you should never suffer from indigestion after eating *carnitas*. (Unless, of course, you follow my example and overeat.)

Carnitas can be ordered by the weight (*kilo, medio kilo, 100 gramos*, etc.) or by the amount you want to spend. There is no savings by buying large quantities.

Start by ordering *cien gramos* per person (Steve comments, "*Cien gramos*?? I order at least a kilo if I'm by myself! But then look at my waistline!") Keep in mind that *carnitas* wrapped in tortillas will make very filling tacos. If you eat chilies, the vendor usually throws them in, free of charge. Chilies help digest the grease. Ask where you can buy tortillas and get about *un cuarto* (one-fourth of a kilo) per person, or less if you're not really famished. Those who don't care for tortillas can buy *bolillos* instead. If you'd like something to drink with your meal, it is considered proper to take your food into a small restaurant, *fonda* or *cantina* and order beverages. They will often offer you a plate, napkins and salt for your meal.

Around a *carnita* or *barbacoa* stand you'll frequently see ladies selling tortillas, chiles, *salsas* and *nopalitos* to those buying meat. *Nopalitos* are chopped cactus leaves often mixed with onion, garlic, herbs and lime juice. They are naturally slimy but have an agreeable flavor and mix well with *carnitas*. They also make a nourishing vegetarian taco by themselves.

Chicharrones (pig skins or cracklings) are sold in meat shops, *carnitas* stands and on the street by wandering vendors. I prefer to buy *chicharrones* from the *carnitas* stand, on the assumption that they were probably cooked with the meat and therefore should be fresh. A large piece makes a handy improvised plate for your *carnitas*. When you've finished the meat, you can eat the plate, salty and soaked in chili juice and pork drippings.

There are many other kinds of meat sold for immediate street eating. One of my favorite choices is to visit a stand with a charcoal brazier over which the vendor or the customer cooks raw meat, usually strips of beef.

Armadillo, venison, fish and other less identifiable animals are also sold precooked, most commonly in markets and small towns with a strong Indian influence.

In southern Mexico you may be offered *tepescuintle*. It is a delicious meat, even if it is from the *agouti*, a raccoon-sized rodent. I've yet to meet a hungry carnivore who didn't love it.

Liver is served as *hígado encebollado* (liver with onions) or *hígado entomatado* (with tomatoes).

Menudo, a very popular dish, might best be translated as the "interior odds and ends" of whatever poor beast fell under the axe, along with its feet, paws or hooves. This stuff is put into something, usually a piece of intestine, and cooked. *Menudo* is a classic Mexican hangover cure and is often sold by vendors around *cantinas*. It is gaining immense popularity in the United States, for reasons completely beyond my understanding.

Mondongo is stomach and intestines, often filled with blood and spices. *Tripas* is tripe.

Pollo (chicken) is much better than chicken sold in the U.S., which usually, as Steve's father used to say, "tastes pasteurized." Mexicans serve chicken in many ways: *pollo asado* (grilled), *pollo frito* (fried), *pollo con arroz* (with rice), *pollo en mole* (in *mole* sauce) and *caldo de pollo* (soup).

Cold cuts (*carnes frías*) are usually offered in sandwiches or *tortas*, but are sometimes served on a snack plate. The most common are *queso de puerco* (head cheese), *jamón* (pressed ham) and *salami*.

Chorizo, the famous Mexican sausage, may be served as a side dish, but it usually comes with eggs or in tacos.

Patas de puerco are pig's feet. They gain a lot when fried in a thick batter.

Seafood

The Aztec Emperor Moctezuma set a precedent for Mexican seafood lovers when he established a system of runners from Tenochtitlán (Mexico City to us) to the Gulf of Mexico. Life for these relay teams must have been like perpetual Olympic Games, with the runner's baton substituted by red snappers, fresh mangrove oysters and steamer clams.

The tradition continues, though the runners have been replaced by fast trucks. *Mariscos* (seafood) are extremely popular, and towns of any size, even far from the coast, will have at least one seafood restaurant.

Because of these fast trucks, many refrigerated and others using ice, there's rarely any worry about being served something spoiled or overripe. If you're in doubt, however, don't eat it. This is especially true when eating seafood from street vendors.

As a general rule I only eat street vendor's seafood when within sight or smell of the ocean. Even then I avoid the less prosperous stands (which can't afford to throw anything away if it's marginal) and prefer to eat seafood before the heat of the afternoon. Most *mariscos* are delivered early in the morning, and several hours out of water or ice is more than enough to reduce their flavor and increase the chance of spoiling.

Pescado frito (fried fish) is usually a whole fish, head and all, deep fried. Unfortunately, Mexicans tend to overcook fish and some positively cremate them. Look at what someone else is eating before you order and you'll get a good idea of what's going on in the kitchen. If they are eating a fish and it sounds like the crunching of potato chips, you'll probably want to order something else, like *mondongo*. (Watch out for stale grease. You can smell it.)

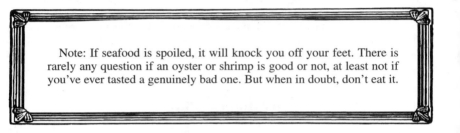

Note: If seafood is spoiled, it will knock you off your feet. There is rarely any question if an oyster or shrimp is good or not, at least not if you've ever tasted a genuinely bad one. But when in doubt, don't eat it.

Filete de pescado (filet) is fish without the head, tail and most of the bones. It is served *frito* (fried) unless you order it specifically cooked otherwise. *Pescado al mojo de ajo* is fish fried in butter and garlic. It is fabulous.

Huachinango a la veracruzana (red snapper Veracruz-style) is justifiably famous. Anyone who can eat a whole red snapper smothered in an elaborate tomato sauce (with olives too) and not groan with pleasure needs help.

Other fine fish are also served: *pargo* (sea bass or snapper), *mero* (grouper), *cabrilla* (excellent rock fish), *robalo* (snook, among the best), *sierra* (mackerel) and *mojarra*, a general word used for any perch-like fish, usually pan-sized.

Camarones (shrimp) are available throughout the country, in both restaurants and at sidewalk stands. They are most often served in a cocktail (*coctel de camerones*) that is doused with sauces and various condiments. If you don't want your cocktail *con todo* (with everything), just point to the things that you want or take it *natural* ("natural," naturally). Some of the sauces are quite *picante* (spicy hot).

Boiled shrimp are often sold by street vendors on the coast and are called *camarones naturales*. They are sold by the kilo. The price of shrimp in Mexico has skyrocketed in recent years due to the insatiable demand from the American market. This is a point of great distress to Mexican seafood lovers, and justifiably so.

Camarones gigantes (prawns) are prepared in various delicious ways; among the best are *camarones en alambres* (shish-ka-bob), *camarones al mojo de ajo* (garlic and butter sauce) and *camarones a la diabla* (fried, deviled shrimp). Great! *Camarones en gabardinas* are batter fried.

Ostiones (oysters) are almost always eaten raw, in cocktails (*coctel de ostiones*) or on the half-shell (*en sus conchas*). They are spiced up the same as shrimp.

Langosta (spiny lobster) is served steamed, broiled or *al mojo de ajo*. *Langostinas* are small crayfish. They are sometimes called "river shrimp" (*camarones del río*) and "cockroaches" (*cucarachas*).

Many seafood restaurants offer fish and lobster by the size, with the price varying accordingly. Keep in mind, therefore, that fried snapper may be low-priced because it's really just a red minnow. If you're in doubt, ask before ordering. Seafood cocktails also vary in size and condiments. Some of the more elaborate cost as much as a full meal.

Caracol (conch) are usually prepared in soup or *ceviche*. *Ceviche* is any type of raw seafood marinated with lime juice, chilies, onions, tomatoes and garlic. The best *ceviche* is made from *sierra* (mackerel) and young shark (*cazón*). It's a popular snack in *cantinas*. (Beware of wandering *ceviche* vendors; their wares are often half-spoiled.)

Calamares and *pulpos* (squid and octopus) are most often served *en su tinta* (in their ink). They are tasty, but something like eating tough spaghetti soaked in India ink. Both are also popular when served as cocktails.

Almejas (clams), *abulón* (abalone) and *lapa* (giant limpet similar to abalone but not as tasty) are not widely available, but when they are, they're usually served in cocktails or as *ceviche*.

Jaibas are very small crabs that make excellent soup. *Cangrejos* are larger crabs often served in rice, cooked whole.

Tiburón or *cazón* (shark, baby hammerhead) is served in tomato sauce and is very good.

Tortuga and *huevos de tortuga* (turtle, also known as *caguama*, and turtle eggs) are sold in many restaurants and cocktail stands. (See *Meats*, above.)

Seafood Sunday

During the Christmas season, Lent and especially Easter Week, millions of seafood-hungry Mexicans head for the coasts. Their minds are dazed with visions of golden fried *huachinango*, tall cocktail glasses brimming with *camarones* and *pulpo* and topped with slices of fresh lime and thick chunks of avocado, bottles of cold beer sweating damp rings onto the tablecloths . . . oh, it's almost too much to bear!

I used to observe these seafood orgies with mixed awe and admiration, tempered by a good measure of disbelief. How could they eat so much? How could they afford the bill, usually running to several pages? Why did they even do it, especially those who drove hundreds of miles to the beach and then spent most of their time in a restaurant?

I decided to find the answer to these mysteries. I knew that like any strange custom, it wouldn't be solved by logic: I'd have to try it for myself. First, a group of people with a similar curiosity had to be assembled, since it would be impossible to round up enough members of my own family to create the crowd needed. And money . . . lots of money. . . .

"Do you want shrimp in garlic sauce or deviled?" Steve asked the group seated at our end of the assembled row of enameled metal tables.

"Both," I answered, "and a few orders of *ceviche* and some tostadas and a bowl of fish soup . . ."

"Hey!" he interrupted. "Isn't that an awful lot?"

". . . and a plate of oysters and . . ." The waiter was scribbling furiously.

"And some crackers," Steve added, eyes glazing over, "and a shrimp cocktail, *large*, and let's see . . . oh yeah, another menu; I want to be able to study it in detail."

Our friends soon succumbed to our mood and barraged another waiter with similar orders. A group of *mariachis* wandered over and were immediately hired.

"Not bad, eh?" Steve asked, giving me a big wink as he drained the last drops of his second shrimp cocktail and waved the band to continue playing. A large family of Mexicans at a nearby table engaged another group of *mariachis* and the sound level soared. The long table was littered with dishes and cocktail glasses, half-eaten pineapples, cracker wrappers and a row of assorted liquor bottles. Some of our group had sent out for strong spirits before embarking on the main courses.

"I think I'll have a . . ." Steve's voice faded into indecision, ". . . a medium, no, make that a *gigante* fried snapper and maybe I ought to . . ." He looked over at me and added, "Carl, do you think I ought to have a lobster, too?"

"Sure, have *two*." I said, "Why be so conservative?"

His eyes widened. "Gee, I don't know . . . two lobsters all by myself?" The waiter stood patiently, tapping his order book with a pencil. "*Bueno*, give me the fish and lobsters!" Steve said. "And better bring us another bowl of soup."

We'd been in the restaurant for almost three hours, eating and drinking steadily, gossiping and enjoying the music, hiring small boys to dash off for side goodies from local stores, having our sandals polished and watching the passing crowds when it suddenly struck me: I was completely and absolutely relaxed, well fed, and slightly euphoric, surrounded by good company and entertainment. What more could a person want? That was it, the secret of Seafood Sunday!

"The bill, *señor*," the waiter said, laying a sheaf of papers in front of me. I took a tentative peek.

"What's wrong?" Steve asked, waving the band to play another tune. "You look like you just saw a ghost!"

Potatoes

Many dinners, especially orders of meat or fish, are served with *papas fritas* (fried potatoes). Baked, boiled or mashed potatoes are unknown in most traditional restaurants.

Eggs and Breakfast

Huevos (eggs) are cooked in a variety of styles. *Huevos estrellados* or *huevos fritos estrellados* are eggs sunny-side-up. *Huevos fritos duros* are eggs fried hard. Eggs "over easy" are almost impossible to order. However, you can always try; the suspense of waiting to see what you'll get can brighten your morning. (Ask for *huevos estrellados volteados*.)

Eggs are usually fried in oil rather than butter and may be somewhat greasy. If they are, you can do the same as a man I once observed in a small cafe, carefully wiping his fried eggs with a napkin.

It is common to order eggs, especially scrambled, "by the egg." When listed on the menu, the price is almost always for two eggs.

Huevos revueltos (scrambled eggs) are very common but the name is something of a tongue twister. I learned to remember it by thinking of "*huevos revoltos*," which was my impression when I once had them served floating in an inch of cold grease.

Scrambled eggs can be ordered Mexican-style mixed with onion, tomato, garlic and chilies (*huevos revueltos estilo mexicano*), or mixed with refried beans (*huevos revueltos con frijoles*) or sausage (*con chorizo*). Eggs mixed with *chorizo* are often greasy and spicy.

Huevos rancheros (eggs ranch-style) consist of two sunny-side-up eggs placed on tortillas and smothered in sauce. The sauce will be red or green tomatoes mixed with the usual combination of garlic, onion and chili. Although it will occasionally blow the roof off your mouth, this dish is quite tasty and usually tolerably spicy. There are many variations on *huevos rancheros*: a tortilla may cover the eggs and be sprinkled with cheese or served with a ladle of beans on top, my favorite.

Regional variations in egg dishes are common and usually quite good. One of the best I've tried was *huevos albañiles* (bricklayer's eggs), a sort of omelette smothered in a flaming hot sauce. If you're leery of spicy foods, ask before ordering; chiles are often used in egg dishes.

Omelettes may be called *omelet* (or some variation of that spelling), but are most commonly known as *torta de huevo*. *Huevos batidos* (beaten eggs), usually shortened to just *batidos*, are whipped eggs, fried without stirring.

Chilaquiles are a scrambled combination of leftover tortillas, eggs, chilies and sometimes chicken. They are usually quite spicy. There are many variations on this dish and it is one that restaurant-goers would call "dependable." (See *Our Favorite Mexican Recipes*.)

Huevos tibios (soft boiled eggs) should not be ordered if you absolutely insist on a properly timed egg. They are sometimes called *huevos pasados por agua* (eggs passed through water) which is the way they generally come out: raw.

Steve once spent several minutes explaining in detail how he wanted his eggs boiled for four minutes. The cook personally heard the instructions and agreed that it could probably be done.

The eggs arrived and were opened with great ceremony. They oozed, raw but warm, into the dish. The waitress, seeing our looks of disbelief, explained that the cook had placed a pan of cold water on the stove, added the eggs, then "cooked" them for just four minutes.

Huevos hervidos duros (hard boiled) are not common, but easier to explain than soft boiled. If you don't want to risk confusion, order *huevos crudos* (raw); many Mexicans eat them this way. They are another of the classic masochistic Mexican hangover cures, especially effective when served in orange juice with a large dollop of searing hot sauce.

Tocino (bacon) and *jamón* (ham, usually pressed) are common, but may be served scrambled into the eggs. If you want them (or anything else) separate, say, "*al lado*" ("on the side").

Hot kakes (you can guess this one, can't you?), though once rarely seen except at fairs and fiestas, are now served in many restaurants. On the street they are sold individually and are considered a treat rather than a regular food.

Breakfast cereals such as *hojuelas de maíz* (corn flakes) are common. *Avena* or *hojuelas de avena* (oatmeal) is served much thinner than in the U.S. The preferred form for oatmeal is as *atole*. (See *Beverages*, below.)

Beans

Frijoles (beans) are served with almost every meal, including breakfast. *Frijoles refritos* are made by mashing cooked beans and then frying them in oil or lard. They are often served with a piece of cheese.

Frijoles de olla (boiled beans, "of the bowl") may be served drained or floating in a delicious broth.

When beans are combined with corn or flour tortillas, the essential amino acids are balanced and provide a complete protein. Add a chili for vitamin C and you're ready for a long day of sightseeing.

Soups

Sopas (soups) are considered a very important part of both the afternoon and evening meal. They are always served with the *comida corrida* (daily special).

Soups are either *seca* (dry) or *aguada* (wet). The very common *sopa de arroz* (rice soup), for example, is more similar to fried rice. *Sopa de fideo* (noodle soup) is another common dry soup.

Consommé is broth and does not have any solid ingredients. The dish which most closely corresponds to our idea of soup is called *caldo* or *caldillo*. This is a catchall term for anything from pea soup to beef stew.

Although Mexico is noted for its fine soups, many restaurants have degenerated to serving canned. Ask "*¿Es sopa de lata?*" ("Is it canned soup?") and if it is, you might prefer to pass.

Sandwiches

A *torta* is a sandwich made on a split *bolillo* (French roll). They are most commonly made with ham, chicken, cheese, lunch meat, cooked potatoes, beans or *carnitas* (pork). Most *tortas* contain one or more hidden chilies. Americans with a heavy hamburger habit usually find *tortas* to be a good substitute.

Take all of the ingredients of a good *torta* and place them between two slices of *Bimbo* white bread. You now have a sandwich that could have come out of a vending machine in a gas station on an L.A freeway. A toasted sandwich is called a *sandwich dorado*.

Tacos, Enchiladas, Etc.

Tacos are basically one or more tortillas wrapped around one or more ingredients and served either hot or cold. The strangest taco I ever ate was filled with *mondongo de sangre* (fried blood from the loser of the previous day's bullfight). It went down stubbornly, even under a flood of beer, but I eventually managed. The taste was actually quite good.

While street grunting, it is wise to buy tacos from someone who is making them on the spot. This is especially true of fried tacos, which tend to get very funky when allowed to stand for several hours after cooking. If the tacos are being fried in old grease—which makes them very dark—move on until you find something more digestible.

Enchiladas are tortillas dipped in hot sauce (the name literally means "chilied"), filled with goodies and then fried. After cooking, the enchilada may be served smothered in sauce or sour cream (enchiladas *suizas*) and sprinkled with cheese.

Quesadillas are made by frying various ingredients inside raw tortilla dough. Two of the most delicious are *flor de calabaza* and *huitlacoche* (squash flower and black corn fungus). The latter type looks disgusting but tastes great. A very common *quesadilla* is *queso y rajas* (cheese and strips of mild green chili). A taco *de queso* is made with a precooked tortilla and often will be called a *quesadilla*.

Tostadas are crisply fried tortillas heaped with a variety of chopped vegetables and meat or cheese. When served as *antojitos* and *botanas* (snacks) in *cantinas*, the tostadas are invariably quite spicy. They sell beer.

Gorditas are round cakes of raw *masa* (tortilla dough) stuffed with various goodies and then fried. The most basic *gordita* is fried with no stuffing and then smeared with refried beans.

There are many variations and improvisations on the *gordita* and taco; one of my favorites is the *empanada*, a baked or fried taco-shaped tart (made with wheat flour). They are filled with everything from canned sardines to meat to sweet sauces and cream cheese.

Chalupas are similar to large *gorditas* and in some areas are similar to cupped tostadas. *Flautas* are like tightly rolled enchiladas, fried.

Tamales are steamed corn dough wrapped in a dry corn husk or a banana leaf and filled with meat, vegetables,

beans, chili or a sweet candy-like mixture. Some are solid dough and eaten like bread. In proper Spanish a single tamale is a *tamal*. Some are so big that they're a real meal in themselves. Because the *tamal* is usually served steaming hot, I consider it to be one of the safest and most reliable street foods.

Burritos are found in northern Mexico. If you ask for a "little burro" in the south, you'll probably end up with something sporting two floppy ears. Burritos are large and very thin flour tortillas wrapped around meat and beans. One or two make a full meal.

Mole is a dish that is distinctly Mexican. The most famous type, *mole poblano*, is a mixture of unsweetened chocolate, chilies and a great variety of spices. *Mole con pollo* (with chicken) or *con guajolote* (with turkey, also *pavo*) can usually be found in *fondas*. Turkey in *mole* sauce is considered the national dish.

Chiles rellenos are large *poblano chilies* (mild to hot) stuffed with cheese, meat or seafood, dipped in egg batter, deep fried, then stewed in a sauce of tomatoes, onion and garlic. Eat a *chile relleno* from the small end up. The stem end will be the hottest part and it helps to work into it gradually.

Salads and Snacks

A typical restaurant *ensalada* (salad) is rather disappointing. It rarely consists of more than a small pile of grated or chopped cabbage or lettuce, a slice or two of tomato, a few rings of onion and half of a lime. The lime is squeezed over the salad as a dressing.

Note: Lime juice has been proven to be highly effective against bacteria and should be used liberally on salads and street foods.

If you're desperate for a salad of fresh vegetables and can't seem to find one, try ordering *un surtido de verduras crudas* (an assortment of raw vegetables). We've found that this often brings better results than trying to describe how to make a "real" salad to someone who has never seen one. We discovered this accidentally, when a frustrated woman brought out a large plate of neatly arranged vegetable pieces and said, "Show me how you make a salad." I picked up a slice of lime and squeezed it over the vegetables and said, "Like that!" Her comeback was the solution to our ordering problems: "That's not a salad; that's a plate of raw vegetables!"

Guacamole is one of the few salads typical of Mexico. It is basically (as invented by the Aztecs) a mixture of chopped or mashed avocado, onions and chilies. Tomatoes may be added as well. Some people throw in mustard, spices and who-knows-what. (See *Our Favorite Mexican Recipes*.)

Many restaurants offer a delicious *coctel de frutas* (fruit cocktail) that just about makes up for the skimpy vegetable salads. Lime juice is also squeezed over fruit salad as a dressing.

Street vendors sell many delicious peeled and prepared fruits and vegetables. Most are served garnished with lime juice, chili powder and salt. By all means, try them *con todo* (with everything). The chili powder is rarely too hot, even for a tourist, and does interesting things to the flavor of an orange, cucumber or slice of pineapple. If the vendor has a large selection, try those things that are not familiar at first. The *jícama*, for example, resembles a potato in texture and an apple or pear in flavor.

Elotes (cooked ears of corn) are sold dripping with lime juice and chili powder. They are tougher than sweet corn sold in the States but the flavor is excellent. Some vendors smear mayonnaise on their *elotes*, but considering that it is unrefrigerated, I would advise against it. During the corn harvest season (summer and fall) it seems that everyone on the street is chewing on an *elote*. They are sold boiled and roasted, the price depending on the size of the ear.

Chick peas (*garbanzos*) are also sold steamed. They are served in brown paper cones, covered with lime juice and chili powder. Pop one in your mouth, suck off the spice and then work out the bean with your tongue and teeth. They are as addic-

tive as the peanuts you'll also find on the streets, either roasted or raw, cured in vinegar. It's another of those habits you'll acquire in Mexico and then never be able to satisfy at home.

Pepitas are squash and melon seeds, toasted and sometimes salted and sprinkled lightly with chili powder. They are a national pastime and a favorite of movie goers. The seed is popped whole into the mouth, sucked briefly and then cracked open with the front teeth. A good *pepita* snapper can eat them as fast as peanuts, one handed.

Mangos, when in season (spring through summer), are sold on sticks, like ice cream bars. Try one with chili. While still green they are eaten with lime and chili, an interesting and tart combination.

Junk Food, Desserts and Candy

The national *postre* (dessert) is *flan*, a sweet, caramel-flavored egg custard. It is sold and eaten everywhere, from restaurants to street corners. Because street *flan* is prepared under rather dubious hygienic conditions (most is made at home by poor people), think twice.

Gelatinas are similar to Jello. Take my word for it, street vendor *gelatinas* aren't worth the risk.

Nieve ("snow") looks very much like ice cream (*helado*), but it's actually made from flavored water. The street vendor who sells *nieves* is popularly known as "*el abominable hombre de las nieves*" (the abominable snowman).

In most towns you can hardly walk down the street without being run over by a *paleta* cart. A *paleta* is a piece of flavored ice on a stick. If you are nervous about water, *paletas* will give you uncontrollable palsies. The best flavor, in my opinion, is *tuna*—not tuna fish but *tuna* cactus fruits.

You'll see *paleta* salesmen pushing their heavy two-wheeled carts *everywhere*, from beaches to deserted stretches of scorching highway to fog-shrouded mountain passes. The distribution of these carts is something to marvel at, which I do whenever I see one sitting on the side of the road, hundreds of miles from nowhere.

Ice cream is very popular and the flavors made with fresh fruits are outstanding. Large ice cream shops are quite common.

Pastel (cake) is common but pie is not. When she can find it, Lorena's weakness is fresh *pay de coco* or *pay de nuez* (coconut or nut pie). By the way, *pay* is pronounced just like its English equivalent, pie.

Buñuelos are molded fried dough served hot or cold, sprinkled with sugar or honey. They come in various shapes and sizes. Pastry lovers often lose their self-control over fresh *buñuelos* and suffer from indigestion. This rarely stops them from doing it again and again.

Churros are also made of fried dough, but the shape is quite different: long, narrow and usually ruffled. The raw dough is squeezed through a paper tube or metal pastry shaper and fried in long coils. These are cut into smaller lengths, dusted with sugar and sold like tiny stacks of cord wood by street vendors.

Polvorones are crumbly cookies, sometimes made with lard, easy to overdose on.

Camotes (sweet potatoes) are a Mexican favorite; they are sold by itinerant vendors who announce their passing by signaling on a flute or with steam whistles. Most *camotes* are cooked in brown sugar and sold hot or cold, to be eaten with the fingers. In restaurants they may be served in a bowl with milk. *Camotes* come in a wide variety of shapes, sizes and colors; my favorite is bright purple.

Many excellent candies are homemade or unpackaged. These are commonly sold from large stalls. Among the best of these are *ates*. *Ates* are jellied fruit bars (some

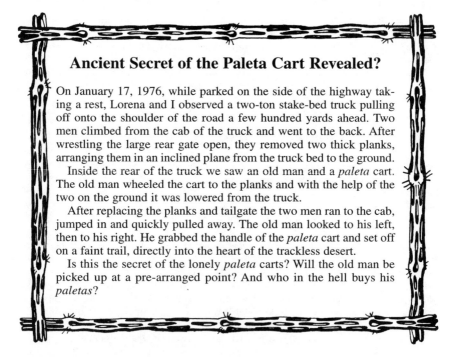

Ancient Secret of the Paleta Cart Revealed?

On January 17, 1976, while parked on the side of the highway taking a rest, Lorena and I observed a two-ton stake-bed truck pulling off onto the shoulder of the road a few hundred yards ahead. Two men climbed from the cab of the truck and went to the back. After wrestling the large rear gate open, they removed two thick planks, arranging them in an inclined plane from the truck bed to the ground.

Inside the rear of the truck we saw an old man and a *paleta* cart. The old man wheeled the cart to the planks and with the help of the two on the ground it was lowered from the truck.

After replacing the planks and tailgate the two men ran to the cab, jumped in and quickly pulled away. The old man looked to his left, then to his right. He grabbed the handle of the *paleta* cart and set off on a faint trail, directly into the heart of the trackless desert.

Is this the secret of the lonely *paleta* carts? Will the old man be picked up at a pre-arranged point? And who in the hell buys his *paletas*?

as big as an adobe brick) sold by the weight and by the piece. Some have been cooked until hard and broken into lumps, others can be sliced like cheese. They are usually made of tropical and semi-tropical fruits. You may be offered a sample. Some stands offer sampler packages of *ate* and these make interesting gifts for people back home.

Along with *ate* you'll see bricks, bars and balls of *cocada*, an incredibly sweet candy made from shredded coconut. There's nothing more pitiful than a tourist strung out on *cocada*, constantly licking sugar from his fingers and probing cavities to dislodge bits of coconut. *Cocada* comes in a variety of colors; try the pink.

Cajeta is a toffee candy made in the city of Celaya and sold in many parts of the country. It usually comes in jars and has the consistency of cold honey. *Cajeta* is also made into candies. Anyone traveling near Celaya will see *cajeta* stands, *cajeta* signs, *cajeta* shops, *cajeta* hawkers and discarded *cajeta* candy wrappers at every turn. Needless to say, you will want to try some.

Obleas come in various sizes and shapes, but are basically a sandwich of *cajeta* between two thin flour wafers—a Mexican version of the Eskimo Pie.

Pepitorias are thin flour wafers folded over a filling of *cajeta* and *pepitas* (toasted squash and melon seeds).

Chongos are a custard-like sweet similar to *flan* but usually of a thicker consistency. They are not too common.

Mezcal is not only the name of a liquor but is also a type of homemade candy, the baked heart of the maguey plant. *Mezcal* is sold by the chunk. Chew the fibrous stuff until you've got the sweetness out and then spit it out.

Peeled sugar cane (*caña de azúcar*) is sold by the length or in bags of small sections; another chew-and-spit candy.

Dulce de tamarindo is tamarind fruit combined with sugar or with salt and chili powder. It is sold in flat cakes or long rolls. The sugar variety is mixed with water to make a refreshing drink, *agua de tamarindo*. The fruit is high in vitamin C.

Plátanos prensados (pressed bananas) are cooked bananas (*machos*) that have been steamed and pressed together in blocks. The natural sugar content of the bananas makes the candy very sweet.

Dulce de tojocotes en almíbar is a favorite mouthful at Christmas time. It is squash, cooked in *piloncillo* (crude brown sugar). *Tojocotes* is often served in *fondas*, usually drenched in sweet cream or milk.

Curtidos are candied fruits soaked in alcohol. They are sold in jars or individually. Kids love them.

Fruits crystallized with sugar are called *frutas cristalizadas*. Candied fruit peels are *cascaras*. Among the more common candied fruits are oranges, limes, mangoes, pears, peaches, apricots, apples, figs and *arrayones* (a type of berry). *Calabaza* and *chilacayote* (squashes) are also candied. Candied plums (*ciruelas*) are called *jobos*.

An interesting variation of crystallized fruits is *limones rellenos de coco*, an entire candied lime, hollowed and stuffed with shredded coconut or *cocada*.

A candy that is very similar to peanut brittle is called *palanqueta*. Peanuts are formed into bars and blocks by cooking them with *piloncillo* (medium hard texture), sugar (very brittle) or honey (very flexible). Some vendors make large blocks of candy and then saw them into smaller pieces.

Candies of this type are also made from melon and squash seeds. Another type, called *alegrías*, looks almost identical to sesame seed bars (and cakes), but is actually not a seed at all. Whatever it is, it has a rather bland flavor.

Anyone with a real sweet tooth should try *jamoncillo*. It is something of a cross between a milk candy and a fruit bar. A friend calls it "Mexican halvah."

Gaznates (gullets) are for hopeless junk food fiends: a pastry tube or cone plugged with stiff sweet cream. Not far behind are *merengues*, a very hard mixture of sugar and egg whites formed into a lump.

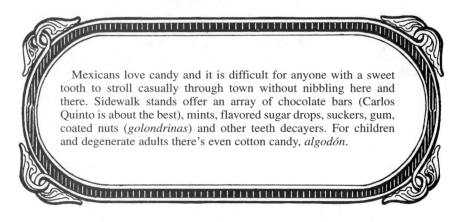

Mexicans love candy and it is difficult for anyone with a sweet tooth to stroll casually through town without nibbling here and there. Sidewalk stands offer an array of chocolate bars (Carlos Quinto is about the best), mints, flavored sugar drops, suckers, gum, coated nuts (*golondrinas*) and other teeth decayers. For children and degenerate adults there's even cotton candy, *algodón*.

Morelianas are pastry-like tortillas smeared with milk candy.

Trompadas are similar to taffy, though made from *piloncillo* and anise seeds. I'm sure you can see the connection. Another taffy candy, very popular on the Day of the Dead, is called *charamuscas*. It is sold in twisted lengths, sometimes covered with nuts.

Beverages

Coffee and Tea

"My frank admiration for Mexico stops just this side of the coffee. To our taste, at least, it is terrible. They do not grind the berries as we do. They pulverize them until they become a brown talcum powder. This they boil until it is like lye. . . .

"In some of the larger Mexican cities they ask you if you would like to have café americano. *Say 'Yes!' Say '¡Sí!' Yell it! Don't let there be any mistake."*
—Harry Carr, *Old Mother Mexico* (1931)

As a serious fan of good coffee, I'm afraid that Harry's grim assessment of Mexican *café* isn't all bluster. Though rich in coffee plantations, Mexico exports its finest beans to Europe and the United States. What's left isn't quite the dregs, but it won't win many awards.

Three types of coffee are commonly served: Nescafé, *café americano* and *cafe de olla*. Nescafé is a brand name of instant coffee, but Mexicans typically call all instant coffee by this name. *Americano* is real coffee, brewed gringo-style. (Regrettably, espresso and cappuchino are found only in resorts and larger cities.) The most traditional brew, *café de olla* or "pot coffee" is simmered in a special earthenware jug. *Café de olla* is sweetened with crude brown sugar and laced with cinnamon. It is potent, delicious stuff, but relatively hard to find.

Tragically, instant coffee will be your caffeine-of-choice in most restaurants. This is how it is typically served: a cup of plain hot water is brought to your table, along with a jar of Nescafé and sugar. Because many Mexicans believe that it is unhealthy to drink liquids that are very cold or very hot, your cup of water may not be steaming. If it isn't hot enough for you, say *"Qué hierva el agua, por favor."* ("Let the water boil, please.")

Once the cup returns, stir in Nescafé and enjoy. (A Mexican friend jokes bitterly that Nescafé is an abbreviation for *"No es café"*—"It is not coffee.")

If available, decaffeinated coffee is almost always *instantaneo* as well. Ask, *"¿Hay decaf?"* ("Is there decaf?") The brewing ritual is the same.

Urgent Note to Coffee Drinkers: The popular Mexican drink *café con leche* (coffee with milk) is hot milk with a shot or two of coffee or Nescafé added, not American-style black coffee with a touch of milk. To get a "regular" cup of black coffee, order *café americano* or *café negro*. If cream isn't provided, ask for *"crema para café."* Don't be surprised if the "cream" you're served is condensed or even powdered milk.

You won't have to ask for *azúcar* (sugar); Mexicans use it lavishly. Some restaurants buy their coffee with sugar already added to the beans and you don't have any choice. Don't expect sugar substitutes, however. (If you need them, bring your own supply from home.)

It is not the custom to drink coffee until the meal is finished. If you want your coffee right away, just say, *"El café ahorita, por favor."*

Free refills are uncommon, though most tourist restaurants loosen their grip on the coffee pot, especially at breakfast. *"Tantito más café, por favor"* ("A bit more coffee, please") is a polite way to beg for more. If you order *"Más café"* ("More coffee") and the waitress responds, *"¿Otro?"* ("Another?") it means just that—you're ordering another cup, at full price. Again this is the prevailing custom, so don't be irritated if you're charged for a second cup.

Té negro (**black tea**) is not as common in small restaurants as herbal tea. If you are a heavy tea drinker, it is best to carry your own tea bags and order a cup of hot water. Don't be surprised if they charge you for a cup of coffee; after all, they have no way of knowing whether you used the Nescafé on the table or not.

Try Mexican **herbal teas**; they're widely available, pleasant-tasting and very soothing. In fact, *té de manzanilla* (camomile) is commonly used for upset nerves and stomachs. Other popular flavors are *té de limón* (lemon grass), *té de canela* (cinnamon) and *yerba buena* (mint).

Chocolate is a very popular drink but it is not always available in cheaper places. An excellent drink can be made by adding instant coffee to hot chocolate.

Juices and Fruit Drinks

Tired of too many sweet sodas? Throughout Mexico bright, clean shops dispense fresh-squeezed juices and mixed punches from oranges, pineapple, grapefruit, watermelon, papaya and sugar cane. Vegetables are also juiced, especially carrot, beet and alfalfa, all the old favorites. A juice stand may offer more flavors and combinations than one could sample in a lifetime: alfalfa and carrot juice, beet and grapefruit or, Lorena's favorite, a potent cocktail of carrot, celery, beet, parsley and lime.

Before ordering a *jugo*, give the stand a quick appraisal. There are plenty of stands that understand the value of health precautions. A good juice stand will be busy *and* clean. I always look for a water purifying filter on the tap or a jug of bottled water close at hand. When in doubt, stick with natural undiluted juices.

Juice vendors also prepare delicious designer drinks with combinations of fruit, milk, ice, sugar, yogurt, granola and raw eggs. The national favorite is the *licuado*, a rich, milkshake-like smoothee of milk or water, sugar, ice, fruit and optional prepared flavors. *Licuados* can also be made from a base of orange juice. This is my favorite: orange juice, one raw egg, banana and ice, or try orange juice with a chunk of papaya and a ripe banana. For variations add vanilla, papaya, strawberries, pineapple and a dash of cinnamon. You'll never want to go home again.

Chocomil is powdered-milk-based drink that vaguely resembles a milkshake. It comes in various flavors, but the most common are chocolate and strawberry.

Esquimales are thicker and creamier than *licuados*, but otherwise very similar. An *esquimal* is made by adding a prepared dry mix (chocolate, strawberry or vanilla flavored) to milk and blending it with chunks of fresh fruit.

Atole and *horchata* are distinctly Mexican drinks. *Atole* is basically fresh ground corn or corn starch, water and sugar. It is served hot or cold with a variety of spices and flavorings. *Atole* is quite nourishing and inexpensive, two good reasons to learn to like it. (*Atole* is also made from wheat flour, rice flour or oatmeal.) *Horchata* is made from ground rice or melon seeds and water. It took me a while to get used to *horchata*, but once I did, I was hooked.

Pinole is finely ground toasted corn. It is mixed with water, sugar and cinnamon or with chile peppers. *Pinole* is a staple of the Tarahumara Indians of northwestern Mexico. It is an excellent high-energy food, lightweight, inexpensive and virtually indestructible.

Aguas or *aguas frescas* (fresh waters) are made by adding a small amount of fresh fruit juice and sugar to a large amount of water. *Aguas* made from flowers, cactus fruits and other exotic ingredients are especially worth sampling. They are refreshing and ridiculously cheap.

Many travelers find that by making *agua fresca* at home (cantaloupe is great), they can wean their families away from expensive and unhealthy soft drinks.

Cocos (coconuts) are sold both as a drink and as a snack. The milk of the coconut is naturally pure and tends to plug up your bowels, but don't eat too much of the meat—it has the opposite effect. After drinking the liquid, hand the nut back to the vendor, who'll whack it open and remove the meat for you.

Soft Drinks

"After the U.S., Mexico is the world's largest market for both Coca-Cola and Pepsi-Cola."

—Alan Riding, ***Distant Neighbors*** (1984)

Soft drinks are very common. Those that are *not* made by large American companies are the best. Soft drinks are generally knows as *refrescos*, but they may be referred to as *aguas* or *gaseosas*.

Some of the better *refrescos* are *Sidral*, *Manzanita*, *Imperial* (all apple flavored and much like cider) and *Sangria* (mixed fruit). Mineral water with fruit flavors is sold under the brand names *Tehuacán*, *Del Valle*, *Lourdes* and others.

Some other common brands and flavors are:

7-Up	*7-Up* or *Seven*
Coca-Cola	*Coca-Cola*, *Coca* or derisively, *Choca-Chola*
Pepsi-Cola	*Pepsi-Cola* or just *Pepsi*
Squirt	*Squirt* (pronounced "ess-squirt")
Orange Crush	*Naranja* or *Crush*
Lemonade	*Limonada*
Lime	*Limón*
Grapefruit	*Toronja*
Pineapple	*Piña*
Strawberry	*Fresa*
Cherry	*Cereza*
Cream soda	*Cebada*
Banana	*Sidra negro* (Yucatán)
Mineral water	*Agua mineral* or *Tehuacán* (*con gas* or *sin gas:* "without gas," i.e., noncarbonated)
Quinine water	*Agua quinina*
Pure water	*Agua puro*, *sin gas* (noncarbonated)

If none of these excite you, almost every restaurant, gas station, grocery store and sidewalk food stand will have *cerveza* (beer). There is a wide variety of mildly alcoholic drinks that are often served at street stands, fiestas and fairs. For details see *Booze and Cantinas*.

When ordering a *refresco* or *cerveza*, especially in a traditional, modest restaurant, you may be asked if you want it cold or warm. Many Mexicans drink beverages *al tiempo* (room temperature) rather than *fría* or *helada* (cold). (For more on beer, see *Booze and Cantinas*.)

I flung open the front door and staggered across the room. "That's it! The end! Never again!" I fell backward onto the cot, trying to massage away the headache that raged behind my inflamed eyeballs. Lorena crouched over the makeshift stove we'd rigged from a five-gallon tin can, stirring the daily pot of beans.

"Was it that bad?"

I sat up. "Bad? *Bad?* Are you kidding? You're lucky to see me alive! Do you know what it's like to drive fifty miles over a washboard dirt road with a load of slopping gasoline drums?" I could still taste the fumes, the awful mixture of dust and raw gas clogged my nostrils and coated my tongue.

"It wasn't the gas spilling all over the van or crawling along at five miles an hour," I said, "or the 150-degree heat or the flat tire." I paused, groping under the cot for a warm beer. "It wasn't even Vincente's damn kid playing his radio full blast the whole way." I took a long foamy swallow. "It was Vincente smoking one cigarette after another, not two feet from the gas, laughing that they'd see the explosion in Guadalajara if anything went wrong!" It was still almost too much to believe; I'd risked my life and the van to earn the price of a tank of gas with maybe enough left over for a few kilos of tortillas.

"Did you say anything to Don Alfredo?" she asked, slowly chopping an onion.

"Of course not," I snapped. "He did us a favor getting me the job in the first place. It would make him feel bad if I griped." Don Alfredo, landlord and friend, had offered to help us ride out a long period of poverty by getting me jobs *fleteando*. "Arrowing," more commonly known as "light hauling," could be a lucrative sideline for the discreet tourist who didn't sweat such trivialities as breaking the law by working in Mexico or delivering dynamite, gasoline, not-quite-mature bulls, bananas, squealing porkers and other local freight. The messes left were indescribable. Fortunately it wasn't our van; we'd borrowed it for a few months from my brother.

"Actually," I continued, "I'd like to find something that doesn't require so much driving. It's been interesting but the wear and tear are really terrible. Rob will kill me if we have to push his van over a cliff somewhere."

Lorena got up from the stove and moved across the room. "You know, we might be able to help out in the restaurant," she said, easing into the hammock with a great sigh of relief. "Don Alfredo keeps saying that Christmas is a real mob scene. He knows we can cook. In fact, he said something the other day about wanting to learn some new recipes."

"That's not a bad idea," I yawned. "What could be easier than cooking?"

"Three shrimp spaghettis, two plates of garlic bread, a vegetarian poor-boy, one bowl of beans and a large fried fish!" Don Alfredo called out the latest orders as he edged through the crowded kitchen toward the beer cooler. He plunged his hands into the dark icy water, muttering "*¡Híjole!*" as he lifted out the brown bottles of beer, wiping them carefully on his white apron. When the round enameled tray had been filled, he hoisted it over his head in approved waiter fashion. With a cry of "*¡Ay voy!*" he shooed a path through to the low doorway.

"Was that three orders of shrimp spaghetti or two?" Lorena reached for a large earthenware bowl brimming with shrimp and began peeling them expertly.

"Three," I answered, giving the Coleman stove a few extra pumps. "Build up the fire, Carmen," I ordered, "and someone cut more bread." The girl slipped out the back door to the woodpile while her older brother, Ramón, began slicing *bolillos*. His younger brother, Juanito, complained that Ramón was crowding him from the table. "Just clean the fish," I said, "and then cut more garlic." The boys fell silent and worked obediently side by side.

"Carlitos!" Don Alfredo called, sticking his head just inside the doorway, "*Lo siento mucho*, but those gringos changed their order. Now they want three orders of beef stew instead of shrimp . . ."

"Oh, hell!" I sighed, going to the refrigerator for the pot of stew. Don Alfredo shook his head sympathetically.

The sound of quarreling voices suddenly rose from near the stoves. "How can I heat the bread if you take the stove?" Carmen wailed, trying to push past her sister, Ofelia.

Ofelia stood firm, brandishing a large spatula. "Use the fire, *tonta!*" she hissed. "I need this one for the fish."

Carmen turned angrily, "*Señor* Carlos, Ofelia won't let me . . ."

"OK! OK!" I said. "Just wait a moment. There's plenty of time for everything." I searched through the littered table, finally unearthing my beer behind a cluster of hot-sauce bottles. I drained it in one long gulp and rolled the empty bottle beneath the counter. It clinked against several others.

We'd presented our scheme to help out in the restaurant just two weeks ago, the same afternoon I'd hauled the leaking barrel of gasoline. Don Alfredo himself provided the opening I needed.

"Even at Christmastime," he said, "we get very few of the gringos in here. They always ask for things we don't have. Then they drink a beer or two and leave."

"Please don't be offended," I said. "But the fact is that many tourists get tired of eating tacos and refried beans after a while. Most of them would get very excited about something familiar, like a hamburger or a hot dog."

"Really?" he answered, running a hand over his chin, scratching thoughtfully at his perpetual three-day stubble. "But if they won't eat something as delicious as *camarones rancheros*, what can we possibly offer?"

As if on cue, Marigenia, his wife, set a long platter on the table between us. It was covered with large pink shrimp, smothered in onion, tomato and chili sauce. As usual he couldn't stand to have us visit without a *botana*, though by his reckoning a snack might be two kilos of shrimp or fried fish.

"Don Alfredo," I said, spearing a tasty morsel with my fork. "If you put this on spaghetti as a sauce it would be perfect."

He looked skeptical; turn ranch-style shrimp into spaghetti? No, it just didn't add up.

I went into detail, explaining how the noodles were cooked and the sauce poured over them. He grinned. Leave it to these crazy gringos to come up with impractical ideas. I became insistent; the more he resisted the more I realized that with shrimp spaghetti on the menu, his business would enjoy an immediate boom.

"Garlic bread!" I said. "That's what you need to go with the spaghetti!" As I explained how he could produce this additional treat, Lorena chimed in with: "And three-bean salad. We've got the beans, all we need is a little celery and . . ."

"*Bueno*," Don Alfredo interrupted, a look of genuine interest spreading over his face, "But do you think others . . . other gringos would like those things?"

"Certainly!" Lorena and I answered in unison.

He began to smile. "Would it be possible . . . could you perhaps teach me? One day, God forbid, when you are gone from here, I would have to . . ."

I interrupted him with a friendly laugh and a pat on the shoulder. "Don't worry, Don Alfredo!" I said. "This will be child's play!"

I sagged against the counter, trying to ease the shooting pains that stabbed through my legs and lower back. My eyes streamed with tears; no matter how often I chided her, Carmen could not seem to keep the wood-fire burning properly. Smoke hung beneath the blackened rafters in a thick acrid fog, cutting down the normally weak light until it seemed that we worked in perpetual twilight. We had tried candles but they toppled into the salad or gave off crazy flickering lights that were worse than none at all. Don Alfredo had promised a lamp, but first it was necessary to locate his brother-in-law. . .

Lorena collapsed onto one of the beds jammed into the narrow room, to sip a cup of tea and chat with Don Alfredo's wife. Marigenia had been ill during most of the two weeks we'd been cooking in their restaurant. It was frustrating for a woman who normally commanded the operation of the restaurant and the practical management of their large family to be confined to her bed. When things got especially hectic or one of the children balked at the task we had given them, her voice would rise over the general din, striking the offenders dumb with her wrath. "Juan, when Carlos tells you to go to the village for more chili YOU GO IMMEDIATELY! *¿Entiendes?* Ofelia! Chop those carrots the way *Señora* Lorena wants them or I'll . . ."

These instructions carried sufficient weight to whip everyone into line for at least an hour. It was only rarely that a situation arose that required direct intervention by Don Alfredo himself.

"Ramón, bring Carlos a beer, he looks nervous!"

Ramón hustled to the beer cooler. Though it was only ten in the morning, Don Alfredo believed that without a beer in my hand I could not cook. I took the bottle, shocked to see that Ramón had another in his hand and was taking a tentative sip. He grinned at me proudly, wiping the mouth of the bottle with the palm of his hand.

"*¿Qué? ¿Qué? ¿Qué?*" Don Alfredo shouted, confronting the fifteen-year-old boy with an outraged glare. Ramón dropped the bottle from his lips, backing away a few steps, giving us a guilty smile.

"What are you doing?" his father roared. "Put that beer down at once!"

Ramón set the bottle on the table, turning back defiantly. "Why does he drink beer all the time and I can't?"

I struggled not to laugh. Don Alfredo caught my eye and winked. He grabbed Ramón by the shoulders and gave him a few hard shakes.

"You're just a child, that's why. Carlos is a gringo and gringos drink beer all the time. You're not a gringo. It is very simple. *¿Entiendes?*"

I started to protest.

"Beer is a vitamin," he continued, "and you are too young to need vitamins."

Ramón's face cleared. Here was something that made clear sense! He grinned bashfully and went back to his morning job of cleaning fish.

As Don Alfredo returned to the dining room he stopped for a moment and called back, "I don't know how children get these crazy ideas!"

The orders were coming too fast; Don Alfredo dispatched one of the kids to the village for more supplies and a pair of idle nieces. Marigenia had risen from her sickbed and now sat near the stove, making garlic bread. Don Alfredo hustled in and out, passing along orders and shouting encouragement to the kitchen crew. The jukebox raged near the doorway, blasting out a *mariachi* rendition of "White Christmas." I could hear drunken voices demanding more beef stew, more shrimp spaghetti, more garlic bread. Carmen burned her hand on a hot coal and began crying; Juanito complained that he wanted to go play soccer; and the grandmother, drafted back to work after years of undoubtedly well-deserved retirement, sang Revolutionary tunes in a shrill quavery voice as she labored over a tortilla press.

I caught occasional glimpses of Lorena hustling from one table to the next, taking orders in a mixture of Spanish, English and sign language. She had found it easier to help Don Alfredo in the dining room than to decipher the garbled orders he took from tourists. The sight of a six-foot gringa waiting tables left most of the customers gaping until they realized it wasn't a joke and began clamoring for service.

The suffocating heat from three stoves and an open wood-fire finally drove me to the doorway of the kitchen for a gasp of fresh air. As I leaned against the door and sucked at my beer, I caught the attention of two Mexican men at a nearby table. I had barely registered their amazed stares when Carmen called out for help with the spaghetti pot. I waved to them and dove back into the maelstrom.

"Know what day this is?" Lorena asked, mopping her forehead with a damp dish-towel. She had taken advantage of a lull to catch up on the pile of dirty dishes that threatened to avalanche into the family living area.

"I give up," I yawned, wishing that it was quitting time and we could stagger back to our house for a few moments of peace and quiet. Was it weeks or months since we'd come to the beach for a vacation?

"It's Christmas Eve," she said, reaching for another bucket of water. "You know, the night before Christmas and all through the house . . . ?"

I shook my head; no, it couldn't be! Christmas? I looked around the room, suddenly noticing the bits of colored paper and tinsel. The family altar, perched precariously on top of the refrigerator, was decorated with fresh flowers and sprigs of pine. And there, right in full view on the door I'd opened at least 200 times that day, were big paper letters spelling out *"Feliz Navidad."*

"We ought to be sitting around a tree, opening presents in front of a crackling fire," I sighed. "And thinking about a big turkey dinner tomorrow afternoon." Lorena brushed a strand of hair from her eyes and began laughing wildly.

I was about to start singing "Jingle Bells" when Don Alfredo rushed into the kitchen, crying, "Two orders of . . . two orders of . . . of . . ." he stopped, looking around the room in confusion, "Two orders of . . ." He slapped his forehead with the palm of a hand, trying to dislodge the words. "Two orders of. . . *¡ay pues!*" he groaned. "Let's have two orders of beer!" He walked wearily to the cooler and stuck his arm into the freezing water, not bothering to roll up the sleeve of his shirt.

"Here we are!" he said, handing us each a beer and then suddenly grabbing more, popping the caps off with a vigorous snap and passing them around the room, to grandmother, children and all. When everyone had a bottle he raised his arm dramatically and shouted, *"¡Feliz Navidad y dos ordenes de espaghetti!"*

MARKETS AND STORES

Markets and tianguis • Ins and outs of bartering • Shopping suggestions • Stores: tiendas, Conasupo, supermarkets, roadside stores, stores on wheels • The shopping list: alfalfa to zucchini and everything in between • A typical marketing trip • Market days in Mexico

Markets and *Tianguis*

Mexico has thousands of traditional markets, including many *tianguis* (Indian markets) that date back centuries before the arrival of the Spanish. A town of any size has at least one permanent market, as well as a weekly or biweekly street market. In addition, temporary markets often spring up like nomadic tent cities during special holidays, fiestas and fairs.

Large permanent markets are jammed with people from surrounding towns and villages on one or two days of the week. They do not close completely on less active days, and many stalls remain open to accommodate regular customers and wholesale dealers.

Temporary markets are found in small *pueblos*, rural areas, on the outskirts of larger towns and occasionally at major crossroads. Temporary markets are especially active during Christmas and Lent. However, even an average market day is something of an event, with a festive, carnival mood.

Shipments of fresh fruits and vegetables are scheduled to reach the market just before large crowds of shoppers, so quality and selection vary greatly from one day to the next, with the best offered on market day (*día del mercado, día de* plaza or just *tianguis*).

Many tourists mistakenly head for the market at the crack of dawn. This isn't necessary; in fact, the main hours of business are later, from about 9 a.m. to 1 p.m. It is at this time, when the food is still fresh and not picked over, the sun is not too hot and both vendors and customers are feeling friendly and energetic, that the market is at its peak.

The best markets for variety and quality of food are located in large cities or towns with a resident gringo community or prosperous tourist trade. Small markets, on the other hand, away from tourist influences, are often much more interesting in themselves. This is particularly true of *tianguis*.

Locating the market is usually not difficult; just walk or drive near the central plaza and look for concentrations of buses and trucks, or pedestrians carrying shopping bags and baskets. You can ask for directions to *el mercado*, but in some areas the market is more commonly known as *la plaza* or *la plaza commercial*. In smaller towns and villages the old custom of gathering in the central plaza to buy and sell is still observed. If you are driving, park a few blocks from the market. When all parking places have been filled, the heavy cargo trucks will still be rolling in with loads of corn, bananas and chilies. You might be hemmed in for hours.

Ins and Outs of Bartering

Bartering is a time-honored custom in Mexico's markets, one that I urge you to practice. Bartering for food and small goods isn't a long involved process. Unless you enjoy drawing it out by diverging into friendly conversation or exchanging tales, the average transaction will take only a few seconds.

Gringos who say that haggling isn't worth the effort aren't doing their math. Anyone who barters competently should save ten, twenty or even thirty percent on an average market trip.

Bartering well also earns you a certain amount of respect from the people you deal with. First and most important, you are not disdaining social contact with them; you are willing and eager to communicate and to acknowledge their customs. The person who pays the first price without question may be laughed at, sometimes to their face. Vendors have little respect for the customer who throws money away.

Bartering in a tourist-town market can be frustrating; vendors often have a "take it or leave it" attitude that is difficult to break through. Haggling is still practiced, however, by people in from the country for market day, by vendors in smaller stalls and those dealing in damaged or slightly inferior goods (which in Mexico often just means "small").

Truck bumper graffiti: At the Glitter of Gold I Won't Come Down

Bartering is not an argument—it is a polite discussion of price—and should be conducted calmly and with respect for the other person. As it is not an argument, you will not offend anyone by trying to barter.

Begin by greeting the vendor. Mexicans are polite to an extreme, even if they hate each other's guts. Examine whatever it is that you're interested in. Squeezing, smelling, hefting are all acceptable but don't overdo it. Many vendors urge you to sample their wares.

The next step is to ask the price. The most easily remembered and overworked word is *"¿Cuánto?"* ("How much?"). Try other expressions like: *"¿Cuánto cuesta?"* ("How much does it cost?"), *"¿A cómo lo da?"* ("At what price do you give it?"), *"¿Cuánto vale?"* ("What is it worth?") or *"¿Cuánto es?"* ("How much is it?"). Each of these should be followed by *"por favor"* ("please").

After you're told the *asking* price, make a counteroffer. This can be the amount you're willing to pay or less: *"No sale en . . .* (amount)?" ("Won't it go for . . . ?"), *"No me da en . . .* (offer)?" ("Won't you give it to me for . . . ?") or *"Lo llevo en . . . pesos"* ("I'll take it for . . . pesos").

Mark-ups for food are usually much less than those for handicrafts. Shop around various stalls. I generally offer two-thirds of the asking price and see what happens. A sad smile and a wagging forefinger means you were too low, but if you are handed the item instantly you were too high. With practice you'll soon learn to quickly judge the proper offer and selling price.

Never try to lower the price by acting as if the merchandise is so foul, so inferior or so unappetizing that the vendor would be better off giving it to you for nothing. This is true for both the craftsman who takes great pride in his crude wood carvings and the *campesina* who laboriously grew a crop of withered squashes on a dry mountain side.

Let's imagine that you want to buy a papaya. An old man seems to have read your mind because he's winking suggestively at several large ones heaped in front of him, attractively ringed with bananas and oranges. This is to be the first test of your newly acquired bartering skill.

You approach with a friendly smile and a greeting. He smiles back. You wipe the smile from your face and become inscrutable. His hand stops stroking the papaya and comes to rest on a pile of potatoes. You make an offer after hearing his initial demand. He appears to think it over as you stand there patiently, humming *El Rancho Grande*.

The old man rubs his chin reflectively, then turns to another customer with a cheery *"¿Qué le damos, señora?"* The woman scowls at a heap of carrots, selecting only the best. You consider the possibility that negotiations have broken off, but notice that his eyes follow you craftily.

You reach into your pocket and pull out a handful of change. His attention is fixed on the money. Are you yielding or just checking for rare coins? He takes money for the carrots, distractedly shoveling them into a plastic sack. You give your coins a tempting jingle and quietly repeat your last offer. There is a questioning note in your voice, as if you might have mistaken his counteroffer for acceptance.

He sighs, *"No es posible,"* but you signal by a cynical twitch of your lips that he'd better deal fast. You lean toward the next stall, squinting toward a competitor's display of fruit.

He makes another counteroffer, good but not quite good enough. You slip the money back into your pocket with a shrug. There are other papayas, your attitude tells him, and other vendors who understand profit and loss.

You wonder what to do next; he is matching you shrug for shrug. The dilemma is solved when the old man points to a slightly smaller papaya and repeats your last offer. You quickly accept, wondering if he'll go home and gloat to his grandchildren that he took you for a ride. He drops the fruit into your shopping bag, then tosses in an orange. You exchange more smiles, silently vowing to renew the contest another day, perhaps over a pineapple or a watermelon.

Many people believe that walking away after the last rock-bottom offer has been made is the best technique. This is often effective, but in some instances it's best to hang around, waiting for the vendor to make a decision. If you leave too soon, they may not bother, especially on small purchases, to yell after you and accept. Always say, *"Gracias, adiós,"* as you leave. This brings attention to your departure. Drag your feet a bit; the vendor knows that many customers have turned back and given in first.

Haggling can involve a complicated juggling of number, size and quality of the items being discussed rather than a sum of money. You offer five pesos for three large oranges. The vendor says she'll give you two oranges for that price.

"No," you say. "I'll give you three pesos for two." She laughs and says, *"¡Bueno!* I'll let you have three oranges, but small ones, for five pesos."

You smile. "Oh, no! You give me four small ones or three large ones for four pesos."

She laughs and says, "I'll give you three small ones and two handfuls of peanuts for five pesos."

You accept.

• Hard-nosed shopping can sometimes backfire, particularly if you want to save money and eat well at the same time. Beans, for example, vary in price depending on age and quality. Cheaper beans are often last year's crop: tough and requiring long cooking (more fuel), they are not as tasty and probably not as nutritious as the more expensive ones.

Shopping Suggestions

• Always carry a good supply of change when shopping for food, particularly in Indian markets where few of the vendors have much money. When they can't come up with the proper change, you'll get it in merchandise. This isn't desirable if you've already got as much as you need.

• Don't be surprised if your money is carefully scrutinized or subjected to the classic counterfeit test of dropping coins to hear them ring. Torn or extremely dirty bills may be rejected, even though the person waving the money away could obviously use your business. Mexicans, especially poorer ones, are extremely suspicious of counterfeit money. A vendor once refused to accept a brand-new bill from me because it was a design that he had not yet seen. Although a helpful passerby assured the man that my money was perfectly good, he just apologized and said, "I can't afford to take chances." Which was undoubtedly true.

Damaged or dirty money must be exchanged at the bank or foisted off on a harried supermarket cashier or gas station attendant.

If someone tries to pass *you* a ripped or badly worn bill, just shake your head and point to the damage. You'll be understood.

• Weights are measured in kilograms (2.2 pounds) and volume in *litros* (1.1 quarts). This system confuses many tourists and they tend to buy in units larger than they normally would.

"¿Un kilo?" the lady asks, filling the measuring tray with twice as many tomatoes as you actually need. With a flick of the wrist she balances out the scale and you pay obediently.

Try to think in terms of *medio* kilo (half a kilogram—1.1 pounds). For example, one and a half kilos is equivalent to three *medios*—which is just over three pounds (math wizards can multiply 2.2 kilograms by 1.5). *Un cuarto* (one-fourth kilo) is very close to half a pound.

Since few foods are sold in packages, this also confuses those accustomed to buying a box of this and a bag of that. How many grams of bulk macaroni are equivalent to the amount you used to get in the local supermarket in a plastic sack? The only way to relearn how to buy correct amounts is by trial and error and a heavy dose of self-restraint.

When I'm in doubt about how much I want of something I always start low. No sensible merchant will be offended if you change your mind and ask for more.

• Many vendors sell their goods by other measures. The most common of these are the *mano* (a handful) and *manojo* (bunch or handful). *Manos* range in size from tiny piles to large handfuls, or sometimes five items. Any food arranged in small heaps, piles, mounds, or pyramids is probably being sold by the *mano*, from seeds to melons.

"Son manos de cinco pesos" ("They're five-peso piles"), a vendor says, noticing your interest in his peanuts. Closer inspection reveals that another pile of equal size costs seven pesos. In this case, it's the quality that changed, not the basic *mano* measurement.

Other common measures are by the can (usually a liter or fraction of a liter), the *jícara* (gourd bowl or dipper), the piece, the bundle (especially herbs and fresh greens), the bunch, the length (sugar cane), the *costal* (large sack) and the *montón*. *Montón* means a pile or heap and can vary from a handful to a truckload.

The word *bola* (ball) may be used to name any fruit or vegetable that remotely looks round or rounded. The term *bola* is frequently heard in Indian markets where many of the vendors do not know the proper Spanish names themselves.

• When buying produce keep in mind that big is beautiful—and therefore more expensive. Large tomatoes and potatoes, for example, cost more per kilo than equally tasty smaller ones.

Produce is sold by the piece and also by the part: a quarter of a cabbage, a slice of melon, half a papaya, etc. Many stalls offer plastic sacks stuffed with grated cabbage, carrot, onion and radish: a pre-mixed salad; just buy a lime and squeeze. You'll also see bags of assorted raw vegetables for soups.

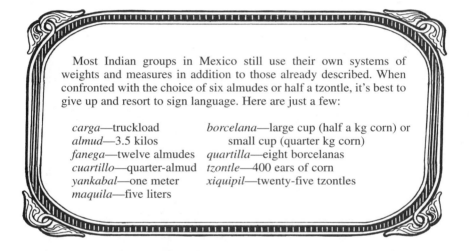

Most Indian groups in Mexico still use their own systems of weights and measures in addition to those already described. When confronted with the choice of six almudes or half a tzontle, it's best to give up and resort to sign language. Here are just a few:

carga—truckload	*borcelana*—large cup (half a kg corn) or
almud—3.5 kilos	small cup (quarter kg corn)
fanega—twelve almudes	*quartilla*—eight borcelanas
cuartillo—quarter-almud	*tzontle*—400 ears of corn
yankabal—one meter	*xiquipil*—twenty-five tzontles
maquila—five liters	

When measuring something a vendor may say *"¡Ya cabal!"* to indicate a full or completed amount. This is an old-fashioned term most often encountered in *tianguis* and rural areas.

If a vendor cannot afford a fancy scale to weigh goods a homemade *balanza* may be used. Your purchase is put in one side of the balance (a pair of baskets or matching tin cans) and a known weight in the other. This "known weight" can be anything from a rock to coins to scraps of metal.

• Because Mexican produce is seldom treated with artificial coloring agents and preservatives, the customer must learn to judge ripeness. A papaya vendor will ask you *"¿Para hoy?"* ("For today?") or *"¿Para mañana?"* ("For tomorrow?"). Other commonly used terms are *madura* (mature, ripe) and *tierna* (tender, soft). A coconut that is *tiernito*, for example, is one with tender meat inside rather than hard. (The diminutive ending—*ito*—means it's really soft.) *Suave* and *suavecito* (soft, smooth) are also commonly heard.

Once untreated foods reach maturity, they go quickly. When a vendor says that something is ripe, be prepared to eat it immediately. Large bunches of bananas, for example, all seem to ripen on the same day and begin rotting on the next.

Overripe fruit is not considered rotten or at all inferior by most Mexicans. To gringos, however, a melon or pineapple that is judged to be *bien bien madura* (well matured) may appear downright soggy. The wise shopper will buy some produce that is ready for immediate eating and some that isn't, for tomorrow.

• Waste not, want not: Smaller stores and markets have yet to adopt prepackaging to the point where you must buy a tube of six tomatoes in order to get one or two pounds of dry pasta when all you need is a single serving. Many stores will even break open packages to sell a single razor blade, a couple of cigarettes or a few saltines. This makes it easier to avoid over-buying. When you just need a small amount don't be afraid to ask for it. Many foods are deliberately packaged in small jars, cans, bags or boxes. This not only keeps the individual price to within a poor person's means, but eliminates leftovers, an important consideration for those who do not have refrigerators.

• Plastic bags: *Bolsas de plástico* flutter across the Mexican landscape like some sort of modern plague, hanging up on cactuses, fluttering and flapping until a curious burro mistakes them for a snack.

When any other container is not available, a plastic bag will be used. Do you need a few ounces of grain alcohol to see you through the day? Sack it up! Large orange juice or a Coca-Cola "to go"? Into the bag for no additional charge. Flavored ices, sliced fruit, dried paint powders, coffee, honey, milk, bulk cough syrup, cloth, birdseed and—why not?—a sack of baby chicks to take to the *rancho*. When it rains, a plastic bag makes a fine hat and a full raincoat for the kids. If it gets deep, buy two more and wear them for boots.

It's much better to invest a few pesos in a well-made shopping bag (*bolsa*) of tightly woven plastic. These bags also make great souvenir-gifts, and have many uses around the house.

Child Labor

While marketing you may be approached by children who offer to assist you with your bundles: *"¿Ayudo? ¿Ayudo? ¿Ayudo? . . ."* ("Help?"). Most of these kids hardly look able to carry a sack of bread.

Before you say, "No!" remember that shopping bags tend to get heavier by the minute. These self-employed "bag boys" can also guide you to the best bargains, search out foods you can't seem to find, teach you a little Spanish and anything else they can think of to please you. The money saved as the result of this advice will pay for their services.

Restrooms

Permanent market buildings are equipped with restrooms, most of which aren't places you'd care to visit except out of real necessity. They are usually located near rear loading docks. Ask for *sanitarios*, *excusados*, *baños* or *mingatoria* (pisser). The fee to pee can be as much as 25 cents, more if you want enough paper to barely cover the palm of your hand. Don't forget that used toilet paper goes into the bucket or waste can, not the toilet.

Stores

The average shopping trip in Mexico often turns into a snipe hunt. You begin by filling two shopping bags with fresh vegetables and fruit at the local market. A piece of beef would be nice, but there was something about the meat stalls along one dark wall that . . . well, there's always a butcher shop nearby, one with better air circulation. But first you need to buy rice. You dash across the street toward a store, arms straining, deftly sidestepping speeding handcarts loaded with crates of carrots, bulging sacks of grain that seem to stagger by on legs of their own and cargo trucks that back up carelessly to the loading docks.

Without once slipping on discarded fruit peels or blackened lettuce leaves, you pass an old man sitting Buddha-like next to half a dozen scrawny chickens as you duck into the doorway of a small *tienda*, a grocery store. At first it appears that there's a run on the stock, but you soon realize that it is just the usual confusion of impatient customers and harried clerks.

"Give me two kilos of tar!"

"I would like seventeen eggs and fresh ones!"

"Put ten pesos of elbow macaroni on my bill!"

"I want a razor blade, two aspirin and five candles!"

You manage to buy your rice in less than ten minutes. You call out "*¡Gracias!*" and slip back outside, pocketing the change. There's a shop selling fresh chicken a few doors away that's not too crowded, so you forget about steak and buy a fryer instead.

"Don't you want the feet?" The lady wielding the cleaver asks, raising her eyebrows in surprise. You generously decline—she can keep the head, too—and push back onto the sidewalk. By the time you locate the bakery, your shoulders are sagging. Was it ever this exhausting at Safeway?

• For translations of food terms and more information and advice on specific items, please turn to *The Shopping List*, later in this chapter.

Tiendas

Anything not available in the market can usually be found in old-fashioned grocery stores, called *tiendas*, that stock everything from fresh capers to firewood. *Tiendas* are everywhere, but those with the best selection and prices are usually found near the market place and central plaza.

Some *tiendas* serve multiple functions, especially in small towns where the most prosperous store owner is also the local government, bootlegger or professional man (or all three). He is assisted in his duties by a confusion of relatives, friends and loungers.

Like the popular image of the American general store, with its group of local characters seated around a glowing potbelly stove, the *tienda* also serves as a social center. Instead of a stove, the gossiping is done around the beer cooler.

One of the most enjoyable ways to learn Spanish is to join the regular loungers in a friendly neighborhood *tienda*. Sit on a rough wooden bench or a sack of dried corn with your soda or beer and watch the locals file in and out for their daily purchases. Before long, you'll be an accepted fixture, included in the jokes and conversations and turned to for authoritative comment should the topic under discussion drift outside of Mexico.

After you've spent some time sitting in the corner, sipping your warm drink and saying, "*¡Buenos días!*" about a hundred times a day, you'll notice something very important: much of the stock isn't in plain view. Customers frequently ask for whatever they want. The owner reaches under the counter, into a bag, box or can or disappears into the back room to produce the item requested. It may be something quite startling: a leg of venison, a car muffler or an umbrella. Always ask, even though you are *almost* sure that they won't have what you are looking for.

Produce and eggs are more expensive in the *tienda* than in the market. This is because the store owner isn't paying much less for these items than you would. The quality of fresh food is often poorer; the owner is reluctant to throw anything to the pig unless it absolutely can't be sold.

Haggling isn't common in *tiendas*. You might try to get the price lowered if the item is damaged or spoiled, but in general the owner sets the price.

Prices vary between these stores, sometimes dramatically. Most have regular clients and a good customer will stop in a favorite *tienda* even though it might cost a bit more than in another place.

Conasupo

The Mexican government provides an alternative to shopping in private stores by operating its own *tiendas*, called *CONASUPO* (which is the acronym of the agency: *Compañía Nacional de Subsistencias Populares*).

Conasupo stores were originally designed to handle basic staples at controlled prices. Their success, however, has led them to expand into *ConaSupers*, offering a much larger variety of goods. In areas too remote or thinly populated to make a permanent store practical, the government dispatches mobile *Conasupos*, usually a large stake truck or semi-trailer rig. Tourists may also shop in these traveling stores. Considering that stocks are limited, it would be polite to buy only what you absolutely need. Local people may rely on the *Conasupo* for their only relief from beans, tortillas and Coca-Cola.

Dry goods stores, pharmacies and supermarkets are also operated by federal health agencies such as IMSS and ISSSTE. Their prices are very good and they're open to everyone.

Supermarkets

The term *supermercado* is loosely applied to any store that allows you to pick groceries off the shelves yourself. In small towns, the "super" may be nothing more—or even less—than a large *tienda*. Full-service, American-style supermarkets are common in larger towns and tourist resorts, complete with ATM machines, bag boys and free cups of coffee.

The biggest supermarkets offer everything from sporting goods, clothing, drugs, hardware and books to furniture; not to mention fresh seafood, imported wines, smoked ham, cheeses, cold beer, canned frog legs and other staples. Supermarket produce is not as choice as in the market, but they may have uncommon things such as eggplant, mushrooms and imported foods.

Supermarkets may not be as interesting or colorful as the open-air *mercado* or Indian *tianguis*, but their prices are competitive and may even beat smaller stores and markets. Supermarkets have frequent sales. Look for signs saying *"OFERTA," "GANGA"* or *"ESPECIAL."*

A supermarket quirk: your cheese, deli items, fruit, and vegetables may have to be bagged, weighed, and priced in their respective departments rather than at the front of the store.

I always make one reconnaissance pass by the cheese and deli section; they frequently give away tasty samples. Samples are also offered if you show interest in a particular cheese or sandwich meat.

Prices are usually marked, but check them closely if you're in doubt, especially if the item is imported. A small can of smoked salmon, for example, may cost as much as an entire armload of groceries. Mexicans love to splurge and the prices they pay for treats can be absolutely astounding.

Most supermarkets do not allow shoppers to carry bags (other than purses) into the store. Look for a check stand near the entrance. The person behind the counter will keep your things while you shop. They usually issue a claim ticket or marker.

Supermarkets often give good exchange rates on traveler's checks and many accept Visa and MasterCard. Confirm this at the checkout stand, however, before you fill a cart.

It is customary to tip bag boys and girls if they help you beyond the check-out stands.

Roadside Stores

When we're on the road, Lorena and I watch carefully for bakeries and tortilla factories. Look for lines of women holding buckets and towels (to carry their fresh tortillas in) or just sniff the air for the unforgettable aroma of roasting corn. Wrap the tortillas in a cloth and eat as soon as possible. Corn tortillas should not be stored in a plastic bag for more than several hours or they'll go sour. (If you find tortillas boring, smear them with your secret stash of peanut butter.)

We also make frequent stops at roadside fruit stands and food vendors. All it takes to lure us in is in a sign tacked to a farmer's hut advertising *"miel de abeja"* (bee's honey) or *"elotes"* (fresh ears of corn). These are golden opportunities not only to buy and eat local treats, but to meet people on a person-to-person basis. Once you've tucked a homegrown papaya or a bunch of bananas into your bag, just ask, *"Qué otra cosa hay?"* ("What else is there?") You might get a shrug for an answer—or an invitation to check out the family garden and orchard for something that interests you. Nothing breaks the ice quicker than expressing friendly curiosity.

When I asked a Baja farmer selling cheeses from his front door, "What is this tree? Can the fruit be eaten?" he loaded me down with grapefruit-like samples, then threw in a squash and a handful of dried figs for good measure. By the time we'd toured his goat pens and admired the family hog, our brief stop to buy cheese had turned into a memorable experience.

Stores on Wheels

In Baja, the Yucatán Peninsula and other remote areas of Mexico, you may see shops-on-wheels, usually a broken-down pickup truck overflowing with fresh produce, cooking oil, tortilla flour, hard candies, candles, eggs and other staples. Some trucks sell fresh meat, ice and cheese. By all means, make use of their services. Most of these trucks have regular routes and timetables. We've camped in places where the driver was happy to include us on his rounds, and literally brought our groceries to the door of our van. On the Michoacán coast, one man was kind enough to fill out his own limited stock by taking our shopping list into town and buying on special order.

The people who live along Mexico's rivers, lagoons and remote sea coasts are also served by an irregular fleet of freight canoes and supply boats. While kayaking north of La Paz in the Sea of Cortez, Lorena and I chanced to meet one of these floating stores. It had been several weeks since we'd launched our boat and fresh foods were just a mouth-watering memory. Once the crew of this fifty-foot "tramp" got over the shock of two sunburned gringos frantically chasing them down in a kayak, they seemed to delight in waving delicacies under our noses. Before our shopping spree was over, we'd packed our Klepper with cooking oil, beans, flour, eggs, fresh jalapeño chilies and even a sack of red, ripe tomatoes. The final treat was presented to us with great ceremony by the captain—a two-pound brick of homemade *panocha*, a rich, dark confection of homemade brown sugar and fruit that made my sweet tooth sing.

THE SHOPPING LIST

Alfalfa
Alfalfa: Fresh alfalfa is popular in mixed juices. Alfalfa seeds often are sprouted for ornament, but almost all are chemically treated and should not be eaten.

Allspice   *Pimienta gorda*

Almonds   *Almendras*

Aluminum foil
Papel aluminio: Supermarket

Anatto   *Achiote*

Anise   *Anís*

Apples
Manzanas: Most are imported from the U.S. but the tastiest apples in Mexico are grown in Chihuahua.

Apricots
Chabacanos, chavacanos

Artichokes   *Alcachofas*

Asparagus   *Espárrago*

Avocado
Aguacate: Avocados were cultivated by the Aztecs, who believed them to be an aphrodisiac. Judging from some people's craving for guacamole salad, this may well be true.

Avocados come in many shapes and sizes, from plum-like to as fat as grapefruits to long crooked-neck types. Some have paper-thin skins that are eaten along with the pulp. This type is preferred for a favorite Mexican snack: smeared like butter on bread or tortillas, then doused with lime juice and a pinch of salt.

Avocados tend to be cheapest in late summer, when back yard trees begin to produce. I once met a traveler who claimed to live on nothing but avocado sandwiches: inexpensive and nourishing.

Baby food
Alimento infantil: American brands of baby food are sold in supermarkets. Many types of baby food and formulas are available in drugstores.

Baking powder
Polvo para hornear: More commonly known by the brand name *Royal*.

Baking soda
Bicarbonato sódico, bicarbonato de sodio or *de sosa*.

Banana
Plátano or *banana*: There are several types, including one that must be cooked, *plátano macho*. Stalks of bananas (*racino*) are sold in roadside stands in the lowlands. Always ask what type of bananas they are to avoid accidentally buying *machos*. The *colima* is an average banana, *tabascos* are large and *dominicos* are quite small, what we call "finger" bananas. A very sweet and plump reddish-purple variety is called *plátano morado*.

In Yucatán, bananas are call *manzanas* or *manzanos*. Since *manzana* means apple in the rest of Mexico, this often leads to confusion.

Basil   *Albahaca, albahacar*

Bay leaves   *Laurel*

Beans
Frijol: The word for cooked beans, *frijoles*, is often mistakenly used by gringos for dry beans. Beans have been cultivated in Mexico for about 7,000 years, so it's not surprising that there are so many types and ways of preparation. Mexicans rate beans according to subtle differences and preferences that are difficult for a gringo to detect or appreciate. In some areas, for example, black beans are considered to be *corriente* (common, mediocre) while in southern

Mexico and the Yucatán they are preferred over all others. White navy-type beans (*fríjol blanco*), thought to be ordinary in the U.S., are reserved for special occasions in Mexico.

The most common beans (other than black beans) are *Bayo* or *Bayo Gordo*, similar to kidney beans, and *Flor de Mayo* (May Flower). The *Flor de Mayo* costs more but has a tendency to break down if cooked too long. Another tasty variety is called *Ojo de Liebre* (Hare's Eye).

When shopping for beans avoid *fríjol viejo* (old beans). This is last year's crop; they are tough, take longer to cook and are not as flavorful as *fríjol nuevo* (new beans). When two apparently identical bins of beans are different in price, the cheaper will be *viejo*.

Always wash beans thoroughly before cooking and watch for small stones, even in packaged beans. (See *Our Favorite Mexican Recipes*.)

If you don't have the time or the patience to cook whole beans, you might like to try canned refried beans. Even Steve is surprised at how good these are. Also, try instant beans, *fríjol instantáneo*. With a bit of practice it is possible to turn this unappetizing brown dust into quite tolerable *refritos*. Look for boxes of instant beans in the supermarket. A good emergency food. (See also *Lima beans* and *Garbanzos*.)

Bean sprouts

Nacidos: Available in some health food stores, but if you eat them often, plan to grow your own.

Beef   *Carne de res*: See *Meat*.

Beets   *Betabeles*, *remolacha*

Bell pepper

imienta, *pimienta dulce*: A Mexican chili, *chile poblano*, is often confused by gringos with bell peppers. (See *Chilies*.)

Berries

Frambuesas, *fresas*, *fresas del monte* and *moras* are commonly used to describe various berries, whether accurate or not.

Black pepper

Pimienta negra: Sold in tiny cellophane packets in *tiendas*. Peppercorns are *pimientas*. They are sometimes sold in bulk. Cans and small bottles of ground pepper are found in the supermarket.

Bleach   *Blanqueador* or *cloro*

Bouillon

Cubitos de Maggi (brand name) or just *cubitos*: Chicken bouillon cubes are as common in Mexico as tortillas. Plain tomato is becoming very popular, but beef bouillon is scarce. Cubes are sold individually, in boxes, cans and plastic jars.

Bread, Bakeries

Pan, *Panaderías*: Many tourists are pleasantly surprised to find that although tortillas are a staple food, *pan* (bread) is also common and very good. *Panaderías* (bakeries) can be found in almost every town.

Bolillos (French-style rolls) are the most common type of bread. Most other baked goods, regardless of their appearance, are slightly sweet. Ask, "*¿Es dulce?*" ("Is it sweet?"). *Panaderías* generally bake only in the morning and offer fresh things in the early afternoon. It's best to be there just after the baking has been done or you may go without. They rarely prepare more than can be quickly sold that same day. Other than American-style products, baked goods do not contain preservatives and should be eaten within a day or two.

Shopping in a *panaderías* is very simple; just grab a tray or basket and a pair of tongs and select more than you can possibly eat. Baked goods are very cheap.

Some bakeries prepare special things on certain days of the week. *Empanadas* are a favorite. They are made by cooking a tart-like shell of dough filled with fresh fruits, vegetables, fish or meat.

At fairs, carnivals and fiestas, you'll see vendors selling an incredible variety of special cookies, breads and cakes. Those that aren't sold will be repacked and taken to another town. This is why most of these baked goods look a hell of a lot better than they taste. Free samples are frequently offered to passersby, which is probably a mistake on the vendor's part.

Bimbo is the trademark for a variety of baked goods that are faithful imitations of the stuff manufactured in the U.S. Their sliced bread probably has even less food value than it does flavor. *Bimbo's pan integral* is a feeble attempt at whole wheat. Other products include *bollos* (hamburger buns) and *medianoches* (hot dog buns, "midnights").

A better mass-produced bread, bearing the unfortunate brand name of *Filler*, tastes like a cross between rye and pumpernickel.

A delicious French-style bread, *pan francés*, is baked in the Yucatán.

Broccoli   *Brécol* or *brócoli*

Brussels sprouts
Col de Bruselas

Butter
Mantequilla: See *Dairy Products*.

Cabbage   *Col* or *repollo*

Cactus
Nopales, nopalitos: The young leaves of the nopal cactus are a very popular food in Mexico. They are sold fresh in the market, cleaned of their spines. Canned *nopalitos* are available in supermarkets and *tiendas*.

The fruit of the nopal, *tuna*, is also an important food, especially to those who live in arid areas and cannot afford imported fruits. *Tunas* (also known as *higo de nopal, higo de chumbo, chumbos* and *xoconostli*) come in a variety of colors, including yellow, green, red and purple, the most common. The fruits are covered with tiny hair-like spines that must be removed with a sharp knife before eating. Anyone who has tried to eat a *tuna* complete with spines (me) can testify that it is a painful experience.

The flavor, a tasty sweet-sourness, is very refreshing. The fruit is high in vitamins and mineral salts. *Tunas* are widely used in candies, *agua fresca* (flavored water) and ices.

The *pitahaya* is a similar fruit from another type of cactus. It is reddish purple with spines.

Cactus fruits have a lot of seeds inside; they are swallowed or spit out, depending on how hungry you are.

Camomile
Manzanilla: *Té de manzanilla* is a classic Mexican drink. It is widely used to calm upset nerves and stomachs. Sold everywhere in tea bags, bulk dried and fresh.

Candles
Velas: Very ornate candles are sold in funeral parlors and coffin shops (often a lumberyard). They make interesting souvenirs. Real beeswax candles are sold in and around the market place.

Candy
Dulces: Sold individually and in bulk. A Mexico City newspaper warned parents that caramel eating was a sure sign of drug addiction. Be careful. (See *Restaurants and Typical Foods: Junk Food*.)

Cantaloupe
Melón: This word is used for all types of melon except *sandías*, watermelons. The peak of the harvest is mid- to late spring, when cantaloupe lovers are struck with melon madness.

Capers
Alcaparrones: Sold in bulk in most large *tiendas*.

Caraway seeds
Semillas de alcaravea

Cardamom *Cardamomo*

Carrot *Zanahoria*

Cashew *Marañon*

Catsup
Salsa de tomate catsup: In Yucatán there is a concoction called *Catzuut* that looks like catsup but tastes like mincemeat pie.

Cauliflower *Coliflor*

Celery *Apio*

Celery salt
Sal de apio: Supermarket

Cereals
Corn flakes: Dry breakfast cereals are sold by their English names. The most common cooked cereals are oatmeal (*ojuelas de avena*) and cream of wheat (*crema de trigo*). Read the cooking directions carefully; many people make *atole*, a watery drink, from these cereals.

Chayote
Chayote: This vegetable looks like a hairy squash. They are vaguely obscene in appearance but taste great. (See *Our Favorite Mexican Recipes*.)

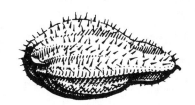

Cheese
Queso: See *Dairy Products*.

Cherries
Cerezas: There is a small native cherry called *capulín*.

Chervil *Perifollo*

Chia seeds
Chia, semillas de chia: *Chia* seeds are used in breads, candies and *agua fresca* (flavored water drinks), and medicinally for diarrhea and to calm upset stomachs. *Chia* was used as a quick energizing food by the Aztecs and is being rediscovered by modern-day athletes and hikers. One or two teaspoonsful is said to be a hefty portion. When mixed with liquids the seeds produce a sticky gelatin that is soothing to the digestive tract. This gelatin is so thick that I once plugged a soda bottle by dropping in a teaspoonful of chia seeds.

Chia is also know in English as the lime-leafed sage.

Chick peas See *Garbanzo beans*.

Chicken
Chicken and turkey are prized by Mexicans, and most private fiestas and celebrations require the sacrifice of at least a few birds. If you want to give someone a simple gift and can't imagine what they'd appreciate, try a chicken, dead or alive. You'll probably be invited to help eat it.

Dressed poultry is sold in meat markets and in small shops specializing in birds and eggs. Live birds can be purchased in and around the market place, but it takes an astute type to avoid getting something old, skinny or tough as rubber. Bartering with *campesinos* for a hen or rooster requires skill; it helps if your Spanish is good enough to say, "His wattles look a little pale."

A few shops sell live birds at fixed rates. The first time I visited one of these I noticed that a nice impersonal, already plucked chicken was displayed on the counter. It lay "in state" on an attractive bier of shaved ice, surrounded by sprigs of bright green parsley. It looked good.

"I'll take that *pollo*," I said to the man behind the counter.

He looked at me for a few moments. "A chicken *like* that one?" he answered.

I hesitated. There was a row of wooden cages behind, crowded with live chickens, clucking and cackling contentedly. A sort of minor egg-laying operation, I assumed.

"Sure, like that one," I said.

With no further comment he stepped to a nearby cage, flipped open the door and grabbed a startled chicken by the neck. Before I could protest he turned the squawking bird upside down and jammed it, head first, into a metal cylinder mounted on the wall. The cylinder ended in a funnel-like device. The instant the bird's head came out of the opening, the man drew a razor-sharp knife across its throat.

There was a crimson spurt of blood, neatly funneled into a metal trough already running with water, and a final frantic rustling. With equal efficiency he removed the chicken, stripped off the feathers and reduced it to a cut fryer in a few strokes of his cleaver.

"Just like that one," he smiled, nodding toward the peacefully resting display bird. I took the body and hurried away; other customers were waiting their turn.

Pollo (chicken) is sold whole and then cut up upon request (make hacking motions with your hand). Some vendors also sell individual parts, usually for about the same price per kilo as an entire bird. These parts are *pechuga* (breast), *pierna* (thigh and drumstick), *alas* (wings), *higado* (liver) and *cabeza* (head). If you don't want the feet and head to eat, take them anyway and bestow them upon some beggar; he'll be delighted.

A chicken that has a golden tone to the skin is considered superior to a pale bird. A *pollo de oro* (gold chicken) usually gets that way by being fed marigold flowers, rather than by lounging around in the sun or eating an especially good diet.

Pollo de leche (milk chicken) is for frying or broiling.

Chilies

Chilies are a very important food in Mexico. A fresh *chile* is an excellent source of vitamin C and minerals. They are popularly believed to stimulate the appetite and improve digestion, at least when eaten in moderate amounts.

Mexicans take their *chile* fresh, dried, pickled, cooked or raw in sauces, stews, soups, desserts (*capirotada*), mixed drinks, with fruit and in a variety of ways for medicinal purposes. The ways of preparing and eating chilies are as numerous as the types: chilies have the ability to cross-fertilize themselves, making the variations infinite.

Contrary to popular belief, chilies are not peppers. They are actually capsicums. Columbus made the initial error in identification when he spotted what he thought was a pepper in Haiti.

Chilies are not only a source of food and vitamins, but play an important role in Mexican humor. *Chile* is synonymous with penis and the jokes are limitless. A classic song, *La Llorona* (The Weeper), has gradually evolved verses far spicier than the original:

"Soy como chile verde Llorona,
Picoso pero sabroso."
"I'm like the green chile Weeper,
Hot but tasty."

A brand of canned chilies is called *"El Lloron"*; the label shows a Mexican *charro* (cowboy) biting a large chili as tears stream down his face. The double meanings are as interwoven as a basket.

• **General chili lore:** The tip of the chili is the coolest part. A particular type of chili can vary greatly in spiciness depending on what stage of growth it was picked at and the conditions it was grown under (temperature, humidity, etc.). One *poblano* in a batch of *chiles rellenos* might go down as easily as a bell pepper while the next will snap your neck.

To impress your friends without searing the skin from the throat, bite off the whole chili just above the stem and quickly move it to the rear molars. Use only the back teeth to keep the hotness away from sensitive taste buds in the front of your mouth and tongue.

Now chew it up quickly, with great ecstatic smacking sounds, and swallow. If you did it correctly the burning sensation will be within tolerable limits. Your friends will be impressed and want to match your feat.

A chili can be cooled by removing the seeds and veins. When using them for cooked dishes or sauces, try soaking the chilies in hot milk or water first; they should cool down even more.

A pinch of salt taken on the tip of the tongue and allowed to dissolve before eating a *chile* will raise a protective coating of saliva that helps resist burning.

A person who has overdosed on chili is *enchilado(a)*. The symptoms are a noisy, desperate sucking of air, head thrown violently backwards, copious sweating, runny nose, and hands clawing at the throat or groping frantically for water. There is no certain cure, but the symptoms can be relieved by eating salt and bread. If this isn't sufficient, try sugar, then milk, sodas and/or beer. Mexicans purse their lips when *enchilados* and inhale forcefully.

For chili in the eyes (I won't bother to describe the agony), immediate and liberal washing with cold water is advised. Lightly rubbing or brushing human hair over the eyes will also give relief.

Cooks often get chili burns on their fingers. This doesn't sound serious unless you get a genuine case of fingers *enchilados*. I once spent three hours with my hands in a bucket of ice water after cleaning a large number of fresh *jalapeños*. It felt like an acid burn. The Mexican women I was helping almost fainted from laughter; their ribald comments got downright boring. For serious chili handling, I now wear rubber gloves.

Chilies are *picante* (spicy hot) and not *caliente* (warm, hot temperature). *"¡Sí, pica!"* means "Yes, it bites! It's hot!" *Picoso* is also commonly heard in place of *picante*.

Ancho
Dried *poblano;* not too hot, very popular for sauces. Add one or more *anchos* to beans as you're cooking them. Powdered chili *ancho* is excellent on popcorn. We always buy half a kilo to take home.

Cambray
Small, green or red and quite hot.

Cascabel
Two to three inches long, dry, red and medium hot. Excellent for hot sauces. (See *Our Favorite Mexican Recipes*.)

Chile del árbol
The "tree chili" is small, green or red and quite hot. They are sometimes offered fresh in restaurants.

Chile negro
Also called *chilaca*. It is long and dark and hot. Dried it is called *pasilla*.

Chiltepin
A very hot, pea-sized *chile* harvested wild in Chihuahua.

Chiltepiquin
Small, green and very hot.

Chipotle
Dried, smoked *jalapeños*. Available canned in *adobo* sauce.

Guajillo
Long, narrow and light red. Mild.

Güero
The "blonde" is light green or yellow, similar in shape and size to a *poblano* and hotter. They are sometimes used as a substitute for *poblanos* when preparing *chile rellenos*. Seasonal.

Habanero
The dreaded and deadly Yucatán killer, known by the Mayas as "crying tongue." The hottest chili in Mexico and not one to fool with lightly. A piece the size of a pea will transform your soup into liquid fire. I once overdosed on *habaneros* in a small restaurant in Quintana Roo. I fainted right into my plate of food. I like to keep some around to offer friends who brag they can eat anything. Instant humility. Bottled sauces made with *habaneros* are popular in Yucatecan restaurants. Handle with care. *Habaneros* are red, green and yellow and generally small.

Jalapeño
The most commonly canned and pickled chili. Up to two inches long, fat and meaty, and tolerable to scorching. Often sold in bulk in *tiendas*. A favorite Mexican snack consists of a fresh *bolillo* with a pickled *jalapeño* stuffed inside. *Jalapeños en escabeche* (pickled) should be stored in a glass container. *Jalapeños rellenos* are stuffed, usually with mackerel or shrimp, and canned. *Rajas de jalapeños en escabeche* are strips of chili without seeds. They make excellent tidbits for those not up to biting into a whole one. Fresh *jalapeños* will be green, yellow or reddish. Dried and smoked *jalapeños* are called *chipotles*. They are hot and have an excellent flavor. Canned *chipotles* are also tasty.

Pasilla
Dried *chile negro* (*chilaca*).

Piquín
Also known as *tipín*. Quite small (berry-sized), quite hot and red in color.

Poblano
A reasonably mild, dark green chili, four to five inches long. It is preferred above all others for making *chile rellenos*. *Poblanos* are what I call a "Mexican bell pepper"; compared to others they are downright cool. When dried the poblano is called an *ancho*.

Serrano
Smaller and thinner than *jalapeños* and preferred by Mexican cooks for sauces, guacamole and *ceviche*. Red or green and quite hot, with a sharper bite than *jalapeños*. They are often served fresh in restaurants. Start with a tiny nip off the small end. Serranos are commonly prepared *en escabeche*. When buying canned peppers try the tiniest size of both *jalapeños* and *serranos;* most gringos prefer the former.

Chili powder
Chile molido: Many types of chilies are dried and ground, but for all-purpose use the *cascabel* and *ancho* are best. The *ancho* isn't as hot as the *cascabel*. Both blend well into sauces.

Pipían is a ground mixture of squash seeds, cornmeal and *chile*.

Chile molido con especías is like the ground chili sold in the U.S.

Various ground chilies are sold in bulk in the market; when in doubt ask for a taste before buying.

Chili sauce
Salsa picante: Bottled hot sauces of various types and blends of *chiles* are very common. Try local concoctions; some are quite memorable.

Canned sauces of chopped chilies and other ingredients are also very good. Our favorite is called *salsa casera* (homemade sauce). It is reasonably spicy and inexpensive. For an instant meal open a can of *salsa casera*, a can of refried beans and a package of saltine crackers.

Chinese parsley
Cilantro or *culantro*: Very important in Mexican cooking, particularly soups and sauces. Many people can't stand the stuff.

Chirimoya
Chirimoya (*Anona glabra*): A greenish fruit that appears to be covered with large scales. The inner pulp is white with many black seeds. Tasty.

Chocolate

Chocolate: A sacred Aztec beverage. Hard chocolate is sold in *tiendas* and the market, cut with crude sugar.

Cigarettes, cigars

Cigarros: A pack is a *cajetilla*, a carton is a *cartón*. You can buy waterproof cigarettes in Mexico. Dunk one in a glass of water to simulate the rain falling on a farmer's head, then light up. The paper won't burn but the tobacco will—well, almost.

Common U.S. brands are also made in Mexico but Mexican cigarettes are cheaper: *Fiesta*, *Baronet*, *Del Prado* and *Record*. Non-filters are cheaper yet: *Alas*, *Casinos* and *Delicados*. And then there are *Faros* (Lighthouses), worth the price just for the picture on the package.

Both *filtros* and *sin filtros* (non-filtered) come regular and *mentolado*.

Cigars (*puros*) are relatively inexpensive but common only in larger towns. Very crude cigars are sold in Indian markets. The classic coffin nail.

Cinnamon

Canela: Sold in powder (*molida*) and stick form (*canela en rama*). Very common.

Cloves

Clavos de especia are whole cloves and *clavos molidos* are ground. If you ask for just *clavos*, the word for nails, that's what you'll get.

Cocoa

Chocolate: The chocolate that comes in cakes is excellent. *Chocomíl* (flavored powdered milk) is very popular, but don't be misled by the name; it comes in flavors other than chocolate: *Chocomíl de fresa* (strawberry), *de vainilla*, etc.

Coconut

Coco: Sold dried and shredded in supermarkets. Much better quality coconut is available in the market and from street vendors. All you need is a straw—to drink the *agua* (water, not milk as we call it)—and a shredder. Whole *cocos* are sold throughout Mexico, usually pared down to the hard inner shell. If you don't want a whole one just ask for *carne* (meat).

Cocos that are grown especially for drinking are *coco de agua*.

Coffee

Café: Many large supermarkets and stores near the market grind coffee beans. If the beans are very dark and shiny they have been coated with sugar. Ask for *café sin azúcar* or *café estilo americano* if you want sugarless coffee. Have it ground *regular*. Coffee that has been ground *fino* is like flour and will go through a percolator.

Instant coffee is called by the most common brand name, Nescafé. The best buy in instant coffee is the CONASUPO house brand, said to actually be Nescafé.

Coffee is sold in one-pound cans, almost always ground *regular*. Look for *estilo americano* on the label.

I always stock up on whole bean coffee (cheaper) when heading back to the U.S. Try to give it a taste test before buying quantity; flavor varies from one area to another. Most large towns have shops that carry fresh beans from around the country. When asking for a blend, the safest is *export* if you prefer American-style.

Coffee is also sold in small packets, just enough to make a couple of cups. It is finely ground and usually mixed with sugar; don't mistake it for instant.

Coffee, canned or bulk, can legally be imported into the U.S. Don't forget, however, to declare it at Customs.

Cookies

Galletas: Sold in bulk in *tiendas* and the market. Animal crackers are very cheap when purchased by the handy, economical gunnysack. Probably not very nutritious, but you can make a lot of kids happy. Fancy cookie assortments are sold in supermarkets.

Coriander seeds

Semillas de cilantro: Fresh coriander (Chinese parsley) is called *cilantro* or *culantro*.

Corn   *Maíz*

Corn on the cob

Elotes: They tend to be tough but tasty. Ask for *tiernito* (tender) and you might get one that is. Try an *elote con todo*: lime juice and chili powder.

A hard, dried ear of corn is a *mazorka*.

Corn starch

Maizena, the most common brand name.

Cornmeal

Harina de maíz amarilla: Supermarket. If you want cornmeal to make tortillas, see *Masa*.

Crackers

Galletas saladas (salted cookies): Crackers are very big in Mexico. A favorite snack, available from street vendors and in most *tiendas*, is a saltine

doused with bottled hot sauce or a squirt of juice from the pickled *chile* jar.

An excellent, and addictive, brand of slightly sweetened crackers is called *Pan Cremas*.

Cream

Crema: See *Dairy Products*.

Cream cheese

Queso crema: See *Dairy Products*.

Cream of tartar

Crémor tártaro

Cucumber   *Pepino*

Cumin seeds

Cominos: Indispensable in creating authentically flavored Mexican bean dishes. Most common whole.

Currants   *Grosellas*

Curry powder

Polvo de curry: Supermarket

Custard

Flan: The national dessert; sold as a mix everywhere.

Dairy Products

There have been so many hysterical scare stories about food and drink in Mexico, many tourists approach dairy products (*productos lacteos*) as if they'd been handled by Madame Borgia herself. People who categorically refuse to touch any milk, cheese or cream are not only unrealistic, but put themselves into the position of not being able to eat much of anything typically Mexican. In fact, pasteurized dairy products are found virtually everywhere in Mexico except for remote villages.

Dairy products are perhaps more important to Mexican cuisine than chicken and beef. For many meat is a luxury, but milk (for *café con leche*), cheese (for *enchiladas*) and cream (to pour over strawberries) are vital necessities.

This doesn't mean that precautions shouldn't be observed. Unhealthy animals do occur, but they aren't the only reason dairy products can be hazardous at times. A piece of cheese may be perfectly safe until the woman in the market cuts off a slice for you with a knife that hasn't been washed with soap and water for a week. Milk may be contaminated by dirt on the cow, in the milk can, in the cup it is measured out with or by adulteration with impure water.

The Mexican government is attempting to educate people, especially those in rural areas, to handle dairy products with care. This means that a homemade cheese may be made under very hygienic conditions or then again, it may not. It all depends on the awareness and attitude of the person who makes it. Which also means that you can never tell.

When in doubt about any dairy product, cook it well. This should make it safe. The so-called dangerous dairy products are those that have not been carefully pasteurized (cooked) and packaged. You should have no problems at all if you avoid uncooked ranch cheeses and raw milk or cook them yourself. Mexico's dairies and processing facilities are generally modern and sanitary; pasteurized products, from butter to cheese to yogurt, can be found in most towns.

Butter

Mantequilla: Sold in *tiendas* and supermarkets in *barras* (sticks, bars). Bulk butter sold in some markets and *tiendas* is usually unsalted and sweet and may not be pasteurized (*pasteurizada*).

Cheese

Queso: Many cheeses are sold under familiar names: Camembert, Gouda, Parmesan, etc. Mexicans prefer to buy cheese in bulk, rather than packaged. Samples are offered in stores that sell cheeses. Just say *"Quiero probarlo"* ("I want to try it") and you'll be given a small piece.

Chihuahua cheese is one of the most well-known cheeses and also among the best. It was originally introduced by Mennonite immigrants, many of whom still live in isolated farming communities in the northern states. *Chihuahua* is pale (Mexican cheeses are rarely dyed) and tastes much like a mild cheddar. When comparing two pieces of *Chihuahua* I prefer the flavor of the darker yellow. This is a good cheese for tacos, enchiladas, toasted sandwiches and other cooked dishes. It keeps well, even without refrigeration, though it should be carefully wrapped in brown paper or cloth.

Oaxaca cheese is also very well known throughout the country. It is sometimes called *quesillo*. It is a very white cheese, formed into balls about the size of a fist and stringy. It is sometimes shaped into small round cakes and can be confused with ranch cheese. *Oaxaca* cheese that is homemade is cooked. If the vendor handles it properly it should be safe even if not labeled "pasteurized." *Oaxaca* is a good substitute for mozzarella.

White or ranch cheese (*queso blanco* or *queso del rancho*, also *queso ranchero*) is almost always homemade. Wrapped in fresh green leaves, it is commonly sold in the market, or door to door. Much of it is made from goat's milk. Ranch cheese has a crumbly texture and is very white. It is rarely cooked in processing. Ranch cheese should be avoided until it has been well cooked.

Queso amarillo, yellow cheese, is more commonly known by the brand name *Queso Club*. I call this stuff rat cheese; compared to *Chihuahua* or *Oaxaca* cheeses it just doesn't seem worth the price. Kids love it.

Other yellow cheeses are either Mexican cheeses that have been dyed, or imported and very expensive.

Queso suizo, Swiss cheese, is found in larger stores and is both safe and costly.

Queso estilo parmesano or just *parmesano*, Parmesan, is fairly common and quite good. Much of it is imported from South America. The type sold grated in cans is much more expensive than bulk. It is sometimes called *queso añejo* (aged).

Queso crema, cream cheese, is sold

Garlic salt

Sal de ajo: Supermarket.

Ginger

Jengibre: Ground ginger is sold in supermarkets; fresh can sometimes be found in the market, from herbalists and in supermarkets. We always bring some from home.

Grapes

Uvas: Mexico produces a quantity of grapes, most of which are converted to brandy and wine. The grape season is late summer to fall, at other times they are expensive. Pale green grapes are called *blancas* (white) and dark grapes are *negras* (black).

Fresh-squeezed grape juice (*jugo de uva*) is available in grape-growing areas during the harvest.

Grapefruit   *Toronja*

Greens

Quelites: Includes a wide variety of green leafy vegetables, many of them gathered wild. Among the most common are *verdolagas* (purslane), *romeritos*, *tintoniles* or *quelites*, a general term that covers many plants with regional names. When in doubt, ask how they are prepared.

Green beans   *Ejotes*

Groceries   *Abarrotes*

Guava

Guayaba: This tasty fruit looks very much like a yellow or pink crabapple, but is soft and sweet. *Guayaba* is used for *agua frescas* and it also makes good wine.

Herbs

Hierbas, yerbas: Herbs and spices (*especías, olores*) are available in most *tiendas* and from vendors in the market place. Some stalls have an amazing variety of fresh herbs and spices, including various medicinal teas.

Imported spices from the U.S., as well as U.S. brands made in Mexico, are sold in most supermarkets.

The best way to find spices is to ask for them. Many are sold in bulk or fresh and are not easily recognizable. A *tienda* often has several types of spices in tiny cellophane bags and others growing in the back yard. It is common to see people ask for a particular spice in a *tienda* and then wait while the woman of the house scrounges through her garden to see if the plant can be trimmed for the customer.

Hibiscus

Jamaica: The dried flowers are sold in bulk in *tiendas* and the market. They make an excellent tea or *agua fresca*; very refreshing.

Honey

Miel de abeja: The Yucatán is famous for its honey, most of which is sold long before it is even harvested. Local honey is available throughout Mexico. It is sold in bulk in some *tiendas* or direct from the beekeeper. Take your own container.

Honey sold in the market by *campesinos* will vary in color, quality and price. Some people aren't above cutting their honey with cheap sugar. Good honey should be fragrant and clear, though even the best does crystallize.

The word *miel* is a general term for honey, molasses and syrups. When buying honey be sure to specify *miel de abeja* (honey of bees). If the label on a jar of honey doesn't say *de abeja*, it may well be molasses.

Jam, jelly

Mermelada, jalea: Because sugar is kept cheap in Mexico by government control, the price of jams and jellies is fairly reasonable. The best bargains are in CONASUPOS. Jam lovers will be particularly attracted to types made with tropical fruits.

Jicama

Jícama: A very popular root vegetable (it grows like a potato) that can be used as a substitute for water chestnuts. It is eaten raw or cooked. Jicamas are a very common street snack: try one peeled and doused with lime juice, salt and chili. The flavor is something like a cross between an apple, pear and potato. Excellent in salads.

Juice

Jugo: Excellent fresh juices are available in the market (see *Restaurants and Typical Foods*). Canned juices (*jugo de lata*) are sold everywhere, almost as commonly as Coca-Cola. They are cheapest in the CONASUPO. Try the tropical fruits: *guayaba* and *mango* are especially good. *Jugo de fresa* (strawberry) is the only one I don't like; it is very sweet.

Bottled fruit juices are sold in *tiendas* and supermarkets. They aren't too expensive and are sometimes on sale in the super.

Carton juices, usually orange, are actually just water and flavors. *Anaranjada* (orange-colored) is a good description of how they taste.

Lard

Manteca de cerdo: Sold in bulk by the peso. *Cebo* is beef lard, i.e., grease.

Lavender   *Espiliego, lavanda*

Leek   *Puerro* or *poro*

Lemon

Lima: This word is forever being confused with *limón* (lime). The yellow lemon used in the U.S. is not common in Mexico. Almost all of the many types of limes and lemons are collectively called *limones*.

Lemon grass

Té de limón: Looks like large pieces of grass and makes a very tasty tea. Try a combination with hibiscus.

Lentils

Lentejas: Good for making sprouts. Clean lentils carefully; even packaged ones are rocky.

Lettuce

Lechuga: Includes both head and Romain lettuce (*lechuga romana*).

Light bulbs

Focos: Same wattage as in the U.S. and cheapest in the CONASUPO.

Lima beans

Habas verdes: Usually sold dried. A traditional Lenten soup is made with lima beans.

Lime

Limón: There are sweet limes and sour limes (*limones dulces* and *limones agrios*). They may look exactly like a lemon, but the taste is definitely lime. The standard lime is small and either green or yellow. Very important medicinally. (See *Staying Healthy*.)

Macaroni

Macarrones, fideos, pasta: Fideos covers many types of macaroni, from elbows, stars and clams (*codos, easterlies* and *almejas*) to a very thin, vermicelli-like noodle that is just called *fideo* or *fideo delgado*. Fideos are very common in Mexican cooking, usually served as a dry soup (*sopa*).

Thicker noodles are not too commonly used. The soft Mexican wheat works best in thinner macaroni. Supermarkets sometimes have good quality spaghetti and fettuccine noodles, though they are much more expensive than the average *fideo*. Fideos are usually sold by the weight rather than the package.

Mace   *Macis*

Mamey

Mamey: An oval-shaped fruit with a brown pebbly skin. The pulp is reddish purple around a large seed and has a very exotic flavor.

Mango

Mango: Whoever introduced the mango to Mexico from the East should be canonized. Mexicans talk of mango season (late spring to fall) in reverent but slightly hysterical tones. In their eager anticipation, in fact, they even eat green mangoes. The hard fruit is speared on a sharp stick, sliced petal-like and covered with lime juice and chili. Slices of similarly garnished mango are sometimes served as snacks in *cantinas*. Never have cheap *mezcal* and tequila been more delicately mellowed than with a sour mango.

There are more than 500 types of mangoes. The most commonly eaten in Mexico is the *manila*. The *manila* is green on the outside or yellow with black spots, depending on its maturity. It is not stringy (coarse varieties are). An average *manila* is about four inches long. They are best when firm. The finest *manilas* come from Veracruz.

The *manila de Guerrero* is orange on the inside rather than yellow.

The *petacón* (from *petaca*—buttock), also known as *criollo* or *indio*, brings blissful sighs from mango fanciers. It is big, as the name implies, red to reddish orange, very sweet and not at all stringy. A *petacón* is large enough to carve, like a small melon.

The latest rage in areas of Mexico where mangoes are grown is the *Tome Arkins*. This mango, perhaps named after some dedicated gringo grower, is even bigger than the *petacón*, which it resembles.

Another huge mango, as large as a cantaloupe, is called *Kent*. It comes in a range of pastels: pale green, yellow, pink and red. The *Kent* has a dreamy perfume flavor that goes well with sunsets and liqueurs.

In contrast to the big mangoes, there's the tiny *obo*, sweet but stringy.

For those not yet indoctrinated into the Mango Mystique, here are a few suggestions:
• Don't eat different types at the same sitting or you'll get a gut ache.
• Watch out for overripe mangoes; they don't digest well.
• Don't try to eat the skin; it's bitter.
• Mangoes are best eaten in the nude or wearing a bib and rain gear. Better yet, in fact the absolute best, is to eat them chin deep in the surf, just as the sun is coming up or going down.

Margarine
Margarina: Cheaper brands taste awful—buy familiar U.S. labels made in Mexico.

Marjoram *Mejorana*

Masa harina
Tortilla flour: sold everywhere.

Matches
Cerillos: The Spanish word *fósforo* is rarely used in Mexico.

Mayonnaise
Mayonesa: A good fake mayonnaise that is much cheaper is called *aderezo para ensaladas* (salad dressing).

Meat Shops
A trip to the average *carnicería* (meat shop) separates the true carnivores from the vegetarians.

If meat markets were graded as movies are, on the basis of the acts portrayed in them, all those in the U.S. would be rated "GP" or "family entertainment." The average Mexican meat market would get an "X" rating, "for hardened adults only." The only stage of

the meat-cutting process not usually done before your eyes is the killing.

To select a meat shop (most are actually tiny stalls) use your eyes and nose. The stalls inside the market place itself are frequently the goriest and least appetizing.

Large markets will often arrange the stalls by the type of meat they are selling. Ten stalls in a row will have beef, the next ten pig meat and the rest goat, chicken, etc.

Although the appearance of the raw meat and the shop itself might be disturbing to those unaccustomed to the sight of pig heads lolling from iron hooks or coils of entrails draped like Christmas decorations over the counter, the meat is almost always very fresh.

In fact, it is often *too fresh*. When an animal is butchered, it is not hung in a cool room or locker to be aged; it's sold that very day. Unaged meat is tougher and may taste stronger than most tourists are used to.

Anyone can become a qualified meat cutter in Mexico as long as they have a strong arm and a big knife. "Cuts" are made by repeated blows on the meat; when it has reached manageable proportions, it's ready to be sold. Although butchering is more refined in shops that cater to foreigners and particular Mexicans, there are just a few basic cuts: steaks, chops, ground meat and stew meat.

Such things as roasts and T-bones are not used by the average Mexican cook. To get them, you'll have to find a butcher who understands the subtleties of meat cutting or else explain it yourself. This can be very difficult.

My first experience with ordering a specific cut ended in disaster. We were having a birthday feast and decided to splurge with a barbecue. I was elected to buy the meat.

After touring the market and looking over the selection, I finally located a good slab of pork ribs. The butcher weighed the meat, then shoved it over the counter for a closer inspection.

"Perfect," I drooled. "I'll take it."

He picked up the ribs and flipped them onto a large wooden block behind him. Before I realized what was happening, he grabbed a razor-sharp machete and dexterously reduced the meat to bite-sized pieces.

As the butcher wrapped the ribs in newspaper, I explained that I wanted to have a barbecue, not a stew. His face darkened. Before I could say more, he walked into the rear of the stall and dragged a freshly killed pig from a dark corner.

Fifteen minutes later, after an exhibition of savage meat cutting, he handed me another sizable slab of ribs. "*¡Pedazo entero!*" ("Whole piece!") he said emphatically, using the words that I could have avoided trouble with in the beginning.

When ordering meat, fish or poultry specify that you want it whole (*pedazo entero*, *trozo* or *entero*) or it may be chopped up.

Because the distinction between cuts of meat is vague, there is no great value attached to specific pieces and parts. The loin may be ground into hamburger rather than cut into more expensive tenderloin steaks. When you do pay more for a particular piece, the extra cost is small.

Prices are government controlled and should be posted in the shop.

Meat is sold by the kilo, but it is more common to order by the amount you wish to spend. The average customer doesn't buy very much; 50 cents' worth of stew meat is a typical order. This is an excellent way to shop as you tend to spend less.

To make meat shopping less complicated, buy all of your meat in one place. Tell the butcher how you want it cut; before long, certain cuts will be saved for you, especially if you spend as much money as most gringo carnivores do. If you're queasy, supermarkets have a large section of packaged meats.

Meat
Carne: Always specify what kind of meat you want: *carne de res*, *carne de puerco*, etc.

Bacon
Tocino: Mexican bacon is delicious. Sliced, it is called *tocino rebanado*.

Beef   *Res, carne de res*

Cecina
This is a curing process used on many types of meat. It is spicy but very tasty.

Chops
Chuleta: *Chuleta de puerco* is the familiar pork chop. Smoked pork chops are *chuletas de puerco ahumadas*.

Dog bones
Huesos para perros: This is just stew meat with bones.

Goat
Cabrito: Tourists may be shocked to see cute little goats trussed together by the hind feet and thrown over a man's shoulder or the handlebars of a bicycle. They aren't being sold for pets, either.

Ground meat
Carne molida, pulpa: Once again, it is important to specify *de res* if you want hamburger or you might get ground pork. Unlike American hamburger, Mexican hamburger is made of meat. Ask the butcher to add a bit of *grasa* (fat) to the meat being ground or it may be too lean to make a proper pattie. If the meat is tough, and much of it is, the hamburger will be coarse and pellet-like. Avoid this by asking for *carne de res doble molida* (beef ground twice).

Ham
Jamón: This usually refers to pressed ham rather than a whole piece of pork.

Organs and innards
As in the U.S., some of the more nutritious meats are also the most inexpensive.

liver	*hígado*	kidneys	*riñones*
heart	*corazón*	brains	*sesos*
tongue	*lengua*	tripe	*tripas*

Lamb   *Carnero*

Pork   *Puerco, carne de puerco*

Ribs
Costillas: About as expensive as pure meat.

Roast
Trozo: Any word or gesture that communicates "whole piece" might result in a roast. Some butchers actually recognize the word *rosbif*.

Sandwich meat
Carnes frias (cold meats): The most common types are pressed ham (*jamón*), *queso de puerco* (head cheese) and salami. *Zwan* brand sandwich meats are generally superior to *FUD* brand. They make especially good hot dogs (*salchichas vienés, perros calientes, salchichas coctel* or just *ot dog*.) Large supermarkets have the best selection and quality.

Sausage
Salchicha: Salami is the only common sausage that does not require cooking. Supermarkets may have locally made sausages or imported. The standard Mexican sausages are *chorizo* and *longaniza*. *Chorizo* comes in links and *longaniza* is long. Both must be cooked, and cheaper varieties are very greasy. They are sometimes quite spicy. Some restaurants and meat shops offer their own *chorizo*. The best are smoked or specially cured and invariably quite tasty. Beans with *chorizo* is excellent.

Steak
Bistec or *filete* (*de res, de puerco*, etc.): The meat is thinly sliced, usually without a bone. It is almost always pounded flat for tenderizing. If you don't want your steak *aplanada* (flattened), say so immediately or you'll get it that way. Some butchers convert all of their chunks of meat to flattened *bistec* and sell almost nothing else. To order a gringo-style beefsteak, ask for *bistec de res muy grueso* (very thick—indicate how thick with your fingers). A steak with bone is commonly referred to as a *chuleta*

(chop). Should you order *chuleta de res*, you'll probably get a rib steak of whatever thickness you indicate.

Stew meat
Carne para caldo: Stew meat is sold *con hueso* or *sin hueso* (with bone or without). It is usually quite tough and stringy.

Tenderloin
Lomo (also *filete*): This cut costs a bit more, but it's usually well worth it.

Veal   *Ternero*

Venison
Venado: Yucatán is famous for its venison. It is often the only meat available in small towns and villages.

Meat tenderizer
Suavizador or *ablandedor de carne*: Supermarkets. Papaya juice is a natural meat tenderizer.

Melon
Melón: A general term used for all melons other than *sandías*, watermelons.

Milk   *Leche*: See *Dairy Products.*

Mint   *Menta* or *yerba buena*

Molasses
Melaza or *miel de sorgo*

Mushrooms
Champiñones or *hongos*: The same type of fresh mushrooms sold in the U.S. are available in most Mexican supermarkets. Canned mushrooms are common.

Mustard
Mostaza: Dry mustard is *mostaza moilida en polvo*. *Mostaza amarilla* is prepared in a jar. Good imported mustards are available in better supers. The common Mexican prepared mustard is vinegary and sharp.

Napkins   *Servilletas*

Noodles
Fideos: Sold in bulk in *tiendas* or packaged in the supermarket. (See *Macaroni*.)

Nopal cactus
Nopales or *nopalitos*: Cactus leaves, flat, thin and broad with the spines carefully shaved off, are sold throughout the country. (See *Cactus*, above, and *Our Favorite Mexican Recipes* chapter.)

Nut
Nuez (plural—*nueces*): Cleaned nuts, salted nuts and nut and seed assortments are sold in grocery and liquor stores.

Some are suprisingly inexpensive. Nuts and seeds are excellent traveling food; they keep you occupied and are nice to offer to fellow passengers on buses and trains.

Nutmeg   *Nuez moscada*

Oil
Aceite comestible: Bulk cooking oil is sold in *tiendas* by the peso or by the measure. It is slightly cheaper if you have your own container; if you don't want to pay the bottle deposit, get it in a plastic bag. Sesame oil (*aceite de ajonjolí*) is very common and costs about the same as other oils. *Cartamo* (safflower) is widely available but usually not in bulk.

Olive oil (*aceite de oliva*) is expensive but good. Be very careful that you don't buy ordinary vegetable oil that has been packaged in what looks exactly like an olive oil can or bottle. This unscrupulous packaging is very common.

Olives
Aceitunas: Green olives with seeds are sold in bulk and are inexpensive. Always taste bulk olives before buying them and be careful to sample one from the jar you intend to purchase. Crafty owners of roadside stands sometimes save on vinegar by using only water to pack their olives. Others put a layer of cured olives on top and plain ones underneath. Stuffed or pitted olives are very expensive.

Onion

Cebolla: When buying large onions by the kilo, select those without large green tops or you'll get as much stem as onion. Purple onions are very mild and can be eaten raw.

Onion salt

Sal de cebolla: Supermarket.

Oranges

Naranjas: Oranges are not dyed and they are rarely a bright orange color. A green or yellow orange will be as ripe and sweet as anything painted up for the A & P. Very juicy oranges (*naranjas para jugo*) are sold for squeezing. In Yucatán, oranges are called *chinos*. Discounts are usually given if you buy them by the dozen or by the *costal* (gunnysack).

Orange leaf tea

Hojas de naranjo: Made of fresh leaves from orange trees.

Oregano

Orégano: Common in bulk form.

Papaya

Papaya: To avoid buying an over- or under-ripe papaya, you can buy just part of one. Most vendors open up a papaya or two to show how nice the inside is. Papayas are especially good covered with lime juice and salt. They aid digestion.

Paper plates

Platos de cartón: Supermarket.

Paper towels

Toallas de papel: Supermarket.

Paprika   *Pimentón dulce*

Parsley

Perejil, peregil: Sold dried and fresh.

Paw Paw   *Papaya*

Peach

Durazno: They tend to be small but tasty.

Peanuts

Cacahuates: Peanuts are priced according to quality. It's usually worth it to buy the best, called *bolas* (balls). *Crillos* (Creoles) cost much less. They taste good but have a higher rate of rotten nuts and are much smaller. (See *Nuts*.)

Peanut butter

Crema de cacahuates: Supermarket. Bring some if you're hooked; Mexican peanut butter isn't very good.

Peas

Chícharos: Often tough, but they taste good.

Pear   *Pera*

Pecan

Nuez: The word *nuez* (nut) covers many nuts, similar to the use of the word *bola* for rounded fruits and vegetables.

Peppers

Pimientas: Chilies are not peppers. (See *Chilies*.)

Pet food

Alimento para perros, gatos and *pajaros*: Food for dogs, cats and birds is sold in supermarkets, Purina stores and veterinary supply stores—expensive. Bird food is also sold in *tiendas* and in the market.

Pickles

Pepinos: Supermarket, *pepinos dulces* (sweet pickles), *pepinos agrios* (dill pickles) and *picados aderezados* (pickle relish).

Pine nuts   *Piñones*

Pineapple

Piña: A ripe pineapple will smell very sweet and aromatic and the inner top leaves should come out with a light tug. Darker-skinned pineapples are often sweeter than pale-skinned ones.

Plum   *Ciruela*

Pomegranate   *Granada*

Popcorn
Maíz palomero: Sold in bulk in *tiendas*. It is called *palomitas* ("little doves") when already popped.

Poppy seed
Semillas de amapola: Hard to find these days, perhaps because of what they use the rest of the plant for.

Pork   *Carne de puerco*: See *Meat*.

Potatoes
Papas: Large potatoes cost more than small ones.

Poultry
Aves: See *Chicken and Turkey*.

Prickly pear   *Tuna*: See *Cactus*.

Prunes
Ciruela pasa: Many types of dried fruits are sold in bulk in the market, on the street and in *tiendas*.

Pumpkin   *Calabaza*

Pumpkin seeds   *Pepitas*

Purselane
Verdolagas: See *Greens*.

Quince
Membrillo: Makes excellent wine or jelly.

Radish
Rábano: Oaxaca is famous for a Christmas radish fiesta. Giant long radishes are common in the south.

Razor blades
Hojas de afeitar: Can buy them individually if you prefer.

Rice
Arroz: Brown rice (*arroz moreno*) is difficult to locate; look for it in health food stores or buy it right from the mill (*molino*).

When buying rice, get the best. Cheap rice may be old, full of rocks and bugs, and not very tasty.

Rosemary   *Romero*

Saffron   *Azafrán española*

Sage   *Salvia*

Salad dressing
Aderezo para ensaladas

Salt   *Sal*

Sauerkraut
Col agria: Supermarket

Savory   *Ajedrea*

Seafood
Most large markets have a *mariscos* (seafood) section. It is wise to do your seafood shopping early in the morning, both on the coast and inland. Fish that have been properly iced for shipment will be almost as good as those freshly caught and dressed. During Lent seafood may be sold from the backs of trucks. This is the best time of year for the Mexican fisherman.

Fish tastes better and is more nutritious when fresh, but it won't kill you if it's slightly old. Bad seafood smells ghastly, but it all smells slightly. I've seen people sniff a fish and say, "Smells kind of fishy to me. Probably no good." What do they want, lilacs?

Abalone
Abulón: *Lapa* are similar and much more common.

Barracuda   *Barracuda, pecuda*

Catfish   *Bagre, gato*

Clams   *Almejas*

Cod
Bacalao: Usually sold dried and salted. Imported *bacalao* is very expensive.

Conch   *Caracol*

Crab
Cangrejo or jaiba: Sold live with their claws tied with twine or pieces of grass.

Crayfish   *Langostinas, cucarachas*

Fish
Pescado: A live fish is a *pez*. Whole fish is *pescado entero*, filets are *filetes*. The price of fish is most often for whole uncleaned fish. It will be cleaned free of charge after weighing. Ask them to remove only the guts and gills. A fish will last much longer if the scales, head and fins are left intact.

Poke the fish with your finger. If the flesh springs back, the fish is probably good. However, should the dent remain or should your finger go into the flesh, it isn't so good.

Look at the gills. They should be dark red. If they are greyish or white, it is a good indication that the fish is old. Now give it the sniff test. If the fish fails again, move on to the poultry shops.

Dried, salted fish, especially shark and ray, are very popular. They are generally called *pescado seco*.

Giant limpet   *Lapa*

Lobster
Langosta: Mexican lobsters are the spiny variety, without the huge front claws of the Maine lobster.

Mackerel
Sierra: A premium fish for *ceviche*. (See *Our Favorite Mexican Recipes*.)

Mullet   *Lisa*

Octopus   *Pulpo*

Oysters
Ostiones: Oysters should be purchased alive, in the shell, whenever possible. If you can partially open the shell with your fingers, the oyster is either dead or dying. A live oyster keeps its shell firmly closed when handled.

Many seafood vendors sell cleaned oysters in bottles, plastic bags and jars. We often buy these when we can't find live ones and they are usually reasonably fresh.

Prawns
Camarones gigantes or *azules*: Very expensive.

Red snapper
Huachinango: Includes many types of snapper.

Salmon
Salmón: Common canned, but not often seen fresh.

Sardines
Sardinas: Canned are most common and very popular.

Shark   *Cazón, tiburón*

Shrimp
Camarones: *Camarones secos* (dried) are excellent and very common.

Fresh shrimp are sold by the kilo, with or without the heads. Vendors may remove the heads as they tend to spoil faster than the bodies. Many shrimp fishermen do this on the boat. With or without heads, the best indications of the freshness of shrimp are general appearance and smell. They should be brightly colored and not mushy.

Shrimp are priced according to their size. *Azules*, the most expensive, are huge prawns. *Cristales* are large and *regulares* are average. The price of these will increase if they've been beheaded.

Tourists sometimes buy shrimp direct from the boats, but this is actually illegal (for the fisherman). The price may or may not be a bargain. I've found that a trade is preferred over cash: fresh fruit, clothing or tools. One crew gave me a crate of shrimp in exchange for a crate of oranges. If they refuse to sell or trade shrimp, be gracious—they may be low or worried about the authorities.

Squid   *Calamares*

Tuna
Atún: Sold fresh and canned. Canned tuna is a favorite *cantina* snack.

Seafood, canned
Canned seafood makes good traveling food. Canned mackerel is often sold in cans labeled *Salmón* in large letters with a picture of a salmon completing the deception. Look for the microscopic words *macerel estilo salmón* (mackerel salmon style). The most common canned seafoods are *atún* (tuna), *sardinas* (sardines), *almejas* (clams) and *camarones* (shrimp). Canned seafood is becoming more expensive because of the demand from the States.

A Mexican picnic or impromptu celebration is not complete without a can or two of some seafood and salted crackers.

Seasoned pepper
Pimienta condimentada: Supermarket

Seasoned salt
Sal para sazonar: Supermarket

Seeds
Semillas

Sesame seeds
Semillas de ajonjolí

Shampoo
Shampoo: *Jabón de coco* (coconut soap) is sold in CONASUPOS, *tiendas* and drugstores. It makes great shampoo and lathers in salt water. American brands are expensive. If you have a favorite shampoo, take a supply with you.

Soap   *Jabón*

Soups, canned and dry
Sopa en lata: Campbell's soups are sold in most stores.

Dried soups are sold under the brand name *Maggi*. They are inexpensive and pretty good. Bouillon cubes are very common. (See *Bouillon*.)

Sour Cream
Crema ácida or *crema agria*: See *Dairy Products*.

Soy sauce
Salsa soya, *salsa china* or *salsa japonesa*: Supermarket. Expensive and not very tasty.

Spaghetti
Spaghetti, *macarrones delgados* or *pasta*: See *Macaroni*.

Spices
Especias, *olores*: See *Herbs*.

Spinach   *Espinaca*

Squash
Calabaza: Covers all types and sizes. *Chilacayote* is a common primitive squash. *Calabacitas* (little squashes) is used for small zucchinis.

Squash flowers
Flores de calabaza: Excellent in soups, deep fried in egg batter or in *quesadillas*.

Squash seeds
Pepitas: Covers almost all seeds, including pumpkin and melon. *Pepitas* are sold roasted in the market and on the street.

Straws   *Popotes*

Strawberries
Fresas: Very common and inexpensive in some parts of the country. *Fresas con crema* is a popular dessert, usually associated with the wealthy. "They eat *fresas con crema*" can be a sarcastic put-down of people who are stuck up.

Sugar
Azúcar: Brown sugar is sold in molded chunks called *piloncillo* or *panucho*. The price is controlled by the government to keep people happy. Raw sugar is *azúcar moreno*.

Sugar cane

Caña, caña de azúcar: The harvest is called *la zafra*.

Sunflower seeds

Semillas de girasol: Most easily located in bird food stores in and around the market. Many good eating seeds are sold as bird food. Ask if they can be eaten in case they're chemically treated. "*¿Se puede comerlas?*"

Sweet potato

Camote: Some are purple.

Swiss chard

Acelgas: You can also use the general term for greens—*quelites*.

Tamarind

Tamarindo: This fruit looks like a giant brown bean pod. The seeds inside are covered with a brownish stuff that is sour but tasty. Good with tequila.

Tangerine

Mandarina: Very cheap around Christmas.

Tarragon   *Estragón*

Tea

Té: Snobs call it *the*. Black tea is *té negro*. Imported teas are sold in supermarkets.

Thyme   *Tomillo*

Toilet paper

Papel sanitario: It's easier to ask for it by the most common brand names, *Pétalo* and *Regio*.

Tomatoes

Jitomates: It varies by region, but red tomatoes are called *jitomates* or *tomates*. I can never remember which is which, so expect to be confused. *Tomatillos* (also known as *tomates verdes*) are smallish and green, with a leafy membrane. They are nice in sauces (see *Our Favorite Mexican Recipes*).

Tomato puree

Puré de tomate: Thinner than puree sold in the U.S.

Tomato sauce

Salse de tomate: It will be hotter than hell if the can has a picture of a chili on it or warnings such as *estilo español* or *estilo mexicano*.

Toothpaste

Crema dental: Very cheap in the CONASUPO.

Tortillas

See *Restaurants and Typical Foods*.

Turkey

Guajolote: The Indian name is more commonly used than the Spanish *pavo*. Turkeys are usually sold live.

Turmeric   *Cúrcuma*

Turnip   *Nabo*

Vanilla

Vainilla: Mexico is famous for its vanilla.

Vegetables

Verduras or *Legumbres*

Vinegar

Vinagre: Homemade vinegar is sold in bulk in the *tiendas*.

Walnut

Nuez castilla or *nogal*

Watercress   *Berro*

Watermelon

Sandía: If you are going to travel back in the sticks and have the opportunity, buy several *sandías*. They keep well, are usually inexpensive and make wonderful treats to offer guests.

Waxed paper

Papel encerado

Wheat germ

Germen de trigo: Sold in some super-markets and health food stores.

White pepper   *Pimienta blanca*

Worchestershire sauce

Salsa inglesa: Supermarket.

Worm seed

Epazote: The leaves of this plant give excellent flavor to soups and are important medicinally. (See *Staying Healthy*.)

Yam   *Camote*

Yeast

Levadura: Dry yeast is sold in super-markets. Bakeries will often sell cakes of fresh yeast if you ask. Brewer's yeast (*levadura de cerveza*) is sold in some drugstores and health food stores, but if you use it often bring some from home.

Yogurt

Yogurt or *bulgara*: See *Dairy Products*.

Zapotes

Zapotes: A very common and interest-ing fruit. Both the *zapote blanco* and *zapote borracho* have sleep-inducing properties. The *borracho* ("drunken") *zapote* is yellow on the outside and red-dish inside, with a few large seeds. The seeds are supposedly narcotic, though they don't have to be eaten to get the sleep-inducing effects of the fruit.

Zucchini

Calabacitas: Mexicans eat an amazing amount of this squash. It is harvested young, when no more than three to six inches in length.

A Typical Marketing Trip

I never cease to be amazed at how much time and effort marketing requires, no matter how much experience the marketer has. You don't just run down for the week's gro-ceries. You form an expedition. As Steve says, "Let's make a foray to the market." To me the implication is that one or more of us may not make it back.

Before we enter the market, Steve issues the shopping bags. (Food is seldom pack-aged and you're expected to provide your own containers.)

"Who's got the list?" he asks impatiently, drawn like a magnet to this great mine of food.

"Not me," I say. "Lorena must have it."

"Where is she?" Steve asks, looking wildly from side to side. She has disappeared, as usual, before the plan of attack can be drawn up.

"I don't know, but before I look for her, we'd better agree on a meeting place."

"How about the *fondas?*" he suggests, thinking ahead as usual to lunch. I agree and set off in pursuit of Lorena.

The main building of the market place is very old, the roof and supporting beams dark-ened by hundreds of years of smoke from the cooking fires below. It is a huge structure and today, on market day, it is literally jammed with people and their goods. Vendors are crammed into every available corner and some have usurped space normally used for walking. Tiny Indian ladies seem able to occupy no more space than could be covered by a handkerchief. Their inventory is worth perhaps 50 cents, if anyone were expansive enough to buy it all. It's doubtful, however, that they would part with everything at one blow; there's far too much gossiping to be done with neighbors to justify that.

An old man stumbles by, pushing an ancient wheelbarrow loaded with freshly butchered meat. He forces his way through the crowded aisles, shouting warnings to ladies haggling loudly over a few pesos' worth of onions or *chiles*. They sidestep his gory load without a glance, a bloody joint of meat barely missing a clean white dress.

On a front corner of the wheelbarrow, the old man has bolted the left arm of some long discarded baby doll. Its hand waves grotesquely at the crowd, fingernails bright with fresh polish.

Following in the wake the old man has cleared through the mass of shoppers, vendors, delivery boys and beggars, I plunge into the long narrow entrance. It is hot and

stuffy, smelling of blood, onions and oranges, and I have a headache. Steve is skirting the main building, confining his purchases to the vendors who have erected their temporary stalls in the surrounding streets.

I see Lorena a short way ahead, but we are rapidly being separated by the crowd. As usual, I cannot bring myself to employ an elbow against these women who use it so liberally on me. Lorena towers over the people around her, attracting a good deal of attention and a stream of comments.

"Hey, blonde, buy my tomatoes!" a cackling old shrew yells. "Give them a squeeze!"

"Look at that tall one!" the woman in front of me says to a friend. "She looks like a Tehuana* to me!"

Lorena is rapidly moving ahead, so I shout over the crowd and ask her what I should buy. "Tomatoes and onions!" she yells back, ignoring a few friendly mocking cries from the stalls nearby. Then she spots a tiny bunch of fresh herbs—or rather is stopped by a bunch of herbs thrust into her face by a grinning Indian woman. She smiles and asks the price. Five fingers are displayed, two times. The old woman evidently does not speak much Spanish. Lorena looks at the herbs, sniffs them, then nods her head.

The bundle is laboriously wrapped in a piece of old newspaper and tucked safely in the huge shopping bag. Lorena hands her a small coin and politely accepts a very withered green onion as a bonus. As she begins to move on, the old lady grabs her long blonde hair with a giggle and gives it a tug for luck. Everyone laughs. I am hit in the back with some type of tiny fruit. More laughter.

---

*Tehuana women, from the Isthmus of Tehuantepec, are famous both for their stature and matriarchal society. They are, perhaps, the only women in Mexico who enjoy a form of women's liberation.

A few feet further on, I spot a likely looking heap of tomatoes. Before I can inspect them, however, someone pushes me and I find myself standing next to a lady selling onions. Rather than push back, I admire the onions.

She shyly names a price, three times more than the going rate, as she carefully observes my face for a reaction.

I make a much lower counteroffer but she just grins and turns her head slightly. She would probably let them go for that, but she is too embarrassed to talk to a foreigner. Her stubbornness irritates me slightly, but before I say anything, someone grabs my ankle and shouts, "Buy my onions, *marchante* (customer)! Smell them! Fresh today! I picked them myself!"

The other vendors giggle at this hard-sell approach, but the lady with the onions is not about to be fazed by her neighbors' comments. She thrusts a bunch at me and waggles it seductively.

After a quick exchange of offers and counteroffers, I stick the onions in my bag. Heads nod and shake as the price I paid is passed on, both behind me to tell others what they missed out on and ahead to warn of what I'm willing to pay. In seconds, every onion in the area is converging on me. I escape down a side alley into Tomatoland.

Everyone in this row is selling tomatoes; there are tens of thousands of them and all look and cost about the same. The vendors loudly proclaim the merits of their wares, as if all the other tomatoes were fakes, only skins wrapped cleverly around hollow frames.

After buying half a kilo from a very serious and dignified elderly gentleman, I make my way slowly to the fruit section. There are a hundred more vegetable stalls, but I am willing to leave them to Lorena; she enjoys searching out strange-tasting treasures packed in from distant farms.

The odors in the fruit section are almost obscenely rich and heavy, fragrant with memories of the hot coastal country and bubbling asphalt roads. Even the vendors look slightly dissipated, as if the goods they sold corrupted them with ripeness and thick maturity.

In a large market such as this one, the selection is excellent, even though many of the fruits available are grown hundreds of miles away. Pineapples seem to be particularly abundant today, their heavy sweet fragrance masks even the strong scents of bananas and papayas. Almost every vendor is busily stacking them in attractive mounds.

Pineapples are being peeled dexterously with razor-sharp knives, sliced, then arranged on trays of ice to attract customers. One nearby vendor spears a juicy piece with the tip of his blade and extends it toward me. As I reach for the sample, momentarily forgetting the rush of people, a young boy piled high with crates of bananas crashes into me. One of the wooden slats hooks my shirt and tears it slightly.

"*¡Aguas! ¡Aguas!*" ("Careful! Careful!") he shouts, swaying dangerously under the tottering load. I curse at the hole in my shirt, but apologize for being in the way; the responsibility to avoid such collisions always rests on the shopper.

When I turn back, the sample is still being offered and the vendor is laughing with amusement over my clumsiness. After tasting the pineapple, pale and slightly sour, I tell him, "*No, gracias,*" and move on. He shrugs his shoulders; there will be more customers and the fruit will ripen.

After a tasty sample in another stall, I finally select a large ripe pineapple and begin to barter.

The huge smiling woman behind the counter asks for a price that seems quite reasonable. I offer her quite a bit less, hoping against hope to get a real bargain. She shakes her head impatiently. I increase my offer. Another head shake. I raise my offer once more, almost matching her original price.

The pineapple is handed to me without a word, though she scans the surrounding crowd quickly to see if anyone has overheard the final price and will know beforehand how far down it can be pushed.

As I slip the pineapple into my shopping bag, I notice a deep bruise on one side. Rather hesitantly I point out this previous unnoticed defect to the woman who had so deftly juggled it out of sight during the bartering. I half expect her to tell me to go to hell, but instead she smiles good-naturedly and indicates that I can select any pineapple I want.

The damaged fruit is being waved brazenly in another customer's face before I am ten feet away.

Once out of the fruit section, I steer a course toward the hardware and leather goods area. Real treasures can often be picked up there for just a few pesos. Junk, secondhand tools, comic books, antiques that almost work, bags handwoven from string and grass and all the other essential things we can do so well without are arranged in tempting displays.

Walking past the leather stalls, I inhale the earthy odor of cured hides and oil. *Huaraches* (sandals) hang in pungent rows, their tire-tread soles turned to display such names as B.F. Goodrich, Atlas and General Popo.

Quickly scanning the various soles for real gems—a particularly good white sidewall or a name that has been accidentally altered by the cut of a sandal maker's knife (. . . rich Tire Co., Fire . . ., etc.)—I spot a pair of Michelins. The owner of the stall quickly seats me on a tiny chair, whips the sandals off the wall and lays them in front of me. Unfortunately, they are too small and he regrets to say that the only thing he has in my size is a white-walled General Popo. He too, appreciates a *huarache* with more class than just a plain black sole.

Next I enter the narrow alleyways of metalware. There are hammers made from iron reinforcing rods, lamps from beer cans, dust pans from oil cans, stoves from gas cans; anything, in fact, made from cans, rebar, scrap tin or license plates that you might imagine.

A few stalls farther on an old man is meticulously arranging keys, broken scissors, a light bulb, bits of iron and tin, washers, nuts, screws, bent nails and other such valuable stuff in neat piles and rows. While watching him, I spot an ancient clothing iron.

It is solid metal, obviously an antique, but not long out of use—the bottom is still smooth and shiny. This is just what we need, I think to myself guiltily, hefting the heavy iron and wondering how I can justify it.

The old man takes his business seriously. He begins to describe exactly how to use the iron; there's no doubt in his mind that I really need it. We discuss the temperature it should be heated to, the best type of fire to warm it on, how to dampen the clothing properly, etc. He is willing to tell me all this valuable information and include the iron for just 50 cents.

I add two very camp-looking old comic books to the deal and we part friends, the old man still muttering about ironing and charcoal as I wander on.

Around the corner I see Lorena examining something on the ground in front of her, at a similar junk stall. By craning my neck, I am just barely able to see past the crowd to the object that is attracting her attention. It is an iron, identical to mine.

The people jammed in front of me make it impossible to force my way through. Now she is bending intently over the iron and I can tell that she has made an offer because the vendor is wagging a forefinger back and forth in front of his nose.

This signal means, "No deal," so I still have time.

Just as I manage to attract her attention, the iron disappears into a piece of newspaper. She turns to me with a grin of triumph and says, "Do you have any pesos? It was only a dollar."

On the way to the *fondas*, we decide to tell Steve that antique irons are worth a fortune in the States. He'll fall for it if it seems we stand to make a huge profit, but we'll have to be convincing; both irons together weigh several pounds. Overloading the van—or how to avoid it—is one of his favorite sermons.

He is sitting impatiently in a dark food stall.

"How'd it go?" I ask sympathetically, ordering a cold beer.

"Oh, God! What an ordeal!" he moans, chugging down half a bottle in one gulp. "Did you see Lorena? I almost caught up with her once near the oranges, but she disappeared again."

"She just stopped to buy some pottery."

"Great!" Steve says. "It'll probably be hours before she shows up."

Lorena emerges as if on cue from a nearby stall. She is carrying a new piece of pottery, a handful of candles and what appears to be a full sack of fresh parsley.

"What did you get, Steve?" I interrupt hastily. "It looks to me like you've got quite a bit of stuff there."

"Just the usual," he sighs. "Onions, tomatoes, potatoes, cabbage, lettuce, a small squash, mangoes, rice, limes, greens, milk, oranges, bananas, half a papaya, some peanuts for the birds, a few chilies, bread, cooking oil, avocados, half a kilo of green beans . . ."

"Forget anything?" I interrupt sarcastically. "Sounds to me like you did pretty well even without the list."

Steve looks up, a mixed expression of bewilderment and injury on his face. "We can't go hungry," he says quietly. "These are *just the basics*; you know that."

Lorena looks at the list and checks a few things in Steve's bag against it. "You got it all," she announces.

"Get a pineapple?" I ask casually.

"Yeah," They answer in unison.

Market Days in Mexico

Acambaro, Gto.	Daily except Thurs.
Acatlan (de Osorio), Pue.	Sun. & Tues.
Acatzingo, Pue.	Tues.
Acayucan, Ver.	Daily
Acaxochitlan, Hgo.	Sun & Wed.
Acolman, Méx.	Wed.
Actopan, Hgo	Wed.
Aguascalientes, Ags.	Daily
Agulilla, Mich.	Fri.
Alamos, Son.	Sun.
Alfajayucan, Hgo.	Sun.
Almoloya de Juárez, Méx.	Sun.
Alvarado, Ver.	Sun.
Amecameca, Méx.	Sun.
Amozoc de Mota, Pue.	Sun.
Angangueo, Mich.	Sat. & Sun.
Apan, Hgo.	Sun.
Apatzingán, Mich.	Sat. & Sun.
Apizaco, Tlax.	Sun.
Arriaga, Chis.	Daily
Atlacomulco, Méx.	Sun.
Atlixco, Pue.	Tues. & Sat.
Banderilla,Ver.	Sun.
Cadereyta, Que.	Sun.
Camargo, Chih.	Mon. & Sat.
Capulhuac, Méx.	Tues.
Celaya, Gto.	Tues. & Sat.
Chalco, Méx.	Fri.
Chetumal, Q.R.	Daily
Chiconcuac, Méx.	Sun. & Tues.
Chicuautla, Hgo.	Sat.
Chilapa, Gro.	Sun.
Cholula, Pue.	Sun. & Wed.
Cd. Hidalgo, Mich.	Sun.
Cd. Lopez Mateos, Méx.	Sun.
Cd. Mante, Tamps.	Sat. & Sun.
Cd. Serdán, Pue.	Sun. & Mon.
Concepcion del Oro, Zac	Sat. & Sun.
Cosamaloapan, Ver.	Sat. & Sun.
Cotija, Mich.	Sat. & Sun.
Cuauhtemoc, Chih	Daily
Cuernavaca, Mor.	Sun.
Cuetzalan, Pue.	Sun.
Dolores Hidalgo, Gto.	Sun.

Ejutla, Oax.	Wed.	Nochixtlán, Oax.	Sun.
Etla, Oax.	Wed.	Nuevo Casas Grandes, Chih.	Daily
Fortín, Ver.	Sun.	Oaxaca, Oax.	Sat.
Fresnillo, Zac.	Sun.	Ocotlán, Jal.	Sat. & Sun.
		Ocotlán, Oax.	Fri.
Gómez Palacio, Dgo.	Daily	Ocoyoacac, Méx.	Wed.
Guadalajara, Jal.	Daily, Sun.	Ozumba de Alzate, Méx.	Tues. & Fri.
Guanajuato, Gto.	Sun.		
Guasave, Sin.	Daily		
		Papantla, Ver.	Sun.
Huajuapan de León, Oax.	Sun.	Parras, Coah.	Sat. & Sun.
		Pátzcuaro, Mich	Sun., Tues. & Fri.
Huamantla, Tlax.	Sun. & Wed,	Perote, Ver.	Sun.
Huachinango, Pue.	Sat.	Poza Rica, Ver.	Daily
Huejotzingo, Pue.	Thurs. & Sat.	Puebla, Pue.	Thurs. & Sun.
Huichapan, Hgo.	Sun.	Puerto Penasco, Son.	Daily
		Puerto Vallarta, Jal.	Sun.
Iguala, Gro.	Sun. & Sat.		
Irapuato, Gto.	Tues. & Sun.	Querétaro, Qro.	Daily
Ixmiquilpan, Hgo.	Mon.	Quiroga, Mich.	Sun.
Ixtapan de la Sal, Méx.	Sun.		
Izucar de Matamoros, Pue.	Sun. & Mon.	Sabinas, Coah.	Sat. & Sun.
		Sahuayo, Mich.	Sun.
		Salamanca, Gto.	Sun. & Tues.
Jacala, Hgo.	Sun.	Saltillo, Coah.	Daily
Jilotepec, Méx.	Fri.	Santiago de Anaya, Hgo.	Thurs.
Jiquilpan, Mich.	Sat.		
Jocotepec. Jal.	Sun.	Santiago Tianguistenco, Méx.	Tues.
Juchitan, Oax.	Sun.		
Juchitepec, Méx.	Wed.	San Bartolo Naucalpan, Méx.	Sat.
La Peidad Cavadas, Mich.	Sun.	San Cristobal de las Casas, Chis.	Daily except Sun.
León, Gto.	Mon. & Tues.	San Fransisco del Rincon, Gto.	Tues. & Sun.
Lerma, Méx.	Sat.		
Luis Moya, Zac.	Sun.	San José Purua, Mich.	Sun.
		San Juan de los Lagos, Jal.	Daily
Manzanillo, Col.	Sat. & Sun.		
Martínez de la Torre, Ver.	Sun.	San Juan del Río, Qro.	Sun.
		San Martín Texmelucan, Pue.	Tues. & Fri.
Matehuala, S.L.P.	Daily		
Mérida, Yuc.	Daily	San Miguel de Allende, Gto.	Sun. & Tues.
Métepec, Mex.	Mon.		
Metztitlan, Hgo.	Sun.	Sayula, Hgo.	Mon.
Miahuatlán, Oax.	Mon.	Silao, Gto	Tues. & Sun.
Mitla, Oax.	Sun.		
Morelia, Mich.	Thurs. & Sun.	Tabasco, Zac.	Sun.
Moroleón, Gto.	Sun. & Mon.	Tamazunchale, S.L.P.	Sun.
Motul, Yúc.	Mon.	Tasquillo, Hgo.	Sun.

Taxco, Gro.	Thurs. & Sun.
Tecali, Pue.	Tues. & Fri.
Tecamachalco, Pue.	Sat.
Tecozuatla, Hgo.	Thurs.
Tehuacán, Pue.	Sat.
Tehuantepec, Oax.	Sun.
Temascalapa, Méx.	Thurs. & Sun.
Tenencingo, Méx.	Sun. & Thurs.
Tenango, Méx.	Thurs. & Sun.
Tepeaca, Pue.	Fri.
Tepeji del Río, Hgo.	Mon.
Tepetlixpa, Méx	Mon.
Tepotzlán, Mor.	Sun. & Wed.
Tequisquiapan, Qro.	Sun.
Tetela de Ocampo, Pue.	Sun.
Texcoco, Méx.	Sun.
Teziutlán, Pue.	Fri. & Sun.
Texmelucan, Oax.	Tues.
Tierra Blanca, Ver.	Daily
Tinguidin, Mich.	Sun.
Tlacolula, Oax.	Sun.
Tlahuelilpa, Hgo.	Tues.
Tlalnepantla, Méx.	Fri. & Sun.
Tlaxcala, Tlax.	Sat.
Toluca, Méx.	Fri.
Tonalá, Chis.	Daily
Tula, Hgo.	Sun.
Tulancingo, Hgo.	Thurs. & Mon.
Tuxtla Gutíerrez, Chis.	Daily
Uruapan, Mich.	Daily
Valle de Bravo, Méx.	Sun. & Thurs.
Veracruz, Ver.	Daily
Villa del Carbón, Méx.	Sun. & Thurs.
Villahermosa, Tab.	Daily
Xicotepec, Pue.	Sun.
Xochimilco, DF	Sat. & Thurs.
Xuchitlan, Hgo.	Mon.
Zachila, Oax.	Mon.
Zacapu, Mich.	Sun.
Zacatlan, Pue.	Sun. & Fri.
Zacualtipan, Hgo.	Sat. & Sun.
Zimapan, Hgo.	Sat. & Sun.
Zitácuaro, Mich.	Sun.

OUR FAVORITE MEXICAN RECIPES

Valuable cooking tips • Our favorite Mexican recipes • The Great Grunt-a-Rama

Tomato salsa is never better than its tomatoes.
—Mexican proverb

When Steve isn't roaming through Mexico and Central America in search of esoteric enchilada ingredients, he can usually be found laboring over a stove at Rancho Deadwood, his family *querencia* in rain-soaked Oregon. Inside a sprawling, weather-beaten cedar cabin sheltered by big leaf maples and dripping fir trees, Steve holds court as he stuffs dry sticks into the open maw of Lucifer, a huge, fire-breathing cast-iron kitchen range. On this particular day, when he'd judged the humidity ideal for rolling out a batch of blue corn tortillas, I pumped him for the inside scoop on Mexican cooking.

"It's so hard to fix really good Mexican food at home," I said, "especially simple dishes with those authentic flavors you rarely get in restaurants north of the border. Not that superheated TexMex stuff, covered with an inch of cheese. You know what I mean: refried beans with a little crust on top and slightly scorched tortillas with crispy edges and those sweet, smoky *chiles* that bite just right. . . ." I felt a rush of saliva.

"Steve!" I continued, "*People's Guide* readers are literally clamoring for help. They know you've sacrificed your waistline in appreciation of Mexican food. Now all they ask is that *el maestro* hand down a few of his favorite recipes."

If I was laying it on a bit thick, Steve didn't seem to mind. With gobs of raw sticky tortilla *masa* clinging from elbows to eyebrows, he preened modestly. "Remember those incredible *chile rellenos* I made at the beach in Mazatlán?" He scattered a handful of long green Anaheim peppers across the stove top. "Man! Was that thirty years ago?" Steve shook his head in disbelief. "I still think about the snook in *salsa verde* we ate in Vera Cruz and that recipe of Teresa's for lima bean soup. . . ."

Eyes glazing with nostalgic hunger, Steve absentmindedly turned the hot sputtering *chiles* with his bare fingers. Turning from the stove he pawed through a counter top piled with utensils, cookbooks, paperback novels, hot pads, discarded paper towels and food-stained notes. "Here we go!" he said. "You want recipes that are completely authentic but easy to follow, right?" He held up a sheet of stained paper.

"I think people will love this Campeche-style duck stewed in *pulque*, followed by tender cactus leaves stuffed with *huitlachoche* and *capirotada* bread pudding smothered in honey, raisins and . . ."

"No! No!" I shouted. "Save that for your memoirs. Give me something *easy!*"

As I'd feared, reducing Steve to simple recipes would be as traumatic as reducing several inches from his ample waistline. "A Yucatán barbecue?" he countered desperately, wiping at a fleck of saliva. "It doesn't get much easier or more authentic than this. First you dig a giant pit and then you get a big pig, two turkeys, a fresh deer, some . . ."

"No!" I interrupted. "I said simple, reliable and healthy!"

"This barbecue is very healthy," Steve said, obviously peeved, ". . . once you dig the pit and find enough banana leaves you take the first turkey and . . ."

I held very firm.

Conceding defeat, Steve grudgingly unearthed a thick, cheaply bound notebook of the type used by schoolchildren throughout Mexico. After flipping through the pages for several minutes, he finally confessed. "As it happens, I've been writing down some thoughts on Mexican-style beans and basic tortilla lore that might be helpful. I've also got a dynamite green salsa recipe that is so simple even you might be able to make it."

"Of course, there are a lot of cookbooks already available," Steve added quickly. "Diana Kennedy's books are nothing less than fantastic." Speaking in hushed, reverent tones his eyes darted toward the porch, as if the world-famous food writer just might be eavesdropping. "But as much as I love *Cuisines of Mexico*, I'm afraid her recipes tend to be pretty time-consuming and complex, especially for novices."

"Your recipes are a lot more down to earth," I flattered. "People who enjoy good food in Mexico often want to try their hand at fixing something similar when they get home, dishes that are simple, tasty, *and* authentic. John Muir probably would have called it 'Mexican cooking for the compleat idiot.'" There was a moment's pause to commemorate our departed friend's appetite for enchiladas drenched in sour cream.

"Okay," I said. "Now where do we start?"

Steve's hand crept toward the guacamole. In the brief course of our conversation he'd managed to do away with most of the tortilla chips and virtually all of the dip. "Well," he said, "if we're going to do this right, we obviously have to start at the beginning, where all life begins—that means breakfast. It's a little late in the day, but how about trying a plate of my *huevos rancheros* along with a side of refried beans and maybe just a dab or two of *chilaquiles*?"

Valuable Cooking Tips

• When in doubt use *more* butter, cream, cheese, eggs and garlic, but *less* cooking oil, heat, salt, chili and cumin.

• Lard is the traditional fat in Mexico. Contrary to what visitors often believe, most restaurants and Mexican cooks now use cooking oil. Even though they probably prefer lard's flavor, cooking oil is cheaper and more readily available. Lard is most often used in rural areas and in restaurants that specialize in traditional dishes. If you wish, lard may be substituted for butter and oil in these recipes.

• Do not use glazed pottery for acidic foods and beverages. If you use a glazed bowl for salad don't add the dressing until right before serving or, better yet, after the salad is on the plate. (See *Shopping: Pottery and Lead Poisoning*.)

• For maximum flavor and authenticity, serve these dishes at moderate temperatures rather than molten hot. Mexican cooks rarely serve food that is bubbling hot. In fact, it is generally believed that scalding or icy cold foods aren't good for us. Unless you eat in tourist restaurants in Mexico, you'll rarely hear the familiar TexMex warning, "Watch out, this plate is very hot!"

Our Favorite Mexican Recipes

1. Huevos a la Mexicana (Mexican Scrambled Eggs)

Heat about a cup of *salsa ranchera* (see recipe below) in a frying pan with a little cooking oil. When the sauce has comes to a boil, add several beaten eggs and scramble.

2. *Huevos Rancheros* (Ranch-Style Eggs)

Fry a pair of eggs sunny-side-up or over-easy. Slide the eggs gently onto one or two warm tortillas and cover with a warm sauce (either *chile colorado salsa* or *salsa verde*; see recipes below).

For softer and more flavorful tortillas, fry them briefly in oil or butter and then dip them into the sauce.

Options: Cover the eggs with another warm tortilla and a generous sprinkle of crumbled white or grated yellow cheese. (It is hardly traditional but parmesan or Greek feta cheese on huevos rancheros is wonderful.) My favorite variation is to smother my *huevos rancheros* in well-drained beans.

Try this: For two eggs, thin a cup of Francisca's *salsa verde* (see recipe below) with a splash of water and sauté it in a little oil. Dip two corn tortillas in the heated *salsa* and stack them on a plate. Spread a layer of warm refried beans over the tortillas, add the fried eggs and then douse everything liberally with the remaining green *salsa* and grated dry cheese.

3. *Chilaquiles*

This dish is a great way to use up leftover tortillas. The regional variations are numerous, but *chilaquiles* are commonly served for breakfast throughout Mexico. I've eaten them soggy with *salsa* and dry to the point of being crunchy, with deboned chicken or grated cheese, and roaring hot with *chiles* or meek and mild. In other words, with a little imagination your *chilaquiles* will undoubtedly be delicious.

> *1 dozen tortillas:* cut into one-inch-wide strips, then cut the strips into thirds. (Use fresh or stale tortillas.)
> *¼ cup vegetable oil (you may need more as you go along)*
> *2 cups or so of salsa (a green tomatillo salsa is traditional, but any salsa will do)*
> *1 large onion: cut in half and slice into thin rings*
> *1 to 3 cups of cheese: a fresh white cheese, queso de rancho or aged queso añejo is traditional but most any white cheese, romano or parmesan is fine*
> *1 sprig of fresh epazote if you have it*
> *sour cream to taste*

Sauté the tortilla pieces in oil until they have softened (or if you prefer more texture, until they are crisp). Drain on paper towels. Now fry half of the sliced onion until soft. Return the fried tortillas to the pan and add the *salsa* and salt to taste. Mix well. You may have to add a little more liquid of some kind—either salsa, tomato juice or vegetable stock.

You want the tortillas to soak up the liquid. Cook this mixture for a few minutes. Add some of the cheese or wait and sprinkle it on top with the remaining raw sliced onions. Dribble sour cream over the *chilaquiles* and serve. I agree with Steve that the sum of this amazing dish is far better than its parts.

Instant *chilaquiles***:** This is probably heresy, but instead of frying pieces of real corn tortilla, substitute a bag of the thickest tortilla chips you can find, especially blue or yellow corn.

4. *Frijoles de la Olla* (Classic Mexican Beans)

Steve says: "Beans, tortillas and *chile* are the great trilogy of the Mexican diet. The majority of people in Mexico live on these staples and they've spent thousands of years learning how to prepare them well. I've had meals with nothing more than beans, tortillas and *chile* that were so good it was hard to believe."

There are many varieties of beans in Mexico and several cooking methods. Generally speaking, light-colored beans are preferred from the northern border south to Mexico City, and black beans are the norm all the way from Mexico City down through Central America.

Essential bean lore: Cheaper beans are usually old and take forever to cook, so get the best. Fresher, good quality beans will usually be fully cooked within two hours, without pre-soaking. However, soaking beans in cold water for a few hours (or even overnight) does decrease cooking time and also reduces stomach gas. (Wash away the loose skins and discard the soaking water.)

One cup of dry beans is a reasonable amount for one meal for three or four people. Wash the beans thoroughly and remove tiny sticks, stones, fragments of brick and other teeth-cracking junk that comes with them in Mexico.

If you don't have a pressure cooker, use a kettle or unglazed clay bean pot. Cover the beans with an inch or more of water or vegetable stock—be generous; it will cook down. ***Don't use salt!*** Salt toughens the beans and they'll never be tender. Bring the beans to a good boil and then turn down to simmer. Watch carefully or your beans will go dry! Don't let the water level get below the top of the beans or you might as well toss them out or resign yourself to eating bullets. If you're forgetful, cover the pot loosely with a lid and cook the beans very slowly.

Important tip: Always add *boiling water* when more is needed, not cold or even warm water. Sudden temperature changes will harden the beans or make them grainy.

Once the beans are soft, mash or blend a few spoonfuls with broth and stir this back in to enrichen the broth. Traditionally, beans should be soupy, so serve them Mexican style, in a shallow bowl.

Variations: Classic *frijoles de la olla* ("pot beans") probably owe as much of their wonderful flavor to careful cooking as they do to herbs and other ingredients. On the other hand . . . as your beans simmer, you might want to add a few pinches of ground cumin, garlic, onion, *chile* (try one dry *ancho* or *pasilla* without seeds) and oregano. One of our favorite variations is to cook the beans with a coarsely chopped onion, one or two dried *chipotles* (smoked *jalapeños*) and a tablespoon or two of olive oil.

In southern Mexico, a sprig or two of fresh, pungent *epazote* is added to black beans when they are nearly cooked.

It's strictly "gringo," but for an excellent vegetarian chili, sauté a can of chopped tomatoes with onion, garlic, celery, green pepper, dry *chiles* to taste and oregano—add them to your pot when the beans are almost done. Once the beans are tender, stir in a generous tablespoon of yellow mustard and another of honey, plus a dash or two of Worcestershire sauce. *¡Qué rico!*

5. *Frijoles Refritos* (Refried Beans)

I'll start by revealing some ancient secrets that have eluded gringo cooks in their never-ending quest for authentic refried beans: first, you can't refry just any old bean, you've got to start with genuine *frijoles de la olla*. Second, for true Mexican flavor and consistency, you have to actually fry the beans, not just reheat and smash them into paste. You must also use a lot of oil or fat, far more than your family doctor recommends. (In the interests of good health, however, our recipe is for low-fat, "lite" refried beans.)

A word about consistency: I've been served *refritos* in Mexico that were baby-food soft and smooth, and I've had them fried until the beans had a crust and were thick enough to stand a spoon in. It all depends on how much fat you add and how long you cook your beans.

We'll go for a moderately firm batch of refried beans: drain your *frijoles de la olla* (save the broth!) and heat oil, butter, margarine or lard in a frying pan. Use two tablespoons of fat—or more—for each cup of drained beans.

Now fry the beans over a medium-hot fire, mashing and stirring constantly. Use a strong fork, or better yet, a potato or bean masher (indispensable, so get one the next time you're in Mexico). After a few minutes add a slosh of the bean broth to the pan and continue mashing and stirring. If the molten beans spit at you a lot, lower the temperature. Fry until almost dry—add more broth, fry, more broth, fry, etc. Continue until the reserve broth is gone and the beans are the consistency of a thick paste, not runny. They'll thicken even more as they cool.

Serve refried beans smeared on tortillas, garnished with chopped tomatoes, onion, avocado, lettuce and sour cream. If you feel really decadent, refry your beans in butter until the edges are brown and crumbly. Though hardly traditional, I love refried beans smeared on toasted French bread with slices of sweet onion and fresh tomato.

Enfrijoladas: This traditional recipe from our friend Doña Mica is a wonderful example of northern Mexico's ranch-style fast food:

Fry corn tortillas lightly in hot oil and drain quickly. Now soak the tortillas for a minute or two in *frijol caldudo*, soupy refried beans. (You can make this very fast by mixing a can of refried beans with vegetable stock or water.) Depending on your appetite, stack two, three or more tortillas on a plate and layer them with finely chopped onion, *jalapeño*, and crumbled white cheese. Top it all off with more cheese and serve, if possible, with a side of stewed *nopalitos* (nopal cactus).

6. *Sopa de Arroz* (Mexican Fried Rice)

This is truly a classic—a delicious and versatile one-pan meal. Don't be confused by the name *sopa de arroz*. This is a Mexican "dry soup," where the liquid has been absorbed by the rice. We'd probably call it a stovetop casserole.

1 cup dry rice	*a handful or small can of peas*
2 to 3 tbs. oil	*1 carrot, diced or sliced*
1 small onion, chopped	*1 tomato, chopped (or canned or*
1 cup of water or stock	*tomato sauce)*
salt	*celery, green pepper, mushrooms or*
	whatever you have, chopped

Heat the oil and fry the uncooked rice until the grains are golden and translucent. Add the vegetables, stirring constantly. Before the rice gets too dark—a few minutes—add the liquid, cover and simmer. The rice will be done in about twenty minutes. If it looks too wet, leave the lid off the pan for the last few minutes of cooking. Avoid stirring the rice as it cooks or it may become gummy.

7. Corn Tortillas

Steve's homemade corn tortillas have passed the Ultimate Test: Mexicans living in Oregon regularly drop by his cabin and try to beg or buy these tortillas. Here are his instructions, to the letter:

The press: You will need a metal or wooden tortilla press (available at kitchen supply stores in the U.S. or buy one in Mexico) and a thin, clear polyethylene bag to line the press. Get the kind used for produce in supermarkets. Slice the bag along both sides, leaving the bottom seam intact. Cookbooks always tell you to use waxed paper, but Mexicans use *clear* plastic bags (not colored) and they do work much better.

Tortilla flour: By far the best *masa harina* (dry tortilla flour) I have found in the U.S. is sold in natural food stores in bulk. If you're lucky enough to have a Mexican food store nearby, use *masa harina* imported from Mexico. The Quaker Oats *masa* sold in U.S. supermarkets is hard to work. Use it if you have to.

Cooking griddle: Mexicans prefer a sheet metal or clay *comal* (griddle), but a cast iron frying pan or pancake griddle will do. Dry metal griddles and iron skillets are preferable to Teflon pans or coated griddles. Tortillas look simple but believe me, details are important!

Prepare the *masa*: Combine two cups of *masa harina* with lukewarm water, a little at a time, mixing it with your hands into a stiff dough. Let the dough *reposar* (rest) at room temperature for about twenty minutes. It should then break cleanly but still be damp enough to hold together—but without being sticky. You'll probably have to experiment to get just the right consistency.

Your dough is too dry if the tortillas crack and tear when you peel them off the plastic after being pressed. If they stick to the plastic, however, the dough is too wet. Depending on the problem, return the *masa* to the mixing bowl and add just a little more water or dry masa flour.

Shape and press: To make a tortilla, pinch off a chunk of *masa* dough and roll it to the size of a Ping-Pong ball between the palms of your hands. Place this ball in the center of your open press, with its plastic liner in place. (Put the bottom seam of the bag toward the hinge of the press.) Close the press and flatten the tortilla with firm, moderate, steady pressure. If the tortilla comes out too thin, roll it back up and try again, but don't press so hard.

Make the tortilla balls one at a time as you cook them. Cover your *masa* between tortillas. If the dough dries out, knead in more water.

To remove the tortilla from the plastic bag, hold the pressed tortilla flat-out on the palm of one hand and carefully peel back the top layer of plastic. Now quickly invert the tortilla onto your other hand and peel that side. Your next trick is to expertly flop the limp, raw tortilla onto the hot griddle without folding or wrinkling it. Win a few, lose a few. . . .

Cook the tortilla: Your griddle or cast iron pan should be dry—no oil at all—and quite hot, but definitely not red hot. Again, you'll have to experiment and adjust the temperature as the tortillas cook. At the perfect temperature, the tortillas won't stick—and if they smoke or scorch, it shouldn't be too much.

OK, flop a raw tortilla onto the griddle. When you see that it has begun to stiffen and cook through, flip it with a spatula (Mexican women use bare fingers!). Cook the second side for an equal amount of time. Some smoking and scorching is OK, but not too much. Now flip it back to side #1 and hold your breath: steam inside a perfect tortilla will cause it to inflate, cooking the inside of the tortilla. *¡Se infla!* This inflation separates the authentic tortilla from mere fakes.

Wait a few seconds and then remove the tortilla and tuck it carefully between the folds of a clean, dry cloth or inside an insulated tortilla basket. Repeat this process several thousand times, or until you get it just right.

In fact, making real tortillas at home isn't all that difficult, especially if you already know something about cooking. The real "trick" is to observe what is happening and make the necessary adjustments in temperature, cooking time and dough consistency. Good tortillas are worth the effort!

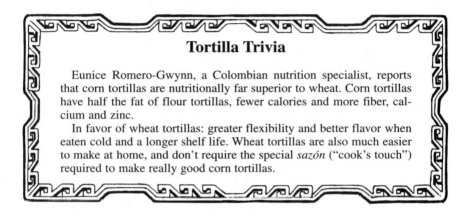

Tortilla Trivia

Eunice Romero-Gwynn, a Colombian nutrition specialist, reports that corn tortillas are nutritionally far superior to wheat. Corn tortillas have half the fat of flour tortillas, fewer calories and more fiber, calcium and zinc.

In favor of wheat tortillas: greater flexibility and better flavor when eaten cold and a longer shelf life. Wheat tortillas are also much easier to make at home, and don't require the special *sazón* ("cook's touch") required to make really good corn tortillas.

8. Flour Tortillas

Flour tortillas probably qualify as the signature food of northern Mexico and the Baja Peninsula. Many first-time visitors prefer the flavor and bread-like texture of flour tortillas over those made from corn. In fact, there are many incarnations of the *tortilla de harina*, varying from thin, platter-sized disks to small thick saucers. I've eaten flour tortillas that were translucent with fat and as flaky as pie crust. Others are tough and chewy; as usual, it all depends on regional tastes and the cook's mood.

The following recipe is for a basic, no-frills Baja ranch tortilla. Lorena and I depend on these durable tortillas for extended camping and kayaking trips, but we also eat them at home, especially for snacks and quick meals. We often make a more bread-like tortilla by adding whole wheat flour, and we use oil rather than shortening or lard, but these are relatively minor adjustments.

Utensils: Instead of a tortilla press, you'll need a rolling pin and a clean, dry surface to work on.

4 cups of flour (we use equal parts of white and whole wheat)
2 to 4 tbs. oil, shortening, butter or lard
½ to 1½ tsp. salt
1 tbs. baking power or dry yeast
1 to 1¼ cups of warm water

Mix the dough: Mix three cups of the flour with the salt, oil, leavening and water in a large bowl. If you use yeast, let the dough mixture rest and rise for at least fifteen minutes in a warm place.

Knead the remaining flour into the dough. Give it a good five- or ten-minute workout. You want a dough that won't quite stick to your bowl or fingers, so adjust the flour and water as necessary. Experiment; this definitely isn't rocket science.

Once the dough is ready, shape it into a ball and return it to the bowl (oil the bowl a little to keep it from sticking). Cover the bowl and let the dough rest and rise for fifteen minutes (baking powder) to an hour (yeast).

The griddle: Cooking the tortilla is the most critical part of the process. As with corn tortillas, you want to use a dry heavy griddle of iron, sheet metal or clay. Then again, almost any frying pan will do in a pinch. Get it hot but not smoking.

Roll it out: As the pan heats, flour your hands and squeeze off a lump of dough about the size of an egg. Flatten the dough ball with the palms of your hands against a well-floured cutting board or even a plastic bag. Once it is flat, continue using a rolling pin, bottle or what-have-you (also well floured) to shape the dough into a more-or-less round disk, ⅛ inch to ¼ inch thick. By the way, if the dough is too sticky to roll out, knead in more flour. Too stiff? Add a little water to the dough.

Once you've got it shaped, pick up the tortilla and slap it back and forth to dust off excess flour. Don't worry; raw flour tortillas are tough and flexible, much like pizza dough.

Place the raw tortilla on the hot griddle. There is a knack to this but how can I describe it? To avoid unsightly wrinkles, I give the tortilla a little top spin and fling it onto the griddle. If the temperature is just right, bubbles will pop up in about thirty seconds. Regardless, once the tortilla begins to smoke, flip it over. A well-made tortilla will soon begin to inflate. Don't pop it; the steam inside is cooking the dough to perfection.

When the inflated tortilla begins to sag or starts scorching, pull it off and wrap it in a clean, dry cloth. Repeatedly flipping the tortilla from one side to the other makes the tortilla tough and stiff, so try to get the griddle temperature adjusted so that they cook with just one turning.

Flour tortillas keep a long time. Even though they'll stiffen, you can easily rejuvenate your tortillas by sprinkling a few drops of water on them and reheating them.

Buñuelos taste a lot like doughnuts or sweet frybread. To make them, just add three beaten eggs to your basic flour tortilla dough. Fry the raw tortillas in lots of hot oil until they're brown and crisp. Now sprinkle them liberally with sugar and cinnamon, or smear the *buñuelos* with butter and honey. Serve these with hot chocolate.

9. Tortilla Snacks and Leftovers

Until you develop a Mexican's awesome appetite for tortillas, you'll undoubtedly have leftover tortillas kicking around. They very quickly turn hard, but don't think they're not still useful and tasty. Here are some suggestions:

• Keep tortillas wrapped in cloth or paper, not plastic. If they can't breathe, they'll go sour.

• Sun-dried tortillas can be used for snacks. Garnish with refried beans, hot sauce, cheese, vegetables or even peanut butter.

• Bake tortillas in a warm (not hot) oven until brittle.

• Fried chips: sprinkle the tortilla with salted water and dry. Cut or break into pieces and fry until golden in hot oil. Fried tortilla "chips" require lots of oil and are less nutritious than baked or sun-dried.

• Sauté hard tortillas in butter. When soft, sprinkle grated cheese on top, roll tightly and eat like a breadstick.

• Add hard tortilla pieces to soups just before serving or bake in casseroles.

10. *Quesadillas*

Purists may argue that these are actually *tacos de queso*, but while they talk I suggest you eat their share. Mix the cheese, onion, tomato and *epazote* (several sprigs). Put two heaping spoonsful in a tortilla and fold it over. If your tortillas are stiff, they can be sprinkled with water and wrapped in a warm cloth for a while. Fry the filled tortilla in hot oil or butter until golden, then turn it and fry the other side. Drain on paper and garnish with lettuce or cabbage and hot sauce.

tortillas	*onion, chopped*	*salt*
oil or butter	*tomato, chopped*	*lettuce, cabbage*
cheese, grated	*epazote*	*chile sauce*

11. *Ceviche*

Mexico has made *ceviche* internationally famous. This excellent snack of marinated seafood is often prepared by fishermen right at the water's edge. It is usually accompanied with salted crackers and beer or tequila.

The type of *ceviche* you prepare depends on the available seafood. In Mexico, *ceviche* never seems to be the same twice. Before committing yourself to a large batch of *ceviche*, experiment with a modest amount, noting the proportions of the ingredients.

Cut two cups of raw seafood into bite-sized pieces. Skinned and boned *sierra* mackerel and shark are good but most any fish will do. Use oysters, tenderized conch, clams, shrimp or whatever else you can scrape off the beach. Put the seafood in a bowl and cover it with lime juice—you'll need a lot of limes. Stir and set aside.

Chop very finely:

1 white onion	*2 seeded jalapeño peppers*
1 tomato	*(canned or fresh)*
salt	*2 cloves of garlic*

Add this to the seafood. Optional: a shot of bottled hot sauce, black pepper, oregano, cilantro or parsley.

Allow the *ceviche* to marinate for at least ten minutes before serving. Many people recommend hours of marinating, but this is usually impractical; no one seems willing to wait that long. *Ceviche* is customarily eaten with toothpicks.

12. *Pepitas* (Toasted Seeds)

Pepitas, toasted squash and melon seeds, are a favorite Mexican snack. They're both nutritious and quite inexpensive. To make your own either buy seeds in the market or scrape them from a squash and clean thoroughly. Soak one cup of seeds in ¼ cup of heavily salted water for several minutes. Drain the seeds and roast them in a dry unoiled pan over a fairly hot flame, stirring constantly. The *pepitas* are done when they're well browned and begin popping open. I cook mine until the shell is crisp and can be eaten; it's lazier than opening them with your teeth.

Variations: Soak the seeds in a fifty-fifty mixture of soy sauce and water; add garlic and/or chili powder while toasting or after.

13. Avocado Dips

The most popular avocado dip in the world is Mexico's guacamole. The easiest way to prepare guacamole is to simply peel and mash a firm ripe avocado together with *salsa picante* (see recipe below). Drain any excess liquid from the tomato *salsa*, and use a fork to combine it with the avocado. Be creative: you can also use *pico de gallo* (see recipe below) for a chunkier guacamole, or most any hot sauce that appeals to you. Steve's favorite is garlic guacamole: mince several fresh garlic cloves and mash them up with a firm ripe avocado. You might also add a tablespoon of mayonnaise or a squeeze of fresh lime juice. Simple but very tasty.

14. *Salsa Picante* (Hot Sauce)

As Lorena points out, there are basically two kinds of Mexican *salsas*: red (tomato) and green (*tomatillo*). As simple as this appears, traditional *salsas* also vary by the type of peppers used, whether the *salsa* is fresh or cooked, coarse or finely chopped, mashed in a *molcajete* or blended smooth. In other words, there are thousands of possible *salsa* combinations. By using additional ingredients, the potential is limitless. On the other hand, if you want *salsas* that are simple, easy to prepare and more delicious than almost anything you can buy at the store, try the traditional recipes below.

The secret to preparing mouth-watering tomato *salsa* is to use fresh, vine-ripened tomatoes, preferably homegrown or organic. Steve lays down the law on this: "There is no substitute. If you can't get fresh, high quality tomatoes, use a good brand of canned whole tomatoes such as Italian Romas. Under no circumstances should you use tasteless supermarket tomatoes. You would be better off buying prepared *salsa*.

"My favorite tomato *salsa* was taught to me while visiting Huichol Indian friends at their small *rancho* in the state of Nayarit. It only has four ingredients but it's the best salsa I've ever tasted." Here it is:

> *a big handful of fresh, red ripe tomatoes*
> *small white onion*
> *2 or more fresh green chiles (jalapeño or serrano)*
> *salt to taste, preferably kosher or sea salt*

For the most authentic flavor you'll also need a campfire, barbecue grill or, if you have to, a gas stove burner.

Roast a couple of good-sized tomatoes until the skin is heavily blistered and blackened but not totally cremated. Roast the *chiles* in the same manner (a pair of tongs really helps) and chop both the tomatoes and *chiles* coarsely. Don't remove the blackened skin on the *chiles*; it adds an important flavor.

Now grind the *chiles* and salt with the *molcajete* (stone mortar and pestle). If you don't have a *molcajete* yet, any good sized mortar and pestle will do. You can use a food processor or blender on "chop" but the salsa just won't be as good. The usual *molcajete* technique is to grind each ingredient for several seconds, then add another and grind it, and so on until everything is mixed together. Don't ask us why, but using a *molcajete* rather than a blender really does seem to improve flavor.

Mince the onion and grind it into the *chiles*; finally, grind in the chopped tomatoes, blackened skins and all. Add cold water as necessary to keep the *salsa* well moistened.

Don't overdo this; you want a chunky salsa, not a blended puree. Adjust the salt and water if necessary. That's it!

For a quintessential *campesino* meal, serve your tomato *salsa* with homemade corn tortillas and *frijoles de la olla.*

Salsa **ideas:** For a slightly more elaborate red table *salsa* add any of the following:

> a small handful of finely chopped cilantro or parsley
> a clove or two of crushed fresh garlic
> one or two squeezes of fresh lime or lemon juice

Steve prefers the simple version but he stresses that the ingredients must be the best. If your tomatoes and *chiles* aren't up to his standards, the extra ingredients will help.

15. *Salsa Ranchera* (Ranch Sauce)

Salsa ranchera is simply a cooked version of fresh red tomato *salsa*. Anything on a menu prepared *ranchero*-style, from eggs to beefsteak or shrimp, uses a version of this *salsa*.

> *1 large white onion, halved and sliced thinly in half rounds*
> *2 to 3 ripe red tomatoes, roughly chopped. Blanch and peel them first if you like but the skin is usually left on in Mexico.*
> *Fresh green serrano or jalapeño chiles, sliced in thin rounds. Remove the seeds and veins if you want a milder salsa.*
> *2 to 3 cloves of garlic, thinly sliced*
> *cooking oil*
> *salt to taste*

Sauté the sliced onion and garlic in a little oil until the onion just begins to brown. Add the chopped tomatoes, *chiles* and salt. Cook over medium heat until everything is tender and well done. Add water as needed to prevent sticking. The *salsa* should be fairly soupy.

Bistec Ranchero: Sauté or grill thin slices of beef until just cooked, then smother the beef in *salsa ranchera* and simmer for several more minutes, adding water as necessary. This recipe is also excellent with prawns, fish or tofu.

16. *Felicia's Salsa Cascabel* (Rattlesnake Sauce)

Sauces made with dried *chiles* are quite different from those calling for fresh. This sauce uses *chile cascabel* (rattlesnake), but try it with most any dried *chile*. With practice you can make a batch in a few minutes. It keeps for weeks if refrigerated. Excellent on enchiladas!

> *10 dried cascabel chiles (a handful)*   *salt to taste*
> *6 to 8 green tomatoes (tomatillos),*   *garlic, several cloves*
> *membrane covered*

Toast the *chiles* over an open flame or in a pan. Avoid breathing the fumes; they are quite irritating. Using rubber gloves to protect yourself from the potent *chile* oil; remove the seeds. (I do this under running water.)

Peel the papery husk from the *tomatillos* and drop them into a pot of boiling water.

(Or roast them over an open fire.) Cook the *tomatillos* for three to four minutes or until soft, then remove and drain them. If you can't get *tomatillos*, regular unripe greenish tomatoes can be used. Just be sure to cook the green tomatoes well, as they can be slightly poisonous.

Mash everything in a *molcajete* or a strong bowl, or use a blender. The flavor is best if your Rattlesnake Sauce is served at room temperature.

Variations: Use red tomatoes or fresh *chiles*. If fresh *chiles* are used, decrease the number to about two or three.

17. *Chile Colorado Salsa* (Red Sauce)

At Doña Mica's table in Batopilas, *chile colorado* is the "house" *salsa*. Red sauce is more common than ketchup in northern Mexico. It is excellent on everything from fried eggs and potatoes to steamed vegetables, enchiladas and refried beans. For a quick, eye-opening snack smear this versatile *salsa* on fresh fruit, plain tortillas or crispy saltines. Don't choke—I once watched a very tough Mexican moonshiner use *chile colorado* as a dip for sweet animal crackers!

The recipe is remarkably simple but as with other salsas, the secret is in the quality of the ingredients. Look for long, dark red dried *chiles* in a large supermarket or specialty food store. You can also use a substitute such as *chile ancho* or *chile poblano*. If you're feeling frisky, add canned or dried *chipotles* to taste. The flavorful *chipotle* (smoked *jalapeño*) is one of my personal favorites, but be careful, they can bite like a pit bull. Whatever *chile* you choose, the sauce will be interesting.

> *2 big handfuls of dried chile colorado: remove the stems and seeds*
> *salt*
> *water*

Rinse the *chiles* and remove the stems, then cover with water in a saucepan and boil for five to ten minutes, or until the *chiles* are easily pierced with a fork.

Drain the water and grind the *chiles* in a *molcajete* (mortar) or a blender. Add enough fresh water to make a thick *salsa* or even a paste. Salt to taste and serve.

Options: For a smoother sauce that's also somewhat easier on your internal plumbing, strain out the *chile* seeds.

Further options: Add garlic, lime juice, oregano, etc.

Chile colorado sauce will last for weeks when refrigerated.

18. Francisca's *Salsa Verde* (Green Sauce)

Salsa verde is served hot or cold, on fish, pork, eggs, potatoes, rice, meat, beans, etc. Green sauce has a distinctive tart taste and does not have to be spicy unless you wish it to be.

1 lb. fresh tomatillos (green husk tomatoes) or 1 can tomatillos
salt
1 medium onion, chopped
½ cup fresh cilantro
1 to 2 fresh green chiles (jalapeño or serrano), seeded and roughly
*   chopped—or for a milder sauce, 1 canned jalapeño pepper*
2 or more cloves of fresh garlic

Cover the *tomatillos* with water and boil until just tender. Drain them but save the water.

Grind or blend the cooked *tomatillos* and chopped onion with some of the cooking liquid (if the *tomatillos* are canned use that liquid). Add the garlic, salt, fresh cilantro and *chiles*, and continue to grind or blend. Don't over-process; the *salsa* should be slightly chunky. If you like your salsa very green, blend in a leaf or two of Romaine lettuce.

19. *Pico de Gallo*

Pico de Gallo ("rooster beak") is really just a chunky form of fresh red tomato salsa (that happens to be outrageously delicious). The main difference is that the tomatoes and *chiles* are not toasted, and *pico de gallo* is not mashed or blended. From such small variations, great recipes are born!

Dice the following into ¼-inch pieces and combine: a small or medium white onion, a couple of firm ripe tomatoes, fresh *jalapeño* or *serrano chiles* (to taste), and some minced cilantro (optional but highly recommended). Douse these ingredients with a few generous squeezes of fresh lime juice, add salt to taste and *voilá, pico de gallo.* But remember, no mashing!

20. Red Chile Enchilada Sauce

Success is virtually guaranteed if you prepare your enchiladas with this sauce. The effort to get good *chiles* for this sauce is more than worth it. The most common dried *chiles* found in U.S. supermarkets are the *ancho*, the *pasilla* and the *guajillo*. The *ancho* and *pasilla* are quite similar, but the *guajillo* has a unique flavor. For a dynamite flavor that isn't too spicy, combine *guajillo* or dried New Mexico red *chiles* with *ancho* or *pasilla*.

10 dried chiles (half guajillo or New Mexico Red, and half ancho or pasilla)
5 to 6 garlic cloves
one medium onion, chopped
2 to 2½ cups water (for even more flavor, use ½ cup of the water you soaked
*   the chiles in or substitute one cup of stock in place of one cup of water)*
salt to taste

Remove the *chile* stem, seeds and veins. This stuff is potent, so use rubber gloves when handling *chiles*. Take my word for it; a *chile* pepper skin burn really hurts!

Tear the *chiles* into pieces and toast both sides on a medium-hot griddle or cast iron frying pan. The acrid, stinging *chile* smoke will drive your family wild, so use an exhaust fan—or follow Steve's example and toast the *chiles* outside, on a campstove. While you're at it, roast the unpeeled garlic cloves too.

Put the toasted *chiles* in a bowl and cover them with hot water. Cover the *chiles* with a heavy saucer and keep them submerged for an hour or more.

When the *chiles* have soaked, peel the toasted garlic. Combine all the ingredients in a *molcajete*, blender or food processor. Grind them to a smooth paste. The sauce should be soupy, so add water as needed.

You are now ready to make unforgettable enchiladas!

21. Enchiladas

The word *enchilada* means to "en-chile." There are endless variations, but the basic idea is to bathe a corn tortilla in *chile* sauce and then wrap it around something delicious. The oven-baked enchiladas smothered in yellow cheese that we find in the U.S. are definitely not typical of Mexico.

There are two basic methods to make authentic, can't-get-enough-of-these enchiladas:

Enchilada #1: Prepare a traditional thin red *chile* sauce (see recipe above). Using tongs, dip each side of a corn tortilla into the sauce, coating it well, then briefly fry the dripping tortilla in ¼ inch or more of hot oil. The mess created by hot sauce spattering in hot oil can be awesome, but this method has our vote for the tastiest enchiladas.

Enchilada #2: Fry the corn tortillas in oil—lightly, just enough to make them soft and pliable—then dip them in a red sauce or green *tomatillo* sauce. We're not snobs, so if push comes to shove, just about any sauce you find hidden in the back of the refrigerator will probably work.

In both methods, the next step is to spread a few spoonfuls of filling down the center of the tortilla. This can be anything and everything from grated cheese or mashed potatoes to steamed greens, shredded cooked chicken or meat, refried beans, etc.

Add a sprinkling of minced raw onion and a spoonful or two of *salsa* to the filling, then roll the tortilla into a fat tube. Arrange the filled enchiladas side by side on a plate. Garnish the dish with crumbled white cheese and thinly sliced raw onion rings. Serve with beans and more *salsa*.

You can warm the enchilada plate in the oven, but don't bake them very long or the tortillas will dissolve. Should this happen, don't panic; just call the dish *caserola ranchera* and no one will be the wiser.

Enchiladas *Suizas* (Swiss Style): In Mexico, "Swiss style" is a good excuse to use dairy products. Be aware that the combination of spicy red enchiladas and sour cream often causes a runaway appetite.

To make enchiladas *Suizas*, just follow the instructions above, adding an extra generous measure of any good melting cheese (jack, mozzarella, Oaxaca, Chihuahua or cheddar) to your filling. Top the garnished enchiladas with an additional dollop of sour cream and drizzle everything with salsa.

22. Steve's *Chiles Rellenos con Queso*

Sometime back through the mists of time I recall a Mexican woman teaching Lorena and me how to make *chiles rellenos*. My memory of the recipe is much clearer than the circumstances, but I believe we were camped north of Mazatlán, in an area of hotels, stores and condos now known as the "Zona Dorada." At the time of our cooking lesson this was a free camping beach dotted with a few thatched-roofed seafood restaurants.

The preparation of this recipe is rather involved, but the resulting *chile rellenos* are worth every minute. It is much easier with a helper or two.

The *chiles*: In Mexico the *chile* of choice for this recipe is the *poblano*, a dark green, triangular-shaped chili three to four inches in length. It varies in hotness from mild to quite *picante*. Here in Oregon, *poblanos* are available in supermarkets. A large green Anaheim pepper makes an acceptable substitute as do any of the long green *chiles* from New Mexico. Bell peppers won't do—the flesh is too thick.

Use two or more *chiles* per person. Leftover *chile rellenos* are delicious for breakfast the next day so I make a few extra just to be safe. To peel the tough skin from the *chiles*, roast them directly in the flame of a gas stove, under a broiler, in a toaster oven or, best yet, over an open fire or barbecue. However you do it, keep turning the peppers until they are evenly blackened over the entire surface—but without burning through or overcooking. As the *chiles* become black and blistered, place them in a plastic bag of the type used for produce in supermarkets.

Keep the bag closed for twenty to thirty minutes, then start peeling peppers. If you roasted the peppers well and left them long enough in the plastic bag, the skin comes off easily.

After they are peeled, make an incision with a sharp paring knife in the side of the pepper. Start at the bigger stem end and go down a couple of inches. Use the knife to sever the main seed pod inside the *chile* and beneath the stem. Pull out the seed pod carefully to avoid ripping the *chile*.

Now rinse the *chile* with cold water. Remove any remaining ribs and seeds and rinse again. Handle the *chile* carefully; you can use torn *chiles* but intact ones are better.

After rinsing, blot or drain the *chiles*, roll them in white flour and set aside.

The cheese: In Mexico, *chiles* are stuffed with *panela*, a fresh ricotta-like cheese. Oaxaca or Chihuahua cheese is also very good but any cheese that melts will do. The tastier the cheese, the better the *chile rellenos*.

Cut the cheese into thin strips the length of your *chiles*. Insert the cheese through the slit in the *chile*. Use plenty of cheese but don't overstuff or the *chile* will burst as the cheese melts and expands. Seal the slit in the *chile* with wooden toothpicks. Now roll the *chiles* in flour again and set them aside.

The tomato sauce: Prepare a couple of quarts, enough to fill a ten-inch Dutch oven or big saucepan at least three inches deep.

> *2 pounds fresh, peeled whole tomatoes, or at least one 28 oz. can tomato*
> *juice or water to thin the sauce. Don't use tomato purees or tomato*
> *paste; your sauce will be too thick. The sauce should be the consistency*
> *of chunky tomato juice.*
> *1 to 2 medium to large onions, thinly sliced*
> *fresh garlic to taste, minced*
> *salt to taste*
> *vegetable or olive oil*

Sauté the onions and garlic in oil. When the onions just begin to brown, stir in the tomatoes. Mash them up and add juice or water to thin the sauce. Add salt and keep it at a low simmer while you fry the *chiles*.

The egg batter: For every two *chiles*, separate the yolk and white of one egg. Beat the whites until stiff. Beat the yolk a little and fold it into the beaten whites.

The frying: Heat cooking oil one inch to two inches deep in a large frying pan. The ideal temperature is about 375° F—very hot but not smoking.

Grasp a *chile* by the stem and dip it into the egg batter. If the entire *chile* isn't well coated, use a rubber spatula to spread the batter.

Holding the batter-covered *chile* by the stem again, slip it into the hot oil, rotating the *chile* slowly until it is lightly and evenly browned. You can fry two or three at a time but it gets tricky and requires asbestos fingers.

As each *chile* is browned, place it carefully in the pan of tomato sauce, ladling sauce to completely cover the pepper. Keep the sauce on very low heat. Heat the *chiles* in the sauce until the cheese stuffing melts, at least fifteen minutes. It doesn't hurt to cook them longer as they'll soak up flavor from the sauce.

The eating: Serve your *chiles rellenos* with rice, beans, salad and plenty of napkins.

23. Meat or Seafood in *Salsa Verde*

The traditional version of this dish is made with pork. Sauté bite-sized pieces of boneless pork in a large frying pan or Dutch oven until the meat begins to brown. Add a large, thickly sliced onion, minced fresh garlic to taste, a good bit of dried leaf oregano (preferably Mexican), salt and black pepper. Stir occasionally until the onions just begin to brown.

If the pork is loin or a tender, center cut chop that will cook quickly, go ahead and add Francisca's green sauce now (see recipe above). (*Salsa verde* tastes better if you don't overcook it. The sauce should be fairly thick at serving time.) Cook it uncovered at medium heat until the sauce thickens and the pork is thoroughly done. Add water or stock if the sauce needs thinning.

Steve often uses a cheaper cut of pork for this dish. If you do, add water or chicken stock when the onions begin to brown, cover the pan and cook over medium heat until the meat is very tender. When the pork is done, remove the lid and if there's a lot of liquid left, let it cook down to reduce the broth, then add the *salsa verde* and cook a few minutes more.

Chicken and turkey: The recipe is the same—just substitute boned skinless turkey breast or skinless chicken with or without bones. Always remove the skin or the dish will be greasy.

Fish in green sauce: Use a firm white-meated filet of halibut, cod or rock fish. Again, the recipe is the same as for pork or chicken with the exception that you do not need to cook the fish in water. Instead, sauté the fish (or prawns) with onions, then add Francisca's *salsa verde* and cook just until the fish is done.

Serve all of the above with rice.

24. *Huachinango a la Veracruzana*

At the rate I've seen Steve go through a large *huachinango*, fins and all, I'm inclined to agree with his claim that the red snapper is one of the most delicious fish in the ocean. The traditional recipe for Veracruz-style snapper calls for a whole fish, including the head and tail. However, any firm, white-fleshed fish, whole or filleted, will do.

If you have small whole snappers, allow one fish (ten to twelve inches long) per person. (In a Mexico City restaurant, I once saw a group of politicians served an entire yard-long snapper on a platter, smothered in sauce.)

Wash and dry whole fish, then cut deep diagonal slashes in both sides. Salt the fish and brown it lightly in three tablespoons of olive oil (use a large frying pan). Don't cook the fish completely, just brown it for flavor and to seal in the juices, then remove it from the pan. It will be cooked later in the sauce.

> *1 large onion sliced into thin rings*
> *2 to 3 cloves of thinly sliced garlic*
> *1 green or red bell pepper cut into long thin strips*

Using the same pan sauté the ingredients above (add more olive oil if needed) until the onion turns translucent and just begins to brown. Add:

> *4 to 5 large tomatoes with the skin removed or blackened.*

Cut the tomatoes into sections or use a 28-ounce can of whole peeled tomatoes, including their juice. Mash the tomatoes up a bit and add:

> *2 thinly sliced canned jalapeño chiles (seeds removed) and a couple of*
> *tablespoons of the juice from the can*
> *1 small cinnamon stick*
> *small jar of green olives (in Mexico the pits are usually left in but it*
> *doesn't matter)*
> *¼ cup capers and a couple of tablespoons of caper juice*
> *salt to taste*
> *1 large bay leaf*
> *freshly ground black pepper to taste*

This should make a somewhat soupy mixture. If not, add water or tomato juice until you have at least an inch of liquid in the pan. Cook covered over low heat until the vegetables are tender (fifteen to twenty minutes), uncover and return the fish to the pan. Smother the fish in the sauce and finish cooking over medium heat. Be careful not to overcook the fish. Add more liquid as needed.

Remove the bay leaf and cinnamon stick. There should be some liquid left when the dish is served. Garnish with fresh cilantro or parsley and homemade mayonnaise (traditional but optional). Serve with rice and hot tortillas.

25. Cactus and Squash

Slice a few fresh young *nopal* cactus leaves (without spines) into thin strips. Rinse them thoroughly, then drop the cactus into boiling water along with garlic and a sliced onion.

Cook for ten minutes and then drain well. Wash and drain them again to remove the slime. Now chop:

> *1 small zucchini squash or chayote*
> *herbs (oregano, basil and thyme)*
> *2 tomatoes*
> *1 onion*
> *garlic*
> *salt and pepper*

Combine everything in a saucepan and simmer until tender. If the tomatoes don't provide enough liquid, add a little water.

26. *Chayote*

Steamed *chayote*: Peel *chayotes* if the spines are tough and sharp or just scrub them well with a brush if the spines are small and hair-like.

Chop one medium *chayote*, including the seed, into bite-sized pieces and steam with:

½ onion, sliced or chopped	*garlic*
herbs (rosemary, basil)	*salt*

When tender serve with sweet cream, butter or yogurt.

Chayote **sandwiches with cheese:** Cut the *chayote* into slices about ¼-inch thick. Fry in butter or oil until tender. Take two of the slices and make a sandwich with cheese. Round slices of Oaxaca-style cheese taste best, but any melting cheese or cheddar is fine.
   Chop and mix:

2 tomatoes	*thyme*
1 medium onion	*oregano*
garlic	*salt*

Arrange alternate layers of *chayote* and cheese with the tomato mixture in a saucepan or bean pot. Simmer or bake for twenty to thirty minutes.

27. *Sopa de Ajo* (Garlic Soup)

Eat enough of this Mexican favorite and it will protect you from stomach troubles, mosquitoes and unwanted company.

peeled garlic cloves, 1 cup!	*1 or 2 tomatoes, chopped*
2 tbs. butter or oil	*¼ onion, minced (optional)*
1 liter water or light stock	*2 bolillos (large buns of*
(chicken or vegetable)	*French-style bread)*

Sauté the whole, peeled cloves of garlic with the onion over low heat until tender. The garlic should be cooked but not brown. Add the tomato and liquid. Simmer for ten minutes. While the soup cooks, slice the *bolillos* (regular bread can also be used) and toast them well. Cut the toast into bite-sized pieces and float them on the soup when it is served. Traditionally, a raw egg is broken into each bowl of hot soup as it is served. We prefer it without the egg.

28. Aztec Tortilla Soup

Served under many names, this traditional dish is often the "house" soup in tourist restaurants.

2 ripe tomatoes
½ white onion
2 to 3 cloves garlic
vegetable stock or light chicken stock
several stale tortillas, cut into eighths and fried until lightly browned
   but not yet crisp
grated fresh white cheese such as mozzarella, jack or Chihuahua
avocado (optional)
salt to taste

Chop the onion, tomatoes and garlic and grind them to a smooth consistency in a blender, food processor or *molcajete*. Fry this sauce in a little oil. Meanwhile, bring the stock to a boil. Stir in the fried blended vegetables. Turn down the heat and simmer for a few minutes, then add the fried tortilla pieces and cook the soup for two more minutes.

Serve with a sprinkle of cheese on top, chunks of avocado, a teaspoon of raw minced onion and a squirt of fresh lime juice.

29. Doña Mica's *Sopa de Papas* (Potato Soup)

This is an easily prepared and very traditional soup from northern Mexico.

> ½ cup chopped onion
> 7 cloves of garlic
> 1 to 2 chopped fresh jalapeño chiles
> 1 to 2 chopped tomatoes
> Optional (but highly recommended): strips of mild green Anaheim-style
> chiles or bell pepper

Sauté the above ingredients in oil or butter until tender. Add:

> 2 cups raw potato: sliced, cubed or grated (using finely grated potato virtually
> makes this an "instant" dish)
> a pinch of salt
> hot water: enough to cover the ingredients

Simmer until the potatoes are tender.

Options: When the potatoes are tender, stir in half a cup of milk and heat the soup until it *almost* boils. Add a handful of cubed cheese or half a cup of *carne machaca* or finely shredded beef jerky.

30. Teresa's *Sopa De Habas* (Lima Bean Soup)

I'd always considered lima beans rather "blah" until I tried this Lenten recipe. This is a simple dish with one vital ingredient: Chinese parsley (cilantro). Some people love cilantro but others hate it. If its distinctive flavor is too much for you, substitute regular parsley.

> ½ lb. dry lima beans
> water or unsalted broth for cooking the beans
> 1 small onion, chopped
> 1 tomato, chopped
> garlic (don't hold back)
> pinch of cumin
> 1 small chile, canned or fresh, or chili powder to taste
> 1 sprig of cilantro
> salt
> **Additions:** crumbled or grated white cheese

Cook the lima beans according to the basic procedures for regular beans (see *Frijoles de la Olla*, above). (Try to use a hearty vegetable or chicken stock as the liquid for this soup.) Combine the vegetables, spices and cooked lima beans and simmer for at least fifteen minutes. Add the cilantro with the vegetables or sprinkle it over the soup as it is served. Crumble cheese into the soup and eat with hot bread or tortillas.

31. *Café de Olla*

Café de Olla is Mexican-style cowboy coffee. Traditionally brewed in an earthenware pot and served in small earthenware bowls or cups, you will often find *café de olla* in market *fondas* (food stalls). You can make a very passable *café de olla* at home: bring a quart of water to a boil in a stainless steel pan. Add a stick or two of whole cinnamon bark (or half a teaspoon of ground cinnamon) and half a cup or more of sugar—*piloncillo* is used in Mexico but you can substitute a dark brown sugar. (Traditional *café de olla* is quite sweet.) Once the sugar has dissolved, remove the pan from the heat and add half to three-quarters cup of drip grind coffee. Cover the pan and let it steep for a few minutes. Cowboys strain the grounds with their teeth, but you might prefer to use a clean sock or even a fine sieve if you serve the coffee to company.

32. *Agua Fresca* (Fresh Fruit Drinks)

Agua frescas are very easy to prepare, more healthful than soft drinks and quite cheap. They go great with a hot day at the beach.

> *¼ ripe pineapple or 1 small melon or ½ lb. of strawberries*
> *pure water (2 quarts) or ice*
> *honey or sugar*
> *10 limes*

Blend or mash the fruit you've chosen (combinations are good, too). If you're using limes, oranges or grapefruits, peel them first, then use both pulp and juice.

Sweeten to taste. Mexicans prefer their *agua fresca* lightly sweetened, which is more refreshing, especially if ice is added.

33. Coconut Banana Bread

Steve says, "I don't do flan!" so we'll settle for the beach bum's favorite, coconut banana bread. Stir the following in a bowl:

> *2 cups flour (try one white, one whole wheat)*
> *⅓ cup NIDO powdered milk (dry)*
> *1 tsp. baking powder or soda*
> *1 tsp. salt*

Chop up one cup of hard or soft coconut meat or half a cup of any other type of nut. Add the nut and enough coconut milk, cow's milk or water to make a thick heavy batter.

Mash three or four overripe bananas and add them to the mixing bowl along with:

> *3 tbs. vegetable oil*
> *½ cup honey or molasses*

Line the bottom of your baking pan with heavy paper. When you fall asleep in your hammock and burn the bread, this will make it much easier to pry out. Grease the inside of the pan, including the paper. Dump in the mixture. Bake for about forty-five minutes at 350° F. When using an adobe oven, tend the fire carefully to maintain a constant temperature. To test the bread, stab it with a toothpick; it's done when the toothpick comes out clean.

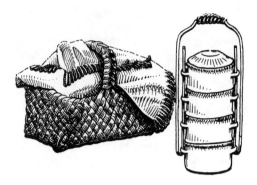

The day began typically enough with bright probing fingers of sunlight urging me out of my hammock. After a short struggle with tangled blankets, I managed to extract myself from my swinging nest. Vague thoughts of an early swim, of fishing, of making coffee or of going back to the hammock were abruptly ended by the sound of curses from our nearby *palapa.*

"That sonnofabitching rat ate my last tomato! I'll kill that bastard if he keeps this up! Aw hell! My very last tomato!"

"Well, " I thought grimly, "looks like Steve is in for a good day."

"I've got to go to town," he said. By the tone of his voice, I knew that arguments were out of the question. He *had* to go to town, even though there was enough food to scrape by for a day or two more.

"Yeah, well," I muttered. "I guess I'll probably stay around here and go fishing or something." The thought of a 150-mile round-trip drive on dirt roads just for food didn't excite me greatly.

"Maybe Fred and Kris would like to go in," I suggested, hoping that our neighbors would accept the wonderful opportunity to make a day long shopping expedition.

Steve left the hut muttering about family loyalty, but I was glad to notice that he headed directly for Fred's van.

He was back within a few minutes, already chanting the food list: "Naturally we need onions, tomatoes, potatoes, bananas, garlic, *chiles,* oranges, cooking oil, flour, rice, sugar, salt, a papaya, a watermelon if they have it, a couple cans of juice, a . . ."

"Wait," I interrupted. "For God's sake, is this a shopping trip or the end of our budget for two months?"

Steve looked at me sadly, "Would you prefer to go instead?"

"Well . . . errh . . . I . . . ah . . . guess not," I answered, shocked that he would say such a cruel thing. "I just thought you might sort of take it easy on the money, you know . . ?"

"Yeah," Steve muttered. "Well, at least Kris has some appreciation for food; she said she'd be glad to go."

As he rummaged through the kitchen area, collecting shopping bags and checking supplies, Lorena wandered in.

"Going to town?" she yawned.

"Thinking about it," Steve answered with forced casualness. "Need anything?"

"Well," she said vaguely, "if you see any purple sewing thread or any of those little brown fruit things or maybe a bunch or two of that greenish herb that lady told us about or . . ."

"OK!" Steve said, scuttling toward the van. "See you guys in a few hours."

As I was about to flop back into the hammock, I heard Steve yelling for me.

"What is it?" I asked, hoping he wasn't going to try to enlist me at the last moment.

"I was thinking that we ought to have a really *substantial* meal when we get back," he said. "Why don't you and Fred see if you can round up a good batch of fish?"

"Sure, Steve!" I agreed, freed now from any lingering sense of guilt at staying behind.

The Great Grunt-A-Rama

"OOrrrfflhh!" Steve moaned, sagging into a hammock and dropping two shopping bags stuffed almost to bursting with food. "God, what a trip!" he sighed, eagerly accepting the beer Kris offered him.

"Blew a tire . . . gasp . . . six inches of dust . . . slurp . . . no tomatoes, except on some rancho . . . cough . . . slurp . . . slurp . . . slurp . . . Kris had diarrhea . . . stopped 2,000 times . . . slurp . . . must have been 150 degrees . . . slurp . . . got another beer? . . . Oh! . . . get any fish? . . . no white onions, got purple instead . . . back killing me . . . slurp, slurp, slurp. . ."

Steve belched, heaving himself out of the hammock. "Time to start cooking!"

"Can't I do something?" Kris yelled after him. "Chop something or . . ." But before she could finish, he disappeared through the low doorway, caught now in the spellbinding thought of intense food fondling and preparation.

"Looks like an impending Grunt-A-Rama to me," I said to Lorena. "Better stay clear of the kitchen."

"What's a Grunt-A-Rama?" Kris asked curiously, for although we had lived side by side for weeks, neither she nor Fred had yet observed this impressive cooking phenomenon. "Why do we have to avoid the kitchen? Can't I help?"

"Look, Kris," I said, "when Steve is in a state that we call a 'food frenzy,' he's like a vicious feeding shark. Anything within range is subject either to dicing, slicing or intense cursing. My advice is to wait until you've seen him in action before deciding to help."

Kris couldn't help looking rather sceptical, so I said, "Let's take in the groceries, have a beer and watch what happens."

"Here you go, Steve," I said, easing my heavy burdens to the ground.

"Yeah, thanks," he muttered absent-mindedly, eyes traveling back and forth over the array of foodstuffs strewn about the hut.

"Oh!" he said suddenly. "How about the fish? Did you get any?"

"Of course," I answered. "Fred speared a really nice hog nosed snapper and we got several smaller fish, too. Also, half a dozen good sized conch and a lobster."

"Then how about some conch soup for starters?" Steve asked. "Sound good?"

"Yeah, sure. Sounds great," I assured him, knowing that on other days he would make it a full meal, but now he considered a huge soup just openers for a larger, more adventurous foray into gluttony.

As I retreated outside I heard him muttering, like strange incantations, the ingredients that would go into the full Grunt-A-Rama.

"Half a cup of onions for the soup . . . better make it a full cup . . . oil . . . lots of garlic . . . I wonder where Lorena put the parsley? . . . ought to have tempera . . . cornstarch . . . stuffed snapper with olives . . . where'd I put the olives? . . . better have Carl fix up this knife, getting dull . . . need another stove . . ."

This last comment caught my attention and I whispered to Kris, "Would you mind getting your stove? This looks like at least a four- or five-burner meal. " While she was gone I began to gather wood. I knew that he would also want a hot campfire for deep frying.

By the time I'd started the fire, Steve had entered into a full food frenzy. Lorena and Kris, giggling as they sipped warm beer, watched furtively from the doorway of the *palapa* as Steve performed before the stoves.

Chopping, cursing, dropping, searching, tasting, sipping, hacking, stuffing, mincing, measuring, burning, smearing, dipping, sticking and making an incredible mess of the kitchen, Steve whipped untold quantities of raw food-stuffs into a symphony of grunting.

With his spatula held baton-like in his left hand and a beer clutched greasily in his right, he induced skillets to musical sputterings and sputterings of hot fat. To add dimension and depth, pungent buds of garlic sent heavy penetrating odors and crisply sauteing sounds out of the hut and into nearby camps.

The staccato chopping of onions, the melodious grinding of peppercorns, the light bubbling of sauces, all held together and given coherence by Steve's rhythmic chanting: "Fry, you bastard . . . why won't that stove get any hotter? . . . Oh, hell! I cut myself . . . where's the hot pad? . . . Use my shirt . . . . ouch! Damn that thing! . . . Wonder if that's going to be enough? . . . Looks like a lot . . . should have got more onions . . . where's the garlic press? . . . My back is killing me . . . "

"Shall I invite those people down the beach?" I asked quietly, dodging a handful of potato peels being thrown blindly away from the cooking area.

"I don't know!" he cried, furiously opening a can of pickled peppers. " If you think there's going to be enough . . . "

T.W.

"What all are we having besides conch soup, fruit salad, cole slaw, stuffed snapper, vegetable and fish tempera, french fries, lobster, tortillas and banana nut bread?" I asked. "Of course, if that isn't enough for five of us, we could always cook up some beans."

"Beans?" Steve said. "Do you think there's time?"

"No," I answered. "I do think, though, that there'll be plenty for a few extra people."

"Whatever you say," he agreed, obviously pleased at the thought. "Just so there's enough for everyone to get really full."

Lorena had overheard our conversation and was already on her way down the beach to the many camps hidden among the palms, spreading word of the impending feast. Odors had preceded her and within minutes, hungry, undernourished travelers were drooling toward our hut.

"This is going to be a good one," I thought ruefully, "and I can imagine who will end up doing the dishes."

The Eating

"Did you try any of this?" I dodged a hot, dripping spatula just as Steve dropped a huge piece of deep fried fish onto my already overflowing plate.

"Oh, man!" I complained, "I can't eat all that!"

"Well, at least give it a try," he urged, moving on to another person who had paused to breathe between bites, encouraging, cajoling and even whining in order to increase the per capita consumption.

The uninitiated loudly praised each bite and were rewarded with unasked-for portions while Lorena and I, veterans of many overfeedings, confined our praise to those dishes we knew were running low or were already exhausted.

As the bottom of pans were scraped for the final morsels and plates dropped empty into the sand, Steve sagged like a bloated walrus, his beer drooping dangerously from a limp hand, eyes wandering vaguely in search of a resting place.

When his grease-spattered bulk had been eased into a vacant hammock, he uttered the immortal words that signal the end of the Grunt-A-Rama: "I don't know why I feel so tired all of a sudden!!"

And with that, he lapsed into a state of semi-hibernation that would last until breakfast.

The Cleanup

There was nothing funny about it at all.

SPEAKING SPANISH

It's worth the effort • Greetings and salutations • Hand signals • Formalities and titles • A typical polite letter • Slang • Nicknames • The Mexican media: books, newspapers, magazines and comics, radio, TV, movies • Speaking Spanish: where do I start? osmosis, self-study, Spanish language schools

"It would be idle to speculate as to the effect of language upon life, but Spanish, I believe, has enriched life for me at least one hundred percent."
—Wallace Gillpatrick, **The Man Who Likes Mexico** (1911)

It's Worth the Effort

English is spoken in major Mexican cities and resorts, but anyone who travels beyond the most popular tourist routes soon learns that Spanish is definitely the "password" to the best of Latin America. On the other hand, most visitors get by surprisingly well with little or no Spanish. Those who do make the effort, however, find that even the most basic grasp of the language increases their enjoyment of Mexico tremendously. In addition to making more meaningful and personal contacts with the local people, speaking a little Spanish offers very practical rewards. Travel is made up of a series of small chores— from ordering meals and finding a hotel room, to catching taxis and buying bus tickets. Being able to conduct routine business in passable Spanish will greatly enhance your self-confidence and undoubtedly save you money as well. Don't be afraid of Spanish; with this book, sign language and a sense of humor, you'll be pleasantly surprised how easy it is to get along in Mexico.

Mexicans are not only very tolerant of novice Spanish speakers, but in most cases they're actually flattered by your attempts to speak their language. In fact, the worst mistake you can make is not trying to speak Spanish at all. Even when you blow it— and mistakes are a natural part of learning a language—they'll listen with patience, encouraging smiles and genuine appreciation. When Mexicans laugh at your most outrageous bloopers, it's "with you," not "at you."

On my first trip to Mexico I brought down the house in a crowded restaurant by loudly ordering a *sandwich de jabón*—a "soap sandwich." The waiter gave me a startled double-take, then grinned and disappeared into the kitchen. He soon returned, however, and gave me a Spanish lesson I'll never forget.

"This is *jabón*," he smiled, lifting a bucket of soapy water to table level, "and this is . . . *jamón!*" In the other hand, he held out a plate of sliced meat. "Now, which sandwich do you prefer?"

I chose the ham.

A friend matched my blunder by ordering a ham sandwich with "*mucho hueso*" ("a lot of bone") instead of a lot of *queso* (cheese).

That mistake was small potatoes, however, compared to my confession to a scowling motorcycle cop that I was "*muy embarasada*" (very pregnant) for failing to use my turn signal, instead of saying "*apenada*" (embarrassed). Once he recovered from the initial shock, the officer leaped to his motorcycle and radioed the big news to the entire Mexico City police force. Then, in obvious appreciation for making his day, the cop let me off with a sly warning, "Be more careful!" and a sympathetic pat on the back.

If communications were nothing more than learning the language, things would be greatly simplified; we could all unearth high school Spanish texts and start parroting phrases. The fact that this doesn't work is demonstrated by the number of people who go to Mexico right out of a formal Spanish course and find themselves faced with that frustrating stare that says so eloquently, "What the hell are you trying to tell me?"

The problem of "proper Spanish" versus "street Spanish" was illustrated by the experience of some friends. When they went to Mexico, the woman had a degree in Spanish from a large university and her boyfriend knew several obscenities and no grammar—good "whorehouse" Spanish. Within two weeks, she felt her nerves straining every time she was forced to speak Spanish, caught between the rigid grammatical training of school and the sloppy everyday speech of the people. He was right in there, waving arms, laughing, gesticulating over this and that, throwing in an occasional inappropriate obscenity and generally making himself understood and liked.

Before you toss your Spanish book out the window, remember that personality and attitude can communicate general ideas and moods quite well, but vocabulary, and to a lesser extent grammar, are necessary for explicit information. You can laugh and stand on your head, but if you want a prophylactic, you'll prefer to know the word rather than having to rely on sign language.

A friend told us that he'd spent several months in Mexico without bothering to learn more than a few words of Spanish. "For example," he said, "all I ever said in gas stations was '*cielo*' and they filled the tank right up." It wasn't until he told us this story that anyone bothered to inform him that *cielo* means heaven and *lleno* full.

Fear of looking stupid chokes up many people. It is very unsettling for adults to be unable to communicate on what they feel is an intelligent and dignified level. No wonder the college graduate feels defensive when forced to say, "Want eat!" in order to find a restaurant. Nonetheless, I urge you to swallow your pride and start talking; it's the only way you'll succeed. I've never felt that remaining silent was preferable to a fumbling but honest attempt to speak Spanish.

Once your initial nervousness subsides, the real fun begins. Mexicans are such easygoing tutors that almost everything you do, whether buying *helado de piña* (pineapple ice cream) to having your shoes shined, becomes an opportunity to practice Spanish.

Being able to say something as simple as, "*Soy carpintero*," ("I'm a carpenter") to a cab driver or casual acquaintance can magically transform you from "just another tourist" into a real person. Before you know it, the conversation is well beyond your grasp of the language—but that doesn't matter. You'll soon get back to the basics: "The weather is warm," "Prices are high," "How do you like Mexico?"

There are times, of course, when your efforts to speak Spanish will draw a blank. When you simply aren't getting through, the most common response will be a polite "*¿Mande?*" or a more blunt "*¿Qué?*" ("What?"). At first, you might feel that some people are deliberately misunderstanding you because it seems that "*¿Qué?*" is heard far too often. If you listen to English conversation, however, you'll notice that "What?" "Huh?" and "What did you say?" are also used far too often and often without reason.

Should this happen, either try another word or phrase or repeat your first statement slowly, clearly and in a normal tone of voice. Don't fall back on English words, especially English words shouted at the top of your lungs. Do you think that a Spanish word would be more understandable to you at full volume and repeated several times in quick succession? It is not polite or reasonable to get mad just because you can't make yourself understood.

In spite of the best intentions, your questions or comments in Spanish may sometimes draw giggles, blank stares or a dull shrug. This is especially true when trying to ask questions of children, tongue-tied teenagers and shy adults. Don't be discouraged. Even if you speak clearly and correctly, there's always someone who won't quite understand what you've said. (An unusually outspoken Mexican once told me, "Don't be offended, Carlos, but after twenty minutes, your Spanish gives me a headache!")

Keep in mind that some people can't understand what you say even when you know without a doubt that it was correct. Anyone who hasn't heard their own language spoken by a foreigner may find it difficult to follow what has been said. Others are hard of hearing or just dumb.

In remote areas of Mexico, the average person might not speak much Spanish. Indigenous languages are very common and you'll find yourself in the rather odd position of speaking better Spanish than the Mexicans. In this situation, sign language is important.

While wandering through an isolated village on the west coast of Mexico, we were approached by an old man who asked if we would sell him clothing.

"We're tourists," we answered, having often been mistaken for traveling vendors in areas where strangers were rare.

"Ah!" the old man exclaimed. "Then you must be Americans! I knew an American here several years ago. He came here to talk with us, to learn our customs."

"Was he an anthropologist?" I asked politely.

"*¿Quién sabe? señor,*" the old man chuckled. "He said that he wanted to learn all about us, but first he would go to the hills," and he motioned with a wrinkled hand toward a distant range of forbidding mountains, "to learn the language."

"What happened then?" Steve asked. From the seriousness with which the old man looked toward the mountains, we felt certain that the American had encountered something unexpected.

"He came back here after six months and tried to talk to us. He tried for a long time, but he finally left."

"Why?" I asked. "Was there trouble?"

The old man looked at us with a toothless grin, then chuckled. "No, of course not. He left because none of us here are Indians. We couldn't understand a word of what he said. Only the people over there," and he waved again toward the mountains, "could talk to him."

The Mexicans, surprisingly enough, are perhaps the greatest obstacle to overcome when learning Spanish. They are so helpful and understanding that they seem able to anticipate whatever word or phrase you've so diligently practiced and you often don't get a chance to say it.

Throughout this book you'll find lots of common Spanish words and useful phrases. Note which ones you might need in Mexico and repeat them often, either aloud or to yourself. If you know, for example, that you'll be ordering breakfast tomorrow morning, loosen your tongue with a few practice sentences. Imagine the look of astonishment on your friend's face when you casually tell the waiter, *"Para mi, un café, por favor"* ("Coffee for me, please").

At the very least, learn to say *gracias* (thank you), *por favor* (please) and *¿Cuánto es?* (How much is it?). Once you've broken the ice, you'll be amazed at how easy it is to gradually expand your vocabulary—and your self-confidence.

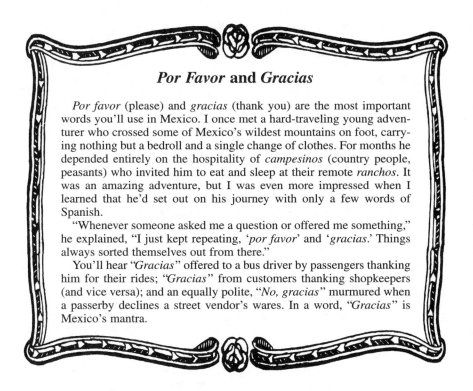

Por Favor and *Gracias*

Por favor (please) and *gracias* (thank you) are the most important words you'll use in Mexico. I once met a hard-traveling young adventurer who crossed some of Mexico's wildest mountains on foot, carrying nothing but a bedroll and a single change of clothes. For months he depended entirely on the hospitality of *campesinos* (country people, peasants) who invited him to eat and sleep at their remote *ranchos*. It was an amazing adventure, but I was even more impressed when I learned that he'd set out on his journey with only a few words of Spanish.

"Whenever someone asked me a question or offered me something," he explained, "I just kept repeating, *'por favor'* and *'gracias.'* Things always sorted themselves out from there."

You'll hear *"Gracias"* offered to a bus driver by passengers thanking him for their rides; *"Gracias"* from customers thanking shopkeepers (and vice versa); and an equally polite, *"No, gracias"* murmured when a passerby declines a street vendor's wares. In a word, *"Gracias"* is Mexico's mantra.

Greetings and Salutations

By American standards, Mexicans can be almost tediously polite. Friends who haven't seen each other for five minutes exchange several greetings, counter-greetings, handshakes and assorted pleasantries.

The tourist often wonders if his Mexican acquaintance isn't putting him on with the apparent intensity of his feeling at each casual meeting. *"¡Qué milagro!"* ("What a miracle!") the Mexican cries, though they are meeting as usual in their regular *cantina*. With a warm handshake he inquires after his friend's family and health, a ritual he also follows day after day.

Although these pleasantries may seem superficial or unnecessary, their importance cannot be discounted. To a Mexican, these formalities all add up to an American "Hi!" and their absence is as awkward and uncomfortable as a cold silent stare.

Effusive greetings between strangers are common. There's hardly any Mexican so impassive that he won't instinctively respond to a polite expression.

Don't worry about such common errors as saying, "Good afternoon" instead of "Good morning" (*Buenas tardes* vs. *Buenos días*). No one expects you to speak Spanish perfectly, but they do expect to hear something, even if it's incorrect. A mistake is usually better than a nervous or impolite silence.

The word *adiós* is a handy greeting that covers many situations. Though *adiós* does mean "goodbye," it is also used extensively to mean "hello." Because it does not convey any sense of time, as does "Good day" or "Good afternoon," *adiós* is always correct when used as a greeting, as long as you're passing someone and not greeting them with the intention of stopping to talk with them. If you intend to stop, you should use one of the regular greetings such as *buenos días*.

If you're greeting someone and don't know the time of day, you can just say, "*Buenas*," and leave off the last word of the expression.

"For a long time it puzzled us why they should say 'good-nights' and 'good-days' instead of 'good-night' and 'good-day,' until we realized that 'Buenas noches' *is an abbreviation of a phrase meaning 'God give you good nights' . . . not to be stingy with the good measure."*

—Harry Carr, **Old Mother Mexico** (1931)

When you're ready to excuse yourself from a person or a group, say, "*Con permiso*" ("With your permission"). The response will be, "*¡Sí, como no!*" ("Yes, of course"), "*Andele*" ("Go on your way"), "*Es propio*" ("It is yours") or some other brief courtesy.

In Mexico, *con permiso* has a very important second meaning: "Excuse me." Whenever you're passing through a crowd or stepping around someone, use "*Con permiso*." The response is, "*Pase usted*" ("Go on by").

A friend tells the story of a young American who worked his way through a badly crowded bank lobby in record time simply by repeating, "*Excusado! Excusado!*" He thought he was saying "Excuse me" but in fact, he was urgently chanting the Mexican word "restroom." Like magic, the throng parted before him. (Again, the correct password for slipping through a crowd is actually "*Con permiso*.")

The following expressions are commonly used as greetings:

¡Hola!	Hi!
¡Hola amigo!	Hi, friend!
¿Cómo está?	How are you? The usual response, even when the stock market crashes, is *Muy bien, gracias ¿y Usted?*" (Very well, thanks, and you?). Other responses: *Regular* or *Así, así* (So-so).
¿Qué tal?	Same as *¿Cómo está?*
¿Cómo le va?	How goes it? Response: *Muy bien, gracias.*
¿Qué hay de nuevo?	What's new? Response: *No mucho* (not much) or *Nada* (nothing).
¡Qué milagro!	What a miracle! Which is meant as, "What a miracle to see you!"

The following words and polite expressions cover a variety of situations, from meeting someone to stepping on their toes. Anyone interested in speaking with Mexicans should learn them as quickly as possible and use them liberally.

Sí	Yes.
No	No.
OK	Becoming quite common in many parts of Mexico.
Por favor	Please.
Gracias	Thanks. Response: *A usted* (You, too) or *Igualmente* (Equally).
Está bien, Bien, Bueno	It is well (fine), OK, good, etc.
Muy bien	Very well. To indicate approval. Someone offers you something and you accept by saying *Muy bien.*
Dispénseme	Excuse me.
Perdón	Pardon.
Perdóneme	Pardon me.
Con permiso	With (your) permission.
Andele	Go ahead.
¡Cómo no!	Why not? Sure, of course.
Lo siento	I'm sorry.
No le hace. *No hay de que.*	Don't let it bother you. It isn't important.
No importa.	It's nothing. Not important.
Al contrario.	On the contrary.
Pase adelante.	Come in.
Pase.	Go ahead. Pass. Response: *Gracias.*
Quiero presentarle a (name).	I want to introduce you to (name).
Mucho gusto.	Pleased. A response to being introduced to someone.
El gusto es mio.	The pleasure is mine. (Similar *to* "*al contrario.*")
¡Nos vemos!	We'll see you! Be seeing you!
¡Qué le vaya bien!	May you go well! This is a very common way to say goodbye to someone whom you may not see for a while or if they're about to take a trip. The response is *Gracias.*
Está en su casa.	You're in your house. An expression that many people unfamiliar with Mexico take too literally. "Make yourself at home" is a more practical translation.
¿Qué? ¿Mande?	What? *Mande* is much more polite than *Qué*, which sounds as dull and abrupt as "Huh?"
¡Salud!	*Gesunheit!* Response: *Gracias.* Also used as a drinking toast, "Health!"

Hand Signals

If a picture is worth a thousand words, the expressive hand signals and eye-catching gestures so loved by Mexicans must rate as novellas. Although some are not used in polite company, many gestures are seen everywhere. Anyone who spends time in the country usually begins to use these signals, too.

    1. *Pintar un violín* (to paint a violin). Favored by loud-mouthed school kids. It is an insult and a taunt, like "Up yours!"

    2. *Colmillo* (eyetooth). Shrewd, crafty. Used to warn someone about a third party.

    3. *¡Ojo!* (Eye!). The meaning depends on the situation. In reference to another person, "Watch out for him," "Be careful" or as a compliment, "He's sharp!"

    4. *¿Quién sabe?* (Who knows?). The classic, "I take no responsibility for anything

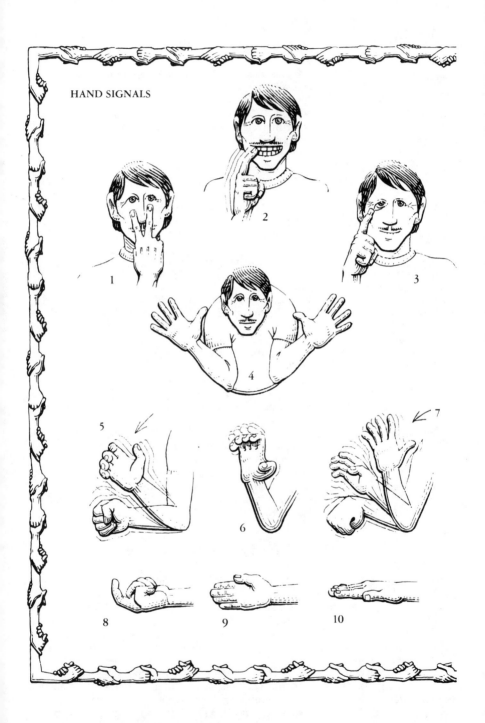

HAND SIGNALS

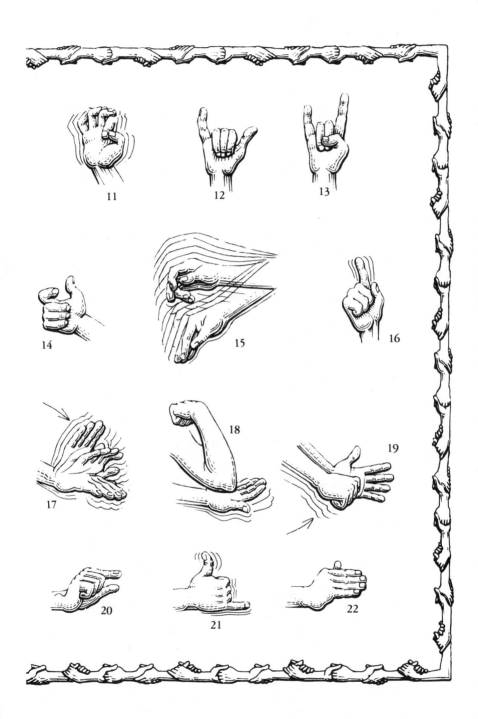

past, present or future." Accompanied by meaningless grunts, moans, eyebrow twisting and general facial contortions.

5. *¡Orale! ¡Simón!* (Right on!). You suggest visiting a disco and your friends enthusiastically make this sort of whistle-pulling affirmation.

6. *Las uñas* (fingernails). Thief or theft. A warning signal if someone nearby is a rip-off artist. "Where's your bicycle?" might bring *"uñas"* if it was stolen.

7. Same as *uñas.*

8. To indicate the height of people. (It can be insulting to use the wrong gesture.)

9. Height of animals.

10. Height of inanimate objects, things.

11. *Mocoso* (snotty). Another schoolyard taunt.

12 and 13. *Cuernos* (horns). Means both "screw you" and cuckold.

14. *Lana* (wool, money). Typical situations: "Have you got the *lana?*" "You'll need a lot of *lana.*" "Expensive!"

15. *¡Híjole!* (Wow!). The fingers flick downward and should make a noticeable pop! If you do it wrong, it hurts like hell.

16. *No, ni modo* (No, no way). Can mean, "No, that's not right," "Cool it," "I've had about enough" or "Lay off, I'm losing my patience." A baleful stare and a wagging forefinger will discourage pesky shoeshine boys faster than anything else.

17. *Adelante* (ahead). "Move forward" or "Come here" looks to gringos like "Go back." Very common and very confusing.

18. *Codo* (elbow). Cheapskate. Saying that a person is "from Monterrey" is equivalent to "very Scottish" (stingy). When done emphatically it means "Up yours!"

19. Sock it to 'em! Right on!

20. *Momentito, ahoritita* (a moment). Be right back, not much, little bit, etc. Used extensively instead of a verbal promise that can't be fulfilled.

21. *El infle* (drinking). "Let's have one," "Down the hatch" or, when speaking of a third person, "a boozer."

22. *No, gracias* (No, thank you). Very commonly used to take the sting out of a refusal of food, drink, smoke and so on.

Formalities and Titles

Students of Spanish are often confused by the use of *tú* and *usted* (you-familiar and you-formal). When greeting a stranger, do you say, *"Cómo estas?"* or *"Cómo está usted?"* When in doubt use the formal. The familiar form is used between family members, friends and people speaking casually with strangers of their own age or social class.

When I took high school Spanish the teacher told us that "the use of the familiar form has taken over in Mexico. Don't worry about learning the formal." This really isn't true; the inappropriate use of *tú* can be both impolite and offensive, since it may imply a lack of respect (for example, a younger person addressing someone older, when speaking with someone of authority or high position, and so on).

The Mexican love of pomp and ceremony always makes it more advisable to lean toward formality, both in words and actions, rather than the studied and deliberate casualness affected by so many gringos.

Titles are frequently used by Mexicans. Some of the most common are *maestro, licenciado, don, doña, profesor, doctor, ingeniero* and *arquitecto.*

A *maestro* loosely translates as a "master" or accomplished tradesperson, technician, skilled laborer or anyone else who is good at something. The woman who runs the *farmacia* can be a *maestra* at pill-pushing and on-the-spot diagnoses, while the old man next door, hammering together sandals, is a *maestro* at his humble trade. The term is also used between friends as a form of respect and affection.

Licenciado(a) (lawyer) is shortened to *lic* between friends.

Ingeniero(a) and *arquitecto(a)* (*arqui* between friends) are used for engineers and architects.

Profesor(a) (shortened to *profe* and *profa*) is a teacher or a person who is well educated or appears to be. *Profe* is used sarcastically for people who put on airs of superior knowledge.

Doctor(a) is sometimes shortened to *doc*.

Don and *Doña* are terms of respect. The word is used before the person's first name or entire name but not their last name. Pedro Gomez, for example, becomes Don Pedro or Don Pedro Gomez, not Don Gomez. Traditional Mexicans use Don and Doña extensively.

When addressing women use *señorita* if they are not married and *señora* if they are (or were). "How do you tell a *señora* from a *señorita*?" A Mexican friend explains that, "Women dressed in black or wearing rings are almost always *señoras*. Girls who giggle or flirt are usually *señoritas*."

When in doubt, address a woman as *seño* (Ms.). This handy term is both convenient and polite.

Joven (young man) is commonly used. When applied to a person who is obviously not young, however, such as a bartender or waitress, the word is rather offensive, similar to the use of "boy" in English.

Señor is commonly used for men, and although *caballero* is quite formal. "*¡Gracias caballero!*" has a nice ring to it when giving thanks for a favor or good deed.

Fulano(a) is used both as John or Jane Doe (*Fulano-a de tal*) and as "so-and-so" or "that person." "*Ese fulano*" is the equivalent of saying "that guy." The terms *vato* and *ese* are street slang, roughly, "guy"

A Typical Polite Letter

While traveling we often meet people we'd like to drop a line to once we return home. The problem is what to say and how to say it, especially if your Spanish is weak. It's amazing what can be communicated with sign language, facial expressions and other signals, none of which are available when faced with a blank sheet of paper.

The following letter can be used, either by itself or in parts, to at least say to a Mexican friend, "Here I am. How are you? We haven't forgotten." Don't worry about the seemingly excessively formal tone; that's just the way Mexicans talk in their letters. If you have more to say, forget grammar and spell it out as clearly as possible. Everyone knows how to read between the lines.

Most large greeting card companies offer foreign language cards for all occasions. Sending one of these to friends and acquaintances you've made during your travels will make a great hit.

Addresses: Print the person's full name and if you don't have the exact address write *Domicilio Conocido* (house or address known) with whatever part of the address you do have. Many people, particularly in the country, will receive mail with just their name, that of their village or *municipio* (county) and *Domicilio Conocido*. Someone will deliver the letter or advise them it is at the post office.

Queridos Amigos:

Nuestros estimados y apreciables amigos: por medio de la presente les saludamos y les decimos lo siguiente: Hemos estado pensando mucho en Ustedes y es posible que podamos visitarles tan pronto como sea posible.

Realmente deseamos que llegue el momento de saludarlos personalmente otra vez y platicar ampliamente con Ustedes. Es por demás desearles que estén bien de salud, puesto que estén bien.
Nosotros estamos bien, gracias a Dios.
Muchos saludos a toda la familia y unos grandes abrazos.

Sus Amigos,

Dear Friends,

Our esteemed and valued friends: by means of this letter (card, correspondence, etc.) we greet you and say the following: We have been thinking of you a great deal and it is possible that we can visit you as soon as possible.
We really hope that the moment arrives to greet you personally again and to talk extensively with you. It is needless to hope that you are in good health since you know that it is our greatest wish that you are well.
We are well, thanks to God.
Many regards to all the family and some great *abrazos* (hugs).

Your Friends,

Slang

"The classroom is the only place where the classroom form of the language will be found."

— Edward T. Hall, **Beyond Culture** (1976)

The use of slang and "body Spanish" is as essential to a Mexican as a toothy smile and firm handshake are to an ambitious politician. There seem to be several ways to say everything. The good old U.S.-of-A. becomes *el otro lado* (the other side), *el norte*, *los united* or *Gringolandia*. Children are *escuincles* (after the Aztec word for dog), beers are *las buenas* (good ones), cars are *naves* (ships), money is *lana* (wool) and life is just *a todas emes* (at full m's—mothers, good!). Mexican slang can be simple and logical, as in *jaula* (cage) for the jail, slightly more complicated with *lucas* replacing *loco* (crazy) and downright obscure as *¡Calmantes montes, pájaros cantantes y alicantes pintos!* (Calm down, man, singing birds and spotted snakes!), an involved way of saying, "Be cool."

There are three major forms of Mexican slang: *caló*, almost another language used in Mexico City and the underworld; regular everyday words and expressions, from innocent to obscene heard around the country; and hip or *de la onda* (of the wave, vibe), preferred by younger people. The three overlap, but for the average tourist the last two types are the most often heard.

An effort to speak the common language, without the stilted and archaic sound of a textbook, may lead you to dangerous areas of speech—namely obscenities.

A Mexican friend who spoke beautiful textbook English asked me to teach him some appropriate obscenities. I wrote down a few, explained their general meaning and use and then forgot about it.

Some time later, we were sitting in his room, talking and drinking beer, when he suddenly began lacing his sentences heavily with profanity. He seemed particularly fond of dramatic endings to simple statements. "I'm going to take a trip next month, shit." His poor timing and improper emphasis on the profane words had me rolling on the floor and quickly ended his attempt to Americanize his English.

Nothing is worse than a really foul obscenity dropped into a conversation at the wrong time or with the wrong person. The only way I know to avoid this is to forget about learning profanities or keep them out of your conversations until you have good control.

The best way to relax your Spanish is to use innocuous—but safe—phrases that you'll hear wherever you go. "*¿De veras?*" ("Really?") will do quite well instead of the more exciting, "*¡Hijo de la Gran Puta!*" ("Son of the Great Whore!"). The use of obscenities is especially risky in situations where it would be better to say nothing at all.

Many years ago, a friend who spoke virtually no Spanish was deported from Mexico as the result of a conversation with a cop about his long hair. Our friend couldn't understand what was happening so he got mad and repeatedly used his most powerful Spanish word—a gross obscenity. Instead of dropping the matter, the cop arrested him.

The Mexican sense of humor is strongly based on the *doble sentido* (double meaning). These may be quite obvious or subtle to the point of complete mystification. Because of their frequent use, either as obvious jokes or traps for the unwary, you should learn to avoid certain words and expressions. Don't panic—in ordinary conversation there are only a few words that you'll want to use with special care.

In a restaurant you'll probably want to order eggs. You innocently ask a respectable looking young waiter, "*¿Tiene huevos?*" ("Do you have eggs?"). Immediately everyone within earshot begins to grin wickedly, savoring an inside joke that is obviously at your expense. You fight down anger (or panic) and look beseechingly at the fellow, hoping for a little compassion.

He answers calmly, "Yes, I do. Two big ones." If this doesn't bring down the house, your flustered exit will.

The use of the word *huevos* should by now be of obvious double meaning. You've just asked the guy if he "has balls" and he's proudly confirmed that he does. The safest words for eggs are *blanquillos* (little white ones) or *yemas* (yolks).

Grammatical constructions can prevent trouble or lead you directly into it. Although technically correct, asking someone a direct question such as, "*¿Tiene huevos?*" ("Do you have eggs?") makes the question personal. You would have avoided embarrassment by making the question indirect and impersonal, as in "*¿Hay huevos?*" ("Are there eggs?") This might seem like a fine distinction, but to Mexicans the use of the "impersonal" is very important.

Other words to avoid with *tiene* are *leche* (milk) and *chile* (chili pepper). I had the misfortune to ask a young woman tending a store, obviously about to give birth, if she had milk. The reaction of the other customers and the look on the girl's face took a year off my conversational ability in Spanish.

To ask a woman if she has milk isn't likely to lead to trouble of the sort involved with asking a man if he "has chili" ("*¿Tiene chile?*"). The *chile* is always synonymous with penis and the jokes surrounding it are innumerable.

When I suspect that something I've said may be impolite or grossly incorrect, I either ask someone immediately for an explanation or note down the word or phrase to ask a friend later.

Note: In the following discussion on slang, words which may or may not be judged obscene are included not to spice up your vocabulary, but to make you more aware of multiple uses and meanings. A word that is profane in Mexico can be quite ordinary in another Spanish-speaking country. It is important to know when to open your mouth and when not to; slang and obscenities are powerful communicators.

• *Chingar*: This is the Big One, the word that gringos mistakenly translate only as "to fuck," but which, in fact, can mean everything from that to merely "messed up" or "Get moving!" The meaning depends on who says it, in what mood, for what purpose and to whom it is directed. As Octavio Paz said: "The word *chingar* with all its

Who Is a Mexican?

The word *mestizo* (or *mestiza*) is commonly applied to anyone of mixed Spanish and Indian blood. Class-conscious Mexicans, however, prefer the far grander term, *gente de razón*, "people of reason or right." On the opposite end of the scale are *gente indígena*, the indigenous, native Indians. Most Mexican Indians, however, do not want to be called *indios*; it is better to use *mexicanos*, *indigenas*, or their "proper" name (Yaqui, Maya, etc.). Rural *mestizos* may refer to themselves as *cristianos*. The message here is, "I am not an Indian."

Who Is a Gringo(a)?

A puzzling word game in Spanish involves the identification of nationalities and ethnicity. Are citizens of the U.S. properly called *gringos*, *norteamericanos*, *americanos*, or *yanquis*? In fact, we are known by all of these terms in Mexico, though the most technically correct word is *estadounidense*, a term that tongue-ties even native Spanish speakers. (Linguistically, *canadienses* get off much easier.) Spanish-speaking U.S. citizens generally agree that the term *hispano americanos*, Hispanic Americans, is preferable to "Latin American," but that term still doesn't identify exact citizenship or heritage. A new term, Indo-Hispanic, presumably includes mixed Indian-Hispanic peoples regardless of nationality.

The potential for resentment lies in the fact that all of us who share this continent—including Mexicans and Canadians—are technically from both America and North America. On the other hand, if a U.S. citizen doesn't have a monopoly on being an American, the only easily pronounceable words left are *gringo* and *yanqui*. Though neither term offends me personally, they are sometimes used in a derogatory sense and aren't appreciated in "polite" company. In the end, I find these distinctions to be interesting but ultimately very tiring.

Gringo isn't the opposite of greaser and many people, particularly those with less education, will call you a gringo without the slightest intent of insult. (A Mexican dictionary defines gringo: "Foreigner, especially the English, Greek, unintelligible language. In Mexico and Central America, 'North American'; in Argentina and Uruguay, 'Italian.' ") The word *güero* (blond, paleface) is also popular and you'll hear it often, particularly in the market place.

Finally, a *pocho*(a) is a derogatory term for a person of Mexican descent (living in the U.S. or Canada) who returns to Mexico and puts on airs.

multiple meanings, defines a great part of our life and classifies our relations with the rest of our friends and fellow citizens."

Some typical uses of *chingar* are:

¡Chinga tú madre!: This is the worst insult of all, fighting words to be sure. "Rape your mother!" just doesn't convey the feeling of the Spanish, but gives the idea.

¡Vete a la chingada!: Used as "Go to hell!" (*Vete a la tiznada*, "dirty, sooty" is similar). A *chingada* is a screw-up and a *chingadera* is a gizmo or thing-a-ma-jig, something you don't really know the name of.

Chingón is usually a compliment. "*El es muy chingón!*" means "He's really something!"

• *Pinche*: Usually combined with obscenities. It means "worthless" or "damned," though the dictionary says, "assistant cook"!

• *Cabrón*: A male goat or cuckold. Calling someone who is not a good friend a *cabrón* can be detrimental to your health.

• *Buey*: An ox, cuckold or generally cloddish person.

• *Pendejo*: A pubic hair. A popular synonym for a fink, square, creep, idiot, wet blanket, knothead, lout, party pooper, asshole or jerk.

• *Pedo*: A fart. "*No hay pedos en el ejido*" is a hick way of saying, "Don't worry about it, don't pay attention."

Nicknames

Apodos are used lavishly in Mexico. The most common nicknames are contractions of proper names (Tonio from Antonio, María from María de la Luz). No opportunity, however, is missed to create a name from a person's physical characteristics, employment, personality or misfortune. Gringos are sometimes offended by nicknames they hear used for others or even themselves. *Gordo* (Fatty) will inevitably be used for the overweight, *Negro* or *Prieto* (Black, Dark) for dark complexions and *Chato* if the nose is not sharp and long, in which case they'd probably use *Nostrils*. Between younger people, nicknames are almost required. (For a sampling of common nicknames see *Appendices*.)

The Mexican Media

One of the best ways to learn Spanish is through the Mexican media. Many travelers tend to isolate themselves from Spanish-language publications, movies, radio and television because of a lack of confidence that they'll find anything interesting or comprehensible.

Since avoiding the media, especially radio, is about as easy as avoiding the water, it's best to make an effort to become familiar with it. Written material is especially helpful. Listening to Spanish on the radio or combined with pictures in movies and television can greatly increase your overall comprehension and "feel" for the language.

• **Books:** Books translated from English are almost always easier to read than books originally written in Spanish or other foreign languages. There are fewer idiomatic expressions and the sentence structure tends to be simpler. If you're interested in works by contemporary Mexican authors, ask for advice in a bookstore; the employees are usually eager to help out.

You'll find that straightforward writing, especially adventures, mystery and historical novels, biographies, etc., is much easier to read and maintain interest in than philosophical or "far out" works.

Read short books to build up your confidence and don't be embarrassed to read children's books and school texts; after all, they are designed for beginners and may be just what you need. The more books you can plow through, the more you'll tend to continue trying. There's nothing quite as frustrating as tackling a book far beyond your abilities.

A good dictionary is essential. Try to find one with Mexican and Latin American Spanish. Dictionaries published in Spain are often aimed at students of "pure" Spanish and don't include important words and phrases used in Mexico. If you speak any Spanish at all, you'll find an all-Spanish dictionary very useful and not at all difficult to use. They are widely available in cheap editions in Mexico.

In towns where gringos congregate you may find lending libraries of English-language books. For a few pesos, you can have access to a great deal of reading material. Large cities have bookstores that handle English, French and German books. In Mexico City you can find a selection of international newspapers and magazines, both in large book-stores and fancy hotels.

• **Newspapers:** Regardless of language, the style and vocabulary of most newspa-pers is unlike the spoken word. Nonetheless, Mexican newspapers are an excellent way to build up your vocabulary. With patience and a dictionary, you'll soon get at least a basic idea of what's going on.

Not surprisingly, most newspapers are heavily weighted toward local and national politics, social events, sports, comics and lurid accounts of murder and violence. *Excelsior*, a national daily often called *"The New York Times* of Mexico," is excellent but almost too detailed and thorough for casual reading. For all-around news and Spanish practice, my favorite daily is *La Jornada*, a more concise, liberal tabloid.

Scandal sheets and lurid tabloids don't even bother to hide behind a front page of world news but specialize entirely in sex, violence and stomach-turning photographs. They are especially fond of bus wrecks and dope busts. These papers are morbidly fas-cinating and I read them with disgust.

Two English dailies, *The News* and *The Mexico City Times*, are published in Mexico City and sold wherever gringos congregate.

• **Magazines:** *Time* and *Newsweek* in English are available in resorts and large cities. The Spanish edition of *Reader's Digest*, called *Selecciones*, is one of the most popu-lar magazines in Mexico. Both *Selecciones* and *Contenido*, a weekly news magazine, are excellent practice for Spanish students. If you're interested in Mexican politics and social issues, *Proceso* is highly regarded. Spanish students who burn out on literary works will find that magazine kiosks offer a variety of easy reading magazines on top-ics ranging from popular science to computers and home decorating.

Comic books are a national passion. They are printed in a variety of sizes, down to mini-comics the size of a pack of cigarettes. Comic books range in content from soft-porno to Donald Duck and Sir Lancelot. Satirical comics are on a higher intellectual level, but may be difficult to understand. Among the best, *Los Agachados* attempts to educate people on everything from personal hygiene to politics. Adult satirical comics are often grossly hilarious, full of slang and slightly off-color jokes.

For those who prefer the Super Hero, *Kaliman* is a household word. The same heroes found on newsstands in the U.S. are also available, from Batman to Buck Rogers. You can enrich your vocabulary with words like "intergalactic travel" or, for aficionados of the classic comic, "Raise the drawbridge, knave!"

Comics are great to share with fellow bus passengers and plaza bench warmers. I like to pass them around and ask for explanations of slang and idiomatic expressions. Kids think it's fun to show off their reading abilities and it gives me a good opportunity to hear the words read aloud. Comics are handy when you feel vaguely like reading, but don't want to get too involved. Those translated from English are amazingly easy to read.

• **Radio:** Although the "*tele*" now ranks as the top Mexican media, radio is still very important, especially to poorer people and those who live in rural areas. In the most remote *sierras* you'll see people listening to cheap transistor sets, receiving nothing more than an occasional song or word through the static.

The radio cult can't be fully appreciated until you've heard the type of broadcasting inflicted upon the eager audience. The most maudlin soap operas are followed by millions of avid listeners, and disc jockeys read off lists of song dedications that sound like census rolls for entire villages. When a news program interrupts this continuous bedlam, it is accompanied by a series of electronic sounds simulating urgency and importance that more often than not obscures the rapid-fire delivery of the newscaster and makes comprehension next to impossible.

You'll also find some English programming, usually from very large AM and FM stations in Mexico City, Guadalajara, Oaxaca, Puebla and other major cities. At night, when long-distance reception is best, you'll pick up a few powerful American stations even on a small radio. Their programming runs heavily toward Salvation and talk shows, but beggars can't be choosers.

• **Television:** Television offers the opportunity of hearing Spanish while watching related action. It is a very effective method for learning the language, though it might strike you odd to hear, as I did one night, "*¡Vámonos muchachos, hay pieles rojos!*" ("Let's go, boys, redskins!") dubbed from the mouth of Daniel Boone.

Closed circuit video, cable and satellite television are available in many hotels and on large screens in "Sports Bars."

• **Movies:** Mexicans are movie goers. Small town *cines* charge very little for admission, and even first-run flicks in Mexico City and other large cities are quite reasonable. Many excellent movies from around the world are shown at universities and cultural centers.

The best movies, especially in Mexico City, often sell out in advance. Buy your ticket as soon as possible for the performance you want.

Prices for the *balcón* (balcony) are cheaper than those for the *luneta* (ground floor). Children under fifteen cannot legally attend any movie considered "adult" (almost all of them), but in most cases the rule isn't enforced, especially if an older person is along.

If you're near a small town that has no theater and suddenly everyone's talking about going to the movies, you're in for a real treat: traveling movies. These "theaters" (actually a portable screen) are erected in the open air by hilarious people (usually *hungaros*, gypsies) who roam the countryside in old trucks, showing their ancient movies to enthusiastic crowds of *campesinos*. This is the ultimate movie experience; don't miss it.

Speaking Spanish: Where Do I Start?

There are three basic ways to learn Spanish from scratch: through osmosis, gradually soaking up the language through contact with Spanish-speaking friends, television shows and casual conversation; by self-study, usually aided with books or cassettes; and in a classroom or "immersion" program.

• **Osmosis:** Wishful thinking for most of us; unless you're quite young or have a natural aptitude for languages, this learn-as-you-live method takes anywhere from five to fifty years to produce results.

• **Self-study:** It took me eight months to complete a university-accredited correspondence course in basic Spanish, and about eight more days to forget most of what I learned. Self-study language courses are a wonderful concept: unfortunately most of us find them as difficult to follow as a do-it-yourself weight loss program. Worse yet, self-study teaching materials are usually based on the much more formal "Spain Spanish," rather than the colloquial, ever-changing Mexican version of the language.

Self-study can work in Mexico, but it still requires a lot of discipline and some basic texts. See my suggestions on learning "*Tienda* Spanish," later in this discussion.

Spanish Language Schools: A Difficult Choice

The most efficient way to learn Spanish is almost undoubtedly by studying in a Spanish-speaking country, in a classroom or similar well-structured environment. As a second choice, try classes at a local community college or adult education program, or one-on-one tutoring. Look for instruction from a native Spanish speaker, preferably Mexican. Last but not least, you can combine either of these methods with travel in Mexico and continued self-study.

It seems that wherever three or more educated Mexicans gather, a school is formed. Add a footloose gringo with a college diploma to the faculty and you've got an international academy. Although most of the schools listed here are for Spanish language study, others have a broader curriculum. The easy-going lifestyle of Mexico, combined with favorable climate and low cost of living, make studying easier and more rewarding. A study-vacation isn't the same as trying to make up a few badly needed credits in some underheated, overcrowded lecture hall in the north. (If you'd like to send your child to school in Mexico see *Traveling: Traveling with Kids: Language*.)

Teaching Spanish has become a minor industry in Mexico and Central America, but choosing a good school takes careful thought. Before we discuss this, however, take a brief look at my ideal two- to three-month travel/study program. This is for people who are intent on learning Spanish but can't afford or tolerate too much formal class time:

Start your program by hitting the books hard in a "serious" school for the first month. Do a "homestay" with a Mexican family rather than hanging out with fellow English-speaking students. Once you've got a good grasp of basic grammar and conversation skills, take off for two to four weeks of travel or volunteer work. During this time make a deliberate effort to practice your conversational skills. Read at least one newspaper and a few comic books or magazines every day. Wrap up your trip and return to school for another two to four weeks of classroom study. Once you go home again, continue reading in Spanish and, if you have cable or satellite TV, try to catch the news in Spanish on a regular basis. Before you know it you'll speak Spanish with real fluency.

• **Student discounts:** Students holding valid Mexican student ID cards are eligible for discounts on everything from hotel rooms to museum tickets. For details ask at the school you are attending or write to the nearest Mexican consul.

How to Find a Good Spanish Language School

Rather than select a school at random from a guidebook or rely on luck, I suggest you try the following:

• Use a referral/booking service such as NCRSA, Language Link or AmeriSpan. This is especially recommended if: 1. You need college credit for your language course; 2. Your goal is to become as fluent as possible in a limited time, yet you don't need credit; or 3. You are nervous and undecided about a school, or somewhat timid about traveling south.

• Ask for a recommendation from a local language teacher, friend or someone you trust who has attended a school. Keep in mind that every school has a distinct style and personality. I prefer small classes with teachers who hold our noses to the grindstone; Lorena is much more comfortable with one-on-one instruction and self-directed study.

• Head south and shop for a school in person by visiting a place with many Spanish language schools. Try Mexico City, Guadalajara, Cuernavaca, Morelia, Oaxaca, San Miguel de Allende, Guanajuato or San Cristóbal de las Casas. In Guatemala, start with Antigua, Quetzaltenango (Xela) and Huehuetenango.

If you're on a budget or have very limited time, pick the place you'd enjoy visiting and then enroll in a language school as a "walk-in."

Mexico, Guatemala or . . . ?

When I travel in Central America people often remark that I speak Spanish with a distinct Mexican accent. As well-educated Mexicans themselves have sometimes confided, my accent also has strong *campesino* (peasant farmer) overtones. I know from their slightly bemused smiles that my occasional use of outmoded, old-fashioned slang makes me sound curiously like someone's hick uncle from the deep *sierra*. This is hardly surprising, since I picked up most of my Spanish over the years while hanging out with muleskinners, farmers, Indians, prospectors, fishermen and tradespeople.

On the other hand, gringos who learn classroom Spanish in Mexico or Guatemala will undoubtedly speak a much more "proper" form of the language. Don't worry about these subtle distinctions; unless you're planning a career as a linguist, one flavor of Spanish is as good as another.

The real decision is whether to study in Mexico or Guatemala. Each country has its advantages—but if you're serious about learning Spanish and enjoy travel, I'd take the easy way out and study in both countries.

Study in Mexico: Many Mexican language schools legitimately boast of higher academic standards than the average school in Guatemala. Mexico is far more prosperous than Guatemala, and it is natural that teachers there tend to be better educated. Language instruction for foreigners has been popular in Mexico for decades, and most schools have a well-developed curriculum, better texts and more complete reference libraries. Teachers in Mexico are better paid than in Guatemala, and therefore more likely to consider their work to be a career, rather than just temporary or part-time employment.

Although the cost of study is higher in Mexico than in Guatemala, the value is usually greater. If you're not on a strict budget, the difference in the cost of living between the two countries isn't that important.

Mexico has the advantage of easy, less expensive access from the U.S. and Canada. You also have the choice of studying Spanish at the beach, in the mountains, in a number of large and small cities, or even in villages.

Study in Guatemala: It costs more to get there but on average you'll pay less for tuition and homestays in Guatemala. Guatemalan language programs also tend to have one-on-one instruction. Unfortunately, costs are often held down by hiring young, inexperienced teachers at ridiculously low wages. As a result, in a school with amazingly low rates an instructor might be excellent and highly motivated on Monday, frustrated by Wednesday, and looking for a better job on Friday.

When studying one on one, it is vitally important to have an instructor who gives more than just token attention to your work. I wasted three long days with a teacher who was also a full-time law student. He spent most of our time holding forth in eloquent Spanish on the intricacies of the Guatemalan legal system. When I finally asked to be assigned another teacher, the school administrator said, "Why didn't you say something sooner?"

Guatemala has excellent language schools but some are merely OK. I'd definitely shop around before signing up, or use an established referral service.

Language schools are concentrated in fewer places than in Mexico, but on the other hand Guatemala has an especially interesting culture and outrageously beautiful countryside. The country is also small, and you'll have no problem filling your spare time with wonderful side trips.

Homestays

The advantages of combining classroom Spanish study with living in a Spanish-speaking household (a "homestay") seem so obvious that I'll concentrate instead on some possible drawbacks. The most successful homestays often result in genuine, long-term friendships between a student and their "adopted" family. For this reason alone, it is worth your time to make the best possible arrangements.

If possible, visit the home and carefully look over your accommodations and prospective family before making a commitment. As with cheap, one-on-one language instruction, some so-called "homestays" are nothing more than private homes operating as student boarding houses. The meals, accommodations and atmosphere might be perfectly acceptable, but if you're looking for a personal family experience, you'll be better off in a homestay situation as a family's "only child."

Every homestay is unique. If nothing else, living with a local family is an excellent introduction to the amazing variation in contemporary *latinoamericano* lifestyles. One of our readers found himself living like a recluse in a spare room of an upper-middle-class family's huge house. Virtually his only human contact was with a maid, who served his meals and tidied his room. In contrast, when I visited our friend Jody, her traditional, highly protective *"madre"* wouldn't allow me to enter Jody's room without a chaperone. Jody complained good-naturedly that her family expected her to live and act like a nun, including being in bed by 11 p.m. and up at the crack of dawn. She adapted well but by the end of a month, Jody was happy to move to a much less restrictive boarding house.

In Guatemala, Lorena and I lived with Doña Lily and Don Eduardo, her forgetful, senile husband. Whenever we sat down to eat together—which was often—the old geezer would give me a thoroughly startled look, as if to ask, "Where did this strange gringo come from?" With a fresh audience for her life story, Doña Lily served our meals along with bottomless portions of gossip, tear-stained tragedies and glowing family triumphs. She doted on Lorena and went to great lengths to prepare interesting vegetarian dishes for her. My role in the family seemed to be that of a slightly wayward, overgrown son-in-law, who desperately needed to be brought up to date on Lily's favorite soap operas.

On the downside, our room in this modest house was indistinguishable from a typical, cheap Guatemalan hotel room: a small, freshly plastered cinderblock cubicle with an unscreened window and single light bulb. The bed was slightly softer than the floor and the bath was one flight down, tucked under the stairs. Don Eduardo could often be found there, dozing contentedly on the throne.

In another memorable household, our host was fond of waking us in the middle of the night and reciting epic poetry between tearful gulps of tequila.

My favorite homestay was with a lower-middle-class family in northwestern Mexico. During the day, I'd sit around the kitchen table with the middle-aged ladies of the house and their female neighbors, drinking endless cups of coffee and discussing everything from politics to *chile relleno* recipes. I learned more around that table than in any classroom or grammar book.

Speaking of food: when evaluating a homestay consider how many meals you'll be taking "at home." If you enjoy good food, eating out in Mexico can change your life. Rather than committing yourself to full board, try a "bed-and-breakfast" agreement.

School Referral Services and Agencies

Referral agencies act as U.S. representatives for language schools in Spain and Latin America. They not only book students in specific schools, but a good agency offers related services such as insurance, college accreditation, postal and email contacts abroad, orientation and the like. Perhaps their most important service, however, is the considerable task of identifying the best language schools and sorting out the very good from the truly bad. Unless you're willing to invest a fair amount of time visiting schools in person and quizzing their administrators, it can be very difficult to tell a good, established school from one with a freshly painted sign.

Teaching Spanish to foreigners is a fast-growing, highly competitive business. It also tends to be unregulated. This is especially true in Guatemala, where the supply of incoming students attracted by low prices can exceed the demand for qualified teachers. Schools not only change their names, locations and staff at a dizzying rate, but as soon as teachers feel capable they often bolt to create their own overnight "language institute" or "linguistic academy."

The best way to use a referral agency is to first request information on their schools. If you have Internet access, visit the agency's website. Once you've narrowed down

Tips For Learning Spanish

• **Challenge yourself to improve.** Rather than accept the status quo, make an effort to identify and correct your most common mistakes in grammar and pronunciation. Most Mexicans are too polite to offer corrections. When speaking Spanish, watch other people's faces for flickers of doubt, surprise, shock, dismay or even disgust. These valuable clues indicate that you may be committing errors or fracturing the laws of grammar.

• **Make word lists.** Jot down phrases you overhear and don't understand. Keep a list of new words and questions and periodically ask a native speaker to go over these with you.

• **Take chances.** In spite of the previous points, don't be afraid to make mistakes. To strengthen your vocabulary and loosen your tongue, you'll have to "exercise" new words and grammatical forms in real-life situations.

• **Read in Spanish!** I started with comic books and children's schoolbooks, then graduated to the daily newspaper, non-fiction and, finally, mystery novels. Reading is the key to unlocking Spanish.

• **Talk to yourself.** One of my favorite methods of self-study is to imagine common situations—buying a bus ticket or arguing politics. I then "script" the imaginary conversation in Spanish, line by line and quip by clever quip.

• **Repeat yourself.** Simple conversations with native Spanish speakers are invaluable aids toward speaking naturally. Repetitious exchanges about the weather, jobs, food, or cost of living may not be intellectually challenging, but you'll learn to speak without having to think about each word.

your choices, review this chapter and prepare a list of detailed questions about each school. Do this several months in advance, especially if you're looking for a serious study program. The best schools sometimes have waiting lists.

Agencies should be compensated by the schools they represent, rather than by tacking an extra fee onto the tuition you'll pay. (It is fair to charge additional fees if you need accreditation for your study or other services, however.)

Finding a School Yourself

There are three reasons you might not want to use a referral agency when searching for a language school. The first is to save money. Keep in mind, however, that when it comes to selecting a school, "you get what you pay for."

The second reason is to stay flexible. If you're like us, your travel plans are vague and you don't quite know where you're headed or when you'll want to start studying.

The third reason not to use an agency is because you want to study Spanish casually, and don't really care all that much about a school's academic standards. This is perfectly legitimate—many schools depend on spur-of-the-moment walk-ins and offer short, informal programs on "kitchen Spanish," "travel Spanish" or even "snowbird Spanish."

Walk-ins

Schools that depend on casual "walk-ins" almost always begin a fresh cycle of classes every Monday morning. If possible, plan on registering by the previous Friday. Some schools are open on Saturday but almost all of them close up tight on Sunday.

Using the dozens of language schools in Antigua, Guatemala, as an example, where do you start?

Visit the local tourist office: they maintain a reasonably up-to-date list of language schools, as well as a good supply of brochures, business cards and school posters. I'd grab a handful and start checking them out in person, taking careful notes along the way. Don't depend on memory; once you've visited half a dozen schools, this will become mind-boggling.

You'll see schools in beautifully restored colonial mansions, and entire "institutes" that scarcely fill a modest family living room. One I visited seemed to have more video movies and bottles of booze on its shelves than grammar books, whereas a neighboring school was filled with bookish, bright-eyed social activists. (Frankly, if your interests are more social than studious, I'd probably skip school entirely. After all, it's rarely difficult to find a good time in Mexico or Guatemala.)

Schools that qualify as "very studious" often have specialized programs designed for diplomats, missionaries, teachers and business people. The curriculum will be intense and challenging, with several hours a day of classroom instruction and an equal amount of self-study. Unlike party schools, where everyone is welcome, serious schools rarely allow a student to simply walk in and immediately attend classes. You'll probably also find that your time is too occupied with studying to make many side trips.

The most popular type of language school is one that has good standards of instruction and an interesting, meaningful program of elective activities. The stress in these schools will usually be conversation and contemporary culture. Students often have the opportunity for volunteer work/study or to make field trips with a social-action theme. The variety of electives is endless, with everything from cooking classes and creative writing to music, archaeology, permaculture and gay and lesbian Spanish studies.

Involving students in real-life activities rather than just grammar drills and books often fires a deep interest in both the language and cultures of Latin America. On the other hand, a student who really wants to learn Spanish will have to be careful of so many fascinating distractions.

LIVE AND RETIRE IN MEXICO

Don't burn bridges or make "pink cloud" decisions • What will it really cost? • A few words from friends and readers living in Mexico • Disconnecting from the "real" world • Can a tourist or a foreigner own land?

"Changes in latitudes
Changes in attitudes
Nothing ever looks quite the same."
—Jerry Jeff Walker

We once met an American police officer who retired to western Mexico on a disability pension. His move was based on simple arithmetic: "Once I paid my rent and utilities in San Francisco, I was lucky to have enough money left over to see a movie, let alone enjoy myself."

After visiting several cities in Mexico, he settled in a small farming town near the Pacific Ocean, a long day's travel from the U.S. by bus. He summed up the first year of retirement in Mexico like this: "I can eat in restaurants whenever I choose, travel, relax in the sun and generally live the life of Riley—and still put money in the bank every month." Did he miss San Francisco? "Not yet," he said firmly, "and maybe not ever."

If you're like me, your fantasies of life in Mexico go something like this: it is January and you're basking in a sunny garden patio, barefoot, sipping fresh papaya juice while reviewing your monthly bills: heating—$0, maid and laundry—$125, food—$200, utilities—$50, rent—$350, miscellaneous—$150. Grand total for the month: $875!

Fantastic? Impossible? Unbelievable? Are you guilty of daydreaming under the influence of too much sun and fresh fruit juice? On the contrary; as many of our readers confirm, a peso-pinching couple can get by in Mexico on even less. I want to emphasize, however, that while saving money can be one of the perks of living in Mexico, the dollar's buying power should never be your main motive.

Don't Burn Bridges or Make "Pink Cloud" Decisions

In my opinion, the single greatest mistake made by people who move to Mexico is a failure to explore the country and experience living there before making a final commitment. In particular, I would never buy a house or make a substantial investment until I'd lived in Mexico for at least several months, and preferably a year or more. "This is paradise, where do I sign?" just isn't good planning. Avoid an all-or-nothing approach by moving into Mexico carefully, one step at a time.

Don't mistake me for a conservative: I suggest this "go slow" approach because there are so many wonderful places to choose from. Lorena and I continue to explore Mexico with eventual retirement in mind, but when the time comes, we won't settle in just one place. Why choose papayas over mangoes when you can have both, and pineapple, too? Our ideal retirement scenario includes summer and autumn in the cooler, forested highlands, and winter and spring on a mid-Pacific beach or lowland jungle. Our artist friend, Bill, keeps a modest house in Puerto Vallarta during the winter, then sublets it for the summer and moves to a rented place in cooler San Miguel de Allende. Bill's been following this flexible lifestyle for decades, successfully enjoying the best of two completely different places.

Renting a place may not be your final goal, but it offers many advantages. After all, why tie yourself down when you're just getting a fresh start? Why rush to buy a house, condo or crumbling hacienda, only to discover a year or two later that another area of Mexico appeals to you more. Instead of buying, use a rental (or even an RV) as a base for a leisurely exploration of the country. Once you've looked Mexico over, and more thoroughly learned the ropes, you'll have a much firmer basis for long-term decisions.

Don't be surprised if your daydreams change as you settle into Mexico. Once you've staked out a favorite place in the plaza and swapped your best lies with fellow bench warmers, now what? Classic "Type A" *norteamericanos* often need a mellowing out period before they can really appreciate Mexico's more relaxed pace. Retirees looking for the "good life" may find that they actually prefer action rather than constant relaxation, or community involvement over voluntary vegetation.

Yet another good reason to go slow is to better understand Mexico's investment regulations and real estate laws. Fortunately, excellent resources are available, including *The Gringo's Investment Guide*, "Every legal thing you need to know about buying real estate in Mexico." (See *For More Information.*)

• **Study Spanish:** Many travelers and resident gringos get by in Mexico without learning Spanish, but you'll save money and feel much more comfortable with a basic working knowledge of the language. Start now, rather than later.

Look before you leap: Use our suggested itineraries (see *The Best of Mexico*) to design a do-it-yourself survey of potential places to live in Mexico or join a tour designed for would-be retirees. (Eisenhower Tours, 734 Mesa Hills Drive, West Town 151, El Paso, TX 79912, offers "Retirement Exploration" tours in conjunction with the American-Canadian Club of Guadalajara.)

One or more survey trips can also help smooth any ruffled feathers among your family and friends. Don't be surprised if your proposed move shocks your loved ones and brings hints that you've finally slipped over the edge. Their concerns and fears will have to be dealt with sooner or later.

• **Popular retirement centers:** Rather than re-invent the wheel, start by visiting some of the most popular (and populous) gringo retirement centers. The Guadalajara–Lake Chapala area is definitely worth a serious look, as it already has more than a hundred thousand American and Canadian residents. I'd also devote a few days to San Miguel de Allende, Cuernavaca, Taxco and Oaxaca. You could easily visit all of these places on a relaxed two-week itinerary, with a beach thrown in for good measure.

Speaking of beaches, the flashier, well-publicized resorts all have small communities of resident gringos, but don't ignore the older, less obvious places such as Mazatlán, Guaymas, La Paz and Veracruz. If the resort pace is a bit too frantic for you, peace and a lot more quiet can be found in outlying coastal villages and small towns.

According to my crystal ball, Mexico has countless yet-to-be discovered places that will eventually attract foreign residents. Mérida is a pleasant, overlooked city, especially if you like its year-round warmth and mellow Mayan people. Other likely choices are Puebla and nearby Cholula, Jalapa (near Veracruz), Zacatecas and Morelia. If you broaden your search to include every pleasant, small-to-midsized city in Mexico, the choices become overwhelming.

Another example of Mexico's untapped retirement potential is the entire northern portion of the country. If you'll be a snowbird, migrating northward in the summer, virtually all of northern Mexico below 5,000 feet offers a temperate winter retreat. This region is convenient to the U.S., vast in area, prosperous and relatively low-priced. The *norteño* culture is also more Americanized than that of southern Mexico and you might find it easier to fit in.

It may be a worn-out cliché, but Mexico is definitely the "land of contrasts." Be sure to visit the places you're considering moving to during the same season of the year you would be living there. During the dry, windy spring and hot summer months Chihuahua City doesn't appeal to me, but by late autumn the weather is much more agreeable.

• **Check it out!** Once you've made a tentative choice, the next step is to rent an apartment or a hotel room for at least a month. Use the time to explore your potential home carefully and to make detailed notes of what you find. We all have our own likes, dislikes, and personal priorities, but here are some of the factors you'll want to consider before making a final decision:

Health care
Services: phone, Internet, bank, cable or satellite TV
Arts and entertainment: English-language library, Internet access, concerts, familiar
　　magazines, movies and video rental, television
Cost of living, especially rents and real estate
Shopping, quality and selection of important foods and staples
Community activities and civic organizations, especially English speaking
Recreation and activities: clubs, side trips, swimming, fishing, hiking, birding, etc.
Schools: bilingual instruction and/or tutoring may be available.
Access to home and/or the U.S. border

• **Talk with like-minded people:** They may bend your ear to the breaking point, but conversation with resident foreigners in Mexico is invaluable. Don't be shy about approaching strangers and asking for their advice and suggestions. "Excuse me, but do you live here?" is often all the encouragement an idle snowbird needs to describe life in Mexico.

In popular retirement communities you'll also find invaluable information and contacts through English-language libraries and familiar organizations, from Alcoholics Anonymous to the Veterans of Foreign Wars. Charitable groups, social clubs and "birds-of-a-feather" associations also welcome out-of-town visitors and potential new members. Check with your group's headquarters for addresses and meetings within Mexico.

As you explore, watch for interesting people and activities. Are there conversation groups, concerts and theater performances, lectures, art films, language schools or museums? Though you may not currently have time to practice flamenco guitar or yoga, the longer you live in Mexico, the more important these opportunities will become.

Tour the city and countryside by local bus and cab. How noisy is it and what areas are quietest? Look at apartments and rental houses you can afford. Are they close to bus lines? Does the neighborhood feel safe to you, even after dark? Are your potential neighbors friendly or distant? Keep in mind that your relationships with the local people will be very different as a neighbor than as a tourist.

Don't depend on wishful thinking or last year's edition of a retirement guide to plan your future. Visit the markets and shopping malls: can you find your favorite, "must-have" foods, or acceptable substitutes? Be honest, practical and realistic. What are your essential must-haves, and what are the things you can definitely do without?

Try to learn what others are paying for rent, food and utilities. Even if you can't read much Spanish, check the classified ads in the newspaper and puzzle out what the locals are asking for rents.

Once you've done your research and crunched the numbers, take a long, completely subjective look around and ask yourself, "Do I really like this place or not?" If serious drawbacks come to mind or if you just feel vague and unsure, don't worry about it. Look upon the time you've spent here as a learning vacation. Move on to another part of Mexico and repeat this exploratory exercise.

What Will It *Really* Cost?

I have several retirement guides to Mexico on my shelves, some dating back to the early Fifties and Sixties. Almost without exception, their authors present Mexico as a bargain hunter's dream, a warm, inviting "paradise for peanuts." For some retirees, however, the promise of living cheap turns out to be misleading, if not entirely false. Why? Because they innocently believed they could uproot their American life, with all of its comforts and conveniences, and transplant it to Mexican soil—with the help of a full-time gardener and maid thrown in for good measure, and all this for very few pesos.

Yes, it is possible to live in Mexico on far less than the average person spends in the U.S. The big question, of course, is *how*? In our experience, the answer to that question is to learn to live like your Mexican neighbors. To enjoy the best of Mexico, including the financial bargains it offers, you must adopt a more Mexican style of living. This might seem obvious, but when you're in the "pink cloud" planning stage this fact is easy to overlook.

Lorena and I have lived for months at a time in a number of small Mexican towns and villages. At today's prices, I'm sure we could find a simple but quite adequate (by our standards) house or apartment for no more than $150 a month and probably even less. Add a generous $3 a day for food we'll cook ourselves and another $2 a day for restaurant meals and beverages. Figure $100 a month for utilities, miscellaneous and local bus rides. Add this all up and I've got the perfect title for my next book: *HOW TO LIVE LIKE ROYALTY IN MEXICO ON $400 A MONTH!* (If we wanted to squeeze, I'd find a $75 house and trim our other expenses, for a stingy total of $300 a month. Imagine the headlines!)

If this figure sounds fantastic, remember that to many Mexicans, even this modest sum would seem generous.

Before you tear up your contract to buy a beachfront condo, consider this: if you were to visit us in this hypothetical village, you'd find us sitting around a cheap pine table, eating the vegetarian dinner we'd cooked ourselves on a tiny gas stove; or lounging on lumpy beds, reading by a naked 60 watt light bulb; or washing our own dishes and laundry. In other words, we'd be enjoying a lifestyle shared by our Mexican neighbors (which is much like we live in our cabin in the U.S.).

One of the best ways to forecast what it will cost you to live in Mexico is to first calculate how much you spend now, in familiar, comfortable circumstances at home.
Using these figures, here are some very rough "ballpark" figures on the cost of living
in Mexico's popular retirement communities. Keep in mind that these figures are moderate rather than "budget."

 • **Housing:** Fifty percent of whatever you're paying now. If you rent a small house
or apartment for $800 a month, $400 should get you an equivalent place—or even better—in Mexico. For this price, however, you shouldn't expect a lavish beachfront
condo or a swimming pool in a gated community. In areas that don't see many tourists
or foreign residents—which is most of Mexico—your housing costs might go as low
as twenty-five percent.

 • **Food:** Eating out becomes an important form of entertainment, so I'll be conservative and guess-timate that you'll trim about twenty-five percent from your current
food bill. On the other hand, diligent do-it-yourself cooks and tortilla lovers will probably cut at least fifty percent.

 • **Alcohol:** Liquor costs less in Mexico but it also goes down easier. I might as well
warn you now: heavy partying is a major expense for many retirees, and alcoholism is
a very real hazard. *Cerveza* costs about the same as premium U.S. beer, and middle-
shelf Mexican wines and hard liquor are fifty percent (or less).

 • **Heating:** Negligible unless you'll be in the highlands above 5,000 feet in winter.
If so, better add $10 to $20 per winter month for gas and electric space heaters.

 • **Utilities:** Mexicans gripe that *la luz* (lights, power) is expensive, but by U.S. standards it is not. Figure an average of $10 a month or $50 if you must have air conditioning. Gas for cooking and hot water will cost $10 to $30 a month. Water may be
free or just a few dollars a month. Mexico is perennially short on water so if you have
a green lawn fetish, get over it.

 • **Telephone:** Basic service is affordable, but long-distance international calls will be
a painful drain on your checkbook. Call your long-distance phone company and get
their rates to Mexico. If they seem high, expect to pay even more for international calls
made from Mexico. Plan on using email and a fax machine if you make many calls or
need to keep tabs on a business.

 • **Internet connections:** $20 to $30 a month is average, not including set-up fees.
Email at pay-for-messages services runs $1 to $2 per message, and Internet café computer use is $3 to $6 an hour.

 • **Laundry:** About double whatever it costs at your local laundromat.

 • **Hired help:** $2 or $3 an hour is probably "generous" for occasional houseclean-
ing and yard work.

 • **Visits to home:** Include the cost of round-trip travel to visit your family and old
home in your projected cost of living in Mexico.

 These on-the-spot figures will give a much more realistic estimate of your actual cost
to live comfortably in Mexico. Don't forget inflation: in Mexico it often runs fifteen percent or more a year. How far will your money stretch in one, two and five years?

A Few Words from Friends and Readers
Living in Mexico

We regularly receive letters and email from Americans and Canadians who have successfully relocated to or retired in Mexico. In sharing the details of their new lives with
us, a common theme emerges: these are people with an unusual spirit of independence
and self-reliance. This doesn't mean they're reckless—more than a few confess that it
took years of visiting Mexico before they took the final plunge and moved there.

Overall, however, these people have devoted serious thought and often quite a bit of study to the challenge of living in a foreign country.

Some of these people might strike you as unconventional, but they all share success and satisfaction in their new lives. You don't have to imitate Milo's semi-nomadic RV lifestyle, but his strategy of dividing his time between northern Mexico and the American Southwest makes a lot of sense, especially on a very modest income.

• Although technically not allowed to work in Mexico, Helen got by for many years on a modest but unpredictable income as an independent clothing designer. Like many other self-supporting foreigners, Helen benefited from the tolerance Mexicans have for those who work in the creative arts. Learning Spanish, hiring Mexican friends and making local contacts also helped. By the time she began collecting Social Security, Helen had pared her needs down to the essentials. Having thoroughly adopted Latin America as her home, her time is now devoted to reading, writing and bilingual tutoring.

• After dropping out of a highly paid, highly stressful career, Alan combined a modest investment income with Social Security to underwrite a comfortable, laid-back life in a popular Mexican retirement town. In spite of health problems, Alan seems very satisfied and has few, if any second thoughts about his move. On most days Alan can be found enjoying the morning sun in the town plaza, reading a newspaper or visiting with fellow retirees. If you're a newcomer and have questions about Mexican doctors or medical insurance, or just want to know the going price of a two-bedroom apartment, Alan is your man.

• Lynne and Harold retired from well-paid civil service jobs. To their children's horror, the couple immediately moved to Mexico. They've rented a very comfortable garden apartment for well over ten years and claim to be perfectly happy. Well into their seventies, both Lynne and Harold are very active in local clubs and charities. In addition to Harold's weekly poker game, their main entertainments are reading, cable television and visiting with friends. They also make frequent sightseeing trips around Mexico, both on their own and in organized groups.

• Jim and Rhonda took early retirement and moved to a comfortable rental house in San Miguel de Allende. A trial period of a year convinced the couple that they could be happy in Mexico. Jim and Rhonda continue to rent and although they have FM2 status, they've imported only their most useful household goods: stereo, computer and television. "Nothing else was worth the shipping cost or hassle," Jim says. "Everything we need is available here, either new or at garage sales." In addition to frequent side trips, both are involved in various classes, hobbies and civic activities. They've made a number of good Mexican friends who share their interests in art, music, archaeology and architecture. Their lives are busy yet they set aside personal time for painting, writing, yoga and reading. Rhonda keeps close track of their spending, which averages $800 a month (not including trips to the U.S.).

• Hazel and Armand retired on a small disability pension, supplemented by odd jobs and a talent for turning flea market junk into salable treasures. Using Salvation Army furniture and used home appliances, they converted an old school bus into a wonderfully cozy motor home and headed for Mexico. They lived half of each year on a little-known Mexican beach or parked among the papaya trees at a friend's *rancho*. Replacing furniture and appliances was their major expense: every spring Hazel and Armand would give away most of their possessions before returning north. Although they lived well below the American poverty line, their generosity to friends and Mexican neighbors was legendary. They're gone now but definitely not forgotten!

• Milo is a lean, middle-aged bachelor with a deep distrust of the government and an equally strong aversion to holding down a regular job. An athlete and dedicated outdoorsman, Milo explores Mexico in the winter and summers in the American Southwest. He has his own small service business, which he insists that I not describe. "There's no paper on me," Milo explains. "I don't pay taxes or social security. Everything I own is in someone else's name. I charge fair prices and I work hard. I also work strictly for cash." Milo's annual income of $12,000 to $15,000 just covers his expenses, which include a small, self-contained RV.

• Jane lives in a small mobile home in Arizona. Twice a year she stuffs her favorite books and most important belongings into the backseat of her beat-up Japanese sedan and heads for Mexico. Jane has several places in Mexico she favors; depending on her mood and savings from a small pension, she'll wander as far south as Oaxaca or settle down for a few months in the state of Chihuahua. Jane's needs are as small as her budget—$500 a month.

• Modest pensions from military and civilian careers allow Ken and his Mexican wife Rosa to live comfortably—but carefully. They live in a large but unpretentious house in an outlying neighborhood of a popular retirement community. As Mexico's cost of living increases, however, the former enlisted man frets about the future. Ken and Rosa talk seriously about moving to a less expensive (and more Mexican) place, preferably somewhere rural. The couple is deeply committed to volunteer work and they seldom socialize within the English-speaking community. Ken has learned Spanish and continues to study seriously. Their monthly expenses, including an annual trip to the States, are consistently less than $1,000.

• We've forgotten their real names, but the amazing couple we knew as "Mr. and Mrs. Around-the-World" were among the very first pioneers to buy a retirement home in Arizona's Sun City. This well-ordered existence soon grew stale, however, and against the protests of their middle-aged children, the couple traded their Caddy in on a VW camper van, rented out the house and hit the road. When we met them in Guatemala seven years and two VWs later, they were on their second circumnavigation of the world. Well into their eighties, Mr. and Mrs. Around-the-World were arguing about whether they should buy a sailboat and return to the Greek Isles or build a house on Lake Atitlán. "We sold everything or gave it to the kids," they smiled. "And now we're living off what's left of their inheritance."

Disconnecting from the "Real" World

After overcoming your nervousness about moving to Mexico, your next challenge will be "pulling the plug" on your present life. How do you gracefully disconnect from your family, friends and faithful creditors? Who will answer the phone while you're in Mexico and water the philodendron? What if . . . the roof leaks? The kids get sick? The stock market crashes? The sky falls?

I assume you'll take my advice and make one or more exploratory trips to Mexico. At the same time, you can use these trips to practice the fine art of disconnecting from your old life. This means finding some reliable person to pay the bills while you're gone, collect the mail and feed the canary. Don't ignore these chores or put them off until the last moment. Once you're living in Mexico, those untended molehills you left behind will have a tendency to turn into mountains, or even volcanoes.

Here are just a few of the steps Lorena and I have taken to help us make a more graceful getaway and a less painful return:

• Arrange automatic deposits and bill paying whenever possible. Visit your bank and explain what you are doing. Ask that someone be your designated contact person. Will they arrange bank-to-bank transfers of funds and accept your collect calls from Mexico? What kind of "long-distance" banking procedures is your bank most comfortable with?

• If a friend or relative pays your bills, consider giving them a registered power-of-attorney for emergencies. List every bill and ask yourself, "What is the easiest way to pay this?" The small expense to have a bank automatically pay some or even all of your bills is better than overburdening a friend.

• Now that ATM machines are common in Mexico, you'll really appreciate having a major credit card, preferably Visa or MasterCard, and a bank debit card.

• Is your health insurance valid in Mexico? Talk to your agent and if the answer is vague, get it in writing.

• Arrange for mail pickup or forwarding to a friend. Consider using a private postal service.

• Homeowners: if you leave it empty, freeze-proof the house (an unseasonal cold snap once shattered the toilet in our unheated bathroom). Have someone walk through the house every week or two. Do you need a lawn service? Consider finding a caretaker or housesitter, even if you have to pay them something.

• Write down all instructions, addresses, phone numbers and contact information as neatly as possible. Make a detailed itinerary and time schedule on a separate sheet. Give everyone you can think of two copies of each.

• Quit stalling and accept that technology can be your best friend. If you don't have a computer, Internet connection and email address, get them soon and learn how to use them. No matter what you think of computers, there is simply no cheaper, more reliable way to keep in touch from Mexico than via email. As a second choice, buy a simple fax machine and install it in a friend's or relative's house. You can send a fax from virtually any town, airport or large bus station in Mexico.

• Reward the people who help you by offering something for their services, be it cash, gifts, souvenirs or some other real compensation. When we return from a long trip, Lorena passes out traditional Mexican candies and small Christmas ornaments at the bank—you can bet they'll accept the charges the next time they get her collect call from Topolobampo.

Last but not least, travel writers and expats have a tendency to speak of Mexico in all-or-nothing, "love-it-or-leave-it" terms. The fact is, when the honeymoon ends, some people find they simply can't stand Mexico. The language is too confusing, the red tape is too thick and the sun is always in their eyes. Though they may only admit it after several margaritas, others resent being minority members of Mexican society. These people often adopt an attitude of condescension or amused tolerance to disguise their bitterness. To keep your equilibrium steady, accept Mexico for what it is, rather than chewing on what you think it could be or ought to become.

Plaza pundits also love to predict major social upheavals, revolutions and other dire events. As much as I enjoy reading the daily newspaper, I maintain a discreet distance from Mexican politics and current events. Like every country, Mexico has its incredible inefficiencies and irritating contradictions. If I took this stuff too seriously, however, I'd probably move to Winnipeg.

Can a Tourist or a Foreigner Own Land?

Tourists can legally buy land in any part of Mexico other than the Prohibited Zone (within fifty kilometers of any coast and a hundred kilometers of borders). To buy land within the Prohibited Zone, you must apply for a lease—via a bank trust.

The trust lasts for thirty years (automatically renewable for another thirty years) and is an agreement between the seller, the bank and the beneficiary (the buyer). The tourist can use the land, improve it, rent it and transfer or sell the rights to it. It can also be passed on in a will.

In the past, members of *ejidos* (rural land cooperatives) did not own their communal land, nor could they sell it. In actual practice, however, *ejidos* made illegal deals with tourists that sometimes led to complex lawsuits. The federal government now allows *ejido* members to sell land legally, although there is still oversight of such sales.

Tourists who fall head over heels for Mexico may impulsively buy a house, condominium or land. The price seems good, the people and climate agreeable and the style of living attractive, if not irresistible. Many of these sudden purchases, however, are regretted later. *Don't rush into anything.* If you think you'd like to buy a place, try living there first. Rent a house and wait a minimum of six months before making a final decision. You might well find that the easy life is dull, or that familiar faces and surroundings are too important to do without.

For advice on buying land and real estate trusts write to:

Banco Nacional de Mexico, S.A.
Trust Department, Head Office
Isabel Catolica No. 44
Mexico 1, DF

or

Banco de Comercio, S.A.
Venustiano Carianza 44
Mexico, DF

GUATEMALA AND BELIZE

Guatemala: Red tape • Money and measurements • Driving and roads • Accom-modations • Restaurants • Food shopping and stores • Booze and cantinas • Services • Arts, crafts and souvenirs • Customs and traditions • Back to Mexico • Market days in Guatemala • Belize

Many travelers mistakenly assume that Guatemala is just a smaller version of Mexico. This is not the case; Guatemala is very different, not only from its northern neighbor, but from the rest of Central America as well. There's no doubt that a large Mayan Indian population contributes greatly to the distinct change in *ambiente* (mood, atmos-phere) that one feels after crossing the border.

The best preparations you can make for traveling in Guatemala are mental. Because it is such a small country, it is possible to miss much by traveling more than a few miles or hours a day. Distances become almost irrelevant, especially in the highlands where two villages separated by a mountain may have different languages and cus-toms. Paved highways and fast buses make it possible to start your day in a chilly, mist-shrouded Mayan village and end it under a palm tree at the beach. (For Guatemalan itineraries see *The Best of Mexico: The Ruta Maya in Guatemala*.)

Red Tape

Virtually every Guatemalan border official we've dealt with in recent years has been refreshingly courteous and businesslike. It took one fellow an hour to type out my car permit, but he managed a smile even while correcting six fuzzy carbon copies. Notorious border hassles for travelers with backpacks and beards have now mellowed to a virtual cakewalk. "Tips" are sometimes requested, but the rate is seldom excessive.

• **Tourist cards and visas:** Guatemala issues both tourist cards and visas. You'll need proof of citizenship, preferably a passport, birth certificate or other good ID. The cost of a tourist card is modest and it takes just a few minutes to fill out the form once you arrive in Guatemala. Tourist cards are limited to thirty days, however, and are a hassle to renew.

A visa must be issued by a Guatemalan consulate, before you enter the country. If you definitely need to be in Guatemala for more than thirty days, a visa is probably worthwhile, as you can often talk them into a ninety-day stay when you enter the country.

Minors on their own must have written permission from *both* parents, notarized by a Guatemalan consul.

• **Car papers:** Drivers will need the usual: registration and proof of ownership. There is a fee for a vehicle permit, which is valid for thirty days, no matter how long your tourist card or visa may be valid. Before the end of thirty days, you must go to the *Aduana* in Guatemala City (hard to find) to have your tourist card and car papers renewed. The alternative is to leave and re-enter only after you have been out of the country for at least thirty days. As Steve says, "This leaves little choice but to dive into 'Guat City' and do the *Aduana* boogie-woogie." The renewed car paper is only valid for the amount of time left on your visa. In other words, if you were given ninety days at the border, the new car permit will be good for sixty more days. Should you neglect to renew your car papers, you are liable for an import duty based on the value of the vehicle, a considerable sum.

Renewing car papers is a complicated procedure that takes about two weeks. It is often done by tourists, but your best bet is to find someone who knows the ropes and will give you detailed advice on where to go and whom to see. Steve says that he has had to do it differently every time.

• **Car insurance** is not required in Guatemala, but it can be purchased in Mexico City, Oaxaca, Tapachula or inside Guatemala.

• **For pets**, you'll need a current rabies vaccination certificate and official health certificate (see a vet). Have these stamped (visa-ed) by a Guatemalan consul before reaching the Guatemalan border. (You can usually get a pet into Guatemala without this paperwork, but there's no guarantee.)

• **Baggage searches** are common going into Guatemala and may be extensive. Usually you'll be asked to carry a few large items—suitcases, duffel bags, guitar cases—into the Customs house for a perfunctory inspection. Do this willingly, but don't take anything out of your car that you aren't specifically told to remove. The officials don't enjoy the inspections much more than you, so there's no need to encourage them.

It's possible that the health inspector will confiscate certain kinds of food. (Lorena lost her entire collection of herb teas.)

After the baggage search, someone will swab your car's wheels and spray the inside of your vehicle with disinfectant. This is required to remove all Mexican bacteria and pests. Do not laugh; you pay a small fee for the service.

• **Tip:** It is advisable to have a few loose dollars on hand to facilitate your crossing. Steve crosses into Guatemala frequently with his van. He budgets $20 U.S. for socalled tips and official fees.

Warning: Don't smuggle firearms; should you be caught, you'll be in very serious trouble.

• **Safety—a return to peace:** After thirty-seven years of "low-intensity" conflict, a peace treaty was finally signed in 1996 between the Guatemalan government and a coalition of rebel groups. By the time it ended, the civil war had taken tens of thousands of lives and forced legions of Guatemalans into refugee camps in Mexico and Belize.

Although the peace accords supposedly increased tourism, Guatemala's turmoil has by no means ended. There is no doubt, at least in my mind, that the deep fear and anxiety the Guatemalan people suffered during so many years of "subterranean" civil war will take many years to heal. As in most countries, common crime is a growing problem, especially in larger towns and cities.

Take the usual precautions, especially at night, and use common sense. With the exception of Guatemala City, the country is probably safer (for you) than your hometown. On the other hand, there's no point in being complacent.

Warning! Be especially wary of pickpockets in any crowd, bus or market. Also, because of repeated armed assaults against tourists, we strongly advise you not to climb the Pacaya volcano, even in an escorted group.

Money and Measurements

Guatemala's money is based on the *quetzal*, named for the national bird, the rare and extravagantly feathered resplendent quetzal. Each quetzal is worth 100 pennies (*centavos*). Coins come in five, ten and twenty-five centavo denominations. Bills are fifty centavos, one quetzal, five quetzals, ten and higher.

Unfortunately for Guatemalans, their currency is just about as endangered as its namesake and much less resplendent. From a once-solid exchange of one-quetzal-for-one-American-dollar, the rate has fallen to less than six quetzals to the dollar at this writing.

In recent trips, we've found prices for typical Guatemalan-style accommodations and meals to be about the same as in Mexico. By learning to love tamales, starvation budget travelers will spend even less.

• **Banks:** U.S. dollars and traveler's checks can be exchanged in banks from 8:30 a.m. to 2 p.m. Monday through Thursday, Friday until 2:30 p.m. and occasionally on weekdays to 8 p.m. and Saturday mornings. Private businesses also exchange money, often at a slightly better rate than banks. On the street, I'd use freelance money changers with caution, especially in Guatemala City. If you must exchange money on the street or at the border, get just enough to tide you over until you can find a bank or private exchange house.

Banks will not exchange Mexican pesos. Change your pesos with money changers at the border, a *casa de cambio*, or in the International Airport in Guatemala City.

Visa and MasterCard cards (credit and debit) can be used for cash advances from banks and ATMs in the largest cities and tourist towns. However, steep surcharges and taxes can total up to fifteen percent on cash withdrawals (and some purchases; when in doubt, ask). Banco Industrial, however, charges no commission. You can draw up to the limit of your credit card—in quetzals. Except at banks, it can be expensive or even impossible to cash traveler's checks outside of the largest cities, especially on weekends. When visiting tempting Indian market towns, for example, carry enough quetzals (in a money belt; pickpockets are common!) to tide you over.

Guatemalan Indians who don't deal frequently with tourists rarely accept foreign money and are very reluctant to make change. In the market place, be well prepared with small bills and coins. The Indian words *pisto* (money) and *leng* (centavos) are often used.

In town and at the border, small denomination American bills are commonly accepted in lieu of quetzals.

Weights are measured in pounds (*libras*), but distances are measured in both miles and kilometers. Liquids are usually, but not always, based on the liter. Altitudes are in feet.

Driving and Roads

Major highways are almost entirely two-lane and paved. Unfortunately, the pavement on many highways is heavily potholed and in terrible condition. Expect narrow-to-nonexistent shoulders, slow traffic, sharp curves and steep grades, especially around Lake Atitlán and mountainous highlands. Because of the high cost of cars and gasoline, traffic volumes tend to be relatively light. Drivers arriving from Mexico often breathe a sigh of relief, at least until they reach Guatemala City, where the traffic congestion and carbon monoxide reach hysterical levels.

Unpaved roads make up much of the Guatemalan highway system. We enjoy exploring these roads, but you'll want to be prepared. Maps are scarce and inadequate, and gasoline and services are rare. Expect dust, mud, steep grades, rickety bridges and sudden road closures, especially during the rainy season.

Note: The legendary Petén highway of bottomless ruts and chuckholes between the Río Dulce and Tikal is now being tamed by pavement. At last word, the road has been paved to Poptun. Expect pavement all the way to Tikal sometime before the next millennium. Vans, pickups and most passenger cars can still make it, but take your time; this is no place to bust a shock or a tie rod.

During the civil war, Army, militia and police checkpoints were common on Guatemalan roads. Guerrilla units also blocked traffic to solicit "donations" from sympathetic motorists. Although the war is officially over, I wouldn't be surprised if you still find an occasional checkpoint. If you do, no matter who it is, *never run through or ignore a checkpoint.* It is extremely unlikely that you'll be hassled or delayed for more than a token inspection of your documents and luggage.

Wandering livestock is seldom seen on Guatemala's highways—farm animals are too valuable to risk. Sadly, drunken pedestrians, usually poor or fiesta-befuddled Indians, are a real hazard at all hours of the day and night.

As in Mexico, the rule for driving at night in Guatemala is simple: don't; it's just too dangerous.

• **Gas stations and repairs:** Familiar American gas stations are a welcome, if rather incongruous, sight in Guatemala. Gas stations are not abundant, however, so top off your tank and carry extra fuel on long side roads. Gasoline is unleaded, even though the pump may be labeled "regular." Prices are about the same as gasoline in Mexico.

Small back yard garages are not as common as in Mexico. Car parts and agencies for most common American and foreign-made cars are found only in major cities.

• **Public transportation and rental cars:** Second-class "chicken bus" service is both cheap and colorful. For anyone over 5' 4" tall and without steel hips, it is also crowded and uncomfortable. "Learn to go with the flow," Steve advises, at least until you can find a first-class coach or cab.

Though infrequent, and limited to a handful of routes, first-class bus service is often worth waiting for. Amenities include one person per well-padded seat and genuine legroom. Some routes have attendants and on-board refreshments.

Tourists and aging hippies who can't face another second-class bus adventure will take comfort in reasonably priced cabs and co-op style mini-vans. Shared among four to eight people, the cost of a van and driver is quite reasonable.

Rental cars are available in the largest cities. Rates are reasonable, though I'd take a careful look at the cost of hiring both a vehicle and driver. Wages are so low that a chauffeur/guide can be a bargain—and an interesting companion as well.

Good deals for day trips (and longer) can also be struck with independent cab drivers. In Guatemala City, unmetered cabs are relatively expensive. Expect to bargain with them or you could be overcharged.

We're sorry to report that the wonderful, old-fashioned train between Guatemala City and Puerto Barrios has been discontinued.

Accommodations

• **Hotels:** Prices are comparable to Mexico, though Guatemala also offers great deals on luxury places. Budget travelers and those seeking the "real" Guatemala will find bargains in clean, Spartan hotels and boarding houses.

• **House rentals:** Anyone who intends to spend more than a few weeks in Guatemala should certainly consider renting a house. Rents vary widely, from fancy vacation homes with all the mod-cons to Indian-style houses of adobe or wood.

• **Camping:** Though once considered a strange and even threatening activity, Guatemalans have become more or less accustomed to campers. Facilities are still scarce, but as the country expands its system of parks and reserves, the situation is gradually improving.

As is always the custom when camping south of the border, be friendly, open and generous. Ask permission and don't leave a mess. Guatemalans are much more sensitive about litter than their neighbors to the north.

Avoid camping beside highways or on the street in larger towns.

Restaurants

Guatemala's cuisine reflects the country's sharp cultural divisions. *Comida típica*, "typical food," is traditional Indian fare, heavily dependent on the New World staples of corn, beans, chilies, squash and onions. Unlike Mexico, where regional variations can be quite dramatic, meals offered in Guatemalan *comedores* and restaurants tend to be very similar. A typical budget menu (breakfast, lunch and dinner) includes chicken and/or beef, eggs, rice, tortillas and cabbage. For a beverage, choose soda pop, sweetened coffee, or Goat or Rooster brand beer.

The saving grace of such limited fare is the care and skill with which most Indian women prepare your food (virtually every *típica* cook is a woman). Add the secret ingredients of wood smoke and *sazón* (the "cook's touch"), and you have a soul-satisfying, unmistakably Guatemalan feast.

On the other end of the spectrum are restaurants that offer a wide variety of European and North American dishes, from pizza and pasta to hamburgers, weinerschnitzel, crêpes and yogurt smoothees. Naturally, these restaurants cater to affluent Guatemalans and tourists. In Panajachel, where Steve once groused that the only food available was "red meat with gray sauce or gray meat with red sauce," the restaurant scene is a virtual international food circus. In fact, competition keeps prices reasonable and the quality high. Steve now gripes that he can't possibly lose weight in Guatemala and still fulfill his obligation to research such "wonderful grunts."

One other cuisine deserves mention: good, economical Chinese food is available in most towns.

Unfortunately, street food is not common, which rates as a tragedy when compared to the temptations available in Mexico.

Food Shopping and Stores

Guatemala's colorful Indian *tianguis* (markets) attract visitors from around the world. To experience these markets at their best, however, it is necessary to participate as a *marchante* (customer) rather than as a tourist. In other words, don't just gawk, buy something, even if you don't need it or haven't the faintest notion what it is. At the very least, buy a small shopping bag and fill it with fruit, peanuts, a carved gourd or two, an avocado and a handful of garlic. Take your time; you'll soon notice that vendors (especially shy Indians) will be glad to talk with you, either in sign language or basic Spanish. Ask simple questions and haggle politely, even for the smallest purchase. You'll find that a few quetzals will buy a good picnic lunch—and a memorable experience. (If you don't want your purchases, give them to the nearest needy person.)

The peak activity in a typical market is around 9 a.m. and may be all but finished by noon. Carry small change. Extra merchandise—a few peanuts or a banana—is often given in lieu of change. Torn or defaced bills or disfigured coins are rarely accepted.

As in Mexico, small *tiendas* are the principal everyday source of food, dry goods, liquor and tools. Supermarkets are found only in the largest towns. The relatively high prices of imported and processed foods put them completely out of the reach of most Guatemalans.

A red flag outside a doorway means "Fresh meat." Regular meat shops are also found in and around the town market. Shop early for a better selection.

Excellent dairy products, including yogurt and pasteurized cheeses, are available in larger towns and tourist areas.

Booze and *Cantinas*

For those who imbibe, perhaps the best thing to be said about Guatemalan-made liquor, beer and wine is that it is "interesting." Check that wine label very carefully. Though it may look like grapes, the fine print often reveals the principal ingredient to be oranges or cashews. The novelty of a "vintage" cashew is worth the price, at least for the first bottle.

Choosing a beer is easy: *Cabra* (Goat) and *Gallo* (Rooster) dominate the national market. Imported beers and specialty brews are found only in larger towns and tourist watering holes.

For the majority of Guatemalans, who can't afford imported liquor, the national drink is *aguardiente* (firewater). Quetzalteca brand is typical: raw, unaged cane alcohol with just enough anise flavor to distract your outraged taste buds. In the lowlands, cane liquors are flavored to resemble rum and brandy (*caña, habanero, brandi*, etc.).

Guatemalan versions of scotch, whiskey and other liquors are relatively inexpensive, proving once again that "you get what you pay for." Alcoholic beverages are sold in *tiendas*, supermarkets and *cantinas*.

Guatemalan Indians practice a custom known as "ritual drinking." In simple terms, ritual drinking is done by the elders and officials of an Indian community, making intoxication a regular part of their duties. Through most of his adult life, a man can be appointed to serve brief terms as constable, secretary, bailiff, sacristan, fiesta organizer, mayor or other important civic or religious *cargo* (post, literally "burden"). These *cargoes* include ceremonial drinking of *aguardiente* at frequent ceremonies, fiestas and councils. Not surprisingly, many Indian men (and some women) become alcoholics.

As a result of ritual drinking, the color, excitement and pageantry of a Guatemalan fiesta can also become a scene of widespread drunkenness. If this occurs, it is important to remember that as a visitor you shouldn't show disapproval. Though you'll most likely be ignored, never insult a drunk, especially in public.

Services

• **Water, ice and fuels:** Purified water is available in many grocery stores in quart or gallon plastic jugs. Once you get away from the "gringo trail," however, carry a supply of iodine or otherwise treat your drinking water. (See *Mexico A to Z: Water: Purify It!*)

Ice is not easily located outside of the larger towns and cities. Your best bet is unpurified homemade ice. Look for hand-lettered "*hielo*" signs on private homes and small shops.

Bottled gas is scarce in the hinterlands. Propane is sold in Guatemala City and at several places along the highway to Quetzaltenango after leaving the Pan American Highway at the *Cuatro Caminos* intersection.

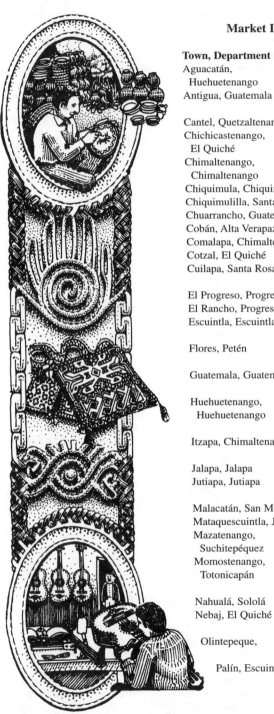

Market Days in Guatemala

Town, Department (State)

Aguacatán, Huehuetenango	Thurs. & Sun.
Antigua, Guatemala	Mon., Thurs. & Sun.
Cantel, Quetzaltenango	Sun.
Chichicastenango, El Quiché	Thurs. & Sun.
Chimaltenango, Chimaltenango	Wed. & Fri.
Chiquimula, Chiquimula	Daily
Chiquimulilla, Santa Rosa	Daily
Chuarrancho, Guatemala	Thurs. & Sun.
Cobán, Alta Verapaz	Daily
Comalapa, Chimaltenango	Sun.
Cotzal, El Quiché	Sat.
Cuilapa, Santa Rosa	Daily
El Progreso, Progreso	Daily
El Rancho, Progreso	Daily
Escuintla, Escuintla	Daily
Flores, Petén	Daily
Guatemala, Guatemala	Daily
Huehuetenango, Huehuetenango	Daily
Itzapa, Chimaltenango	Fri. & Sun.
Jalapa, Jalapa	Daily
Jutiapa, Jutiapa	Thurs. & Sun.
Malacatán, San Marcos	Sun.
Mataquescuintla, Jalapa	Wed.
Mazatenango, Suchitepéquez	Sat. & Thurs.
Momostenango, Totonicapán	Sun.
Nahualá, Sololá	Sun.
Nebaj, El Quiché	Thurs. & Sun.
Olintepeque,	Tues.
Palín, Escuintla	Sun. & Wed.

Panajachel, Sololá	Sun.
Patzicía,	Wed.
Chimaltenango	
Patzún, Chimaltenango	Sun.
Quetzaltenango,	Daily
Quetzal	
Rabinal, Baja Verapaz	Daily
Sacapulas, El Quiché	Thurs. & Sun.
Salamá, Baja Verapaz	Daily
Salcajá, Quetzaltenango	Sun.
San Andres Semetabaj,	Tues.
Sololá	
San Antonio las Flores,	Tues.
Guatemala	
San Cristóbal Verapaz,	Tues.
Alta Verapaz	
San Francisco el Alto,	Fri.
Totonicapán	
San José Nacahuil,	Thurs.
Guatemala	
San Juan Chamelco,	Sun.
Alta Verapaz	
San Juan Ostuncalco,	Sun.
Quetzaltenango	
San Juan Sacatepéquez,	Daily
Guatemal	
San Lucas Tolimán,	Thurs. & Sun.
Sololá	
San Marcos, San Marcos	Tues.

San Martín Jilotepeque,	Tues.
Chimaltenango	
San Martin, Sacatepéquez,	Fri.
Quetzaltenango	
San Pedro Carchá,	Daily
Alta Verapaz	
San Pedro la Laguna,	Thurs. & Sun.
Sololá	
San Pedro Sacatepéquez,	Sun. & Fri.
Guatemala	
San Pedro Sacatepéquez,	Sun. & Fri.
San Marcos	
San Raimundo,	Thurs. & Sun.
Guatemala	
Santa Cruz del Quiché,	Thurs. & Sun.
El Quiché	
Santa Lucía Utatlán,	Thurs.
Sololá	
Santiago Atitlán, Sololá	Thurs. & Sun
Santiago Sacatepéquez,	Wed.
Sacatepéquez	
Sololá, Sololá	Fri.
Tactic, Alta Verapaz	Thurs. & Sun.
Tamahú, Alta Verapaz	Wed. & Sat.
Tecpán, Chimaltenango	Thurs.
Todos Santos, Cuchumatán,	Sun.
Totonicapán, Totonicapán	Tues. & Sat.
Tucurú, Alta Verapaz	Thurs. & Sun.
Zacapa, Zacapa	Sun.
Zunil, Quetzaltenango	Mon.

Pitahaya

• **Post office, telegraph, phones, email:** These services are very similar to those in Mexico. The *telégrafos* office is often located in or adjacent to the post office.

It's now easy to use calling cards to call home from Guatemala (and is cheaper than calling from Mexico). To reach operators in the U.S., dial MCI, 1-89; AT&T, 1-90; Sprint, 1-95. Give your calling card number or make it collect. Many hotels will let you use their front desk phone. Otherwise, the offices of Guatel, the national phone company, are located in cities and small-to-midsized towns. Many private businesses offer satellite phone connections that are reputed to be considerably cheaper than Guatel's expensive rates. Fax services are everywhere and quite inexpensive. By the time you read this, email connections will probably be available in most cities and tourist towns.

Arts, Crafts and Souvenirs

For the traveler who has stubbornly resisted stuffing a suitcase in Mexico's fine craft markets, Guatemala is the final, wallet-loosening straw. Intricately handloomed textiles, embroidered clothing, brocade and leather *bolsa* handbags, quilts, wall hangings, wool blankets, tie-dyes, ceremonial masks, Mayan flutes and wooden drums are just the beginning of a typical tourist shopping spree. If the outstanding selection and quality of these crafts isn't enough temptation, the prices can be distressingly low. Distressing because the artisans are working for pitiful wages and because you'll have to jettison your beach towel and travel iron to get these treasures home. (To temporarily salve your conscience on both points, buy a large duffel-sized *bolsa* directly from an artisan, using symbolic rather than hard-nosed bartering.)

Típica is a term broadly used for Indian textiles, clothing and crafts. The village of Panajachel, on Lake Atitlán, is world-famous for "Típica Street," an irresistible gauntlet of tiny stalls, shops and streetside vendors. Thousands of international travelers have been dazzled by Guatemala's markets, inspired to make their "fortune" with speculative purchases of *típica*. Many have made modest profits, some have gone broke and others have filled relatives' attics from Amsterdam to Anaheim with unsold inventory. Look carefully before leaping into the highly competitive *típica* business, especially if you're betting your travel money on success or failure.

Most travelers will satisfy their buying urges by doing early Christmas and gift shopping. If you're a less experienced shopper looking for personal collectibles or higher quality crafts, visit some of the country's fine specialty shops. Many store owners buy direct from the best Indian artisans or employ buyers who scour the country for the finest work. Unless you're a competent, determined barterer and an excellent judge of quality, you'll find shops hard to beat. (See the *Shopping* chapter.)

Note: Export permits are required for large purchases of *típica*, pre-Columbian artifacts and certain antiquities. Your luggage will probably be inspected when you exit the country, especially if you travel by plane. Export brokers, shop owners and art dealers are the best source of up-to-date information on regulations and permits. (For bringing the items into the U.S., see *Back to the U.S.A.*)

Customs and Traditions

It is important to note that Guatemala is probably the most conservative nation on the North American continent and the least changed by modern "progress." Such factors as the country's isolation, internal political and economic problems, and a large, non-Spanish-speaking Indian population contribute to the feeling that Guatemala is still very much a world of its own.

Sensitive tourists should be aware that in traditional Indian and *ladino* (non-Indian or mixed-blood mestizo) societies, some things just aren't done: at the top of the list are immodest and provocative dress, public nudity or skylarking, and old-fashioned, just-for-the-fun-of-it gringo craziness. Although the situation has relaxed somewhat, it is still possible to wake up in jail, especially if such rudeness involves drugs.

Note: When visiting Indian villages and towns, be aware that local laws apply. In one village, for example, we were barred from entering the church. Some people mistakenly believe (and insist) that churches are public places. This attitude could definitely lead to trouble with Indian authorities.

Other customs to observe: Indian mothers are very afraid of both child-stealing and the evil eye. No matter how cute they are, do not touch their children, photograph them or even admire them. Although strange men, especially with beards, are often distrusted by nervous parents, even the most amiable gringas risk a hysterical, even violent reaction from these superstitious people.

Never photograph Indians without asking permission. When in doubt, point to your camera and ask, "*¿Un foto, por favor?*" If they agree, you will often be asked to pay one or two quetzals.

Because so much violence has been perpetrated against Indians by non-Indians, don't expect a hero's welcome when visiting their communities.

To ease your entry, be relaxed, friendly and very polite. Avoid staring or making a fuss about anything. When you meet people, greet them quietly and shake hands (gently). Avoid laughing when you don't quite understand what someone says or what is happening. A serious, restrained, yet warm manner is the best approach. The chill that sometimes hangs over Guatemala usually thaws once it is known that you are a tourist and not an arrogant *ladino* or suspicious foreigner (such as a plain-clothes cop or military type).

Should you find yourself in a situation where people simply don't respond, or are clearly uncomfortable, it is best to make a polite exit. Don't question things, just leave. For all its beauty and interest, there are wounds in Guatemala that are far from healed.

Back to Mexico

There is a popular saying in Guatemala that goes, "*Salimos de Guatemala y entramos a Guatepeor*" ("We left Guate-bad [*mala*] and we entered Guate-worse [*peor*].") Don't let your trip to Mexico get off to a bad start by repeating this joke at the border.

• **By land:** After exiting Guatemala (and paying the usual tax for the privilege), you'll be issued a tourist card by Mexican authorities. (See *Red Tape and the Law: Tourist Cards* and *Car Papers.*) If there are any potential confusions or discrepancies with your documents, I recommend that you get a tourist card in advance at a Mexican consulate inside Guatemala.

If you kept your Mexican multiple-entry tourist card and car papers when you left Mexico, and if they haven't expired by the time you leave Guatemala, simply use them again when you re-enter Mexico. Be sure, however, that the papers will be valid for as long as you plan to stay in Mexico.

Drivers can avoid a mandatory vehicle fumigation only by presenting a doctor's letter, in Spanish, swearing they are allergic to insecticides. Although bribes won't work (officially), Steve disagrees. "I have been discreetly asked to bribe the Mexican fumigation people almost every time I have gone through. The last guy said, 'I am not asking you for a *mordida*, but if you gave me an extra ten pesos I would not have to spray your van. Now, I didn't ask you for a bribe, did I?'"

• **By air:** The airline will provide a blank tourist card. You'll go through Mexican customs and immigration when you land. Expect the usual baggage inspection.

Note: If you're passing through Mexico but will stay no longer than overnight, you may be given a transit visa. However, the red tape associated with a transit visa can be time-consuming. Always ask for a regular tourist card.

• **Entering Belize:** Though Guatemala officially claims Belize as part of its territory—and includes Belize within the borders of official maps—the days of saber-rattling and border tensions finally seem to have passed. Other than the usual brusque reception that is a trademark of Belizean border officials, your entry into the country from Guatemala should be the same as described in the Belize section later in this chapter.

BELIZE

Language • Culture and customs • Red tape • Money • Food • Driving and transportation • Safety and rip-offs • Camping • Climate • Re-entry into Mexico and Guatemala

Belize (formerly British Honduras) is a small country of less than 9,000 square miles and scarcely 200,000 inhabitants. Sandwiched between Guatemala and the Mexican state of Quintana Roo, this former British colony tends to be overlooked by travelers and tourist agents. Personally, I consider Belize to be an undiscovered jewel: friendly, colorful and unusually interesting.

Belize may be too far off the beaten track for most "fun and sun" seekers, but in an era of heightened environmental awareness, this diminutive country is well positioned to reap the benefits of its isolation and underdevelopment. "Eco-tourists" and adventure travelers in particular will find that although facilities and transportation are still somewhat limited, the potential is tremendous. In an area smaller than most American states, you'll find virtually untouched beaches and cays, jungle rivers, extensive Mayan ruins, caves and one of the world's most extensive barrier reefs. In addition, most of Belize's tropical old-growth rain forests are still intact. The opportunities for camping, bird watching, wildlife photography and Neo-tropical tree hugging are excellent.

Belize's attractions include more than its natural resources. Its people are an exotic blend of cultures and ethnic heritages, including English-speaking Creoles (descended from African slaves), Garifuna (African and Caribe Indians), German-speaking Mennonites, Chinese, Lebanese, East Indians, Mayan Indians, Salvadoran and Guatemalan immigrant-refugees and miscellaneous Caucasians, from Australians and Canadians to Americans and Europeans. Though some groups have concentrated in specific areas, relations among these diverse peoples are unusually harmonious. This is reflected in the typical Belizean's hospitality and tolerance toward visitors. As one Belizean told me, "We so mixed up here, mon, we just got to get along."

Language

English (officially) predominates, supplemented by Spanish, especially in southern Belize and near the Belize-Guatemala border. Many Belizeans also speak Creole, a Caribbean-English dialect with a colorful, often baffling vocabulary ("pink knee"— children; "john crow"—buzzard).

Culture and Customs

Belize is a true potpourri, in everything from laws and manners to religion and architecture. You'll see proper British Colonial government buildings, traditional Mayan stick-and-thatch huts, tin-roofed Creole stilt houses and quasi-suburban "cinder boxes."

As in Mexico or Guatemala, the most important customs to observe in Belize are courtesy, friendliness and self-restraint. When in doubt, smile frequently. Though it is good to express your (genuine) appreciation for Belize, don't overdo it.

Red Tape

Visas of thirty days or less will be issued at the border. Extensions are available at immigration offices within the country. American and British Commonwealth travelers should carry a birth certificate, passport or other good identification. You may be asked to show a reasonable amount of money. Have your documents ready, comb your hair and tuck in your shirt: Belizean border officials tend to be curt and formal.

Money

Belizean currency is relatively stable. In recent years it has traded at a rate of two Belize dollars for one U.S. dollar. The official bank exchange rate is a few pennies less. At border crossings, people will offer to change your American greenbacks, pesos or quetzals into Belizean dollars. This is convenient, but be cautious. Most transactions are honest, but cheating does occur. (Never exchange money on the street or in bars in Belize City.)

• **Cost of living:** Belize is a poor country, with a very small middle class. By *People's Guide* standards, the prices for meals, liquor and hotel accommodations are relatively expensive, especially when compared to Mexico and Guatemala. Gasoline is high (about U.S. $2 a gallon), but bus travel is a bargain.

Travelers sometimes complain that it is difficult to find a balance between comfort and economy in Belize. However, good deals are available, especially on the less developed cays and in small towns. The secret, as usual, is to travel Belizean-style rather than as a typical tourist. Though you may grow slightly weary of "stew beans and rice" and thin mattresses, I can virtually guarantee an interesting and rewarding journey.

Food

I hereby retract my rude comments on Belizean cooking in a previous edition and beg forgiveness from Miss Brenda (for her superb johnnycakes), Miss Jennifer (memorable Creole chilie sauces, fry jacks and lobster rice), Miss Lilly (cole slaw and conch fritters) and Bill (stir fries, chowders and prawn pizza).

To instantly understand at least fifty percent of Belizean menus, memorize these national dishes (served at breakfast, lunch and dinner): rice-and-beans (rice and beans, mixed, cooked and served together) and stew-beans-and-rice (stewed beans served alongside rice, often with chicken). The distinctions between the two dishes are important, at least to Belizeans.

Vegetarians will find that salads, fresh vegetables and fruit are distressingly difficult to locate.

Driving and Transportation

A good two-lane paved highway now traverses Belize from the Mexican border near
Chetumal to Guatemala, at Melchor de Mencos. You can easily drive or bus across the
country in one day, including rest stops. Side roads are another story, and in Belize, all
other routes are definitely side roads: dirt or battered pavement, with very narrow
bridges, tire-busting chuckholes and teeth-rattling washboard. (For many years the
scenic Hummingbird Highway was rudely known as the "Hummingbutt.") In other
words, surface travel in Belize is both exciting and challenging. Fortunately, nothing
is very far away or difficult to find (except gasoline; carry extra and watch for
American-brand filling stations in larger towns).
   • **Insurance:** It is required in Belize, so expect to buy it when you enter the country.
The rates are reasonable. Drivers may be asked to provide proof of insurance at random police checks.
   • **Buses:** Connections from border crossings and between the largest towns are adequate, inexpensive and sometimes quite crowded. On side roads, bus service is much
less frequent: once or twice a day, or perhaps once or twice a week. Ask locally; you'll
find Belizeans to be very helpful.
   • **Cab** service is not expensive for short rides.
   • **Boat** service to the offshore cays is easy to find. In Belize City, ask for
recommendations from a solid citizen or business (Mom's Cafe & Triangle Inn is
the place for travel tips and information). Avoid fast-talking, free-lance skippers and
street touts.
   • **Air travel:** If the adventure of boat and bus travel wears thin, regularly scheduled
small plane service is available throughout the country, with connections to both
Guatemala and Mexico. For some reason, flights from the municipal airport in Belize
City are often cheaper than from the international airport, a few miles outside of town.

Safety and Rip-Offs

For all its charm and natural beauty, a cloud hangs over this country, and it can't be
overlooked. Crime, primarily in Belize City, is a real problem. Though I consider it an
exaggeration, many people I've spoken to see Belize City as an unnerving gauntlet of
hustlers, dopesters, scam artists, muggers and petty thieves. The local tourist industry
tries to downplay the problem, but too many ordinary citizens and tourists fall victim
to these pirates to be ignored.
   Among international travelers, the "word" is to avoid Belize City, especially after
dark. This isn't easy; as the hub of the country's transportation and commerce systems,
all roads lead to it. To complicate matters even more, I like Belize City and consider it
to be an interesting and worthwhile place to visit, *with caution*.
   To minimize the hazards and calm your nerves, follow these suggestions:
   • Don't lump all Belizeans together; most of the people you'll meet in Belize City
are quite honest. Do, however, stay well clear of glib street people offering everything
from dope, sex and submachine guns to "insider" tips on restaurants and hotels.
Decline politely, but don't stop; be brief and firm.
   • Spend more than you might like to on a secure hotel room.
   • Never leave your vehicle unprotected on the street, even in the daytime. Find a
guarded parking lot.

• If you go out at night to eat, stick to the lighted main streets. Try to be tucked in by 9 or 10 p.m.

• If you go out for excitement, you'll find all you can handle and more, usually in the form of R & R & R (rum-reggae-and-reefer). Ask other travelers and reliable Belizeans for the safest places to party; avoid everything else. Go in a group, don't separate, stay sober, quit early . . . be careful!

• Finally, don't let Belize City's reputation prevent you from enjoying the rest of the country. In our experience, small towns and villages are not only safe, but the people are helpful, warm and very hospitable. Travel carefully, but don't overdo it; you'll soon relax and have a great time.

Camping

Organized facilities for camping and RVs are very scarce. Because much of Belize is covered by swamps, savannahs and dense jungle, the choice of "no hookup" campsites is also limited. Your best bets are wildlife reserves, the grounds of hotels or jungle lodges, farms and plantations. Rather than roadside camping, we prefer to ask local people for permission to camp in their fields and yards. You'll not only get open ground and security, but water for drinking and washing, as well as a great chance to meet people. Offer to pay, of course, and don't be shy about asking to buy home-cooked meals.

A word to the wise: Belize is a wet, warm, tropical country. Be prepared for rain and bugs. Better yet, be *well* prepared: have plenty of insect repellent and a tent with ultrafine, no-see-um netting. Use a good rainfly and give serious thought to a folding umbrella or poncho.

Climate

It's almost always warm-to-hot, except in winter and spring, when clouds and wind bring a welcome moderation in temperatures. Expect occasional rain during the "dry" season (usually January through April or May) and plenty of rain the rest of the year.

Re-Entry into Mexico and Guatemala

If you intend to visit Mexico for more than thirty days you must get a visa from the Mexican consulate in Belize City (weekday mornings only). Otherwise, go directly to the border.

Entering Guatemala from Belize is simple and straightforward: after being checked and stamped out of Belize just walk into Guatemala, request a visa (show a passport or good ID), pay a nominal fee and be on your way.

You'll find buses, cabs, snacks and money exchangers at both borders.

BACK TO THE U.S.A.

Searches • Declare your purchases • Duty-free limits • Pets and plants • A typical border crossing?

Searches

Your return to the U.S. may be the most stressful part of your trip. After turning over your tourist card and car papers to Mexican border officials, you must then turn yourself over to American Customs agents. Don't even bother to offer them a few dollars to overlook the baggage inspection; their price, if they have one, is beyond reason.

The inspection that you and your belongings are given can vary from a quick glance into your suitcase to an intimate, embarrassing "strip search." Although most people receive quick courteous treatment, you just can't anticipate anything. Customs officials are well aware that not all crooks and smugglers look like characters from Zap Comix.

Although weird-looking people usually get a closer and more thorough examination, this, too, is unpredictable. An apparently respectable traveler may get a detailed search, complete with sniffing dogs and rude probings, while a very shaggy character is quizzed briefly and sent on his or her way.

Warning: Many unfortunate people, especially first-time travelers, don't take U.S. Customs inspections seriously—until the agent unexpectedly roots through a pile of dirty underwear and pounces on the Acapulco Gold they were going to enjoy that evening. You may simply be waved through U.S. Customs, but what if you aren't? Resist the temptation to smuggle illegal souvenirs of any kind; the penalties are *very harsh*.

When you enter the inspection area, an agent will give you a quick once-over. You'll be asked where you've been and for how long. Since they have no easy way to verify your answer, keep it simple. This may help keep the search and questions to a minimum. Don't say, "I've been gone a year and been just about everywhere."

You will be asked where you were born and if you've ever been arrested. Give straight answers; these facts will be checked by computer and a lie arouses suspicion. Be calm and cool but don't babble; Customs agents are cops—make them ask. The best attitude is one of calm resignation. Arguing, being stubborn or too eager to please will all attract attention.

Baggage inspections for air travelers and those on foot shouldn't take more than a few minutes. If you're detained longer, the agent may ask loaded questions such as, "Ever see anyone smoking marijuana down there?" Give simple "yes" and "no" answers and you'll avoid Dick Tracy traps.

Car searches are equally quick, but again, if you fit the profile as a potential smuggler, the inspection can be lengthy. Everything may have to be unloaded, probed, prodded, squeezed, sniffed, pinched, tapped, hefted, tasted and in some cases, taken inside for laboratory analysis. During the search your reactions will be closely observed. Even if you're completely pure and innocent, a search will be nerve-wracking. "Did that hitchhiker leave something under the seat?" Those who aren't clean will have a hair-raising ordeal. "Oh, God! He's actually sniffing the air from the spare tire valve. Five kilos!"

Although mechanics are available to tear your car right down to the frame, few inspections go this far. A close look into nooks and crannies, from trunk to chassis, is common. Panels will be thumped, the air cleaner removed and possibly the cardboard liners of trunks and dashboards taken out. Three or four agents with a dog can cover an incredible amount of territory in a few short minutes.

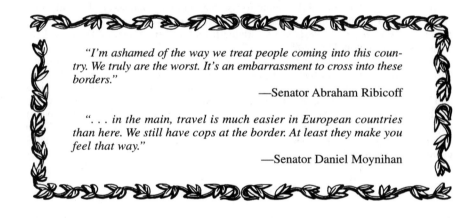

"I'm ashamed of the way we treat people coming into this country. We truly are the worst. It's an embarrassment to cross into these borders."

—Senator Abraham Ribicoff

". . . in the main, travel is much easier in European countries than here. We still have cops at the border. At least they make you feel that way."

—Senator Daniel Moynihan

Declare Your Purchases

You'll be asked if you have anything to declare. Be safe: declare everything, even if you're not sure you still have it with you. As we approach the border we jot down a list of the things we've bought in Mexico, from medicines to food and souvenirs. If you're bringing something back that is prohibited, you aren't liable to legal action or fines if you declare the item. I read of an unfortunate tourist who was convicted of smuggling coffee from Mexico into the U.S. It is not illegal to import coffee; his crime was hiding the coffee and not declaring that he had it. Omissions, however trivial, can raise you to a higher level of suspicion and prolong an inspection. Any violation, intentional or not, can result in an administrative fine—on the spot—or heavy legal action in serious cases. To put it another way, they don't get promoted in the Customs Service for being nice.

Small amounts of medicines accompanied by a valid U.S. prescription or a plausible excuse, are usually allowed to pass. Switchblade knives are prohibited, *unless you only have one arm.* Border states allow tourists to bring in a quart of liquor. They usually won't quibble if it's actually a liter, but be sure to declare it as a liter. There is also a limit of one carton of 200 cigarettes and 100 cigars.

Duty-Free Limits

The duty-free limit on souvenirs and purchases is $400. This includes everything you bought in Mexico. If you go over the limit, duty can be charged at a flat rate of ten percent on the first $1,000 above the $400 allowance. In actual practice, most agents won't question the value of your souvenirs if you don't have a lot of identical items.

Steve notes that most craft and art items are duty-free and don't count towards your $400 limit. "The catch is that if you have too many similar items, even though they may be duty-free, it is presumed that you are going to sell them. You'll have to declare the stuff as commercial. This is a big hassle. If your merchandise is worth $1,250 or more, you'll need to hire a Customs broker to do the paperwork, to the tune of several hundred dollars. The lesson here is to have receipts proving that the value of your stuff is under $1,250. Just don't lie. When I say I'm not commercial and only sell 'some of it,' I am telling the truth, mainly because I never manage to sell it all!"

As you travel, you'll undoubtedly wonder: "Can I get this across?" "What do I need to throw away?" "Do you think I ought to risk buying this?" and so on. The only sure answers are in the current U.S. Customs pamphlet, *Know Before You Go: Customs Hints for Returning U. S. Residents*, available from the Department of Treasury, U.S. Customs, Washington, D.C. 20229

In general, don't bring meat, plants, or anything dangerous, narcotic or obscene. Citrus fruits won't get through, but peanuts, garlic, papayas, coffee beans and most foods not grown in the U.S. are OK. Don't buy anything made from unfortunate birds and beasts—feathers, hides, shells, ivory, hair or skins are almost always prohibited by the Endangered Species Act. Don't believe what they tell you in the Mexican souvenir shop; it's the U.S. Customs regulations at the border that count. If you expect to buy a lot of one thing, write for the General System of Preferences booklet detailing what is currently allowed in duty-free.

Pets and Plants

Your dog will need a rabies vaccination certificate, but your cat, if in good health, probably won't.

For **pets other than birds**, write to: Office of Veterinary Public Health Service, Centers for Disease Control, Atlanta, GA 30333. For psittacine birds larger than parakeets **(parrots)**, contact: Fish and Wildlife Service, P.O. Box 3654, Arlington, VA 22203, and U.S. Dept. of Agriculture, Veterinary Service: Import-Export: Animal, Plant and Health Inspection Service, Hyattsville, MD 20782, 301-734-8687, <http://www.aphis.usda.gov/ppq/ppqpermits.html>.

If you have questions about **plants** (or to obtain permits) contact: USDA APHIS PTQ, 4700 River Rd., Unit 136, Riverdale, MD 20737; tel: 301-734-8332 or 301-734-8645, ext. 3, <http://aphis.usda.gov/ppg/ppgpermits.html>.

A Typical Border Crossing?

"Where you folks coming from?" the Customs agent asked, leaning down to give the inside of the van a quick once-over. His eyes widened.

"Mexico," Steve whispered, his hands gripping the steering wheel, eyes frozen on the inspection area ahead.

"What was that?" the agent said, bending closer.

"Mexico," Steve repeated, glassy-eyed. His breathing was fast and shallow and the complexion beneath his heavy tan was pasty. The agent's attention moved from Steve's face to his hands, clenching and unclenching on the wheel.

"Are you all U.S. citizens?" he continued, glancing back at Lorena and then turning to me. His cheek twitched slightly as he noted my beard, my hair, my sandals. I felt like screaming, "Look at my J.C. Penney sport shirt and slacks! Can't you tell that I'm straight? Steve is just naturally nervous, officer; I swear we're not smugglers!"

"U.S. citizens?" Steve said, running his tongue over dry lips. Sweat beaded his forehead; it had been his idea to cross the border in late afternoon, in the heat of the day. "Day shift will be too hot and tired to tear us apart," he'd said, "and the evening shift won't be in high gear until later." I looked at the Customs man. In spite of Steve's planning, the officer looked as though they'd just lifted him off a coat hanger. The creases in his uniform were sharp enough to cut bread. Sweat began to pour down my chest.

"Yeah, we're U.S. citizens," Steve finally answered. He was about as convincing as if he'd claimed we were Russian ballerinas.

"How long have you been out of the United States?" the agent continued relentlessly. There was a quickening excitement in his voice that made my stomach knot up: these weirdoes were right out of a Customs Service training video. He'd bet his badge against a six-pack of Lone Star that there was enough of *something*, somewhere inside this van, to get everyone on duty promoted on the spot. It would just be a matter of rooting it out.

"Ah . . . well . . . a long time," Steve stammered, giving a sickly grin and shrugging his shoulders helplessly. The agent didn't bother to press for a day by day itinerary; without taking his eyes from us, he backed into the booth and reached for the red phone.

"Man, you really blew it!" I hissed. "I told you to let me drive through! He probably thinks we're the Mexican Connection!" Steve waved his hands in front of his face; this was all too much for him, nothing was going according to The Plan. I stared out my window, grimly remembering all of our preparations, the long hours spent packing, cleaning and sorting. It had all gone to waste in a few moments, a few fumbled answers to simple questions. They'd tear us down to the frame and then sift through the pieces.

"Would you folks mind pulling up over there?" The agent's voice dripped with false sincerity as he pointed to a long metal table in the inspection area. Fluorescent lights cast an unforgiving glare on the shiny metal surface, banishing afternoon shadows. Behind the table stood a group of men and women in Customs uniforms. The entire staff was turning out to welcome us home.

"Yeah, sure," Steve croaked, lifting his foot off the clutch. He maneuvered the van alongside the waiting inspectors and stopped. Contorting his upper lip, he chewed morosely on his thick mustache.

"Mind shutting it off?" a grey-haired agent asked with elaborate patience. Steve fumbled for the key. There was a long silence.

"Now would you please step out of the vehicle?" As Steve reluctantly crept from behind the wheel, the agent gave his comrades a wolfish smile. All he lacked was a podium and a long pointer: "Now this, ladies and gentlemen, is your classic counter-culture smuggler. Please note the dry mouth, the slight trembling around the knees and the furtive eye movements."

The agent waited a few more moments and then said, "Now would you mind opening the doors of your vehicle so we can proceed?" One of the younger agents chuckled, but caught a quick look from the older man and turned it into a discreet cough. "Please take everything out," he added, a note of anticipation in his voice.

"*Everything?*" Steve asked, looking up hopelessly at the long roof rack, piled high with baskets, boxes and unidentifiable lumps and bundles.

"Everything!" the agent repeated. "And lay it all out on that table."

"Is this hashish?" The agent drawled wearily, reaching into the handcarved wooden chest. He gingerly removed a cylindrical bundle of heavy dark lumps wrapped in dried corn husks. After two hours of fruitless searching, his dreams of sudden promotion and banner headlines (*Trio Nabbed in World Record Haul of Zonko Root*) had turned into a sweltering snipe hunt. The high good humor of the first hour, with many wisecracks about the incredible amount of junk we'd collected on our travels, was rapidly changing to a grim determination to find something, anything to justify the blitzkrieg search they'd dropped on us.

"No," I sighed. "That's not hashish. It's incense. Homemade copal incense from Chiapas." He gave me a doubtful look and managed a controlled, "We'll just check that out in the lab." While awaiting the results of the analysis, he pointed to the top of the van and said, "Get that box down, please."

I looked up. A vague premonition stirred in the back of my mind. Wasn't that box actually . . . ?

"Hey, Steve!" I called. "They want to look at your box. You know, the *little one*?" Steve had been leaning against a tall steel stanchion, desperately trying to look casual. Whenever one of Lorena's plastic bags of herbs was sent off to the lab his knees buckled and his breathing became ragged.

At my mention of the box, Steve took a few quick steps toward us and then stopped dead in his tracks, a look of complete panic twisting his face. He moved hesitantly to the van and began climbing slowly to the top, like a condemned man ascending a scaffold to perform his final rope trick. As he handed the box down to me I caught the desperate message pulsing from his eyes: "Think fast, smart ass, this was your idea!"

I cradled the box in my arms and carried it to the table. The agent was busily burrowing through a huge pile of Mexican Indian clothing. "You folks have got enough stuff here to open your own store." He laughed, turning toward us with a weary smile. He looked at the box. The smile faded. "What in the . . . ?" He stopped, eyes bulging slightly. His hand moved cautiously to the lid.

"Hahahaha! Well," I choked, "it's a, it's a sort of a, you know . . . a . . . a coffin." Other inspectors, sensing the kill, gathered around us, abandoning a detailed search of our dirty laundry, moldy tent and coffee cans filled with broken seashells.

"A coffin?" The question was a blend of outrage and disgust. "You mean that's a *baby coffin!*" he yelled, struggling to regain his composure. There were low growls from the assembled agents. How could I explain that it was actually a nicely crafted pine box that we'd bought from a Guatemalan carpenter? That with a bit of wood stain, varnish and some brass hinges we'd converted it into an ideal container for our odds and ends. It was a coffin only in name. It was a simple matter of *perspective.*

"Open!" he barked, sucking a great breath of air in anticipation of some unprecedented horror. His wife had been right; he should have gone into the Postal Service!

I twisted the little brass latch and raised the lid.

"Oh, Lord . . . !"

"You've gotta be . . . !"

"Gross . . . !"

We stood in guilty silence, cries of outrage ringing ominously in our ears. Steve turned to face south, toward Mexico and freedom. I knew what he was thinking: Run! Now! While their attention was on the coffin . . . leap the pipe barricades . . . fast and low, crouching to avoid the .357 magnums . . . into that alley . . . shave head . . . change identity . . .

The officer reached hesitantly into the coffin and began removing the little pink arms, torsos, legs and heads. His hands shook noticeably as he lined the grisly plastic parts along the edge of the inspection table. A miniature morgue.

"It's . . . it's kind of a long story!" I blurted, pulling my eyes away from the gruesome display. "You see we were camped on the Caribbean and every morning I went beachcombing . . ." They didn't seem to be listening; one of the older inspectors, a man who looked like my grandfather, was shaking his head from side to side. "I've seen it all now," his expression said. "It's time to retire!"

". . . and I started noticing, you see, these, uh, pieces of doll babies all along the beach. An arm here, a head there. You know, litter. Doll baby litter. It seemed kind of, well, hilarious."

No one laughed.

"So then I started picking them up. Cleaning the beach, you might say," I hurried on. "And we had the coffin already, got it in Guatemala for a good price. Couldn't pass it up, actually. Seemed, well, natural to put the baby parts in it . . . "

At the word "natural" one of the women inspectors shuddered and steadied herself against the table. Others began drifting away, picking distractedly at the array of junk that had yet to be searched.

"I mean . . . don't you think it's . . . ?" The agent raised his hand, cutting me off. I looked over at Steve and Lorena; they were staring at the corrugated metal roof.

The Customs agents stepped back for a strategy conference. Trying to ignore the occasional hard stare, I quietly scooped up the pitiful remains of the doll babies and dumped them into the coffin, carefully closing the lid. Out of sight and out of mind, I hoped.

"Get ready," Steve muttered. "Here's round two." As the meeting broke up, one officer went to the phone while another hurried into the main building. They looked grim and determined. We had beaten the first team, now they would call in the shock troops.

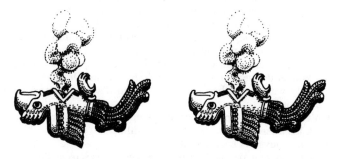

The big black Labrador crouched in the back of the van, head tilted upward, his chest rising and falling as he howled mournfully. The handler turned to the chief inspector with a puzzled look. "I've never seen him do this before," he said, shaking his head worriedly. The handler dragged the moaning dog from the van, glaring at us suspiciously.

"Whatever it is, it's weird!" he said, hustling the dog away. The agent glanced at his watch, then at us. He'd thought of calling in sick, but had come to work in spite of a nasty chest cold. Nights weren't so bad unless you got stuck with a bunch like this . . .

"He probably smelled the coyote," I offered. "We picked up this guy named Ramón, a rancher from around Monterrey. His pickup had broken down and he had his pet coyote with him. Cute little thing, completely tame. He slept back there on the floor for most of the day."

The Customs man smiled knowingly. A clever story, but not quite clever enough! He summoned an agent in coveralls and ordered up a battery of powerful flood lights, a hydraulic jack, floor crawlers, stethoscopes, probes, hammers and whisk brooms.

"Or it could have been the pig," Lorena added helpfully. "It took days just to clean up all of the . . . " Her voice trailed off; if he didn't believe the story of the coyote how would he handle a pregnant 500-pound brood sow?

"It was near Tepic," she continued. "Our landlord said he'd knock something off the rent if we'd take this pig to Guadalajara. His brother has a . . . "

The chief inspector turned his back on her, ending any further explanations. Inside the van, an agent tapped at the paneling with a tiny mallet. He worked as methodically and intently as a master safecracker, but found nothing. A third inspector scrutinized the screw heads attaching the paneling to the interior for scratches or other evidence that we had taken down the thin wood and stuffed the empty spaces with forbidden powders or herbs. Still others removed the headlights, hubcaps, heater ducts and heavy cardboard liners beneath the dashboard. At ground level, agents with wheeled creeper boards and powerful lights examined the chassis for hidden compartments or clever modifications to hide illicit goods.

Though Steve knew as well as I did that the van was immaculately clean, he watched the search with undiminished horror. I wanted to tell them that Steve's paranoia had driven us to check and clean those same spaces the day before. We'd spent hours in the middle of the desert, sweating under a blazing sun, dusting, sweeping and washing every corner in the van. Two miles before the border Steve had suddenly stopped, demanding that we swear an oath that we weren't smuggling anything. Lorena and I had answered with laughter, but Steve had insisted we pledge to be clean and innocent.

"A minute of paranoia is worth a year's detention!" he repeated, time after time, until I was ready to swear to anything just to get moving again.

Another conference was called, the inspectors moving carefully out of earshot. An argument seemed to have developed between those who had given up hope and those still thirsting for the kill. Fate intervened in the form of a brand new white Cadillac. The driver, a huge red-faced man wearing an improbably large cowboy hat, was having trouble understanding what was being asked of him.

"Open the trunk? What for? Some kind of trouble here?" He glared at us from around a thick cigar, as though we had brought this upon him. I looked at the Customs people. Perhaps it was true; they all wore the expression of hungry, frustrated sharks.

The man's wife, a small silver-haired woman, peered suspiciously through the tinted windows, looking at the inspectors as if they were bandits. One of them was standing behind the Caddy, waiting for the trunk to be opened. The rear bumper seemed unusually low to the ground.

"Why don't you folks just pack your things up and go along your way?" the chief inspector said, his interest refocusing on the Cadillac. We sagged with relief and hurried to shovel our souvenirs back into the van.

"And don't forget that damned coffin!" an agent snarled, stalking back into the office.

"Well, that about does it!" Steve said, tying a final knot around the seabag and checking the lashings on the outboard motor. We squeezed into the front of the van, exhausted but triumphant: they hadn't found it! We still had it!

"ONE BOTTLE?! ARE YOU SERIOUS?!"

Steve had just put the van in gear. The man with the cowboy hat was waving his arms wildly, his face dark with anger. There were enough bottles of liquor on the inspection table to stock a large *cantina*.

"Check that out," Steve chuckled, motioning toward the Cadillac. An inspector was removing several large boxes from the rear seat. The sharks had found their prey.

We pulled by them slowly, smiling with relief and amusement. The man in the cowboy hat glared malevolently, then suddenly leveled his smoking cigar at us like a pistol. "What in the hell do you call *that?*" he yelled.

Steve's head jerked forward. It was a classic trick, to turn attention to another when caught red-handed. I held my breath as Steve flicked on the headlights. If they were bright enough they might not . . .

"Hold it right there!" an inspector shouted, moving quickly in front of us. Steve stepped on the brake, then slumped over the wheel, nervously probing his teeth with a long thumbnail. I could imagine what he was thinking: "almost" only counts in horseshoes. They had us.

We got out of the van, silently joining the group of agents at the front bumper.

"OK, what is it? the chief inspector asked, shining the beam of his flashlight onto the black fuzzy ball.

"It's a . . . " Steve hesitated. "It's a duck," he confessed. "The *Pato de Paz*."

"The Peace Duck?" someone sputtered.

I groaned. After the coffin, I would have thought they'd take a souvenir duck in stride.

"Well, you see . . . " Steve hesitated again; these people just didn't seem to understand the offbeat humor that is so dear to Mexicans. But maybe, once they heard the story . . .

"Carl had this terrific attack of diarrhea last year in Baja and . . . "

"You mean to say that this duck is from Baja California?" a stern voice interrupted, "and that you have had it in your possession for more than a year?"

"Well, yeah," Steve continued, "but like I said, Carl had this attack and

wandered off into the bushes. That's how he found the duck. In a bush. It was dead, you see, but it had got hung up in this bush. Perfectly dried out. Dehydrated, just like a mummy."

Heads nodded. Mummy, doll parts, baby coffin. Oh, yes; it all added up.

Steve hurried on with the story. "You see it occurred to us that it would be neat to wire the duck to the front bumper, like a hood ornament or a mascot. Mexicans loved it. Every time we stopped it drew a crowd. Nobody has ever tried to steal it. We don't even have to take it in at night."

Heads nodded again. Yes, they could certainly understand why we didn't have to take it in at night. Steve began to elaborate on the tale, but the words weren't coming out quite right. He choked, stammered and then suddenly buckled forward. He jammed a fist into his mouth as great bellows of nervous laughter reverberated off the metal ceiling overhead. Several hours of tension had taken their toll; Lorena and I joined him, tears streaming down our faces. The Customs agent grew more and more impassive.

As our fits gradually subsided, one of the inspectors stepped forward and between tightly clenched jaws said: "Under the Endangered Species Act . . . of . . . 1973 . . . I hereby . . . confiscate . . . this duck!" Before we could protest he grabbed the Peace Duck and jerked it toward him.

Steve looked sadly at the empty bumper. The duck had seen a good many miles, from northern Baja to El Salvador and back, through deserts, jungles, mountains and cities, spreading peace and good will to millions. Well, hundreds at least. He reached down and gently pried the skinny little legs from the piece of twisted coat hanger. After carefully brushing the brittle black feet against his shirt to clean off the dust and road grime, Steve handed them solemnly to the seething Customs man. "Don't forget his feet; they're endangered, too."

As we climbed back into the van, the inspectors were slowly converging on the Cadillac. Their shoulders were slumped, their pace weary. It had been such a long day.

FOR MORE INFORMATION

Cyber cafes • The best of Mexico: Weather, Baja, Copper Canyon and Northern Mexico, Pacific Beaches, Central Mexico, Gulf Coast, Oaxaca and Chiapas, Yucatán Peninsula, Ruta Maya • Getting around • Driving • Travel clubs • RV and camping • Packing up and travel supplies • Mexico: A to Z • Health • Shopping • Speaking Spanish • Live and retire in Mexico • Central America • Back to the U.S.A.• Newsletters • Magazines and newspapers • Books • Maps

As I recall, reading for my first trip was limited to a paperback Spanish/English dictionary and a very battered secondhand copy of *Mexico on $5 A Day*. In fact, it wasn't until I'd actually experienced Mexico that a serious curiosity to know more about the country and its people infected me. Excellent books such as *Incidents of Travel in Yucatán and Chiapas* really came alive for me after I'd been over the ground and personally acquainted myself with the Maya.

The books and periodicals included here represent just a portion of the growing number of excellent publications on Mexico and Central America. We don't claim that this list is complete or even objective—in fact, it tends to represent favorite titles from our personal libraries, including many older, out-of-print books that are well worth searching for. I also have a definite soft spot for self-published books, "desktop" newsletters and small press publications that rarely get mentioned by most reviewers. I've even included a few books that I haven't yet read; they either sounded especially noteworthy or a trusted traveler gave me an enthusiastic, "Carl-you've-got-to-read-this!" recommendation.

For even more reviews of books, publications and websites, please see *The People's Guide Travel Letter* and our website, **<http://www.peoplesguide.com/mexico>.**

Books will always be my favorite source for background reading on Mexico and inspiring armchair adventures. There's little doubt in my mind, however, that the Internet is now the world's best resource for up-to-the-minute travel reports and first-hand communication with people living in Mexico and Central America.

When I'm planning a trip to Mexico, I can view current satellite weather photographs, query people who actually live in Mexico about hotels and restaurants, book discount air tickets, gather background on everything from local history to bird watching, read Mexican newspapers in Spanish and English, and, last but not least, discuss my plans in minute detail with travelers who have just returned from Mexico. This is such a far cry from the days when the only information that leaked out of Mexico were reports of killer earthquakes or Cancún beauty pageants that I'm still in a daze.

In order to include as many entries as possible, I've kept these reviews quite brief. Don't be surprised if you can't connect with one of the websites described here. Cyberspace is vast and websites tend to come and go according to their creator's whims. Others move, leaving you stranded with no forwarding address. If this happens, check back with us at **<http://www.peoplesguide.com/mexico>**. We are constantly updating and expanding our extensive list of recommended sites, with links to the best web pages on Latin America.

The following book reviews and websites follow the order of the chapters in the book, with a few additional sections. A special *"¡Gracias!"* for suggesting and reviewing some of the books and websites discussed here to David Eidell, Dr. Linda Nyquist, Ron Mader, Kay Rafool, Stan Gotlieb and "Mexico" Mike Nelson. Their names are in parentheses after their recommendations.

Guidebooks, Websites and General Information

Mexico & Central American Handbook edited by Ben Box. This well-respected book has much to recommend it: consistent and logical organization, tremendous nuts-and-bolts travel details, a broad range of reliable food and hotel suggestions, plus a degree of accuracy consistently higher than other guidebooks I've tried. A remarkably compact 926 pages, spanning nine countries, the *Mexico & Central American Handbook* is downright marvelous.

Mexico Handbook by Joe Cummings and Chicki Mallan, 1996, Moon Publications, Inc., 1457 pages! This brick-sized guidebook could have used more attentive updating, but considering its scope and awesome size, flaws are inevitable. All in all, *Mexico Handbook* lives up to Moon Publications' reputation for thoroughly researched books with plentiful maps.

Mexico Insight Guide by Kal Muller. Tim Crump, a book-loving ex-Border Patrol officer with an extensive library on Mexico, says, "Aptly named, this book is full of interesting information by many authors, mostly Hispanics, each familiar with his or her subject. The style is slightly 'textbook' but easy to read. The photography is excellent."

Northern Mexico Handbook: The Sea of Cortez to the Gulf of Mexico by Joe Cummings, 1994, Moon Publications. Covering nine very large northern states (over 50% of Mexico's territory), veteran travel writer Joe Cummings leaves very few stones unturned. Brief but well-researched descriptions of cities, historical sites, hiking trails, highways, hotels and restaurants, beaches and especially interesting "biotic communities" are combined with easy-to-follow maps "to every city, region and park." Joe Cummings and Moon Publications are to be commended for offering such a substantial work on a region that is too-often ignored by both tourists and travel writers.

Spas & Hot Springs of Mexico by "Mexico" Mike Nelson, Roads Scholar Press, $16.95, tel: (956) 580-7760 or webpage: **<http://www.mexicomike.com>**. Details and directions for spas, spiritual retreats and simple mineral water hot springs that help arthritis, psoriasis and depression. "Mexico" Mike says, "I've had personal experience with most of them."

Mexico City by Andrew Coe, 1994, Passport Books. A concise, highly readable mixture of history, archaeology and culture, lightened by interesting excerpts, offbeat detail and beautiful photos by Kal Muller. Includes maps, restaurant and hotel lists and basic how-to information.

Mexico: Places and Pleasures by Kate Simon, Harper & Row. The author's intelligence, wry humor and witty insights into Mexican life keep this dated guidebook high on my personal favorites list.

The Rough Guide to Guatemala and Belize by Mark Whatmore and Peter Eltringham, Rough Guides Ltd. Having used this book from one remote corner of Guatemala to another, I don't think you'll find anything better for offbeat, budget travel. The full text is also available on *HotWired*, <http://www.hot wired.com /rough/mexico/>.

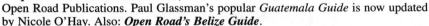

Open Road's Guatemala Guide, Open Road Publications. Paul Glassman's popular *Guatemala Guide* is now updated by Nicole O'Hay. Also: *Open Road's Belize Guide*.

Henry's Hint$ On Guatemala by Henry Gall, 1993. Between clichés (Huehuetenango is "a sleepy town"—yawn), Henry's terse travel information can be quite thorough and useful. Whereas one author describes Lake Atitlán as "a gem in its natural beauty," Henry flatly declares, "It would be a crime not to see it." This mildly cranky approach appeals to me.

MexConnect, <http://www.mex connect.com>. This site and *@migo* (**Mexico OnLine**) <http://www.mex online.com> are among the oldest and most reliable sources of information on Mexico.

Nerd World, <http://www.nerdworld.com/travel.html>. With a name like "Nerd World" these guys just have to overcompensate by putting up a very good website. I especially enjoy their off-the-wall Mexico links, including Tijuana's Industrial Park, the Catholic Church of Yucatán and Fernando's Home Page. A quick pass at this link-filled site is worth a thousand words.

Consulate General of Mexico in New York, <http://www.quicklink.com/mexico /ingles/ing.htm>. Compared to most "official" government websites, this one is definitely worth a second look.

Free Time, "tiempo libre," <http://www.tiempolibre.com.mx/>. A weekly "lifestyles" online magazine, in Spanish, with articles on movies, books, dance, music, tourism, nightlife and so on. This is an excellent place to casually hone your Spanish skills. Also, a wide range of links to gay bars, services, organizations and a glossary of gay Spanish.

Wide Wired World, <http://www.worldworks.net/widewiredworld/index.html>. This hard-to-pigeonhole website is like stepping through the looking glass—follow the links and wherever you end up . . . there you are!

University of Texas, <lanic.utexas.edu>. "Superb site with links to everything about Latin America—arts and humanities, discussion groups, magazines, popular culture—not just the academic areas." (Kay Rafool)

Azteca Web Page, <http://www.azteca.net/aztec/>. I'm enjoying Azteca's ongoing discussion on ethnicity, "Are we Chicanos/Mexicanos or Hispanics?" The site includes, "What is Mexico's Indian population?", a Pre-Hispanic calendar, U.S. Immigration info, Chiapas updates, Art & Dance.

Mexican Government Information, <http://serpiente.dgsca.unam.mx/caleidoscopio /gobierno/>. A Spanish-only site loaded with official documents, links and many dry but useful resources.

Excite Travel, Mexico, **<http://city.net/countries/mexico/>.** Enough travel and information resource links on Mexico and Latin America to overload a Cray Super Computer. Open the institutional size bag of tortilla chips before you visit this one.

Latin America on the Net, **<http://www.latinworld.com/norte/mexico/>.** Extensive links to Mexican magazines, media and personal web pages in Spanish and English. A genuine cyber-crapshoot.

Central America Today, **<http://www.centramerica.com>.** An attractive business site with good links for Central America.

NACLA - North American Congress on Latin America, **<http://www.nacla.org/>.** Information on major trends in Latin America and its relations with the U.S. Outstanding links of special interest to scholars, activists, Spanish students and serious aficionados of Latin America.

Be There Now: a zine of budget travel and beating the rat race, **<http://www. apocalypse.org/pub/u/x/zines/>.** Dedicated to "Life, Liberty and the Pursuit of Slack," this is exactly the kind of irreverent travel rag that makes the Internet so entertaining.

Art of Travel.com, **<http://www.artoftravel.com/>.** Barnes & Nobles' worst nightmare: an author self-publishes an entire book on how to travel cheap and then has the gall not to charge us a cent for the information. Chapter 4, "How To Get Cheap Flights" is an excellent overview of how to shop for a bargain air ticket.

Britannica Internet Guide, **<www.ebig.com>.** Rather than grab everything in cyberspace, Britannica highgrades the Web for the most interesting pages on Mexico and Latin America. Real humans review these web sites and award stars only to the very best-of-the-best. I've used Britannica for all kinds of searches and find it to be consistently excellent.

CyberTravel: Talk About Mexico and Latin America

I've already mentioned newsgroups, but you may find it easier, especially at first, to join a discussion based at a website. The sites listed below host excellent discussions (also called message boards or forums). Many of the participants are knowledgeable travelers or have special skills and information that they share generously. (Chat groups are yet another format—live, "real time" group conversations via computer. As an information addict, I have to say that the chat sessions I've tried haven't impressed me.)

Before you jump in, keep in mind that there is a definite etiquette that must be observed, especially if you want to avoid being "flamed" (chewed out, often graphically). Most groups welcome "newbies" and offer them a list of FAQs—Frequently Asked Questions. Read the FAQs and follow the exchange of messages for a session or two before you participate. This break-in period helps to avoid cluttering the discussion with repetitious messages and questions.

By the way, in discussion group cyber-jargon, the term "thread" is used to describe a series of messages or an ongoing exchange on a certain topic.

Discussion Groups

MexConnect, **<http://www.mexconnect.com/wwwboard/index.html>.** My first choice for thoughtful answers to questions about living and retiring, with lots of good input from gringos actually living in Mexico.

@migo! Mexico Chat And Message Center, **<http://www.mexonline.com /amigobbs.htm>.** An interesting and talkative group hosted by *Mexico OnLine*, **<http://www.mexonline.com>**, one of the oldest and best websites for general travel and Mexico business information.

UseNet Travel Newsgroups

Travel discussion groups based on Web sites tend to be relatively sedate and well-mannered. In contrast, some unmoderated UseNet groups are one step away from total chaos and clamor. A prime example is <soc.culture.mexican>. The conversation in this unmoderated newsgroup is a cross between an overcrowded singles bar, a political protest rally and a Mexican *carnaval*. Enter at your own risk!

Not all groups are so disorganized. Here are several that I follow regularly and with great enjoyment. (Newsgroups can be accessed from your web browser, I much prefer to use a stand-alone "news reader" program.)

<rec.travel.latin-america>: My first choice, especially if I'm looking for up-to-the-minute information and responses from people who are actually in Latin America.

<soc.culture.honduras>: Light traffic and (mostly) on-topic, polite discussion.

<sci.archaeology.mesoamerican>: Since I'm not really qualified to discuss archaeology with real experts, I tend to "lurk" in this group, trolling for interesting travel crumbs. When I needed a list of reading material on the indigenous people of Honduras, one of this group's regular participants sent me an incredible bibliography.

<rec.outdoors.camping, rec.backcountry, rec.outdoors.rv-travel>: Rather than wade through all of the talk about Yosemite and Winnebagos on these groups, I use the search function to look for "Mexico" and other key words in the titles of messages.

<rec.photo.digital>: If you're as excited about the potential of digital cameras for travel photography as I am, you'll find reams of valuable info here.

<soc.subculture.expatriate>: A place for expatriates to compare notes and trade recipes to cure homesickness.

<rec.travel.budget.backpack>: If you're traveling cheap. . . .

Cyber Cafes and Traveler's Email Services

Travelers Message Service Bulletin Board, **<http://www.weblane.com/experiecia /bb/>.** If you don't have an email account that can be used while on the road, you can access the Travelers Message website from any Internet connected computer (such as a cybercafe). Post your message—and look for messages that friends and family have posted there for you. Like any community bulletin board, this one is completely open to the public—in other words, there's absolutely no privacy.

Cybercafes on Eco Travels, **<http://www2.planeta.com/mader/ecotravel/coffeeag /cybercafe.html>.** An index of Mexican and Latin American cybercafes.

Cyber Cafes, Asociación Latin America **<http://www.amcc.org.mx/>.** Cybercafes listed by state.

The Best of Mexico

Weather

Weather, **<http://www.solar.ifa.hawaii.edu/Tropical.StrikeProb/me>.** Tropical storms and hurricanes that affect Mexico, with "probability of impact" for key coastal cities. (David Eidell)

WeatherPost, **<http://www.weatherpost.com/>.** Weather reports for thousands of cities worldwide. (Tom Rodriguez)

Baja

So many books have been published on Baja that I can't possibly keep up. For a budget-busting selection that includes some difficult to locate titles, try searching for "Baja" at Amazon's online bookstore, **<http://www.amazon.com>.**

Baja Handbook: Mexico's Western Peninsula, Including Cabo San Lucas by Joe Cummings, 1994, Moon Publications, Inc. The *Baja Handbook* tries to do the impossible, which is to deliver all the information that a traveler to Baja may require in just 362 pages. The surprise is that to a very high degree, the author actually succeeds. For instance, Joe Cummings describes "Playa El Burro" as "A public beach with *palapas* and trash barrels next to a scrappy-looking residential section" This is an excellent description of my favorite beach. But sadly, Joe didn't have room for the best part: camping costs just two dollars a day and the girl-crazy young caretaker often forgets to come around and collect. All-in-all, the *Baja Handbook* is the best informational book that I've seen on Baja to date. (David Eidell)

Discover Baja Newsletter: A bimonthly publication of the Discover Baja Travel Club. Good articles and many ads, but if you're a serious Baja traveler, the ads are of interest. Subscriptions included with club membership of $39 a year. Call (800) 727-BAJA (see *Travel Clubs*).

Baja Life Magazine: Slick and attractive, four issues are $24. Call (714) 376-2252 or go to **<http://www.bajalife.com>**.

The Baja Book III by Tom Miller and Carol Hoffman, Baja Trail Publications. Though still worthwhile, *The Baja Book*, long a reliable companion for untold numbers of Baja travelers, has not been kept up-to-date since the death of its author, Tom Miller. Also by Tom: *Angler's Guide To Baja California* and *Mexico West Book: A Road and Recreation Guide to Today's West Coast of Mexico*, listed under books on driving.

A Desert Country Near the Sea by Ann Zwinger, Harper & Row. Prize-winning naturalist Ann Zwinger takes a close look at the flora, fauna, marine biology and geology of Baja's southern tip, with detailed observations on the region's history and geography. A wonderful combination of field guide, travelogue and personal adventure.

Baja California Information Pages, **<http://math.ucr.edu/~ftm/baja.html#TOP>**. This is my kind of site: straightforward, no frills, with lots of well organized, well researched information. Includes road, weather, gas station reports, bus info, hotels, books, tides and so forth. The site is heroically maintained as a non-commercial public service by Fred Metcalf. Well done!

Latitude 38, **<http://www.latitude38.com/>**. The "Baja Ha-ha" is an annual disorganized gaggle of 500 or so cruising sailboats that departs San Diego every fall for a giant party in Cabo San Lucas before dispersing worldwide. (David "El Codo" Eidell)

BajaLinks, **<http://www.bajalinks.com/>**, and *Guide to Mulege and Concepcion Bay Mexico,* **<http://members.home.net/mulegebaja/mulege.htm>**. Excellent Baja resources, with "highgrade" links to equally good Baja sites.

Baja, San Felipe, **<http://www.sanfelipe.net/>**. San Felipe is a small town on the northern shore of the Sea of Cortez. This website was suggested by Vee Weber and others as very community oriented.

Baja Sun Newspaper, **<http://www.mexonline.com/mexinfo/bajasun1.htm>**.

Amigos de Baja Discussion Group, **<http://www.geocities.com/TheTropics /4888/>**. The hardcore Baja Rats gather here to plan their adventures, lie about fish and chew over favorite topics. Fishing is prominent on this excellent site but don't panic, there's a lot more here than boats and bait: They've got ocean temperature charts! (I know, but some of us weather geeks eat this stuff up). There's also lots of valuable Baja info such as road conditions, recipes, photos, a very spirited discussion forum and the Baja Breeze online newsletter.

Baja California Discussion Group, **<http://math.ucr.edu/~ftm/bajaPages /MsgBoard/MsgBoard.html>**. A public, non-commercial message board and discussion forum on Baja. Maintained by Fred Metcalf as part of his excellent Baja Information Pages site.

The Copper Canyon and Northern Mexico

Mexico's Copper Canyon Country: A Hiking and Backpacking Guide by M. John Fayhee, 1994, Cordillera Press. John Fayhee has definitely covered a lot of ground in the Copper Canyon. Unfortunately, the book too often reads as though the author suffered from an overdose of his favorite fermented beverages (the Spanish is riddled with errors.), Fayhee does best when he drops his mock-macho style and applies himself to the job at hand, namely, providing useful information about hiking. The "Particulars" section at the end of most chapters is usually a clear-headed summary of practical tips, contacts and need-to-know information.

Mexico's Copper Canyon: Barranca del Cobre by Richard D. Fisher, Sunracer Publications, P.O. Box 86492, Tucson, AZ 85754-6492 . This large format book offers an excellent pictorial review of the region, useful "tourist tidbits," interesting essays, maps and a point-by-point log for the trans-canyon rail trip.

Tarahumara of the Sierra Madre: Survivors on the Canyon's Edge by John G. Kennedy, Professor Emeritus, UCLA, Asilomar Press, 1199 Forest Avenue, #321, Pacific Grove, CA 93950, $17.95. A description of the life of the most isolated Indian tribe in North America by a noted expert on the Tarahumara.

Life Through the Eyes of a Tarahumara by Romayne Wheeler, 1993, Editorial Camino. A book of wisdom, poetry and personal experience by an internationally recognized composer and musician who lives among the Tarahumara. Available in Creel at the Tarahumara Mission bookstore.

Trails of the Sierra Madre by Eugene Boudreau, 1973, Capra Press and Pleasant Hill Press. Like other thoughtful writers on Mexico's backcountry, Boudreau's out-of-print books are timeless. Also good: *Ways of the Sierra Madre, R.F. Grigsby's Sierra Madre Journal: 1864* and *Move Over Don Porfirio: Tales from the Sierra Madre.*

Unknown Mexico: Explorations in the Sierra Madre and Other Regions, 1890-1898 Vol. 1 by Carl Lumholtz, 1898, Dover Publications, Inc. One of my all-time favorites, a turn-of-the-century classic detailing explorations in the Sierra Madre of Northern Mexico. It is a measure of how isolated the Tarahumara have been that Lumholtz's observations on their customs and ways of life are still valid today.

Mata Ortiz—A Mexican Village of Potters,<http://mindspring.com/~mataort /matahp.htm>. This site celebrates the amazing potters of Mata Ortiz.

El Paso City Guide, <http://www.elpasocvb.com>. For more El Paso information see <http://www.citi-guide.com/ep> and *The El Paso Infopage,* <http://www.ElPasoInfo .com>.

Pacific Beaches

Mazatlán, <http://www.mazcity.com.mx/> and <http://www.maztravel.com/>.

Acapulco Newspaper, <http://www.aca.novenet.com.mx/ingles.html>. The emphasis at this slick Spanish/English site is on tourism info, entertainment, services and shopping. Also: *Acapulco Travel Net,* <http://acapulco-travel.com>.

Central Mexico

Ajijic, Lake Chapala, Guadalajara, <http://www.ajijic.com/default.htm>.

Gulf Coast

Adventuring Along the Gulf of Mexico by Donald G. Schueler, Sierra Club Books. Outdated but still a "must read." Schueler's description of Gulf Coast wildlife, parks, beaches, accommodations and tourist attractions is presented in a knowledgeable, highly readable narrative style. I only wish he'd keep it current.

Oaxaca and Chiapas

Oaxaca: Crafts and Sightseeing by Barbara Hopkins, drawings by Alberto Beltrán, 1992, Editorial Minutiae Mexicana, distributed in the U.S. by Jean Stenzel, MEX/ICS, 124 Av. Cota, San Clemente, CA 92672. Barbara Hopkins shares an intimate, expert knowledge of Oaxaca City and its environs. The author offers us everything from detailed shopping suggestions for crafts and folk art to fascinating historical tidbits, fiesta dates (and backgrounds), local foods and delicacies, costumes and nearby side trips. Her suggested walking tour takes in the city's most interesting streets and byways, markets, museums and colonial monuments.

Oaxaca, Pacific Coast of Mexico, **<http://www.eden.com/~tomzap/>** Tom Penick covers hotels, travel, food, surfing, snorkeling, scuba diving, fish, turtles, history, native dances and the Spanish language. Information is also available on the beach towns of Jalisco.

Oaxaca, State Tourist Guide, **<http://www.oaxaca-travel.gob.mx/>**. This tourist-oriented site manages to overcome its "official" nature and provides some interesting and useful information as well as a good list of links: mezcal distillers, folk art, tours, articles, orphanage, museums and more.

Oaxaca Discussion Group, **<http://oaxaca travel.gob.mx/wwwboard/>**. A slow to load but quite active message board with many interesting "threads" of conversation.

San Cristobal Las Casas, Chiapas, **<http://www.sancristobal.podernet.com/>**. A good community resource site with info on schools, hotels, local newspapers, services, cybercafes, tour operators, airlines, etc.

Chiapas Massacre and What is Really Happening in Mexico, **<http://www .criscenzo.com/jaguar/chiapas.html>**. Reports from Chiapas on the liberation struggle of the Mayan people.

Zapatista & EZLN home page, **<http://www.peak.org/~justin/ezln/ezln.html>**. Also: *Zapatista Action,* **<http://www.utexas.edu/ftp/student/nave/>**.

The Yucatán Peninsula

Adventure Guide to the Yucatán by Bruce & June Conord, 1998, Hunter Travel Guides, Hunter Publishing, Inc. This attractive, well-researched book is definitely a "cut above" the usual, all-too-familiar guidebooks.

The Lost World of Quintana Roo by Michel Peissel, 1963, E.P. Dutton and Co. A few years before my own introduction to the Yucatán Peninsula, Peissel set off on a risky one-man jungle-bashing expedition down the Caribbean coast of Quintana Roo. His story is now a cult classic among Mexico travelers and do-it-yourself explorers.

Diario de Yucatán, **<http://www .sureste.com/noticias/primie.hts>**. A daily roundup of Mexican and international news, in Spanish, from a very good newspaper.

The Ruta Maya

Incidents of Travel in Central America, Chiapas, and Yucatán by John L. Stephens, 1843, Dover Publications, Inc. Don't be put off by this book's age—it remains one of the best adventure travel sagas ever written. Exploration and archaeology at their finest, with incredible drawings by Frederick Catherwood.

The Last Lords of Palenque: The Lacandon Mayas of the Mexican Rain Forest by Robert D. Bruce and Victor Perera, 1982, Little, Brown and Company, Boston. Noted Mayanist Robert Bruce became embroiled in scandal when his nephew Leo was charged with murdering his Lacandon

wife. Freed in the Zapatista uprising, Leo immediately vanished, leaving his uncle to explain reports of alcoholism, pornography and human rights abuses to his fellow anthropologists. Remember: this is not a novel. (Dr. Linda Nyquist)

The Heart of the Sky: Travels Among the Maya by Peter Canby, 1992, Harper Collins.

Time Among the Maya: Travels in Belize, Guatemala, and Mexico: by Wright, Weidenfeld and Nicolson, 1989.

A Forest of Kings by Linda Schele and David Freidel, William Morrow. The authors are leading scholars in the deciphering and interpretation of Mayan hieroglyphic texts. As dry and intimidating as that may sound, this book brings ancient cities back to life for archaeology buffs and Ruta Maya travelers.

The Maya by Michael Coe. Archaeologist Coe has a talent for explaining pre-Columbian history in terms that even I understand. Good overviews of the Mayan world.

The Caste War of the Yucatán by Nelson Reed. This book might change your view of the "peaceful" Maya. Illuminating history and good reading on this bloody, forgotten war.

La Ruta Maya: Yucatán, Guatemala & Belize by Tom Brosnahan, Lonely Planet Publications. Brosnahan is a veteran travel writer who seldom takes a wrong turn. His eye for bargains and his no-nonsense reporting make this a very popular book.

Archaeology of Mesoamerica, **<http://www.criscenzo.com/jaguar/>.** Jeeni Criscenzo, author of *Place Of Mirrors,* a self-published, new-age style novel about the ancient Maya, has created a visually striking website on the Maya region of mesoamerica: maps, Mayan glossary, history and more.

Los Loros, a Mayan jungle community, **<http://www.wjh.harvard.edu/~ctennant/ EthnoWeb/home.htm>.** Created by anthropologist Chris Tennant, this outstanding website is an inspiring blend of ecology, archaeology, history and community action. The site skillfully presents an educational theme with excellent art, photography and an online museum of Mayan artifacts.

Getting Around

For information on Mexican bus lines, try: *El Uno Line,* **<http://mexplaza .udg.mx/uno>** or *ADO,* **<http://mexplaza.udg.mx/ado/gleng1.html>.**

For information on air travel: *Airlines Of The Web - Information, Reservations, Aviation,* **<http://www.itn.net /cgi/get?itn/cb/aow/index:XX-AIRLINES>.**

Driving

How To Keep Your Volkswagen Alive: A Manual of Step-by-Step Procedures for the Compleat Idiot by John Muir, John Muir Publications, P.O. Box 613, Santa Fe, NM 87504. In the early seventies, we met John and Eve Muir while camping on a remote Mexican beach. John had a parrot named "Hey Man!" on his shoulder and a stack of self-published "Idiot Guides" in his VW van. "Take this," he said, giving us a copy. "You'll need it." John was right; if you're driving a VW to Mexico, his classic do-it-yourself guide to repair and maintenance is as indispensable as a spare tire and a road map, if only to check what that mechanic is doing.

Mexico Mike, **<http://www.mexicomike.com/>.** "Mexico" Mike Nelson, former editor of Sanborn's Travelog (see below) has written books on Mexican spas, living in Mexico, touring and god-only-knows-what else. Mike is restless and irreverent, and he writes about Mexico with a sharp eye and a self-deprecating sense of humor. He also gets so enthused about Mexico that he tends to drift over the centerline sometimes, but that's the risk you take on a road trip with Mikey (as he calls himself).

Sanborn's Mexico Travelog by Sanborn's Mexico Insurance, (800) 222-0158. Sanborn's sweetens their insurance policies for Mexico drivers by throwing in a free copy of the looseleaf Mexico Travelog. Designed to guide motorists along Mexico's major highways, the detail is awesome: "VW agency at right and Coca Cola bottling plant at left. Start working your way to right lane." Is the Travelog accurate? "Mostly yes . . . and sometimes no." The maps and simplified road plans of how to bypass major cities are especially valuable. The RV and campground information is useful but scanty. To get the most out of your road log, take it with a grain of salt.

Mexico West Book: A Road and Recreation Guide to Today's West Coast of Mexico by Tom Miller and Carol Hoffman, 1991, Baja Trail Publications. Tom Miller explored Baja and western Mexico for decades, sharing his expertise and discoveries with a prolific output of books, newspaper columns and magazine articles. Shortly before his death, Tom told me, "I haven't had to wear shoes to work since '73." *Mexico West Book* is a detailed milepost-style log of highways, back roads and beaches from northwestern Mexico to the Guatemala border. Tom's personal observations on everything from fishing and Mexican food to camping (and restaurants), history (and taco stands) and even coconut oil production, add a very personal flavor to this book.

Travel Clubs

Discover Baja Travel Club, San Diego, CA, (800) 727-BAJA. In addition to a monthly newsletter focusing on Baja, this club features discounts on everything from Mexican insurance and guidebooks to special member rates for participating hotels and restaurants. Discover Baja also sells Mexican fishing and boat licenses. **<http://www. discoverbaja.com>**, email: discovbaja@aol.com.

Club Vagabundos del Mar, (800) 47-4-BAJA. This nonprofit club is distinguished by its emphasis on boating and cruising. It also holds club functions, with fiesta-meetings in southern California and the Southwest. Vagabonds was founded in the sixties.

RV and Camping

Traveler's Guide to Mexican Camping: Explore Mexico with your RV or Tent by Mike & Terri Church, 1997, Rolling Homes Press. A comprehensive, no-frills directory of every RV park we've heard of in Mexico, plus an abundance of very useful maps.

The People's Guide to Camping, Backpacking & Boating in Mexico by Carl Franz and Lorena Havens, 1981, John Muir Publications, and The *People's Guide to RV Camping in Mexico* by Carl Franz and Steve Rogers, edited by Lorena Havens, 1989, John Muir Publications. Both of our earlier books on camping are still out of print, but copies can sometimes be found in used bookstores. We'll also be posting excerpts from both books on our website, **<http://www.peoplesguide.com/mexico>**.

RVing in Mexico, Central America and Panama by John and Liz Plaxton, 1995, $18.95, P.O. Box 21104, Kelowna, B.C., V1Y 9N8 Canada. A self-published account of a long RV trip through Latin America with many useful suggestions and insights.

Backcountry Mexico by Bob Burleson and David H. Riskind, 1986, University of Texas Press. Much of this book is down-to-earth Spanish-English vocabularies and sample conversations, making it both a self-contained dictionary and language guide. There are brief but useful discussions of driving, health, hiking, canoeing and mule trekking. Anyone interested in life and travel in Mexico's backcountry or colloquial, everyday Spanish will enjoy this book.

A Hiker's Guide to Mexico's Natural History by Jim Conrad, 1995, The Mountaineers.

Mexico's National Parks (GORP), <http://www.gorp.com/gorp/location/latamer/Mexico/pks_intr.htm>.

Happy Campers, <http://www.hcampers.com/>. Good travel information and online maps for RV'ers headed for the Southwestern U.S. and northern Mexico.

Packing Up and Travel Supplies

Walkabout Travel Gear, <http://www.walkabouttravelgear.com>, (800) 852-7085. Essential gear and information for independent travelers.

Europe Through the Back Door, <http://www.ricksteves.com/services/accmenu.htm>, (425) 771-8303. Rick Steves sells a good money belt, an excellent carry-on travel pack and other travel accessories.

Magellan's, <http://www.magellans.com/>. A major travel accessories catalog, now online.

Roadnews.com, <http://www.roadnews.com/>. Accessories and support for laptop computer users worldwide. I'll definitely be checking back here before I take my Mac PowerBook on the road again.

Mexico: A to Z

Money

Peso Exchange Rates, <http://www.quicklink.com/mexico/tabla.sec/tcc/htm>. Graphs of today's exchange rate with a ten day history curve and an archive of exchange rates from past years. The easiest site I have yet found. (David "Cheapskate" Eidell)

Volunteer & Social Action Groups

Action Without Borders: <http://www.idealist.org/>. A site for those seriously interested in volunteer work, humanitarian organizations and social action projects. *Action Without Borders* is a nonprofit organization that promotes the sharing of ideas, information and resources to help build a world where all people can live free, dignified and productive lives. For general questions and information, send an email to info@idealist.org, or contact at: Action Without Borders, Inc., 350 Fifth Avenue, Suite 6614, New York, NY 10118, (212) 843-3973, fax: (212) 564-3377.

Global Volunteers, <http://www.globalvlntrs.org/>, (800) 487-1074, email: Globalvol@aol.com. "Adventures in Service" volunteers pay their own way and lend a hand with construction, education, health care and environmental projects.

Institute for Global Communications, <http://www.igc.org/igc/>. A "community" of progressive organizations and individuals, including five "Nets": Peace, Eco, Conflict, Women and Labor.

Pastors For Peace: "IFCO" Interreligious Foundation for Community Organization, <http://www.ifconews.org/>, email: p4p@igc.apc.org. Pastors For Peace reports on Peace Caravans to Chiapas and other social action projects in Latin America. (Stan Gotlieb)

PeaceNet, <http://www.igc.org/igc/peacenet/index.html>. "information and work for positive social change in the areas of peace, social and economic justice, human rights and the struggle against racism." Action Alerts, Headlines and Features include updates on the conflict in Chiapas. (Stan Gotlieb)

Pina Palmera, <http://wombat.eden.com/~tomzap/pina.html>. Pina Palmera is an organization that provides shelter, meals, training and support for children and people with physical disabilities.

Doctors Without Borders, <http://www.dwb.org>. (888) 392-0392. This highly respected international relief group sends volunteers to over 80 countries.

Hands Across The Border Foundation, 4323 North 12 St., Suite 201, Phoenix, AZ 85014, (602) 277-1344. A wonderful exchange program for thousands of American and Mexican schoolchildren.

Health

Where There Is No Doctor by David Werner, The Hesperian Foundation. A truly great book: readable, practical advice designed to keep you healthy with a minimum of treatment and expense. Used extensively in the Third World and originally written on the basis of the author's extensive experience in Mexico's backcountry. A non-profit publication, also available in Spanish. Take at least one extra copy in Spanish to give away to someone who needs it.

Staying Healthy In Asia, Africa, and Latin America by Dirk G. Schroeder, ScD, MPH., Volunteers In Asia and Moon Publications. This compact book is based on actual traveler's experiences, including considerable input from David Werner, author of *Where There Is No Doctor*. Chapters on diagnosis and treatment of illness, common health problems, and infections and diseases are especially valuable. (Pay close attention to Schroeder's advice on malaria and his warnings about Third World antibiotics.)

Mexico Health Profile, <http://www.paho.org/english/mexico.htm>. Information and statistics of special interest to health professionals and traveling hypochondriacs. In a similar vein: **ProMED,** <http://www.healthnet.org/programs/promedhma /9706/>.

Traditional Medicine Project, <http://www.halcyon.com/FWDP/medicine /tmp.html>. The Center for Traditional Medicine in Yelapa, Jalisco (south of Puerto Vallarta) collaborates with traditional village herbalists to provide free local health care and fee-for-service holistic health services to travelers. They seek to increase understanding of the role women and traditional medicine play in strengthening, stabilizing and nurturing human society. Dr. Leslie Korn also publishes a newsletter, *La Curandera* (The Healer) and sponsors an Internship Program.

Shopping

The Shoppers Guide to Mexico by Steve Rogers and Tina Rosa, John Muir Publications (out of print). Our *compadre*s Steve and Tina operate Amerind Arts, a home-grown business featuring unusual crafts and indigenous art from Mexico and Central America. The *Shopper's Guide* gives invaluable advice on buying a wide range of Mexican crafts: ceramics, leather, silver, metalwork, furniture, *pâpier-mâché*, toys, jewelry, glassware and pottery. Steve and Tina also share their personal experiences of shopping and exploring Mexico, along with techniques for bartering, judging quality, packing and shipping and dealing with U.S. Customs.

Mexican Art Sale, <http://www.folkart.com/~latitude/home/mex.htm>. Mexican folk art and crafts for sale. The colorful online catalog gives a great preview of some of Mexico's fine *artesania*.

Speaking Spanish

I recently met a young Danish traveler in northern Mexico who wished to learn Spanish in "three or four days." He was in a hurry to get to South America, but felt that achieving fluency in the language was worth such a delay. According to people who do not speak it, the Spanish language is as easy to pick up as the common cold. Don't believe it!

Breaking Out of Beginner's Spanish by Joseph J. Keenan, 1994, University of Texas Press. A journalist and long-time resident of Mexico, Keenan confesses that he learned Spanish just like the rest of us, by studying, practicing and trial-and-error. In a style that is both instructive and a delight to read, the author shares hundreds of hard-earned tips on correcting grammatical errors, improving fluency and understanding the subtleties of spoken Spanish. If you want to tune your Spanish to Latin American ears, or try for genuine fluency, get this book.

Cassell's Colloquial Spanish: A Handbook of Idiomatic Usage, Including Latin-American Spanish by A. Bryson Gerrard, 1980, Collier Books, Macmillan Publishing Co., New York. Subtitled "A

Handbook Of Idiomatic Usage," Cassell's is more dictionary than language instruction book. The author explains "the pitfalls and difficulties inherent in colloquial, colorful, or idiomatic usage. . . . a valuable source of reference but also an entertaining and absorbing portrait of the current state of the language." Particular attention is given to the vocabularies of cars, courtesy, food, household items, lectures and conferences, office matters, telephones and other practical situations. Beyond that, Cassell's wry humor is great fun, especially on long bus rides across northern Mexico.

Mexican Slang, A !*#@&%+! Guide by Linton H. Robinson, 1992, Bueno Books, In One Ear Publications, P.O. Box 637, Campo, CA 91906-1128, $6.95. Beginning with a humorous "Sleazy Moral Disclaimer" that warns readers of coarse language ahead, this tiny volume neatly covers everything from "The Obligatory Boring Scholarly Introduction" to Translated Americanisms, Major Mexicanisms, Sex, Drugs, Rock and Roll, Nicknames, Border Slang and even body parts. The writing is skillful and entertaining and the author's translations are "right on." It is a cold day in Coatzacoalcos when I am unable to put down a Spanish text book. *Mexican Slang* is absolutely *padrisimo!*

Larousse Diccionario Moderno: English/Spanish Dictionary by Garcia-Pelayo, 1983, Larousse. Buy this one in Mexico.

Langenscheidt's Pocket Spanish Dictionary Langenscheidt Publishers, N.Y. This plump, pocket-sized dictionary has been my personal favorite for many years. Unlike cheap dictionaries that self-destruct with even average use, Langenscheidt's bright yellow plastic cover is made for hard travel. Better yet, the paper is white and the crisp typeface is readable even in dim, back-of-the-bus conditions. With over 40,000 entries I find that my Langenscheidt easily sees me through non-fiction books, daily newspapers and Spanish magazines.

The Spanish Language Home Page, **<http://www.el-castellano.com/>**. A treasure trove for Spanish students, educators, translators and travelers, with links to online dictionaries, language courses, newspapers and literature.

Spanish on CD, **<http://www.learningco.com/learningco/products/foreign /speak1.html>**.

Learn Spanish, **<http://www.lingolex.com/spanish.htm>**. Useful expressions, live "Espanglish Chat," lots of links to very useful Spanish resources, bookshop and more.

Language Link, **<http://www.langlink.com/>**, (800) 552-2051. A very reliable broker for academic Spanish programs and language schools in Guatemala, Mexico, Costa Rica, Ecuador, Peru and Spain. Kay Rafool is also an enthusiastic People's Guide reader and has given us many valuable suggestions.

NRCSA - The National Registration Center For Study Abroad, **<http://www .nrcsa.com/>**, (414) 278-7410. One of the oldest, largest and most respected booking services for language schools around the world. Includes Spanish, Mayan and Garifuna.

AmeriSpan, **<http://www.amerispan.com/>**, (800) 879-6640. Spanish immersion and educational travel programs throughout Mexico and Latin America.

Latin America Traveler, **<http://www.goodnet.com/~crowdpub/>**. "A Latin America travel and Spanish language school resource, with a subscription-only newsletter.

La Pagina del Idioma Español, **<http://www.pobox.com/~hispano>**.

Live and Retire in Mexico

Choose Mexico: Live Well On $600 A Month, by John Howells and Don Merwin, 1998, The Globe Pequot Press, (800) 243-0495. Though the $600-a-month subtitle might seem difficult to achieve in today's economy, co-author Don Merwin correctly points out that there are literally two sides to every coin in Mexico. As he told us, "We agree that there is a wider disparity than ever before between the prices paid by tourists and by residents (both native and foreign). But the country still has plenty of places where Mexicans and anyone else living there (or smart enough to get off the tourist track) can get accommodations and food of similar quality at a fraction of the cost." The only thing I can add to that is, *Bravo!* On the web, **<http://www.discoverypress. com/mexico.html>**. Also, *Choose Costa Rica,* **<http://www.discoverypress.com /costa.html>**.

Under the Tabachín Tree by Celia Wakefield, 1997, Creative Arts Book Company, Berkeley, CA. Unlike many people who never move beyond daydreams of retiring to some unspoiled corner of Mexico, Celia and Bill Wakefield move to the little-known colonial city of Colima. In describing the personal warmth and rich texture of daily life they enjoy in Mexico, Celia gives reassuring confirmation that life under the Tabachín tree does indeed include both adventure and deep satisfaction.

Mexico Living and Travel by Jean and John D. Bryant, 1994, Mexico Retirement and Travel Assistance, P.O. Box 2190-23, Pahrump, NV 89041-2190. The Bryants are veteran retiree/residents of Guadalajara, who also publish a quarterly retirement newsletter ($25 a year), maps, video and a basic Spanish language guide. *Mexico Living and Travel* offers information on the ever-popular "retirement triangle" of Guadalajara-Ajijic-Chapala, with contributions from about three dozen writers, photographers and artists. The book is an interesting hodgepodge, with short articles on everything from golf in Mexico to descriptions of a wholesale food market, a brief history of Guadalajara, a list of neighborhood-by-neighborhood suggestions for Lake Chapala house rentals and a 25 page advertising section.

Retiring in Guadalajara, Apdo Postal 5-409, Guadalajara, 45000, Jalisco, Mexico. The long-running Furton retirement newsletter gives good detail on prices and homespun advice on life in and around Guadalajara.

AIM: a newsletter on retirement and travel in Mexico, published bimonthly by Adventures in Mexico, Apdo Postal 31-70, Guadalajara, 45050, Jalisco, Mexico. Subscriptions are $16.00 U.S. and $25 in Canada. Detailed information and first-hand reports make this one of the most popular retirement newsletters.

The Gringo's Investment Guide by Ginger Combs-Ramirez, 1994, Monmex Publishing, (406) 682-4967. This book more than fulfills the promise of its subtitle—"Every legal thing you need to know about buying real estate in Mexico." In addition to Ginger Combs-Ramirez considerable experience as an American selling real estate in Mexico, one of the book's strengths is the legal expertise provided by her brother-in-law, a Mexican attorney, and her husband, an attorney and estate planning accountant. The result is an invaluable combination of personal experience and clear, step-by-step legal advice that should give readers the answers they need about owning Mexican real estate.

The Teach English in Mexico Employment Guide, **<http://www.employnow.com/ Mexico.htm>**. Teachers, this site sells a book that will tell you how to teach in Mexico and what you will get paid. This site also sells many good maps of Mexico. (Ron Mader)

Central America

Guatemala Living and Retirement Newsletter, PO Box 669004, A-192, Miami Springs, FL 33266. This recently launched bimonthly newsletter promises articles, encouragement and tips for retirees and wannabe "expats." Their booklet, The Guatemala Bus Traveler's Little Helper is crammed full of bus routes, schedules, travel tips and even hotel information. Email: lifestyles@centramerica.com, and a promise of a website at **<http://www.goguatemala.com>**.

Guatemalan Journey by Stephen Benz, University of Texas Press. Our friend Gary Bevington says, "Benz is a writer and English professor who speaks Spanish and obviously devoted himself to exploring Guatemala and writing about it in a way different from but reminiscent of what you did."

Sweet Waist of America: Journeys around Guatemala by Anthony Daniels, 1990, Hutchinson. Daniels approaches a very difficult topic—making sense of modern Guatemala—with remarkable clarity and objectivity.

I...Rigoberta Menchu: An Indian Woman in Guatemala by Rigoberta Menchu, 1984, Verso Editions. A very disturbing autobiography of the Nobel Prize winning Mayan activist.

Belize First: Your Guide to Travel and Life in Belize by Lan Sluder, Equator Travel Publications, Inc., 280 Beaverdam Road, Candler, NC 28715. Fax: (704) 667-1717. This newsletter in booklet format offers everything from lists of recommended hotels and offbeat news tidbits (my favorite section) to articles on retirement, camping, cheap living, laws and customs, real estate listings, fishing, road conditions, history and whatever else editor/publisher Lan Sluder can shoehorn into 60+ pages. Subscriptions are U.S. $29 a year in the U.S., Canada and Belize, and include an excellent color road map to Belize. Also try: *Caribbean Coast Catalog,* **<http://207.136.90.57/equator/>**. "Hard-to-find books, maps, retirement info and cool Belize stuff."

Belize: Adventures in Nature by Richard Mahler and Steele Wotkyns, John Muir Publications. Everything you need to know about Belize and its natural attractions, from bus travel and jungle lodges to birdwatching and waterfalls.

Belize Retirement Guide: How to live in a Tropical Paradise on $450 a Month, 4th Edition 1998 by Bill and Claire Gray, Preview Publishing, Box 107, Corozal, Belize. $19.95. Email: prepub@btl.net. A nice place to vacation, but would you want to actually live there? As the authors warn, Belize is not for everyone and an exploratory trip is an absolute must. I was impressed by the Grays' frank, down-to-earth assessment of Belize, "warts" and all. The authors obviously take a positive view of the country, but there's no feeling that they're trying to pull the wool over anyone's eyes. All in all, this book nicely fulfills the Grays' purpose of informing their friends of the exciting discovery they've made, while sharing the down-to-earth details of their enviable new life.

Honduras This Week Online, <**http://www.marrder.com/htw/>.** An online weekly magazine of Honduran news, travel, business, environment and culture.

Back to the U.S.A

"Parrot Papers," <**http://www.aphis.usda.gov/oa/petbird.html>.** The official rules and procedures for importing a pet bird into the U.S. from APHIS, the Animal and Plant Health Inspection Service of the U.S. Department of Agriculture.

Plant Protection and Quarantine Permits, <**http://www.aphis.usda.gov/ppq /ppqpermits.html>.** Download U.S.DA permits to legally import plants into the U.S. Information on regulations, plant pests, etc.

Newsletters

The People's Guide Travel Letter: Wherever You Go . . . There You Are! Our own 64-page newsletter on travel, living and study in Mexico and Central America. Published "whenever it's ready," subscriptions are $15 for 4 issues and $5 for a sample: send a check to People's Guide Press, Box 179, Acme, WA 98220. Our email address is mexco@peoplesguide.com. Website: <**http://www.peoplesguide.com/mexico>.** We're often traveling, so please be patient!

After more than 30 years spent knocking around south of the border, my notebooks are bulging with unpublished stories and interesting travel tidbits. In typical *People's Guide* style, both the Travel Letter and our web site document our relentless search for everything that's interesting, offbeat, amazing or just plain weird in Mexico and Central America. Our readers pitch in by sharing their letters, recipes, jokes, articles, misadventures, gripes and hard-earned advice. We do our best to keep the Travel Letter and website <**peoplesguide.com/mexico>** informative and informal. In other words, "This ain't the *New York Times!*"

Mexican Meanderings: A Newsletter of Explorations in an Enchanted Land, by the Felsteds, P.O. Box 33057, Austin, TX 78764, 6 issues a year, $18. In *Mexican Meanderings*, the Felsteds successfully focus each six-page issue on a specific place or region, emphasizing history, architecture, culture and cuisine. Articles are clearly written, thoughtful and well-researched. Simple maps and well-composed black and white photographs add just the right touch. Website: <**http://www.greenbuilder. com /mader/ecotravel/resources/mmex.html>,** email: mexplore @aol. com.

The Mexico File by David Simmonds, Simmonds Publications, (800) 5MEXFILE. "The Newsletter for Mexicophiles" is well-written and definitely worth a look.

Letters from Mexico: Mexico as Seen Through the Eyes of an Expatriate Gringo by Stan Gotlieb, 1996, B & W Enterprises, 707 Kingston Blvd., McHenry, IL 60050. Stan Gotlieb is accurately described as an irreverent, itinerant ne'er-do-well gringo malcontent who has discovered home, patience and a positive attitude while sitting in the sidewalk cafes of Oaxaca. His book, *Letters From Mexico,* is a mixed bag of advice, humor, politics, culture and history. Stan's writing is highly personal and personalized. From the Zapatista uprising to the current status of Mexican bathrooms, his commentaries are meant to remind old visitors of what they might otherwise forget, and to captivate and mobilize the new reader to come and find out for her/him self. Stan's website <**http://www.mexconnect.com/ letters_from_mexico/lettersindex .html>** offers monthly musings, hosted by

MexConnect. For information on his subscription-only email newsletter, contact Stan at stan@mexconnect.com.

Magazines and Newspapers

Mexico Desconocido/Unknown Mexico, Editorial México Desconocido, Monte Pelvoux 110, Planta Jardín, Lomas de Chapultepec, CP 11000 Mexico, DF, Mexico. Fax: 011 52 (5) 540 1771, email: 74052.2055@compuserve.com. Subscriptions in the U.S. and Canada are $65. *Unknown Mexico* is a colorful bilingual magazine that literally covers the map. Typical issues include everything from an article on an island bird sanctuary, the highlands of Zacatecas, the Mexican black bear, pottery in Patambán, *rebozo* weaving, baroque stucco adornment, jade, medicine women and magic among the native Huichol. Over the years, *Mexico Desconocido* has compiled a unique inventory of Mexico's fascinating natural and cultural treasures. Now on the Web, in English, at **<http://www.mexdesco.com/indice.htm>**. View their outstanding links at **<http://www.mexdesco.com/enlace.htm>**.

Transitions Abroad: The Guide to Learning, Living, and Working Overseas, P.O. Box 3000, Denville, NJ 07834-9767. (413) 256-3414. "Alternatives to mass tourism: work, study, travel." This magazine and its related website are both a resource guide and a global how-to-travel information network. If *Transitions Abroad* sounds too serious, don't be fooled; the tone is spirited, with personal accounts of travel, study and work in fascinating places. **<http://www.transabroad.com>**, email: trabroad @aol .com.

MediaINFO Links, **<http://www.mediainfo.com/emedia/>**. A searchable database with links to thousands of newspapers, magazines, radio & television stations and city guide. Also *Newspapers,* **<http://www.explore-mex.com/noticias/periodicos/>**.

e.Traveler! Magazine & Resource Guide, **<http://www.empg.com/etraveler/index .html>**. An online travel magazine & travel resource guide. Interesting links to other travel publications.

One World News, **<http://www.oneworld.org/news/centralam/>**. News of human rights and justice.

Infosel En Linea, **<http://www.infosel.com/>**. *Infosel* (Spanish) is a slick way to check out the headline news.

Connected Traveler, **<http://www.travelmedia.com/connected/index1.html>**. The Connected Traveler has little to say (so far) about Latin America, but with writing as spirited as the following, who can resist? "Just a few years ago, Nepalese gourmet food was an oxymoron. More often than not you were faced with a plate of buffalo meat, a side of lentils, a tough roll and a tub of yak butter."

Books

Armchair Adventures and Fiction

As a wannabe writer, one of the first tips I got on career planning was a succinct, "Whatever you do, don't write about Mexico. Nobody cares." This warning from a successful writer who had lived in Mexico for decades was based on the New York publishing industry's historical lack of interest in anything south of the border. There are exceptions, of course—especially in guidebooks and academic titles—but if we look at the tens of thousands of new books released each year, Mexico-related publications are definitely scarce.

Why do many publishers ignore or avoid Mexico? I really don't have a clue. In fact, given the strong affection so many of us have for Mexico, I would expect readers to jump on books about the country. Putting aside a possible conspiracy theory for the moment, I want to bring your attention to the following interesting and undeservedly obscure titles on Mexico.

Quest For The Lost City by Dana and Ginger Lamb, Santa Barbara Press. When I first began exploring Mexico I was strongly influenced by the Lamb's gutsy yet humorous approach to adventure. The Lambs set off for Mexico in 1937 with $10.16 in their pockets and an unerring, outrageous nose for adventure. Wear a pith helmet and sharpen your machete for this one. Also: *Enchanted Vagabonds* by Lamb and Cleveland, 1938, Harper and Brothers Publishers.

A Small Mexican World (originally entitled *Little Mexico*) by Spratling, 1932, Little, Brown and Company.

A Vagabond in Mexico, by S. Guzmán-C., 1993, Nomads Press, (604) 621-3911. In 1975, S. Guzmán-C. left a "meaningless job and a rather insipid life" and headed for western Mexico. As a tourist Guzmán cannot legally work in Mexico, but nonetheless takes a succession of jobs with fishermen, chicken ranchers, janitors, farmers and leather workers. If finding work does not seem all that difficult in Mexico, the same can't be said for a decent wage. Like millions of Mexicans, Guzmán's initial hopes of a "good living" are gradually replaced by a life of poverty. The author eventually confronts the wrenching dilemma that so many hardworking, impoverished Mexicans face today—that of leaving their friends and family behind and heading north, toward the elusive promise of a better life. *A Vagabond In Mexico* is an unusual, thought-provoking book. In particular, anyone who thinks that Mexican "illegals" are easily drawn over the border should find it instructive.

Viva Mexico! a Traveller's Account of Life in Mexico by Charles Flandrau, 1990, Eland & Hippocrene. First published in 1908, this humorous but compassionate account of five years on a remote coffee plantation is probably my favorite book on Mexico. Flandrau's insights into the customs and character of rural Mexicans—and expatriate *gringos*—still apply today.

Face to Face with the Mexicans by Francis Gardiner Gooch, 1887, reprint by Southern Illinois University Press.

Judas at the Jockey Club and Other Episodes of Porfirian Mexico by William H. Beezley, 1987, University of Nebraska Press. The author's scholarly credentials and the odd title almost diverted me from a most illuminating and delightful "read." Where else would you find the history of bicycling in Mexico? This book is a goldmine of trivia, fascinating anecdotes and unusual historical tidbits.

Old Mother Mexico by Harry Carr, 1931, Houghton Mifflin Company.

Terry's Guide by T. Philip Terry, later editions by James Norman. (Older editions of this classic guide 1906 to 1938 are prized by collectors.)

Stones for Ibarra by Harriet Doerr is a bright, moving account of Americans living in a small Mexican village. (fiction)

Under the Volcano by Malcolm Lowry. A dark, introspective and powerfully written *cantina*-crawl that probably isn't for everyone. (fiction)

Gringos by Charles Portis, author of *True Grit*, presents an entertaining saga of expatriate escapades among the Maya. Also good: *The Dog of the South* (fiction).

The Long Night of White Chickens by Goldman, 1992, Atlantic Monthly Press (fiction).

The Man Who Likes Mexico by Wallace Gillpatrick, 1912, The Century Co.

The Mexicans: A Personal Portrait of a People by Patrick Oster, 1989, Harper and Row Publishers.

Aztec by Gary Jennings. A complete "hammock book," this thick, sexy historical saga oozes blood and pre-Columbian details. (fiction)

The Treasure of the Sierra Madre by Bruno Traven. You've seen the movie, now try the book. (fiction)

The Volcanoes from Puebla by Kenneth Gangemi, 1979, Marion Boyars

Publishers Inc., 99 Main St., Salem, NH 03079, $9.95. A long series of topics and observations neatly arranged in alphabetical order. From Acapulco and Bakery, through Cerveza . . . and Mangoes . . ., Gangemi's attention shifts from Political Notes . . . to Street Snacks . . . and finally, Zocalo. "I considered it an achievement, for someone of my background, to be able to sit quietly in a plaza and do absolutely nothing. When I lived in Mexico I had the time for such a worthwhile activity. Sitting in the plaza I had the time to think about the really important things, such as the differences between the morning and afternoon sunshine." Highly recommended!

Travelers' Tales: Mexico by James O'Reilly and Larry Habegger, 1994, Travelers' Tales Inc. An anthology of articles, stories and musings from a wide variety of authors.

Where the Strange Roads Go Down by del Villar, 1953.

The Bakery of the Three Whores (poetry) by James, 1994, InkPot Press,

The Three Pigs: Los Tres Cerdos by Bobbi Salinas, 1998, Piñata Publications. An illustrated bilingual fable by the author of *Indo Hispanic Folk Traditions*.

Culture

The Art of Crossing Cultures by Craig Storti, 1990, Intercultural Press, Inc. If you've dreamed of living in Mexico but wondered how you'd adapt, this book analyzes the causes of culture shock and gives how-to-cope suggestions that really work. Storti avoids lecturing and tempers practical advice on dealing with foreign cultures with illuminating examples and entertaining excerpts from an illustrious field of writers.

Distant Neighbors by Alan Riding. A fascinating look at the inner workings of Mexico, from popular customs to its complex political systems. Highly praised, even by Mexicans.

Beyond Culture by Edward Hall, 1981, Anchor Books, Doubleday. The author examines the roots of culture and suggests why Mexicans are so uniquely . . . *Mexican.*

A Treasury of Mexican Folkways: The Customs, Myths, Folklore, Traditions, Beliefs, Fiestas, Dances, and Songs of the Mexican People by Toor, 1985, Bonanza Books. *Mexico South: The Isthmus of Tehuantepec* by Covarrubias, 1946, Alfred A. Knopf. Two classic works on Mexican culture and folkways.

Indo-Hispanic Folk Art Traditions (2 volumes) by Bobbi Salinas-Norman, 1991, Piñata Publications. A combination of classroom and home projects, essays and illustrations that makes an excellent introduction to the cultural spirit of Hispanic America.

Indigenous Peoples of Mexico, <http://www.indians.org/welker/mex_main .htm>. Native American traditions, history, art and literature presented by tribe as well as by geographical region.

Mexican Heritage Almanac, <http://www.ironhorse.com/~nagual/alma.html>. Pre-columbian calendars, folk music, Mexican news and more. Don't miss Victor's modestly presented but impressive credentials, as well as some excellent resources, available by clicking on "feedback" at the bottom of the home page. Wonderful!

Mariachis, <http://www.geocities.com/~puro_mariachi/>. This is it! Your all-in-one site for mariachi music, including lyrics, performance dates, history, books, CDs and so forth.

Mexican Dance, Music, Art & Culture Web Sites, <http://www.alegria.org /mxother.html>. A feast of Mexican dance companies, folk dance information and discussion, regional dances, plus links to music, art and culture sites.

Chupacabra, The Official Home Page, <princeton.edu/~accion/chupa.html>. It's a hoot, and I've even heard the *chupacabra* described as a deliberate government attempt to keep Mexicans' mind off the economy! (Kay Rafool)

Contemporary Culture and Entertainment, <http://udgftp.cencar.udg.mx/ingles/ cultura/cultura.html>. Interesting and refreshingly off-the-wall web pages from the First University of Guadalajara.

Esquizofrenia Comics: El Webzine del Comic y los Eventos Mexicanos,

<http://www.geocities.com/Area51/Dimension/8638/>. Tune up your hip, streetwise Spanish on these online comix. Also: *Yaoyotl Teteo,* <http://udgftp.cencar.udg.mx /ingles/teteo/iintro.html>.
La Chingada, <http://csgwww.uwaterloo.ca/~dmg>. They don't teach this kind of Spanish at the local high school. . . .
Mexico Arts: Universes in Universe, <http://www.kulturbox.de/univers/america /mex/english.htm>. A major collection of Mexican art links and online resources.
Mummy Museum, <http://www.sirius.com/~dbh/mummies/>. The Museo de las Momias is not for viewers with a weak stomach. If you've never heard of Guanajuato's famous mummies, you may want to skip this site and remain blissfully ignorant.
University of Guadalajara, <http://udgftp.cencar.udg.mx/ingles/CUAADINGLES .html>.

History
The Conquest of Mexico by Hugh Thomas, 1993, Random House. Using previously unpublished material gleaned from ancient archives, the author has created the only history book I simply couldn't put down. His story of the Conquest is a fantastic accomplishment that outdoes fiction.
Many Mexicos by Lesly Byrd Simpson. The author untangles several confusing revolutions and throws in the strange-but-true story of Santa Anna's missing leg for good measure.

Nature & EcoTravel
Gathering the Desert by Gary Nabhan, 1985, The University of Arizona Press. Nabhan's talent for nature writing puts all of his books high on my "favorites" list.
Handbook of Indian Foods and Fibers of Arid America by Ebeling, 1986, University of California Press. If you're interested in the life of pre-Columbian Americans, this ponderous tome is well worth reading.
Birds of Mexico and Central America by L. Irby Davis, U of Texas Press. Lorena's favorite!
On the Road to Tetlama: Mexican Adventures of a Wandering Naturalist by Jim Conrad, 1991, Walker Publishing Co. A quiet, introspective account of the author's solo journey.
A Handbook of Mexican Roadside Flora by Charles T. Mason Jr. and Patricia B. Mason, 1987, The University of Arizona Press. Shortly after tearing my hair out over a mysterious but common plant in western Chihuahua, I was mercifully given a copy of *Mexican Roadside Flora* by Mary Lou Wilcox, a botanist and natural history book dealer. As she noted, my tantrum over a dusty specimen of Randia echinocarpa is all-too-common when ignorant "greenhorn" botanists like myself attempt to identify many common Mexican plants. In addition to a brief overview of Mexico's geography and vegetation, this excellent book has a simple plant key, a basic botanical glossary, a good reference list and many line drawings.
Volcano World, <volcano.und.nodak.edu>. Eruption alerts and good things for children. Everything you ever wanted to know about volcanoes. (Kay Rafool)
Green-Travel, <http://www.green-travel.com>. Marcus Endicott introduced me to the amazing world of Internet travel several years ago when he suggested that I subscribe to an email list that discussed eco-travel. Marcus offers an exceptionally rich website with an almost overwhelming link list.
Eco Travels in Latin America, <http://www2.planeta.com/mader/>. Ron Mader's Eco Travels ranks near the top of my personal WWW favorites. ". . . the Internet's foremost clearinghouse of environmental news and ecotourism information for the Americas. You'll find short articles and in-depth reports, book reviews, lists of travel providers and Spanish language schools. The best news - all of this is free." Includes

the *Planeta Platica* environmental newsletter, an excellent Directory of Spanish Language Schools and other education resources, as well as one of the most interesting eco-oriented travel archives on the Web.

Book Stores and Sources

To locate a particular book on Mexico, consult *Books in Print* at your local library, ask a bookstore to do a computer search by title or author, or, if you have Internet access, you can do the search yourself at one of the suggested websites below.

If you're a serious reader, request catalogs from regional and university presses in the American Southwest and California (ask your librarian for addresses). Most publications on Mexico are considered regional or special-interest and won't be distributed nationwide. *Index of Periodicals* is another excellent source of information on camping in Mexico. This reference source lists virtually every magazine article ever written. Don't overlook used bookstores; I recently found a dusty first edition (signed by the author) of a fine 1930s travel book on Mexico for $3.

Book Searches

Bibliofind, **<http://www.bibliofind.com>**. Used book searches. "Five million old, used and rare books offered here for sale by 1750 booksellers around the world make this the largest and possibly the most interesting bookselling site on the Web." This is the place to look for out-of-print books such as our 1981 *People's Guide To Camping, Backpacking & Boating in Mexico.*

Book Exchange, Used & Rare, **<http://www.abebooks.com/>**. Suggested by Jerry at Thaddeus Books as his first choice for finding used, rare and out-of-print books on the Web. Includes a list of used bookstores with links to browse each store's inventory.

Bookdatabase, **<http://www.interloc.com/bookdata.htm>**. A searchable book database—simple and fast.

Books Con Salsa, etc., **<http://www.brainiac.com/gordon/>**. Antiquarian, out-of-print and scarce books, ephemera and other items, with particular emphasis on Latin America.

Biblioteca digital (Digital Library), **<http://sunsite.unam.mx/biblioteca.htm>**. UNAM's extensive links to online books, magazines, museums, newspapers and more. Most are in Spanish.

Book Stores

Wide World Books & Maps, **<http://www.travelbooksandmaps.com/>**, Seattle, WA, (888) 534-3453, email: travel@speakeasy.org. The first travel-only book and map store in the U.S. Excellent bookstore with mind-boggling selection. Phone orders and recommendations.

Powell's Travel Books, **<http://www.powells.com/>**, Portland, OR, (800) 878-7323. Another justifiably famous bookstore.

Book Passage! **<http://www.bookpassage.com/>**. "The Bay Area's Liveliest

Bookstore" offers a lively web page with an excellent selection of travel books and maps.

Bon Voyage! Fresno, CA, (800) 995-9716. Books, maps and accessories such as PUR water filters, luggage tags and locks, travel packs and . . . *biodegradable toilet seat covers*?

Tolliver's Books, Los Angeles, CA, (213) 939-6054. New, used and out-of-print books on travel and natural history, archaeology, Mexican antiquities, Baja and the Sea of Cortez. Tell them your interest and they'll send you a specific catalog that will drive you wild with temptation.

Art Books of Latin America, **<http://www.cts.com/~karnobks>**, Valley Center, CA, (800) 34-KARN0. . email: karnobooks@cts.com. New, out-of-print and rare books, catalogs and monographs.

Central America Resource Center, PO Box 2327, Austin, TX 78768. Books on social and political activism, economics, refugees and peace programs in Mexico and Central America.

Flora & Fauna Books, Seattle, WA, (206) 623-4727. "Natural History Book & Print Specialists." Looking for a cassette tape of Belizean bird songs or the book, *A Naturalist's Mexico*? Ask for a book list.

Curious Cat Travel Books, **<http://www.curiouscat.com/travel>**, email: travel@ curiouscat.com. Imagine how dull cyberspace would be with just one gigantic Amazon-sized bookstore. Curious Cat has a good selection of travel books at 20 to 30 percent off.

Amazon.com, **<http://www.amazon.com>**. Millions of titles, so little time. . . . I use Amazon.com to search for off-the-wall, out of print and hard to find travel titles. Their reader's reviews are also a good feature.

World Wide of Books and Maps: Vancouver, Canada. (604) 687-3320.

Maps and Sources

Don't expect to find road maps in Mexican gas stations—or even in Mexican book stores. In fact, it's best to buy maps before you leave home, unless you want map hunting to be your first errand in Mexico. Road maps of Mexico are usually available in the U.S. at gas stations near the border, tourist agencies, large hotels, insurance offices, and Mexican Consulate and National Tourism offices. Get two copies; you'll lose or loan one map almost immediately.

Campers, birdwatchers and amateur explorers will want something better than a gas-station map. The most reliable sources I know of Mexican topographic maps, sea charts and other specialized maps are listed below. Topos and specialty maps are published and sold in Mexico by various government agencies, but like most such bureaucratic enterprises, you can grow old trying to track them down. Again, it is far easier to use a map service in the U.S.

In general, our experience has been that topo maps aren't nearly as accurate as those in the U.S., especially if you need several to cover a proposed trip or an area of interest. Major foot trails may not be shown, rivers are missing, villages misplaced and so on. If a river is shown on two out of three maps, there's a reasonable chance that it actually exists.

INEGI: Mexico's mapping agency is the National Institute of Statistics, Geography and Information. My first stop when flying into Mexico City is INEGI's excellent hole-in-the-wall shop in the airport's main concourse. They sell topographic and relief maps, Carta Turistica road maps and charts. Their prices are very fair. The selection, especially of topos, is broad but unpredictable. If you need a specific topo badly, I'd query sources in the U.S. first. INEGI's website is loaded with maps, statistics, economic info, census figures, international events and on and on. Unfortunately, I still can't figure out how to order anything from the online catalog: **<http://www.inegi .gob.mx/homeing/homeinegi/homeing.html>.**

Geocentro is a Mexico City map store that has aerial photos, topos, road maps, atlases and books. San Francisco 1375 Esquina Tlacoquemecatl, Colonia del Valle, Mexico, DF.

State and countrywide maps are also available in larger bookstores, sidewalk newsstands and magazine kiosks throughout Mexico. Prices are low but the selection is poor. Don't expect to find maps of the entire country in local tourist offices or travel agencies.

The best road atlas of Mexico ever published, by Pemex (the government oil monopoly), is called *Atlas de Carreteras*. For unknown reasons this best-selling atlas is still out of print. If you find a copy, buy it and don't loan it out.

Guia Roji, <guiaroji.com.mx>, is Mexico's largest publisher of highly detailed city maps and state road maps. Unless you've got 20/20 vision, however, their maps are notoriously difficult to read. Drawbacks aside, Roji maps are inexpensive in Mexico, well-researched, reliable and widely available. By the way, most gringos mistakenly call these maps Guia Roja (Red Guide). Roji Guides are named for their illustrious founder, Seusly diffiA complete **geographical atlas** published by Porrua *(Nuevo Atlas de la Republica Mexicana)* is sold in some Mexican bookstores. It is inexpensive and well worth having.

Carta Turistica: There are eight "Tourist" maps in this outdated but still useful series, including seven regional maps and a single sheet map of the entire country. Large and easy to read, with some topographic shading. (scale 1:1,000,000). Look for the *Carta Turista* in Mexico or try U.S. map stores.

Topo maps for the Copper Canyon (1:50,000) are sold at the Tarahumara Mission Store near the train station in Creel. (This is also the best source of books, postcards and Tarahumara crafts. Profits benefit the Tarahumara health clinic.)

Guatemala

Road maps of Guatemala are hard to find and topos are even worse; because of military paranoia, most of Guatemala is "classified" and detailed maps are not sold to the public. Ironically, you can buy Guatemalan topo maps by ordering from the U.S. Write to the **Instituto Geographico Nacional**, Avenida las Americas 5-76, Zona 13, Guatemala, C.A.

The best map I've ever used in Central America is the *Traveller's Reference Map of Guatemala and El Salvador,* by Kevin Healy, from **ITM** (see below).

If you're not a member of AAA (American Automobile Association) and eligible for free maps, your best bet is a road map and city guide by the **Instituto Geográfico Militar** (Avenida Las Americas 5-76, Zona 13, Guatemala City). They also sell detailed maps for back country explorers. Some maps are restricted and can be studied in their offices but not purchased, presumably to keep them out of the hands of guerrillas.

A fairly good road map co-published by **ESSO** and **INGUAT**, the Guatemalan Tourist Commission, is sold in some tourist shops and bookstores. INGUAT'S main office is in Guatemala City at 7a Avenida 1-17, Centro Civico. In the U.S., write them at P.O. Box 144351, Coral Gables, FL 33114-4351.

Map Dealers

Traveller's Reference Series, International Travel Map Production, Vancouver, Canada, (604) 687-3320. They publish our favorite travel maps, including Mexico, Baja, Southern Mexico and the Yucatán, a street map of Mexico City, Central America, Belize, plus great maps of Guatemala and El Salvador, and Honduras. Typical **ITM**

maps are large, with crisp definition and sharp lettering, and are quite readable in low-light hotel rooms and bouncing buses. Multicolored topographical features make it easy to distinguish major mountain ranges and river drainages. Unlike maps that go blank at borders, these include portions of the adjoining countries.

Wide World Books & Maps, Seattle, WA, (206) 634-3453, email: travel@ speakeasy.org, web: **<http://www.travelbooksandmaps.com>**. Carta Turistica, Guia Roji, Baja Atlases (north & south), ITMB and even Edwin Raisz's famous hand drawn geological relief map.

San Diego Map Centre, (619) 291-3830. A very good stock of maps, charts, cruising guides and books. Their imported map prices are very fair. Ask for a catalog.

Map World, <http://www.mapworld.com/maps/>, San Diego, CA. Maps, topos, books and globes.

Map Link, <http://www.maplink.com/>, Santa Barbara, CA, (805) 965-4402. Mexican topographic maps, the Pronto Mexico City atlas, excellent maps of Belize and Guatemala (and other Central American countries).

Tucson Map and Flag Center, Tucson, AZ, (800) 473-1204. Topos, travel maps, books.

Wide World of Maps, Phoenix, AZ, (602) 279-2323. Maps, charts and books.

Tucson Blueprint, PO Box 27266, Tucson, AZ 85726. Topos and historical maps of Mexico.

US Geological Survey, <http://mapping.usgs.gov/esic/to_order.html>. Online ordering.

Southtrek, <http://www.southtrek.com>. Southtrek sells a huge variety of maps of Mexico, as well as other Latin American countries. Be warned—the Shockwave noise is somewhat irritating for an otherwise excellent commercial site. (Jennifer Rose)

Aeronautical Charts: Large scale aeronautical charts are published by the U.S. Department of Commerce, National Oceanic and Atmospheric Administration, National Ocean Survey C-44, Riverdale, MD 20840. Four big charts cover all of Mexico, Guatemala and Belize.

Sea Charts: Charts of Mexican waters designed for ship navigation are published by the U.S. Defense Mapping Agency, 5801 Tabor Avenue, Philadelphia, PA 19120. Ask for their catalog. They are slow, so do it early.

Cruising Charts, P.O. Box 976, Patagonia, AZ 85624, (602) 394-2393.

If you've discovered a worthwhile, book, map, website or other information source on Latin America, please share it by writing us at PO Box 179, Acme, WA 98220 or email: mexico@peoplesguide.com.

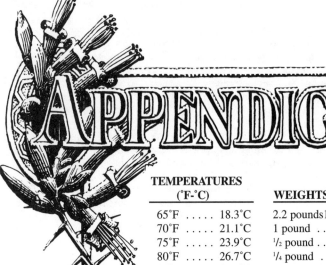

APPENDICES

TEMPERATURES
(°F-°C)

°F	°C
65°F	18.3°C
70°F	21.1°C
75°F	23.9°C
80°F	26.7°C
85°F	29.4°C
90°F	32 2°C
95°F	35.0°C
98.6°F	37.0°C
99.0°F	37.2°C
99.5°F	37.5°C
100.0°F	37.8°C
100.5°F	38.1°C
101.0°F	38.3°C
101.5°F	38.6°C
102.0°F	38.9°C
103.0°F	39.4°C
104.0°F	40.0°C
105.0°F	40.6°C
106.0°F	41.1°C

°F	°C
250°F	121°C
275°F	135°C
300°F	149°C
325°F	163°C
350°F	177°C
375°F	191°C
400°F	204°C
450°F	232°C
500 F	260°C
550°F	288°C

WEIGHTS AND MEASURES

2.2 pounds	1,000 grams (1 kilo)
1 pound	454 grams
½ pound	227 grams
¼ pound	113.5 grams
1 ounce	28.35 grams

1 quart	.95 liters
1 gallon	3.875 liters
5 gallons	19.4 liters
10 gallons	38.75 liters
15 gallons	58.1 liters
20 gallons	77.5 liters
25 gallons	96.9 liters

1 inch	2.54 centimeters
1 foot	30.5 centimeters
1 yard	91.5 centimeters
	or .915 meters
1 mile	1.61 kilometers

centimeter	39 inches
meter	3.28 feet
kilometer	.62 miles

TO CONVERT:

• Temperature in degrees F to Centigrade:
  °F - 32 x .55 = °C
• Temperature in degrees C to Fahrenheit:
  °C + 17.8 x 1.8 = °F
• Multiply *liters* by .26 to get *gallons*.
• Multiply *gallons* by 3.8 to get *liters*.

VOCABULARY

GETTING AROUND

Ticket window	*Caja, taquilla*	First class	*Primera clase*
Reservation	*Reservación*	Second class	*Segunda clase*
Reserved seat	*Asiento reservado*	Taxi	*Taxi, Libre, Coche*
Arrivals & Departures (posted on 24 hour time system)	*Llegadas y Salidas*	Taxi stand	*Sitio*
		Boat	*Lancha*
		Canoe	*Canoa*
		Pack animal	*Bestia*
On the hour	*Cada hora*	Bus station	*Terminal* or *estación de autobuses*
Every half hour	*Cada media hora*		
Daily	*Diario*		
Passenger	*Pasajero*	Bus stop	*Parada*
Driver	*Chófer*	Train station	*Estación de ferrocarril*
Line or company	*Línea* or *compañía*		
To get aboard	*Subir*	Ticket	*Boleto*
To get off	*Bajar*	Ride	*Aventón, Ride*
Airport	*Aeropuerto*	I'm going to	*Me voy a . . .*
Bus	*Autobús, camión*	Where are you going?	*¿Dónde va?*
City bus	*Servicio urbano*		
Train	*Ferrocarril, Tren*	Get in	*Sube*
Airplane	*Avión*		

I want a ticket to . . . ? — *Quiero un boleto a . . .*

How much is a ticket to . . . ? — *¿Cuánto cuesta un boleto a . . .?*

What bus line goes to . . . ? — *¿Qué línea tiene servico a . . .?*

What is the number of the bus? — *¿Qué is el número del autobús?*

What time does the bus leave for . . . ? — *¿A qué hora sale el camión a . . . ?*

Where does it leave from?— *¿De dónde sale?*

Where does this bus go? — *¿Dónde va este autobús?*

How many hours is it to . . . ? — *¿Cuántas horas a...?*

I lost my baggage. — *Se me perdió mi equipaje.*

How much time do we have here? — *¿Cuánto tiempo tenemos aquí?*

Let me off at the corner (off here). — *Quiero bajar en la esquina (aquí).*

Will you give me a ride to . . . ? — *¿Me da un aventón a . . . ?*

I'm traveling by thumb. — *Viajo por aventón.*

What will you charge to take me to . . . ? — *¿Cuánto me cobra llevarme a . . .?*

HOTELS AND HOUSES

Hotel	*Hotel*	Extra bed	*Cama extra*
Motel	*Motel*	Blanket	*Cobija, cubierta*
Inn	*Posada*	Cot	*Catre*
Hammock	*Hamaca*	Shower	*Regador, Regadera*
Bathroom	*Baño*	Hot water	*Agua caliente*
Bath	*Baño*	Fan	*Ventilador, abanico*
Boarding house,	*Casa de huéspedes,*	Air conditioned	*Aire acondicionado*
Guest house	*Pensión*	Manager	*Gerente, Dueño*
Room, double	*Cuarto doble*	Dining room	*Comedor*
Key	*Llave*	Bar	*Bar*
Bed	*Cama*	Swimming pool	*Alberca, Piscina*
Double bed	*Cama matrimonial*	Noise	*Ruido*

Do you know of a cheap hotel? — *¿Conoce usted un hotel económico?*
Do you have a room for two? — *¿Hay un cuarto para dos personas?*
Do you have a room with bath?— *¿Hay un cuarto con baño?*
with meals — *con comidas*
without meals — *sin comidas*
Is the car safe?—*¿Está seguro el coche?*
Is there a night watchman at the parking lot. — *¿Hay un velador en el estacionamiento?*
Do you have ice? — *¿Hay heilo?*
Please put in a cot for the child. — *Favor de poner un catre para el niño.*
The toilet is stopped up. — *Está tapada la taza.*

House	*Casa*	Furnished	*Amueblada*
To rent	*Alquilar, Rentar*	Electricity	*Electricidad*
For rent	*Se renta,*	Room	*Cuarto*
	Se alquila	Bedroom	*Recamara*
To sell	*Vender*	Living room	*Sala*
For sale	*Se vende*	Kitchen	*Cocina*
By the week, month	*Por la semana,*	Stove	*Estufa*
	el mes	Refrigerator	*Refrigerador*
Landlord, owner	*Dueño-a*	Maid	*Criada*

Is this house for rent? — *¿Está de renta la casa?*
Who owns this house? — *¿Quién es el dueño de esta casa?*
Where does s/he live? — *¿Dónde vive?*
How much is it per month? — *¿Cuánto es por mes?*

FOOD AND DRINK

Restaurant	*Restaurante,*	Dessert	*Postre*
	Comedor	Beverage	*Bebida*
	Lonchería,	Fork	*Tenedor*
	Fonda	Spoon	*Cuchara*
Daily special	*Comida corrida*	Knife	*Cuchillo*
Menu	*Menú*	Cup	*Taza*
An order	*Un orden*	Glass	*Vaso*

Meal	*Comida*	Napkin	*Servilleta*
Plate	*Plato*	Toothpick	*Palillo*
Snack	*Antojito, Botana*	The bill	*La cuenta*

What is there to eat? (to drink?) — *¿Que hay de comer? (de tomar?)*
Are there . . . ? (beans, eggs) — *¿Hay . . . ? (frijoles, huevos)*
I want . . . — *Quiero . . .*
We want . . . — *Queremos . . .*
The bill, please — *La cuenta por favor.*
We want to pay separately. — *Queremos pagar aparte*
The meal was very good. — *La comida estuvo muy sabrosa.*

Liquor	*Licor*	Draft beer	*Cerveza de barril*
Drink	*Copita*	Wine	*Vino*
Cocktail	*Coctel, Jaibol*	Sweet	*Dulce*
Glass	*Vaso*	Dry	*Seco*
Aged	*Añejo*	Case	*Cartón*
Soda water	*Agua mineral (con gas)*	Bottle opener	*Destapador*
		Bottle cap	*Ficha*
Ice cubes	*Cubitos de heilo*	Ice pick	*Picahielos*
Bottle	*Botella*	Opened	*Destapada*
Beer	*Cerveza*	Room temperature	*Al tiempo*
Dark beer	*Cerveza oscura, negra*		

I'm really drunk. — *Estoy bien pedo.*
I have a terrible hangover. — *Estoy muy crudo.*
I'd like to buy you a beer. — *Le invito a una cheve (cerveza).*

POST OFFICE, TELEGRAPH, TELEPHONE, BANK

Post office	*Correo*	Special handling	*Entrega Inmediata*
General Delivery	*Lista de Correos*	Registered	*Registrado*
Letter	*Carta*	Certified	*Certificado*
Address	*Direción*	Postal money order	*Giro*
Return address	*Direción del remitente*	Package, box	*Paquette, caja*
		Wrapped	*Envuelto*
Return to . . .	*Remite a . . .*	String	*Cuerda*
Envelope	*Sobre*	Glue	*Pegamento*
Stamp	*Estampilla, timbre*	Duty, tax	*Impuesto*
Postcard	*Tarjeta*	Weight	*Peso*
Airgram	*Aereogramo*	Change of address card	*Tarjeta de cambiar direccíon*
Airmail	*Correo aereo*		
Regular mail	*Ordinario*		

Is there any mail in General Delivery for Joe Blow?—*¿Hay algo en la lista para Joe Blow?*
Weigh it, please. — *Péselo, por favor.*
Does it need more postage?—*¿Necesita más estampillas?*
Three airmail envelopes, please. — *Tres sobres aereos, por favor.*

Telegraph office	*Telégrafos*	Regular	*Ordinario*

Telegram	*Telegrama*	Night letter	*Carta nocturna,*
Urgent	*Urgente*		*Carta de noche*

I would like to send a telegram to . . . — *Quiero mandar una telegrama a . . .*

Telephone	*Teléfono*	Long distance	*Larga distancia*
Telephone office	*Oficina de teléfonos*	Collect	*Al cobrar*
To call	*Llamar*	Person to person	*Persona a persona*
A call	*Una llamada*	Station to station	*A quien contesta*
Number	*Número*	Credit card	*Tarjeta de crédito*
Operator	*Operador*	Hello!	*¡Ola!, ¡Bueno!*

I want to call the United States, please. The number is . . . — *Quiero llamar a los Estados Unidos. El número es . . .*

Money	*Dinero, lana*	Dollar	*Dólar*
Change	*Cambio, feria,*	Bill	*Billete*
	suelto	To cash, change	*Cambiar*
Check	*Cheque*	Bank	*Banco*
Personal check	*Cheque personal*	Teller's window	*Caja*
Traveler's check	*Cheque de viajero*	Signature	*Firma*
Bank draft	*Cheque del banco*		
Money order	*Giro*		
Mexican currency	*Moneda Nacional (MN)*		

Can you cash a traveler's check? — *¿Se puede cambiar un cheque de viajero?*

HEALTH

Health	*Salud*	Pill	*Pastilla*
Doctor	*Medico, Doctor*	Capsule	*Capsula*
Hospital	*Hospital*	Aspirin	*Aspirina*
Drugstore	*Farmacia*	Salve, ointment	*Pomada*
Sick	*Enfermo*	Bandage	*Venda*
Pain	*Dolor*	Adhesive Tape	*Cinta adhesiva*
Fever	*Fiebre*	Cotton	*Algodón*
Headache	*Dolor de cabeza*	Vitamin	*Vitamina*
Cold, Flu	*Gripe*	Birth control pills	*Pastillas*
Stomach-ache	*Dolor de estómago*		*contraceptivas*
Diarrhea	*Diarrea*	Kotex, Tampax	Use brand name
Cough	*Tos*	Dentist	*Dentista,*
Burn	*Quemadura*		*sacamuelas*
Sunburn	*Quemadura del sol*		(molar puller)
Cramp	*Calambre*	Toothache	*Dolor de muelas*
Medicine	*Medicina*	Shot, injection	*Inyección*
Antibiotic	*Antibiótico*	Toothbrush	*Cepillo dental*
Cough syrup	*Jarabe para tos*	Toothpaste	*Crema dental*

I have a headache, stomach-ache, etc. — *Me duele la cabeza, estómago, etc.*
I have a cold, flu, cough, etc. — *Tengo gripe, tos, etc.*
I need medicine for diarrhea. — *Necesito medicina para diarrea.*
Do you know a good doctor?—*¿Conoce un buen medico?*

GAS STATIONS, CAR PARTS, TERMS

Gas station	*Gasolinera*	Grease	*Grasa*
Pump	*Bomba*	To grease	*Engrasar*
Gas cap	*Tapón, tapa*	Grease job	*Lubricación, grasa*
Tank	*Tanque*	Oil change	*Cambio de aceite*
Gasoline	*Gasolina*	Oil	*Aceite*

Fill it up, please. — *Lleno, por favor.*
Check the oil and water, please. — *Vea el aceite y agua, por favor.*
I want an oil change and grease job. — *Quiero un cambio de aceite y lubricatión.*
Check the oil in the transmission and differential. — *Vea el aceite en la caja y diferencial.*
Put in a liter of 30 weight oil, please. — *Eche un litro de aceite número treinta, por favor.*
Put 30 pounds of air in the tires. — *Ponga treinta libras de aire en las llantas.*
Where is the restroom? — *¿Dónde está el baño?*
Do you have a map of Mexico? — *¿Hay un mapa de la republica?*

Accelerator	*Acelerador*	Bumper	*Defensa*
Adjust	*Ajustar*	Bus	*Autobús, camión*
Adjusting stars	*Ajustadores de*	Bushing	*Bushing, buje*
(brakes)	*frenos*	Cable	*Cable*
A-frame	*Horguilla*	Camshaft	*Arbol de levas*
Air filter	*Filtro de aire*	Camshaft bearings	*Metales de árbol*
Air filter cartridge	*Cartucho del filtro*		*de levas*
	de aire	Car	*Coche, automóvil,*
Alternator	*Alternador*		*carro*
Armature	*Rotor*	Carburetor	*Carburador*
Assemble	*Armar*	Carburetor float	*Flotador*
Auto electric shop	*Taller auto-*	Carburetor jet	*Esprea*
	eléctrico	Choke	*Ahogador*
Auto parts	*Refacciones*	Clutch	*Clutch*
Auto parts store	*Refaccionería*	Clutch disc	*Disco de clutch*
Axle	*Eje*	Clutch pedal	*Pedal de clutch*
Brake shoe	*Zapata*	Coil	*Bobina*
Ball bearings	*Baleros*	Condenser	*Condensador*
Ball joints	*Rótulas*	Coil springs	*Resortes*
Battery	*Acumulador,*	Crankcase	*Monoblock*
	batería	Crankshaft	*Cigüeñal*
Battery cable	*Cable de*	Cylinder	*Cilindro*
	acumulador	Cylinder sleeve	*Camisa*
Block	*Monoblock*	Differential	*Diferencial*
Body and paint	*Hojalatería y*	Dismantle	*Desarmar*
shop	*Pintura*	Distributor	*Distribuidor*
Boot (tire)	*Huarache*	Distributor cap	*Tapa de*
Brakes	*Frenos*		*distribuidor*
Brake drum	*Tambor*	Drive	*Manejar*
Brake fluid	*Líquido de frenos*	Drive shaft	*Flecha cardán*
Brake line	*Mangera de frenos*	Electrical system	*Sistema eléctrica*
Brake lining	*Balata*	Fan	*Ventilador*
Brake pedal	*Pedal de frenos*	Fan belt	*Banda de*
Brake plate	*Plato de frenos*		*ventilador*
Gas tank	*Tanque de gasolina*	Fender	*Guardabarro*
Brushes	*Carbones*	Fields	*Campos*

Fly wheel	*Engrane volante*	Panel truck	*Camioneta, panel*
Frame	*Bastidor*	Parking lot	*Estacionamiento*
Front wheel	*Alineación*	Patch	*Parche*
alignment		Pickup truck	*Camioneta*
Front wheel	*Baleros de las*	Piston	*Pistón*
bearings	*reudas adelantes*	Pitman arm	*Brazo Pitman*
Front wheel spindle	*Mango*	Points	*Platinos*
Fuel pump	*Bomba de gasolina*	Pressure plate	*Plato de presión*
Fuse	*Fusible*	Pulley	*Polea*
Garage (repair)	*Taller mecánico,*	Push rod	*Levador, puntería*
	taller automotriz	Radiator	*Radiador*
Gas cap	*Tapón de gasolina*	Radiator cap	*Tapón de radiador*
Gas line	*Tubo, mangera de*	Radiator hose	*Mangera de*
	gasolina		*radiador*
Gas tank	*Tanque de gasolina*	Re-cap (tire)	*Recubierta*
Gasket	*Empaque, junta*	Relay	*Relé*
Gasket set	*Juego de empaques*	Rings	*Anillos*
Gear	*Engrane*	Compression ring	*Anillo de*
Gear shift lever	*Palanca de cambios*		*compresión*
Generator	*Generador*	Oil ring	*Anillo de aceite*
Ground	*Tierra*	Rocker arm	*Balancín*
Hand brake	*Freno de mano*	Rod	*Biela*
Head	*Cabeza*	Rod bearing (insert)	*Metales de bielas*
Head gasket	*Empaque de cabeza*	Rotor	*Rotor*
Headlights	*Focos*	Seal	*Retén*
Horn	*Klaxón, bocina*	Shaft	*Flecha*
Hose	*Mangera*	Shock absorber	*Amortiguador*
Hose clamp	*Abrazadera*	Solenoid	*Solenoide*
Ignition key	*Llave de switch*	Spark plug	*Bujía (Candela in*
Ignition switch	*Switch*		*Guatemala)*
Jack	*Gato*	Spark plug wire	*Cable de bujía*
Kingpin	*Perno, pivote de*	Starter	*Marcha*
	dirección	Starter ring gear	*Cremallera*
Kingpin carrier	*Portamango*	Steering gear	*Caja de dirección*
Leaf springs	*Muelles*	Steering wheel	*Volante*
Lever	*Palanca*	Stop light	*Luz de stop*
Main bearings	*Metales de bancada*	Stud	*Birlo, perno*
Manifold	*Múltiple*		*prisionero*
Exhaust	*Múltiple de*	Tail pipe	*Tubo de escape*
	escape	Thermostat	*Toma de agua,*
Intake	*Múltiple de*		*termósi*
	admisión	Throw out bearing	*Cojarín*
Master cylinder	*Cilindro maestro*	Tie rod	*Barrilla de*
	de frenos		*dirección*
Mechanic	*Mecánico, Maestro*	Tie rod end	*Terminal de barrilla*
Motor	*Motor, máquina*		*de dirección*
Muffler	*Mofle*	Tighten	*Apretar*
Oil	*Aceite*	Timing gear	*Engrange de árbol*
Oil filter	*Filtro de aceite*		*de levas*
Oil pump	*Bomba de aceite*	Tire	*Llanta*
Tire balancing	*Balanceo*	Valve cover	*Tapa de pulerías*
Tire gauge	*Calibrador*	Valve guide	*Guía de válvula*
Tire repair shop	*Vulcanízadora*		

Tire tube	*Camara* or *Tubo*	Valve lifter	*Buso, levanta válvulas*
Tire, tubeless	*Llanta sin cámara*	Valve springs	*Resorte de válvula*
Tire valve	*Válvula*	Valve spring keeper	*Cazuela de válvula*
Tow truck	*Grúa*	Valve stem	*Vastigo de válvula*
Torsion bar	*Barra de torsión*	Van	*Camioneta*
Transmission	*Transmisión, Caja* (box)	Voltage regulator	*Regulador de voltage*
Truck	*Camión*	Water pump	*Bomba de agua*
Tune	*Afinar*	Weld	*Soldar*
Tune up	*Afinación*	Wheel	*Rueda*
Turn signals	*Direccionales*	Wheel cylinder	*Cilindro de frenos*
Turn signal flasher	*Destallador*	Windshield	*Parabrisas*
Universal joint	*Cruceta y yugo, cardán*	Windshield wiper	*Limpia parabrisas* or *Limpiadores*
Upholstery shop (auto)	*Cubreasientos*	Windshield wiper blade	*Pluma*
Vacuum advance	*Avance*	Wire	*Alambre*
Valves	*Válvulas*	Wrist pin	*Perno, Pasador de émbolo*
exhaust	*válvula de escape*		
intake	*válvula de admisión*		

It's bent — *Está doblado*

Adjust the clutch — *Ajuste el clutch*

Adjust the brakes — *Ajuste los frenos*

To bleed the brakes — *Purgar los frenos*

To rebuild the wheel cylinders — *Cambiar las gomas*

To turn the brake drums — *Rectificar los tambores*

Adjust the valves — *Ajuste las válvulas*

To grind the valves — *Asentar las válvulas*

Engine overhaul — *Ajuste general*

To turn the crankshaft — *Rectificar la cigüeñal*

To charge the battery — *Cargar la acumulador*

The engine is knocking — *Suena la máquina*

The engine is overheating — *El motor se calienta*

The engine is throwing oil — *La máquina está tirando aceite*

The engine is burning oil — *La máquina está quemando aceite.*

The radiator is leaking — *Esta tirando la radiador*

I want a major tune-up — *Quiero una afinación mayor*

Pack the front wheel bearings — *Engrace los baleros de las ruedas adelantes*

The tire is punctured — *Está ponchada la llanta*

The tire has a slow leak — *La llanta está bajando poco a poco*

Put a boot in the tire — *Vucanice la llanta.*

Put 30 pounds of air in the tires — *Ponga treinta libras de aire en las llantas.*

TOOLS, HARDWARE & ODDS AND ENDS

Acetylene torch	*Soplete oxiacetilenico, Equipo de autógeno*
Allen wrench	*Llave de alán*
Axe	*Hacha*
Bag	*Bolsa*
Bolt	*Tornillo*
Box end wrench	*Llave ástria*
Bucket	*Cubo*
Can opener	*Abrelatas*
Chisel	*Cincel*
Compression guage	*Compresión metro*
Cotter pin	*Chaveta*
Crescent wrench	*Perico*
Crowbar	*Barra*
Drill and bits	*Taladro y brocas*
Emery paper	*Lija de esmeril*
Extension (socket)	*Extensión*
Feeler guage	*Culibrador*
File	*Lima*
Flashlight	*Foco de mano*
Flashlight batteries	*Pilas*
Funnel	*Embudo*
Gasket cement	*Shelac*
Gear puller	*Extractor de engranes*
Glue	*Pegamento* (white glue-*Resistol*, brand name; epoxy glue-*Pegamento Epoxy*)
Grease	*Grasa*
Grease gun	*Inyector de grasa*
Grill (cooking)	*parilla*
Hack saw	*Cegeta*
Hammer	*Martillo*
Hardware store	*Ferretería*
Hatchet	*Hacha*
Hose	*Mangera*
Iron rods	*Barras de fierro*
Jack	*Gato*
Juice squeezer	*Exprimidera*
Key	*Llave* (Woodruff key-*Cuña*)
Liquid wrench	*Afloja todo* (brand name)

Lug wrench	*Llave de cruz*
Needle (sewing)	*Aguja*
Nail	*Clavo*
Needle nose pliers	*Alicates*
Nut	*Tuerca*
Open end wrench	*Llave española*
Phillips screwdriver	*Desarmador de cruz*
Pin	*Perno*
Pipe wrench	*Llave Stillson*
Pliers	*Pinzas*
Pottery	*Cosas de barro*
Ratchet	*Matraca, Llave de trinquete*
Rope	*Soga*
Sandpaper	*Papel de lija*
Scissors	*Tijeras*
Screw	*Tornillo*
Screwdriver	*Desarmador*
Sharpening stone	*Afiladera*
Shoelaces	*Agujetas*
Shovel	*Pala*
Socket wrench	*Llave de dado*
Solder	*Soldadura*
Soldering iron	*Soldador*
Spark plug wrench	*Llave de bujias*
Spring	*Resorte*
String, cord, twine	*Cuerda*
Tape	*Cinta* (Plastic electrical tape-*cinta de plástico*)
Thread	*Hilo*
Timing light	*Lampara de tiempo*
Tin snips	*Tijeras de cortar lámina*
Tools	*Herramientas*
Torque wrench	*Llave de torque*
Vise	*Tornillo*
Vise grip pliers	*Pinzas de presión*
Washer	*Rondana*
Water pump pliers	*Pinzas de extensión*
Wire	*Alambre* (electrical wire-*alambre eléctrico*
Wrench	*Llave*
Zipper	*Cierre, zípper*

RED TAPE

Tourist card	*Tarjeta de turista*	Married	*Casado (a)*
Passport	*Pasaporte*	Widowed	*Viudo (a)*
Vaccination Certificate	*Certificado de Vacunación*	Car permit	*Permiso de automóvil*
Immigration	*Migración*	Driver's license	*Licencia de manejar*
Inspection	*Revisión*		
Suitcase	*Maleta*	Car owner	*Propetario de automóvil*
Minor	*Menor de edad*		
Single	*Soltero (a)*	Title	*Título (de propiedad)*
Divorced	*Divorciado (a)*		
Profession or occupation	*Profesión or ocupación*	Motorcycle	*Moto*
		Pets	*Mascotas*
Registration	*Registratión*	Rabies vaccination	*Vacunación de rabia*
Insurance	*Seguros*		
License plates	*Placas*	Boat	*Lancha*
Border	*Frontera*	Outboard motor	*Motor de fuera borda*
Customs	*Aduana*		
Baggage	*Equipaje*	Guns	*Armas*
Age	*Edad*	Hunting license	*Licencia de cazar*
Marital status	*Estado civil*	Fishing license	*Licencia de pescar*

Is there no other way of arranging this problem?—*¿No habría modo de resolver el problema de otra manera?*

FISHING & DIVING

Fishing rod	*Caña (de pescar)*	Spearhead	*Punta*
Line	*Cuerda*	Swim fins	*Aletas*
Hook	*Anzuelo*	Diving mask	*Visor*
Bait	*Carnada*	Snorkle	*Snorkle*
Sinker	*Plomo*	Diving equipment	*Equipo de bucear*
Lure	*Curricán*	To dive	*Bucear*
Speargun	*Arpón, pistola*	To fish	*Pescar*
Spear shaft	*Flecha*		

SLANG

¡Aguas!	Careful!	*buey*	cold, fool
agua de riñon	beer	*buque*	car
alivianar	help out	*caco*	thief
aliviane	aid	*café*	marijuana
apañar	to arrest	*cante*	squeal
azul	cop	*caño*	a joint
baboso	fool	*carcacha*	old car
banquetazo	big meal	*carnal*	brother
bolo	drunk	*carrujos*	smoking papers
bravo	tough	*chavo-a*	guy, girl
bruja	broke, poor	*chelas*	beers

chota	cop	marmaja	change, money
chupar	to drink	mear	to piss
coco	head	¡Mecacho!	Wow!
codo	cheap, stingy	mocoso	snot-nosed
conchudo	insensitive	moler	to bother, bug
conectar	get with it	mordelón	cop
cuete	drunk	mordida	bribe, bite
dineral	lots of money	mota	marijuana
desmadre	screw-up, mess	muerto	broke, poor
esquincle	kid, brat	naco	thug
¡Entrale!	Get it on!	nave	car
fachas	Chicle sellers	nieves	no
fregar	screw up	nones	no
frías	beer	nortearse	beat it, scram
forjar	roll joints	onda	vibe
gandalla	ass (person)	padre	very good
gañan	thug	la papa	food
gasofia	gasoline	papear	to eat
gerolan	drunk	pedo	drunk
gorrón	cheapskate	pelarse	escape, avoid
huevón	lazy	pendejo	creep
¡Hiole!	Oh, wow!	pinche	damned, useless
infle	a drink	pintarse	escape, avoid
jetear	play the fool	pomos	wine, booze
la julia	the cops, paddy wagon	ponchado	husky
lana	money	quemacoco	convertible
libar	to drink	quemarse	to be silly, stupid
ligar	to score (sex)	regarla	screw up
loco	stoned	el rol	the vibe
lorenzo	crazy, nuts	sábanas	rolling papers
lucas	crazy, nuts	simón	yes, right on
luz	money	suave	really nice
madre	good, great	suelto	change, money
mafufo	stoned	tamarindo	traffic cop
mamacita	little mama	tira	cop
mamosota	big mama	toque	toke
mamón	sucker	troca	truck
mango	pretty woman	yerba	marijuana
mano	"brother"	zoquete	knothead

NICKNAMES FROM PROPER NAMES

Beto	Alberto, Roberto	Chepito	José
Bety	Beatriz	Chico	Francisco
Billy	Guillermo	Chivio	Silvia
Chabela	Isabel	Chole	Soledad
Chala	Rosalía	Chon, Chona	Concepción
Charo	Rosario	Chucho	Jesús
Chela	Gaciela	Chuy	Jesús
Chelo	Lucero, Cielo	Cleto	Anacleto
Concha	Concepción	Memo	Guillermo
Cuca	Refugia	Mima	Irma

Curro	Francisco	Moy	Moises
Fallo Fello	Rafael	Mundo	Edmundo
Foncho	Alfonso	Nacho	Ignacio
Güicho	Luis	Nando	Fernando
Gus	Gustavo	Nardo	Leonardo
Juancho	Juan	Neto	Ernesto
Lacho	Horacio	Nico	Nicolas
Lalo	Abelardo, Eduardo	Paco	Francisco
Lencho	Lorenzo	Pancho	Francisco
Lety	Leticia	Panta	Pantaleona
Licha	Alicia	Pepe	Jose
Lola	Dolores	Pita	Guadalupe
Lucha	Maria de la Luz	Queta	Eriqueta
Lupe	Guadalupe	Quique	Enrique
Lupita	Guadalupe	Rico, Ricky	Ricardo
Luz	Maria de la Luz	Tacho	Anastasio
Manolo	Manuel	Tere, Teté	Teresa
Mari, Maruca	Maria	Tina	Florentina
Mariquita	Maria	Toño, Tony	Antonio
Mayté	Maria Teresa	Vicky	Victoria
Mela	Carmela	Willi	Wilfrido
Melu	Manuel		

SLANG NICKNAMES

Bruja-o	Witch	Huevo	Baldy, Ballsy
Chaparra-o	Shorty	Mocho	Square, Fink
Chata-o	Pugnose	Negro-a	Blackie
La Chilindrina	Naughty girl	Ero-a	Pal
Chino	Curly, Chinaman	Orejón	Big ears
Chiquis	Squirt	Pachuco	Punk
Chiva	Goat	Pecoso	Freckles
Chula	Cutie	Pelón	Baldy
Colocho	Curly	Pelos	Hairy
Cuatro Lamparas	Four eyes	Perico-a	Parrot
Dandy	Dandy	Pinolillo	"Dennis the Menace"
Diablo	Devil	Pirinola	Spinning top
Enano	Dwarf (also Giant)	Pistolón	Big Pistol
Fede	Ugly	Pollo	Chicken
Flaco-a	Skinny	Prieta-o	Darky
Gachupín	Pale	Puas	Unshaved
Gorda-o	Fatty	Puerco-a	Pig
Greñas	Messy Hair	Rorra	Doll
Gringo	Gringo	Tigre	Tiger
Guero-a	Blondie	Tuercas	Bolts
Hijín	Sonny	Yaqui	Yaqui

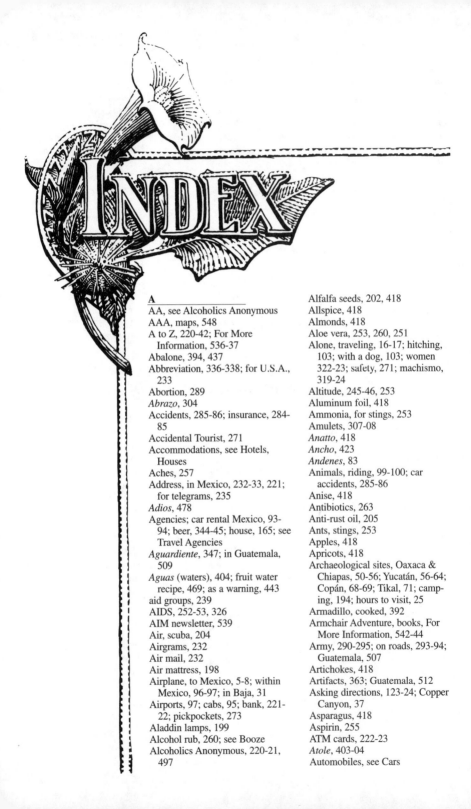

INDEX

ABOUT THE AUTHORS

Carl Franz and Lorena Havens have been exploring Mexico and Central America since the early 1960s. A writer/editor team, their warm, easy-going style and personal insights have inspired generations of travelers. When not on the road, they live in a pioneer-era log cabin in the North Cascade Mountains.

Also by Carl Franz and Lorena Havens: *The People's Guide to Camping, Backpacking & Boating in Mexico*; *The On & Off the Road Cookbook*; *The People's Guide to RV Camping in Mexico* (with Steve Rogers); and *The People's Guide Travel Letter*. Their articles have appeared in *America*, *New West*, *Outside*, *Amistad*, *Backpacker*, *Pacific Northwest*, *Adventure Road* and other magazines.

People's Guide collaborator **Steve Rogers** is a serious student of Mexican customs and cuisine. Steve and his partner, Tina Rosa, are the authors of *The Shopper's Guide to Mexico* and *Mexico in 22 Days*.

ABOUT THE ILLUSTRATOR

Glen Strock has studied painting and exhibited his art in both the United States and Mexico. His recent work focuses on capturing the regional flavor of Northern New Mexico and has been used for cards, posters, books, and magazines. Glen and his family live in Santa Fe, New Mexico.

THE PEOPLE'S GUIDE TRAVEL LETTER

Try as we might, it's impossible to squeeze everything we've learned about life and travel south of the border between the covers of a single book. As our "People's Guide" adventures and discoveries continue, however, my notebooks are literally overflowing with good material. We also get a lot of great mail from People's Guide readers, sharing information and hard-earned tips. This stuff is invaluable—the title of a great new book on the Maya, the name of a particularly choice *cantina* in Oaxaca, unusual foods and special recipes, hotel bargains in Mexico City, Spanish school recommendations, favorite beaches, jokes and songs—for diehard *aficionados* like us, virtually everything about Mexico and Central America is worth looking at.

Hence, we've created ***The People's Guide Travel Letter***, a twice-a-year newsletter devoted entirely to travel and life in Mexico and Central America. Each issue is stuffed with articles, letters, illustrations, and our usual grab bag of irresistible trivia and tidbits. More than anything, however, the newsletter is our way to compare notes and stay in touch with other People's Guide travelers. With this in mind, we do our best not to sound like a magazine or a "serious" travel publication. The *Travel Letter* is informative, but it's also informal and fun—and when necessary, even off the wall.

Subscriptions to ***The People's Guide Travel Letter*** are $15 for four issues (two years), or $5 for one sample issue. Please make your check out to The People's Guide to Mexico and send it to People's Guide Press, Box 179, Acme, WA 98220.

We welcome your comments and contributions to both the *Travel Letter* and *The People's Guide to Mexico.* You can write us directly at the address listed above, send us an email at **mexico@peoplesguide.com** or visit our website: **<http://www.peoplesguide.com/mexico>**.

Cater to Your Interests on Your Next Vacation